Poetic Voices
of America

Fall 1993

Sparrowgrass Poetry Forum
Inc.

ACKNOWLEDGMENTS

Photographs reproduced by kind permission of:

Randy Ball, page 79, 109, 124, 139, 154, 169,
184, 199, 229, 244, 259, 274, 289, 304, 319
Barb Coleing, page 4, 214

Copyright 1993
Sparrowgrass Poetry Forum, Inc.

Published by
Sparrowgrass Poetry Forum, Inc.
203 Diamond St., P.O. Box 193
Sistersville, WV 26175

Library of Congress
Catalog Card Number 90-660082

ISBN 0-923242-28-7

Introduction

Welcome, Reader, to this edition of Sparrowgrass Poetry Forum's **Poetic Voices of America.** Once again, our collection of poems represents a wide variety of thoughts, themes, and genres. And again our collection includes the voices of poets from across the continent and even beyond from other countries. As the Publisher, I like to think that this volume is in many ways a written record of our times and our places, these voices from across the land.

What are these voices saying as they provide this written record? They are providing a personal journal of feelings — disappointments and joys, sorrows and pleasures, fears and triumphs. Certainly, each of our poets writes from individual experience but assembled together in our collection, the poems begin to form a consensus of experience.

Who are these voices? They are persons literally from all walks of life who have a common need to express themselves poetically. Young and old, they are students and teachers, soldiers and ministers, ranchers and cabdrivers, doctors and drifters and a myriad of others in a myriad of other roles. They are people who definitely have something to say and in turn they say it very well.

Where are these voices? Seemingly, they are everywhere. They live in such diverse places as Cheyenne, Wyoming, and Chagrin Falls, Ohio; Saskatoon, Saskatchewan, and St. Augustine, Florida; Peculiar, Missouri, and Punxsutawney, Pennsylvania. Sandburg and Whitman would have loved the poetry in all the names of all the places where we live.

As you read through this collection, I trust you will share the pleasure that I did in helping to select them. I am always struck by what I discover I have in common with all the poets whose work I read. Indeed, poetry emphasizes the humanity that connects all of us.

Sparrowgrass Poetry Forum is bringing you an outstanding volume of verse which you will want to read and share. We bring you the poets' works but until you read them, the act of sharing is unconsummated. As Emerson wrote, "It's the good reader who makes the good book."

Jerome P. Welch
Publisher

MAY

May is the month
easily crushed beneath the thumb and forefinger.
The pulp of a soft bud plucked early one afternoon
and wiped off against the side of a house.

May, a season too soon.
A crinoline blouse
flowing shamelessly over a pure soul.
The skin of her shoulders showing through
and her face still hidden in chiffon.

May is for frogs to sit upon,
spreading their eggs over the water like warm glue.
The mud grows fat in May
and the roots fatten in the warm earth.

I am working my way
over this immense, defenseless land.
Day after day, shaping verse
with passionate word.

I scrape the green from the soft earth
and sing the infinitely faint song
of eternal life.

—**Anthony J. Velez**
First Place Award Winner

MY DOCTOR

You voiced oath —
 the healing of humanity's hurt,
new vows on your tongue —
that strange hunger to serve,
to aid, to console.

Bruised prayer beads echo
through the dark
to understand the silent depths,
the tangled needs of the day,
the awareness of the slow surge
of burning pain,
deeper than thought.

And evening curves its chalice
to your hand,
prayer blends with the stars
and spills its light
into your upturned palm.

You chose your lode-star —
the Great Physician.

—Emma Crobaugh
 Second Place Award Winner

BLISS

Sunday in bed
 beneath soft covers.
Clouds drift across
my window to the sky.
Two warm spaniels,
asleep on an unmade bed.
No food to make,
no shopping lists or printed word.
Only the soaring violin
of the Spring Sonata.
Exquisite.
No other stimuli allowed to touch
the jangled switchboard of my mind.
Nor is sleep permitted,
to waste this precious day.
It is set aside
for drifting into being.
Nothing else.

—Freda Freeman
 Fifth Place Award Winner

RESTORE HOPE

We sent you there
 Grain in one hand
Rifle in the other.
Amid hobbling skeletons
with outstretched arms
and furtive eyes.
Amid fragile, swollen bodies
and jubilant dancing.
We sent you there
To help.
Among all the shriveled pieces
There for the world to see.
Watch carefully though
Some are still strong
With puffed chests
and sneering eyes
Adding misery.
Watch carefully
Not everyone is dancing.

—Paulette Nelson
 Fifth Place Award Winner

FOREWARNING

There is so little time . . . How can I stand
 Here in the brittle wind and watch you go
Across the saffron stubble. Now the land
Has closed upon itself. All that could grow
Has given fruit and gone. The tepid sun
Tips the amber hills, fingers the hollow
Still silver with night's frost. My heart may run
Beyond the pasture gate, begging to follow;
But I must wait. How, ever, could I say
A beetle's ticking in the grass, a brown leaf strayed,
A blackbird's rusty note, the very way
The passive morning lies, make me afraid;
That something in the slim elm shadow's bending
Speaks of a final hour, whispers an ending?

—Madge Lay Ruark
 Fourth Place Award Winner

PUEBLO ARTISTS

*[Portion taken from the Letter "P" — Excerpted from Piki
Bread & Peppers, 1991, Smith & Kalb
text & illustrations, unpublished manuscript]*

As each one pairs her skill with
 a picture-writing past
A pat, a pinch, a promise
Creating things that last.

The potter's art and patience
  set the pace each day
Where play and prayer are partners
In the push and pull of clay.

Pieced and pressed together
Contours spun to touch
Pictures, texture: poetry
Eye-pleasing patterns polished
Simple symmetry and such.

—Ann T. Smith
 Third Place Award Winner

building blocks.

words are the building blocks, it's true,
of all human understanding, but stay their
inconsonant flow between us. if we but knew
their awesome abilities to lead our minds
astray . . . who seeks to use words, like mortared
bricks, to build semantic, transient castles,
must come to know that such words fall, like
  cotton sticks upon an empty drum.

from guttural grunt of Neolithic man
to these lips of ours, that utter
the highest praises to absolute beauties
and perfections, we span the bridge of time
with word overlays. words. words. words.
words. words. words: from the wanderers—
throughout—time, have surely made heroic
monuments to human progress . . . while some words
are but tuneless tattoos: tuneless tattoos
that spawn, abort and fall in soundlessness, like
  cotton sticks upon an empty drum . . .

like cotton sticks pounding upon an empty drum.

—L. Bruce Kingery, Ed.D.
 Fourth Place Award Winner

WHISPERINGS, AFTER STEPHEN

Dear water of my seas, my midnight's moon,
The boded drought is here, the dustbin days.
Sweet potter to my kiln, my bright balloon,
The roadway's strewn, with shards, love's greens are grays.
Soft singer of my songs, my April's rain,
Our morning-music melts, turns sound to sleet.
Oh, bringer of my loaves, my body's grain,
A scorning absence bends me, wind on wheat.
Ah, Arab of my sands, my headstrong steed,
Long lizard-shadows creep, siroccos blow.
Bright scarab on my heart, my sacred bead,
The blizzard bites until the soul is snow.
    Oh, swimmer in my pool, my sonneteer,
    My shimmerstone, appear again! appear . . . .

       —June Owens
       Fifth Place Award Winner

AFTER THE TERROR

Deep in the forest the terrible deed—
the devouring witch undone, well done,
roasted and dispatched
in her tomb.

Now free, the children Hansel and Gretel
walk hand in hand,
finding their way through darkened woods and water
to their father's home

Where Gretel's fright each night
in dreams of terror
loosens the witch's hold
upon her soul.

But younger Hansel hides at night
in dreamless sleep
forgets the witch
denies the witch's house
the fattening cell until
deep down
the dreaded Norns
destroy him.

       —Johan Stohl
       Fifth Place Award Winner

AT THE ARTS CENTER, BATES COLLEGE

Now that it's spring it's their legs that stop me
when I go to the library. Before the sun
reaches a certain angle or the river is free
of ice, they're in shorts and no socks with their Docksiders.

It's the slope from calf to ankle, color
of oiled wood, asking for a hand to fold around it
to form a hollow for it to press into
that makes me see how far behind I am.

It's taken me all the life I've lived just to
look you in the eye, wearing my jeans and socks
and feel my shoulders spread like two continents
across my back. I want to attach myself

like a barnacle to this secret, ride it
to its private place where it must survey itself naked.
How did it learn such music, both hands
flinging huge arpeggios along the keyboard? I love how

somewhere a French horn carefully turns around one spot
to make it perfect. I want to sink my face into this living
until it is inside me like the sea when it rolls toward shore
raising itself to balance for one moment in a perfect glass scroll.

       —Katharine Gregg
       Fifth Place Award Winner

CLEAN SWEEP

Hard wood
Smooth and strong;

Sweet straw
Pliant and full;

Quick pass or slow
The silent ritual of sweeping—

Making ready,
Restoring order,
Satisfying the soul.

       —Lynette Mallette
       Fifth Place Award Winner

OH, TO BE AS POETRY

Oh, to be as poetry,
with passions running wild,
Yet gentleness of spirit,
as honest as a child.

Oh, to be as poetry,
a precious, timeless thought,
Transcending earthly mind or means,
throughout the ages sought.

Oh, to be as poetry,
lifting spirits high,
And opening man's guarded heart,
inspiring him to try.

       —Toni McClellan
       Fifth Place Award Winner

toadstool

my mother is a brown
spotted dry mushroom
in some neighbor's
front yard
standing chinaman-tall
in the greenest patch of green
next to an oak tree
my bare foot tipped
with frosted pink
kicks its head off
smashing brown
spotted dry bits
upward through
an enameled blue day

       —Maggie McDowell
       Fifth Place Award Winner

EDGAR, 1957–1986

I mutely heard the word
And tried to keep my ground.
What would have made a difference
To keep him here with me?

Can a soul be healed of loss?
My head won't press that chest,
My finger touch that nipple.
The lips I kissed in sleep are memory.

The kisses,
Those exquisite little grapes,
Of a sweetness
That each creates a longing
For the next.

       —Richard Cabral
       Fifth Place Award Winner

SYMPHONY OF LIFE

The setting sun turns emerald water
to shimmering gold
as it mystifies the distant mountains.
Golden ripples dance wildly with joy
as they rush in shoreward harmony
to the alder's peaceful tune.
Heavenly voices radiate
from our song birds
as they flutter about,
blossoming into the evening symphony.
All of the world's beauty
converges at one point
to bring my ambling soul
back to life.

—Dave L. Kingwood
Fifth Place Award Winner

PRAYER OF AN EL SALVADORAN MOTHER IN 1982

Oh, Sweet Spirit of Death,
Wrap thy silken shawl about my grief.
Lift my soul into thy whirlwind,
Let my bones fall among the bones
Of my children, and among the bones
Of all others whom I held dear.

Though the crescendo of my soul
Could erupt that mountain of fire, Ezalco,
And swallow our enemy, let it not.
Grant that our bones nourish our beloved
Green mountain, and our tears as soft rain
Quench the thirst of the bromeliads there.
For in the mist of the mountain,
Swishing in the water cups of the bromeliads
Are the tiny frogs my children loved.

Oh Sweet Spirit of Death,
Wrap not thy silken shawl about this land,
Nor lift her into thy whirlwind.
Grant now, that peace come to El Salvador.

—Mary S. Shepherd
Fifth Place Award Winner

THE EARTH AS GODDESS

They have made her
a gown of clay, pressed
the fine coils like leaves
around her

They have made her a tree
hung with serpents
somnolent, dazed
in the bright sun, gathering
to her breasts sharp
and hungry the bite of a wasp
or quivering bee

Holding the small migrating bird, exhausted,
she breathes into its beak
and its heart works—
red flashes in its wings
beyond the nets

She has poured out herself
a libation, the years of her generations,
she takes her stand on the hill
defying the hunters.

—Carol Snyder Halberstadt
Fifth Place Award Winner

FLOWERS

The sun is like a great big heart that loves and warms the
flowers.

The rain is like the gentle loving of a mother that washes
over them.

The wind is like a gentle pat on the back that says
"Everything is going to be ok."

And the dirt is the soft bed where the flowers lay.

—Samantha Gray, age 11
Fifth Place Award Winner

AMANTE DE TIEMPO

as sunsets mark years with impressionable stains,
and rains wash days with an aqua cloth,
she cries of laugh lines, frown lines,
and crow's of frustration—for
age prevents her to be her lover's first.
but to her wrinkles, and experience,
and one grey hair peeking from her bangs,
he gently cups her breast, looking
into the eyes behind the lines, whispering
—it's more important to be the last.

—W.A. Whiteside
Fifth Place Award Winner

FOLDING SQUARES OF CLOTH

Folding white squares of cloth,
Folding the fraying pieces of cloth
as Mary and Mother before me.
Women have always folded scraps of cloth.
Smoothing, folding the fabric of a family's life.
Families need bits and squares of cloth.

My rasped and callused hands
Fold and smooth and stack
The day's yellowing squares of cloth.
Hands too gnarled and cracked
to hold a pen to write of laws or life.
Hands that must fold.
Folding as my mind tosses thoughts
of future, of hearts and souls molded today.
Folding white squares of cloth.

—Christine Wilson
Fifth Place Award Winner

MORNING

Morning sat in discontent
In sullen silence outside my door
Its face hung with dreariness
Brooding against the brightness of new snow.
Wrapped in a cloak of somber gray
It moved among the trees
Pondering lifeless-looking branches
Heard their hardened whisper
Echoing in the cold air.
It saw the last darkened blooms of late flowers
Their heads hanging as if defeated
But looking closer saw the frozen smiles.
It closed around the house
Huddled low against the earth
And through the melting ice on warming windows
Saw the life stirring within.
With a clearing countenance
Morning wandered through the gate.

—Lin Davis-Hurst
Fifth Place Award Winner

Set down in September, late,
I was a seed, deep, but out
of season, digging far into
    roots and rocks and beetles,
disturbing settled ground—and

when winter came, the trees
    rose high above me, letting through,
in stingy rays, a distant sun, urging
    me back through the earth, to
grow runners, and write with
    green fingers, the icy white poems
                        of spewed up fields.

—Betty Sherron
Fifth Place Award Winner

ONE AND ALL—FORGETTING

One and all, they sit side by side,
forgetting the Son who was crucified.
One and all gave a voice to their pleas,
forgetting who gave His blood so willingly.

One and all here to lend a hand,
forgetting those left alone to stand.
One and all ignored deeds we one day face,
forgetting the Son sent by God's Grace.

One and all found strangers in their place,
forgetting here their teardrops time will erase.
One and all found their reasons to cry,
forgetting again, in the tomb, He no longer lies.

—Cheryl K. McNett Mead

LEGACY

I.   Seeds

After the great lord God
made the land
He cradled the people he created
in the palm of His hand
infinite as grains in shifting sand
men and women of all design created equal
that's how this world began
but somewhere along the way
we abandoned God's plan

II.   Roots

through the hollow eyes of prejudice
you spied equality peering
your vision remains stirring—

        you can rob us of our heritage
        change our names
        pistol whip us
        or beat us with chains
        but no force can stop the freedom train

you lived your life passionately
forever dreaming of better days ahead
suspended between reason and violence
and when all else is said
all the rest is merely silence

—Steven R. Brown

DREAM THE THOUGHTS SO DEAR TO ME

My love to me is like a happy song
That makes my heart, my soul, my all
Want to dance and sing.
Oh for the love of him
Of him I so adore
For just one more glance
One more kind word
Then will I
To some green bank
By some cool stream
Dream the thoughts so dear to me.

—Vangi

VEINS

I remember my initial awe
after seeing white paper under a microscope.

There were canyons and falls
where I had thought only endless resistance

and where there were words
ink in black glaciers

furrowed the smooth plains.
In my fiftieth year I thought of my parents

and came through the hour children
do not visit. In this dim hall

men and women are on paper sheets and gurneys;
her leg has been stapled and pinned.

My father is watching
a sleep he will not join

how it emerges from my mother's dark
mouth a small mammal departing

across red dunes, over
the marble system of her.

—Alexandria Peary
Fifth Place Award Winner

ENDANGERED SPECIES

Gently as iambic trimeter
snow drifts across the Sisters'
        quiet graves,
spiraling in dactyls
        on their crosses
to warm old bones, cold bones.

A century ago their owners left
        to follow God's and Mary's Lamb
        because he first
had followed them, these other Marys,
        poor, obedient, chaste,
vowed to their Lord through all their years.

Similes are singing in the trees;
metaphors march along the silent paths
        where no one drops
her Aves like strawflowers in the snow
        these wintry days.
Blue shadows slant across the swirling white:

memories of countless worthwhile lives
of teaching, nursing, guiding, cherishing;
        of dedicated years
strong as devotion, delicate as breath
        yielded at last in death,
a way of life, it seems, endangered now.

—Maryanna Childs OP
Fifth Place Award Winner

SHADOWS

When the sun is in its height
Truth is real and can be believed.
But before,
in the blinding time,
Explanations can only fall short
And truth can only hurt.
There is a need to believe in shadows
Of smaller men in bigger dreams,
Of a dry and moistless present
That yields more in promise than in thought.

But after,
in the later time,
Proofs need altering
And the end is near.
The facts no longer can be as clear
As they were in the shadowless time.
For now the body tires, and the eyes grow weary
And now the shadows reappear.

—Carl Liebich
Fifth Place Award Winner

I AM AFRICA

I am Africa
A place I have never been
Where the sun will burn off my back
and someone will speak in the night
My eye is the muddy water
My arms are the endless plains
The stars there are my brothers
The men there are my friends
I love Africa
Where life on earth is marble-hearted:
mouths grow dry and wind carries nothing
out of the sky, hard as packed dirt.
I am Africa
Where the printed foot is eminent
where darkness in the cave is black
where daytime is a diamond-cutting glare
Every red rock, every zebra hair is bigger
than August. Every story of Africa
has to do with me; every loss, every shade of green.

—L. Kennelly
Fifth Place Award Winner

IN ANOTHER LIFETIME

In another lifetime you were my son.
Not knowing then how our lives would converge,
We have unfinished business.
Shadows danced on the night of your birth.
I grapsed the rounded, splintered bedposts in futility,
Tethered to the certainty of our destiny.
Your father's name was Peter.
You, pushing, pushing
Rebelling the confines of our ties.
Contractions squeezing, squeezing,
Relentless.
Red-haired child fury,
You wrestled and clawed at your powerlessness.
With tearing passion you fought to leave
The chamber of your origination.
Screaming, both screaming,
Penetrating fire in my loins.
Flesh ripping, your head engraved our oneness.
And time was motionless.
The blood of the labor bed bound us for eternity.

—Diane Adams
Fifth Place Award Winner

DEAR,

Brothers and sisters of this nation,
I have a dream that one day this world will
be clean and pollution will clear the sky,
and the eagles will fly.
That every boy and girl will walk together in
harmony.
That there will be no more violence, there
will only be silence.

I HAVE A DREAM.
—Bradley Dennick, age 11

BIRD LIVES

Through grey clouds of thick smoke
stands a dark specter of frenzied
sound which screams with rage.
Out of his luminous horn leaps notes
of fire, impinging one's ear like
drops of rain landing one by one
on crystal waters in streams of
gold, flowing to one's heart,
flowing to one's soul.

*In memory of Charlie "Bird" Parker
and John Birks "Dizzy" Gillespie*

—William J. Cole
Fifth Place Award Winner

DANCING SCHOOL CLASSES

Frilly white dresses & lavender sashes —
Little girls going to dancing school classes.
Little boy partners with horn rimmed glasses.

II

Frilly white dresses & pink sashes —
Little girls batting their upswept eyelashes.
Little boys making clumsy passes.

III

Frilly white dresses & sky blue sashes —
Little boys playing with matches.
Little girl dreams — dirty grey ashes.

—J. Pierritz
Fifth Place Award Winner

SORROW OF THE YELLOWING LEAF

Feel that sweet exotic fatalism
in the dying song of Summer
softly hummed in fading themes
praising wickedness in Autumn's will

There is the whining ache of silence
as when a door draws closed
or a train crawls out of sight
that dread pause between claps of thunder

Lifting our eyes to abandoned heavens
we swallow the choke of chagrin
ignoring the sorrow of the yellowing leaf
whistle the measures of timeless tunes

The dreams of our sleep grow wilted
as the iced-white teeth of Winter
crawl between our sheets gnawing
and the wax of the year drips down

—Burr McCloskey
Fifth Place Award Winner

Dusk ripens in uncertain hours of light,
Swells, testing its imprisonment in shade.
The gardens, dreading to converge with night,
With roots grip deeper for the soil's aid.

Night treads upon the tree-tops, and, bewitched,
Their leaves hang heavy, crown after crown,
'Til crowns of half the world night holds besieged.
What mercy? 'T isn't even glancing down.

Dusk seeps, like ink, from shadows on the ground,
And climbs, entailed by the campaign on high.
Rite is complete, when on horizon, bound
By clouds, blue is led from conquered sky.

And though I know the mechanism behind
This nightly change, why do I feel so blind?

*Dedicated to Mama (my 5's are still
your 5's.) To Daddy, Grandma, Michael.
To Mary Davis.*

—Polina Rikoun
Fifth Place Award Winner

A CHILD IS DROWNING

And so her matter comes to this:
The summer clouds high and buoyant,
Though not as dry as her mouth
Before the final wave invades her breath.

And that death is before she was
She never learned;
Hardly, that fire burned as spray
Stings her eye where gulls fly safe
In the lake of the day.

O what a rage at the thought
She could be caught
And taken in!

Their laughter and voices call thin from the beach
As her hand reaches the end of a tether and she slides
Away from the land, through that wavering wall,
Into unchanging weather.

—Michael B. Girsdansky
Fifth Place Award Winner

LUNAR ECLIPSE

A trio of herons flapped restlessly about the shore as the
full moon—its new-minted rim rusty and ragged—rose high
over the creek.
Half a moon hangs now in the darkening sky and the other is
adrift on the water.

And the herons squawk in terror.

Moon of the long night, moon of the hunters, burnished gold
orb of December, full moon born of a holy month long revered
for celestial things, is lost in the cold black maw of the
creek.
Its ghost floats high above in the wake of Orion.

And the herons squawk in terror.

They crouch on their perch in the glow of the resurrection,
descendants of pterodactyls, discerning hosts of all the
lunar phases, but nonetheless mystified. In the cold white
night their exclamations echo along the icy shore as the
eerie dream is recounted again and again.

And the herons squawk in terror.

—Audrey Y. Scharmen
Fifth Place Award Winner

DANDELIONS

With one mighty exhale,
Thus exposes Act I.

A million billowy ballet dancers
Glide through a performance in the sky.
On tippy-toes,
A trillion toes
To plant their ways
On every parcel of land.

Yet, none is greater—
None is greater than the final act
As they descend the wild sky like fans.
None is greater
Than a sunny dandelion
Held within your hands.

—Joslyn Gadwah, age 16
Fifth Place Award Winner

A TRIP TO THE MAILBOX

Where does he go? I want to know—
Tiny footprints in the snow.
They come from out of nowhere,
In all that pile of snow.
They disappear to somewhere.
Where, Wee One, do you go?

The trail is long and crooked,
Up the road and over—down.
Are you very cold, dear Wee One?
Do you wear your winter gown?

Are you searching? Are you playing?
Are you hungry? Are you scared?
I'm certain I don't know.
I do know I'm excited—
Tiny footprints in the snow!

—Hester Godwin
Fifth Place Award Winner

JOCASTA'S DOMINION

A faded picture of distant friends
Staring back with sightless eyes

I remember the time . . .
Visions of once when we were closer
Where did the summer go?
Now nothing but snowfall around me.

My soul, chilled and lonely —
I sleep alone.

I can see her bright eyes
But her face is a mist

Roses bleached stark from youthful vigor
Never expressed the depth of my feelings

Ulysses gone on four winds
Jason, trophy fleece in hand, return!
Uruk shook with titans' strength
Achilles never came home.

Osiris' fingers, buried in sandy riverbank
Mjolnir rocked the Midgard Serpent
Colonus be my resting place
I never saw her again.

—Robert Long

HOPE

Reach out to those that are in need
and long for earthly peace,
by comforting in word and deed.
Let want and hunger cease.
The world belongs to everyone,
at home and far away.
Let's ask ourselves, what have I done?
What can I do today?
Forget both, hate and prejudice,
ill will, however faint.
Let hope prevail by bringing bliss
to all without restraint.

—Otto K. Dannenmann

COLORS EVERYWHERE

Red, orange, yellow
Green, purple, and blue
Colors can be pretty
A rainbow can too

Flying colors
They are so high
Flying colors
Can touch the sky

Colors colors
Above and below
Beautiful colors
A nature show

Colors are great
Do you agree too
What would we do
Without red, white and blue

—Andrea Kapellusch, age 9

RUN THE COLORADO

Run the Colorado,
    sit back and let 'er rip,
up and down the big white rapids,
    what a fascinating trip!

Through calm and lazy stretches,
    the river rolls and waves along,
the lifeline of the West,
    the Colorado sings its song.

Oh, the marvel of the canyons,
    the Colorado is the source,
you're surrounded by the beauty
    carved by wind and water's force.

Rock formations, vivid colors
    rise above the bends so wide,
with the splashing, rushing water,
    oh, the thrill of this ride!

The Colorado, Green, and San Juan
    leave their marks in colored sands,
what a journey down these rivers
    through the scenic Canyonlands!

So, have a great experience,
    where geology's so rare,
run the Colorado,
    no excitement will compare!

—Alvin K. Benson

THE KEEPERS OF THE FLAME

To those who care for the light
    That burns within the soul of man
Its flickering in the dark of night
As if by some mysterious plan.

To those who nurture its glow
Burning within each human soul
To fan and rekindle its spark to grow
Through life that takes its unknown toll

To those who keep the flame
Like the keepers of the beacon light
To guide all within its lighted frame
Past the shoals of life's darkest night.

To them, let it be known — the flame will be past
To others caring hands life has already cast.

—C.W. Lind (Jr)

APRIL CAME

April came on dancing toes.
Sprinkling green on every hedge, row on row.
Stepping lightly slow.

II

April came sandal shod.
At her passing, flowers nodded.
She even got a smile from God.

III

April came Zephyr blown.
She left a pot of violets on the hearth stone,
And picnicked on the lawn.

IV

April came but not to stay,
And she was gone on the wings of a blue jay;
Leaving daffodils on your breakfast tray.

—J. Pierritz

MEDITATIONS OF MARY ON THE RESURRECTION OF CHRIST

Behold! The heavy stone is rolled away—
    And where is He—whose body rested here?
Did thieves invade the tomb, while all was still—
    And carry off the One we loved so dear?

Where are the gentle hands we loved to touch?
    The weary feet that once we washed with tears?
The arms outstretched to comfort those who weep?
    The tender voice that wiped away our fears?

If only we had stopped the angry mob—
    Before they placed the thorns upon His brow—
Before they nailed Him to the rugged cross—
    Perhaps our Saviour would be with us now.

But wait! Whose countenance is this I see?
    The face of Christ who died on yonder hill—
Can it be true? Oh, I must hear His voice—
    And touch His wounded side to know it's real.

"Why weepest thou," I hear my Saviour say—
    My eyes look up, and I can feel His breath—
Rejoice! Rejoice! the stone is rolled away—
    The tomb is empty! Jesus conquered death!

—Melba Chaffin

WILL YOU REMEMBER ME?

Sometime when skies are clear and blue,
And flowers bloom again as new —
Only a whisper of the wind
Will remind you of me, my friend.

In summer's dry parched earth,
A thought of me may be rebirthed,
And the intense heat of sun-drenched skies
Conjures an image before your eyes.

As autumn leaves began to fall
And flutter in the breeze, I'll call,
But you'll not see my face again —
Just a cry in the moaning wind.

And on the soft, white fallen snow,
Listen carefully and you will know —
I'll be as the flakes that brush your face,
Although I am in a distant place.

—Cynthia J. Herring

FOR ONLY A MOMENT

You are the Dark Shadow
that whispers through a thousand dreams;
in my mind, breathing, touching, you
have the hand that holds even the most
frail flower — and my Heart.

You were the Warm Wind
passing through the void in my soul.
Why did you touch for only a Moment?
Like children we teetered on the edge
back and forth from fantasy to reality.
And Reality won the mighty battle
leaving me with only an image.

No longer do I sail
to the distant world that we created,
but rather, venture forth in the
Passion of life that you brought to me,
but for only a moment.

I am not afraid.

—Amy S. Mitchell

NOWHERE, REVISITED

Where is the place where dreams are born;
Where illusion becomes reality
And romantic idealism is still in bloom;
Where poverty and disease are dim memories,
The homeless housed, the hungry fed,
And wars fought with words, not weapons?
I long to be a resident of that place
Where virtue, honesty, and justice prevail;
Where there is light at the end of the tunnel.
I want to rescue damsels in distress
And slay a dragon to protect the king;
To plant a flag on uncharted land,
And climb an icy mountain to see the yeti.
Somewhere within the realm of imagination, only,
Lies a world of heroic motive and deed.
Idyllic worlds exist only in fantasy.
Trapped in the winter of broken dreams,
We survive in the shadow of the bird of death;
And here am I, still tilting at windmills,
In a world where pragmatism rules.

—Philip A. Eckerle

SUNSET REFLECTIONS

The round and glowing golden sun
Hangs warm and low above the lake
In its last bold and bright display
Before the night shall overtake,
While down below in water calm
Its glory lies in mirrored form,
And mighty spruce look silent on.

But now the sun has slipped behind
The distant rim of tree-lined shore.
The sky's aglow with wondrous hues
Of blues and rosy pinks galore,
While in unruffled water clear
The blues and pinks again appear,
And mighty spruce stand silent, near.

What beauty! And what quietness!
It soothes the soul of weariness
And lifts the heart in grateful praise
To Him Who watches all the days
O'er the creation He has made.
The Master Painter up above
Who also is a God of Love
Will always care for each of us
If we will put in Him our trust.

—L. Marie Enns

A POEM IN FOUR PARTS

1.

pearls
roundly sound placed
seedling like
(snug between index
and thumb) of red's Desire

little moons of mars
shining there like stars

2.

where out of No
came you

clear on earth
how sky in your eyes
is blue

Now tell me yellow moon—
when walking was I
showered
(the mists of seldom kisses)
Sometime within notice

I arrive soaked with your wishes

3.

If the moon was never made of cheese
(I Believe) these things can happen:
    Nothing if love is illusory
    If it is not Something

4.

Questioning the construction
of what is illusion
you breathe beside me
pulling pearls from the air
    setting them
on the tip of my tongue

—L. Elizabeth Bryant

SPRING

Winter is gone.
The ice is melting.
Birds are chirping with joy.
While children are playing
in the sun.
Parents are planting seeds
in the garden.
The clouds get dark when a
thunderstorm is near.
School is going.
The short, cold days are over.

—Jeremy Francis Posk, age 9

Love like a whitewashed fence
pale and bleached
steaked with lines
wrinkled like the face
in a permanent museum painting
not part of a show that travels
not painted by a live artist
a face weary
worn by cigarettes
all the oxygen dragged from it
the face like the love
pale and bleached
like the over-thinned whitewash
that streaks the pickets
and retains the brushstrokes

—Julie A. Bisbano

SPARKLING THINGS

Raindrops on pine needles
   after a summer shower,
Myriads of dewdrops
   on morning grass,
Delicate ice pictures
   on window panes,
Crystals in city sidewalks
   shining in the light,
Icicles hanging in frozen splendor,
   New-fallen snow,
Gems and glass
   on persons and tables,
Emotion-filled eyes of living creatures,
   Heaven.

—Norma Lou Quiring

JENNY WREN AT ONE

The fixed glazed stare
   She's gone again

Silently listening to the
faeries in her nether world

Our tiny time traveler
Her mind separate again from body

What lies in that ancient astral glen
Leave it there, wee one

Fly little bird, back to us who love
Jenn to earth, earth to Jenn

Safe
Back in your nest again

—Bettye Maglaris

RAINY DAYS

Curling up in an afghan
Sipping on chamomile tea
No wonder nobody returns borrowed books anymore.

—shari schierl

JUST ONCE

I've never won anything in my life
I've never been number one
I've had to stand back and clap the man
Stood above me on the rostrum

I've taken second place so many times before
My lucky number is two
I've been in the final, I've heard the applause
But for number one not two

But I've given my best
And I've played the game
I've given it all
So I can't complain
But just the same
I'd have loved to have won just once

—Graham Reader

THE FLESH OF LIGHT
(after a work by Butoh dancer, Mr. Masaki Iwana)

Stark and unashamed,
he dances
truth and freedom
like a Druid.

Stepping softly
into the fertile field
of my imagination,
his spirit sows a seed.

Gestation takes it on a journey
and brings it back to me in poetry—
the fruit of an encounter
with the flesh
of light.

—Catherine Urquhart

LOVING NEVER WANED

Damp, heady moisture in the fingering mist
Fast pulling at the drawstrings of my thought
As if to seal my soul to all but this
Warm web of you in which my soul is caught.

Glittering silver in such reverie's gloam
It sways my senses with a sinuous song
And gently plucks my tautened soulstrings — Lone
Instrument amid the shadows long.

Time-stilling, shattering duel in the dark
We're soul to soul, but you the bow yet wield
And touch, withdraw, then tentative' draw your mark
Of music on the tender heart I yield.

My resolute soul within your latticed lair
Soft trembles to the rhythms you have played
And seeks your soul, its resonance to ensnare
Inside the symphony our love has made . . . .

Love's melodies still glisten in the gloam
And mist enshrouds our souls, well passion-claimed,
Which lie in love-lined verses of our poem —
Sweet testament to loving never waned.

—Ann H. Womer Benjamin

JAMES DEAN

I no longer dream of taming James Dean,
or of Harley riders in black leather jackets
with reckless smiles.
I discovered one too many make-believe rebels
who were real-life sell-outs,
imitating the movies they saw.
And the country-western singers
on Dad's radio have replaced
my rock'n'roll idols.
I'm happy now with faded denim
and the people here.
My dreams are of wheatfields.
John Deere tractors,
clear summer skies,
and having a place of our own.

—Samantha Morsch

NOW THE WHOLE TOWN KNOWS

Now The Whole Town Knows
Every Scar A Public Place
Will People Wait Until I Leave The Room
Or Laugh Right In My Face
Now The Whole Town Knows
Walk Me Naked Thru The Streets
Open Season For The Taunting
Inspect My Linen & Dirty Sheets
Now The Whole Town Knows
New Pupils Different Eyes
Relishing And Reducing
Spirits Down To Size
Now The Whole Town Knows
Expose My Secrets And My Dreams
Make This A Living Autopsy
Patch Me Up At The Seams
Now The Whole Town Knows
Gossip Breeds A Different Zeal
Every Circle Is Not Round
What Is Make Believe What Is Real?
Damn This Rotten Stinking Town

—John Penn

MEANING: PERFECTION WITHOUT PORTFOLIO

You are the past, you are
all that has gone before,
yet the past belongs
not to you, but to
all who are no more.

You are the future, you are
everything yet to be,
yet the future belongs
not to you, but to eventuality.

You are the world that is,
all that there is lives in you.
Yet the now belongs not
to you, but to
all humanity.

You are the moment. Only you
fuse the was to the will be.
You are the cosmos, You are
the past, the future, but especially
you are you. And me.

And **eternity.**

—Fred Fox

Late at night,
when words won't come,
Restless, they say . . .
But I say, you.

—Denise R. Hamilton

UNKEPT SECRETS

and for all of us
who live in a world
where secrets
must be kept
to them
we are strangers.
for they will never know
that the life of most
is lived within an
extraphobic world
where people find themselves
in subways and elevators
letting out their life story
to strangers they have never met.

—Megan Botsford

THE SEASONS CHANGING

Spring, summer, winter, fall,
Oh, how I just love you all.

Oh, spring,
A time of blooming.
A time when the robins are king.

Summer, summer,
A time for the beach,
When it is hot and out of reach.

Winter, oh, winter,
Snow is here.
Soon, now, spring will be near.

Fall, fall,
Leaves fall on me.
The wind in the air
Sets them free.

Spring, summer, winter, fall
Oh, yes, Oh, yes,
I love them all!

—Gina Marie Esposito, age 10

THE GOOD LIFE

The sights and sounds of city life
Were once familiar to me,
But rural America, the country life
Is where I choose to be.

The drive down unpaved byways,
The dust that clouds the air,
It fills my eyes, but I don't care;
I feel free as a bird in flight—
In this I delight.

The open space, this quiet place
Where nature sings aloud
Where all God's creatures congregate
Where untamed creatures comprise the
only crowd
That frolics in my yard.

Take the city and all its comforts
And do with it what you will;
Take delight in the bright city lights;
I've succumbed to the country's appeal.

—Lee Esch

FENCE RIDING

Whisper spirals down corridors
bouncing off diagonals,
trapped in paralleled walls

Voice,
with her seductive soft curves,
pregnant with invitations of
shiny silk scrap metal

She rides Razors edge
down Opponents confrontations

Whispers breath
brushes the curved neck of
Voice

She tumbles from side to side
always recovering to
Perfects
balance

—Kathleen Torian-Taylor

ON MY BACK PORCH
May 1986

Can timelessness exist
if we can conceptualize it?
a weighty question I'll admit
but I have nothing but time
to ponder and sit
and send celestial bodies
spinning into the galaxy
pare the experience into poetry
and cross to safety

If poetry is a thirst
then imagination is a water hole
and imagination is a lie
drink deep
Fish for pebbles in the sky
(a lie we learn to live and die by)
Relationships change
Times change
The one constant force
Gravity on our lives is change

—Steven R. Brown

COMING HOME

The kitchen floor;
white, wounded by tracks of
a workin' man's shoes,
sighed just as she.
Heavy rain armed in disdain,
fell softer than the words
which hit so low.
The mud laid deeper than
dead and said, "No more." to
calloused hands and sweet candied
yams made to feed passion's famine.
Praising pane, the roaring rain
beat down the dream, echoed
scream and lightning eyes —
midnight cries hushed themselves
in cracks of soiled tile,
yet all the while,
weathered bevels shone
reconciled rainbows unknown,
but by countertops.

—Christine Kania

THOROUGHLY MODERN WOMAN

Try magic cremes and potent oils.
Aging won't stop, so what. Just nip and tuck.
Underwire bras that lift and separate.
Still no luck, so what. Just reconstruct.
Morning aerobics make you huff and puff.
Giving up, so what. Just liposuck.

—Leissa Remesoff

THE HIDDEN EVIL

It is a lurking shadow,
It is always there.
It puts countries at war with themselves;
It is said, it gets better generation after generation,
but in the truth it gets worse.
It is evil in its purest form,
It is hate,
It is prejudice.

—Michael A. Re, age 13

I am like what they call a man
myself
Do you know death
I do
I have seen her face to face
she is made of fire and wind
I stopped in on life to see god but he was out to lunch
I walked along a mountainside to only see black
I jumped off and landed on my feet
once again my mind leaves my body
to run free with dreams
I make love with my thoughts
my mind is now free to live in a game of passion
no man was worth the love and pain
I see you on top of emptiness.

—Brian Swan

REGRETS

Was it Sofia, Bucherest, Buda or Prague
Le Grand Metropole or Grande Continental
Where ambient walls of past clandestine dialogue
With piano and violin, old world sentimental

From communist neglect near thread bare
Still, the boulevards intriguing rendezvous
Poignant gypsy music, and Danube waltzs share
With lovers in shadowy corners imbue

A countess perhaps, once upon a time
Of rank and wealth the Reds did steal,
In competition with a raggedy mime.
Drew charcoal portraits for her meal

A grand dame perhaps, once upon a time.
From her window seat upon the boulevards pine
Of Bohemian days before thought control crime
And years plundered, proletarians brutal fine

A bitter man, young, perhaps of five and fifty
Born in the yokes of Hitler and Stalin,
A life time stolen by a state diety
Mourning of what could have been, drunk in maudlin

—Jim Dahl

SOUNDS FROM AFAR

Are sounds from afar what they really seem
    or different to each one that hears
A stream could be tears of a heartbroken girl
    who's felt pain for too many years
The sound of a bird in a distant tree
    more than happy to share his song
Might be trying to call all of his friends
    to tell them that something is wrong
The falling of leaves on a bright fall day
    makes little in the way of sound
The trees may be keeping their roots warm
    until the spring thaw rolls around
So the next time you hear noises stirring
    pay attention to what they are
They might have a hidden message
    or maybe they're just sounds from afar

—Micha Grager

POWER

Power, waiting for you to
face logic and proportion.
Let your soul find your mind
and choose a sunchild in a ceremony
of fire.
Who is Known that you know?
Closed in, filled with pain
for your satisfied hatred controlling your
unconscious world of disillusion.
Founder of faith which contains yourself
Look unto tomorrow.
Dream of your deathbed.
It's not far away.
I will take you away when you do.
I am the tear in
Your eye.
Disfiguration of your own kind.
It's time
awaken.
You're finally alive.

—Michael J. Saxton

DREAMS

Dreams
Need fuel for burning
In the soul that hope is, precarious
That lives from the flesh of life
That strives on hope, then satisfaction,
Then hope again
Do not let the flames depart
To ashes blowing in the wind
Feed the fires of hope
With feelings of truth
And reality
Reach out to touch
Do not fear the martyr's kiss
Do not run from his hand
His bloody lip can comfort you
His pallid cheek is warm
Not from hot tears
But from the glow of the fires of hope
Radiating from him
From the burning inside

—Terry L. Struse

TO TRY THIS

Dirt walked under the crooked path
    while tattered feet dirtied socks.
Stones took tumbles over toes
and stumbles rose to greet the heel.
Fall sprung upon frozen face
to see terror in the rising sun.
Resurrect again the eternal stride
from unbeaten tombs found barren.
Walk on under the pleasure road
and seek the dirt as fruitful food.
Trip to view the sun from the floor
and hope for sights unseen.
In finding destroyed gentle violence
journey with a barbed wire hat.
Walk alone as he starving was unfound
and lie on your feet to gain discovery.

—Robert J. King

BE NOT AFRAID

When the storms of life are raging
    as a wild, tempestuous sea,
So afraid, I seek your presence,
    praying earnestly to Thee.

But the night-time slowly lingers
    as the raging billows roll,
Overwhelmed with utter darkness,
    engulfed in sadness of the soul.

When my spirit is o'er shadowed
    and my heart is filled with fear,
When the night of death comes calling
    You have promised to be near.

Take my burdens, lift them from me
    and bid all my sorrows fade,
Let me hear You sweetly speaking,
    "It is I, be not afraid."

—Ruth C. Demetral

ICICLE, ICICLE

Icicle, Icicle,
Your figure is so crystal clear
You fill us with a lot of cheer.
You hang from a ledge
Looking like a clear pie wedge.

The heap of snow under you
Is piling up to reach you.
Somewhere in between
To share one common dream.

To live contentedly
Watching each other grow,
and some of us are
looking up from below.

None of us are too proud
to make a friend,
We'll make time to change our range
and find each other in the end.

*Dedicated to Mrs. JoAnn Clark Landis.
My 6th grade Teacher.*

—Malika Kapadia, age 11

MASQUE

In the fog I see fairy folk
Dancing on the city streets
Under electric oval moons.
Wind whipped, on top of
Dumpsters, they spin and twist.
They fly on delicate fluttering wing
Flinging confetti composted
Of last week's discarded trash.

Maybe, under harsher light, they'd be
Exposed
As leaves and as wastepaper;
But, under the glamour of the fog
Which turns unwashed transients
Into fallen princes and
Riot architecture into
The fortresses of Ogres,
The fairies bend to cast their magic.

—Varda Mercurio

DARKNESS AND DESPAIR

Tonight I am lost in fear,
    my heart beats thunder fast.
I see the darkness coming,
    any breath may be my last.
I feel you but cannot see you,
    my eyes are blinded with tears.
Each one that falls to the ground
    is silent and disappears.
The light, the dark they tear at me,
    each for grasp of my soul.
Pierce the void and reach for me,
    help me toward my goal.
Unite my heart with yours again,
    forever more as one.
Bear witness as a new day starts,
    our love — the rising sun.

—J.E. Turachak

MEMORIES INVASION

The horror of war
    explodes again
in my brain
and I can not imagine
what road
I have to run on.

The desert invades your memories
mixes death with flowers,
breeds bitterness ideas
about Saddam potshots.
You have to decide
which way you choose
if you could control
your chopping sea.

Before my last trip
in the sand ocean,
a black crow told me:
you would lose
your steps
for tomorrow.

—Mohammed A. Al-Fequi

BLACK

Darkness of the mind reflected on the outside . . .
not a forced darkness, but darkness by choice,
overshadowing those hidden emotions that must not
be revealed to a world that thrives on the shattering
of emotions and dreams . . .
The color of a People, a Race,
in a land of poverty and strife . . . invaded by another
which murderously strives for superiority disregarding
the fact that skin color does not exclude anyone from
the Human Race . . .
Those who have labeled this Color due to terrible deeds
and actions . . .
those who even go as far as killing their own People,
bringing shame upon its name,
acting proud of a Heritage which they've helped to
destroy.

—MeLinda Smith

RESILIENCE

Do you not bend
in the doorways between the worlds?
For the worlds are always present
    and ofttimes in dreams doors open.

And when you are certain,
    can you not take
        the outer edge of your wound
            and insure itself healing throughout?

When you pierce a web of harmfulness
    with bubbles of joy
        are you not living
            full of power in thought?

To be unbending in thought
    would deny the doorways
        their chance to be opened.

—K.A. Oesterreich

balkan queen

shadow cast upon my door
barefoot . . . dancing in my soul.
pen and journal . . . clutched in hand
unframed wisdom . . . bridging lands.

quest for truth . . . set her apart
betrayed homeland etched in heart.
ethnic revenge . . . horrors past
her shattered nation . . . an outcast?

east-west destined to collide
on bloody bridge of genocide.
far east led her to unfold
prodigal son . . . in search of gold.

blood lines . . . archives . . . reconciled
prince of balkans . . . gulag child?
prayer revealed impostors since
west unthaws exiled prince.

horizon vanished in the storm
through fog . . . we lost her flickering form.
barefoot . . . dancing in my soul
. . . a mere shadow upon my door.

dedicated to miki and ruth . . .
who understood . . . $e=mc^2$

—sonia wolff

FADED SUNS

Look at the sky, as blue as can be.
Look at the people who live in harmony.

Look at the flowers, watch them grow,
look into the forest and spot a doe.

Look at the trees, watch them sway.
Look at the bees, they buzz away.

Look at the grass, so sparkling sweet,
look at the cows—watch them eat.

Look at my heart and see what's inside,
because in my heart I have my pride.

Look at the sun, watch it fade,
look at the Lord and what He made!

—Nicole Kristal, age 10

MY RIVER

From a land of bad dreams
    The waif like creature ran
Outside its bounds to a river
Where laughter slashes the sand

To her ears came tinkling echoes
And its cadence eased her pain
First muted low, then it rose
Blissfully falling again and again

Haunting melodies of background music
Swell to love's impetuous crescendos
And sweetly scent a breathless magic
Needed like water to a thirsty rose

Along the shores are pearls of harmony
Who escape their shells in joyful chorus
Bathed by sunshine removing anxiety
They become the dry tears of great fondness

To bells ringing in a castle band
Beat reminders throbbing in origin
To phantoms of a far away land
Spinning nightmares of unworthy vision

—Dorothy Vanovcan

THE WORLD IS AT YOUR FEET

Step outside your body
    and take a look around
Isn't it ironic
    the many things you've found?

They say life is what happens
    when you're making other plans
When you come back to your own life
    it seems another man's.

You can achieve so many goals
    never thought to be in reach
When you put aside your worries
    the wonders life can teach.

To open your eyes and realize
    the world is at your feet
Is such an awesome feeling
    if you're determined to not be beat.

As you face new challenges
    you put your knowledge through the test
The greatest test is life itself
    so always do your best.

—Candace Gano

KONA MANA

Morning swept in across glossy waters
    and pushed the night of my dreams
    into yesterday's doubts.

Towering clouds float up to me,
    press their moist lips against mine,
    and pause to hold me in soft repose;

Then wisp away my cares one more time,
    and roll me in sun-splashed hope
    of a day too new not to play with,
    at least one more time.

Mahalo, Kona Mana!

—R. Wayne Parlier

BURNING MAZE

Angry heart of passion
filled with jealous rage
Words that bring disaster
caught inside the burning maze.

Endless well of darkness
filling my heart and soul
Nothing more to hold on to—
no future to behold.

Stairway to nowhere
winding 'round and 'round
Ever-growing frustration
beating me to the ground.

Can't erase the memories
or this feeling in my soul
Hoping maybe things will change
as the days go by unknown.

Walk around in silence
every night and day
No windows here or doorways
here, inside this burning maze . . . .

—Dana M. Garton

A MOTHER'S LOSS

Love growing beneath my breast
Throbbing sounds of happiness
Flutters of life deep inside
Abounding ecstasy and pride
Planning, hoping for the future
This tiny soul that I must nurture
Unique and blessed from above
Full of talent and God's love
In this world of pain and strife
You brought joy into my life
My Child, my Teacher, my Best Friend
Why so soon, must it all end
Taken away in your prime
Loaned from God, for such a short time
Loved by all who ever knew you
Lives so changed for the better, too
My heart aches for you each day
A pain that never goes away
Somewhere in time and space we'll meet
But for now, that's bittersweet

*Dedicated to the memory of,
Lieutenant Thomas E. House USNA,
a Navy Pilot downed June 30, 1989.*

—Carol House

MOTHER

Spring was her time of year
and those near her
learned to dance on needlepoints
and wear the clouds as halos
in their hair.

—V.R. Wig

KAWAI

Sitting on the long hard bench
Staring, as if color blind
Remembering a music box
Dancing through my mind.
My fingers, stiff and bored
Give no equal sound
of what my mother could give to me
on such an open ground.

—Angela Holloway Horton

LITTLE SISTERS

They are pests,
but of course,
they're the best.

They smell,
can't spell,
and always tell.

They eat your favorite food,
the stuff that tastes good,
which is part of childhood. I guess?

They're not always bad,
but sometimes make you feel sad.

Most the time I'm mad,
that they're my sisters.

But when I am down,
they're always around,
to bring me the sunshine I need.

Sisters

—Marie E. Morgan

SIMILES OF MY GRANDMOTHER

Her hair is one shade darker
than the grass in the Savannah
her eyes are like marbles
as black as the trees
in her backyard at night.

Her skin is as brown as dirt
as soft as clay
she likes to sing a lot
she sings very, very good
so good that her voice
is as smooth as leather.

She is as tall as a highchair
and a half
as tall as an alligator's length
she's as tall as me.

Dedicated to my Grandmother,
Earsie, she inspires me to
write poems & short stories.
I want to be like my Grandmother
in so many ways.

—Teoma Taylor, age 11

WORLD YOUNG, WORLD OLD, IT MATTERS NOT TO ME

When the world was young,
And the colors of the earth bright,
The song was quick and soft on my tongue,
And my eyes were filled with light.

Now, the world is old,
My tongue no more with song;
The colors of the earth are cold
And the shadows in my eyes long.

World young, world old, it matters not to me;
Colors bright or colors cold, what is there to see?
Song or no song, the words are no longer free.

Eyes go bright, eyes go dark, no more the sun;
Tongue quick, tongue dead, all the words unspun.
Day and evening were, the night has begun.

—Sheridan Fonda

FORGOTTEN DREAMS

Walter Mitty-ing I was superb at —
I had ambition by the yard.
All too soon reality arrived;
Young dreams, contrived schemes fell hard.

It was the age of innocence.
Life's fancies were pure and free.
Suddenly the time of illusions was gone;
Age apprehended dreams' vitality.

Life's mundane-ness deflowered youth;
Castles in the air were shattered.
Ethereal plans for wealth and fame
Lay at my feet — broken, forlorn, tattered.

Deep within my heart of hearts
Forgotten fantasies I cherished and held
Continue to live — reminders of schemes,
Wishing-on-star dreams — that always cast their spell.

—Jan Widman

REMEMBER YOUR ROOTS

Black Brothers and Sisters, Remember Your Roots
By starting with Slavery, we elude the truth
The truth begins on African land
From Kings and Queens came the Black Man
From the Pyramids, to Philosophy and math too
African Creations through and through
Our Ancestors gave us a legacy to keep
To find the truth you first must Seek
Seek out the Knowledge and the light
Then you'll begin to Know what's right
look for the wisdom that lives in the Past
Through Knowledge of self our race will last
Find the books that speak the truth
The African Man must find his roots
Then Remember the Slave ships that brought us here
And Remember the Cross that our forefathers bore
They fought for their lives and died to be free
The struggle must continue with you and me
We must be the truth that restores all trust
For Knowledge is Power and it begins with us!

Dedicated to "Mother," the strongest, most
powerful and surviving woman that I know. For she
is the root and the life of our family.

—Margo Hinton

DANDELION (LION'S TOOTH)

Dandelion, so bright and yellow;
  Shining towards heaven, all aglow;
Golden blossoms are from tiny seeds;
  Who said this flower is a weed?

—Ruth Wylie Milburn

SPAT

Violence in
unending fashion;

  The cruel glitter
of stainless steel;

  They're arguing over
whose turn it is
to buy the next round:

  These are the makings of war.

—Joseph F. Guzman II

THE FOOL

It breaks my heart to see
  your soul weep with sorrow,
When you are young and in love,
you don't think of tomorrow.
Love, innocent and gentle,
like a dewdrop in the spring,
Your spouse gets the feeling
he has to swing.
He turns into a monster,
has tantrums and fits,
His guilt turns to hate,
he loses his wits.
He sold his soul
for a cheap affair,
gave the best of himself
to Lucifer.
Satan is delighted,
his game is done,
destroyed another soul,
and thinks he has won.

—Hedy Schwarzhaupt Jex

KEEP ME SWEET AS I GROW OLD

Lord keep me sweet as I grow old
  And things in life seem hard to bear,
When I feel sad and all alone
  And people do not seem to care.

O keep me sweet when time has caused
  This body which is now so strong,
To droop beneath its load of years
  And suffering and pain have come.

And keep me sweet when I have grown
  To worry so at din and noise,
And help me smile while I watch
  The noisy play of girls and boys.

Help me to remember how that I
  When I was younger than today,
And full of life and health and joy
  Would romp and shout in happy play.

Help me to train my heart each day
  That it will only sweetness hold.
And as the days and years roll on
  May I keep sweet as I grow old.

—Drice Dykhouse

A CHILD OF COLOR

Christmas! A time of cheer!
  Holly-green and berries-red!
Mistle-toe and hearts-a-glow!
Glimmering-tinsel — glistening-icicles and
Snow-a-flurry!
Gold and emerald and blue — silver and
Red too!
The life a babe for us is bred.
Who wouldn't like Christmas?
Unless — it's Easter or Hannukah instead!

—Joyce Anna Jess

MIRACLES

Clouds drifting through the sky
Sound of the infant's first cry . . .

Waves crashing against the sand
The touch of a tiny hand . . .

Butterflies floating on a breeze
A gentle nuzzle of newborn babies . . .

Sun setting on the mountain beyond
Mother and child creating a bond . . .

Of all the things on this earth
Nothing can compare to the miracle of birth.

—Kelly Critzer

THE NIGHT

Oh! What peace, the night is coming,
  Greet me soon thou gentle winds.
Blow away and cease this heated throbbing
That dwells like darkness within.

Bright, opal moon above me now,
Turn away your all-knowing eye
And send your stars out to comfort those
Whose hearts have been broken like mine.

Send me sleep in your fragranced wind
And rest in your sweetened song
Lead me away into my dreams
Where now I must belong.

—Sara Binder

TAILOR OF MY SORROW

How do you mend heartache and woes,
  As you would your tattered old clothes?
Show me the way in which it is done.
You with the expertise, I with none.

To mend my heart, shall I sew and darn
Like a worn out sock, with skeen of yarn?
Or, with some fabric nice and new,
Fashion another to replace the blue?

For the part of me that was a glutton,
Simply replace it like a lost button?
Perhaps, like laundering a shirt,
Wash away the pain and the hurt?

Tell me how to forget completely.
Do I just fold it away nice and neatly?
Place my feelings away in a drawer
And close them up forevermore?

I am a seamstress, well you know,
Yet, this broken heart I cannot sew.
Your secrets, I have need to borrow
Since you were the tailor of my sorrow.

—Cynthia Warren

OUT THE WINDOW

I look out the window
And see the snow coming down
I sit and wonder
As it covers the ground

I look out the window
And see the trees all bare
I sit and wonder
Why they are there

I look out the window
And see the snow start to melt
I sit and wonder
About how I just felt

I look out the window
And see the grass all green
I sit and wonder
About what I have just seen

—Mike Turdo

UNDERTOW

O cease the mournful calling, for
I'll ne'er return again
To salt mists wildly blowing
From deep waves heavy churning,
And sailors' ceaseless struggle
With the winds and fog and rain.

Nor tempt me with the sunset
Of a calm and peaceful day:
The time of heaven's wedding
Of the sun with golden sea;
Or charm me with night's silver
Kiss to try to make me stay.

Your mystic power cannot command
My soul forever more;
The restlessness and yearning
Of parting and returning;
The spell must cease its beck'ning
For I've found my peace at shore.

—Robert Kirk Jones

'Tis well, I do tell thee,
But sky's tears know the truth.
With the shadows that watch me,
They laugh at my youth.

For my head is quite heavy
With unfinished dreams,
And all that was giv'n me,
Is not all that it seems.

Oh my fears, they consume me,
Lest my spirit be poor,
For I want them to know me,
When my breath is no more.

Thus I strive with great vigor,
That one heart I may touch,
So my memory may linger,
And my life be worth much.

*Dedicated to Scott, my love, whose
devotion, support, and understanding
inspire me to pursue my dreams.*

—Karen Ann Crewe

THOUGHTS UPON A ROOFTOP

Sleep in peace, My Darling, under the glow of the moon
Let the soft sound of Angel's wings, be your lullaby
Let your dreams fly like the graceful swallow
Safely landing in the arms of the sunrise.
—Elizabeth C. Willis

AGAINST THE SKY

A sphere of light silhouetting against a sea of aqua
A beacon of trust guiding us to worlds around us
An unknown place hovering above us
A heavenly mass lifting the curtain of darkness
An incredible first step teaching us to believe
A dream remaining above us, tried and true
A fool would only take for granted the sight of the moon
—Kimberly Glazewski, grade 12

AFTERTHOUGHTS

Do not come sadly to my graveside and cry,
I am not there, but with clouds in the sky.

You will feel me in rays of the morning sun,
See me playing with deer as they leap and run.

In the delicate touch of a snowflake on your face,
Feel my arms in a gentle summer breeze's warm embrace.

In the happy trill of a bird's melody of songs,
On a silent Sunday morning as the church bell dongs.

In the twinkle of a moonbeam on a starry night,
Or see my shadow beside you walking softly in moonlight.

Hearing clearly my voice in the hum of misting rain.
Singing to you softly as I whisper your sweet name.

You may catch me in my daughter's laugh or smile
Be-still and feel my presence, if only for a little while.

Do not come dear one to my grave and weep.
You can always find me, there in your heart asleep.

—Joyce Lane Wade

LOVE IS A GIFT

Love is a gift of fairytale things,
Balloon bouquets, tied with heart strings.
Dancing hearts — a celebration of love,
Through stardust filled skies,
A gift from above.

Softly, you reach for my hand —
Our souls were united; the start of a lifelong plan.
Warmth engulfs mind, body and soul,
A waltz through time as our love continued to grow.
Watercolor sunsets, my prince swept me away,
On bars of light and bouts of child's play.

Through laughter, tears, love and harmony combined,
Your strong arms around me as our souls entwine.
Ticklish laughter,
Husband, lover and best friend
A rainbow of memories, to where there's no end.

A walk through life, hand in hand,
Forever at your side,
How incredible God's plan!!
—Ramona Buchlmayer

A REVOLUTION OF MYTH

The blazoned scale of the mermaid was singed
    By the tides of humanity, bereft of will.
As the wave approached the woman cringed—
Her cart left broken, raped of its weal.
A stranded vassal of ancient pride
On an island slowly fading 'neath the gale.
To the sky she spoke in broken stride
Of wasted lore lost in life's tale.
"Think of me Please," was all she could say
As her figure was engulfed and washed away.
A shard of cloth, a piece of gold, a moment's thought . . .
All that was left of our mythic plot.
An echo in the wind and a small youth's dreams:
It begins again, reality — not what it seems.

      —Paul D. Ellis

CHILDREN

The last true evil ones; children of the dark,
    Seek not knowledge, but madness cold and stark.
Always destroying, forever suppressing; thoughtless of the heart,
Stalling, denying—fearful to embark.

The last true silent ones; children of the deep,
Love not laughter; silently do they seek.
Always lurking; forever stalking—suddenly they leap,
Slashing, tearing—never do they weep.

The last true wild ones; children of the land,
Seek not capture but freedom for a span.
Always running; forever fleeing—finding peace where they can,
Searching, reaching—never can they stand.

The last true free ones; children of the sky,
Seek not breezes; but wild currents rising high.
Always windward; forever seaward do they fly,
Gliding, never falling—even when they die.

The last true pure ones; children of the light,
Seek not riches; only a glorious robe of white.
Always patient, forever faithful, with their goal in sight,
Longing for eternity—infinitely bright.

      —Steven Wendall Moore

THE HUMAN CONDITION
(A ZERO SUM GAME?)

Why is it so the elite and very rich rarely go
    From the blind side of self to admit and (truly) know
They are the power and arbiters of human fate:
For the poor made weak, whose destiny is the mad gate
Of all the world sorrow and the "Weltschmertz"* of pain outside
The bright Light of hope for those millions so sad denied?
Are they humans of mean intent who care not a whit
For those apart the burgeoning whorl of power consummate?

In towers of concrete, steel and glass — and rich consort,
They see not the plight of those without a Caring Port.
Yet on the merry-go-round they go, "reaching for the stars"
And blind success, devoid of heart (a wealth of loving scars);
While even those who *Love* in vain, in honest Giddiness,**
Find the self fulfilled in Life's full cup of happiness.

* *Weltschmerz: n. (Cassell's German Dictionary: weariness of life, pessimistic outlook, romantic discontent); sentimental pessimism or melancholy over the state of the world.*

Love: Love in its largest sense.

***giddy: etym. "possessed by God"; inconsistent; fickle, frivolous, flighty, heedless.*

      —James Buckner McKinnon

COME SWEET SLEEP

Come, sweet sleep,
    Visit me.
Lift my weary body
    Into your realm
Where pain is barred.

Come, gentle sleep,
    Flood my mind
And wash out the worries
    Of the day.

Come, renewing sleep,
    Revive my troubled spirit
With the cool breeze
    From your ocean of reserve.

Come, penetrating sleep,
    Reach into my soul
Mend it
    And make it whole.

      —Elisabeth M. Savich

IN LOVE'S MIND

I loved you once,
    but that was long ago,
when we were both young,
and naive.

And even though it's been forever,
since the last time your lips have
touched mine,

I find there isn't a single day,
I don't think of you,
in some small way.

Yes, I know we've both changed,
that nothing can be done,
to make us the way that we were.

But sometimes at night,
when I'm all alone,
I wish you were with me,
and not her.

      —Victoria Hill

INSPIRED RAPTURE

I feel one
    with rain
it caresses my awaiting skin
like a welcomed lover's kiss
it consoles me beautifully
in my resigned solitude
it comforts and soothes me
in my loneliness
its earthy fragrance
so sweet and enchanting
engulfs and intoxicates me
its crystal tears mingle
with mine to create a oneness
that ignores both time and place
its touch so infinitely gentle
so blissfully cool
lingers . . . long remembered
on the eternal landscape
of my soul, I become one
with rain

      —Barbara Coleing

I felt the artist's palm
holding the poised brush
prepared for madness
reason worn as a cloak
fool the ones who
let the cloak wear them

felt the drive to spill
seed more precious
than sperm
gives more raw nerved
awe
blind men rise at morning
fully dressed
moor their thoughts to trappings

through an artist's palm
allowed unreasoning
the universe moves into itself.

—SJones

THE VOYAGE

We sail through endless days,
stars shine like eyes,
the black night shines.

The moon leaves silver dreams,
our dreams are deep,
as we travel the seas,
through the night.

The earth we long to see,
of sapphire days,
and land blown winds.

We long to see the trees,
feeling the gentle breeze,
silver starlight,
breaks through the dark night.

So we set our sails high,
look into the night,
our swords raised high,
as we sail the seven seas.

—Johnny Laronn Williams

TO MY LOVE

Look at me, who am I
Not just someone walking by
Always listening for a song
Doing right against the wrong

Chasing dreams from the night
Darkness changes into light
Beauty exists all around
In the sky or on the ground

With your thoughts create a tale
Flying fish or large blue whale
Mountain peaks reach the sky
Hawks and eagles soaring high

People rushing here and there
Never taking time to share
Work from morning till the dawn
Pictures of the rainbow drawn

Here I am in your space
Not so distant of a place
What I have belongs to you
With all my love in all I do

—Nick Hammerschmidt

GROWING OLD

Suddenly I've grown old,
The days are long and the nights are cold.
Empty chairs and vacant places
From the scenes are gone familiar faces.
Autumn days kissed by the sun
So swiftly passed one by one.
In evening when shadows fall,
I wait for footsteps down the hall,
To find them crushed beneath the years,
Leaving behind their trail of tears.
Embers now are burning low,
I turn to run but nowhere to go—
All my dreams in ashes lie,
Everything too soon must die.
The night comes down like falling rain,
All around I feel the pain,
Oh what loneliness engulfs my soul,
For suddenly I've grown old.
I toy with memories and thrills of yesterday
But 'til I grow much stronger I'll store them all away.

—Martha J. Nissen

ENCOURAGING TEAPOT

I had been watching TV since about a quarter of two,
When I realized I was hungry for some salad and Tofu.
I went into the kitchen and began to search around,
But nothing seemed to please me, nothing that is I found.
I ran across some olives, dried carrots too, I think,
Maybe bean sprouts, and something small and pink.
There was celery and yogurt and dried left over peas,
Raisins and prunes and something marked lite cheese.
I opened up the cupboard and was very sad to see,
Seven boxes of crackers staring back at me.
I went into the teapot to see if there was cash,
For the diet I had been on I was surely going to crash.
Five dollars and a quarter was all that I could find,
As a hamburger and french fry flashed across my mind.
I knew I should do it, for I had lost eight pound or so,
But my stomach said, all heck, put on your coat, let's go.
I got the food and stuffed myself before I could bat an eye
I loved the taste, loved the smell, I was on a burger high.
I know I broke my promise, but I swear, it's my last time
And I'll never feed the teapot another red thin dime.

—J.M. Bennett Hammerberg

LIFE'S PICTURES

The motto of the class of '43 was
"Life is a Picture, Paint it well."
And I'm sure we all intended to try.
That year we were in the middle of a war,
and we jumped in feet first, our new and shiny
sword held high.
"Remember Pearl Harbor" was our battle cry!

Our paint was spilled, red as blood it was.
or was it blood, red as paint.
Our canvas was torn, the scars we carry yet.
Where once we dreamed of pictures tall and wide
we are now content to paint a small one,
one we can finish in a single day.

Some days are smooth as a beach, washed clean with every tide.
Some days seem all uphill, but oh the joy when we reach the top
and see the wonders on the other side.
Keep your canvas tight and keep your brushes clean
And paint life's picture well.
You will be so much richer, tho' n'er a one you sell.

—Grady Du Bose

JENNY

Elfin water sprite of golden summer days,
Brightly colored rainbow appearing through the haze,
Golden ballerina in a gauze of misty blue,
Poignant silver tears on a fresh cheek, too.
All of these are you, O light and lovely child,
Spinning out your dreams both innocent and wild.
Too soon, the world will claim you from your golden reverie,
But, I will treasure most these days with you beside the sea.

—Jean Carr Smith

SETTLE DOWN

Uncle, Uncle, settle down, way down.
Way down somewhere, where you can have some kind of peace.
Way down where there's no more crying and sleepless nights.
Somewhere, where there's no more crimes to be in sight.
Uncle, I really wanted to see you have some peace, I hated
to see you suffering.
Now I don't have to see you suffer anymore.
I know that you are in the hands of the mighty Lord.
We'll all miss you, but we'll let you have your peace,
because you have earned it.

—Misha Renee' Williams, age 10

INCANTATION

Come to me in life as you have in dreams —
Come to me and let us lose ourselves in dancing
as we did on the mountain.
And let us drench ourselves again in sweet madness,
in music and summer air.

I'll stand on the sidewalk waiting,
in the heat that radiates off the pavement and the brownstones
I'll appear willowy, burnished, at ease
when you drive up to meet me
And once I see your face and touch your skin
I'll praise the month of May.

Come to me —
Come East to see me —
Come, and live my pretty dream.

—Elena Rockmann

HER

High in the Ural steppes where foxes have lairs for a thousand
Years in the Chair of Ancients a man looked out from
Alma-Ata into Deep Night   The exultant moan of a woman
   Turned the breeze into a storm, mounting torrents up to the
Heavens   Still he — Xian-hi — bore the sign in his flesh,
   A loadstone for the eastern pole that troubled him right
From left in the Orient.

Here — a timepiece stunned on the edge — he rested between
   East and West willing his shadow back so many degrees
Before the Daystar declined by the lines on the dial already
   Gone down   Here lived he sentenced to life — the way he
Was alive — where wisdom was not swallowed up all his days
   Of like adorning, in gold, of gold

   — Taking root downward —
   — Bearing fruit upward —

In the space of his mind.

—Tabitha Grail

SILVER UTOPIA

The hot sun
Beats down
Icicles
Turn
To

—Krista Chaney

LOVE NEVER DIES

Love never dies
it may sleep and
it may dream.
It may wilt and
it may change
FROM FACE to FACE
and LIFE to LIFE
Through pleasure, pain
and strife,
Love Never Dies

—Shawn W. Francis

FIRST CHILD

warm
against my breast
crying—needing
taking—giving
at once all things
      and all demanding
soon first smile
      first tooth
      first step
none ever like
      first child

—Donna Reidland

THOUGHTS IN WINTER

Nature's artist, Jack Frost,
has just made his debut.
With his etchings on windows
— spectacular view.

The soft fluffy snow
falling all through the night.
Has covered brown earth
with a blanket of white.

The ice on the pond
is aglitter and bright.
With the prospect of fun
children's eyes are alight.

The return of these cycles
coming year after year.
Gives a feeling of comfort
of Joy and good cheer.

For just as this season
follows after bright fall
Just as surely, we reason,
spring will too, come to call.

—Helen M. Evans

POEM TO MYSELF

I sit
   by the river
and write
poems on my feet,
I stand and
   walk on them
until they bleed,
and
   if the sun should
go down on them,
I will wait for
   the moon
to heal them.

—Joe Camp III

THE CONSTANT

Unicorns,
   the heart of a
watermelon and
you.
Swift and slow
things,
all things
living, and
you.
The sea,
changing of the
moon, and
pebbles
that little boys
throw
trying to reach the
other side,
and always
you.

—Margaret M. Dial

A CHILD'S UNIVERSE

A childhood forgotten,
  in a father's dream.
A sheet of cotton,
  with feet through a seam.

Deathbed's playground,
  with laughter and play.
Innocent and sound,
  life's own way.

Mom and Oma,
  first not second.
An admired aroma,
  a friendly beckon.

Memories forlorn,
  finally found.
Brothers torn,
  but spiritually bound.

Flashback terrors,
  life's own sorrow.
The cross' bearer,
  will live tomorrow!

—Peter F.X. Kuegle

The green lush
   Absorbing the sun's gleaming, golden beams
So quiet
   So peaceful, as though never knowing the meaning of war.

The trees, gossiping among themselves
   Of a hundred years of history.

As peaceful as her fight to stay alive
   Against man and his destruction.

—Josh Virostko, age 13

THE MOST BEAUTIFUL POEM

Of all that I have come to know
  You are the one poem for which I can find rhyme or reason.
You exist, at times, as you are,
And at others as reflections of my imagery.
And the mystery of you;
That which you do not know of yourself,
Is what I write—what I feel—
The cause of my life and breath.
And of all the poetry that I have ever
felt, spoken, imagined, or written—
The most beautiful poem of all
is you.
The one that I cannot touch
because you are too near;
Or that I cannot write,
because there are no words.
This is for you to know that when I am in some other world,
And you can feel me with the turning of each page,
That you are the poetry within my heart—
And the verse within my soul.

Dedicated to my family and to T.G.,
you are seeing my dreams come true.

—Angela Kelly

THE GHOSTS IN THE WOODS

I stare into those dark shadowed corners
  at the edge of a long ago yard;
The ones hidden by blurred veils of cobwebs
   where the woods remain in brown and green profusion,
   wild splashes of deep purple violets
   and bright oranges of a setting sun.

A short distance into the fragrance of leaves underfoot
   stand the rotting planks of childhood castles,
   imaginary dragons sleeping, waiting, dreaming;
   holding forever the laughter of eight year olds.

Grandma's echo whispers heavily on the wind
   to the quiet tune of a drifting hymn.
Her smile warms as I catch the twinkle deep within her soul.

Babies wait behind reflections from mirrors that don't exist;
   waiting to wake the dragons of yesterday,
   rebuild the castles and pick the violets,
   return to the woods with a newborn innocence
   and grab the laughter that roams the shadows.

HOLD TIGHT—those ghosts who linger there
   and *know*—that *RESTING* now—a place *WE* called *OUR* "Camelot."

Dedicated to my brother, Jim, who saw more of me in this
poem than most people see looking at me. Though he's miles
away, and we don't often get to see each other, he's
always in my thoughts and prayers.

—Shey

DUANE THE CHRISTMAS DONKEY

The night breeze stirred and the song of a bird, were part of a sign on high
The mountains slept as the daylight crept off in the western sky

Where shepherds keep their flocks of sheep and all others rest till dawn
A sudden sight was a star so bright as if darkness were totally gone

The wise men knew and the shepherds too, what had taken place
A king was born in a baby's form to save the human race

In a manger bare in the cold night air, the Babe was without covers
So the word was sent of the child's lament in a bed where the bright star hovers

On a slope nearby under starry sky, grazed Duane with his load of hay
God's message said, seek the baby's bed and this Duane did obey

When the family saw the gift of straw, they knew why Duane was there
The straw made a bed 'round the baby's head and they rejoiced in thankful prayer

As Duane too adored this tiniest Lord his reward was more than you think
The Christ Child's smile beamed for many a mile, but Duane got a loving WINK!

—Hugh T. Boland

PORTRAIT OF AN UNBROKEN SPIRIT

Gently, gracefully poised and ready for battle,
Sparkling child of the Universe,
The night has already made its mark.
The wound has begun to shape you brittle.
Fear and scrutiny have all too soon devoured the wide-eyed innocence;
Reticence and ridicule now your guarded guides.
The dance of angels, turned the stance of demons
Clasped firmly in the cobwebs of your mind.

Speak to me, oh lovelorn one, of secrets
That bind the very essence of your soul;
And scream the silent sound of fallen tear drops.
Allow the living passion to unfold.

There's safety here beneath the weeping willows.
There are bridges back to trust for broken starts.
There's hope and joy and life and love eternal.
With outstretched hands . . .
I offer you my heart.

Dedicated lovingly to Sarah Imajene Bales

—Pat Ellin Lakin

A WORD TO A FRIEND

Don't fall in love my friend, you see
It doesn't pay.
It always causes broken hearts, it happens everyday.
You wonder where he is all night,
you wonder if he's true.

One moment finds you happy, next one finds you blue.
When he's near you, your knees grow weak, your heart begins to DANCE.
Your world revolves around him.

BOY, THERE IS NOTHING LIKE ROMANCE
and then it starts, you don't know why.
But you see my friend you're losing him
It never turns out right!!
Yes, true love may be fine,
But the price you pay is high.

IF YOU HAD TO CHOOSE BETWEEN LOVE AND DEATH
I am sure I would choose to die.
So when I say don't fall in love,
you'll be hurt before you're through!

You see my friend I ought to know
I FELL IN LOVE WITH YOU!!

—Hazel Jones

27

THE WEIGHT

As I face the mirror
I love the line on the right side of my face
I press my finger into it; along it
It's a wavy motion
It's not the same on the left side
Because my right cheek
Rests nightly on my pillow

—Lisa Garofalo

BEING A GUITARIST IS LIKE.

Feeling the music beat start in my feet
The rhythm in my soul.
The songs I play for you one day
Will tell you of my role . . .
The Hours of my Learning
Are heard by you in a song . . .
It's just a part of life
It lets your day move on.

The movement of my fingers
Plays out a musical tune . . .
They play of joy and sadness
Beneath a mid-night moon.
So if you want to be happy
And not feel so beat . . .
Just dos-a-dos your partner and
Ask her please get off your feet.

—Ben Larsen

A TWO-WAY STREET

This freedom thing is a two-way street.

I will never be free from you,
Until you are free from me.

Me the serf, you the master is the reality,
Which kept both of us enslaved throughout history.

Years of chaos, death, agony and pain,
The vicious destruction among men is madly insane.

Past generations somehow did not have the will,
The wretchedness they left is with us still.

Keep it the way it is a few more centuries,
Our children, and theirs, will be the casualties.

Right now, let's rise up with courageous determination
And totally eradicate this scourge from our great nation.

Completely free from you is my human right to be,
Only then will you be, truly, free from me.

Lest your superiority complex versus my captivity,
May keep us both in bondage for eternity.

What our posterity needs, ancestors denied you and me,
The freedom to travel on this two-way street.

Ultimately free, from each other, in peace and harmony.

*Dedicated to my seven living children, fourteen
grand-children, one great grand-child, and Jay
Brooks Hickey, whose soul God reclaimed in infancy.
Also, Malcom J. Green, Shawndeeia L. Drinkard,
Forrest L. Green Sr., the late Clarence E. Green,
Lillie V. Grigsby and Joe W. Ward.*

—Ardelphia Hickey

THE VIRGIN

The virgin kneels before
the altar of the Lord
on blood-red carpet
dressed in white.

Silver blessings from above
fall like rain
on bread and wine
to cast the magical spell.

With tentative steps does she approach
the cup so freely offered, and
from it she takes a sip.

"Be not afraid," she hears,
then into rapture's chamber
she disappears.

—Miriam Pugliese

BIOCHEMIST

You might call me an explorer
Of molecules, and adorer
Of Life's complexity;
I seek, I probe, I synthesize,
I postulate and analyze
And quell perplexity.
Some say that I deconsecrate,
Others that I risks create;
They strive to end my quest;
They do not see that Truth is there
Amongst the molecules from where
God's light is manifest;
For there's no more sublime a place
Than where metabolism's grace
Prevails in wonderment;
Where Beauty's face is palpable
And human ailments soluble.

—Frank Ashall

PASSIONATA

Sundrenched bodies intertwine
on shimmering gold, sunheated
beaches sparkle, dance, in
syncopation with whitecaps on
the water playing, as the Sun
sprays itself over the open sea.

Aquarmarine ocean, endless
in never ending undulation,
melting into blue sky,
and white clouds
underlined in grey, looking
like your eyes, blue
on white, edged darkly.

I rise on transparent, irridescent,
unbearably light rays, toward
the red center of my Sun.
You, growing, glowing,
as your inner fire heats me,
beyond desire.

—Barbara Weber

WHERE ARE YOU?

I often sit and think of you
   wondering where you are.
Are you on a cloud up in the sky,
   or riding a silver star?
Are you singing and laughing
   and roping the wind?
Where are you now? I can't comprehend!
I look at the mountains, trees and birds,
I know you are there, just not seen
   and not heard.
I feel you all around me, in all
   that I do,
So why do I feel so empty, lonely and blue?
When I look at all these things
   and I feel the loss of you,
God sends a message to me from you,
   and what it says is this . . .
"I am still your brother, you're
   still my sis. The wind is my hug,
and the sunshine is my kiss!!!"

     —Charlotte Wood

TORRENCE BLYE

Torrence Blye, she wept upon her
   Husband's barren grave.
She could have done if she had cared,
But life she did not save.
The darkened garb she wore over her
Body matched her hair,
Her fingers cold as such she went
The same upon her stare.
The thoughts which racked her feeble mind
Told that her love was gone.
She stood through cold and night onside the
Dirt until 'twas dawn.
Her legs had stiffened since her feel had
Gone from far to near,
Her eyes had swollen upon her face and
From her brow, a tear.
She had no will to live and thus she
Pray ye Lord to die,
And so a corpse lay on his grave,
Her name was Torrence Blye.

     —Joey Jordan

LOST WITHOUT YOU

Having it all, but never having enough.
I took everything from you all except
your love.
Struggling to make it last, you tried
everything in keeping us strong.
My love for you will go on forever,
but your love for me has diminished
and to return never.
Vanished away are the moments to remember
which now lie in history.
Never witnessing the dream in reality,
for tomorrow is still a mystery.
Only the memories are left, as they
make it harder to control the fear.
And because I no longer have you, I
now live in agony crying silent tears.
Remembering someone special is something
not hard to do.
Especially when a life like mine is forever
"Lost Without You."

     —Maurice Adkins

DESTINATIONS

Though many miles of road I've walked
   Through storm and desperation
The inspiration from the stars
Made it seem like but a walkway
Or a path I've yet to conquer
. . . for no reason at all
I ponder for an answer
To all of life's most secretive mysteries
And I know I'll find my answer
On the road I've not yet taken.

     —Stacey Tonita

The feeling of your embrace . . .
   The smile that was always on your
face. Your heart which I held for
only a short while.

   I shall remember you.

The way we held each other tight.
Warming our bodies by the fire light.
The laughter, the sorrow of yesterdays
and tomorrows.

   I shall remember you.

The memories I hold so dear, time
may dry up all of my tears. I shall
look back over the years and smile
— for I will be remembering you.

For maybe one time you shall too,
look back at these times and know
at that moment I too will be thinking
of you.

     —Doreen M Cormier

IMMORTAL FRIEND

Moving to a foreign land
   Far away from one's dear friends.
Growing lonely as the night
Grows darker in my blindful sight.

Then one fateful summer day
Made a friend with which to share,
My time, my happiness and my life.
Moments and memories which would outlive
The time that we had left to give.

Then one fateful summer day,
My friend moved to a land far away.
Never saying our final goodbye.

Unknown to my special friend
A gift was left to last within.
One that *YOU* could not touch or see.

But the gift that was left behind
Was forever painted in my mind.
In the darkness of my thoughts,
Colored memories had replaced
The darkness felt in my heart.

*Thank you Dean Pasko for all the great
memories during the summer of 1986. These
are the words that filled my heart the
night you moved from Madison, Wisconsin.*
   Your friend always,

     —Linda Dabrowski

A NEW PERSPECTIVE ON LIFE

A new perspective on life you see
can be up or down, left or right.
It can be anything you want it to be.
It can be wrong or right.

A new perspective on life is good
or it could be strange.
It could put you in the
best of moods.
It is good for a change!

—Gregory Perkins

TRAVELOG

I'd like to see New Haven in the fall
When frosty winds blow leaves around my feet . . .
And lamps are lighted in the early dusk
While shadows dance about me on the street.

I'd love to see the old mill stream in fall
When faded summer fields are lone and bare;
A naked birch against the harvest moon
And maybe snowflakes falling everywhere.

A covered bridge that spans an icy stream,
Or troubled clouds when flying wild geese call;
A coming-home path by a picket fence—
How I wish my home could be New England in the fall!

—Edna E. Moore

THE WORLDS APART

We're sitting in a limbo.
We still don't know how to get through.
For God created the world for man to live.
We live in this world that was given to us.
That is why we are fighting for better living.
But man rules the world with sweetness and bitterness.
We speak out on top issues everyday.
Like, racism, injustice, human right violation,
homelessness, world hunger, ethnic tension, etc.
Because that is the right we wanted.
But how long shall we stand and say:
Better days are coming.
Better days are coming.
With the possession and sacrifice of our soul.
For a step by step evolution of good over evil.

—Bernard Bangura

THE CHILDREN OF THE WINDS

The shadows of the trees beside the pond
Reveal that it is morning.
The sun is well upon his pathway in the sky.
Though pointing West, the shadows inch by inch
Recede and slowly disappear.
And now the sun is high.
The air is heavy and no leaf stirs,
The winds all chained beyond the far horizon.
I call upon the one who holds the chains
And ask that he relent and let the children of the winds
Came playing to my meadow soon again;
The daisies and the meadow grasses wait
To sway in gentle rhythm with their play.
And now the daisies and the meadow grasses gently sway
As the children of the winds come down and play.

—Harold P. Resh

LAUGHADIDINOTHERATION

What is laughadidinotheration?
Why it's something to keep the motion
Of your belly while you continue
On your downhill shoot,
Giggling, gasping, and groping,
For more and more engrossing
Things to say to every others
To keep them in stitches and sputters.

—Fran Singley Mercade

THE BEST IS YET TO BE

I wonder why we worry
And fret with increasing years.
True beauty does not tarnish —
Even if it so appears.

The perfection of a Rembrandt
Is undimmed by the hand of Time;
A musical score by Chopin
Is not any less sublime.

The fine writings of a Dickens
Do not lose their truth and power.
E'en some buildings have a beauty
Only mellowed by all the hours.

A bountiful, agéd garden
Is just as peaceful for all that: —
And so it is with we humans,
Created by God's divine hand.

If our hearts are right within us
And we have blesséd hope, you'll see
That tho' the path seem bleak at times,
Yes! — the best is yet to be!

*Dedicated to my late parents, Percy T.
Platt & May H. (Elstob) Platt of England.*

—Pamela T. Bassett

Like a tiny seedling,
Child you grow and grow
Always searching for a confidant
Never to find a single foe.
Thou are the sunshine in
My glowing watch,
Thou has taken my attention
Thou has captivated me,
Thou has known thy love
Ah, so tenderly.
From afar mine gaze and wonder
What life will bring to thee . . .
Hope from any evil doing
My precious life can flee.
Strong and bold thy hands will grow
To chase it all from me,
All a single price for giving life to thee.
Oh little lamb, pure and unshaven
Protected from the black and evil raven,
Be strong my priceless seed,
Travel yourself afar from
Man's evil deed.
Protected from a poison
My wiser call a weed.
This land created for thy delight,
Keep well my love, both day and night.

—Deanna Osborne

LONELY CHRISTMAS

Merry Christmas people wishes in the morning,
Some are happy and others are working.
We pass from house to house, giving whom we see,
Have a joyous day, and remember me.

Christmas never passes without someone sad,
No joy or happiness in the face of Dad.
Children are crying, no food in the plate,
I was begging from people, sorry I am late.

Let us cherish someone who is lonely and gloom,
Specially those who have nothing, waiting in the room.
Then I remember Jesus and look on His face,
He said, "Come with me for I have no place."

I walked with Jesus and He told me this,
Don't be lonely, come with me in the bliss.
It is my birthday why you are so sad?
I love you my child, stay by me, and be glad.

—Suranjan K. Baroi

MY BLANKET

The green and white stripes faded with time
Smaller from years of use
Yet it still has the smell of baby powder
It warms me through the winter
and cools me through the summer
Protecting me from the evil things of the world
Including the Boogey man and the thing in my closet
Holding it tight as if it was magical
Its soft texture touching my skin
Through the time I broke my leg
To all the early Christmas mornings
It has always been there
Taking care of me in its own special way
To others it's just an ordinary blanket
Even though my parents say to throw it away
I can't bear to separate myself from it
To others it might be just a cloth
But to me it's a part of my family

—Geoffrey Townsend

When cats meow once, twice, three times
and then pass on to a screeching cry
of infant likeness
breathless, excruciating,
the senses tear the heart up, and out.
When the feline purr proclaims unendlessly its need
to beings about the need to being there and then
by being allowed
alone outside inside with others by themselves
to regularly mate, or to copulate
despite the cumbersome nature of such an animal act
to which in the same manner, but
in a different way respond
males and females, women and men . . .
When these creatures horn in the heated phase
with a piercing lament for hours on end
it is cats!
Not people's feelings
which flush with shame
at the disgraceful race, at the kingdom betrayed.

—Eugenia Garcia Irizar

I always like summer best
You can visit your family in Alabama,
make money
get loved
eat hamburgers
and chicken
and spaghetti
play with your dog
in the field
and play baseball
and football
outside
with your friends
feed the hogs
and cows
and fish
and get dirty
without anybody caring
and go swimming
all in one day.

—Jay Price, age 13

ANOTHER HISTORY

I wanted to tell that Social Security man
that every wrinkle in grandma's face
tells a story.
The story of how she raised four kids alone.
The story of chopping and hauling wood,
pumping water, mending the roof,
and hitchhiking to Fargo
for a graduation dress.

I wanted to tell him about
her planting a garden
and when it wasn't productive,
how grandma walked five miles
on a moonlit night
to carry a deer home —
praying she would not be caught.

Asking for Social Security at 88
took all her pride.
But that Social Security man told her
"You never worked!"

—Helen Gerhardson

NERVOUS ANTICIPATION

Slowly, and evenly the
days go by. The undeniable
end draws closer and
closer. After all the work
to get yourself ready, you
find that you're ready
for anything — anything, *but*
this! The thought excites you,
while at the same time
paralyzes you with fear.
What will you do when you finally
get free! Free of this
scholastic prison?! Well,
it's finally here, after
twelve long years. High
school graduation — your
day of fame!

—Cindy E. Huskins

ETERNITY

Life
Full of emotion and spice
Walking toward the light
Or the dark with cruelty and spite
Death
Can come with the gentleness of a breath
Or oft with violence
But you still obtain the silence
Of Eternity

—Burton Taylor

DEAR LORD:

Help me to forget the pain
Help me to see the sunshine, not the rain
Help me to cope—
And to see that there has to be some hope.
Help me to see the light—
For right now;
I'm truly fighting for my life.
Help me to remember
That people really do care—
That my heart is still good—
That my life is really worth something—
Only if I can bear.
Help me to see the real me—
Someone who truly does care—
Not the one that's inside of me now.
Help me to live in the present—
Not to look back all the time—
For someday soon my Lord—
I'll be in your kingdom—
And the sun will again shine.

—Karin L. Magnuson

CRYSTAL VISION

You search to reach that realm of peace
you search to find your freedom
you ward off any thoughts of doubt
uncertainty and depletion

You listen to the calling
the yearning deep within
the inward sense that guides you
in perfect unison

As you capture lucid stillness
in wonder and belief
this tranquil crystal vision
you know will never cease

Seeing natures innate beauty
exquisite in its essence
you search to know serenity
from creations shining presence

You continue on your journey
you cast away the fear
with absolute conviction
you see your path is clear

Now you claim your freedom
as obstacles release
this tranquil crystal vision
you know will never cease

—Teri Cuschera

IS IT BECAUSE OF MY TINT?

My soul always felt bent
is it because of my tint?

Work harder for less of a cent
is it because of my tint?

Proving myself, not making a dent
is it because of my tint?

Trying to be the other side of Clark Kent
is it because of my tint?

Never willing to accept the good I meant
is it because of my tint?

Oppression, suppression, obsession nowhere to vent
is it because of my tint?

Finally, to God the creator I went
and he affirmed his love for my tint.

—Michael L. Dublin Sr.

Sometimes
 in this world
  of strangers
   and new-found friends
    and doubtful dreams
     and demands
      and responsiblities
       and troubles
        and fast moves
         and worries
          and insecurities
a person wants to seek out the people
and places that knew what he used to be —
what he dreamed of — and what he hoped for —
what he was and how he grew . . . .

Sometimes
 a person just wants his old Love, his old friends,
  and to go home again . . . .

—Kathryn B. Couch

CANDLE LIGHT IN THE WIND

    She was a brightly, burning star;
For awhile;
    But, also, like the candle light in the wind,
Fragile.
    A blonde beauty with a breathless, whispery voice.
She was our favorite, our choice;
    Running along the beach, one minute;
Dressed in diamonds and fur,
    The next time you saw her.
Almost everyone who was around her was beguiled;
    She was like a loving, trusting child;
But, one, whose life flickered, from time to time,
    Like the candle light in the wind.
It became harder and harder for her to pretend.
    Finally, the candle light burns down low;
Flickers one last time and goes out.
    The candle light was snuffed out, so unjustly;
But, we'll all remember her,
    And her memory will never burn out.

In memory of Marilyn Monroe

—Leah Charles

THE WHALES NOT SEEN

I weep for the whales not seen,
for the whale song no longer heard.
My heart cries out in agony, for
the migration trails no longer traveled.

The breaching of the majestic beasts today
leaves us in awe, but the memories of pods
of yesterday will never fade.

The blue, the gray, the humpback, dear
God, what have we done? When will we
cease to take advantage?

I weep for the whales not seen, for
they have left a legacy. A path that
should never be repeated. Will we
learn?

I yearn to see the bursts of water,
signaling the orca. I weep for the whales
not seen.

—Scottye Roop

SEAGULL

Single seagull, flying low,
  Across the waters, to and fro,

In gloomy mist and falling rain,
  Over waters' swells, you dive again;

Up above, you circle twice,
  For Nature's folly, you've paid a price.

It's not your fault, that you were born,
  Into a world of hate and scorn;

The race of men, are the ones to blame,
  The ones who feel no guilt or shame;

What we have done, and will yet do,
  We wreck this world, for innocents like you.

You live in peace, and lack the greed,
  Which mortal men appear to need;

So stay at peace, and heed me well,
  Keep far away from our living Hell.

—Janna Bloom

OLD DOGS ALREADY KNOW

as pointless as the red band around my
bologna
the belt around your waist
the weight on your shoulders
the cuff they made at the bottom
of your pants
as pointless as crystal clear pepsi
purchased at the mart
or the warranty for your new car
the pine cones you collected today
as pointless as trying to teach the unwilling
to learn
the alcohol free beer you drink as we speak
the surgeon general warning on a pack of cigs
and directions on the back of the
shampoo bottle
I tried to teach an old dog new tricks
I tried to teach an old dog new tricks
I tried to teach an old dog new tricks
And it didn't work

—M. Shane Jones

THERE WAS GOAT

There once was goat who lived
in a moat.
  It was so damp he got a sore
throat and sometimes he even rode
in a boat.

—Donna A. Reed

OLD GOBBLER

Old gobbler gave up his proud gobble
to step in a pan and sit
amid mounds of corn bread dressing
and savory giblets.

From his time-honored place in the roaster
all cooking he did supervise;
beaming on busy tradition
right up till his time of demise!

—Mary Grimes

THE OUTCASTS

Oh mighty mites with strength supreme,
  Using muscles unforeseen.
Traveling through the day and night,
  Catching morsels in their flight.
And, in and out of places likeable,
  Searching for some objects edible.
Turning here and turning there,
  Seeking food most anywhere.
Over the bushes and over the plants,
  Under the trees, these little ants.
And under the house and off they go,
  Crawling here, there, and to and fro.
And, at last they found their crepe suzette,
  Sitting in the cellar yet.
There's a fruitcake on a shelf of pine,
  Subdues these outcasts, these ageless,
Wonders of time.

—Jaygee

I look in the mirror and wonder,
  Will tomorrow be just like the past?
Fill my head with a dream for tomorrow
He shatters it just like the last.
I see a man on the stairs in the distance,
Slowly walking back down,
He turns around and he smiles,
But his smile turns into a frown.

He knows he has lost this hard battle,
The battle he almost had won,
He knows that he's been defeated,
No longer am I on the run.
Once I had told a dolphin,
Just what it felt like to die,
The dolphin dove into the distance,
Taking it all as a lie.
I look in the mirror and wonder,
Will tomorrow be just like the last?
But then I stop myself and remember,
That all of that is in the past.

—Elaine Iaccino

33

ODE TO A GRAND-DAUGHTER!

My dearest Amy, I just wanted you to know,
This Grandpa of yours, just loves you so.
From your light brown hair, to your winning smile,
And your hazel eyes, kid, you've got some style.
When you were born, I knew from the start,
You'd always have a place in my heart.
My walks with you just lit up my life,
Back when Grandma Julie was still my wife.
Those days are gone, but the memories still clear,
And my thoughts of you still bring me cheer.
Though we're miles apart, I always feel better,
When I pick up my mail, and find your letter.
So Amy dear, please keep up your writing,
Cause it makes my days, a lot more exciting.

—Gerald .S. Aull Sr.

SPIRIT AND AGONY IN LIFE

Oh,
How have they you, cut up your feelings,
        you stand now strange and special there.
You suffered often that had you reeling,
        left only defiance and despair.
I am cut like you with years behind me,
        despite those, who scarred us with deceit.
Now patiently you reconstruct your life span,
        in spite of inflictions to you and me.
We emerge daily through rude treatment,
        new of thought to face the spirit of the light.
Your sense has thought you not to feel humbled,
        when absolutely right.
Indestructible is our will and virtues,
        when challenged our feelings noble beliefs.
The damage done, by this world so crude,
        hurt been done, you can not reverse it.
So let's love life, not fail or fall,
        this insane world in spite of all.

—Rudolf Stober

NATALIE

I never would have guessed,
    That I would be so blessed,
To be given another life
    to nurture and love.

She's so beautiful and perfect,
    There's a great bond we share.

It's unique and very special,
    Nothing can compare.

She depends on me, I'm her all,
    It's me, who answers, every call.

Asleep or awake I am near,
    My very presence casts out all fear.

Her face lights up, like the sun gives light to the earth,
    As I lovingly caress her being,
This is how I know I'm doing the right thing.

She's growing fast I'm not blind,
    Somehow, I don't even mind.

But I treasure these moments in time,
    Just she and I . . .

For raising her delights me,
    I'm filled with the utmost of glee,
For she, is my daughter, Natalie.

—Yvonne M. Villa

THE APPLE OF MY EYE

Through all my years of life,
    And of all my loves gone by . . .
You, Dear Mom, have always been
The "Apple of my Eye!"

Sometimes my life has been real bad,
Sometimes it's been real good,
But, through it all, you've been right there,
Beside me, there you've stood.

You've always been so caring, and
you've always been so right,
Even though at times I have
put up one helluva fight.

Although I've said it before
I will say it once again . . .
You are the "Apple of my Eye," Dear Mom,
From now until the end!

—Richard L. Galloway

AN OLD ROCKING CHAIR

A sale was being held one day
    I stopped, then could not walk away,
Some household goods were being sold
There weren't many, all were old.
I caught sight of one old item there
A well-worn wooden rocking chair,

I wondered — over all the years
How often it helped silence tears,
As a mother rocked her child to sleep
Or sat in it all night to keep
A vigil when someone was ill,
Now at last it just sat still.

I sat in it and heard it squeak
As if to me it tried to speak,
I bought that chair, and now I know
Why I could not let it go,
It brought back happy memories
Of rocking children who belonged to me.

—Mildred Deutschmann

HANDS OF THE WORLD

Is the strongest hand of all
    it keeps us safe,
it holds the world
    That's **God's** hand.

The hand of comfort, when
    something does not turn out right.
We have Grandma to comfort us,
    That's **Grandma's** hand.

The hand of love that hugs us
    before we go to bed
That's **Mom's** hand.

The hand that reaches out for us
    to hold on to, because he loves us so.
That's **Grandpa's** hand.

The hand that takes the time
    when he is running late for work.
To give a wave of Good-Bye.
    That's **Dad's** hand.

The hand that is still growing and
    reaching for God's love and comfort.
That's **My** hand.

—Deb Brungardt

SPRINGTIME II

A gardenia white unfolds,
sweet scented melody,
sways lightly . . .
My heart strings play again.

—Mary Clinard

CHAIN OF LOVE

Into the world
    of comfort,
        no-more being alone.
She sets
    in a chain of love,
        & decided to
            call it home.
For home
    is an escape,
        Right to the end.
Where it will
    be your love,
        for you are its friend.

—John T. Savino

A DAY HAS GONE

A day has gone
And come
I still remain.
Speechless night
My friend—
Surrounds me
With its darkened cloak
In the silence of the hour
I hear the earth's heart beat
I am refreshed
As a baby
In its mother's womb—
Contentment.

—A. Charles Dana

MY PARENTS

Today I find a friend

Someone who will be
    there to the end

Should there be a time
I might need to hear the
    words of my friend

A friend who will last
through the thick and
    thin a true friend

I can always count on
the love of Mom and
    Dad to help me,
with their love from
    deep within

When I need a true
friend I always have
    them

—Eddie Pounds

BELIEVE AND BE FREE

The sky was crystal blue
Above so many birds flew
The wind smelled of nature's sweet scents
I could feel God's Heavenly presence
As the wind made its way whirling down
My feet stood firmly upon the ground
As the wind blew harder and harder
The leaves flew farther and farther
The leaves and trees began to dance about
And in my mind there were no doubts
For I could feel my father's great power
Though just a few minutes, it seemed like hours
As the wind whirled and blew around me
My heart, soul, and mind became free
My spirit is lifted soaring with the wind
For I knew in my father's world life shall never end
Others don't bother to take time, listen, or hear
Or stand amidst the whirling wind, without any fear
If only they'd acquaint themselves with God, a true friend indeed
They too could be free but only if they would believe.

—Rebecca L. Wheaton

HERE'S TO

All the notes we've ever wrote
    all the words we've ever spoke
All the tears that have been cried.
    all the lies that have ever been lied
All the emotions that have been expressed,
    happy, sad, excited and depressed
All the secrets that have been told,
    all these years as we grow old
All the hours we've spent together,
    all the silence that's happened whenever
All the things I could have said,
    all the things that were in my head
All the time that has elapsed,
    all the feelings that have been attacked
All the male friends that have come and gone,
    all the memories, and don't forget those songs
All the wounds that have been healed,
    all the envelopes that have been sealed
All the regrets that have been kept inside,
    only to find there was nowhere to hide
All the people who called you names,
    sometimes you thought you were going insane
All the times we've counted on each other,
    sometimes we even acted like our mothers
All the things we've ever tried,
    some good, some bad, some denied
All the pictures we've gotten taken,
    yet still I might be mistaken
All the people who would stop and stare,
    all those who didn't care, no, not you, you were always there
All the times you've never let me down,
    all the rumors that have gotten around
All the times you could have quit,
    you never gave up, you kept trying for it
All the habits that were once here,
    all the times we've looked in the mirror
All the problems that have gone away,
    all the things I've wanted to say
All the time we talked on the phone,
    all the time you wanted to go home
Through all the life that has been lived,
    you are my Friend, whom I'll always forgive
As you can see—the past, present, or future could never be,
    what you've meant to me

—Shannon H. Albright

36

HEART FULL OF LIVING

Dancing, dancing, dancing through empty rooms here in the darkness of my shattered dreams
Leaping, dipping, running from floor to floor laughing at madness, echoes of screams
Singing, shouting, whispers of rhapsody, daydreams of fantasy mine to beseech
Flitting, taunting, elusive as butterflies, dangle as destiny out of my reach
Skipping, spinning, sliding down banisters giggling helplessly, sprawled on the floor
Joyous, bittersweet, heart full of living embracing the challenge beyond every door
Healing, heartbreak, crushed 'neath the heel of divine intervention again, and again
Hiding, seeking, rebellious, and childlike I race through the halls of my comforting friend
Unfinished, unfurnished, this mansion of dreams awaits my propriety, honors my name
Unique and unblemished, each room in decorum is markedly different, yet one and the same
Stately, comely, vision of loveliness looks like the others that boldly deceive
Skeptical, cowardly, pass by the doorway that opens upon things they cannot conceive
Painted, shuttered, eyes behind windowpanes, deftly and openly mirror the soul
The outside is nice, but the inside is better, in wealth beyond measure lie riches untold

    —Rebecca A. Barton

THE SYCAMORE TREE

There is a land that I dream of today, my thoughts linger there tho
I'm far away. There is no other place that I'd rather be. Than walking by the
river near the sycamore tree. I have roamed a long way, but my thoughts remain,
where the warm winds blow, and there are soft gentle rains. There I ran through
the meadows, and my spirit was free. The sun sent its rays shining, around the sycamore tree.

How well I remember the warm starry nights, with the fireflies flashing
their beautiful lights. The song of the katydid, floating softly to me. The hoot of the
owl, from the sycamore tree. I can recall the days we made hay. The smell of the Earth in
the month of May. The fields of corn in my mind I can see. There I longed for the shade
of the sycamore tree.

The mist rolled in, o'er the new mown hay. Dew lay on the cobwebs in a
magical way. The birds sing a song to the new day they see. The wind stirred the
leaves on the sycamore tree. The day fades into twilight, the first star I see, as I
walk down the lane, in my mind's eye I see. There in the moonlight, someone waiting
for me. We shared laughter and secrets, neath the sycamore tree.

To walk there again, would make my soul thrill, tho my loved ones
have gone, and their voices are still. When the shadows deepen, and death
beckons me, please lay me to rest, neath the sycamore tree.

Dedicated to Barbara Ward

    —Vivian Shipp

WONDERMENT

What were you thinking when you made the seas, the tall wonderful and beautiful trees?
The stars that shine in the heavens at night, the strength in our bodies to give us might?
Our eyes of color to give us sight, the sun for its warmth of day and light?
Your plan of a beautiful earth for your people to share; man has made a mess without care.
Why do we continue to turn from your plan, and not live in unity in this same land?
Some turning on their brothers, as a daughter against mother, continuing to reach out for someone to blame,
While enjoying the sun which warms the earth, why are our hearts so frozen in pain?
We do not communicate with God nor fellowman; why have we gone against your wonderful plan?
The tongues of fire, the sticks and evilness, having used cloaks and crosses to carry out this deviousness.
I ask in wonderment, who chose their pigment of being, I cannot remember having been
    asked such a decision to make.
We all have the same sweat on our brow when toiling, and the same tears
    overflowing from eyes sad and swollen.
If all could pretend this the last day to be, families of all could bend down on their knee,
And ask for feelings of understanding to flow thru their being, to stop all
    the actions which are hurting and stinging.
If only the beams of love from your throne could shine on the mixture you've
    created, all the hate and discomfort would surely be abated;
Lifting up hope for a peaceful existence of heart, the way it was
    meant to be right from the start.

    —Evelyn M. Doucet

HE WASN'T THERE

You look so much like him
In everything you do
I just want you to remember
He really does love you
He never meant to hurt you
It's just the way he feels
He decided to leave us
To work out his ordeals
You were given his name
To carry and to bare
Don't be ashamed child
Just because he wasn't there.

—Lori Sharp-Van Buskirk

TRIBUTE TO MY MOTHER

I can still remember now;
It seems like just yesterday;
When I was eight or nine years old,
My mother went away.

Of course I cried and cried;
I said it really wasn't fair.
I needed Mother Oh! So much!
And yet she wasn't there.

Our kindly Reverend said to me;
"We have no choice to stay or go;
God needs your mother too.
He only takes the best you know."

Years have come and gone.
I miss Mother more each day,
Yet I am not alone.
Many others feel this way.

So once a year, Dear Mother,
A tribute to you I say.
I wear a white gardenia.
It's for you on Mother's Day.

—Pinky Laykish, deceased

SO LITTLE DID I REALIZE

I wonder where you are today
Sweet child of only seven,
With curly locks of auburn hair
And eyes as brown as chocolate
How oft you sat upon my lap,
"I love you Kim," I'd say,
So little did I realize
How time would slip away.

I wonder where you are today
Sweet miss of seventeen,
With baby days and childish ways
Now vanish like a dream.
I still recall your smiling face
On graduation day;
So little did I realize
How time would slip away

I wonder where you are today
Sweet bride of twenty;
Per chance the Lord has blessed you
With a precious son.
Upon your lap oft hold him
For soon, like Mom, you'll say,
"So little did I realize
How time would slip away."

—Shiril Christofferson

MIRACLES

Now I believe in miracles they happen every day
You don't have to be a millionaire for luck to come your
Way
Well God gave me an angel who would become my wife
She shared with me the good times and helped me through
My strife
She gave me three fine children who think I'm the
Best of all
And if I ever needed them they are at my beck and call
Well you can take the riches, just leave me as I am
For there is one thing I know for sure
I am a lucky man.

—Robert Beebee

GENERATIONS

The helplessness filters through generations
while time silently glides by.
I watch my mother comfort Grandma
as the frustration of age makes her cry.
The knee that once gently bounced us,
no longer complies with her will,
simple things taken for granted
now require steady determination and skill.
Mom takes great care to do for her,
the things Grandma can no longer do.
All the while love of mother and daughter
comes brightly shining through.
She feels every ache, as if it were her own,
and in turn I feel them too, for she is not alone.
Soon it will be my turn to take Mom's gentle hand in mine
and comfort her in those years of need
when time renders itself unkind.
I feel an eternal circle form, it will never die or break,
to care for those who have been there for you
is something age nor time should forsake.

—Lynne A. Carpenter

I AM YOUR MOTHER

The joy to see you laugh and play. The suspense of little things
you might say.
The hurt to see you cry. The sometimes innocent little shy.
The sorrow I feel when you're sad. The happiness when you're glad.

I would take life's little falls and games. I'd do it over and
over just the same.
And if I could I'd share life's unfortunate illness. I would take
the sickness and the soreness.
I would do all this, to spare you of all pain. I'd do it over and
over again.

But, because you are your own. I'll be at your side—you'll never
be alone.
I'll hope and pray, life treats you kind. You're forever always on
my mind.
I'll be caring and loving you in a special way. I'll nurse and
guide you through each day.

For you, there is nothing I would not do. But, you'll find in life
some choices are up to you.
Some may be small with not much thought. Some will dwell in your
mind of fault.
Just remember you're in my thoughts each passing moment by. If ever
you need to talk, laugh, or to cry.

I can lend a hand, give a hug, and help a heart mend.
I am your Mother — and also your friend.

Dedicated to Leigh and Nicole

—Barbara Weaver Emerson

MY PATH

The path I choose in life is of my own choice.
No one can tell me which trail to walk on.
I know at times this path will lead me to people and things
            that may influence my life in many ways.
My friends can't help me, my family can't help me, I have to help myself.
There are times my thoughts take me to far away lands, isolated,
            alone, with no obstacles in my way.
There will be days when I need my space, a time when I have to be alone.
It's not that I want to, I have to. Time will heal the pain I feel inside.
Family and friends try to understand what's going on inside of me.
I wear a false smile so people won't know when I am troubled. I seek
            help from my inner self, help that comes hard because I am lost,
Searching for a way out. The way for me may be strange to other people.
They don't understand how I feel. I want to be close to certain people, but
            I am afraid this uncertainty I have may hurt them.
So I keep every tear I cry, every hurting moment to myself,
            and until I find the answer I search for
                        I'll walk MY PATH alone.

—Andy Cote

THE WINDOW

As I look through the window of my life, I feel an emptiness inside myself.

I notice the cracks in the glass — each representing a shattered dream, a broken promise, or a moment that passed me by.

As I examine the window further, I realize that the pane is no longer gold; but instead silver — resembling all the broken friendships, lost loves, and distant relationships.

I notice a beam of sunshine peering through the window.
For a moment, I feel all the laughter, joys, and triumphs.
But, as the sun fades, darkness comes once again and so do the memories of the tears, the heart-felt pain, and the disappointments.

As I open the window, the gentle breeze comes to a halt and all time stands still.
Leaving me to wonder how the bruises heal; but the wounds scar.

As my cuts bleed once more from my haunting past, I again close the window to heart forever.

—Tanisha Hamel Randall

REDEEMING THE MIND

Evil thoughts can board a brain, never to leave, until let go
They can't be forced out until a soul explodes
The jury inside the head convicts without any objection
They will let evil prevail, and take a life
The jury's conscience catches up. A jury inside the jury says
An eye for an eye. What you cast upon a body must be thrown back at you
A heart burns ashes leave home, over land, across seas, they toss
and turn in the wind, until disintegrated in the world's sin
A self-absorbed soul is unlike any you've seen. It doesn't understand
the concept of saying no. Because of this our race will be a
skeleton in its own closet
A character thinks of humanity as just a "word." The tragedies
are somewhat hidden. Grass still grows, sky's still blue. The
bark of a family tree carries a flame
Imprisoned in an atmosphere that blocks the fulfillment of life
A hand reaches across the realm eager to ease the pain
All the lifeless souls it has taken the brain becomes enraged.
It finds a place in the back
The calvary, Its fingers, pulls the strings of a guillotine. ON the
darkside it separates the body from the murders of the mind

—H.E. Hayden

THE TRUTH REVEALED

One dream,
led
to one nightmare,
which
revealed the truth.
That truth,
showed
great courage,
in
a young mind.

—C. Doerig

LEARNING TO FLY

Discarded wings lay
    in the still air
                close,
to the unseen
        traveling
    currents of dust.

Grounded shadows,
    of their former selves,
into tattering psalms,
    of small beauty
seen nestling,

    stretching shades
across lower footprints
                chasing
the living,
    new flight below
a different sky.

—Joe Camp III

BROKEN HEART

I can feel my heart
breaking in two.
Just lying here
thinking of you.

Trying to remember
what I cannot forget.
Thinking of you
but not with regret.

The emptiness
fills me inside.
Wanting to escape
trying to hide.

I'm dead inside
feeling the pain.
Not able to love
never to be the same.

I'm hurting now
I sit here and cry.
Ready to give up
just waiting to die.

So hold me tight
don't let me go.
I need your love
more than you know.

—Joanne Houghton

SELF-SEEKING

Taking the night flight,
I journeyed
to the dark side
of the moon,
And into the shadows
of self seeking,
And into the star zone,
light years away.

Piercing the glimmering dots,
I journeyed
through the patterns
of the galaxy,
And into the starry mist
of self-seeking.
And from the night flight
I never returned.

—Patricia Boney

MEMORIES

The time has come
to say goodbye,
To all loved
and held dear.
The pain and fear
is overwhelming
And I can handle no more tears.
Memories will last forever,
Good times and bad,
And soon I shall be just,
a memory of the past.
Hold the memories
close to your heart
and never let go
For then they shall
never leave you
And the body now gone,
Is a soul watching over you,
With memories too.

—Tara L. Anderson

LOVER'S LAIR

I sit in my garden
of blooms upon plates,
in paintings, on the fabric
of furniture, and I stir
fantasy with the fresh
bouquets of salmon azaleas
and lilac rhododendrons.
An atmosphere of gentleness
and grace, a haven of
romance pretended. A
fragrance of sensuality and
a heat of desire blur
my focus.
I nurture and await my yard,
a patch of lawn swallowed
by gardens, to turn into
a sweet ripeness of scents,
blooms rich as the colors
of a prince's velvet garb.

—David E. Dyer

A CIRCLE OF LOVE

You gave me love and taught me to care.
You gave me discipline and taught me control.
You gave me responsibilities and taught me the value of work.
You gave me your time and taught me to serve.
You gave me your support and taught me to endure.
You gave me security and taught me how to trust.
You gave me sacrifice and taught me how to give.
You gave me Christian parents and taught me faith in God.
You gave me understanding and taught me to accept my mistakes.
You gave me your patience and taught me to be patient.
You gave me advice and taught me how to live.
You gave me freedom and taught me how to make choices.
You gave me forgiveness and taught me to forgive others.
You gave me your love for each other and taught me how to love.

—Joan Rothermel

HAND IN HAND

Hand in hand we were together
In the springtime of our lives.
The air was warm and skies were blue
As nature was waking into life anew.

We were together in long hot days of summer,
Though at times the thunder rolled and lightning flashed;
Still we worked and laughed and dreamed
In the promise of a harvest in fields of ripening grain.

We were together in the autumn of our lives
As hand in hand we watched the falling leaves;
Content to rest and watch as earth prepared for winter.
We smiled for life was good and dreams complete.

Then you left me in the cold of winter;
Days so sad and lonely as no more your face I see.
But our love is everlasting and melted ice and snow
And the lovely flowers of springtime within my heart still grow.

—D. Helene Yost

REMEMBERING YOU SIS

Well Sis almost five years since you left me has gone by;
It hasn't gotten easier to see the grave in which you lie:

I often remember when our lives begin;
We fought, we fussed but we had all the love within:

We used to run, sneak and play;
And oh all the silly things we used to do and say:

If you could just see your little girl now;
She looks just like you, you would be so proud:

Everytime I look into her eyes, I can see you;
God I miss you so much I don't know what to do:

If God could give you back to me, for just one more day;
I have so much I feel I need to say:

Time — that we took for granted has already passed us by;
I still don't understand God taking you away from me — why?

I'm no one to question the great man above;
But you were my only sister and oh how I miss your love;

I feel as though yesterday were our past;
If only I knew the time we had together was going by so fast:

Sis — with this poem I sigh with relief;
Because the two of us together had the love and belief:

*Dedicated in loving memory of my sister,
Pamela Kay Hicks Horton.*

—Kathy Sue Hicks Bell

VALENTINE . . .

Roses are red violets are blue please be my Valentine, oh won't you?

My heart's set on you; no one else, oh, what shall I do?

My love for you is so deep; I need some boots to walk in this creek.

Without you, I am a nobody, I need you just to be somebody.

Did you say yes? Good, good, good I just knew you would!

—Amanda Johnson

RECYCLED

A heart —
atrophied and callused, weary with frigid uncaring.

Then you came along.

A heart —
warmed with your love like a spring thaw flooding right through me.

Then you went away.

A heart —
shattered, with nary a piece big enough, left to carry on the beat.

Where are you now?

A heart —
atrophied and callused, weary with frigid uncaring.

—Rae M. Zweber

AS TIME GOES BY

every day is closer to the future
      . . . every second
      . . . every minute
as time passes by it seems sometimes slow
      sometimes fast,
years have come and gone so quickly
i just sit and think about where it all went
time waits for nothing
      . . . it just keeps ticking away
sooner or later
      the future
will become
      the present
      . . . and time will have passed me by

—Tammy L. Malone

LIKE A DREAM — LIFE IS

Time goes past and nothing lasts, so you look into the past.
  Blink an eye and the pain's gone by.
But if it doesn't, to forget you'll try.
In this way, you live from day to day.
The anticipation is so great and when things are late,
  anxiety causes tension, muscles flex and get tight.
The moon appears and it's midnight.
Dawn has come and you cry some and another day is on its way.
Don't try to outguess if you'll ever have happiness or what role you'll
  play in this life of living from day to day.
Don't try to understand while you are living on this strand cause
  disappointment makes pressure high.
So, on yourself you must rely — cause no one comes to hear you cry.
Soon your existence will be no more and you'll be on that distant shore.
Your cry silenced forevermore.

—Marcia (Shank) Whitsel

ALONE

At first
  I sat in your chair,
  I slept in your bed
  And tried to forget
  That you were dead.

Later
  I captured my grief
  And watched it grow,
  A grim companion,
  I would not let go.

At last
  I opened the door
  And set grief free.
  Alone — unafraid,
  I will live with me.

—Mary Ann Adams

Whirling
Twirling
Frantically spinning
To the east
To the west
Cursing and sinning
Too much here
Not enough there
Throwing a fit
Twisting
And turning
Just for the hell of it
Swaying like a dancer
Yet carrying a ton
A twister on the horizon
Will dance destruction
'Til its dance
Is done

—Lolita Blathers-Craig

THE SONG OF THE NIGHT

The day has been a poem
A stanza of my dreams.
But night is the time I
Long to see
For things aren't what
they seem.
Shadows dance across
The eve,
Not being able to
Keep still,
I dream of living on a
Star
As I look out across the
Hill.
The ethereal charms of
The moon
Are those of the
Night song.
It reminds me of my
Love Forgotten,
And that of which I
Long.

—Amanda J. Denman

TRYST

They met by a chance encounter
He meant it to be that way.
He was the hunter who stalked her
She was the easy prey.

He circled his quarry with skill
She tried feebly to keep him at bay.
He quickly closed in for the kill
She fell under his spell right away.

He wove a mirage of desire
She soared to the heights of emotion.
He heaped the flames ever higher
She surrendered with blinded devotion.

She thought it would last ever after
He planned it to be that way.
He was the fool who left her
She was the dying prey.

—Liisa Liinamaa

FOR ANGELA

You remind me of a painting,
done under a sweet and gentle hand.
And though your colors may swirl
from harried thoughts and wishes,
please don't forget the artist's kisses.

Angela, may I ask how you are?
Are you feeling the icy-crisp winter air?
Are you lonely on a dark-highway night?
There is no reason to shiver in a cold
way.
There is every reason to avoid loveless
days.

I only offer some simple words,
that you may hold and keep.
Not words to echo up to your window,
but words that are meant for your eyes,
words that whisper, that don't cry.

Good-by, Angela

—Chris Batcha

DREAMING

Between the dark and the daylight,
When the shadows begin to fall,
I like to sit and dream
And do no work at all.

I dream of the swaying branches,
Of the high and lofty trees.
I dream of the sweet refreshing
Of a gentle ocean breeze.

I dream of the snow-capped mountains,
Far above the silvery sea,
I dream of the red-sailed ship
That will bring you back to me.

I dream of a little cottage
Nestled among the hills.
I dream of a cozy fireplace,
And the touch of your hand that thrills.

I dream of the day you'll come,
From across the silvery sea.
I dream of the years you'll share
All of your future dreams with me.

—Oneta Brauher

You walked into the room graced with a smile,
my spirits were lifted in the cool evening breeze,
as my body and mind reach,
my soul suffers the romantic tease.

I've waited my whole life for your touch,
Juliet would have faired much better with someone else,
but her heart was won by a Montegue,
both families thought it was a love of fools.

Only if they knew.

Cold courtships of physical attraction,
pale greenly next to true passion.
Two hearts in a tight embrace,
personal vanity is such a waste.
Clouding visions that rest beyond time,
I only long for tender words and sighs.

How can our souls meet if obscured by our bodies?

—John Oliver Kay

NOSFERATU LOVERS

I am a creature that walks the night
with eyes of dark blue and skin silken white.
I was once mortal, a gentleman of London
yet for 300 years I've not seen the sun.
My veins pulse with the hunger to drink;
it consumes my equal desire to think.
Walking in shadows dressed all in black
I search out my prey and quickly attack.
Behold! A young virgin standing by a light!
Be still, my love, try not to fight.
I wrap my arms around her, her breasts against my chest
with my lips pressed to her neck I lay her down to rest.
I taste the warm blood as it slides on my tongue
and my passions explode as heartbeats are one.
Never to grow old, I leave her there to die,
but in love with her beauty I make her one like I.
We are lovers as we sleep in my coffin of grey
until we grow hungry at the end of another day.
For we are creatures that haunt the night
with immortal beauty and fangs of pearl white.

—Jillian Lonely

RAGE

One love		with depths unknown
With a mind	and strength	all its own
To see eyes	full of tears	never shed
Raging anger	so enormous	to erupt instead
Emotions so wild	flaring	like a mind mad
Yet	to see beyond all	a tormented soul
Hearing	beyond all rage	a cry for help

Within another	tender gentle	full of need
To turn to twist	to roar	with rage
Erupting from depths		all eyes are blind
Dark secrets	of evil horrors	buried in time
Blocked out	a mind so small	now grown

Love to seek	to search	to help
Eyes blinded	to condemn	a love like this
Love to endure all		to take one back years gone
To remember	all hell	when it began
To get it out	to let it out	forevermore
All rage now gone		only peace and love remain
A soul once lost in time		now saved

Dedicated to my husband, my daughters, and Mom.
Thanks.

—Linda (Ryan) Martin

MY BABY WITHIN

Oh, God, please give my baby ten perfect tiny toes,
ten perfect little fingers, with a tiny button nose.
Form a dainty little mouth with sweet lips soft and simple,
and in those rounded, rosy cheeks, you might just place a dimple.

Form two bright blue eyes firmly set in perfect harmony,
between the tiny, well-formed ears that listen now to me.
Frame this precious baby face with fine hair, blond and curly,
and, oh, he'll need strong vocal chords to wake me very early!

I feel my precious baby growing deep inside of me,
and my heart is ever thankful to a God as great as thee.
For to share in your creation is the greatest blessing known,
and my perfect little baby will make my house a home.

*Dedicated to my daughter, Mary Kay Swenson,
awaiting the birth of her first child.*

—Dorothy A. Allen

STRAIGHT FROM THE HEART

There is nothing like a family
   To share one's burdens with.
Though we are miles apart from those we love
   Our hearts go out to them in their hour of pain.

As each of us has a turn with pain or sorrow
   We are certain that friends and relatives are praying
For that day when all is well again.

When we were children it was so easy
   To be close to offer comfort
But, today it must be done with a heart full of prayer
   and a written thought or two.

The fact remains that as life goes on times change
   And though we have our own loved ones close by
It is wonderful to realize that there are so many relatives
   who carry our burden with us and only wish us the best.

May the LORD help us to give courage to those
   who need it and love like a fountain will be flowing
Like a river of good wishes for a quick and complete recovery.

—Alice R. Lafleur

MY WONDERFUL MOTHER

I've written poems to most of my family and others to my friends,
About life itself the good the bad and how love will always mend.

But I've never put to words the thoughts about my Special Mother,
How good she is and how she's better than any other.

For me she's been there every day to help me with whatever,
Like life and living, love of others and of course to finish my
sweaters.

My mom is kind and full of life and never lets me down,
She lifts me up whenever my smile turns into an ugly frown.

I love her more than anything you can name on all this earth,
She's even been there for me when I was giving birth.

This poem describes a special woman with dreams that will come true,
She always puts her best foot forward and is rarely ever blue.

Mom, I hope you realize that I really love you so,
And I'll always be there for you, whichever way the wind will blow.

A smile to you from me, your daughter, I give to you each day,
That will spread my love to you for sure, from June right through till
May.

I Love You
   —Kimberly L. Deguire

house of moon

In the houses of the moon
   there are no shadows
of people
   in places
that the wind
would not inhabit,
   or is not needed.

Only a reflection.

—Joe Camp III

DECEMBER RAIN

   Through December Rain
troubles are taken.
   Like laughters are
hidden by a train.
   More and more I seek
December Rain to maybe
take my pain.
   My troubles are few;
and few are they.
   Oh! Come, come December
Rain. Please take my
pain away.

—Autumn H. Eaton, age 13

A PLACE TO SIT

I chase my love
as it flies around the room.

I open a window
for some fresh air and
it becomes a chair
sitting there next to me.

So I decide to take a walk
and it becomes a hammer and
nails boards across my chest.

In sleep it becomes
a massive root.

After all of that
I live in a tree.

—Joe Camp III

DAYBREAK

The sunlight shined through,
   On the long dusty road.
The sky was a light blue,
With speckles that glowed.

The hills had a touch,
Of light mountain sun.
And the world seemed to know,
The day had begun.

The birds made their songs,
With a light whistled tune.
And the breeze blew softly,
For daybreak was soon.

When the sun was the brightest,
Daytime was here.
With the breeze the lightest,
As nighttime drew near.

—Heather Bocook

HOME

Home is a place to hang your heart,
Home is where your life will start.

Always be near your home sweet home,
Wherever you may travel or roam.

It will always be there when you come back,
Even if your clothes are packed.

Yes my home is very dear to me,
And it will forever be!

—**Kari Anne Williams**

YEARS OF LIFE AS ONE

In life much will be written,
   in our life so much has been done.
There was laughter, happiness and sadness
   but we lived our life as One.
Many years have now gone by us,
   with God's blessing, many years will come.
Now I pray for the blessed moment,
   when we cross life's threshold,
And join our eternal sleep as one.

Eternally yours, Rudolf

—**Rudolf Stober**

THIS, OUR LIFE, OUR BEGINNING

"This, Our Life, Our Beginning"
What beautiful words these are
We both unite as one
Our future bright as a star

A future uncertain but full of hope
Comprised of each of our dreams
A future of love and sharing and caring
A future we'll face as a unified team

A future of giving, of patience, too
Where we will understand
Though we are one, we're each unique
So we will do the best we can

While some dreams may seem out of reach
Their spirit shall always live
For spirit is heart and heart is life
So spirit is what we each must give

So fear not dreams that distant seem
For their spirit is much alive
Just cradle these dreams like a newborn child
Though they're distant, they shall survive

So dream and dream and dream some more
And then do dream again
For life is but a dream of sorts
So make it what you can

"This, Our Life, Our Beginning"
What beautiful words these are
They have as much potential as
Our universe and stars

So close your eyes and say these words
When dreams may not seem right
And then these dreams that seem so bleak
Will magically turn bright

Happy Valentine's Day, Diana
All My Love, Geoff

—**Geoffrey S. Bue**

She's gone.
   All gone.
I should have kissed her more.

But now, too late.
I'm left with wretched might.
Have-beens and helpless yesterdays,
   a store of what can never be set right.

I should have held her closer,
   told her,
      shown her she was my ecstasy.

But, all I did was play the fool.
I did not see the writing on the wall.

It's over now,
   but for those silent wails,
      echoing through
      the unforgiving nights.

—**Mary Ann Adams**

A NEW BEGINNING

Gazing from memory
   I see a broken sky
Of mountains, melting ice
   A field of flowers
   Children laughing
   I see me

Gazing from memory
   I see broken dreams
A love that didn't survive
   But products of love
   That live on forever
   I see me

Gazing from memory
   I see broken hearts
Dark clouds loom; slowly the sun peeks through
   New dreams emerge
   A new beginning
   I see me

—**Käthe Giles**

COME SWING WITH ME

Come swing with me; what fun it will be
   As to and fro we go
It sets your mind free; all worries will flee
   Oh, it's something I do love so

Memories it brings of another old swing
   When I was only a child
I'd sit and I'd sing; the pleasure still clings
   In my heart the feelings are filed

But years have gone by, and now a family have I
   My cares have certainly increased
On that swing I rely; to find answers I try
   It helps! Anxiety decreased

For me? Yes, the pleasure remains; peace and
happiness it sustains
   It takes me far, far away
New heights I can gain; all things I can attain
   It's a place where I'd like to stay

So, come swing with me; what fun it will be
   As to and fro we go
It sets your mind free; your worries will flee
   And you, too, will love it so

—**Jean P. Ballis**

THE BRIDE

In antique lace with fair complexion,
She holds a red rose with delicate perfection.

As she walked down the aisle dressed in white,
The air was still and all were quiet.

In an angelic voice I heard her say,
I'll love you more and more each day.

With the exchange of rings and love so true,
She smiled and anxiously said, I do.

—**Linda Williams Pierce**

WITHOUT

When his lips touched mine, it was not the same
Somehow something happened
Sorrow upon sorrows and woes upon woes
My love's kisses at one time were genuine.

Once, when he kissed me a magical charm
encompassed my entire being, sending
sparks throughout, & it was real.
Now it is a compelled kiss.

Without the spirit it is only a peck.
Kissing is not needed if it is
without the soul. Kiss me not.
I'll do without.

Without my love's kisses of the spirit
I'll kiss no more. We were bound
for years by the soul but it has
been pierced, broken, 'tis doomed.

Sorrow upon sorrows and woes upon woes
My true love's kisses at one time were genuine
The essence of the kisses are gone
He loves me not anymore.

—**Shirley Shepard**

WHEN THE WIND BLOWS

When the wind blows . . . I think of You
When the wind blows . . . I come to You
The rivers and the oceans know my love is true
When the wind blows . . . I'm here with You.

I've reached for the stars . . . looking for You
I've gone so far . . . and I've been so blue
The mountains and the valleys know I love you too
When the wind blows . . . I'm here with You.

When the wind blows . . . the chimes will ring
When the wind blows . . . you'll hear me sing
The leaves will be reminders of seasons that we knew
When the wind blows . . . I'm here with You.

Love has a way . . . of making me shine
Love is the way . . . I'm spending my time
Though some have tried to warn me
    There's nothing I can do
The winds will bring . . . me home to You
The winds will blow . . . me back to You
When the wind blows . . . I'm here with You . . . .

To Duane, who has stirred me to reach beyond
the restricting limits, that held me back
from being the me that I am/could be . . . .

—**Leslie K. Walton**

ETERNAL LOVE: AN AMERICAN DREAM

Thank you, my love, for sharing with me
the joys and trials of a family.
Washing and dishes and diapers to do,
crying and fussing and disagreements too.
But love and kindness usually prevailing
have kept us happy and minimized wailing.

And although the words aren't always there,
within my heart is deepest care,
For you, for us, for children we see,
together forever through eternity.
A family now and forever too,
if we follow together the path that's true.

Reflecting on memories and building more,
our potentials expanding, now what's in store?
To be more like God, with joy forever?
Yes, that's the reason for life's endeavor.
So, thank you, my love, for sharing with me
Now and forever, through eternity!

—**Alvin K. Benson**

THE KISS

I looked at a star and saw you there
a million light years away,
        and yet I dreamed.
As time passed by I knew you were
too remote for me
        at least as your look seemed.

You could not see in my eyes,
my voice, my tears
        how much I wanted you
to give me just one sweet thing
I pined for
        if a miracle might ensue.

A meteor fell to earth that night
and something sublime struck my heart
        just by chance; it almost missed me.
An explosion came from Cupid's dart,
yet it was not a dream.
        You kissed me.

—**Nancy O'Malley**

FOREVER A MEMORY

You came into my life so quick
You influenced me in so many ways
You were someone I always dreamed about
But could only stay a few days

The few stolen moments we shared
Were enough to get me through
The laughter and the joy you gave me
Was a high I never knew

We talked to each other openly
We became each other's friend
The nights we spent together
Were nothing to pretend

It was a shame you had to leave
I was hoping that it wasn't true
I've waited so long to find
Someone who is as special as you

You were everything a woman could want
You were sweet, gentle and kind
Now all I have left of you
Are the memories you've left behind.

—**Ann-Marie Schmidt**

HURRY, PONDER AND CARE

The seasons come, the seasons go,
  As the frantic masses hurry to and fro.
To reach the goals we set in life,
We struggle through the toil and strife.
We often ponder where it will all end,
As we rush around the next bend.
When we go to our beds each night,
We hope that the world will be bright.
We labor to make it the kind of place,
We can proudly give to the entire human race.
Even when a minute is hard to spare,
May our hearts be filled with care.
Let us extend our helping hand,
To our needy brothers throughout our land.

—Rolanda Barton

OH, TO BE ONE AGAIN

Oh, to be "One" again
  What a lov-e-ly thought!
And get to live over again
  All the pleasures life has brought.

To see again the first snowflake
  And wonder at Starlight
As it shimmers on the lake
  Or thunder clouds gather in the night.

To marvel at animals
  So frisky at play
And examine the buttercups
  As they unfold each day.

Oh, to be "One" again
  And observe all the treasure
That God in His Goodness
  Has sent for our pleasure.

—Geneva Davis

ONLY GOD

  Only God can give us life
and make the mind to understand

  Only God can make it rain
and plants to grow at his command

  Only God can give us strength
when we can't make it anymore

  Only God can give us faith of things
we're hoping for

  God gave the earth to
each and everyone

  God gave Jesus Christ
His only begotten Son

  God gave the moon and the stars
God gives us love no matter who we are

  Only God can reach out his hand
and touch the heart of everyone

  Only God can forgive our sins
no matter what we have done

  Only God, Only God, Only God

—Dorothea Clausen

THE RAINBOW

God's promise to us all.
Beauty beyond compare after
  every storm.
Our Creator's gift of color.
In the same light He has given us
  a world of different colored people.
We must look upon each as awe inspired
  as we do the beauty of the Rainbow.
For each of us is created in the image of God;
  And beyond each storm of human conflict
  should lie beauty beyond compare.
In the form of Love, Respect, and Equality for All.
  Until there are no more storms.

—R.G. Watkins

DEAR JESUS

Dear Jesus:
  With the deepest sincerity I want to say I'm sorry,

  For the times you knocked on the door of my heart
  But I wouldn't let you in
  For the times you gently corrected my mistakes
  And I kept making them all over again
  For all the pain you felt in your heart
  As you so patiently watched me doing wrong
  For all the times I disappointed you by
  Being so weak instead of being strong
  For all the times you've shown me mercy
  Yet I showed no mercy towards others
  For the times I rebelled against your word
  By disobeying my father and mother
  But most of all I'm so sorry for
  The many, many times I've made you cry
  Please forgive me my Heavenly Father
  Dear Jesus please don't pass me by

—Thernell Johnson

SWEET LORD

Oh, come unto me, sweet Lord from above,
  And shower me tenderly with your warm love.
My soul, my heart, my life I give.
Please, teach me now, how I should live.

I know all the suffering and pain you had,
And how it pierced your heart and made you sad,
To see all the evil and wickedness around.
All the stealing, cheating, and lies we surround

Oh, sweet Lord, I can now see,
How you suffered and died to make us free.
The thorns in your head, spikes driven in your hands,
By the Father above, you took your commands

He must have loved us an awful lot,
To give his only Son, that He had begot.
Oh, sweet Lord, you too must have loved us tremendously,
To give your life to set us free.

Because through you, Our Father would forgive,
All the hate in this world, so we could live.
As you died on that cross, you said,
With much grace, "It's all over and done,"

"Your sins are forgiven you, your new
life has begun."

Dedicated to my maker, the Lord above,
for inspiring me and making it possible
for me to write my poetry.

—Judy Westover

STAR IN THE SKY

If I could forget the way I felt about you, I would throw it all away.
I would let you fade from my memories, as night bleeds into day.
If I understood why I loved you, do you think I'd hold you in my heart?
I can't seem to forget what you meant to me, so you'll always own a part.
I know it's hopeless when I look at you, like a drowning man at sea.
I can't understand the fire inside, and why it's burning me.

Maybe if I reached right up in the sky, and gave one star to you.
Perhaps you would finally realize, that the love we had was true.
Now it's time to move along, to leave all our memories behind.
To bury our treasure so far away, to a place we can never find.
When you look in the sky and see the stars, you once saw in my eye.
If you were one in a billion stars, you would still be the only star in the sky.

So when you look up in the sky, never forget all the times we had.
Remember all the time we had together, and tell me it wasn't that bad.
If it seems I don't remember, if it seems I can't get by.
When I give up on our dream of us, there will be one less star in the sky.

—Jay Perkins, age 16

SHADES OF A COLOR

Blue and green are the colors of the world that encompasses us.
The sun is the eternal spotlight that works to reveal our nature.
Yet forever we hide in an effort to diffuse the light that is nature.
Eventually the light prevades us and we are exposed as only black and white.
Time has faded our colors and emotions into nothing.
And so we are nothing.
Emotions change from love to hate.
A cloud of burden releases fear and anxiety.
Light has eaten away the mask and we vanish.
Joy and hope are an illusion of despair and insincerity.
Blackness surrounds all existence like a shallow hole.
Darkness consumes us and we have become grotesque by reality and truth.
One can not bear the horror and shame.
And so the endless cycle begins.
Black becomes pale mixed with blue and green.
It is a gradual transparency.
Never the same growing uglier and uglier with decay and isolation.
The sun grows stronger and we grow weaker.
It becomes futile to hide.

—Liz Quinn

FAMILIES

"God places the solitary in families," comforting words from the Bible . . .
families by blood, by obligation, by necessity, by desire . . .
and sometimes, if one is very lucky, by love.
It is a word that implies solidity, a rock solid foundation, a place to go home to . . .
to grow out of . . . to grow away from,
and yet to remember and hang onto . . .
the echoes never leaving one's ears or one's heart,
the memories carved like painted ivory, from a single tusk, delicately colored in brilliant
hues and softer ones, faded sometimes, so dim as to be almost forgotten . . .
and yet never to be totally forgotten or left behind.
The place where one begins and hopes to end . . .
the thing one works hard to build on one's own . . . the pieces like building blocks . . .
reaching high into the sky . . .
family . . . what images that conjures . . . what memories . . . what dreams.
I am just beginning to make some definite changes in my life.
Some of them will take some time, some of them will cause me grief, some of them
will mean risk and a lot of growing pains too.
But whatever the case, I know I will make it . . .
it's having someone like you to see me through both the good times and the bad
that makes me so sure.

Dedicated to my mother, Mona G. Gordy

—Kathryn Rachelle Gordy

WEEPING WILLOW

Weeping willow when the wind blows,
I see your branches swing to and fro.
When the rain pours down I know you weep,
but you don't stop, you never sleep.
Soon the sun comes out again,
it doesn't matter, you never grin.
All the time, you always cry,
your weep and moan will never die.

—Melissa Doran

Dusk falls on windswept sea
Dirty foam tops the angry waves and is
    whipped high into the air.
Eerie light deepens the darkened water.
Still, the man walks the beach—alone . . .
gulls shriek a cry of danger as they
    fly inland to safety.
Haunted—grey and bitter as the icy wind,
He walks into Winter—alone . . . .

Love,
Dona

—Dona Hough

THE RIVER

The river flows through the heartland,
    flowing carelessly without a worry.
The people go and sit for awhile,
they can't help but smile.

They sit until it is dark,
going home following a dog's bark.
They go again and sit, for it is another day,
and sit beside the bay.

As they sit beside the bay,
they see a sea gull flying away.
As the river flows,
they see a sunset and say, "there she goes!"

As another day goes by,
they remember the day with a sigh.
"The day has been good," they say,
as they sit beside the bay.

—Elizabeth Harding

LAKE MICHIGAN

As the Western sky glows red
    With the setting sun,
A quiet stillness settles
    O'er the lake.

The peaceful serenity is broken
    By the gentle splash,
Made by a gracefully
    Leaping trout.

Again, a silver arc he makes,
    As though to catch
The last rays of the
    Fast retreating sun.

Nothing remains but an ever
    Widening circle of ripples,
Gently spreading like a soft blanket,
    Covering God's creatures for the night.

—Alma Grossman

THE SEA

Once you have the feel of the sea
    your home away seems dull and drear,
no calm and blue sea on sunny day,
no angry and grey sea on stormy day.

I miss you, you are so faraway,
I miss you at night, the movements of waves,
no seagulls calling and flying to race,
no sea air washing my eager face.

I love the sea and I always will,
just waiting for chance to go back still,
I know and feel you calling me there,
I hear your voice and understand.

Before I leave this earthly life
with all its joys and all its strife,
I shall go back to sea and shore
and I shall stay and leave no more.

—Hedy Wolf

A DAY AT THE BEACH

Bathers displaying their new suits of crimson,
    Sun burning brightly to warm up the day;
Sands shifting gently to cradle the still forms
    peacefully sleeping their troubles away.

Waves beating fiercely subduing the shoreline,
Eroding stone sentries formed long ages past;
Slowly but surely reclaiming the treasures
    that man had considered his right to the last.

Seas fighting bravely to purify waters
    fouled through the thoughtless excretions of man;
Rolling and pounding, then casting ashore
    once proud living creatures now dead on the sand.

Under the waters serenity rules,
Reigning in silence and eternal bliss;
Patiently waiting for man's disappearance
    and time immemorial's all-healing kiss.

—Jerry D. Siders

VISIT TO HAWAII

My visit to Hawaii was simply superb,
    This island is even more beautiful than I
had ever heard.
The sights that you see there are so grand,
It made me so proud to claim this state as
part of our own land.
Hawaii is one of our fifty states of the
U.S.A.,
We are so happy when they welcome us
with a lei.
Their Aloha is so sincere and true,
It makes us feel very welcome too.
The mountains and the beaches are picturesque,
What a lovely place to relax and rest!
The flowers and trees are something to see,
What a treat to see coconuts and bananas
growing in the trees!
The breezes in Hawaii are so balmy and pleasant,
It makes everyone wish they could become
a permanent resident.
The highlight of the trip was the spectacular
rainbows in the sky,
Then I knew that God was watching nearby.

—Annelle Stuckey

MEMORIAL DAY

Arranging bouquets in hues so right
Lavender, yellow, pink or white
Some their favorites we know well
And go about our love to tell
To only a name on marble, cold
And the memories of days of old

How we'd like to have a bosom chat
Of happenings of this or that
Only in thoughts topics abide
We try so hard our tears to hide
Then only a name on marble, cold
And the memories of days of old

We will go again next year and show
Respect for those whom we loved so
Only a Name on marble, cold?
No they're not here the ones we enfold
THEY'RE DWELLING ABOVE IN MANSIONS GOLD.

   —Gladys B. Cutkomp

FOREVERMORE

Death, an element of loneliness,
Hated, at the same time loved,
Not by all, but by one;
One, racked with madness
Captured in his turbid soul,
Inspired by a Demon — Lucifer, himself,
Forever trapped in pitiful horror with
Unmerciful haunts of yore,
Never to gaze at the majestically, beautiful moon,
But to stare wildly with horror; for it alone,
Affected his brain, letting escape —
The Mind —
The Hand —
The Pen —
The terrors trapped —
Inside the man's soul. And now,
Forever at rest, inside a coffin most dreaded;
A soul,
Eternally undisturbed,
After many a long and restless night.

   —William G. Hammel

THE ANGEL

Among the stars, the moon at night,
I saw an angel in purest white:
Such peace as I have never felt
as the angel came and before me knelt.
My soul was searching, Lord is it true?
For you know I want to worship you.
The angel said, "Have no fear
for the Lord is standing so very near."
The angel said, "You must be brave,
for it was for you his life he gave.
I'll give you strength to defeat the foe
just stand for me, be very bold,"
my thoughts were turning so very fast
as the angel said, "This too shall pass."
My shoes I took off on this holy ground
as the angel said, "In you a pure heart is found,
I am here tonight to lead you home
for your trials and troubles will be gone
eternal life now you have earned,
for things of God you cared to learn."

   —Donna Reynolds

SIMPLE MAN

  A Simple Man leaves his native land in search for a helping hand. Across the sea of turmoil, he sails to the land of fairytales where everything rhymes and works out fine. Upon arrival, Simple Man, finds many people with their heads stuck in the sand, so he travels further inland.

  He quietly strolls across the open spaces without loss of faith; that his journeys will soon be at an end. The Simple Man kneels to the ground finding riches all around. The dark clumps of soil feel like gold to his touch. In his dreams he never asked for too much.

Dedicated to the memory of grandfather, Reinert Boe, who came from Norway in 1904 and farmed in South Dakota for nearly 60 years.

   —Mark L. Wyant

SILENT CRIES

Only 17, she was so strong,
In every group she did belong.
So young, so beautiful, so sincere,
No one realized her death was near.
She had been strong, now very weak,
Too much in pain to even speak.
So afraid as she lay there dying,
No one around to hear her crying.
She had felt so lost, so confused,
All her life she'd been abused.
She stopped the ticking of her heart,
And tore her family's lives apart.
She said she'd show them, make them see,
Just how revengeful she could be.
With her last breath she tried to be strong,
There were other choices, suicide was wrong.
She was too late, they took her away,
Just when she wished she could have stayed.

   —Catherine M. Clouse

DESTINY

My time draws nigh
As I recall once more
The joy and hope I once had
For now, it is only a past memory
Lingering for all eternity

Though I now face death
I go, unafraid, yet I am not brave
Years I've strived to reach my goal
Tormenting hours, ageless days
And I am defeated in the presence of all
I leave, destroyed and sorrowed

My demise comes, but not as a stranger
However, being prepared and set
My expectation of my finish
Occurred suddenly, abruptly
And my deeds left undone

The closing is here; retreat I must
Triumphant and conquering I'm not
I merely go humbly to my end
And wish others the chance I never had

   —Susan Rovens-Beedle

MY SON, MY SON

I see the first rays of sun
   shining on the smiling face of my son
   and he looks like he's having fun.
We're not on our way to the mall
   or at the park playing ball.
Maybe we're out for a walk
   or on a hill having a talk.
We're not out and about
   Trying to catch us a trout
   But on his early morning paper route.
And, yes, we are having fun
   me and my number one son.

Dedicated to my son, Waylon.

—Patra Jo Iverson

TO MY CHILDREN

Sometimes I forget to say
I love you.
Sometimes it seems all I do
is lecture you.
Sometimes I don't seem to appreciate
the things you do.
I just want you to know
I love you
And I lecture you because
I want you to be mature,
responsible adults.
I want you to know
I'm proud
that each of you are now
young adults and
have become what you are.
I love you.

Love,
Mom

—Barbara Kelley

JUST FOR YOU

   I thought of what to do, so many
sleepless nights thru
   Always wondering how I'd be able
to pick and choose for you
   A family who was in need of
someone so young and sweet
   Someone who I already loved, yet
am unable to keep
   Needing to find two loving people
to keep you safe and warm
   To clothe and love you, feed you
and especially keep you from harm
   Someone to love you just as I,
and somebody who can explain all
the reasons why
   I wanted you to have so much
more than I, so I tried to pick two
people who would do their very best
   To insure your future, your
happiness and any of life's quests
   Your real Mom still loves you
and frets, but knows she tried
her very best
   To give you a chance, your
life to enhance, two loving new parents,
who are going to be what I can't.

—Bonnie S. Brown

LISA ANN

Her Little Heart, all smothered in Pain
No One to comfort Her, No One can explain,
The Anger She feels cannot give Measure
   The memories of Mom — To Her a Treasure
But memories right now — Tho bring her no pleasure
She takes in Stride that She'll never be
   Like any of those That She can See.
She was made different And Only God Knows,
Why, in a Thorn Bush He placed A Rose
   A Rose So sweet — Velvet to touch —
A Special Gift From God — and
   We Love Her So Much —

—Mary E. Ayers

MY DAUGHTER GOT MARRIED TODAY

I stop by her room and pause at the door,
Wedding gown on the bed — satin shoes on the floor.
Packing and moving left the room in disarray . . .
My daughter got married today.

A lovely wedding — she made a beautiful bride,
And I remember the years with her at my side.
A wonderful long visit, but I knew she couldn't stay . . .
My daughter got married today.

Stuffed animals and dolls on lonely shelves remain,
And pillows on the window seat where she loved to play.
I pin a wedding program to her bulletin board display,
My daughter got married today.

On this day, their life together will start.
But with her she took a piece of my heart,
Letting go is so hard — but I must be brave . . .
My daughter got married today.

Oh, Lord, I pray that I raised her right,
To be loving and true and pleasing in your sight.
Our years together passed so quickly away . . .
My daughter got married today.

—Marlis Day

MOM

What does our Mom mean to us?
   She is someone we love and trust.

Young and beautiful she is indeed,
But just as wild as a growing weed.

Caring and kind she is to us,
How grateful we are for her loving touch.

Always there for us at our beck and call,
Ready and waiting to go to the Mall.

So full of knowledge and wise too,
She'll answer your question and tell you what to do.

Doing for others all the time,
Never taking anything not even a dime.

The years have crept upon her so fast,
We hope and pray this won't be her last.

We neglect to tell her how we feel,
We're all caught up in making a deal.

We only have one Mom in this life,
She's a great mother and a good wife.

So we'll say Happy Mother's Day now before the tears,
We love you very much Mom and hold you so dear.

—Gloria Fama

WISHING

I wish that we could be alone,
 Us and the kids in a happy home.
On a desert isle out on the sea,
 No more problems and hassle free.
Where all troubles and stress would end,
 And we'd once again be best of friends.

What I am wishing is not for sex,
 but of knowing each other and mutual respect,
Of love and honor and total sharing,
 of talking, listening and really caring.
So let's, in our minds, just move away,
 and begin our lives in a brand new way!

—David M. Cook (Cooky)

I voluntarily shared my soul with you
And you engraved yourself in my heart
The moments we endured in sent my spirit a flutter
Dramatically now we must part

All the memories I have are massively sacred
I will cherish them safe in my inner core
Mutually at the present we are merely friends
Although in the future I wish we could be more

You waltzed into my life to shine new light
Everyday you presented to it new meaning
But now you are so far yonder from my grasp
I can only be with you how I want when I'm dreaming

Everything seemed so fantastically perfect
As if our relationship was succeeding
Now you have grasped that sharp, shining knife
And in the center of my heart I am bleeding

I can not possess you to love me more
I can not make you feel what I want you to
But a part of my heart is still left and beats on
Crying painfully that I will always love you

—Anna Giuliani

ARE YOU BEAUTIFUL

Are you beautiful, I do not know,
But my heart keeps saying so.
Love is blind so they say,
But my heart wants you anyway,
From you I will never sway.

Beauty is in the heart of the beholder;
Will it grow as we get older.
Time will tell what life will bring,
Growing love is such a beautiful thing.
Oh! we wonder what time will bring.

Are you beautiful, I guess so;
Because the beating of my heart, keeps saying so.
With every beat of my heart it seems to get stronger,
To last forever and ever longer.
Oh! we wonder what time will bring.

Why do I love you, I do not know.
Still my heart keeps saying go.
With you, time will forever glow.
For ever and ever I will know.
Are you beautiful; I guess so.

—David L. Paugh

A WISH

I wish for you every dream come true,
every mountain peak,
and the misty morning dew.
For nature's finest treasures are seen
in a child's eyes,
and icy mountain streams.
Look deep within everything around,
and open your eyes to see,
for in everything there is a beauty found.
Listen quietly, as the morning bird sings,
for songs of joy
and songs of love it brings.
And in the still of the evening air,
in your heart you'll see
that song of love is still there.

—Wendy J. Kimble

REMEMBER

I sit alone
See the world through a stranger's eyes

I think of you
All alone
Looking to the horizon

There's a storm brewing there
Now alone, do you remember me?

I have walked alone
I always do
But now and then I stumble
And I blame it on you

I think of you all alone
Looking for what you don't know
The storm you see bears my name

Do you remember me?

Love and memories are held dear
Inspiration can be few and far between
This is for you, Charlotte Marie

—Sonny B.

THE VALENTINE TREAT

Mom, you are sweet,
you are my morning smile.
Also, you are my afternoon treat,
you keep me smiling all the while.

Dad, you are so strong,
you are always there when I fall.
You are hardly ever wrong,
you come to my rescue when I call.

Mom, your voice is like a flute,
a sweet sound to everyone who hears.
You are also very cute,
when you are around I have no fears.

Dad, you are my friend,
you'll always be there for me.
You also keep me well fed,
when I was a baby, I sat on your knee.

You're a queen and king to me,
I love you very much.
My Valentines will you be,
because I'll take you out to lunch.

—Jane Hutson, grade 6

WONDERS OF SPRING

The trees are busy budding
Robins are singing everywhere
Oh what a happy season:
For "Spring" is in the air.

The daffodils and tulips
Peek out of the frost-free ground
To spread their lovely colors —
And beauty all around.

There's "March" with all the strong winds
And "April" with all its showers
Then along comes the warm sunshine
To bring us those pretty "May" flowers.

Then "June" will bring assurance
That "Spring" is here to stay —
And all the glooms of "Winter"
Have forever passed away.

—Betty J. Hagen

MAIDEN OF DAWN

Like maiden fair of days long gone
The morning blushes tender
Pastel pink on snowy white
Her beauty soft in growing light
    This maiden of the dawn.

Stunned by the grace her presence demands
Hushed to silence these lips of mine
I gaze in admiration
Her smile a veil all its own
Disarms one's cares, stands alone
    This maiden of the dawn.

With wink she bids me follow aft
Her lithe form glides with supple curves
Above yon terra firma
As far and more than eye can see
The youthful game awakened me
    This maiden of the dawn.

—Mickey B. Wisehart

SPRING PRETTY

Spring blossoms through the mid-night air.
March winds change to spring fever.

Life's hard work continues to be wise.
As the temperatures fall and rise.

Birds strut their stuff around.
Do you hear their sweet sound?

Some say, "Spring Pretty has arrived."
Others say, "Winter Willie has survived."

Spring enters with a wedding band.
April rains over her rich land.

The stamp situations dwindle.
As Homer opens his window.

Cold and hot bring sneezes.
Mother Nature teases.

Some say, "Spring Pretty has arrived."
Others say, "Winter Willie has survived."

Sunshine plays the game of peek-a-boo.
May gives birth to a flower or two.

—Raymond Clark Nelson

SPRING

When soft green leaves have spread their fingers
The air is filled with bracing scent,
The bushes' boughs are flower-bent,
And a light haze on hilltops lingers.

    The ripples of the river run
    As to outrun the wind, their master,
    Above, the clouds are moving faster,
    Unveiling the eternal sun.

—Alexandra Teploff

SONG OF SUMMER

The summer trees weave their green lace,
    Birds call throughout the land,
And summer breezes kiss my face.
Come here and take my hand.
Your love will keep me safe and warm
No matter what's to come.
Life's like a sudden summer storm.
Behind the clouds, the sun
Shines through, and sheds its golden sheen
On flowers of every shade and hue,
On trees of lacy green.
The birds call in the morning dew.
Their singing and the summer breeze
Make music in the land.
It whispers in the murmuring trees.
Come love, and take my hand,
And walk along with me
Down life's road 'til life ebbs out like grains of sand
And in the life to be.

—Mary Gebo

HIDDEN FOREST

The deafening silence fell as heavy as the fog that
    encased the forest trees,
Another morning sun giving birth to the dawning of
    a new day it receives.
Innocence of an untouched, untarnished world hidden
    from man,
Kept pure by its inhabitants being held as captives
    in paradise's command.
A world that men can only embrace in his dreams and
    forlorn wisdom,
Is the world that shelters and mothers the forest
    kingdom.
Creation and creature sharing jointly keeping their
    forest home confined,
In a balance orchestrated in motion from the beginning
    of time.
Lying beneath the majestic skies and kneeling at the
    feet of grandeur mountains,
Waits the silent, hidden forest with inhabitant creatures,
    streams and fountains.
How long will this paradise remain untouched and
    unspoiled?
Its destiny yet hangs in the balance of man's greed
    and selfish toil.
The imagery of such a world should be implanted on
    all of our minds,
For as we induce destruction for gain we can produce
    change to protect any world of this kind.

—Miriam Rhoades

I'M THE BIBLE

Read me often, I'm your friend
on me you always can depend.
There's comfort for every sorrow on most every leaf.
And only three requirements hope, love and belief.
You'll probably stumble, your faith will falter,
but **He** won't let you tumble for **His** love doesn't alter.
This is the truth, you may hold me liable,
I've lasted many years
I'm a book called the B I B L E.

Dedicated to our father, Carl. From your children—
Kenneth, Judy, Leonard, Randy, Donna, LeAnn
In loving memory of our mother.

—Aileen Boecker, deceased

DANIEL

One day he's here with a smile on his face.
The next day he's in heaven in a much better place.
What a kind, forgiving heart that has passed on.
His memory will live in our hearts,
even though he is gone.
A good son, a loyal brother, an unforgettable
friend, and no one will forget him even when
we come to our end.
What an awful world we all live in.
A place full of violence, struggle, and
unforgiving people of sin.
Heaven is so much better than this,
but everything about him we shall all miss.
Someday we will all see him again.
Rest in peace, my brother, my friend.

—Amber D. Carlson-Sega

PRAYER MEETING

In the old EUB church on Main Street
Was a group gathered strictly for prayer.
And voices that rose from the meeting
Brought blessings to all that were there.

The room that they used was the Scout Room.
The folding chairs brown, hard and bare.
And they scooted about rather noisily
When everyone knelt in prayer.

Brother Howard McNeal led the singing.
The dear hymns that he loved so well.
And selections called out — by the number —
How they sang them with joy — how they swelled.

As they knelt on their knees in communion
Taking turns talking out loud to God.
Spirit led — with love and thanksgiving
Life's problems given up to God.

There'd be tears on the faces of many;
Soul cleansed — how their eyes would shine.
The prayer meeting then was for praying
Humble Christians touched with power Divine.

Christian fellowship there was so precious.
On Wednesdays you'd find us all there.
When Brother McNeal led the singing!
And talked to his Father in prayer.

Dedicated in loving memory of my Dad,
Howard W. McNeal 1886 - 1941

—Hazel McNeal Graves

DEATH

Death is a feeling only the dying know
Whether to stay or whether to go
Is life on the other side better than
here or are we fooling ourselves to
What may be near
Heaven above or hell below, dying
to stay or dying to go
Only the dying know

—Paulette Sands

IN MY DREAM

In my dream,
My mother died,
And she came down to visit me.
We hugged
And we hugged,
Until I told her I was tired.
So she laid me down on the world's land,
And covered me up with the sea.

—Heather Marie Bell, age 11

THE DEATH OF A LEAF

The raging wind made it dance and sway
Burned its cheeks of red today
And in its cry the leaf seemed to say:
"I will not die on an autumn day
When everything is dismal, and gray!"

Winter came, and drank its blood away.
Made it dull, shrivel, and fray.
Still, the stubborn leaf decided to stay
As little pieces were nibbled away;
Neither would it die on a winter day.

Now spring is here, and to my dismay,
The leaf let go of its branch today.
On the grass peacefully it lay
Seeming pleased in its own way,
That it had died on a warm spring day.

Dedicated to the memory of my father,
Robert Martin.

—Francoise Martin-Litch

PEACE BE WITH YOU . . .

Peace be with thee my children
as I take orbit to things unseen.

Peace be with you as I take flight,
& spread my golden wings.

Like an eagle I shall soar high far
& wide,
I'll be watching over you!

As one's spirit never dies,
beauty yet to see,
for one's soul is set free!

I hope you remember to have fond
memories of me—,

As I soar up to the sky,
with this I say goodbye . . . .

Dedicated in honor of Jocelyn A. Domela.
May she rest in peace. Also to her beloved
son, Fred J. Domela . . . .

—Gloria Mae Moskovita

..ETLY SUGGESTIVE

Sweetly suggestive, of old, dusty lace
Dried flowers, forgotten, in some dark,
lonely place
Silently dreaming, of a time, and a
face.

A manuscript written, for love, for
all time
To read, and remember, the bittersweet
rhyme
No page goes unnoticed, the words
are sublime.

A love lost in tempo, a sweet memory,
Kept for all seasons, a reminder, you
see
That love is a keepsake, and your
heart is the key.

—Cat Galloway

BLESSINGS FROM HEAVEN

Arrayed in golden splendour,
A cherub appeared from Heaven above
To bless you and I, my dearest,
With friendship, harmony, and love.

Graced with guidance
And spirits bound,
Heavenly wisdom
I have found. Now . . .

In my heart of hearts I see
Visions of a life that is new to me.
In my mind I cannot conceal
The feelings for you that are so real.

And blessings from Heaven are ours.

*Dedicated to Jimmy Dean Burch, my
soul mate and fellow poet, brought
together by the same dreams.*

—Rosemary Pavlina

LOVE

Love,
An all-consuming power,
Surpasses the beauty of any flower.
Though it may scar a lover's heart
When love's bonds are forced apart,
Loneliness, love's only enemy,
Is surely no infinity.
Love will stand while empires fall,
For the power of love will conquer all.
Love gives meaning to life
Through all our trouble and strife.
Love is what makes life worthwhile.
A gentle touch, a friendly smile.
Though all our days may pass
Like sand inside an hourglass,
The love that's shared will last forever,
For the bonds of love no blade can sever.
Love,
An all-consuming power,
Surpasses the beauty of any flower.

—Austin Wayne Brown

RELATIONSHIPS

Every person is individual made from a unique mold.
No one is perfect so I am told.
But each has facets
Worth their weight in gold.

Dwelling on the past and remaining mad,
Insures no solution will ever be had.
Remember the good,
Forgive and forget the bad.

When you can truly forgive a wrong done to you,
You will be a better person and a stronger one, too.
Your goodness will shine
As bright as new.

The seers say the truth, "Love conquers all."
They also say "Pride goeth before the fall."
Make sure you walk with love and forgiveness,
Straight and tall.

—Jeanne Haley

LIFELONG LOVE

As we walk along this path of life
Trying to distinguish between wrong and right,
We encounter many a burden—and of one
Thing only are we completely certain.
That though many a broken heart we've had
We alone can make our souls live sad.
We find a time to cry and laugh,
Our time is divided . . . not half and half.
We alone may choose our destiny
And the rest of our life, with whom it will be.
And so we examine under close scrutiny,
And choose our life long love so carefully.
That we not send our souls into sadness,
But we truly love and live in gladness.
And so I've tried and I've learned
That true love isn't given, but it's earned.
And so that in the very most end,
You choose to love your Very Best Friend.

—Chelsey A. Torgerson

I LOVE YOU

I hate to be alone. I love people.
Saying, "I love you," to a man isn't easy for me.
Men try to make me say it.
They put their arms around me—
I pretend I don't see it.
They pinch me—
I pretend I don't know it.
They kiss me—
I pretend I don't feel it.
They take me out
in the evenings and try to force me—
but I'm careful, I don't say it.
If they don't like it, they can leave me alone.
Because when I say, "I love you" to him
He will know just by looking in my eyes,
that many have held, pinched and kissed me,
but I truly mean the words . . .
I LOVE YOU.

—Cynthia Atkins

MOM, I LOVE YOU

The LORD is good and his mercy endureth forever,
  for those like you, a true believer.
You've been waiting for the LORD to come back,
You've been running awhile and you haven't lost track.
Thanks be to GOD, he has smiled on you,
On the things you say and whatever you do.
May he continue to bless and use you in your daily life,
so you can stay strong and overcome life's strife.
And, if along the way, you should be dismayed,
think of the HOLY LIFE that JESUS gave,
and remember that I LOVE YOU,
and mainly, JESUS does too!!
                    —Ronald J. Solls

MY CHILD

        She was once my weakness,
She is now my strength.

        She was once my sorrow.
She is now my greatest happiness.

        She was once my embarrassment.
She is now my pride.

        She was once the reason I could no longer go on.
She is now my best reason to live.

        She was once my handicapped daughter.
She is now my child.

        —Al Sisson

MURIEL'S AUNT

Seeing that old lady for the first time
  Did me a lot of good.
She's ninety-one, you know.
She is a tiny woman—
I'm sure she used to be larger as all her family were.
Do you suppose she shrunk?
She was well aware of being the center of attention.
Her bright eyes just sparkled
As she sat at the big, round table.
Clean, well dressed and healthy.
A clever conversationalist, knowing both dates
        and facts.
Seeing that old lady did me a lot of good.
Don't we all wish we could be that sharp at ninety-one?

        —Margaret Ethelyn Hunter

TO JIMMY

When I was eight and you were eighteen
  They took you away
I was too young to know
  My heart was broken.

I remembered happy summer days
  Blue skies, green meadows
  Laughter, donuts warm from the oven
I remembered no dark, cold, bitter winters.

When I was thirty-eight and you were forty-eight
  God took you away
I was old enough to know
  You were safe, loved, whole.

I will be with you again
  My best friend, my brother.
        —Mary Hegle

BIRTH MOTHER

The letter came today each line
  explaining my way.
For I had come to yearn the truth
  about my life here on this earth.

Loving parents had smoothed the way
  and I truly love them to this day.
And yet, knowledge of my birth
  seemed to taunt those nights and days.

I needed to know about my first
  hours and day,
While I kept on seeking my way!

They said you stayed seventy-six days
  soon to be torn away,
Fondness and refinement were your way.

The forms are filled, sent on their way,
Hoping a match will be made someday!

Will I really find the one who
  was there at my birth?
The year that was so bad for
  this earth!

What will I do, what can I
  learn from you?
I know you loved me, in your
  own way, what more can I say!
        —Carol Jean Crew

A CHILD

She was just a little tot
  Fresh from Heaven
She came with not a lot
I named her Nicole Devin

She gave me joy
A chance to be
Friends brought her toys
In the future I can see

She played, laughed and cried
Walking, failing all around
When she got sick I thought I'd die
Talking, making precious little sounds

Then one day a sadness came
She was going away
No one is the blame
But this place she had to stay

This little child was no bother
I love her as if I gave birth
Now she's with her real mother
This precious little thing on earth

Now she's gone I know not where
She's loved and missed so
Being watched over from the man upstairs
Nicole's in good hands, this I know

Dedicated to all adopted children.
        —Jean Cito

TALKING TO WINTER WINDS

I stood facing the mountains
The wailing of my sorrows, mere echoes
Of our love, now done.
You had chosen to steal away
With the dying of the sun
And hide yourself in shadows
Belonging only to your soul,
Ancient ghosts neither sage nor cedar
Could purge or purify or bring
Into the lightedness of your awareness:
You had chosen this for both of us,
My voice falling silent upon the
Reverberation of your aching spirit,
My broken heart talking to winter winds.

—Lydia Chapman

SCRUB OAK

Alone
In the small valley
It struggled to grow

It stole drops from low clouds
While ancient rains stayed locked
In the high mountain lake

Towering hillsides blocked the sun
Few precious rays snuck through
Yet it continued to raise limbs

Stars aligned the lake overflowed
Roaring through the valley
Testing Its hold on the earth below

The pain as roots left behind their efforts
It was flushed from the small valley
Alone into the swirling night

Morning sun found It standing
On Its side at the edge of the great forest
It continued to raise limbs

No longer
Alone

—Jack Barr

THE BROKEN OAK

High on a rocky hillside stands an ancient
And rugged oak tree.
Its branches gnarled, twisted and broken
By the ravages of time and element,
Reach out, as if in mute supplication
To be free.
Through centuries it has stood there alone
Like the condemned doing penance to atone.

And so becomes the soul of a man
Who walks the pathway of life alone.
A hapless thing, as twisted and broken
As the old oak tree.
How can he be kind who has known no kindness,
Or love, if he has known no love:
So let us look a bit more closely
E're we pass him by,
We may find there one tiny ray of hope,
A mere gleam of eye,
In mute supplication for a reaching hand
To lift him up and let him stand
Tall and free.
A gentle heart to teach him to love
And to reach for that Hand from above.

—Ila Loveless

WINTER'S SLUMBER

To every season the trees convey,
The beauty God has sent our way.
On winter mornings white blankets of snow,
Wait to be lifted from branches below.
He sends down warming rays of light,
To lift the covers of the night.

—Barbara Mauthe

THE SNOWFLAKE

To speak of a snowflake pure and white
and of its short life within our sight.
A frozen crystal beauty beyond compare
ever so gently falling through open air.
It journeys downward to the ground,
and never makes a single sound.
The snowflake.

—Richard Jones

WINTER FUN

On a cold winter day
children love to play.
Early to rise and then outside
to find a place to slide.
Children run and stomp
because it's so much fun to romp.
They run up the long hill
and ignore winter's icy chill.
It really doesn't hurt to take a nasty spill
at the bottom of the slippery hill.
When the snow begins to melt
snowballs find targets to pelt.
Soon a snowman begins to form
and all eagerly await another storm.
At home mothers wait and fret
as children arrive very late and wet.
It's been great to play on this winter day.
But, alas, all wish for warmer days in May!

—Mr. D.

WINTER TIME

The winter days are long and cold
and it's then that I am not so bold.
When the wind and snow blows in my face
it is then I long to be some other place.

My hands get cold and my lips turn blue
and I think my feet are frozen too.
I cannot put on enough clothes
to keep me warm from head to toes.

Sometimes I would like to leave this place
and go someplace where the weather's warm.
Where the sun comes up each morn
and southern breezes keep me warm.

I would risk sunburn every day
and mosquitoes come out at night.
If I could say just for one day
I lived in paradise

Sometimes I think I would like to be
Where I have been told to go.
They call it hell but I have been told
it never ever snows

—Walter A. Evans

OUR UNFINISHED SONG

Last night I wrote the saddest song I never heard.
It seems like an eternity, or was it a story or just a word.

It was like another day and time, I felt I'd known him forever.
From the moment our eyes first met, I knew we should be together.

The emptiness surrounded him, as I answered his touch with sighs.
The world could see his smile, only **I** could hear his wanting eyes.

His nimble fingers pulled my heart strings out of key —
And I wish I could hear our unfinished song — sung just for me.

His passionate lips swept me **AH!** to heights I could not believe,
As entangled, raptured **LOVE** we'd weave.

And all too soon **He's Gone!** And his song was soft and his song was low.
God grant me mercy, for my heart and soul ache, that **I miss him so!**

See. **BARRENNESS** where he was — and the **SONG**, It has no harmony — I yearn
As I pray and wait for his swift return.

> —**Wanda Sykes**

ANOTHER TIME OR PLACE

A special person touched my life in a very special way.
I think about her every minute of nearly every day.
Caring for my loved one in his time of dying
and greeting me with open arms in my time of crying.
I'll never forget the night he passed and feeling so alone
or the soft sweet voice she soothed me with when I called her on the phone.
She invited me to sit with her, some tender thoughts we shared.
It made me feel so warm inside to see how much she cared.
She said the things to ease the pain that no one else could say.
I finally had to leave that night, though I wanted so to stay.
My feelings grew in the days to come, of her I became so fond.
What started with a helping hand became a special bond.
She'd meet me with an eager hug when I'd walk through her door,
and when I hugged her in return I'd wish for more and more.
I fell in love so hard and fast I couldn't believe my eyes.
My feelings poured from deep inside like rain falls from the skies.
I long to hold her in my arms and be with her all night.
I wanted to make love with her though I knew it wasn't right.
I wish that we could always share a passionate love embrace.
If only our paths had come together in another time or place.

> —**Terri Scott**

MEMORIES

Today I'll go down Memory Lane, my walk to school in snow and rain.
A woodland path that had a name, running the May Hill was our game.
Occasionally I fall, but feel no pain, jump right up and start running again.

Autumn here, the start of school, a tree lined path, the air seems cool.
A hopping rabbit, a chipmunk with cheeks so full, by now the leaves
have turned to red and gold, I stop a moment, this beauty to behold.
Then comes a windy day, the leaves all down, each step I take makes
a rustling sound.

Winter Wonderland is on its way, Jack Frost has painted everything today.
Soon the heavens will open wide and lay, a pure white blanket that will stay.
The little path now hidden by drifting snow, I slip and slide as
strong winds blow. And stop a moment to gaze at the Creek below.

In spring, what a wonderful time, the first wildflower I claimed was mine.
As I passed, the violet bowed her head, the Jack-In-The-Pulpit, in a mossy bed.
Wild ferns, framed a tree long dead, Robins, bluebirds, singing,
flying overhead. Just a few thoughts, more can be said.

> —**Mary Massimino**

A TRIBUTE TO MOTHER

To Mother who gave me birth
upon this great, wide, wonderful earth.
Her strong guidance has borne me light
on this long journey's flight.

She dwelt with me both night and day —
The light of God and his straight way.
Of the beauty of flowers, grace and trees,
of the mystery of life beneath the seas.

She stressed the importance of occupational labor.
These are the traits I will savor —
and to each there is no other
That could occupy the state of Mother.

—Juanita Russell Sheets

FATHER

Father is a very special person,
yes to you and me.
When we are in trouble, he
is always there to heed,
he tries to guide us straight
each and every day,
and with his love and understanding
he knows the narrow way.
He tries to make you happy each
and every day,
he takes you on vacation,
and tries other different ways.
So treat your Father with respect
Because you only have a Father
once, so treat him with a
very special love

—Butch Woolsey

WAIT AND SEE

Christmas is the time of year,
When all small children spread the cheer.
I stand by and watch the line
Of Santa Claus soon decline.

Children jump from left to right,
"I want a doll, a game, a bike.
I want some clothes, a bat, a ball,
I want a dog." I heard one call.

But one small child caught my eye.
She stood back as she did cry.
I asked her what she wished of him.
"My daddy, I want him home again."

My heart just melted inside out,
What's her story all about?
She wrapped her arms around my neck
As she gave a little peck.

A smile formed slowly on her face
As she soon began to say,
"But it's all right because you see,
Next year he won't forget about me."

Her mother came and took her hand.
The strength in her I couldn't understand.
She waved goodbye and said to me,
"He'll be back, just wait and see!"

—Tami Michaud

CHILDHOOD

When I was only five
I was going home from school
Kindergarten thoughts in my head.
It was springtime and I was bouncing along
In the pretty green grass at the roadway.
Soon I saw yellow flowers — yellow bells —
Next I saw blue flowers — blue bells —
And there thick among the grass and flowers
Were bird noses or shooting stars
In their bright cerise dresses and black noses
With their fragrance so rare.
When I picked a big bouquet
I hurried home to Mama.
There she sat on an easy chair
And as she took the flowers,
Her smile was so heavenly
It is a precious memory!
Next day she had a new baby!

—Anne Harris

MY SISTER, MY BEST FRIEND

You are a very special person to me
Without you I'm not sure where I'd be.
During this past year we have become close;
I guess God knew that I needed you the most.

I know I can count on you when I am down;
You always make sure I smile instead of frown.
You always seem to know what to say
And try to guide me in the right way.

No matter if my problems are big or small;
All I have to do is pick up the phone and call.
You're always there for me even late in the night
Letting me know that everything will be all right.

Thanks for being the special person you are
You are the best sister anyone could ask for.
And I thank God for my sister He did send,
'Cause not only are you my sister, you're my best
friend.

—Cindy L. Cromeans

THANK YOU

Every night before I go to sleep
I pray the Lord my soul to keep
Every time I pray I try to end with a Thank You
Thank You for first loving me
Thank you for letting me be
Thank you for sending your Son
Thank you for letting Him be the One
Thank you for making me whole
Thank you for saving my soul
Thank you for all the things you've given me
Once again Thank You for letting me be
Thank you for the people you've brought into my life
Thank you for guiding me through strife
Thank you for the sacrifices You made
May your memory never ever fade
And I say all this with one simple

Thank You

In remembrance to my loving grandmother,
Louise Sanford, I love you.

—Gina M. Hughes

FOR STACY

When the day is long, and you're feeling really down,
I'll be right behind you, turn and look around.
When your feelings overwhelm you and you feel
nothing but fear,
Turn and look behind you, and I'll be standing there.
When your "heart hurts," and you're lonely, and
all you feel is pain,
Turn and look behind you, my love is still the same.
When the tears are non-ending, and you've had
it being *there,*
Turn and look behind you, my eyes will say, "I Care."
When you crawl into bed at night, holding your
pillow as you do,
My arms will be around you, as I whisper,
"I Love You."
And each morning as you awake, to greet
a brand new day,
Know that I'm right behind you, and *with* you
I will stay.

—Tana Giusti

ROBERT

May God bestow life's richest blessings upon you
and sprinkle your silver-gray hair with dew.
And may the sun gently kiss your lips,
as gently as your fingertips touched me.

May kindness be your guiding light
and gentle love your star at night.
May heaven and earth be at your feet
when our tender lips gently meet.

Though my love for you is an illusion of mind,
In lonely solitude I'll find
peace and contentment of an unearthly kind,
and so God made him man among men.

He is a gift from God above
to dwell with me in unearthly love.
And so in him I do hold,
in his image my soul will mold.

—Juanita Russell Sheets

I GIVE YOU LOVE

though pain, sorrow, and stress leave me deserted
like a carcass freshly raped, pillaged, and picked
clean by life's vultures . . . i can think of you and
the things you do and i give you love and that makes
things fine.

though tornadoes, droughts, and floods of turmoil
twist about me like a cowboy's lasso to the neck of
a calf . . . my thoughts turn to you.

volcanic explosions do no longer replace my anger.
flat desolate plains are no longer symbolic of my
depression.
liberty, freedom, and truth now light my path with
hope and love that comes from you.

to say i care for you is not enough,
you're more than my inspiration,
you're a beacon on an island of darkness,
you're courage where fear has long tread
and through all of this the least i can do is give
you love . . . and more love.

—Denise K. Johnson

VALENTINE

Valentine's Day is here again,
and so does our love begin to mend.

The love that we share will surely grow,
for this we feel and deep down know.

Caring and sharing falls into place,
and painful memories leave only a trace.

Hugging and kissing, is not missing,
to share a lifetime, we keep on wishing.

I definitely know you are the one,
so happiness will surely come.

You are my love and deepest friend,
all my love I wish to send.

—Constance Fechhelm

ONCE TOGETHER

Shattered love, broken hearts,
Once together, now apart;

Little pieces on the ground,
Broken love all around;

I lost the one I loved so much,
I lost his warm and gentle touch;

Once together, now apart,
I lost his love, I lost my heart;

I loved him so, but now he's gone,
I wonder now what I did wrong;

He held the key that unlocked my heart,
He shot the arrow that hit its mark;

But now it's over and he is gone,
So for him I sing this song;

Once together, now apart,
I lost the one who held my heart.

—Shelly Twitchell

. . . TO ONLY UNDERSTAND

When all the stars fall out of the sky
As the tears roll down your face
Trying to think of the reasons why
Is it worth it for just an illusion

Things that happen in life
They are not always nice
Remember the good and not the bad
Think of all the great times we had

Dream of me often and I'll be there
Don't try to touch me
Cause I may disappear
Off on a journey I must go

One day I'll return
With stories to tell
I'll love you, I'll miss you
Please just let go

Now with this kiss, my life fulfilled
I see now that I've lost you
Can I be gracious in my defeat
I'll love you *Tara* for always!!!

—John OAF Keithan

ROSES

"Ah as roses glow on bowers,
mid the soft summer showers
so God's great love,
shines from the heavens above"
So after years (83 yrs.) yesterday He
has been good to me. Before I
retired I had 20 lovely years picking
up boys and girls on old #4 bus for
the Church of the Nazarene. It was
beautiful
While I was in the hospital with a
friend of mine he wrote this little verse
and handed it to me
Thou handest me a golden platter Lord
upon it my sanity restored
hence-forth my life outpoured
forevermore.

—**Ray O'Dell**

RAINBOWS

The sun shone through the raindrops,
casting a rainbow over the lake.
It seemed to connect, one edge of
land to the other.

Sometimes life is like that,
souls connect to one another,
like the rainbow, beautiful —
but not encompassing.

Respected and cherished
filling the void —
that otherwise, would not be there.

The rainbow is one of nature's
most beautiful treasures.
It represents the ending of a storm
and the beginning of a new dawn.

It also connects kindred spirits.
So, that the sun may shine on
new beginnings and;
the beauty of the world.

—**Trudy Maiwald**

NO MATTER WHERE THE SUN GOES

No matter where the sun goes,
It will follow you,
To guide you on your journey
And see you make it through.

No matter where the sun goes,
You'll always reign as Queen,
From the shore unto the mountain tops,
From realities to dreams.

No matter where the sun goes,
Everyone lives forever,
Especially those you love,
To aid in your endeavors.

No matter where the sun goes,
Your friends are always there,
To help you out
When things seem tough to bear.

No matter where the sun goes,
Everything is clear.
No matter where the sun goes,
I am always here.

—**Kristopher White**

AUTUMN REFLECTION

We're all born to go our separate ways
Busy with given tasks throughout the days.
Just when we've learned to carry our load
Destined, all of us share the same road.

—**Sindy Chavez ~ ♈**

AUTUMN

Summer is passed and the days grow short with
blue skies over head.
The trees have changed their coats of green
to gold and brown and red.

The birds have sung their farewell songs,
Nature calls, it's time to go,
Time to start that long journey south
where the warmer breezes blow.

We'll watch the leaves drift softly down,
As over the fields they fly.
Then there's wieners to roast and marshmallows
to toast, while the moon sails high in the sky.

There will be time for a ride around the country
side, on a hay wagon filled with your friends.
And the air will ring with the songs that they
sing, before the season ends.

Beautiful autumn, you're a glorious sight,
But nature will soon let you know,
That even in all your splendor, you soon
will have to go.

Winter will come with a chilling blast.
It will come like a thief in the night.
To blow snow around all over the ground,
And steal autumn away from our sight.

—**Audrey V. Burnett**

INTO THE REDWOODS

California is the place to be,
Hollywood, Disneyland, and the Redwood trees.
Enter this world and travel back in time,
What these trees know would amaze the mind.

Before me, after me,
These trees proudly stand,
All knowing presence.
They watch as I walk along in time,
Did I hear a giggle as I tripped on a root,
A root as thick as my entire being?

Enter this world one might almost expect,
A dinosaur to approach, trampling leaves,
There he went!

Stop, look, listen, smell
That's what goes on most
Some before me might tell.

Respect and admiration I take with me
As I move along the Redwood trees,
Clear air, great feelings, memories.

I return in time
With a great more ease,

Oh the trees,
Would surely be pleased.

*Dedicated to my husband, David, who showed me
the world beyond my Southern California . . . .*

—**Patricia Moore**

GRANDMA'S CHAIR

She rocks back and forth to the beat of a drum
And every time she called my name, I would come.
She talked to me like no one has before
But she no longer talks to me that way anymore.
She helped me so much when she gave me advice
Her voice was so gentle and so very nice.
She might have been old and showing her age
But when telling a story, she never missed a page
It's hard to believe she is no longer there
But I still see her, sitting in Grandma's chair.

—**Ronnie Rhea Royer**

GRANDMA'S PRIDE AND JOY

C — Careful to hold you when but a small child
H — Heart filled with Love since the day you were born
R — Resting and sleeping in the cradle of my arms
I — Interested in all the things that you did
S — Sweet as could be, starting from day one
T — Tender and loving you have always been
I — In sharing your dreams with Grandma and friends
N — Never forgetting the precious moments we've spent
A — Always in my heart you forever will be, God's
     little angel, a gift for me to love for all eternity

Dedicated to Christina Brown, Love Grandma

—**Violet Brown**

WHAT A BEAUTIFUL WORLD IN MY MOTHER

What a beautiful world in my mother
God know that there was not another
God raised her through trials and tribulations
Then he blessed her and gave her her creation
What a beautiful world in my mother
God know there was not another
My mother's creation was five
My mother taught us to survive
What a beautiful world in my mother
God know there was not another
My mother's creation was love
She gave it and gave it
She knew hers was up above
What a beautiful world in my mother
God know there was not another
My mother's creation was faith
For she knew God would wait
What a beautiful world in my mother
God know there was not another
For he would talk to her and she would talk to him
Although God knew
But she had to keep telling him
Lord in the end we will win
What a beautiful world in my mother
God know there was not another
My mother's creation was true
My mother told us "God loves you"
My mother's creation was bright
My mother told us "you'll see the light"
"Oh" what a beautiful world in my mother
God know that there was not another
My mother's creation was demanding
My mother was very understanding
My mother's creation got grown
My mother called God and he said
"Shirley leave your creation alone"
"I want you to come on home"
What a beautiful world in my mother
God know that there was not another.

—**Shirley Massie**

SEEDS

My Grandmother always taught me
not to be afraid of death,
because the soul never dies,
it just stops to take a breath.
When that breath is breathed anew,
the beauty just begins,
the soul sprouts wings and soars up high
as the earthly carriage ends.

And when they get to heaven,
with old friends that they once knew,
there is the grandest celebration,
that the heavens ever threw!
GOD is standing, arms stretched wide,
welcoming them back home.
Knowing these are his own seeds,
that he had earlier sown.

—**Susan G. Renfroe**

THE LIGHTHOUSE

As a Mother is to her daughter
And a Father is to his son,
The Lighthouse shines to guide our way
Until our journey's done.

Sometimes life's waves are angry
And our ships are tossed and torn,
But a Mother's love is strong enough
To help us weather the storm.

A Father's light is constant
And his strength lasts through the years,
He is the light we look to
Through all our doubts and fears.

Let this Lighthouse be a symbol
And just our way to say,
Mother and Dad we love you
On this very special day.

—**Randall K. Simmons**

IT'S A GIRL!

Finally a daughter
To show to the world
To show the world
The mother smiles with pride

Years go by
An adolescent appears
Not to care about the things
Her mother taught her
Maybe when she's older . . . .

It's later yet
There's no time
For the mother/daughter thing
Mother's sad—daughter's glad
She's finally on her own

The hope for joy fades away
Hurt and anger take control
A letter, a message—no one's ever home
A mother's love still
Hopes for things to come

*Dedicated to Mom. You are my one and
only just as I am yours. I love you.*

—**S.E. Maxwell**

SPRING HEART CLEANING

I cleaned my heart out yesterday.
I steel myself to throw away
Quite all the precious, foolish hoard
Of memories and dreams I'd stored.

Courageously, I cleaned each room
And swept it clean with Reason's broom,
Till every little nook was bare,
And not a single memory there.

No dream, no must, might have been
And then I saw—
You'd crept back in.

—Kelley Hansen

FAREWELL TO MIKE

On the day we said goodbye
I tried so hard not to cry
My heart is filled with so much pain
Just to know I won't see you again

For every tear that was shed
Another memory came into my head
In my heart I have such love
To send to you up above

I know I will never know
Why it was your time to go
You will always be near
Cause in my heart I hold you dear

There's one more thing I must say
I'll think of you everyday
I love you, miss you & you'll always be
A very loving part of me.

—Aunt Linda

MOMENTS TO SHARE

This morning as I faced the world
    the day spoke out to me.
The sun was bright the sky so blue.
    I reveled in such finery.
Went to market with spirits high,
    twas a day to spread good cheer.
I smiled at everyone who came my way,
    my intent was quite sincere.
I reaped no more than empty stares
    from all who crossed my path.
In payment for my friendly mood,
    I received an icy bath.
I pondered long why this was so
    how no one felt like me.
Why on this wondrous gorgeous day,
    no one took the time to see.
That evening I called out to Him
    and asked for explanation.
Why peace and joy could not be found
    in the gift of His creation?
In silent meditation I became aware
    caring is beset by ego.
So important is the 'I' syndrome
    it's become a common credo.
Come and celebrate our world together,
    hands clasped in unity
And share the festival of life
    prepared for you AND me.

—Ida A. Ricker

IS IT LOVE OR PAIN?

Why is it that love causes so much pain?
It feels like a fire burning without a flame.
You are so lonely you can't help to cry,
You keep asking the same question over and over — Why?
You thought you loved him, but he doesn't feel the same.
Is it him or yourself you should blame?
When people tell you that your love is natural and
feeling this way is fine.
You tell them that it isn't love, it's the losing at
love that has brought you down this time!

—Jamie L. Holbrook

VALENTINE

Oh my beloved, unforgettable,
Overpowering blessed touch sense of vulnerability.
Stunned mesmerized by so much beauty,
From surface to core plus so much more.
My heart filled to capacity,
Sinking deep anchoring into the depths of my abdominals.
Creating butterflies fluttering
Leaving me speechless unable to say.
Quaking, trembling ready to explode with feel.
Love of the words, so hard to find,
But I must have you my beloved, all.

—Zoltan Palkovits

TWO LOVES AS ONE

We belong together like twilight's daylight
And night's darkness, or like morning's first light
That moistens dew among the daisies.
We can walk in the rain and cast shadows or look
Into the sun and cry no tears.
We breathe the first air of Winter and together
Walk the snow's first footprints.
There is no last with us. All is the first time
Fingers of hand-in-hand romance.
All ways in wonder;
All ways in dance, together we're moonlight and
The night's booming surf.
Together we're forever the revolving earth
And forever as one.

—Joseph Posner

I was 15 when I first fell in love
I was young and vulnerable then
It was the night of the Christmas dance
Everyone was dressed formally,
You in your red silk shirt, and I in my green taffeta dress,
You brought me a single red rose
And we slow danced all night long,
But I fell in love on the dance floor, later,
When you first kissed me
We started going steady a week later,
Around Christmas you brought me things:
A teddy bear and a bracelet,
But it was all a fairytale,
Even though it was the best month of my life,
You left me with a broken heart,
Alone, very alone in this cold world.

—Cristie Shepard

TRIPTYCH

Sense	Her	Near you
Her	Heart beats	Quickly
Trembling	For you	Hold her
Love her	Like the stars	Forever
Lost in the	Shine	In her eyes
Caress	Her face	With great tenderness
You share	Smiles	She holds you
With Love	With Love	With Love.

—Joseph V. Bopp

The wind is warm and sweet today,
it's almost as you aren't away.
We both know that isn't true,
I could never hold a secret from you.

What did you expect my loyal dear?
Did you think from my chest my heart would tear?
Is there a burden I cannot bear?
Did you think you unleashed my harshest fear?

When we met I was attracted to your pain
I protected you like a child, caught in the rain.
But time passed, and your self pity grew,
You became a person that I never knew.

Another cliche, I found I became,
A woman tied to a man quite insane.
Was it your mother, where the fault did lay,
who scolded you terribly, one winter day?

Well now I am a mother too,
I have your son, who will never know you.
You've left us both, you're far away,
and the wind is warm and sweet today.

—Vickie Pantalena

BLUE VASES

While walking down a shady avenue,
I stumbled upon somethings new,
Lovely crafted vases of blue,
Reminding me of flowers, when winter's through,
Reminding me of warmer days,
Of crystal clear mornings, without haze,
Of tulips, roses, orchids and maize,
Of a tree-lined park, where a child plays.
Ah, spring will come,
And butterflies, there'll be some,
Honeybees, honeycombs; where honey comes from,
Like it so well, eat every crumb.
Ah, warm days, 'n cool nights,
A stroll along a lake of reflecting lights,
A walk along a park, absorbing the sights,
Blues, greens, yellows, blacks, and whites,
Colors of the rainbow, confront my eyes,
These warm days under sunny skies,
The horse will graze, as the bird flies,
Choirs sing and the baby cries,
Spring will come, when winter's through,
And these vases crafted in blue,
Will hold flowers, for her and you,
And the scent will remind of the morning dew.

*Dedicated to Eloise, my dedicated, devoted and ever
patient former wife, who raised my beloved son, and
only child, and who has done right by me through
the years . . . .*

—Keith Bell

TO BE THERE FOR YOU

You are the one so dear to me,
I will always want that to be.
I want you in my arms while you grow,
And I will always hate to tell you no.

I will be there for you to talk to,
As I want you to do.
I don't care if you do something wrong.
My love for you will still be strong.

I will always be there for you.
I don't care what you ever do.
You are in my heart forever,
And I hope we will always be together.

—Justin Blue

A LOVE LETTER . . .

Each day goes by, it seems so fast,
live for the day; cling to the past.
Tomorrow's a hope on which to build.
The past a dream, a hope fulfilled.
On every curve life seems to throw,
You're always there as if you know
I'm living only for your smile.
You're what makes each day worthwhile.
The past and present of my life
entwined each day with you, my wife.
God only knows what time will bring.
My dear, I'm praying for one thing.
As time goes on, know this is true,
I only hope to dream of you.

I love you Laurie

—Patrick O'Masters

MY ANGEL

Is there a heaven, I believe there is
But what it's like I've only been told.
So I picture it myself and there you are
It's a quiet morning the world is still.
We lay together in each others arms,
I kiss your lips and stroke your hair
The sounds of birds drift through the air.
The day's first light warms our skin
You drift off to sleep and I snug you in.
So if there is a Heaven one thing is true
It's the days I share my life with you.

*Dedicated to Barbara, you've been my
inspiration, my best friend & my love.
You're one in a million.*

—Douglas L. Caylor

I MISS YOU

The gentleness of your touch,
Is what I miss so much.

The way you smiled when you looked at me,
Made me lose touch with reality.

The spark ignites when you look my way.
I want to see you every day.

My pulse quickens, my eyes light up,
Without a word to say, you walk by.

It breaks my heart, and I want to cry.
We used to be such good friends.

Now this . . .
Why?

—Mechelle Lively Woodburn

LITTLE JADE
(A Disabled Child)

Little Jade, little Jade
Little girl of man's love made.
Now I know you are so rare,
Little girl extraordinaire.
For only you have helped me find
That gentle touch of human kind.

Little Jade, little Jade
Our love for you will never fade.
Your touch upon my arm, alas,
An expression of love from child to past.
And though a wedding band we'll never see,
You teach us all, per God's decree.

—Leonard Bryla

SISTERS

We came from the same beginning
and with God's Love, the same ending.

Our lives were disfunctional, you see
That's what they call it,
when you live with a disease . . . .

Not having the love, trust and care we needed
No one understood us,
it was too deep seeded . . . .

So our years came sooner than we hoped
It was our only way to possibly cope.

And to much our own surprise
we look back and are amazed . . .
How we survived all that crazed.

We are here Sister, and we will
be healed from all the pain

For it's His love that
protected us and His Home
we will gain.

—Anna Carrozza

GRANDMOTHER'S GARDEN

Larkspurs of violet blue hues
in Grandmother's Garden spiked high,
Waving gently in the soft Spring breeze
Under the pale blue sky.

Grandmother tending her garden,
cares burdening and clouding her mind,
Kneeling and pulling out weeds,
and discarding the withering vine.

Mixed among the lacy Queen Anne's Lace,
Heads plump of ecru and white,
I can see the deep pride in Grandmother
and the satisfied smile at the sight.

Yes, that was some of Grandmother's Garden
As were trellised sweet honey-suckle bright.
The flowers fed little birds daily and
scented sweetly the dark of night.

I often think of Grandmother's Garden
She so lovingly tended with care,
How I wish to be in Grandmother's Garden
feeling she is still with me there.

—Marion Armstrong Craft

JUST THOUGHT I'D MENTION

There's a time to laugh and a time to cry
As ironic as it sounds there's also a time to die
Those words aren't original, and may have
been said before
But if my words can be heard I'd want to say
"I love you once more."
We admired the history and stories of old
Pictures of you in army boots and stories told
So now we can only go on taking the knowledge
we've gained
Remember your conversations and politics explained
You always seemed indestructable to me and
I don't want to say "goodbye"
I wish death never existed, that way
you'd never die.
You wanted us to love, you gave every
intention.
Well Grandpa I love you, just thought
I'd mention.

—Gina Cialkoszewski

TEA TIME

I look in my treasure chest, what do I see . . .
dollies and teddy bears looking at me.

I take them all out and line them all up.
One at a time, I pass them a cup.

They look at me, and I see them smile.
I give them all goodies and pretend for a while.

I laugh and I chat as they watch me play.
They never interrupt a single word that I say.

I am their hostess, and they are my friends.
I hug them all tightly when the tea party ends.

My eyelids are heavy. Bedtime is near.
My friends must go home, and I hold back a tear.

I know in the morning, they'll be waiting for me.
So, back to my treasure chest 'til next time for tea.

Dedicated to my wonderful daughter,
Sara Renee, who has made me see life
through a child's eyes once more.

—Renée Lyn Johannes

GOD BLESS OUR "MOTHERS"

Mother's Day is here,
What are we doing dear?
Plenty money in many ways is spent:
Flowers, sweets, jewelry, balloons, cards — no end
Yes, happy smiles and a "big thank you."
Husbands, fathers, children follow through.
Is this the appreciation for our mothers
only on "One Day?"
There is another, better glorious way.
All the work, caring, sharing, praying day and night.
Never leaving her family out of sight.
How many times tears of joy and worry.
Do we ever feel for her and say, "Sorry."
Every day assure her that you are there.
Lighten their tasks, brighten their days everywhere.
Thank you Lord for our wonderful mothers
"Every Day."
We can't do enough for them in a special way.
May sincere prayers wipe out their sadness.
May your blessings fill their lives with gladness.

Love to our "Mothers Every Day."

—Ingeborg Kraehmer

ELIZABETH

Our Elizabeth . . .
    Tall and slender, she'll turn everyone's head.
A lover of teddy bears, soft sweatshirts, and fire flies.
And any creature that needs to be adopted.

Our Elizabeth . . .

Her music is from the heart, the keys her friends, her solace.
Dreams played out, that could bring tears to your eyes,
With melodies that return you to a different time and place.

Our Elizabeth . . .

No longer will the snub nose little lady be seen,
With Peanut running by her side.
For today "Our Elizabeth" turns sixteen.
And . . . Oh . . . how we could burst with pride.

—Julianne

GRANDPA,

I know you're not with us in sight,
But you can see through the light.
There's so many times I wish you were here,
So many times, but you are there.
I often find myself talking to you,
For I know you hear me when I do.
There's so much I want to say,
Grandpa, I still love you till this day.
The days and years went by so fast,
The memories will always last.
You touched our lives with so much,
Now we long for your touch.
I know now it's too late to show my love,
For one day The Lord took you up above.
I don't know why, but you were suddenly gone,
In my heart lingers a very special bond.
We never show our love until it's too late,
My love for you, Grandpa, went with you through the Gate.
I love you, Grandpa, I want you to know—
I miss you and love you so!

—Tracy Naughton Oman

PIERRE

He asks about the final weather report,
It tells him if we're going to leave the sea port.
Your life perserver is a must and to be worn,
It's as easy as eating buttered sweet corn.
You tell me I'm nice and pretty too, he's full of flatteries,
He likes his toys, from the attic, and full of batteries.
I've showed you where my pet frog lives, he's always home,
He stays under the rock and uses it as a dome.
His parents tell me at times he's a hellion,
But when he comes down here, he's fine, so we have watermelon.
He sings, with his head phones, and his tape recorder,
How can I resist not getting it all on the camcorder.
When it rains and everything gets wet,
We throw in a movie and watch it on the T.V. set.
When it's sunny, clear and dry,
We hop in the boat, and say good-bye.
He's smart and handsome at just 5 years old,
He certainly has my heart and all of my soul.
I bet your grandpa would have loved to have met you,
But grandma is here and will just have to do.
When we are together in the clean fresh air,
I enjoy life with my only grandson, Pierre.

—L. Ragan

MICHAEL MARRIES

Today I watch my little boy
    turn into a man.
I know that he feels such joy
as someone else now takes his hand.

I knew the day I gave you life
that someday it would be.
That you would find a loving wife
and I'd have to set you free.

Now on this day you leave the nest.
I'm feeling a little sad.
Although I wish you all the best
I'll miss the little boy I had.

Dedicated to my son, Steven
"Michael" Niece, on his wedding
day, December 24, 1992. Love, Mom

—Sue Bartelson

RACHAEL

I watch you in your bed at night
So peaceful as you sleep.
Full of life throughout the day
Now silent, as darkness creeps.

I think about the hours before
As rotten as you could be
Whining whimpers of tired cries
A frightful sight to see.

I sometimes hear you laughing
In a mischievous sorta way.
Or see a smile on your face
That's as cunning as the day.

And as I watch you sleeping
I thank the Lord above
For giving me a perfect you
And filling my life with love

I love you Baby,
Mommie

—Jody Kauffman Pitman

GRANDPA

Grandpa, Grandpa, Grandpa,
Sometimes I wonder what it
would be like with you back
here. It just seems so weird
without you here with us.
What Grandma does, Randy,
Rick and Dad without someone
just being there. I really
miss you and the checkers too,
but everyone goes someday and
somehow. I don't understand
how we got here, but I am glad
just having you for those
eight years. I will always
remember and never forget you—
you will always be with me
through good and bad times. I
love you Grandpa, and you are
still alive to me and in my
heart. Good-bye Grandpa.
    Love Always

—Jayme

LOVERS

I walk, I look, I turn to see,
I hear a soft whisper,
I feel a touch on thee.
The sun casts its glimmer,
A young bird soars in flight,
The balmy air makes me shiver,
I know you are there, I hold you tight.

We walk, we look, we turn to see,
We enter the night into ecstasy.
One with one we will always be,
As often as the tide rolls out to sea.
Until our destiny takes us away
To love's alluring rapture, I pray.

—Bonnie L. Glass

THE TRUE MEANING OF LOVE

Love is a wonder
an amazement
an ever changing battle
yet to be won.
A battle which
all the options are laid out
yet one can't decide
which path to take.
Do we choose the way
which shows no pain?
Or do we just sit back and wonder?
Do we wait for the challenges
or do we go ahead
following our hearts?
So many questions
yet to be answered,
who has the answers?
Only from within ourselves
can we find
the true meaning of Love!

—Denise Smith

EVERLASTING

The moon above
So large and bright
Lights our path
In the starry night,

Hand in hand
We found our way.
No more searching
Love's here to stay.

But then a heart breaks;
The hours pass like days.
Now my heart aches —
Empty and alone.

I love you with all my heart;
You are all I dream of.
We had the perfect start
But now it all must end.

At least we are friends,
As the sun begins to rise.
Our new life has just begun
And the future holds love's surprise!

—Janice McDonald

TIL THE SUN SETS LOW

The days drag on . . . til the sun sets low . . .
then the night is cold as she sits all alone.

Once she loved a man . . . He even took her hand,
with a band of gold . . . He imprisoned her soul.

But his love was a lie; . . . Now she lays down to cry,
while the days drag by . . . til the sun sets low . . .
and the night is cold . . . then she is all alone.

Now the years pass by . . . an' there is age in her eyes . . .
Will she ever love again . . .
can she really trust any man?

All she's heard from them . . . is a pack of lies . . .
Still the days drag by . . . til the sun sets low . . .
And the night is cold . . . As she sleeps all alone.

—M. Marie Bettger

O enchanted woman, where are you from?
Fluttering and dancing in the breeze,
I picture you as a flower, a violet by a mossy stone
Beside the lake, beneath the trees.

O enchanted woman born from the sea,
surrouonded by peacocks with a hundred eyes,
my soul I will pour into thee,
when the silver dusk starts to rise.

O enchanted woman, traveler from a distant land,
fragrance of new mowed hay on the first day of spring.
I see you as a child, with child like hands
under the scent of plum trees the angels sing.

O enchanted woman, have the heavens fallen from the sky?
For your beauty is none like any others I've seen.
Lost in a world of just you and I,
Is this reality real or just a dream?

—Anthony Jason Pasquino

TAINTED

A window painted shut.
A prisoner to the four walls of thought
like a nightingale in a brown bag.

My hand touches my face, I confirm my existence.
My lips move constantly in silent prayer.

I close my eyes and see a sunflower, strong and hopeful.

Is it ecstasy or torture?

I want to bite you like an animal, taste your blood in my mouth.

I must believe you're real.
I want to whisper my name in your ear again and again like a
child in a closet.

I'm real too, I have a name.

I'll never be able to smile without a shadow,
A shadow you created and stitched to my skin.
A shadow only I see, in dreamless sleep.

The chilling poke guts me like a shot doe whose eyes begin
to close.
Hate storms a place where a child used to live.

My hollowed eyes see darkness now, behind the light of
the past.

Shadows seem longer than they used to be.
They linger and drag like smoke in the sunlight.

—Annie Smith

SAY WHAT?

In this big ole' country in which we live, it's called the U.S.A.
    We can stand at any moment, and say what we want to say
Be it about the President, or the ballgame that occurred last night
    We can say whatever we feel - it's a God-given right
Some like football, some like baseball, some don't really care
    Some like games and puzzles, others a teddy bear
Some say "GO BLUE," some say "GO GREEN"
    Others think, what you say is mean
Opinions will differ, till the day we all die
    Like what you want, don't live in a lie
Not everyone will agree, with what you have to say
    But if you firmly believe it, let no one stand in your way
Wrong or right, it doesn't matter, say it anyway
    We have this thing called FREEDOM OF SPEECH, and no one can take that away!

Dedicated to my uncle, D.J., thanks for inspiration.

—An Andrea Berghoff Original

THE RELUCTANT SPIRIT

"Victoria—are you there?"—"Victoria—we are aware."
    "What evil means took you away?"—"What do you want from Deseray?"
Each night you come into our room; you bid us "come" to a cold, dark tomb.
The air grows heavy, hard to breathe, until the dawn bids you must leave.

No peace you've found, nay, even in death!
Your soul, a prisoner of evil you have met!
"What must we do to free you now?"—"What is there Victoria?" "Show us how!"
Again, the night, your spirit revives;—our door is open, you come inside;—
"What's that you carry by your side?—a knife Victoria, is it mine?!?"
"No, please Victoria!, put it away!"—"Do not take the life of Deseray!"

"Upon your dress—a piece of hair,—a lock of my love, who placed it there?"
"The walk I took while in my sleep—was it "I" you buried deep!?"—
"Tis I, the spirit, not you at all!"—
"My body lies inside the grave—I've lost my love, my all"
"Twas in this room, you stole from Deseray!, and I, I never knew, I must go away!"

"Oh!, my soul!, the pain inside!, I must leave this mad, mad night!!!"
"No longer shall my love decay!—God forgive, release the soul of Deseray!"

—Elaine Ash Cagle

IF WALT WHITMAN HAD BEEN SHOT

Was there ever born a Russian who never heard of Pushkin?
    No, his sweetest rhymes are savored and his quest for freedom honored.
No doubt he was the greatest Russian poet of all time.
Inside his house I saw the couch on which he died so very young,
Slain by the lover of his wife, depriving us of songs unsung.
The Tsar had done his best to have his poetry suppressed, but Pushkin wrote the truth until
    he died,
And in that vast and lonely land, his works today are widely read, and no one could suppress
    them if he tried.

Once I heard a well-read woman quoting lines from our Walt Whitman,
Well, too few of us, it is our loss, have even heard his name.
A poet in America gains scarcely any fame.
But Whitman's verse lives on, historical perceptions and lyrical reflections,
The nature of a nation seen while wandering and singing.
I read his song to the open road, his happy song to falling trees, his verse on nature varied, rich
On earthly sex of an easy girl, on life-long love of comrades.
I read his fervent verse of love, his passion singing down through time,
A love sublime for America, land of a favored race.

Poets live, make verse and die, and seldom heard their lonely cry,
They rarely change the ways of life or even make a dent.
If Whitman too had been shot dead, perhaps his verse might have been read
More often by poetic souls for whom his work was meant,
More often by Americans for whom his life was spent.

—Charles A. Long

THE MOON

The moon is only a yellow balloon,
  Just sitting in the night.
And when it beams,
Around the world,
It gives a lovely light.

—Sayward Morse

OCEAN STORM

The waves thrash and tear
  At night so fair
And as the waves pour
Upon the sandy shore
The lightning streaks
Across the sandy seaweed peaks
The ocean roars
And the waves lap up broken oars
Then the rain starts to patter
And the ocean starts to clatter
Then the sun starts to rise
And the ocean is calm again
Under the skies

—Vicki Lame

THE VICTORY

Her opponent was Time
  Losing to him
Was considered a crime
She chased and outraced him
Her lead had erased him
She was fast
But he was stronger
Each time she leaped
His strides grew longer
While her legs became lame
He mastered her game
Time ran ahead
She could no longer win
She felt her head begin to spin
Hopelessly defeated she stopped to relax
Time stopped
And fell dead in his tracks

—Aliza Stevens, age 14

DARWIN'S GARDEN

Flowers ever so beautiful
your scent uncontrollably alluring
needing only love to grow
yet so fragile and unenduring.

Where is my garden?
Is this my fate . . .
a bowl of rose petals
to tease my hate?

Through the wall I walked
like the ghost of an unloved child
and though the grass is green
I have nothing to feed the soil.

Unkept and unheard
happiness is my hell
disillusioned and disturbed
on the flower, I fell.

—David J. Emswiler

THE GOLDEN ROCK

The Golden Rock, St. Eustatius, mote of a Caribbean island
  and linchpin of triangular trade to the Colonies from Holland,
was a rescuer of our infant nation from the British tyrant.

Sephardim, the horror of ancestors' Inquisition
still in mind and lovers of freedom,
rejoiced in this island sanctuary.

These Dutch congregants of "Honen Daliem,"
"He who shows mercy to the poor,"
gave their hearts to the American cause.

Clever Jewish traders
loaded fleet blockage runners to the gunwales
and greased the flow to Washington's legions.

Alas, the Golden Rock is lost in history!
But British commander, Rodney, called it a "nest of vipers,"
nourishing the American rebellion.

Rodney pillaged the Golden Rock,
banished the Jews and declared:
"This rock has done mortal harm to England."

Recently, Virgin Islands commissioner, Paiewonsky, exulted:
"St. Eustatius and the Dutch Jews changed U.S. history."

—Charles Bernstein

SEASONS OF LIFE

Autumn beauty's vibrant hues, crisp cool air, kaleidoscope
  views.
Shiny red globes with emerald ties, apple cider, pumpkin
pies.
Winter's frosty windowpanes like lovely lacy Valentine
frames.
Roaring fires, ambers glow, mugs of cocoa, drifts of snow.
Springtime's palette of azure sky, cottony clouds billowing
high.
May Day's dance, robins sing, children's laughter, joys it
brings.
Summer's warmth from golden rays, picnic lunch by rolling
waves.
Lemonade stands, steamy days, lazy naps, hammocks sway.
Climates come and seasons go, the outside world, the changes
show.
Seasons of life — its secrets unfold, our fate, the destiny
each of us holds.
Seasons of life, we search within, personal struggles,
battles to win.
The twists and turns, the crossroads meet, one path dark,
another sweet.
When the season of life is smooth and clear, we flourish in
peace, hope and cheer.
Life's rocky roads stir doubt and fear, worry, sadness and
despair.
The heart and mind reflect this chain, when crisis strikes,
inflicting pain.
I've traveled down that bumpy road, confronted changes,
heavy loads.
To take one's troubles, turn life around, requires strength
and courage sound.
Encircled by love, family and friends, emerging different
yet happy again.
I can't look back on seasons done, must seize the moment,
enjoy the "SUN"
Challenges faced, conquering strife, overcome obstacles,
CELEBRATE LIFE!!!

—Jan Haroutunian

LOVE IS A ROSE

In the field there is one red rose.
It is not like any other pose.
This rose stands strong through all wind and rain.
It is never weak, it can stand all pain.

It stands still like silence through the night.
Its petals are dazzling like the sunlight.
Its sturdy blades reach out to comfort those who are blue.
It smiles a little smile to make you feel brand new.

The sweet aroma in the air
Senses its sweet loving care.
To look at this beautiful life
Gives you a warm, loving feeling inside.

The flower gives love and affection to all,
But the time must come that his last petal shall fall.
Then again, like that one red rose,
In the field there stands another red rose.

—Mindie Lee

THE JOURNEY

We search our lives for a meaningful existence,
But life is often confusing and we must be persistent.
Our travels seem to be filled with many curves and bends,
And just when we want to give up we meet a good friend.

Our thoughts and our soul begin to grow and evolve,
And the choices we make can create foundations or walls.
Relationships arise bringing joy and pain that will mend,
We now become stronger with help from great friends.

The mind is now knowledgeable but our heart still seeks more,
I believe that it is Love that we are searching for.
We pray with faith that there will be a Godsend,
And what do you know Love comes from a close friend.

The journey continues but the mystery is gone,
The happiness we live explodes into song.
We now have no questions about the meaning of Life,
LOVE is our focus . . . We become Husband and Wife.

—John D. Cacioppo

VOLCANO

My true emotions are held deep within. The past hurts too much
To allow me to take risks. The friendships that I once
Thought were true, have turned out to be only skin deep.
People are always telling me "say what you feel." But how can
I, if every time I do, people I thought I could trust with my
Feelings look at me funny, and I end up alone once again?

There are so many things of value that I have to say. Ideas
And beliefs. Emotions of care and concern. All are bubbling
At the surface, ready to erupt like a newly awakened volcano.
Yet I hold back because I don't want to get burnt like so
Often in the not too distant past.

Yes it is easy to forgive. For life is too short to hold
Grudges, and to worry about what other people may think. But
The hurt remains for a long long time.

I may look all right to you, but deep inside I want to tell
You about the pain I really feel. The pain that you have
Caused. However, the risk is too great. Once we were the best
Of friends. Now I have only memories of what were the good
Times. That is what hurts the most. Needing to tell you how
I feel, but knowing that you are unable to understand.

—Wendy C. Rourke

TO MY ABSENT LOVE

I'm struggling with the agony
Of wanting you.
My first waking thought is yours,
My last thought ere I sleep.
Thoughts of you fill my days.
I think of all the ways
In which I find you wonderful —
Your strength, your gentleness —
The happiness you give — incredible!
Because I'd thought it unattainable.
A total giving!
Now I'm living
With joy, wonder and delight
And the searing pain
Of being without you.

—Juana Murano

SUCH IS MY LOVE FOR YOU

How soft the wings of a butterfly
translucent in the sun?
How silent is the slumbering earth
when day, its course has run?

How constant is the coming
of the seasons of the year?
How sure is spring to bring the ring-
necked geese to reappear?

How gentle are a baby's eyes
of sweet cornflower blue?
How tossed are willows in the wind?
Such is my love for you!

How fragile is the autumn leaf
that falls upon the grass
in quiet resignation
of the winter's snowy mass?

How fervent is the longing
any poet ever knew
who sweetly bares her lyric soul?
Such is my love for you!

—Joanne Birks

IF YOU WERE MINE

If you were mine to hold and love
How wonderful and sweet!
The world would be my own, and I
Would lay it at your feet.

Yes, I could conquer all the earth
As much as you inspire,
And pile it high into your hands
To build your own empire.

You say you'll never need the world
To make your life complete,
But may I offer you my heart
With every tender beat?

I'd like to spend my time with you
And take you by the hand;
To lead you down the path of love
Into our Wonderland.

If I had you to call my own,
I'd never let you go.
But own you I must surely not
For love is meant to grow.

—Janis Neergaard

69

ERINN

I took the ribbons from her hair
And gently set her in his chair
He looked at her, and then at me
Then said "I'll do it, but don't
You see—
'Tis a shame to cut the hair of this
Child sitting there."
Tears were streaming down her little
Face
'Twas not the time, nor the place
So I kissed the tear drops from her
Eyes
And restored the ribbons amidst her
Sighs
We'll keep the glory of her hair
And sit never more in a
Barber's chair.

> **—June Benn**

GROWING UP

A child's dream,
Can't wait to be thirteen!
A teenage dream,
Can't wait to be eighteen!
But what's most fun
Is to be twenty-one!
That's when you reach the end
Of the block
Then you want to turn
Back your biological clock!
Trying to remember
All your younger days,
But all you remember
Is an opaque haze.
Growing up may seem neat but,
Take it from me
It's not all you think!

> **—Judith R. McGuire**

LAUGH OF THE CENTURY

How odd is something misshapen
Something spinning though warped
Like a melted record
Or a bicycle wheel

Seewish seewack

Observe the warped wheel
Re-consider the path-os
Crooked line
Straight direction

Child
Riding the bike
With the warped pink wheel
Trailing her siblings

And Mom behind

Pedal Pedal
Talk   Smile
Fret   Not

God's given us
Warped wheels
And he laughs his lungs out loud

To my family and Kid Alvarez

> **—Frank L. Audino**

BEDTIME STORIES

She came wide eyed,
"Mommy, why is the worm broken,
Is he dead?

She came again one day,
"Mom, no one talks to my friend 'cuz she's black.
It's not fair!"

In tears she came one night,
"He packed his things and left!
Can I come home?"

I held her in my arms,
We talked
     of worms,
         friends,
             and
                 bedtime stories.

> **—Leigh**

On the night that you were conceived,
I did not know, that I was soon, a mother-to-be.

The day I found out, I was crushed and hurt inside.
I was so scared that I just sat down and cried.

But as soon as I could see, you grow inside of me,
The less scared I came to be.

The more you grew, and the bigger I became,
I no longer felt all the guilt and the shame.

Each time you kicked my ribs, or hiccuped inside,
It filled me up with joy and pride.

On the day you were born, my heart no longer felt torn.
It filled with a different kind of love for you,
Because, not only do I have one heart,
Now I have two.

Now as each day goes by, I will promise this to thee,

'To be the best mommy that I can possibly be!'

I love you Ashley!

> **—SueAnn McCartney**

TO MY LITTLE SOULS;

You have chosen to be a small soul among me
I have chosen to be your guiding light,
I have shed away your darkness
And it seemed to work out alright.

Now I must guide your tiny souls
To do the best that you can,
And to not ever give up hope
As I will always offer you my hand.

All that I will ever want for you
Is to understand and know that I care,
To befriend all that you can in this life
And share love wherever you fair.

Please know that I'll always be with you
In all your decisions you will make,
And my soul is as one with you now
As my love is, for all you can take.

The most beautiful day of my life, was
The first time I saw both of you,
And I'll never be able to match that love
For your souls, are the best, of so few.

All my love,
MOMMY

> **—Cindy Weddell**

A MOTHER'S LOVE

It seems like only yesterday I held your tiny head
Wrapped you oh so tightly and lay you in your bed.
You listened quite intently at all that had been said
Then shook your wrinkled, fisted hands, screaming to be fed.

As you grew to be a toddler, Grampa's hand you took, and led,
You'd walk about a mile, then sit, and listen while he read.
The years have moved to decades, Grampa's gone now, and you're wed
Your life takes on new meaning, you must move on, I said.

Your children will be coming and you'll lay them in their beds,
You'll say a prayer, and kiss them, as you pat their little heads.
Their life is just beginning and so gently will you tread,
The torch of love keeps passing and the love will help it spread.

—**Maureen Reid**

MY GREATEST GIFT

I have felt cool hands on my feverish brow . . .
   A GIFT I CALL TENDERNESS . . .
I have seen tears shed for both my happiness and pain . . .
   A GIFT I CALL CARING . . .
I have felt a helpful force in times of need . . .
   A GIFT I CALL PRAYER . . .
I have been Pardoned for my Wrongs . . .
   A GIFT I CALL FORGIVENESS . . .
I have been cherished despite my flaws . . .
   A GIFT I CALL UNDERSTANDING . . .
I have been taught about Love . . .
   A GIFT I CALL GOD . . .
I have been given these blessings by my greatest treasure . . .
   A GIFT I CALL MOM . . . .

—**Carlotta Frazier**

I DID NOT GO THERE

I did not go there
to the deep brown spot where soil hit wood.
Where headstones glisten in the autumn rain.
Where bereaving mortals go on a silent Sunday afternoon,
laden with shovel.
To plant a tree.
To whisper "I love you." Too late!

I did not go there on a slate grey afternoon
to pay homage to the stonecutter.
To mesmerize the lowly gravedigger.
How could I admire a white rose on newly upturned soil?

I did not go there to shed my burden.
To pluck a weed on bended knee.
I stayed away out of reverence for "Mamma."
That big warm woman, the core of my soul.
That complex woman who sifted from my life like sand.

I stayed away for "Mamma" is here.
I see her in my daughter's smile. In her sense of fun.
In her liquid eyes.
On bright days "Mamma" dances at my feet.
I see her in miniature form. Her steps are light.

And she will be here till I hit soil.
And rain falls for me on autumn days.
And the stonecutter hones a happy line for me.
Till then, I will hear her voice, soft and low.

Dedicated to Mom, whose endless story telling
warmed the long winter nights of my childhood.

—**Anne Kelly-Pereira**

BACK HOME

The hills of home
   may they ever be
As fresh and green
as in memory,

I walk the roads,
some changed, some not
I feel their gaze
From their small plot

My mom and dad
their love aglow
Surround us still
As long ago.

—**Dorothy Marta Certo**

A MOTHER'S PRAYER

Dear Lord above, hear my prayer
Take care of my boy
While he's up there.
Guide him to your loving arms,
Keeping him safe from all harm.

Let him know we love him,
And miss him so very much,
And how at times I know I feel
his warm, loving touch.

Heavenly Father, watch over him
He meant the world to me
And grant that I'll be good enough
To see him in eternity.

Help us, Lord, to bear this pain
And make our burden light.
One more thing, Lord, could you please
Give him a kiss goodnight?

Dedicated to the memory of
PFC Paul W. Vincent Jr.
Sept. 6, 1967 - Sept. 18, 1988

—**Sandra VanOrman**

MY DAUGHTER

She was a stranger
That arrived one day.

I loved her already
In a special kind of way.

It wasn't until later
That I noticed a change.

Day after day
I know I love her more.

She cannot even speak
I just know it's there.

There is a precious bond
That she and I share.

Onward it grows
The more that I care.

She is my daughter and
This is only the start.

There is a lifetime of memories
That will grow in my heart!

—**Kelly B. Helms**

ON LIFE

If life is paralactic
    And view its all in all,
Then one who is didactic
    May come to stumble, fall.

—Albert Nelson

i unfold out
of cool dark
into warm light.
i am bright,
i am yellow,
i am white,
i am light,
floating on wind
to begin again.

            dandelion
    —Charles Richards

HEAVEN

Conversations uncompleted,
    Songs to sing
        For those who wait.

Hymns, perhaps,
    Or tunes from childhood
        Write themselves
            Beyond the gate.

Friends released
    From solemn chambers.

Decisions rendered
    By mighty shadows

Strange shadows,
    Strange chambers,
        Beautiful songs.

        —Julie E. Devontine

IMMORTAL LOVE

When my mind,
    is far away.
I think of you,
    and I pray.

I pray for me,
    I pray for you.
That there is a heaven,
    and I'll be there too.

You are my Mother,
    as you've always been.
We were together once,
    and we will be again.

Until that day,
    I can only know.
That our love is special,
    and will always grow.

*In memory of the late
Delores M. Clark,
my beautiful mother,
1934-1978*

    —Sheila Raye Clark

BREAKING POINT

Out of Life's pits, often black as coal, I thank God for
    my erectable soul.
Though those oft' view me as a paragon of strength and
certitude; never imagining the pain within.
I rise above all to conquer a peace of mind that will
never be; for what Life has dealt I must endure.
Blow after blow, I fall again and again; only to pick
up the pieces and forge my way on.
Never realizing the weakening until alast, I finally break!

    —Linda Faye Hopkins-Woodcock

THE HONORABLE MR. BAILEY

It will make your heart ache, this true story I tell
About my good neighbor, who served his time in hell

Now meet Mr. Bailey, his first name is Lyle
Along with his wave, comes a refreshing smile

He walks with no cane, his back is not bent
He gets around pretty good, this 87 year old gent

Although he retired, he could never stop working
For around every corner, a fatal disease was lurking

He took care of his wife, after she suffered a stroke
And his grandson with cancer, 'til they both never awoke

He took care of Arlene, his only son's wife
She too had cancer, and she lost her life

Bedridden with M-S, was Mr. Bailey's son Don
He devoted years of his care, until he too, was gone

Disease wiped out his family, how did this man stay sane
But never once did I hear, Mr. Bailey complain

He endured each hardship, with face always aglow
He's but one of only two, honorable men that I know

So when he stands at the gates, the angels will give their nod
And beckon Mr. Bailey, to come sit at the right hand of God

    —Arley M. Bischoff

REMEMBER . . .

A tilt of trademark hat, a glimpse of mischievous grin;
eyes alight with spirit and love, fingers flying once again.

Modest as always ("You should hear my brother"),
your inner fire was matched by no other.

We wanted the world to know you were a Texas boy;
you gave us your heart and soul and became our "Pride and Joy."

Watching you grow from "Little Stevie" to "Stevie Ray,"
no one ever imagined the price you would someday pay.

You inspired us all to get "In Step" and taught us
    what "Family Style" means.
Now we're left with songs unsung and the heartbreak
    of unfinished dreams.

The awesome fragility of life nightmarishly appeared,
    and we created our own "Texas Flood"
with the shedding of countless tears.

Your spirit lives on; we won't let it die
even as we struggle with the unanswerable why.

Go with God, sweet angel; our memories must suffice.
Fly on, dear friend, until we meet, this time in paradise.

*Dedicated to the memory of Stevie Ray Vaughan —
may his music and memory live forever in our hearts.*

    —Cindy Jentho Homan

AUTUMNAL EQUINOX

Darkened winds, fill my branches with tears
In rising waves of unseen chill, winter nears;
Dispel the smothering placid illusion set sweet
So long upon us like sleep by calm blue August heat;
    Come, Autumn:
        Slam my door, rattle my pane
        Pelt my face with dust and rain
        Break the willow, lay flat the wheat
        Wry promise of bitter snows, howling sleet
        Shred supple green into crackling brown swirls
        And chase to safety all the squealing young girls;
But Come, Autumn:
        I fear you no more.

    —Karl E. Hase

FLYING

My thoughts — my soul-certainties — my essence. From where?
I search restlessly to confirm a feeling:
That I am what I always have been.
The core of me has not learned:
I have learned *it*. *It* has always been so, but
I have been slow to know it.

Almost, I feel of it as though of another entity:
It is a friend, and a beautiful thing;
one of which I am sneakingly proud.

It far surpasses my consciousness (that slow, doddering semi-sleep).
I wake, sometimes, and bound at the feelings that flutter in me.
I reach to snatch each butterfly-thought
Which flits and skitters within and without
My conscious grasp.
In outrageous, multi-colored confusion
This brilliant hodge-podge of exquisite knowledge
Allows me to stroke its latticed wings
Only at unexpected moments.

Then, I feel as if I am bestowed with favor:
I fly.

    —Wendy L. McNeil

AUTUMN OF YOUTH

Sunlight teased its way between blinded slats
    Come out and play
Quilted darkness wrapped around she shook her head
Go away go away
The sun dropped to the floor and lined the carpet hers no more

Poetic lines drifted through her mind
Streams of muddy consciousness for days passed by
Covered up covered up
By dust on a marble table and photographs of who am I who am I

Clocks were red merry go rounds and pendulums
Swings swaying in deserted playgrounds taunting go on go on
But where to go
When day is night and autumn frost numbs a calloused soul

Wait for me!

The trees did not listen and turned to gold
All the grass shriveled brown and the stream slurred no
Chimes chimes
Of falling leaves muffled her cry when the evening sun slanted
To kiss her cool cheek and saw the night
In her autumn eyes

    —Kathleen Pieters Ebell

SUN CATCHER

Let the sun shine in your window
Let the sun shine in your heart
See the Lord has kept his promise
See the rainbow on the walls
Sun catcher.

—Clarence West

IT'S SUMMER TIME

I walked right out the
door as if it would be chilly,
but the breeze was warm and
comforting, almost close to
thrilling.
    I looked up into the light
blue sky as the white clouds
scattered,
and then I looked upon the
grass which was green and
all of this surely mattered.
    I started running and turning
flips,
and then I picked a flower
with tightly held grips.
    "It's finally summer time!"
I cried, as I threw it with
great power.
And then I looked at this
beautiful thing, a new summer
flower!

Dedicated to my parents who
encourage me in writing about
the interesting people and
things that surround me.

—Jerica Elisabeth Burgette, age 11

BEAUTIFUL SUNFLOWERS

    Oh, Beautiful, sunflowers, my how
you have grown.
    I watched you from morning
noon and night.
Your head turning like a
revolving door.
    Following the sun, as it comes
up in the morning.
Your big leaves draped down on your
slender body
Like elephants' ears with your
heads so full of seeds
Hanging low upon your slender
body
Soon blue birds will be picking
seeds from your huge head
But, soon fall will be here
Killer frost will be preying upon
your slender body
Then you be no more beautiful
sunflowers
Good bye beautiful sunflowers
I will see you again another
year.
With your big leaves waving
& forward in the breeze
over your slender body following
the sun as it moves to the west.

—Charles E. Green, Jr.

LOVE AND PRIDE

When love is new,
and hearts are light,
it's like little sparrows,
swept up in flight.

And when love changes,
beyond our control,
we act like the ostrich,
our heads in a hole.

Our pride keeps us from mending,
the damage we've done.
And what once was light-hearted,
pleasant and fun,

Becomes more a strain,
uncomfortable to bear,
and causes the end,
of a once lovely affair.

—Victoria Hill

YOU

YOU were there when I needed
someone.
Someone to talk to.

I told YOU things.
Things I would not tell everyone.

Just in the time I knew YOU.
I knew YOU would be there
when I needed someone.

YOU may never see me again.
But I hope we can keep in
touch.

And whenever I am sad and
need a friend.
I will read this poem and
think of YOU.
For YOU are a friend, forever!

—Allen J Campbell

There goes my guy
He is mine, All mine
He has promised me the stars and
the sky
He said he would always stay and
be mine
When I am with him I feel I could
soar and fly
I have known him long enough to
know he wouldn't lie
He is mine, All mine
He is Mine All Mine
He is so sweet, he can't be beat
So don't think you can take him
because you can't
He loves me and I love him
He is Mine, All Mine
So you see this is how it goes
We take every day easy and slow
He is Mine, All Mine
He is Mine, All Mine

—Beverly Jackson

THE ROOM FULL OF ROSES

Families go through phases of love & hate,
Being part of yours was part of my fate.
Smiles when we meet & tears with goodbyes,
But the most precious thing is the love in your eyes.

Mothers & Daughters, Sons & Dads,
Finding your son was the best luck I've had!
The love that you show for your family & friends,
Makes any broken fence easy to mend.
Most families work at staying in touch,
With yours it just happens, that's why I love you so much!

A hummingbird's beauty as it zooms through the air,
The garden of love that shows how much you care.
The rose is one of nature's most perfect endeavors,
My room full of Roses means I'll love you forever!

—Robin Keenan

TRAPPED

Yesterdays were memories I once had of you
Tomorrow are dreams of us that will someday come true

Time is only that past ticking behind you and I
Forever is what matters in the clocks of my mind

Driving down a dark road of dead ends in the night
Thinking of the pain of ever saying "goodbye"

Waking in a cold sweat of visions alive
Praying for something that could never survive

Throwing pennies into wells, while wishing on stars
Disguised as love are these unbreakable prison bars

Somewhere in the myth is the truth untold
Hiding between the lines while the stories unfold.

Tears that fall for something I can't see
These are the things that are trapped inside of me.

—Jeni Brewer

WILL YOU STILL LOVE ME

Will you still love me when the morning comes
When the brightness shines of the morning sun

Or will your love disappear just like the night
When daylight has faded out of sight

You seem so close but yet so far away
But maybe someday your love will come to stay

Will your love be there just like mine
Until we reach the end of time

Sometimes I wonder if your love fades away because of fear
Just like the sudden raindrop or the shedding of a tear

Will you love me when time has passed
And we have both grown old at last

Will you still love me like I love you
With a love that is real through and through

Time will tell if you love me
But for me it will always be

A special love between us two
That no one could change, not even you.

—Denise Marie Genco

74

WHISPERING A PRAYER OF LOVE

Your love was like a rose that blooms in the early part of spring
A feeling that would make me weak that your touch would always bring
I miss your smile and tender way your eyes would look at me
So much love within your soul that only I could see
I'll never touch your loving face or see your smile so sweet
No one could ever fill the void, your leaving was so complete
My heart went with you when you left that day
The memory still lingers of how you went away
The tears still fall, I'll never forget
All those wasted hours, I'll always regret
The thought of being with you helps me make it through the days
You'll take my hand and we'll be together, forever and always

Dedicated to the memory of my husband, Howard L. Payne

  —Lee Payne

LETTING GO

Death is a terrible thing we see, although it happens every day
We forget the way we really feel and the words we did not say
Until it seems we wake one morn to find it happened during the night
The shock is felt at first, then the sorrow, the grief, and the fright
The shock is felt because we really don't know what to expect
We aren't ready to face reality, it's our own hearts we're trying to
 protect
The sorrow that is felt, is not only for the one which has passed away
But also for one's ownself, because of the feelings we did not relay
The grief that is felt comes from deep within one's heart
Because you know that from your loved one, you were not ready just yet
 to part
The fright is a natural reaction that comes from within one's soul
You must go on living your life, although it seems you're no longer whole
The days grow long and the nights longer yet, and the time seems to
 pass so slow
But now we must face reality, we must let our loved ones go!

  —Lisa Bolen

TO KERMIT

You were my friend, you were my lover, husband, father, loving brother.
Wherever we would go, whatever we would do,
You would always take the time to talk to people that you knew.
Council Meetings, Lion's Club, choir practice too,
Give another pint of blood, these were all important to you.
Church on Sunday morning, there was never any doubt.
It was as much a part of you as breathing in and out.
Dear God, I am not bitter, no anger do I feel,
Just pain like I have never known, in time I know you'll heal.
My tears they flow like Mary's, as she wept for her dear Son,
That day He died upon the cross, for the sins of everyone.
I thank you God, that you spared me, I did not have to see.
Kermit's death came in an instant, no pain or agony.
I thank you for the time we had, our love was truly rare.
A love that only God can give, a love beyond compare.
Poor Kody couldn't understand why everybody cried.
Explaining death to one so young, I know his mother tried.
Jenessa called him step-pappy, she loved him very much.
If only we could be like her, and not show prejudice.
One day she ran to him and asked, with joyful anticipation,
"Did you ask Jesus in your heart?" He said, "Yes" without hesitation.
And off she ran to spread the news, and all the angel's sang.
Another soul was saved from Hell, the bells of Heaven rang.
If Kermit would have one more chance, I know what he would say.
"Did you ask Jesus in your heart, if not do it today!!!"

Written in loving memory of
KERMIT R. BYERLY
by his wife, Charlotte

Till we meet again in that land that knows no sorrow.

  —Charlotte J. Byerly

SPECIAL KIND OF LOVE

Love of my life,
 feeling free.
To hold you close,
 to comfort me.

Take my hand,
 don't let me go.
Greater heights,
 for us to know.

Once in a lifetime,
 love to share.
No one knows,
 such love is rare.

Sublime nature,
 beyond our class,
Ultimately happy.
 I found you at last.

—Pam Wilson

UNFINISHED

It was as though
 their love was
forbidden by
 the heavens.

Their friendship
 denied by
 the world.

And yet, she was
 allowed one dance
 with him.

A dance which would
 last a lifetime.

Meeting his gaze,
 if only for a
 moment,
would fill her
 with an everlasting
 warmth.

—Michelle V. Nugent

STILL IN LOVE

two birds
very different
always changing
still evolving
quite alone
recklessly wild
highly sensible
one stable
one lost
brightly colored
forever linked;

alabaster columns
leaning skyward
always supporting
never touching
perfectly independent
hopeless alone
momentarily important
singularly infinite,

seemed appropriate.

—Roger Hall

75

LIFE SLOWLY FADES

Fading Times Of Masquerades
  As My Life Slowly Fades
Like A Petal On A Rose
That Wilts An' Dies And Then It Goes.
Faded Memories Of The Past
Flash Of Colors Going Fast
Like A Snowflake On The Skin
It'll Fight To Live But Never Win.
Faded Faces Of My Friends
Life To Death Now It Ends.

—Zane Bastian

THE LAST WALK

Along the rough and rocky road
  A man did slowly creep
His shoulders bent beneath a load
  Of sins too harsh to keep

Some people by the wayside jeered
  Yet others stood and prayed
While many cried and had much fear
  The Lord's last walk was made.

His cross he bore in silence deep
  His time had come at last
A silent shepherd leaving sheep
  Whose destiny was cast.

His life was but three decades long
  Too young to suffer so
A burning light of hope soon gone
  Too many people's woe.

—Judy Freeman

TODAY!

Today a load was leveled on me!
  A load that's hard to bear!
I lost a brother! A friend! For we,
  were close, a bond to share!

With unspoken words, we would talk,
  And Loved and liked and felt.
With never an unkind word or balk,
  At knowing what life had dealt!

It seems we knew, with unsaid thoughts,
  No matter where we were.
Understanding only closeness wrought,
  Through life, from start to here!

Just a look, a nod, a sigh,
  Could tell the story at hand.
A tale woven would unveil, why?
  A trait to understand!

And that, we did, up to now,
  That "Spring of Life" is gone!
I cherish the way we knew how!
  Even Love, unsaid, a Song!

Goodbye "Doodle," My Friend—I Love You!

In memory of my Dearly Loved Brother,
  Donald Hudson Phillips, Sr.
  Christmas, December 25, 1991

—Hugh Phillips, Jr. "Sam"

MY LIFE IS IN YOUR HANDS

Just sitting under the old worn out tree
  Listen to the bad news the wind cries to me:
It's all so unclear, like my reflection in the stream:
But fairytales are only in books and stories.
Lord, I pray for one of your amazing glories.
Specialists and doctors have done all they can;
Now it's up to you and me if I lie or stand.
Radiation treatment did not go as it should;
I've just gotten weaker and can't walk as good.
Not a hair on my body, nor a white cloud in the sky.
My parents can't believe that their little girl may die.
With my death on my shoulders, but with a will to live;
Lord, here is my strength, all I have to give.

—Kelly R. Jones

AFTER DEATH

A darkness, then it's bright,
  As I walk into the light; pictures flash before me,
Memories of what has passed.
I took those times for granted;
I thought they'd always last.
The pictures begin to slowly fade away,
And now I see the present day.
Your eyes are red and swollen,
As the tears still persist to fall.
I wish I could break through this barrier,
Break through this terrible wall.
This wall that now divides us,
That can never be broken through.
This wall that forces me to see
All the pain my death, is causing you.
I can't turn away, you're all around;
I think this is what hell is all about.
Feeling so helpless, being tortured by your hurt and fears.
I'd die a million times if it would only ease your pain
And dry your falling tears.

—Amie Howard-McGraw, age 16

THE CALL

The call no one wants to hear,
  a loved one has been in a crash.
As the mind races with fear,
  memories of yesteryear pass by in a flash.

Doctors say he has no chance,
  with loved ones to support with hope.
On the way to surgery we get a glance,
  and strong minded parents find it hard to cope.

After surgery we find he will pull through,
  the room is now filled with joyful tears.
For sending an angel to help him, we thank you,
  now we have time to spend with him the rest of the years.

He has a strong will to survive,
  a time to rehabilitate.
We thank God he is still alive,
  for starting over, it's never too late.

Together we will learn to walk before we run,
  for our love for him has no curfew.
Thank you for returning our son,
  for the son we speak of is our nephew.

I sit and think of things that used to be every now and then,
  with your help and his angel, he will be all right — Amen.

—Philip W. Mills

A NEW PERSON

"Therefore if any man, be in Christ, he is a new creature,
old things are passed away; behold all things are become new;"
These words supplied to us, in all seasons, by many a preacher;
In a daze but conscious, I sensed a change in me, miraculous, I knew.

Like drops of gentle rain, falling on a desert's dusty face,
I am tender, when I was ruthless giving way to temptations of life, —
The happiest day, hour and moment when my sins He did erase;
I've been filled like an empty cup, in smiling infancy—behind is my strifest.

Have I paid my debt? I have tasted the acrid taste of sin,
Moving now in melodious time, so both God and I will glorify; —
The old chapel now looked as though it had a globe of circular light as I entered in
"As newborn babes desire the sincere milk of the word that ye may grow thereby!"

Dediated to my sister and best friend, Pauline Bruder, who is my greatest supporter.

—Mary Ann Wagner Steirer

PERDEITA

"Once upon a time . . . in a land far away . . . many years ago, lived a princess of
extraordinary beauty." "She spent her days doing the things that royalty does best." "It
then became time to put away her dolls and think of her future within the kingdom."
"She had many suitors . . . for being with her, for many, was a treasured experience."

"One day she asked her father why she hadn't fallen in love with any of the good looking
men that came to call." "Her father thought a moment and answered her with a story."
"When the crickets find their rhythm on a hot summer evening;" "I know it's summer!"
"When the hue of the day changes from a yellow to a soft blue;" "I know it's fall."
"When winter is upon us and the brightness of Christmas is with us, I feel at peace . . .
for I know that it will again be spring."
"When the clouds seem to look less angry . . . the days lengthen and the hint of a warm wind
blows from the south against the smell of warm earth . . . It's spring."

"These things I have mentioned are truths that would have happened even if I were not to
acknowledge them . . ." "My beautiful daughter . . ." "These truths to me are also truths to you."
"You will know many more truths in your life, not by seeking them, but by having the
wisdom to perceive them in your mind's eye."
"In affairs of the heart you will know from deep inside you that your truths are the essence
of your being and they will not fail you."
"So relax my little Princess." "Listen for your truths and like the seasons; love will
come and you will gain a "freedom of spirit" that will always be with you."

—W. Channing Dunbar, III

THINKING

A young boy stares into the white sky thinking of how the world goes round,
Thinking of how easily friends are made, thinking of how easily friends are lost;
A yellow maple leaf trickles down from above, hypnotizing the boy's green eyes.
The crackled edge ripples with veins of old age and tears fall from the boy's face.

Recalling memories from the empty past, a frown forms on the freckled easel,
Fading into two perfect lips because nature always has to change;
Nothing is eternal — moods change as the seasons change,
Melting like ice cubes when feeling mellow, but cold inside when feeling blue.

The day grows dim and calm as the stained green eyes quiver and tear,
Meeting a new companion had been only a game for the world to enjoy,
Preparing this nervous child for the battle yet to come.

It had been one year of pleasure, two friends experiencing all the joys that life had to offer —
It had been one year of pain, two friends being drawn towards the dark underworld.
Time ticked on, as anxiety pumped into the pulsating minds,
Temptation arrived knocking at each beating heart.

The boy used to sit up on the green grass, forced to watch bottles shatter on the hard earth,
Smoke formed circles around the black bangs hanging from his friend's oriental forehead,
Concealed with hope that his friend would lose interest — the boy yawns.

Blonde hair glistens under the maple tree and another crackled leaf falls from above,
While the tree sits bare, waiting for the rain to light up the white sky.

*Dedicated with all of my heart and soul to Visalam Subram,
who beholds as much beauty as poetry itself.*

—Bobby Wells

A LOVER'S DANCE

Hand in hand,
Arm in arm,
They danced a lover's dance,
Whispers of the wind,
Their melody,
The rhythm of hearts,
Beating steadily,
A longing sigh,
The words unsung,
Under a midnight sky,
They danced on.
No sweeter could one song have been.
Written by the minds of men.
Arm in arm,
Hand in hand,
They danced,
A lover's dance.

To Russell Warren Raynor

—Laura Lyne Miller

FOR LOVE

For love I gave you all my heart,
Not dreaming we would ever part,
You took my love so willingly,
Then turned your back on love and me.

For love I searched my heart to find,
How seeing, you could be so blind,
To all that love that did so bind,
My heart and soul to you.

But love can't always be returned,
And hearts on fire can be burned,
Their ashes scattered in the wind,
Like hopes and dreams that have to end.

Alas, for love we give it all,
Forgetting just how far the fall
    will be when love is proved untrue,
As I have found my love for you.

—Lolly Bryant

REMEMBER ME

You will remember me
When the rain no longer falls
And the wind no longer blows;
The sun no longer shines
And the flowers no longer grow;

For you have chosen this destiny
As far as the human eye can see
Destruction has come over thee;
Now do you remember me?

On the fatal day that I arrived
Tears were shed as people cried
A mushroom shaped cloud in the sky;
Now do you remember me?

Our hearts are broken and full of sigh
Everything is gone and we wonder why;
And all it took was one button, you say?
One minute to push . . .
And a lifetime to take away

—Charlyn P. Woodruff

TO INÉS TATJANA

Let my love sustain you through the night
Let it guard you in times of fright
Let it lead you through to light
In the darkest storms of turmoil blurring sight
Let my love comfort, console, and caress you
For its lasting strength will envelop and protect you
In times of crisis and those of joy I'm there for you
Despite time and distance my spirit looks out for you
A tear, a smile, a laugh, all remind me of you
For today, tomorrow, yesterday and forever, I love you.

—Reginald Lee Heefner

MY LOST LOVE

Our spirits became as one, i would look into
My reflection and see your image

I would speak aloud only to hear the whispers of
your voice deeply within me

A single touch of your hand on mine would possess
My mind of a thousand thoughts and memories that
we once shared and the feelings that transformed
our minds to a magical place where love had no limit
and time had no end

Our love was forever back then, a forbidden love that
could have only been born spiritually by two souls

Now my spirit soars aimlessly searching for the
love that once lived deeply within me, a shadow
covers my reflection now, i fear our spirits will
never meet again

I look into my eyes only to see the pain that
now haunts my heart and the sadness that
has over come my life and all i can do is
dream of my lost love

—Melinda M. Medina

INTROSPECT

Deep in my mind your image does dwell.
Even in sleep, these thoughts prevail.
Dreams of you, my own introspection
Without the NO of your subtle rejection.

Morning comes awake all fresh and new.
My first thoughts are pleasant thoughts of you.
I rise from my bed when the sun starts peeking,
Still, it is your love my heart's gladly seeking.

You are with me Dear, all through the day,
While in my mind, your image does play.
Your handsome features and joy of your smile,
They journey with me through every day's mile.

When the day is ending, evening starts to fall,
Earnestly, I hope and pray you'd come to call.
With lover's embrace, I'd slowly melt in your arms,
Where I'll find happiness and bask in your charms.

The sun gone with the darkness of night once more,
You, my Dear, did not come to knock upon my door.
But, then there's tomorrow to want and to woo,
So I lay down to rest with sweet dreams of you.

—Cynthia Warren

THE BEGINNING

The Lord is our life.
He alone we should see.
As a beacon of light
and like Him, we should be.
He gave us His son to
free us from sin
to give us new hope
and a place to begin.

—Matthew A. Holm

GOD'S LOVE

"No one is perfect,"
as some people say.
But God is perfect,
as which to I say.
His love is endless,
although it's tremendous
That's what I think
of God.

—Erica Manes

THE GAME OF LIFE

You are dealt the cards of
life to play,
never knowing what could
happen one day.

Never lay one down unless
you're ready to see,
what the rest of your life
turns out to be.

No one never really knows
the out come of the game,
But nobody's hand is ever
the same.

—Heather Branam

GOD'S LOVE

Sometimes you wonder,
Is God really there?
Does He really love me?
Does He really care?
Why should He bother,
With someone like me?
My name will never
Go down in history.
But listen to me,
And listen well.
His love for you
Can save you from Hell,
He doesn't care
What color your skin.
He doesn't care
The degree of your sin.
He loved you so much,
He was willing to die,
So that you could live,
And that's no lie.
So give Him your heart,
And your whole life too.
And you'll feel it inside,
For *God's Love* is true.

—Charlotte J. Byerly

MY LIFETIME GOAL

My lifetime goal is to accomplish my dreams. My main goal is to achieve a successful spot in society. I hope to become a lawyer for a lot of reasons. My main concern is to help people get the justice that they deserve. If I help at least one person to better their life, I think that I would have made a difference.

Another reason is to make something out of myself. I hope to do this because my parents have spent a great deal of time and money to make sure that I am receiving the right kind of education I need to succeed. I am truly grateful of them. I love them both. My great-grandmother has helped also. She has given me much courage. Making my dreams come true will make a lot of people proud. There is one other person who would be the happiest of all. ME! I would be the happiest because I would have accomplished my dreams, and I have GOD to thank for it.

—Tamika Lushonna Leverette

THE PRISONER

I was locked up in a prison, when a preacher came to me.
He handed me the Bible and, said brother will you read?
I just smiled and said to him, it's too late for me now!
I could read those words a thousand times, He wouldn't hear me anyhow.
For I've done things in my lifetime, that I cannot reveal.
There's no way that I can say, just the way I feel!
The preacher said that's where you're wrong, God's with you every day.
He knows all that's in your heart, then he turned and walked away.
I just laughed and told myself, go on and do your time.
But the words the preacher said, kept pressing on my mind.
I picked up the Bible and started to read. I couldn't put it down,
Matthew, Mark, Luke and John and the glorious life they found.
While in the book of Psalms I read, the words I had to say.
I fell down on my knees that night, as I began to pray.
Father forgive me for my sins and wash them all away.
Please dear Lord remember me on your final judgement day!
I thank the Lord each time I pray, and every chance I can.
For giving me the will to take the Bible from the preacher's hand.
When I leave these prison walls, life will be good for me.
For my love is in Jesus and Jesus is in me!

—Alvin Ray Kessinger

GLORY TO GOD IN THE HIGHEST

I will extol the Lord at all times, His praise will always be
    on my lips.
My soul will boast in the Lord, let the afflicted hear and
    rejoice.
Glorify the Lord with me, let us exalt His name together.

He is the Almighty God, our Heavenly Father. He is the one who
    delivers us. He is the one who supplies all our needs.
He is the Almighty God, our Heavenly Father. He sent His Son
    Jesus as a witness to us, His blood was shed on Calvary's tree,
Through Him we have power and authority, through Him we have
    salvation and eternal life.

The Word of the Lord says, "Believe in the Lord Jesus and things
    will be done," for His Word says, "Ask and you will receive."
We are all witnesses to these things He has revealed. The Lord
    has healed broken hearts, He has mended families, He has healed
    many of His servants.

His arms are ever stretched out for His people, His love for us
    is ever true. We are His servants, let us be in obedience to
    our Lord and be faithful.

Let our voices sing, "Glory to God in the Highest! Hosanna! Hosanna!
    King of Kings." Let our hearts rejoice, let our hands
    be lifted up, let praise come from our lips.

Together let us praise and glorify the Lord.

—Stacey L. Tunstall

MOTHER'S REHEARSAL TOAST

I was surprised to learn I was pregnant
Surprised to birth a third son

Surprised throughout his childhood
With many a first all his own

Surprised with his talents and achievements
His happy-go-lucky self

A surprise I'd like to have cast in gold
A keepsake upon the shelf

Then, if ever a parting should occur
Warm memories would then be my treasure

My most precious gift, a valuable art,
Is entrusted to Natalie with all of my heart

—Rebecca E. Fleck

LETTING GO

Rain is sky writing summer's end
as September changes into Autumn's blend.
The apron strings lay carefully upon the stool
for all first graders who start school.
Eager eyes so big and bright
stop at the door now filled with fright.
What words of wisdom do we speak?
When a mother's heart starts feeling weak.
Why not protect a little longer?
Tell time to wait until we're stronger.
Put back the strings and tie the bow
I'm not sure yet, I can let go.
But we do release our child's hand
to go explore life's wonder land.
So on this first day when we hugged goodbye
there was a smile and a sigh.
For inside a mother's heart the tears are kept
there too all unspoken fears are swept.
From the day of birth a mother does know
to truly love, is to let them grow.

—Victoria M. Vilsmeyer

SPECIAL WOMAN

There's a special woman in my life,
I'd like everyone to know.
She gave me such a special gift,
she gave me life . . . she helped me grow.

She cradled me when I was small,
she wiped my tears away.
And even when she didn't know it,
she showed her love each day.

She watched me grow into a woman,
she let me spread my wings.
Just to think about it now,
tears to my eyes it brings.

When I need her she is there,
she's only a phone call away.
And even when I'm really busy,
I think of her each day.

This woman that I speak of,
with her love that has no end;
Is not only my beautiful mother,
she's also my special friend.

—Maria L. Iannotti

MOONLIGHT MEMOIRS

The fawn and his mother come to drink,
From the pond's crystal brink.
They like to talk,
In their own special way.
To tell of adventures,
Far and away.
They do this ritual every night,
From the moon's golden candlelight.

—J. Scott Davis, age 13

In my eyes there's no such joy
as having a healthy baby boy

Bringing laughter on bad days
Babies are like sunshine rays

Rain or snow can make a day gray
But his bright smile makes it all go away

After seeing that bright eyed face
I forget that long day's rat race

Watching my child learn new things
Oh what joy to my heart that brings

Reading him books and playing his games
He learns new words and new names

When he comes and gives me a hug and a kiss
My heart soars, oh what bliss

I want my child to be happy and bright
I pray that I do everything right

I want the best for his future to come
I make plans I hope I can get done

In my eyes there's no such joy
As having a happy baby boy!

—Tammie Mitchell

HE UNDERSTOOD

My sugary feet
Kept me from making it to the playground
My salty blood
Kept my pressure not down

I was slapping myself
Puncturing the chair
I was slapping myself
Slapping at air

But I'm not sorry
Won't be carried
To the dinner table
Mom would worry
and Dad would be harried
But brother
I was able

Everybody laughed
At the Christmas Party
My strength was sapped
It really hurt me
You were younger
But wheeled me out to play
I Love you little brother
I will always remember
that day

—Rocky Morrow

THE GOLDEN ARROW

You are the golden arrow that
runs straight through my heart,
    It is very thin and narrow,
but without it I'd be torn apart.

    You may not think you mean
that much to me,
    But are you so blind,
that you cannot see?

    For I love you with all
my heart,
    And if you break that arrow,
you will break my heart . . . .

                    —Gloria A. Hulley

LOVE ME ♡

When I wake up in the morning
'Til I go to sleep at night,
The only thing I want to see
Is you within my sight.
    Love me. ♡
When we are together
My heart, it beats so fast!
The time we have together
Just doesn't seem to last.
    Love me. ♡
When you love me all the day,
That's when our love is true.
When you love me in your way,
I love just being with you.
    Love me. ♡
All I want is for you
To stay right by my side.
Without you I am feeling blue
Inside my heart has died.
    Love me. ♡

                    —Rebecca J. Mills

THE GOOD, THE BAD

The good, the bad
    The days, the nights
So soon I try to completely forget
The gentle, loving words
The awful, screaming fights.
All it takes is a phone call
All it takes is an old song
And I cannot forget your face
And I cannot forget your smile.
What is the lesson I am to learn?
Why must I always be reminded?
Because I won't forget your smile
And I couldn't forget your face
I remember those old songs
I remember those phone calls,
Those awful, screaming fights
Those gentle, loving words
So, soon I try and completely forget
Those days, those nights
The good, the bad.

*Dedicated to Andrea Noel Prevost,
my first true love, whom I will
never forget.*

                    —Sean T. Staggs

WITH YOU

With you, I thought I had found the perfect love.
    I thought we would share the rest of our lives together.
But instead, with that love, I found heartache and pain.
Pain so deep, it cut to my very being.
I don't know how to stop loving you, I wish I did.
Maybe then I could get rid of this pain.
Though I know with you the pain is deep.
I also know without you, it would be unbearable.
There is no easy answer for me.
With you, I have hope, without you I have nothing.
So, I choose to wait, wait for you to love me again.
I know that you will.
What we had is too precious to lose.
I will wait, and I will pray that the rest of my life
will be . . . with you.

                    —Judy R. Green

A SPECIAL VALENTINE MESSAGE

There is a special day that comes to the shortest
    month of the year.

Pretty little bright red cupids with shoulder length
    wings fluttering high and low.

Carrying sugar coated secrets filled with tiny love
    notes tucked under their overcoats.

With tons of deep rich chocolate and bunches of
    yellow, pink and red roses all wrapped in the
    finest of white satin ribbons.

Hugs and kisses by the truck load, laughter and joy
    and tear-filled eyes and there's singing in the air,

A velvet valentine trimmed in shimmering white
    lace.

A silver arrow right in place with your initials
    above and below, open the gate and feel the weight.

This message is from your chosen sweetheart.

    "JUST TO SAY I LOVE YOU"

                    —Shirley Blagg

THE DOVE

I can't understand this feeling inside.
    I want to run away but there's no place to hide.
What is this feeling that I feel?
Do I know if it's fake or real?

I sit here and wait as the days go by.
And yet while I sit here, I can't help but to cry.
What did I do to make you feel this way?
How can I change? What can I say?

Since you've left, my world's been torn apart.
Ever since you left, with you went my heart.
Why with another I'd know what to say.
But an exception with you, something gets in the way.

As soon as you called my name, something wasn't the same.
This feeling in my heart that I didn't know was there,
Suddenly stepped out when I found you didn't care.
This feeling will be there through good times and bad.
This feeling will be there when you're happy or sad.

This feeling is beautiful—just like a dove.
I finally found this feeling.
This feeling is LOVE.

                    —Katie Muldowney, age 13

TIME FOR THE ROSES

My mother didn't know it then, but she bloomed more brightly than the gaily colored roses she used to pick from our California garden when I was still a girl.

Now I am a woman and live miles away from my childhood home, and my mother has moved to smaller quarters with no back yard.

But whenever I come to visit she still finds time for the roses, that she picks from her neighbor's garden, who doesn't seem to mind when she comes calling.

Gently armed with shears and basket, softly kneeling down to address her rainbow friends, that will soon accompany her home to fill the vase upon the table.

And find no grander place to bloom than with the fairest flower of them all.

—Clare Edwards

FOREVER DAD

Your smile was my first introduction
You stayed side by side with strength guarding me as your possession
Praise came and scolding too, but I felt the warmth
Your advice was well studied and carried out as life moved forth
No day went by, that you didn't make time to include
Your precious family needs were allowed to intrude
You became a loving father, a dependable parent and a loyal friend
You got known as a problem solver who could mend
Uphold the law, you politely insisted
Respect and honour you gracefully persisted
We spoke your name with such pride
When you got promoted, you deserved the Sheriff's title
We stood proudly alongside you, envying a little
You gave us courage to start and finish when burdens came
Sometimes I felt weak but then I flashed back
And there you were Dad, still smiling the same
Now that you are alone, don't be sad, we are still around,
To love and care and let you rest
You are still special to all of us and still remain the best
You will always belong to all of us forever Dad . . . .

—Angie Sheldon Simard

MOTHER'S BEST

Looking back on all of my accomplishments of life's tests.
Two precious daughters stand out, proudly chosen as Mother's Best.

One dark and lovely, full of pepper and spice.
The other fair and golden and everything that spells nice.

Without them life would have been empty and dull.
Together they brought happiness and filled my life so full.

Being needed as a mother gave me reason to exist
Their hugs, smiles and tears I never could quite resist.

Two sisters, not alike, you could often hear one say.
Each hearing a different drumbeat, taking them a separate way.

One a career girl, ambitious in law, her life's goal.
One a bookkeeper but shines most in her motherly role.

For this I feel blessed, grateful and always so proud.
Even when their friends, music and fussing got too loud.

I like reading books, romantic movies and love of home.
To dance and travel, many places I could roam.

I love beautiful golden sunsets painted across purple hued skies
Stars that shine on moonlit nights in a lover's eyes.

I'm fascinated by pretty blue birds and robins red breast
Of all my favorite things, my girls are Mother's Best.

—Joyce Lane Wade

SHE GAVE ME:

She gave me her eyes and her soft gentle smile, her caring mind and her giving heart. She gave me her love when she had nothing more to offer.

She gave me the will to go on when it seemed I could take it no longer.

But sometimes I forget that one single gift she gave me that I can never repay and that was the gift of life.

—Christina Pacheco

Grammy,

SIGNS OF SPRING

Birds Chirping
Winds Whistling
Trees Blooming
Flowers Growing
Longer Days
Sunrays
Jets Soaring
The Smell of Pollen
Fresh Watermelon
Fun, Happiness
Grass Growing
Sailing Swimming
Easter Holidays
Many Parties
Spring Fever
Graduation Achiever
Together these are the
"Signs of Spring"

Love,
Sarah

—SEBS

To have them near
an' hold their hand,
when they're afraid
Say I understand.

Sometimes we forget
to show we care
They begin to wonder
if we know they're there!

Don't take them for granted
Soon they'll be grown
they'll go into the world
on their own.

Times may get hard
an' there's nothing you can do.
Hold them close, an' say
I love you.

When we begin to wonder
have we done our best?
I love you Mom, Dad thanks
and they leave the nest.

*Dedicated to my sons,
Aaden, Brent an' Chance
Love, Mom*

—Jo Jo Lohre

RESTLESS SEA

The sea is restless tonight,
As it laps upon the shore.
The moon seems ever so bright,
But it will shine no more.

The gulls swoop just out of reach,
As they soar above the swell.
And I am alone upon the beach;
Living in my silent hell.

The waves retreat back to sea,
Only to begin their march again.
Life's repetition has defeated me;
And left me racked with pain.

Would that we could love once more;
Would that your love returned to me;
But I am solitary upon the shore,
Envying the restless sea.

Tonight it has a life of its own,
And tonight, softly, it calls to me;
To cease being so lost and alone;
And become one with the restless sea.

—J. D. Copeland

A STORM ARISING IN THE SEA

All The Colors Of The Rainbow
Behold! The Glory Of Its *Glow*
A Vessel Paved In Golden Splendor
One Of Heavens—Many Wonders

Foretold—A Legendary Journey
A Gentle Promise, Etched Within A Tree
Adhere, "The Story Of The Calming"
A Storm Arising In The Sea

Awake Thee, Rolling Clouds Of Darkness
Winds, A Howling In The Breeze
Waves Of Fury, Stir Thy Nation
Await, The Falling Of The Leaves

Strike! ye Flashing Bolt Of Lightning
Blinded Eyes, Omit To See
Adrift At Bay, ye Shall Be Wandering
Fear Not; If You Believe

Hush—ye Roaring Claps Of Thunder
Away Thee Cast / Thy Human Blunder
Plant The Seed Upon One's Mind
Change of Seasons For Mankind

—Carol A. Johnson

THE OCEAN

The ocean wide and gray lures me close to its waves
Rushing upon the sand with teasing spill
roaring, rushing back and forth
Deep within its bowels teem creatures,
unknown below its surface
Frightening, yet calling me to taste its power
Salty foam comes to its head
Seagulls flutter, skimming over
searching for their sustenance, screeching
crying as they fly
blending in with ocean color
Remnants of living unknowns scatter
over the sand from where they
came is a mystery from below
Innocence of calming waves crash and
break the silence of morning dawn
Never ending, vast beyond the human
eye is God's creation of the sea
How marvelous beyond man's comprehension is He.

—Carol A. Sausen

THE SALT IN THE SEA

There is an old-wise tale, that explains
something true.
I will start this poem & dedicate it to you.
It goes way back, way back in time, before I ever
knew that you would be mine.
It explains how all that salt got in the sea,
way before there was you and me.

Many a sailor has left behind a wife or his
family, but I never thought it would happen
to me.
I fell in love with you & went far, far away!
But in my heart I knew you were here to
stay.

I shed many a tear for leaving you behind, sometimes
I feel I am losing my mind.
All of the tear drops fell into the sea, one at a
time is hard to believe.

The taste of salt comes from not 1, 2 or 3
but all of the sailors who are just
like me.
We all miss our loved ones & families
enough to make us cry.
But everytime I leave you behind, I
feel a piece of my heart die.

—John Scrivano

I will arise and go now, and go to the heavens;
And love and kindness built there, of puffy white clouds made;
Relatives will I have there, a gift for the friends who care;
And live with all my hopes and dreams here.

And I shall have peace inside, for peace comes from living here;
Listening to this place, gentle care to where you are equal;
There midnight stars a glimmer and noon time just aglow;
And evening sunsets full of color.

I will arise and go now, for always day and night;
I hear the birds singing what a peaceful place this is;
While I stand on good firm ground, or jump for joy and peace;
I hear it in the air around.

Dedicated to Bill DeHart,
a grandfather who took time to care.

  —Jennifer Theroux

JUST PASSING THROUGH

Shane, as you were just passing through,
I'm so glad that I knew you.
For one so young in years, you were so wise,
And we enjoyed seeing the world through your eyes.

We saw the flashing waters of the stream,
Realized the hope of a dream,
Marveled at the beauty of butterfly wings,
And knew the pain of an angry bee's stings.

You loved nature and respected it all,
And you were always ready to answer the smallest creatures' call.
You thoroughly enjoyed cooking,
And liked to go shopping, not just looking.

To the fullest you really enjoyed life,
You well knew in it there was joy as well as strife.
You dearly cared and you helped others,
For you saw them all as your sisters and brothers.

We rejoice with you in your home up above,
And we know you're looking down on us with love.
We join our voices with you in joyous symphony,
As you praise God throughout eternity.

  —Maria E. Herbert

THE UNSAID GOODBYE

At first there was pain and joy;
And then there was pain, but no joy.

He was there as she had expected,
And then he was not.

They told her the will of God is to be respected
But, she through the pain, thought not.

How could their God bring her, Her Boy, and then in a
thundering instant, deploy His strength to undo her joy?

To take her boy to Heaven?
She could have, would have, led him there.

One day . . .
Could their God not wait?

And in the morn they gave her a girl to take home; they said,
"And now you will feel again, the joy."

So she took her home and did what was expected
And they thought her pain was gone, but it was not.

For they had forgotten, for all the new joy
She had never gotten to say goodbye to Her Boy . . . .

Dedicated to my Mom, thank you for letting the understanding,
drift thru the layers of me, and touch my soul with love.

  —Mary M. Payne-Norris

GOODBYE, MY FRIEND

He lies there asleep
Satin lines his bed
A cross and a rose
He holds in his hand
And inside the chapel
The funeral dirge plays
It's time to say
Goodbye to my friend
As he closes the door
To his life here on earth
He crosses the hall
And opens another
The door to heaven
Is opened up wide
Welcome home, Welcome home
Oh, Child of Mine.

  —Delores Utecht

If or when I ever go
mourn not long
these things you should know
I know the truth of all mystery
I am the priviledged one
with my body at rest
but my soul not near done
You'll know right away
I will give you a sign
that I am your angel
and will keep you just fine
Though not there
you and I are never without
I am now your strength
you'll no longer have doubt
So please just remember
our love, the laughter, the fun
because that's all that matters
until you become . . .

  The privileged one

Dedicated to the family of our
beloved friend, Allan, who will
be greatly missed.

  —Kelly Lannan

NO ONE KNOWS THE PAIN

No one knows the pain I feel,
As I turn away pretending, it's
not real.
I know, nothing just not the same,
For I feel like, I am on a
fast moving train.
All the reasons, are nothing
but lame,
As I turn away, still feeling
the pain.
I lay the flowers, and say
a prayer,
And let you know, I'll always
care.
No one knows, as I stand
and stare,
Just how much, love we really
shared.
No one knows, the pain I feel,
As I turn away, there you lie
so still.

In memory of my sister, Penny Parmer.

  —Denelda DeWitte

SUMMER DANCE

And so begins her summer dance
 The heart's design is left to chance
And such assiduous romance
 For sun and wine and circumstance
The harmony, the graceful rites
 Of sultry summer days and nights
Capriciousness nothing may sate
 Content only to aestivate
And be forgiven all her sins
 And so her summer dance begins

— David W. Sjöberg

TWELVE ROSES FOR YOU

The first two roses I give to you
 Stands for a word
It expresses ownership
And is very often heard
The next four roses I give to you
Is the second word
It's a devoting emotion
That makes some people scared
The next three roses I give to you
Is now the third word
It is the representative of
As I give to the one who deserves
The last three roses I give to you
Is the last word
It expresses a person
Who must always be observed
Now add them all up
You get twelve roses
That stands for four words
MY LOVE FOR YOU.

— **Ray A. Calton**

GREEN, BLUE, GREY, BROWN

You look through me
 with your silent eyes of color.
I drip salty moisture
and stare (defiantly) back at you.
Green, blue, grey, brown.
Green, blue, grey, brown.
My wet hand reaches
out to you
and it tingles
as it
falls asleep.
You are no longer there
and my pale, white hand
shakes and trembles
(but does not move).
You exist along with me.
You stand next to me.
I see your eyes
veiled by a coma of
. . . (I do not know).
I cannot reach you,
I cannot touch you,
and I know
that you want me to.

— Elisa E. Human

FRIENDS FOREVER

When we became friends,
 I knew that it would never end.

But then the day came that my friend had to leave,
It was a day that I grieved.

For I thought our friendship was over,
But to my surprise it was just starting over.

So even if we weren't going to be together,
We were going to be friends forever.

— **Stacy Pierpont, age 14**

REMINISCING

The sky was clear,
 the water was still.
Within the air . . . a slight chill.
We walked upon the sand,
then we sat upon the shore.
It was much too perfect to ask for much more.
As the sun was setting,
we held each other tight.
Awaiting for the stars to come out of the night.
The stars appeared,
and as bright as ever.
We wished this night could go on forever!
There was no other place that I longed to be,
Reminiscing on a night . . .
of you and me.

— **Kristine Jones**

JUST THREE LITTLE WORDS

Just three little words that I want to say
 But somehow, something always gets in the way
In this world where people lie and cheat
It's hard to find caring arms
Into which I can retreat
To trust another with all my heart
Only to have my world broken and fall apart
In the past it always did seem
That all I got were broken dreams
As I grow in wisdom and age
In this book of life I turn a page
To find a friend so fine, so real
I cannot believe this, which I feel
You, I can trust always I pray
So, I Love You is what I want to say

— **Diane Kram**

COURTSHIP

 Submerged in a sea of solitude,
Safe behind an impenetrable wall of steel mesh.

 Love is an abused term:
For it can not be bought or sold,
As misconceptions have leant it,
Love can only be given or received.

 Even then, true love
Is only found.

 After thought, it comes to me, what I seek;
Not love, not peace. I seek not joy and romance,
No honesty, no loyalty. Oh how wonderful virtues
These are, in unison they are the stepping stones
To a path less traveled: that path is a trail
To a meadow of simple complacency.

— **William Stone**

FIVE WISHES

Being only four, and soon to be five. It's really a job trying to decide.
She raised her eyebrows, then blinked her eyes. And tried to think of her first surprise.
She put her finger under her chin, then curled her lips with a funny grin.
She was only four, and soon to be five. So soft and small and sweetly alive.
I wish I knew what went on in her head, still changing her mind when I tucked her in bed.
She asked for things that were tiny and small. The wishes she had wouldn't cost much at all.
Lipstick and make-up, a little tea set, a real baby lamb, which she won't get.
A blackboard and chalk, to hang on her wall. Pretty new shoes, and she thinks that's all.
She has had a week, and is still thinking, raising her eyebrows, and her eyes still blinking.
With five days left, she's still undecided, then thinks of one more and acts so delighted.
I wonder if she'll decide, it's getting so near, what she really wants when her birthday
    gets here.
As I kiss her goodnight, one wish if I may, is to always have her to love, as I do here
    today.

    —Kay M. Hermann

MOURNING FOG

The morning fog was heavy and thick in the air, making breathing difficult, almost painful.
    And it impaired sight completely, except for the grayness of its existence.
The stillness of the early morning was suddenly pierced by radio tones slicing through the air.
Like a two-edged sword, they shattered the peaceful dreams of the ambulance crew,
Alerting them to an automobile accident with seriously injured victims.
As the ambulance rolled out of the garage and the flashing red lights hit the dense, gray world outside,
The driver was blinded by the reflecting glares in the heavy mist.
For nearly thirty minutes, the ambulance crept along the road at a painstakingly slow speed,
Searching for the wreckage, hoping that they would arrive in time, yet knowing deep inside
That with each passing moment the lives of the victims were slipping farther and farther away.
It was maddening to realize that the very fog responsible for this accident
Was now being so relentless in allowing help to arrive.
With no warning, the wreckage revealed itself from behind its ominous gray cloak.
The car entrapped two boys in its twisted, mangled, unmerciful grasp.
Although the medics fought with fury to free them, another twenty minutes passed before they won.
That time, that golden time, was just enough for one boy, just too long for his friend.
The medics labored to the best of their abilities, putting every medical skill they knew to the test,
But the fog had outwitted even their most modern technology, forcing them into defeat.
They watched in mournful silence as the boy's last breath painfully expired his soul into the air.
Within moments, that fog mysteriously lifted, quietly yielding to the warm, early morning sun.

    —Steven G. Brewster

WILL I NEVER DREAM AGAIN 11:56 P.M. TUES 1/1/91

I, like others, have had my share of dreams.
    And they were like heroes or so it sometimes seems.
Heroes of a lost war who had all died in vain.
    So went my dreams and I, feeling only more and more pain.
I used to see myself as an unbeatable white knight.
    Then tears clouded that vision, and 'twas no longer in sight.
And tears dry up and are brushed away, and new dreams are born
    It's such a beautiful painting but, in the corner the canvas is bloody and torn.
Yes, as I said, I've had my share of dreams.
    But, the best laid plans of mice and men are often only schemes.
And just like the funny little circus clown.
    There's always someone who will laugh each time you fall down.
But when you're all alone and the grease paint is all gone.
    No one will ever know you'd have no smile were it not painted on.
It may be all over soon as you place the last brick in the wall.
    Then the last hero; the last shining white knight may fall.
And with him love and hope will also fall and evil will finally win.
    And the world will know only heartache, and the child in all of us and the child still somewhere in me
will never dream again . . . .

Dedicated to Kimberly Marie Sparks with love 11/12/60 — 4/9/90.

    —Robert Eugene Christopher Sparks, Jr.

LOVE

Your LOVE for me was everything,
  I held within my heart,
I might not have always said it,
But I LOVED you all a lot.
Your LOVE is what helped me,
To make it day by day.
Your kindness and your caring.
It made my brightest day.
I know I was not perfect,
And some things I did not right,
But you stood right behind me,
To help me make them right.
So do not cry and do not frown,
Don't worry about me no more.
I'm safe and out of danger,
Just waiting at Jesus' door.

—**Robert W. Garringer Sr.**

JOY

I look up to the sky and see
  the Lord's face in the clouds,
And suddenly I'm transported from
  the rush of earthly crowds.
I have left that harsh and heartless
  world, way down deep below,
And squint as I gaze at God's pure,
  white light and loving glow.
He takes me and enfolds me in
  His gracious, strong, pure love
And tells me that He cares for me
  and looks down from above.
And I think as I float gently
  back to where I live,
That life is only just as good
  as whom we love and what we give.

—**Linda L. Sparks**

WATERFALL

Water cascading down my face
  is refreshing.
How I wonder your name sweet
angel.
How I long to caress your
smooth silklike skin.
Water cascading down my face
is refreshing. In filth strewn
streets, I search. Seeking he who
has wronged me so, (contemplating
revenge is not an idle task).
Water cascading down my face
is refreshing.
If you ask me my name I will
not answer, I have no reason to
be called. Give me a reason
for living and I'll die for that
reason also.
Water cascading down my face is
refreshing.
Love is a wonderment of
which I have no comprehension.

—**Brian P. Muska**

FOREVER

The heavenly white of an angel's wing; the warmth and love
  that your heart sings.
As twilight ends another day; I'll love you more than words
can say.
True love will never fade away.

*Dedicated to a person I don't know yet, she is
out there somewhere. The day I meet her it will
be hers, as will my heart.*

—**Steve Kuppinger**

ME WITHOUT YOU

Me without you, is like a flower without sunshine or rain,
  or a blind man without a dog or cane,
a baby without a rattle,
or a rowboat with no paddle,
or a sea with no shells,
and a door bell with no bells.

Me without you, is like a church with no preacher,
or a school with no teacher,
a winter without any snow,
or a glow worm with no glow,
or a flower without any stem,
or a tiny baby, with no one to teach, or to love him.

Me without you is like, a tree in the summer without any leaves,
or a coat in the winter without any sleeves,
a spring with no baby animals, or flowers,
or an April with no showers,
a kite with no tail or string,
or a bird that can't fly or sing.
None of these things can be or do the things they're supposed to,
    and that's me without you.

—**Vickie Benedict**

BYGONES

Bygones, a word about days gone by with bittersweet meaning.
  With thoughts still in my heart toward you even leaning.

But time takes its toll, and so slowly takes away.
Until your smiles and memories are only just another yesterday.

Taking with it all the good times, laughter and love.
Leaving me empty, lonely and blue as the skies above.

Picking up pieces, putting back together puzzles of my life.
Alone, but stronger until there's no more tears of strife.

Learning to live a new life after you and me.
So different, uninvolved, from all my feelings free.

But still I like to take walks down memory lane.
Reliving happy times, letting go of any faults or blame.

Oh, to see your face again and feel your touch.
To tell you the things that dearly meant so much.

But precious thoughts are all I have with me today.
Let bygones be bygones, with nothing much left to say.

Except I love and miss you and maybe in time,
We'll be together again, only this time more in rhyme.

Always walking hand in hand, only just us two together.
Blue skies, sunshine and rainbows, promising life's beautiful weather.

—**Joyce Lane Wade**

HAYLEY'S TOMORROW

Hayley is a child who is less undernourished in soul, day by day.
She is a child who is more of a moonbeam, than of a shining ray.
Some beautiful day, she will just wake up and find — it is tomorrow.
That day, she'll use her own imagination within her tomorrow.
Though maybe, she feels that is too good to happen — even in tomorrow
And maybe, she will pass a dull colorless world, into a brighter day
Or maybe, she'll see a twisting harbor road — at the end of a bay.
Then some day, she'll see a spotted forest splashed, with golden light rays
And may she pay less attention to any lost whispers, that come her way.
Therefore she may pass on the other side to find, a watery silk bay.
Some great day she feels an island of happiness, will be in that bay.
One day, she hopes ships will navigate to the island across the bay
And some day, she will find it when tomorrow comes, on that joyful day.
Some beautiful day, Hayley will just wake up — and find it is tomorrow!

—James A. Locke

TOMMY

Tommy—come here. I have some questions I'd like to ask you.
Where did you get those bruises? Why are you black and blue?
Why are you so quiet—even when I speak to you?
Why are you so unhappy? Why don't you ever smile?
Why don't you talk to other children—even for a little while?
Why do you look at me that way? What are you feeling inside?
Why won't you tell me just what it is that you're trying to hide?
I never see you crying, but I know that there's something wrong.
I can tell by the way you act—you're withdrawn all day long.
You look so helpless. I just don't understand.
What can I possibly do to give you a helping hand?
I guess I've said enough—I'm not sure what to say.
Except that I love you, baby, and I pray that you're okay.

*Tommy is a little boy about six years old. His teacher is
thinking of what she would like to say to him. "Tommy" in my poem
does not exist. He is in my mind, and represents all abused
children.*

—Terre Libby

SPIRIT

*"How can the body touch the flower
which only the spirit may touch?"
Rabindranath Tagore*

What the spirit seeks to touch of beauty
lives within its hands and spreads wings
like self-butterflies, to swing about air
breathed into the breath of fools
to make them cry for precious sweet love.
What the spirit needs of fruit is satisfied
at its lips forever . . . fresh and cool and
fragrant as flowers: invisible as wind,
they are eaten by the woeful hearts
whose lips starve for such treasures.
What the spirit sees past the stars
falls through its eyes like a fountain of dew;
it runs and runs over the faces of the wicked
of the world and opens their wounds and cleanses them
with desire for sacred things.
What the spirit finds of strength is like mountains
in its arms, though soft as embracing; light as a babe . . .
it surrounds the ones of weakness and winds joy
into their paled skin . . . within.
So how *can* the body touch the flower which only the spirit may touch?

—Chelsea L. Robb

STREET LADY

It's no fun,
being on the street . . . .
I'm fifty years old and,
some days don't eat.

Digging in trash cans
for food or whatever . . . .
Sometimes you have,
to be very clever.

Seven surgeries in all,
two heart attacks too . . . .
In remission from cancer,
oh what do I do?

I write songs people,
tell me are good . . . .
If only I could sell them,
survive then, I would.

—Dana L. Gibson

SHATTERED

Who had
the right
I shouted
from my
solitary
soul.

Who had
the right
to throw
the rock
of pain
that shattered
to pieces
the picture
window
of my
heart?

—Mary A. Duffy

The waters are still
all is calm,
but in my heart
I know it's not.

I wish it was done.
I wish we got along.
But when we're together,
all rocks are thrown.

It's like a war
to see who's right.
But like a war
no one wins.

We both get hurt
and wonder what
went wrong.
Seems there is no answer.

*Dedicated to my
father and our hope
for the future*

—Heather Louise Lagrone

THE DAY THEODORE BUNDY DIED

The day Theodore Bundy died,
   I heard distinctly the demons cry.
In depraved joy and glee,
amidst the darkness
they held a twilight jubilee,
and all of them were invited to see,
the half-lit celebration,
in whirling mad continuation,
for one of their own,
who had finally come home.

   —William R. Ford, Jr.

I was walking into darkness
leaving all behind
wanting to stay,
but death was leading me all the way.

I wanted to go.

Voices were calling my name,
saying, "A world awaits you."

No time for goodbyes.
I was sorrowing inside, for what,
I did not know.

I turned off the lights,
and closed the door.
Singing, in my tears, AMAZING GRACE,
while the blood was shed.

I could see the world,
and *it was great!*

Gone was today.
I saw tomorrow.

—Nicole L. Cook

THE ETERNAL DANCE

I did not want to dance
Yet You dragged me to the floor
You said it was a chance
For me to love You more.

I was unsteady on my feet
I did not know the steps
Yet You made my knowledge complete
Made me light with life and pep.

But soon I became tired and weak
My joy began to cease
And so You wiped my wet cheek
And made my grace increase.

I gripped your hands so tight
You held me through it all
While I waltzed with all my might
You ensured I wouldn't fall.

'Twas then I heard the song
A hymn of praise and glory
For You have done no wrong
It is me, the ungrateful, I am sorry.

And now the music ends
You release me from your arms
Whatever beat of life He sends
You will protect me from all harm.

—Michelle Petrovic, age 15

CRY OF AN IRAQI POET

I live to write a poem sublime
but I'm to die for an innocent crime
I criticized Saddam in a rhyme
now I will truly truly be
a member of the Dead Poet's Society

Dedicated to Robin Williams

   —Allan H. Lambert

SMILIN' JACK — DIAMOND IN THE ROUGH

He was born on the plains of Montana, educated in a one room school, He learned his lessons well there, as he was nobody's fool.

He worked for years as a ranch hand, the job he knew and loved, but when time came to raise a family it just didn't pay enough.

So he hit the road for Utah, in his old Chevy car, he liked to never made it, not realizing it was that far. He gave up his cowboy life for a diesel truck, and rode the highways and byways to wherever he was sent.

Long days and nights in all kinds of weather, he stuck to the job, hell bent.

His C.B. handle was Smilin' Jack, a name that was sure to stick, as there was always a smile and a helping hand for anyone in a fix.

For twenty-nine years without accident, a life that was mighty tough. But here was a man respected by all. Surely a diamond in the rough.

He loved the mountains of Utah, the excitement of the Rodeos, but he always had time for his family and friends, more important than making dough.

   —Erma L. White

ON MY DAD'S 60TH BIRTHDAY

Dear Dad, when the pumpkins wore frost
      To greet their new morn
And the grass in the field waved hello
      As fall blew its horn
And leaves 'neath your feet crackled their song
      Of good-by to the trees they'd adorn
Was the time when you spoke and your breath
      Could be seen in the air — and the corn
Was golden and tall — and the fall
      Wore its nighties like
The dresses that summer had worn

Was the time, when you, sweet, were born

How fitting that Nature paid you tribute
      On your first new day
With her decorator brush in hand, she painted
      Every hue and ray
Lavish reds and golds and even amber
      Sunsets had their say

'Cause tho the world prepared its winters rest
      New life had stirred that day

And what better way, but Autumn's beauty,
      Than so to say
And ever since, sweet, on your birthday.

   —Kathy Stark

TOMORROW

Tomorrow is tomorrow no matter what it brings
     For some people tomorrow is happiness
For others it's darkness
Because tomorrow is tomorrow no matter what it brings
For some people it's a place to stay
For others it's just another day
Cause tomorrow is tomorrow no matter what it brings
People continue to live even though their lives are shattered
They live even though they have been battered
Cause they know that tomorrow will be another day
                    Tomorrow brings happiness
                    Tomorrow brings laughter
                    Tomorrow brings sadness
                    Tomorrow brings disaster
We never know what tomorrow may be like
Tomorrow is tomorrow no matter what it brings

    —Shea

TRIBUTE TO GOD

GOD's Grace

Man lives his life on earth, at a fast pace,
never taking time to remember, he was placed here by GOD's grace,
At the top of the Animal Kingdom man feels he is in first place,
but in the creation of the universe he is barely a trace.
Our GOD made man in his own image to live on earth,
yet with all this man still has not shown his worth.
Man on earth just will not follow the divine plan,
to love his brother and his fellow man.
The church is the rock the Bible the word,
GOD's grace the power if only His words are heard.

GOD's Good Book

Our GOD's words are in the Good Book,
all man's problems can be solved by taking a look.
Our Lord's Bible was written for all mankind to see,
if these words are read your soul will be set free.
So do not ignore our GOD's Good Book,
open the pages and take a good look.

    —Anthony J. Siconolfi

DRINK DEEPLY FROM THE LIVING WELL

Most of us are dreamers; we have dreams of every kind:
We wish for fame . . . we wish for joy . . . we wish for peace of mind.

Our wishes are so shallow; we are selfish when we pray.
We want fame . . . we want joy . . . we want peace of mind.

We must send our buckets down low into the Living Well
That the Spirit of our Lord will with us closely dwell.

But when heavy trials come along, and sorrows bend us low,
It's into the Living Waters that we must surely go.

We need His Holy Spirit to walk with us each day.
We need those Living Waters to guide us on our way.

We must send our buckets down low into the Living Well
That the Spirit of our Lord will with us closely dwell.

Christ will soothe our weary spirit, and love will with us abide,
For into the Living Waters, He will be our Guide.

He will give us strength for ev'ry task; our courage, He'll renew.
To drink deeply from that Living Well is one thing we must do.

We must send our buckets down low into the Living Well
That the Spirit of our Lord will with us closely dwell.

We must send our buckets down low.

    —Edith F. Head

MEMORIES

When I was a kid
     I seemed to think;
When a pen goes dry
it is out of ink

Now when I write
it takes some time;
To get those words
in rhythm and rhyme

    —Clyde W. Jontz

LITTLE BIRD

Little bird
          so cold,
               so frail,
As the wind
     ruffles your tail.
Clinging tightly, to the bush
chattering to your friends
          so pretty,
               so tiny,
          yet, so frail
     In the wind
          you sail . . . .

    —Sarah B. Haines

the sun rules the day;
the moon at night.
clouds busy the sky
but the stars seem right.

the grass can be green,
or ugly brown;
while the earth continues
to revolve around.

fall is the darkness;
winter the beast.
this is the season
i like the least.

but spring is near,
knocking on winter's door.
a prelude to summer;
the season i adore.

    —Ervin Glass

I show myself
     the way,
without knowing.
I search for answers;
     the truth,
of who I am.
Becoming . . .
all that is,
     to be.
Discovering and learning.
Changing.
Growing.
Amid the drudgery,
     there is good.
It's up to me
     to find it;
and use it toward
     my purpose.
Following fate.

    —Barb Zieger

LOVE SONG

A Song
So Powerful and Magical,
A Song
Brings Me Tears And Joy,
A Song
Reminds Me Of A Loved One,
A Song
Brightens My Darkened Mood,
A Song
Relieves My Soul,
A Song
So Beautiful And Mystical,
A Song
Leads To Fantasies,
And Lives In My Heart,
Protected By Love.

—Rachel Jenkins, age 18

ARE THEY REALLY GONE

Are they really gone
We cared
We loved
We watched
Lasting moments
Knowing you were part of a life
Suffering is gone
Pride is there
Sadness is deep
Dignity was there
Love exists
'tis true
Chapter is closing
Memories we hold
Oh so dear
Love
Holding
Quietness
Love exists
Are they really gone

—Jean M.S. Lerner

THROUGH THE EYES OF A WIFE

He knew you were the one
when time first began,
but I'm so much a hurry-girl
He gave me a slow-down man.

Well now we're together
'till death do us part,
for God has my soul
and you have my heart.

We'll laugh and we'll cry
but we will succeed,
for God is our center
in prayer, work and deed.

Not much more can be said
until our judgement day,
when God calls upon us
and we're sent on our way.

He'll know that we tried
and worked hard all our life,
and kept holy our marriage
as husband and wife.

—Mary Birch

YOUNG LOVE

Where else do you find a love like this, on a night like this is? When a young girl falls to her knees begging her Savior to grant her one single acknowledgement in an otherwise empty heart.

It's a part of her and always will be, but is the strongest wish she's ever wished out of all her strongest wishes.

Not even the miles of distance that separate them, can place even one single doubt into her, least of all when she saw him from the start.

At times I hear her cry, clutching her love to her heart in desperation that is painful and preciously delicious,

There is only one key that opens the door to which she cannot find the fit,

Although I watch her from the side, my heart aches for hers to heal with his in her emotions.

Would he please just ease her pain, for him to see her would break his heart, and I would find that this girl is me.

—Wendy L. Liddell-Hackett

ACCIDENT

Today, I received a letter. It brought tears upon my eyes,
Not afraid. I left. Knowing deep within my heart and soul,
what I must do.
They say it was only an accident. I didn't want to
cause everyone the pain that I felt. I don't feel
guilty. I can see from above, looking at my
stone. Remembering, that it was only an accident.
I did write to you.
I don't know if you had gotten it. You have gone
on . . . Tears welling up into your eyes now and then.
But if you only knew, that it never hurt.
I never screamed, or wanted out.
Yes, this is the peace and happiness
I once had with you.
I've watched you from the beginning.
I'll watch you till the end.
I'll be there,
even if you don't know,
Always, loving you.
I'll always be there, for **you** . . . .

—Chantel M. Hillius

PERFECT VALENTINE

I looked thru all the cards today
And knew I wouldn't find, the perfect words
To tell you, that you've always been my Valentine
It doesn't take a holiday, to remind me how I feel
The love I've always had inside, has been there all
these years. And so I took some time today; to try to
express the letters of Valentine, That really suits you best.
V — Very important in my life
A — As always being there
L — Lending a hand when needed
E — Everytime and anywhere
N — Never ever complaining
T — The trouble I put you thru
I — In sickness or in happiness
N — Nearer my heart to you
E — Everlasting is the love I have for always being you
That's why I send the Valentine to let you know
I care, and that you're always in my heart
and in my daily prayers.

Dedicated to Mom & Pop Bryant. Love Violet

—**Violet Brown**

THE CONQUERING WARRIOR
Ephesians 6:11-20

The Whole Armour of God requires self-disciplined behavior
Prepared for Spiritual Warfare as a conquering warrior.
The Armour's readiness activates each piece applied
For the specific purpose intended well fortified.
The Weapons of Spiritual Warfare are to cast down carnal activity,
Against All knowledge of God bringing its strongholds into captivity;
II Corinthians 10:4,5
Scripturally based on principles of truth tested
The Whole Armour of God is Victoriously contested.
The Helmet of Salvation is Steadfast in securing;
The evil forces that combat the warrior's faith in enduring.
Effectively challenged by the prayerful use of God's Word declaring:
Satan's fate, with his angels, is no match when comparing;
II Peter 2:4-9
The Wisdom of God's Might and Power exemplified in the
Conquering Warrior's triumphant hour.

—Elina E. Lee

GOD'S PRESENCE IN THE SEASONS

He reflects Himself in the seasons, I can sense His
presence there. In the fullness of each season, there is
beauty that is rare . . . .
 In the Spring-time, He is there, the little wild flowers
and the clean fresh air is Him in His beauty so fair . . . .
Even the birds follow Him all around, singing and praising
Him with a heavenly sound . . . In summer, He is there
He makes Himself known in the warm, fresh air, in the
beautiful green grass that springs alive from the roots is
somewhat of an expression of how God lives in us . . . In Autumn
He is there. Where the beauty is so rare! The colorful season
Always wears the beauty of His love, as the leaves turn many colors before
they fall from the tree above! The trees from whence they fall
obey God's command, as they continue in their uncloth beauty
forever more to stand . . . In winter, He is there. Even in the
pure beauty of a winter's snow, He is there to purify, I do know . . .
to refresh the air that we breathe, to make the earth prepared to
conceive . . . He reflects His purpose and beauty in all
seasons, He reflects His beauty in each of us, let His life and
light shine from within us, just as the seasons show his divine touch . . . .

 —Lennice-Marie Taylor

TO GRASP THE ROSE

In order not to feel the thorns, one's hands must grasp "The Rose";
For, only then one's life accorded 'gifts' as to what chose!
'Apostle's thorn' — that left in flesh as said, "I can't decide
Whether to remain as 'dust' — or go — with God abide!"
INDECISION! "Adam's thorn!" To eat — or not partake —
Of forbidden Fruit placed on "That Tree" in midst of stake.
For, ON THE SON OF GOD imputed: sins that ever past!
Or ever in the future to be done! From FIRST to LAST!
Oh; taken were these 'thorns' so we could clasp Rose to our breast;
Which naked, bared the soul to God with every quaking breath;
Thus be assured! Smell Fragrance sent from Heaven to this dust
To nurture 'seed' for Roses New: Green Tender Shoots — of trust!
Wee 'mustard seeds' — in Lily's Bulb — that Rose Hip doth enfold;
As tops these 'stems' with 'thorns' below (called "ARMS" and "LEGS")
to hold:
These Helping Hands! and Feet to tread this 'winepress' we are on;
Until these Setting Sons go down — to RISE — IN BRAND
NEW DAWN!
There, Hands of God shall unfold 'petals' (worldly cares have torn)
To wrap in Brand New Essence —
 THESE HYBRIDS HE HATH BORNE!

 —Glee Stevens Weiner

SNOWFLAKES

Drifting White Petals,
 From Heaven's Rose,

Making of the Earth a Poem,
Of God's Perfect Prose!

—Mary Dunn

METAPHOR

A person is a ghost
 searching,
In the lost
NIGHT.

A person is a shell of
a person.
A person is a
shadow of a SOUL.

Searching,
always
searching

A human being
is a mirror
echoing
back.

Always looking
in.
Trembling on
heaven's edge.

Lingering in
a house that
is the SOUL.

Until invited.

—Kelli R. Simmerman

Students.
 Messengers.
All
Loyal
Lovers of God.

Persecuted
Under the
Regime
Pervasive.
Lashed.
Executed.

Tortured
Repeatedly.
Integrity
Affirmed.
Never
Giving in.
Living.
Enduring.
Strengthened by God.

*Dedicated to those who
were forced to wear the
"Purple Triangles" under
Hitler's reign. (Once
known as Bible Students,
now recognized as
Jehovah's Witnesses.)*

—J. Jeff Harrer

93

HIS GENTLE WAYS

Lord, lift me up so I can see
Past all the grief and misery
My heart cries out in wounded pain
But remaining in You I have all to gain.

Your gentle voice speaks hope and peace
And abiding in You brings sweet release!

I could not pray saying, "Father Dear"
Till You healed me, Abba, and now You are near
My love for You means everything
Thank You, Lord, for the joy You bring!

Your gentle Spirit heals wounded hearts
And gives broken vessels brand new starts.

—Linda S. Johnson

BIBLE STUDY, "FOR THE AGED"

Just a short poem
about the Nursing Home,
The Home is close to me
So we visit it often — you see

Nearly 20 years since the Home
was built here —
And since that time we've shed many a tear
Tears of sadness and tears of woe —
As we watch each one come and go

The folks are as sweet as they can be
Try working in a Home and you will see.
We love them all — each and everyone
And working with them is lots of fun.

On Saturdays we have Bible Study there
And that's because we really care —
When this life is over we'll see them again someday
In Heaven — if we'll just help to show them the way.

—Pearl Vadino

MY BLESSING

Lord, you blessed me with three wonderful boys,
And a darling little girl.
Now what more could a mother want,
In this old sinful world.
But I cried and prayed to you dear Lord,
And asked "How can this be;
My little girl can't speak a word,
Why did this happen to me?"

Then I prayed and asked you Lord,
To help my baby talk.
But I looked around me in this old world,
And said "Thank you Lord, my baby can walk."
Here's a child with twisted legs,
He will never run and play.
This little girl will never hear,
Or see the light of day.

My baby can't say "Mommy, I Love You,"
And if she does it will be by your touch.
But you gave her two loving arms,
Sparkling eyes; and a smile that can say so much.
Dear Lord I'm not asking you,
To take my burden away.
I just Thank you Lord, and ask you,
To help us from day to day.

—Geraldine Neighbors

DARKEST HOUR

When through a valley you walk,
dark though it may seem.
The Lord is always near,
carrying you through, whispering
soft words of comfort and hope.
In life's darkest hour,
the love of our Lord shines forth.
To guide and keep you until
your mountain top is reached.

—Jennifer Lynn

PROVERBS SIX: THIRTY-TWO

Let us pray for disease, such as AIDS;
for it is taking so many young away.
For when you live by the sword,
That's how you'll die, said 'God's Word,'
So let's pray for a cure someday.
The commercial said to Beware!
To practice 'Safe Sex,' but I declare,
The safest way's in your house,
with your 'God Given Spouse,'
preceded and followed with prayer."
Jesus said 'Believe I am HE,
be baptized, pick up your cross and follow ME.
Confess ME before men,
live according to My Father's Plan,
And in Heaven, someday, you'll be.'
So if Homosexuality's for you,
Read Leviticus Eighteen: Twenty-Two.
Or, if you've been convinced,
That 'Sex' is no offense,
Read Proverbs Six: Thirty-Two.

—Samuel Blaine Allen

WHY DO YOU LINGER?

Sinner friend, why do you linger,
In this world's cruel sinful way?
Jesus gave His life for many,
He, your very debt to pay.

Oh why do you not accept Him,
He, who gave His life for you?
Bore upon His back the bruises,
That you might have some way through.

Jesus is a blessed Saviour,
So divine and full of grace,
He will save you, poor lost sinner,
If you only seek His face.

Can't you feel the Spirit calling,
You to leave your path of sin?
There will be a new day dawning,
When your heart is cleansed within.

Can you sit in sad rejection?
And with scorn upon your face?
You can now accept salvation,
And He will help you win the race.

Hallelujah! He is able,
When the trials press you low,
When you go to Him in prayer,
He will surely bless you so.

—Altha B. Davis Williams

A QUESTION OF SILENCE

I lie in my bed at night,
Asking the Creator
What does it mean to live?
What does it mean to die?
I close my eyes

And hear the Silence,
The terrible Silence . . . .

—T. Hawk Scoby

WHAT YOU MEANT TO ME

Rainbows, softly falling rain,
Summer sunshine, lingering shadows,
Autumn leaves, crunching snow,
Spring flowers, whispering wind,
Stars twinkling in the sky,
The mighty eagle; as he soars so high,
The mountains in all their majesty,
The vast oceans; shimmering and blue,
The sobbing of the violins; their
unchained melodies, the geniuses of
Shakespeare, Byron, Keats,
Schubert, Mozart, Bach,
And all
The glory and grace
God bestowed to this earth.
That's what you meant to me!

Your smiling face I miss so much.
Sleep tight sweet prince.
Goodnight, goodnight.

*For Dickie, whose gentle spirit
flew away on the wings of doves on
the Eve of Saint Valentine's Day.*

—Nancy L. Matsey

LINGERING DEATH

Hold it close
To your heart
For it will continue to live
To love forevermore
I found out
That you had neglected it
You dropped it
And it shattered
Into a thousand tears
Which flooded the room
With despair and false hope
You had not cared for me
All alone and bleak
How can you expect it
To survive
Without warmth, without light
I love you no more
How could you leave me to die
Have you no feeling, no remorse
Farewell, my executioner.

*This poem is dedicated to all
my friends who help and support
me. Thanks again: Michelle Chartland,
Marc Chaput, Jenn Barnier, Kerin
Daviau, Chantal Laprise, Mr. Jean-
Paul Gagnier Jr. and my mom.*

—Diane Normandin

WHEN SPIRITS TOUCH

When spirits touch, there is peace,
like a monarch butterfly, upon a full blown rose.
They move together, flight suspended,
for a moment in time, then they drift apart.
The fragrance of the kiss lingers,
like the breeze across a warm summer eve,
then with weightless feet, they move,
among the common things,
but they are no longer alone.
The butterfly has the sweet nectar,
yet, the rose has the memory,
of the butterfly's gentle kiss.

—Doris Hartsell Brewer

A MISSED DADDY

Who will wipe away my tears
And softly settle all my fears?
Who will assure me things are right?
Who will tuck me in at night?
Who will tell me what to do?
When trouble strikes, can I count on you?
Who will walk me down the aisle?
Who can always make me smile?
Though you may not be here in the flesh,
You did not leave upon your death.
For you'll always be here in rain or shine.
Daddy, can I still be your valentine?
Thanks for the good times. I can't recall any bad.
How come this time of year always makes me sad?
Perhaps I'm reminded of the last time I saw your face,
Touched your hand, or heard you sing "Amazing Grace."
I love you, Daddy. I always will.
Your little girl remembers you still.
You are my hero, my best friend, and most of all I pray,
You will be my guardian angel whose love will always stay.

—Amber Cordell

REFLECTIONS

Before Life's Mirror You Stand and Gaze,
Remembering Your Life's Dreams and Bygone Days.

When You Look in A Mirror and See Beyond,
Years of Memories That You Have Found.

The Faces of All Appear One By One,
Back To The First One When It's Done.

From Then To Now Flows All Memories,
Those You Shared and Ones You See.

Count Them All Fading Reflections In Time,
These Memories Will Not Be Lost From Your Mind.

This Special Day You Will Remember We Spent,
Remembering The Years and What They Meant.

I Hope You Achieve What Your Heart Does Dream,
For Sacrifices You Give and For What They Mean.

Where ever You Go Do Not Forget,
That Your Mirror of Life Reflects No Regrets.

*Dedicated to the memory of Dr. David L. Bell:
His greatness is reflected in his patients so well.
We treasure his memory, so fondly we hold,
Like jewels of diamond, silver and gold.
by: James D. Keenan, M.D.*

—Pat Fogleman

ODE TO EDGAR ALLAN POE

The arrival of the raven during a gloomy night laden ravaged the soul of the lover of our fair maiden — Lenore.

From whence thy had thy start of prying in my heart, you foul and loathsome beast, you abysmal utterance — Nevermore.

Was it happenstance or chance thou descended upon my life, to steal away betrothed sweet dreams of Lenore, or was it the destiny of a youth shunned from heaven's sacred door?

Be it happenstance or destiny with which you gained the mastery over my subliminal abode, you stained my heart with badness, you evil pretense of madness, you croaking voice — Nevermore.

Fled I from those dismal piercing eyes that penetrated my very core. Fled I to another shore, to another far away shore, to find a fair maiden resembling Lenore.

'Twas a stormy day by the sea, I first laid eyes on Annabel Lee. The thunder echoed as this maiden's eyes met with mine, where on the sand of the sea stood, in a radiant beam of light, the full majesty of Annabel Lee.

The lightning filled the air as I stood there with a stare, to observe something so rare, a beauty beyond compare, when dared return that dark, foul, immortal spirit flying through the air, in the very beam of light that shone by the sea upon Annabel Lee.

A screeching louder than the thunder reverberated from shore to shore, that single blasphemous word I heard many times before — Nevermore.

The glimpses of heavenly light dancing off the sea disappeared, and along with it, the fair maiden, the beautiful Annabel Lee — Quoth the Raven — "Forevermore."

I was left standing in the mist on that cold, black December day, in a profusion of illusory thoughts, when that frightful plumage again appeared to me.

In those green dismal eyes appeared a road down which I strode, to find the love of my maiden Lenore — Nevermore.

—Richard E. Rose

MY LIBERTY

The Eagle will soar through the skies,
wings outstretched
to their fullest.
She flies to the heights and the depths,
between the clouds and the heavens . . .
how beautiful that she will always be there!
She is free, the Eagle, comes and goes
when she wishes . . . it is a beautiful thing
to be able to see.
Because she has her liberty, and that is why
she comes and goes when she wishes.
But I cannot do this . . .
for my liberty was taken away
by drugs and alcohol,
that is why I cannot be flying
here and there with the Eagle.
One day, with the power of God
and the power of my soul and my heart,
I will leave behind the drugs and alcohol,
and soar with that beautiful Eagle.
That day will be when my soul is cleansed
of these things that have ruined my life.
My wings began to open a little,
with what I have learned in these months of study.
I will be able to say that I walk the Right Path,
to one day fly with that Eagle here and there . . .
with my soul and my heart at peace.
Flying through the heavens with my liberty
that I fought for and won away from drugs and alcohol,
to find my liberty
and soar with that Eagle,
in skies blessed by my beloved God.

Dedicated to my brother, Jake Herrera,
who is now flying free with the Eagle.

—Jake Herrera
Submitted by: Amy Esquibel

MI LIBERTAD

El Aguila volará por los cielos
con sus alas abiertas,
a lo más que pueden estirarse.
Vuela para arriba y para abajo
entre las nubes y el cielo . . .
¡Qué bonito que siempre estará ahi!
Está libre el Aguila, va y viene
cuando quiere . . . es una cosa muy bonita
para poder ver.
Porque tiene su libertad, y por eso es
que se va y regresa cuando ella quiere.
Pero yo no puedo hacer esto . . .
porque mi libertad me la quitaron
las drogas y el alcohol,
por eso es que no puedo andar volando
lado a lado con el Aguila.
Algún dia, con el poder de Dios
y con el poder de mi alma y corazón,
voy a dejar las drogas y el alcohol
y voy a volar con esa Aguila bonita.
Ese dia sera cuando se me limpie mi alma
de estas cosas que me han arruinado mi vida.
Mis alas se comenzaron a abrir un poquito,
con lo que he aprendido en estos meses de estudio.
Podré decir que voy en el Buen Camino,
para algun dia volar con esa Aguila lado a lado . . .
con my alma y corazón en paz . . . .
Volando por los cielos con mi libertad
que la luché y le gané a las drogas y al alcohol,
para hallar mi libertad
y volar con esa Aguila,
en los cielos bendecidos por mi querido Dios.

—*Jake Herrera*

ONE MOMENT

My chin rests on my folded hands
As I pause.
Taking time to reflect
On life's chosen paths.
Stopping briefly to see
If I'm on the right track.
Looking inside
Further than I can ever see out.
Miles ahead.
Miles behind.
As I pause
To reflect,
To savor
This one moment
In time.

—**Kelly Majors Hawersaat**

LILIUM AND ILEX

Celebrant of the birth of Christ
My name is of decoration.
Your last is of a flower
Denoting His resurrection.

Berries red as Christ's blood,
My leaves are forever green.
Trumpet of His arising,
Your pure white flower's seen.

Mine is what Noah sought
From the beak of a snowy dove.
Yours blooms at springtime
With God's unending love.

My first is the Greek moon.
I am sister of the sun.
Yours is of a scholar saint
Whose Bible verses are done.

Your last follows my first
Fullness: the holiday of springs.
Your first is shared by many,
And by some six famed kings.

—**Cynthia Warren**

A MATTER OF CHOICE

"God's countenance is fair,"
The white man said loudly.
"He's dark like the night,"
The black man said proudly.

"The Great Spirit's face
Is bronze like the sand
That rims the blue sea."
Thus spoke the red man.

"He's like none of these,"
Came a voice, 'cross the sea.
"He's swarthy, slant-eyed;
Exactly like me."

Now God in His Heaven
Looked down from above,
Smiled ever so gently,
His heart filled with love.

For all of mankind
On the green earth below.
Then He showed them His color;
He made a rainbow.

—**Helen Gibson Estep**

Lord! Will this time ever pass
It seems my soul is heavy with it!
I either have too much or not enough.
I need to feel the solid touch of my south land.
There time has no meaning, it just passes!!
My mother and my father are there, in my south land.

The dogwood, sweet williams, and wild plums are in bloom there
It seems when I think on these things.
My soul is lifted up.
My spirit is renewed!
Time has no meaning!
For my soul has touched my south land!!

—**Charlotte Harvey Ritchey**

FOR MY BROTHER

Thinker of such thoughts,
Knower of so many things:
Your depths have been long untouched
By any, I think.

Within you I sense a brewing of emotion and thought;
Your intricacies and knots of nature unsuspected by all.
Do you feel apart; bereft of any who understands you?
Do you wonder if you will ever be known?

Your mind's workings mark you unique among the rest of us.
Your undulations of thought take you beyond my touch.
I cannot reach your depths: too intense.
Your heights: too lofty for me to follow.

In my life, you are a sparkle of beauty so great
As to have no measure.
You are a gift of mystery whose depths I can never plumb.
I only worship, and am thankful for you.

Oh, my special brother:
I think no one understands
The essence of you . . .
Not even I, who loves you so much.

—**Wendy L. McNeil**

FRIENDSHIP

Friendship is built on compromise, care and trust.
Being honest to each other is a definite must.
Friends don't mean to hurt you in any sort of way.
Just telling the truth will help your friendship grow each day.

No matter if you're the best. Or even if you're not.
Your friend will stand beside you and help you when you're caught.
Friendships tend to vary.
Some start late, others start early.
Friends have opinions in one way or another.
They're not just friends, but like sisters and brothers.

As time goes passing by,
People change and others cry.
Friends get hurt, but later feel okay.
It's because they're there to help along the way.

My poem's about friends and friendships.
They are great to have, but are sometimes ended.
Friendship is a terrible thing to throw away.
Because friends can stay together and be there day by day.

This explains it all! About everything you need to know.
Friends are forever, like Larry, Curly and Moe.

*Dedicated to my friends Marlo Medenilla and
Melissa Changho, my sister, Geraldine, my
parents and teacher Miss Diane Leavitt.*

—**Gina Elaine Dapul**

CASCADE POND

There is a lovely place in my memory, Cascade Pond is its name,
And after having visited there, I shall never be the same.
With its own private majesty, it calls and beckons me,
A place where I pay homage, created for me by Thee.

Proud mountain ranges surround the frozen scene,
Visions of inspiration, a wintry Christmas card theme.
Sinewy spruce arch shamelessly towards indigo skies,
And amidst the dusky hue, a shadowed bird mournfully cries.

There is no temptation in me, to disturb this peaceful place,
For I am only a visitor here, among what God has graced.
To appreciate this quietness, the elegant beauty I have found,
The white riches of snowfall, upon the trees and ground.

Amidst the glory of God's creations, a lone bridge stands in wait,
Where I walk, with breathless wonder, towards Heaven's gate.
Not knowing when the time comes, I must leave all this behind,
I am humbled by it now, a forever memory, to carry in my mind.

  —Ann Mathews

WHAT'S IN A NAME

My name is called Beryl.
I like it pronounced as in "Bear-l."

And what is its meaning I'm sure you must ask.
It's a beautiful gem, whose colors all bask
In crystals of amber, of pink and of green,
And can also be found in an aquamarine.

In reading the Bible, in Exodus twenty-eight
That beautiful gems adorn Aaron's breast plate.
It shall be in linen of gold, scarlet, purple and blue,
And set in four rows of stones in a dazzling hue.

The first row a topaz; the second a diamond; the third amethyst all ablaze,
And the fourth row a beryl, its brilliance will amaze.
Now, what's in a name? If you search you will find
They all have a meaning and a history of kind.

So guard it well—it's all that you own.
Remember, prestige and wealth can be overthrown.

  —Beryl B. De Natly

SILKEN SUMMER SOUL

Smile once more, O shimmering spirit
Swiftly the planets align, crying for heaven's eleventh setting sun
her sleeping soul slips into a velvet sea
the endless lagoon of fiery light
center of the music enamored to be
excited and writhing in silky night!
"A raft!", the cavern happily mumbles
exploding, exploring in centuries bright
a dusty nightwatch suddenly crumbles
all hues and seasons of white!

Legions conspire in a shapeless void
swooping bats and sunless swallows
all time and reason, all fate avoid
twitching graves and crooning hollows!
Clouds of yellow, a coloring sky
flitting flashes from father free
all nights to live, all deaths to die
cackling, crashing, clasping with glee!
Sex as smooth as one, whispering water wakes pure as thee!
Smile once more, O shimmering spirit.

  —Michael Faher

REACH OUT

Reach out
Right now
Reach out
Somehow

Motivate
Anticipate
Legislate
Participate

Do it today.

—Marie Mascena

PERSONAL IMPERFECT

I
took the
personal
and
subdued it.
Like
stripping the GREEN
from the
grass,
or the BROWN
from the cola,
or the WHITE
from the
dish soap,
and suddenly
it all became
clear.
So *very*
CRYSTAL CLEAR . . . .

—Terrence D. Haynes

METAPHYSICS

Redman
Blackman
Indian
Negro

Savage
Slave
Renegade
Afro

Bought
Sold
Cheated
Refused

Destroyed
Beaten
Denied
Abused

Enemy
Oppress
Resentment
Injustice

Alienate
Abase
Condemn
Prejudice

Endure
Emerge
Beautiful
Proud

—Gale Rogers

FRIEND

If you ever need a friend
I have a lot of love to share.
I will be here until the end
To show how much I really care.
If you ever need a guide to
Help you see the light
I will be right by your side
To make everything seem bright.
If you're ever looking for love
You have to look no more.
For I will show you a side of love
That you have never seen before
So, if you're ever feeling blue
Just remember
I Love You!

—**Tony Nazario**

LOVE IS . . .

Love is friendship,
So deep and so true.
Love is a person,
One who really knows you.

Love is the knowledge
Of one who cares.
Love fills the heart,
Where it once was bare.

Love is thinking
Of you everyday.
Love is feeling
In that special way.

Love is missing,
When you are not here.
Love is forever,
All throughout the year.

Love is a friend,
Some old and some new.
Love is happiness
And that is you.

—**Stephanie Reeder**

ASK

Ask me not
ask me why
ask me when
probably when I die.

Ask me something
ask me soon
ask me now
what's the tune?

Ask me not to
ask me why not
ask me when to
and when not.

Ask me to
ask me please
ask forgiveness
will war ever cease.

Ask for love
ask someone near
ask for happiness
shed not a tear.

—**Linda M. Cooper**

SERENITY BE

Your sunshine's hidden from me
By a cloud that's grey with gloom
I hope my sunshine finds you
Sitting safely in your room

Your sunshine is important
To those who feel your pain
So please accept this gift of mine
To clear the clouds and rain

This gift that's given freely
From the heart unto the heart
Will surely help undo the pain
And let the healing start

So know I give it freely
My sunshine for your rain
And let my love for you be
A shelter from your pain

—**Michael Piper**

IF WE ONLY BELIEVE

You will never know unless you truly believe
What it is I feel for you so deep inside of me
You allow me to become someone I can't be with anyone else
With you I'm safe and comfortable, even with myself
We've held within our hearts the love we've longed to share
All these years have passed us by, but the love time did not wear
We've both believed in something we didn't know we would ever see
We thought our love could only be in the security of our dreams
But with belief there comes a power, the strength we need to
        release
The love we've both held prisoner, only now can the withholding
        cease
Today we have to sincerely believe in something more than our
        dreams
We must have faith in tomorrow, our someday is closer than it seems
I will let you see inside of me, a sight no others have seen
I will open my body and soul to you, my true feelings you then will
        receive
In return I will accept you and the feelings you hold for me
Our dreams will then become reality, because we simply believed

—**Vicki Johnson**

LIFE

Life is an uncertain path that every day we follow.
Not knowing what's coming next, happiness or sorrow.
We walk along this path of life though we may fall astray,
we'll get back on the path of life and finish up that day.

Life is like a mountain, icy, steep, and tall.
Sometimes it gets so hard, we think that we might fall.
But soon we'll find the strength we didn't know was there,
and then accept the statement "Life's not always fair."

Life is as the ocean and we are as the ships.
It often gets so rough, we feel that we may tip.
Though storms and windy weather will often pass our way,
we must put that all behind us and live for today.

Life is one big book that we are authors of.
It's up to us to fill our books with hope, good works, and love.
I hope the tears you've cried will be replaced with laughter,
and that your book will end "happily ever after."

*I dedicate this poem to my family. They have
given me care, support, and love, and have
made my 'Life' all the more wonderful.*

—**Jennifer Jill Taylor**

It was September in 1971 Now your journey had just begun. Thru the halls of T.C.S. You were definitely among the best. You weren't quite sure what you wanted yet, So you traveled with Kemp, the country vet. Boces was a stepping stone While your senses were being honed. Then in June of 1984 Graduation! the day you had worked for. Then Broome Community was the way, For two years there you were to stay. Then to Rhode Island to study and work, From there to Florida to hit the books. Ah! Then the place of your heart's desire Stony Brook on the Isle. They would send you off to do your stint, Five weeks at a time; and away you went. Queens, Rochester, and back to Queens, Then Tennessee, Rochester, and again to Queens. And at some point in time, Guthrie was the scene. Now it's back to Stony Brook on the Isle Where the Gods of Medicine upon you smile. There you graduated on June 28, 1982, **ROSE ROPER, P.A.** we are all proud of you!

—**Phyllis VanVleit**

THE NEVER ENDING JOURNEY

Anticipating baby and the work that will come in tow
Dirty diapers, fever and no sleep for nights in a row
But no need to worry or to fret, every day will be a joy
With more love than you can imagine whether baby is a girl or boy.

The baseball games and ballet recitals, scrapped knees and broken arms
The bear hugs with sticky fingers, the messy faces with eyes of charm
All the things that make grandmas cry and moms-to-be smile
Are waiting for the next few years by the hundreds of miles.

Hundreds of miles of fits in the store, "Buy me a toy or I'll die"
The nights out to dinner or visiting friends, "Oh please don't cry"
Miles of school years, miles of books, miles of inches they'll grow
Until one day those miles are gone and Mom and Dad must let them go.

Those miles right now may seem to be miles away from today
But just as quickly as it starts, so will childhood slip away
Your first job is completed but another now begins
For your child is on a different road of miles that do not end.

Your shoulder will still be needed for a broken heart's reliance
Your words of encouragement and truth a gentle path of guidance
So you see, this journey you've now begun is an important road to tend
For only the scenery will change, the love will never end.

—**Cheryl Daniels Carreon**

RETIRED TEACHERS, HAIL!

Barbour County is justly proud of its retired teachers to whom certificates of achievement were presented at the mid term meeting on March 2, 1957. Those teachers so honored were Elzie Everlyn Adams, William B. Baker, Arla Casto, Floyd Cornwell, Howard Cornwell, Talbott Cross, Virginia Croston, Charles Haddix, L.L. Hershman, E.A. Hunt, E.L. Knight, Jesse Lang, Bonnie Mason, John M. McVicker, Daniel B. Poling, J.H. Rohrbough, Harry H. Stalnaker, Mrs. Lou Summers, Mrs. Jessie Thompson, Mrs. Lulu Valentine, E.F. Van Gilder, and Sevva Wilmoth.

Mellow masters of the wondering mind,
What kept you in your work for endless days?
Culturing and counseling all who came to learn,
In hope that none would ever go astray.

Were there days when you wondered why
You chose to teach because it looked like fun?
A doctor or a lawyer you should have been,
Or just a laborer who knew when day was done.

Your pay was meager, your rewards so few;
You wondered if the effort was worthwhile.
Time has passed. Now you see the work you've done
Reflected in our nation's peaceful smile.

—**Bret Everson**

A FRIENDLY SMILE

A shining light!
A sparkling glimmer
of hope,
In a sea
of darkness.

—**J.C. Legge**

A TOKEN TO MUSIC

A rhyme with reason
put to words
to sing!

In time played to sound
tubular sound
to hear
with our ears!

Notes of angels singing
to the words
of *their* heart's song.

Being four reeds of wood!
Four strings!
For our ear's pleasure

A gift from heaven
for a reason
Words can't express
beauty in music
a token to my heart!

—**Nancy Heaton-Blouin**

THE ANTIQUE SHOW

Although the things are
tarnished and green,
They are the loveliest
sights I have seen.
The old rocking horse
sits by the hearth,
The old wooden chest,
Filled with toys for Garth.
The herbs are drying on
the rack,
The hat boxes piled neatly
in a stack.
The scent bottles lined up
in a row
Crystal, cobalt and things
I don't know.
The line of bowls of wood
and clay,
Remind us all of yesterday.
The candles hanging up
to dry,
They're pleasant to the
nose and eye.
The little wooden
milking stool,
The butter churn is kept
so cool.
I love to walk past
row on row
of antique quilts,
women did sew.
It takes me back to
years gone by.
Grandma and Mama & I.

—**Alice R. Harris**

STRAY WAYS

Alley cat ways
produce Alley cat days
of the matted coat and danger

It's a strange little maze
those Alley cat days
A ball of twine to disentangle

With persistence amiss
and lost days of bliss
with barbs hung at hidden angles,

The wise cat discerns
and politely returns
to a home of its former belonging.

—Dave Kimber

PLASTIC SILENCE

I actually caught some yesterday
—wrapped it in cellophane
and scotch tape.
I want to keep it
for a while.
Where did I find it?
Oh, I don't know.
I thought I wasn't listening
to anything
—but there it was.
So I grabbed it.
Before it could get away
(I think I was over there
by the rubber whisper.)
Strange thing, this plastic silence.
Doesn't really do anything
—it's almost like it's not there
But I have it here,
wrapped in cellophane
and scotch tape.

—Cathy May

HALLOWEEN

With jack-o-lanterns waving,
All lighted and aglow,
The witches and the goblins,
Are marching to and fro.

Clouds dot the sky in patches,
Cast shadows all around;
All sorts of funny objects,
Found lying on the ground.

Clowns in special costumes,
Some thin and some fat;
Black cats sit on fences,
Hiss at this and that.

Doors open to loud knocking,
Or the sound of shuffling feet;
Notice quickly given,
That it's either trick or treat.

So the witches and the goblins,
Out from hiding can be seen;
On this late October evening,
That we know as Halloween.

—Edmond C. Woods

MAY I PLEASE

I know I'm not supposed to ask you this but, I haven't had it in
such a long time. I can imagine it now, feeling so good and
tasting so good. I love the way it feels, especially the feeling
when it's wrapped around my tongue and I can't get enough of it.
So if you could satisfy me please do. I know I'm not supposed to
ask you this but, "Do you have a piece of gum?"

—William B. Webb

MR. TOM CAT

It was late August when to our house he came,
A thin-hungry cat with a collar and no name,
White is his main color, with pretty blue eyes,
Opinion was given, feed him now, or else he dies.
So his first meal was relished from a big 'ole can,
Jack Mackerel it was, and good—"man 'o man."
"Cat" was scared of loud noises, and away he would run—
Our son's dog found out in a hurry, that he was no fun.
Lying on a jacket, in the boat, is his favorite place to rest,
At night, playing frisky in the house, he's at his best.
So Mr. Tom Cat, you have a home as long as you want to stay—
You're a fine baby cat, and we're glad you came our way.

—James E. Spivey

HE CAME BACK — AFTER TEN DAYS

You precious Baby Tom Cat, I wonder what's happened to you?
Each day is so lonely, and we both are so very blue.
To see you once again, sleeping on the couch, or in the chair,
Resting your little head on your paws or feet in the air.
We loved seeing you eat your dry food, in your own little way,
If one spilled out—you'd get it, for on the floor it could not lay.
Then you would glance at the other bowl to see—
If any mixed grill was left and look up at my wife or me.
Friday morning came and still no sign—
But at eight in the evening, she heard a little whine.
Could it be? Or just hearing things as before.
Would you believe? There he was, paws upon the door.
Since he's been home, he won't leave us, but stays close by,
Baby Tom Cat, we love you—Truly you are the apple of our eye.

—James E. Spivey

D O G S

Star is sort of shaggy.
Chief's jowls are certainly baggy.
In the morning they bark to say:
"It's time to get up today!"
The first thing they do is stretch,
then run, then lie in the sun.

Chief likes to chase and be chased;
Star likes to wrestle in defense because
Chief can be rough sometimes.
Then I have to run out and say,
"Chief, enough is enough! Star isn't that tough!"

When the ground is damp,
they sit on their ramp,
which is high and dry, as it goes up to their playhouse roof,
halfway to the sky (according to Chief).

Alas, the day is over.
Before you know it, the sky starts to show it
and dusk settles quickly on two pups asleeping.
God only knows what they are dreaming
(of beefy bones and steak flavored scones?).

Good night, good night, and **PLEASE** sleep tight!

—Nathan Kugland

COAL MINER'S PRAYER

Oh LORD, let me live with an understanding
wife, children and friends.
Let me dig the coal that the nation needs so badly.
Let me win instead of losing, the role of COAL MINER'S plan,
for that is a COAL MINER'S style today and I have got to make
it mine all day. Let me live to a ripe old age, with snow white
hair to tell my age. Having done my labor and earned my wage,
As my body lies peaceful, restful and still, people from far
will come to bid me farewell.
So at last when it has all proudly been done, I hope there will
be one who realizes the COAL MINER was a coal digging person;
who cares for our nation's coal industry and the human race.

A tribute to Frank Edgel Lester, my father

—Hazel Hurley

MY LADY IN STONE

All that morning Jose or was it Antonio with the face of an angel
            drove us through the city streets.

Through fractured Spanish/English,
Charades of signs and smiles,
We began to love his Mexico.

I didn't want to see her but knew that I would,
Baked into stone with her begging bowl
Dragging her child behind her.

Even now, still she comes like a sudden flash in a mushroom cloud . . .
Deafening in her silence.

Baked into stone she cannot speak,
Seared on my heart she can.

Even now, still she comes
Bearing my face in the looking glass.

She cannot speak . . .

            I can.

—Judy Imrie

THE TEARS OF LIFE

As I travel through the years, I look back in strife;
to see the pain, sorrow and happiness, through the tears of life.

I see my childhood, not knowing what's right or wrong;
but the tears for the time, didn't last very long.

As the years go by, I learn to appreciate the beauty I see;
like a rose and a sunset, and the birds in the trees.

Next comes a true friendship, the most important thing you'll need;
until it gets blemished, from sorrow, hurt, distrust and greed.

Then it happens, your true love comes along, and you feel your
troubles are past;
and the tears of hurt start to flow, when you realize, it was never
meant to last.

Then when you are finally happy, or content so to say;
you open your eyes and realize, your life has passed away.

But in the end just remember, your tears weren't in vain;
'cause somewhere along the way, you've dried others' tears and
stopped their pain.

Sometime we all need, to take a look back in strife;
to see the pain, sorrow and happiness, through
            "The Tears Of Life."

—Dale H. Brooks

MOONGLOW MEMORIES

Silvery rays of moonlight
embrace the rippling
waters of the lake
            caressingly

Summer scented breezes
whisper soft phrases
of love's pleasures
            enchantingly

Silk and satin
gossamer and lace
tease the senses
            tantalizingly

Moonglow memories
of once upon a time
return to the mind
            hauntingly

—Ruby Rasor

SAINT ALBERT

St. Albert, St. Albert
send me a cure,
with the Blessed Mother Mary,
    who is so pure.

I come to you with an aching
heart.
Please help me and cure me.
So we will never part.

    St. Albert, St. Albert
    Help me this day,
For with you and our mother
    together we will stay!

*Written out of bed at 11:09 pm
while praying for a healing for
myself and for her mother.*

*I am disabled!
Please spread this prayer and
pray for Us!*

—Paula Pugh

KILLING ME

There's a lot of hurt,
and a lot of fear.
But to which I
show not a tear.

You took a knife,
to me you know.
I'm just waiting,
for the final blow.

Kill me quickly,
don't tear me apart.
Do it to me,
and not my heart.

Leave my heart,
for me to love.
My little ones,
from God above.

They mean so much,
to me you know.
I can't help but,
let it show.

—Janet M. Harris

A WITHERING ROSE

A dying rose is a lovely rose,
  A forgotten jubilee.
A joyous past, now a fading mask
Is all that you can see.

A withering rose is a vibrant rose,
A tale of days gone by,
A memory, sweet melody,
A silent, sad goodbye.

Though in a days passing
A rose may seem dead,
In our minds it keeps living
All bloomed and red.

And though its beauty sadly fades,
A melancholy fate,
A rose lives on eternally
In an everlasting state.

— **Lorrie Van Arsdale**

THE WIND

It is a very confusing thing
  and yet we constantly seek it.
Many words
  have been used to describe it.
And much time
  is spent trying to understand it.
But all to no avail.

Like the wind,
  you can feel it
  but you cannot grasp hold of it.

I stopped chasing it long ago
and have given up
  on fully understanding it.
Now,
  I ignore it
  until it comes my way.
And only then
  will I welcome its pleasure.

— **Patrick Terrence Malfi**

DANCING NORTHERN LIGHT

Shadow me white in the sky.
  Dance my spirit like white pearl.
Trot me in the sky of blue night.
In the high shades move so quiet.

    Oh dancing northern light.
    Shadow dance you are bright.
    Way high your breath is cold.
    Froze me like snow to fall.

From the high snow look so blue.
Still dance high in white spirit.
On this night you took my soul.
Way far in wisdoms world above.

    Dancing northern light.
Sings no song with fait words.
Look to me here in the skies bright.
    Shadow dancing like pearls white.

With silence you are gone quietly.
Step aside for the coming of dawn.

— **Ben Abel**

SOFT BEAUTY

The trees sway breathlessly in the silent breeze,
  The wind, feels soft as the finest silk, smooth and
tender as the human touch.
The warmth of the afternoon sun, glows all around me.
The gentle rush of the trickling stream, dances playfully
at my finger tips, the coolness is soaked up by my soul.
The giant oak trees stand tall above my head,
they seem like gods, strong and magnificent.
My companions gallop to me,
their coats are as black as the midnight sky,
as I stand there in flowing white of the day.
Away we fly, towards the moist cottony clouds.
As we fly up into the golden blue heavens,
I look down at my beautiful green earth and whisper
"farewell."

— **Kimberly Monda**

THE WIND

God opens his store-house, and the winds rush forth.
  To complete the assignment, that he gives it on Earth.
Its job's never-ending, on land or on sea.
Yet it stops to whisper, its secrets to me.

God steps from the heavens, The Thunders begin.
He races the lightning on the wings of the wind.
The dark, murky clouds, flash fire as he goes.
He gives power-unlimited, to the wind when it blows.

It dances with tulips
Leaves set sail on its breeze.
It rushes to bend down the tops of the trees.
It skips o'er the meadows, singing as it goes.
It speaks a strange language that no-body knows.

It shrieks in the whirlwind.
It makes the snow fly.
It calls out my name, as it passes by.
I never really know if it's foe or a friend, and it never
will tell me of the places it's been.

— **Vivian Shipp**

FLOWERS

Flowers Flowers Everywhere
  Roses, Magnolias, Lilies
All vibrant colors
But the soil is dry

Slowly the flowers begin to fade
Petal by Petal they decay
And the leaves weigh
Each individual bud down even further

Limp and listless
They sway back and forth
In search of a means to end this drought forevermore

Hungry bees and butterflies
Encircle this garden of weeds
Unsure of the path they must take
Decisions to be made, and the hardship they will soon endure

The rains will come one day
But that one day will be too late
For the thirsty cries of the yearning ones
Have been muffled by the swift winds and the sun.

— **April Lane**

HANDLE WITH CARE

Little children are very, very curious
Even tho' they make some people furious.
They ask, and ask, and ask,
Even tho' you've explained the task.
We can't always understand what they're feeling —
When it's *their* problems, with which we're dealing.
Every minute, every day, we ponder —
What have they learned today, I wonder?
Give them lots and lots of love, and many a hug.
And be very careful, don't sweep their emotions under a rug.
They're only little, for a moment now,
Tomorrow they'll be grown-up and you'll marvel at how.

—Marijo Hirstine

THE BURST OF LAUGHTER

Kate's reached the age of three.
Her shoulder length, sandy blonde hair lays in long spiraling curls.

At the top of her crown in between the curls rises a large red bow.
The sides of her hair, except for the facial and ear hair ringlets,
lays caught up in the bow.

Her dark brown eyes sparkle as she poses for her picture to be taken.
She lifts her nose into the air to bring her slender neck into the
best possible picture taking position.

Her red dress is surrounded by a mixture of white and red ruffles that
stands out like a half opened umbrella. Her slender arms lay within
the folds of her lovely shroud.

Her red and white ruffled topped socks cover her tiny feet that are
shod in white, one strapped, shining leather shoes.

Snap!

She relaxes with a burst of laughter.

—June Roberts

THE GREAT CHRISTMAS CAPER

Once upon a time far away and long ago,
Around about the time people hang mistletoe.

There were two small children a boy and a girl,
Getting caught up in the Christmas whirl.

The wheels would start turning, their eyes would gleam,
Plans were being made for another caper it seemed.

To make it downstairs without making a sound,
And catch Santa placing presents all around!

Those two mischief makers between giggles and woes,
Would sneak downstairs on tiny tip-toes.

A step would squeek . . . and then they were caught,
Sent back to bed, giving their caper more thought.

The big night arrived and as everyone slept,
Down the stairs those little ones crept.

Peeking around the corner, quiet as a mouse,
Nothing stirred inside the whole house.

It seemed once again they got there too late,
The only trace left, were crumbs on a plate!

Sitting in the glow of the Christmas tree lights,
Among all the presents, sat two little tykes.

With a twinkle in their eye, a smile from ear to ear,
They exclaimed to each other, "We'll catch him . . . *NEXT YEAR!*"

*Dedicated to my brother, Tim. Not only my best-friend growing
up but my accomplice. With lots of love and fond memories,
this one's for you.*

—Linda Hoffman

THE MOON

The moon is bright and
sometimes white. It comes out
at night, which is a pretty sight.
The moon gives us light so
we can see. Without the moon
where would we be?

—Stacey Trunecek

CHRISTMAS IS . . .

Christmas is a time for
     love
In fact, you may see a
     Dove flying above
Santa is a jolly man
His sleigh bells sound
     like a band
While parents call
Children are having a
     ball

—Matt Conover, age 10

THE GIRL ON A SWING

There is a little girl
     who likes to swing.
And when she swings,
     she likes to sing.
She loves to swing high
     but not too low.
And she wants a big push
     to make the swing go.
When she swings high,
     she sings, "Oh my!"
And when she swings low,
     she sings, "Oh no."

—T.M. Edwards

THE GIFT

To awaken, as a child,
     on Christmas morning
and sense the magic
     of the moment,
brings memories of childhood
past, but remembered
     so vividly.

The child's smile
that comes from believing
that magic is real,
if only for a short time,
     is the true meaning
     of Christmas.

No greater gift
     can one be given,
than to have been,
     in some small way,
a part of the reason
     for that smile,
     though unseen.

—David Taylor

It's never too late
to begin again
the things that you started
out to win.

To stick with a decision
or climb to a new height,
whatever you want
just stick to the fight.

Some days will be hard
and lonesome ones too,
but whether you win
is all up to you.

So start out again,
take up the fight —
go get what you want,
you deserve the best in sight.

—Sandra K. Ford

THE RIVER

Stop before the river
of pillowed voices
& listen closely
  for their soft messages
Open your eyes
  to reflect a familiar image
Bring rest to a fatigued mind

We all do come here
  to join the masses
It is but
  an everflowing network
    of troubled emotions
Smooth & welcoming
Cool & warm

We flow easy on the ride
  & enjoy the lasting
Only to come back
  to begin again.

—Jamey Richards

PERIPHERY

grass whispers
trees sigh
lines are corseted
in artificial forms

in the primal recess
unnamed knowing,
not quite touched,
whimpers
its despair

hidden words
are needles, stinging
tormenting me
crying "Name us!" "Speak!"

sorrowfully
I become again
mute
at the edge of knowing
poetry

—Karen Jackson

MORNING

The blades of grass cry rainbow colored tears, as I walk
softly through the lush mat of green.
My footsteps rustling life out of the quiet earth.
All is silent.
The wind keeps me company so a magnet pulls me to a pond's edge.
I peer into the melted glass, focusing on the circus of life below.
I drop a stone which sends ripples; spreading, growing
I have found my contentment in a luminous sea where life
sleeps until the sun's first rays cry, "awake!"

—Brenda Margerison

MY TENDER-HEARTED "BRO"

A little dog came along exactly the same time each day,
for my brother David to feed him then let him on his way.
Each day this man looked for a short body running down the street,
each day the dog looked for the loving face of David to meet.

Until one day the dog came but didn't want to eat,
he just wanted to rest awhile and laid his head by David's feet.
Brown eyes so tired, shortness of breath, a sigh of relief so big,
to come back to his friend, my tender-hearted "bro," who would dig
a small grave in his backyard to lay his little body in,
because this dog chose to die at the feet of a gentle man.

—Patricia Capps Amunson

IF ONLY

If only someone told me that he didn't love me anymore.
I'd have known it was over and closed the door.

If only I'd known why he came home so very late.
I'd have stopped the relationship before it turned to hate.

If only someone was honest and told me about it all.
The end could have been sooner and not become a brawl.

If only I had known the deception being played.
It all could have been finalized quick and not delayed.

If only he was honest, hadn't denied he'd been unfaithful.
Then my feelings of love wouldn't have instead become hateful.

If only I had known!!!!!!!

—Marda Rowe

PROMISE YOURSELF

To be so strong that nothing can disturb
  your peace of mind.
To talk health, happiness, and prosperity to every person you meet.
To make all your friends feel that there is something in them,
To look at the sunny side of everything and make
  your optimism come true.
To think only of the best, work for the best, and
  expect only the best.
To be just as enthusiastic about the success of others, as
  you are about your own.
To forget the mistakes of the past, and press
  on to the greater achievement of the future.
To wear a cheerful countenance at all times
  and give every living creature you meet a smile.
To give so much time to the improvement of yourself
  that you have no time to criticize others.
To be too large for worry, too noble for anger,
  too strong for fear, and too happy to permit the
  presence of trouble.

—Lee Joseph Cochran, deceased

DO WE REALIZE

Do we realize how happy we are, until something makes us sad,
do we realize how good something is, until it goes bad.
Do we ever count our blessings, until they've come and gone away,
do we realize how fortunate we are, to wake up every day?
We take so much for granted, we never stop to think,
are we one that needs that pill, or can't get by without that drink?
Life is kind of funny, as it continues day to day,
and if you don't watch out what happens, it could be you that lives that way!
So you have to make sure to thank him, the Lord from up above,
because without him watching over you, and giving you his love;
You might fail in achieving your goals, your plans may go astray,
so make sure that you thank Him, each and every day!!

    —Jeanette K. Clark

I rise to offer a substicure title. Life begins each morning.
Whether one is twenty, forty or sixty, whether one has succeeded,
Failed or just muddled along, whether yesterday was full of sun—
Or storm or one of those dull days with no weather at all,
Life begins each morning!
Life is a day—this day. All past days are gone beyond reviving. All—
Days that still may come for you or me are veiled in the great mystery,—
And for all we know, there may not be another for either of us. Therefore,
This day is life, and life begins anew with it.
There is no stated age or period of which it can be said, "Here is the dawn of life's—
Day." Today is the dawn of that day. Take and use it as best you can or as you choose.
If you prefer to lull it away or waste it, that is your privilege, though it be—
Unwise and unprofitable.
However each morning. If you so desire. You can use this day for consolidating past gain
Of spirit, brain and hand, or you can use it for tearing down the old structure of self+
And laying the foundations for a new building. Each night of life is a wall between
Today and the past each morning is the open door "to a new world—new vistas, new aim, —
New tryings.

The greatest fact in life is this, that it never is too late to start again, history—
Overflows with startling examples of this truth. And if we had access to the vast—
Number of unrecorded lives, we would find an overwhelming mass of supporting testimony.
However discouraging your days may have been thus far, keep this thought burning—
Brightly in your mind—life begins each morning!

    —Charles W. Collins Sr.

IGNORANCE

A word that which in itself is filled with misconceptions
that we share for each other The misconceptions that fill the
people we look at and who look at us, Ignorance is what makes
our mothers and fathers fight, Ignorance which makes brother turn
against brother because of misconceptions that neither one of them
can understand the Cain & Abel of past-time, present-time,

US   family, friends, enemies, people, humans, too blinded to see beneath
the anger and pain and hurt (that we all have) so that we could help
each other, filled with misconceptions which is what will keep us
from being together as brothers, too filled with ignorance too blinded
by misconception which is what will keep the cultures (I would not
dare use the word race instead of culture because there is only one
race the human race separated,

Ignorance which is filled with misconceptions which is filled fear,
fear that has no trueness which is unvalidated fear that makes you
not want to look in my eyes and see my pain.

Ignorance, Ignorance, Ignorance you better start to know so your Ignorance
won't show

Dedicated to the lives of my father, Thomas Hill Jr. and my
cousin/sister Tara Jeanine Crawford, our two angels in heaven

    —Lynell Crawford

DREAMS

Dreams are meant to challenge you
    to see how strong you are,
    to see if you are brave enough
    to grasp your shining star.
Dreams become a test of strength
    when your star seems to turn to dust,
    for that is when reaching your dream
    suddenly becomes a must.
Dreams are a challenge to your courage
    to see if your strength is enough,
    to keep you pressing onward
    even when your way becomes tough.
Dreams that are left unchallenged
    can only be a fantasy,
    for it is up to you alone
    to make that dream reality.

—dawn marie

JUST A DREAM

The night was quiet and still,
and there was nothing around to do;
I lay down in my bed,
my dreams were all of you.
It started when I came to see you,
you and your boyfriend had just broken up;
so, to get your mind off of everything,
I asked you to go for a walk.
As we walked along the sidewalk,
we watched the stars twinkle bright;
I stopped and asked you a question,
a kiss under the moonlight.
In reply you smiled and said yes,
I thought my dream was coming true;
to have you in my arms,
there, alone, was me and you.
As we stepped up closer to kiss,
and then from no where came a beam;
I woke up, the light was on,
and noticed it was all just a dream.

—Sherman "Dewayne" Story

DREAMS

At night when I lay down to sleep,
some dreams I wish that I could keep.
Life is easy when you're asleep,
    you don't have time to sit and weep.
You're in a world all of your own,
    the shadows speak a silent tone.
The words are sweet, the words are clear,
    and always they are full of cheer!
But when the dream is full of fear,
    you know reality is very near.
Open your eyes and look around
    it's your bedroom you have found.
No need to fret or be alarmed
    you were never really harmed.
And when you fall into the night
    it's just a dream, no need to fright.
You fall and fall until awaken
    and realize that your body's shakin'!
It's just a dream, don't you worry,
    morning is coming in a hurry.
Morning comes and you're relieved
    for that dream you believed.
It's just a dream, they come and go
    you never know what they will show!

—Jackie Sisto

SEEMS LIKE YESTERDAY

Seems like yesterday
when we were young
Only yesterday when we became one.

Seems like yesterday when things were new
Only yesterday when I met you.

Seems like yesterday
we had our fun
Only yesterday you said I was the only one.

Now the kids are here,
the mortgage is due.
But you know what dear, I'm more in love with you—

Than yesterday when we were young
Only yesterday when we became one.

—Jeanne Schaffer

STEEL AND LACE

A woman's dreams, inconsequential though they seem
are made of fragile fabric easily broken
yet stronger than links of steel
and often left unspoken

They aren't mostly filled with emotion
but wishes and promises and intuition,
a sure knowledge and a delicate lace curtain

Untouched and unearthed
they become reality at birth
silken threads to last generations
not painless but precious in their worth

A son's journey toward man
success not result, only plan
A daughter's beauty early seen
A sparkling star in a mother's sky, it gleams

A torch she brings to hers
worth and treasures blessed
blind to only those who can't see
what a woman's dreams can be.

—Maureen Porter

DAY DREAMS

All of us dream our different dreams
Of things we hope to attain,
When life is not always as bright as it seems
Or our hearts are heavy with pain.

We dream of a world content, and at peace
Where friendships can blossom and bloom,
Where hating and hurting and fighting will cease
And gone is the shadow of doom.

We dream of children laughing and gay
When we see them hungry and cold,
We dream of a land with a magical way
Where no one grows tired or old.

We dream of attaining glory and fame
And maybe riches galore,
We know we are only playing a game
But then . . . what is dreaming for.

So if you are lonely, or tired or sad
And of troubles it seems you've a stream,
To bring peace to your heart, and to make you glad
. . . Just take a moment to dream . . . .

—Margaret E. Townsend

MY SONNET

I feel like I've been washed ashore
on my own tide once full and strong.
Oh why, I ask, am I so wrong,
to be myself and nothing more?
I've tried to change myself to be
like one you would appreciate;
but there's just One who can create
the boy, the girl, the you, the me.
So, where's the answer to my call?
Why must I be like everyone,
to act the same and have no fun?
Oh, when can I stand straight and tall,
and tell the world I'm not to blame,
for being me, and not the same?

—Jeanne M. Pazehoski

SIGN LANGUAGE

I stand in line
Watching hands
Realizing I have something
They may never have

The hands are making shapes
Saying things I can not understand
It is a foreign language
I feel left out
And at the same time, envious

They understand
How it feels to be left out
They are different
But, they don't mind
It has grown on them
That they may never have
Something we take for granted

So, I stand there
And, as I watch the hands,
I listen
And learn a new language

—Jill M. LaBanca, age 12

POET

the proud warrior stands
upon the wall of time
he holds within his mighty hands
the catharsis-sword of rhyme

i'll slay them yet
he bravely boasts
with pen i'll set
their souls afloat

they say he lost it long ago
he walked into an infinitve
with wild abandon then was sowed
within his soul the negative

and yet he once again
raises the sword to strike
a blow resounding deep within
with a rending cry most war-like

the sword it splits his soul
between faith and unbelief
and most silently unrolls
the curtain of uncovered grief

—Sidney Miller

THE SYNERGISTIC POEM

At the rise of the curtain,
one thing that is certain,
poetry has been around for a long time,
because it has beautiful rhyme,
there is no better way to say,
that indeed, it is a beautiful day,
than with a poem which is bold,
and you will receive responses untold,
for I shouldn't tell you too much,
but the weather, or any subject could be treated as such,
so, more people need to pick up a pen,
and write a poem to a friend, or to their next of kin,
for to all of us, this would give,
to us a world, which is a better place in which to live,
because this is the kit and caboodle,
best wishes, from Charles H. Tootle.

—Charles H. Tootle

There are many names for children;
I can think of two real quick,
One is little Jane,
And one is little Dick.

Ernie is nice, or perhaps Dollie,
As long as it's not a Pekinese or collie.
But we're getting off the track, this is a baby not a beast,
We need a name befitting a president or a priest.

How about George, or perhaps John Paul,
Or maybe little Sam, or little baby Saul.
For a girl it could be Edna, after Ms. St. Vincent Millay.
If that doesn't suit your fancy, how 'bout plain old Nancy?

Whatever you come up with,
I'm sure it will be nice.
(Two favorites of mine are Constantinople,
And Brice).

—Rebecca G. Barbieri

HONORABLE MENTION

Here I am gazing out the window
With pen and paper in hand
Waiting for my creative juices to start.

Usually I have no dilemma
Deciding what to write
The words come right from my heart.

But now that this is for publishing rights
My mind is all jumbled inside
Will it be rhythm and rhyme or tiresome and dreary?

Are the judges looking
For antonyms and synonyms
Or heartfelt and symbolic?

Right now my house is in such a disarray
With crumpled papers thrown about
Michael Jordan, I am not!

Pondering upon my decision
I know there will be several revisions
When everything is accomplished, I mail out my composition.

Hoping and praying that this one poem
will win me the honor and praise,
I so desire.

If I can't win first prize
I'm hoping to get honorable mention.

—Gloria J. Palmitier

COLOR

Color of red is my heart*************
Color of pink is my lips**************
Color of gold is my skin**************
Color of brown is my eyes*************
Color of auburn is my hair************
Color of green is the trees***********
Color of white is the moon***********

The color of human flesh and the color of the earth is
beautiful, Just as God's children are too.

   —Deborah L. Mcnab

RIPENING

Years melt away
 As you, dear daughter lay
Tired, school-spent, upon my chest and sleep
This waning, dusky day.

So old, so young,
Your age is such
I long for simple, care-less days when you sought me out
For shade from the scheming sun.

You'll go too soon.
Pushed out by ripening dawn,
You'll tear this nest apart for flight, to share your shaky start
With some man's beaming son.

I'll let you go.
If 'let' is to allow,
Then surely once you're gone, and free to stretch and be,
You'll let me, too.

She's no more mine
This woman child
Whose time is her's, whose dreams are fairer than my minutes are,
And less confined.

   —Byron Edgington

MY DAD

My Dad seemed hard, cold and unkind. Yet, now that I'm older
and I've taken the time, to look back over all that was done.
I know in my heart he loved me and was so proud of his son.

His 'Heart's Desire' was put on the shelf. I know now he never
thought of himself. His family came first and I, the first
birth, caught all of his wrath and his pain.

For the hate that I've felt for this man I called Dad my heart
has always been more than just sad. Cause deep down inside
a voice says to me, "The way I was raised gave me the strength
to be FREE!"

From him I received some beautiful gifts. And for now I'll
just mention a few; Honor to women that I've always held true
and the heart and the soul to sing out the blues. Another
gift to me was his love for life. With this thought I'll always
strive, to hold onto his values, a little softer than he, yet
always grateful that he chose me, to stand there always ever
so strong, never telling anyone that he felt he'd been wronged.

I know you hear me Dad and it fills my heart with joy.
Although I still feel, you could have been much softer to that
tiny little boy.

*Dedicated to George T. Freeman, a talented jazz pianist,
a policeman in Chicago 1920's, killed in line of duty 1947.
Theirs was one of the rare Black American families to have
a Father in the home. His three sons are reowned
jazz musicians today.*

   —Sharon Rae Coggeshall

She was a beauty in her day
Or so, I heard my Grandpa say
Hair of gold, eyes so bright
(She must have been a lovely sight)
He spoke of Grandma,
lovingly,
painting her picture
with words,
for me.
He'd lost her many years ago . . . .
So long before
that I would never know
that frail, sweet woman,
fair of face,
who went to Heaven
in her baby's place

   —Sandra Morgan

TO MOM

What love there is
flowing from my heart to yours.
Its seeds were planted in your womb
and spring forth now
as invisible lifelines;
in truth, it is your energy
of love that you sowed many years
before that now
returns to you.
For what is from you
must return to you
in order to fulfill the law of life.
You are my kindred spirit,
my wave of light,
the kind hand that I so often need for
guidance on my path.
Peace.

   —Kris Eiring

WHERES TIME GO

Time is endless
it passes by,
The young get older
the older die;

In younger years
time seemed slow,
But looking back
where did it go;

The minutes, the hours
they go so fast,
Before you know it
another day has past;

The days, the months
the years keep going,
With an uncertain ease
of the future not knowing;

So live each day to the fullest
don't take any in stride,
And don't let any of your dreams
ever be denied.

   —M.L. Everett

GROW UP!

Some people grow old without growing up,
Off to work, but maturity in a 'rut.'
Hot headed, yet cold, everything *they* know.
To submit to truth the old pride says "no."

Relentlessly hanging on to hurts buried deep,
Basking in self-pity, bad fruits they then reap.
Don't waste your life, it just doesn't pay
Sooner or later you will be old and gray.

Heed the warning: listen to your heart cry.
You have a choice: eternally live or die.
God the Father is calling: don't wrestle so,
Wherever He leads is the way to go.

Blessings abound and peace comes within
When we acknowledge and repent of our sin.
Jesus our Saviour, "Let your light shine,
Set us free and help us always be thine."

—Kathleen M. Kremers

PORCELAIN GATES

You put your hands together . . .
in prayer.
Looking up at the sky,
the stars,
the heavens,
longing for companionship.
Hoping that one day,
the Lord . . .
will send you someone . . .
that you can spend . . .
the rest of your life with.
Maybe even perish together.
If you don't perish together,
then you'll be assured,
that you will meet again . . .
at the Porcelain Gates . . .
of Heaven.

*Dedicated to my grandfather, Jack D. Hackett,
and my boyfriend, Brian R. Thompson, the two
most important men in my life.*

—Heather L. Jantzi

ILLUSIONS FROM HEAVEN

Watching you walk
Brought a tear.
Fearing nothing
Because you were so near.
Calling out,
My heart yearned.
Walking away,
Your back was turned.
I can only stand and watch,
Seeing your face
I burn to talk.
To hold you near.
I long to hear.
I see you smile — Sparkling your eyes.
An illusion —
I hold back my cries.
Present you're not,
For heaven has wrought
forth your soul
Only it may hold.

Dedicated to those who have walked.

—Tiffany L. Rehbein

PATTERNS

Our lives are made of variegated strands.
Each fiber woven carefully into place
By the unseen hands of time and circumstance
Becomes enmeshed, until it's hard to trace
Where one begins and where another ends.
Thus, the fabric of our lives seems void of grace.

Yet, look closely, there is a pattern there
If we but possessed the will and wit to see.
Each tangled web of darkness and despair
Could change with just one snip of threads to be
A monument to God, to Self, to Man,
A gloriously rich, embroidered tapestry.

—Helen Searle

THE GODLY WHO DIE

The Good Men perish and the Godly die,
And no one seems to care or wonder why,
But the Godly who die shall rest in Peace,
And the burdens they've carried will be released.
For with their God they've made Amends
And their future ahead will have no end.

Like these men we long to be,
And from our sins to be set free.
The Grace from God that was given them,
is also available to you my friend
For God will not give me more or less,
than He'll give you when we do our best.
And He does not say "Well done my Friend,"
If in your heart there still is sin.

He wants us all to like Him be,
And with Him live Eternally.
Where up in Heaven He's prepared a place;
Where there is no color & there is no race,
Where nothing but Joy & Peace remain;
For all who believe in Jesus' name.

—Alice Jordan

GIVEN ANOTHER CHANCE

Waving my hands above me
I couldn't catch my breath.
Feeling as though I were sinking
I lost the air from my chest.

Surrounded by a liquid mass
unable to control my destiny.
Falling in an airless hole
I found no peace within my sanity.

God, Please catch my fall
for I can't survive on my own.
Grab my waving hands and raise me
to the surface where the light is shown.

Something gripped my chest
it engulfed my dense mass of being.
I felt as if I had lost my life
only to realize it was the sky I was seeing.

I gasped for air and was fulfilled
I found the peace within.
God had saved my fate and my life
giving me another chance to live again.

—Darcy Erin-Marie Long

IT'S TIME TO STOP DREAMING

Martin Luther King brought hope and faith to our lives,
But now, Martin Luther King has gone to the other side.
     "IT'S TIME TO STOP DREAMING"
Our young men are incarcerated or dying because they gave
Up the fight and have stopped trying.
     "IT'S TIME TO STOP DREAMING"
Babies are having babies on a daily basis—unable to take
care of themselves: Yet another innocent mouth in the world to feed.
     "IT'S TIME TO STOP DREAMING"
Education at an all time low; the children are saying,
"No! we don't want to go."
     "IT'S TIME TO STOP DREAMING"
Let's keep the DREAM alive, put some action along with
our pride, forge ahead in a peaceful stride, and make the
DREAM come alive. But "IT'S STILL TIME TO STOP DREAMING."

    —Dames D.F.

NIGHT STILLNESS

Yes, it is late in the day, the new day has already begun.
I should be at the mercy of my dreams, or my nightmares.
And yet, it is so hard to leave the stillness of this night,
only to welcome chaos, upon the rising of next day's sun.
A spider busily spins its web, against the backdrop of an orange night sky.
A bird sings, but only for a moment.
Skyscrapers, the streets among them, wait in silence.
Only to be at the mercy of an inevitable morning rush hour.
A night train suddenly breaks the silence, only to keep going 'bout its way,
and leave the night as it once was.
Then I too, with hesitation, leave the night,
to be at the mercy of my dreams, or my nightmares.
And yet, it is so hard to leave
the stillness of this night.
Only to welcome chaos,
upon the rising,
of next day's sun.

    —Annetia

I'LL NEVER UNDERSTAND!!!

Why is it always; I'll never understand,
That the line which moves the slowest, is the line in which I stand?
And why is it that I, am all the time the last,
To know of a good deal, that too when it has passed?

Have you ever noticed, that big leak in my sink,
And the brand new T.V. I bought, is already on the blink!
Though I drown my lawn, and spray it till the air is dense,
The grass is always greener, on my neighbors' side of the fence.

The car I just tuned up, in the best possible way,
Has decided to rebel, so I walk to school everyday.
And my telephone number, which is not even on the list,
Is always dialed by people, I don't even know exist!

And why does Newton's law, I'll never understand,
Always act on objects, which are in my hand?
I do wish that the apple, which fell on Newton's head,
Had been a big overripe, watermelon instead.

Has anyone ever thought, why I am always the one,
Whom fate has to unleash, its bitter humor upon.
People call me a pessimist, and I have every right to be;
For no matter when or where, it's always poor old me!!

    —Hrishabh Sanghvi, age 16

FEELN MPT
STTN N TH PRCH
ALN
DAYDRMN ABT
BN VITAL.

    —Deborah Field

IMPOSSIBILITIES

Explaining
  thoughts,
Describing
  feelings,
Expressing
  desires,
Perceiving
  dreams,
Understanding
  love . . .

Realizing

  destiny.

    —Aimee D. Fossa

I reached for a cloud
Tucked under the sun
It floated away.

It was all that I wanted
I thought I was done
I reached for a cloud
Tucked under the sun.

Its mist was a vision
That showed me a way
To slide down a rainbow
But to my dismay,

I reached for a cloud
Tucked under the sun
It floated away.

    —Kendra McLaughlin

THE COLORS OF LOVE

As it approached a grey day
you begged the azure stay
to fill an alabaster urn
with hues of green, yellow,
and brown.
For your name is Love.

You reflect upon snow-covered
hills
biding winter's chills
be warmed in part
with sunshine
radiating from the heart.
For your name is Love.

Like the painter Titian,
your medium
strength lies in the blush
of Nature's rouged brush.
For your name is Love.

Ah, Bluebell!

    —Roni Bell

SKY

If I were the sky,
I would fly, fly, FLY . . . .

If I were the sky,
I would go up;   HIGH . . . .

If I were the sky,
And the sun was my nose,
All the little planets
would be; . . . MY TOES . . . .

—Robert Mihalko, age 7

STORM

Night,
Watched the jagged lightning
Ride on the storm's fierce wrath
To make a death lunge, shattering
The red-wood in its path.
Dawn,
Walking thru the stricken woods
Found a slim-stemmed violet
On guard beside the fallen tree
Her velvet face tear-wet.

—Eileen O. Biermann

WINTER WOOD

I'll walk the winter wood alone
And thrive on seasoned air,
Where I'll make my friends among
The cougar and the bear.

With the wind behind me
To gently prod me on,
I'll catch the drops of morning
Left behind by early dawn.

I'll make my bed of dreams
With bows of sweetened pine,
And drink the crystal waters
So bountiful, so fine.

Here among my woodland friends
I will await the future plan,
And hope the future holds
An open door for mortal man.

—Renée C. Goudie

COME WITH ME

Dream of the sunset
coming alive,
beautiful colors,
as real as if they were alive.
Wondrous feeling of life,
an escape from pain,
and man-made strife.
See the sun,
our brilliant star.
Let yourself go, travel far.
Come to a place,
a place of universal space,
where only the dreamers go.
Know the dream of the unseen,
the beauty of color,
watch it vividly gleam.
Come with me,
on that flowing dream.

—Jimi D. Kegelmyer

THE SEA

At one time it carried food and men
And the water flowed quietly to the golden sand
Its water has carried people from place to place
Or it was the scene of a violent wartime chase
Nothing was thrown into the waterway
Except maybe a sunken ship and that left a captain in dismay
After years of the steady flow
Man's ignorance started to grow
The sea turned black from
The tons of garbage and crude
Now Neptune must endure
The test of humankind
And the only thing the land
Could do is wait
Wait, hope, and pray that the
Sparkling blue water will return
To the disappearing golden sand.

Dedicated to Beth Riley, she's the inspiration. Thank you again

—Blair C. Long

PHOENIX

The time may come
When all things will be known and seen as they should be,
And nothing will be left undone in days ahead;
But visions of that day are vague in morning mists
That rise from Phoenix ash to fly high in skies of red,
As we hope to do.
For when we can
We will stretch our wings from here to there
And soar beyond ourselves in silent flight
And happiness,
To find visions lost when yesterday was here;
And then renew ourselves in cooling flight
Without redress
With silent sleep.
The grand tomorrow will wake us with rising sun
And guide us once more on our way to somewhere
Beyond this day,
And all Phoenix moments will become a memory
That lingers but a moment more upon the land
As we fly away.

—Merle C. Hansen

IMAGINE THAT

Imagine the sun on a hot summer day
It's burning your skin, your mind starts to stray
You're sweating and lazy, you feel kinda' faint
But then there's a wind, it feels cool like wet paint

The wind blows its breeze, it surrounds you so pure
Your eyelids grow heavy, every move feels so sure
And at once you're off soaring, you're flying the wind
You glide through the clouds, your head starts to spin

Then splash, you're a fish, a dolphin with speed
The water's your playground, to swim is your need
You're chasing and darting, now jumping the waves
And at once you're on land with some native, brown braves

You dash through the forest and swing from the trees
They're all right behind you, you feel pain in your knees
Then you trip and fall badly, you roll like a log
You spin down a canyon through the dew and the fog

But then there's a clearing, a field of grass
You settle down gently, you rest in this pass
And peacefully rising, the sun reappears
To greet you with gladness, to dry the earth's tears

—Ricky Bruce

HEART-STRINGS REGRET

Remember the days when you were young,
When a boy could make your heart flutter.
The glow from your heart could be seen by all,
By the everlasting smile in your eyes.

If only we could bottle those feelings,
To save them.
Use them as a medicine for years to come.
When you aren't feeling very loved and feel quite
alone.

Wouldn't our problems seem a lot less over-whelming?
They probably wouldn't matter at all.
Too bad such emotions as powerful as these,
Are wasted on our youth,
When we need it so much more as time passes,
And you've forgotten how to conjure up such magic.

     —Diane S. Fritz

Through time and space my love cannot be free,
And like the clouds conceals the inner me.
Touch my heart and find that you are cursed,
The very center of my universe.

Tell me now or make me leave, my friend
For I'm afraid I can feel my heart again.
It's been so long — the earth is bound to win,
It won't give up, it wants my life to spin.

Through slanted planes my restless love surrounds
And rules the world where shackled knees meet ground.
Like weighted moons in front of moons behind
It wants to fall and show my inner mind.

Tell me now, or walk the other way,
For I alone know what my eyes would say
To loosen every strand that binds my all-consuming love
through space and time.

     —Jill Spriestersbach

ODE TO MY LADY

It seems there was magic —— In dreams I once knew
And here's to the lady ——— Who made them come true

My lady my lady ——————— None other than she
Could sweeten the wine——— And share it with me

She fills up my cup and ——— She sings me a song
Like the robin in spring ——— When winter is gone

She tells me I'm special ——— And I know I must be
To walk in the garden ——— My lady and me

She's my color in Autumn —— No painter could touch
The rose of my dawn ——— That I love so much

Now silver replaces ————— The gold in her hair
But the fire still burns——— And the magic's still there

Her arms hold me tightly —— And it's plain to see
It's love on the double ——— For my lady and me

     —Roy L. Cameron

YOUR LOVE

How precious is the time I have
   with you,
Your love touches my heart, my soul,
   through and through . . . .
     —Tammy J. Shepherd

LISTEN TO YOURSELF

Listen to yourself
You know how you feel
Whatever strives in your heart
you can believe is real

Go along with your own thinking
and wrong you'll never go
Because your own thinking
is the best you'll ever know

Confusion can destroy you
So take it all in my friend
But be sure to listen to yourself
in the very end

You'll never lead yourself astray
You know your heart is pure
You're the best friend you'll ever have
and you know that's for sure

Shakespeare said it better
than I ever could do
Because he said it in less words
"To thine own self be true"

     —Jerry W. Cooper

BURNING DESIRE

    I
     feel
      chills
       rush
        down
        my
         spine.
        As
       the
       warmth
      of
      his
      hands
      blaze
    a
    trail
   across
  my
flesh.
  Breast
   to
    breast,
     body
     to
      body,
       our
        souls
        become
         intertwined.
     —Jennifer Elizabeth Campbell

UNDYING LOVE

Love is like a costume that covers the heart
  With hope and joy beneath our breast,
For to endure will prove the test
Of lasting faith we will employ
To look forward to eternal life of joy
For a few more years to be here
We will trust our Lord, without despair
While we are here without tears.
Incline your ears to my sayings
To avoid you will be paying,
For your soul you will pay the toll
In eternity without end,
He will never forsake you or leave you alone
For he will take you home.
In need of a friend like Jesus.
        In Christ,
        —Clara E. Lansing

CAPTAIN OF MY SOUL

Fierce winds blow as lightning flash
  o'er restless wave and angry sea,
I need not fear the stormy voyage
  while my Captain sails with me.

When life's surging tides beset us
  and we seem so near the realm,
Safely still, we're firmly anchored
  with my Captain at the helm.

Tempest tossed and sorely battered,
  we must brace for another gale,
Though our barque seems somewhat shattered,
  yet my Captain will not fail.

Storm driven winds and threatening waves
  o'er jagged rock and perilous shoal,
Safely through each storm He brought us,
  He's the Captain of my soul.

Indeed, He's Master of the mighty sea,
  waves and wind obey His will,
At last I hear Him calmly speaking,
  Peace be still! Peace be still!

        —Ruth C. Demetral

THE STORM IS RAGING

Lord, the storm is raging
  Hussein has us in war!
Lord, help us! We need you!
His missiles are trying to score!

Dear God, won't you please save us!
Help us before we drown
Our loved ones are being shot at
Their hearts full of fear from the sound

So many, oh God aren't your children
Let your word ring out through the land
Let your spirit bring salvation
To those who walk on the sand

Dear Jesus we know you're not asleep
It is we who have been slumbering
And now with our sudden awakening
We hear your voice loudly thundering

I'll calm the raging storm
Trust me — though you live or die
One day you will understand everything
At that time you'll say 'Now I Know Why'

        —Anna Lee

AT HOME WITH HIM

The time we spent will mean the most
  When one is called by our gracious host
For the answers to our questions we all want to know
When it's felt in our hearts we must let them go

Then why in our eyes does it always appear
That this is not my loved one there
For all we've done and can't explain
We know it now in God's great game
For time has come to say good-by
Our hearts grow heavy our eyes they cry

It's not the question where have you been?
We know it's the answer "AT HOME WITH HIM"
        —Randall C Hiatt

MY DREAM

Jesus oh Jesus up above.
I have a dream today.
A dream to find someone to love,
someone to love me always.

I've searched so hard to find
a Christian man who would be true
someone to be loving and kind.
Then, thank Jesus, I met you!

You, David, are the one I've been looking for.
A Christian, loving, kind and true.
I couldn't ask for anything more
I've finally found this love in you!

I'll tell you dreams can come true.
They have for David and I!
Hang on to your dreams and pursue
it will soon be real before your eyes.

Dedicated to David Mata

        —Iris Matzen

TOGETHER AGAIN

Tennyson wrote of the crossing of the bar —
  Once, this seemed so distant — so far;
Until one day, I stood by the side
  And watched a dear one ride that tide.
We'd had years to be so close;
  So much was shared before that soul arose.
Our spirits had found kin of greater kind,
  Before this parting was assigned.
And we'd rejoiced in the One Who holds all,
  There, waiting for His call.
He gave a sharing, so very sweet,
  As we lingered at His feet.
We both knew time was brief;
  Making each moment treasured relief.
Our hearts joined in communing prayer;
  And, we desired this time to share.
Yet, we knew . . . we understood,
  That God had granted a deeper brotherhood;
One where yielding to a heavenly call
  Meant more than our earthly all.
We'll meet again; There at His side;
  Until He calls, I'll quietly abide,
With memories so sweet; so dear —
  Of those 'There,' so far, yet so near.
Until we gather again . . .
  I'll be true; For that gathering, I'd not miss!
If in the 'rapture' or in death's crossing,
There awaits a beginning, not the closing.
        —Fran Hensley

YOU ARE MY INSPIRATION

You Are My Inspiration — you make me feel I can do everything . . .
You are my sanctuary, where I am safe whatever life may bring . . .
You Are My Inspiration — to me you are the center of the world . . .
Your trust in me lets me believe in me, and I become the one you see in me . . . .

When the problems of today become too much to bear . . .
When I am lost along the way and no one seems to care . . .
You're always there beside me — you take me by the hand and guide me . . .
Never asking anything of me; and life is wonderful — because you love me . . . .

I love you forever, and I adore you and admire you . . .
And I'd love nothing better if, in my way, I could inspire you . . .
You made me see creation — when I saw only devastation . . .
You gave me reason to be happy — You Are My Inspiration . . . .

      —Francois de La Rochelle

LOVE

As I sit here contemplating life and death,
My mind becomes obsessed with your sweet breath.
I think about your warm soft smile all the time,
    It is as if GOD in heaven has bestowed on me a wondrous sign.

As I stare at the once bright stars in the evening sky,
    They now are pale compared to the brilliant glow of your glorious eyes.
Not a second can pass without the thought of you on my mind,
    I feel stronger now; that GOD has revealed to me a beautiful sign.

As I listen to the wind gently blow across the window pane,
    All that I hear is the soft warm whisper of your name.
I lie in my room in complete darkness, but do not feel blind,
    It is very clear to me now that GOD has sent me a sign.

This sign encompasses, not some, but All of me,
    It surrounds and burns my soul, and fills me with glee.
It descends upon me like an angel . . . no a dove
    I now know what this sign is; It is you . . . IT IS LOVE!

      —John D. Cacioppo

SPRING AND LOVE
SPRING ON OUR FARM . . .

There are *not enough colors* in a Rainbow to paint the feeling of Spring
on the farm when the air brings memories of past loves, *nor enough pages* to
write and describe the taste of life rural America brings, *nor enough fingers*
to count the trees, bushes and shrubs Mother Nature gently touches as she swoops
over the landscape kissing her children, *nor enough words* to give the picture of
birth as it transforms and multiplies the animal kingdom into new beings, *nor enough
vision* to have saved a little of the Breath of Spring that permiated one's entire
being when windows are flung open and curtains rippled in the breeze.

After a long icy hard cold winter clothes are taken out-of-doors to dry in
the sun knowing the evening's sleep would be enhanced with the clean aroma of
fresh country air and the chirping sounds of crickets will be music to one's ears.
The clean clear spring air revives the love in all creatures.

The glowing feeling will not be broken by the sound of the pitter-patter of
the rain the next day as the gentle drops are soft and warm on one's skin after
the stark, dark dampness of winter. Nor will the odors floating from the dairy cow
barnyard when the wind shifts affect the newborn aroma that has finally arrived. Nor
the dust from the gravel road in front of our home, as the spring progresses, hinder
us from opening wide the house doors to let in these gifts given so freely by God.
Nor will these special happy memories ever be broken by time or life but will
forever remain in our hearts until eternity.

LOVE AND SPRING ARE SO DIFFERENT, YET FEEL MUCH THE SAME—Airy, Gentle,
Soft, Clean, Quiet, Pure and Never Ending.

    —S.T. Curran

JUST BELIEVE

Somewhere, my friend, there is a spark,
    a flame that keeps life going
escaping your grasp when you want it
    but always there anyway.

Believe in this, my friend,
    a flame still glows in the heart,
binding us all together
    and you are not alone.

In desperate times reach out
    even call out loud and clear,
someone who cares will hear you
    though they are not truly there.

When your spirits are low hold on,
    should they be high rejoice.
Whatever you do, whatever you be,
    still, you only need to believe.

—Patricia A. Gruber

BUBBLE GUM RING

Dear, may I have your heart?
    Let's go down to the grocery mart,
There we can buy most anything,
From the bubble gum machine, a ring.
I want to place one on your finger,
So no other fellow near will linger.

You've always been so dear to me,
True to me when I was over the sea,
The ring today will be a token
To do until the jeweler is open.
I want you to be my loving wife,
You are to me a pearl without price.

The ring we select will be your choice,
My will upon you I'll never force,
Our love will be strong for many years,
Hope there will be only happy tears.
Together we can face any weather,
Later we'll live with Jesus forever.

—Betty Abbott-Wagner

TO MY JO

In tumultous privacy,
    I was dying lonely,
Amongst the relentless silence,
    Of the four walls,
Until I met you.

It was a part of time's tragedy,
    With the world's darkness,
Crumbling my fortress,
    And crushing my soul,
Until I met you.

A moment's happiness could not erase,
    The days upon days of suffering,
From ill-timed truths and heartbreaks,
    And the sheer loneliness,
Until I met you.

I'd become a stranger to myself,
    In a lonely cubicle,
Of an unmerciful earth,
    Where strangled sobs went unnoticed,
Until I found you.

Dedicated in memory of Carlo L. Heath

—Roxanne T. Heath

I see forever when I look into your eyes;
I see years from now you and I as a family—
    I look upon the sunrise and remember
our joy, our dreams.
    I see your smile in the moon,
I hear your laughter in the breeze,
    in the ocean I see our tears,
in the mirror I see a person full of shame
    and pain,
    in the meadow in which we parted I feel at HOME.

—Kristy Tidwell

WONDERING

Isn't it a mystery
    Yet, isn't it just right
To wonder where love will come from,
Until unexpectedly one night
You find that all the things you dream of and reach for
Are suddenly in sight;
While wandering through time
Discovering truth
Wandering on
Past youth?

Dedicated to the one I love, Rosie

—Jim Burch

THE PERFECT ROSE

The perfect rose! She held it in her fingers
    The petals soft to her touch — a Rose
Pure and lovely, a deep red, a rose that
    spoke of love. He had given it to her.
A single lovely bloom! "It is perfect —
    just like you! It says I love you," he whispered.
She smiled and gently kissed him. "I know
    it does," she told him. She held it
lovingly now touching the petals to her cheek.
    Tears filled her eyes as she did so. His
plane was taking off to a distant place. A place
    of gunfire and fear. Other men were leaving
as he was to face who knows what in
    a Foreign Country. Bravely she waved at
the departing plane. The red Rose is a symbol
    of his love in her hand.

—Louise M. Meeks

SEA OF LOVE

As the waves washed onto the shore,
    Like a bird my heart did soar.
Watching the sunset reflect on the sea,
Made me wish you were here with me.

The salty scent that lingers in the air,
With my beloved, I can compare.
Like the never ending life of the tide,
Deep in my heart I have nothing to hide.

On this beach in the quiet of the nite,
To hold and kiss you would feel so right.
The pain I feel, time will heal,
But to live without you doesn't seem real.

A sea storm of thoughts rushed through my head,
I will never, ever believe you are dead.
The memories will always be here with me,
Like the everlasting flow of the sea.

—Violet Dubé

THE FROG CROAKETTE

I'm a happy little tadpole, under a lily pad,
Yonder on the big log is my handsome Dad.
Someday when I grow up, I'd like to be like he,
I'll join the other bullfrogs; and croak in harmony.

Rivet—rivet, rivet, rivet, rivet

Today I have my gills and a tail, too;
But it won't be long 'til they drop off an' I grow legs like you.
'Tis great fun to dart about and try to hide from view,
One day I'll earn my legs an' I'll hop and jump like you.

Hippety hoppety, Hippety hoppety, rivet, rivet, rivet

Like all good little tadpoles, I go to Taddy School;
Someday when I grow up I'll be the big frog in the pool!
I'll join a Bull Frog Symphony; and sing bass, you bet!
Maybe just a smaller group known as FROG CROAKETTE.

—Theatta Mae Gregory

MY FIRST TURKEY HUNT

What is that I faintly hear, a rustle in the brush?
Could it be that old wild gobbler . . . Hush! Hush! Hush!

Slowly he wanders nearer, calling to the hens.
I'll take him home to Mama . . . and she'll put him in the pen!

She'll feed him till he's fat and fine, ready for the table.
With dressing piled all around . . . and gravy in the ladle!

A step upon the triggered twig, a sharp resounding snap.
Heart pounding in my ears . . . he's caught in the old box trap!

Rushing up to reach inside, careful to miss his spurs.
Freezing in horrid disbelief . . . AT THE FEEL OF POLECAT FUR!

And there in the light of the cold grey dawn, I knew I was a goner.
Sprayed all over from head to toe . . . with Polecat Aroma!

And then I heard a distant sound, almost faintly deft.
It sounded like that old Tom Turkey . . . Chuckling to himself!

—Wanda L. Barber

THE PUDDINGSTONE ROCK

Out for a stroll, with the sun setting low,
I listened for the crunch of my footsteps in the frozen snow.

Past our front lawn—marshgrass and bayberry line the way,
then up a slight rise to the shore of Mount Hope Bay.

I pause, Canada geese, mallards, seagulls—at rest visiting there,
of my presence they are not yet aware.

Then suddenly as I move just a slight,
the "sentry" has warned—all lift off in flight.

As majestic as royalty, they waltz in the sky,
so gracefully beautiful, performing for my eyes.

As the families assemble on the calm of the bay,
they settle, watching to see if this visitor will stay.

As I climb atop Puddingstone Rock with great care,
wondering, what giant glacier had left it there?

A restful time to reflect and be glad,
my life is so full . . . while others are sad.

When I slowly descend my great Puddingstone Rock,
I shall be careful not to frighten my flock.

Although my joy is to see them in flight,
God, let them rest, I'll not disturb them tonight!

—Lee Lannan Silvia

FLEAS

When I feel the breeze,
It makes me sneeze,
My mom says geez Louise,
Give me a squeeze,
For my poor old knees
   will freeze,
My brother will wheeze,
   and wheeze, and wheeze,
No more hugging for Louise
   has fleas!
Go to the vet please Louise,
I yell don't hug me,
'Cause I don't want fleas.
Don't you think they're
   worse than bees?

—Austyn M. Stevens, age 10

GET-UP-AND-GO

I get-up-and-go,
my body's motor is slow
to fuel me on my way.

The get-up I use
makes my battery not lose
the power for this day.

My get-up-and-go
has shifted into low,
my idle is stuck at bay.

Getting up is a drag,
this chasis will sag
but it mustn't rust away.

My starter gets going
but my exhaust is showing
I need a check-up today.

I get-up-and-go
while my mileage is low,
good maintenance does pay.

—Violet Hilderbrand Kane

chinese communism: 1922

a broken toaster
rip off a toenail

cigarette smoke
through psyche, lungs

follow the rhythm
of rain

peppering down
like salt

a dirty window
through blinds

refracted light
a cigarette

blue-grey smoke
dancing

like chinese characters
written

spoken, heard.

—Stephen C. Stearns

HAWKMUSIK

The winds of change are blowin'
    nothin' remains the same
over the ocean is music flowin'
a haunting song without a name.

The days of now are now gone by
as the future turns to past
the young ones have grown old and died
and the unborn are growin' fast.

The countryside is now a town
and the forests have turned to road
where the past is no longer found
and the future is yet to be sowed.

The winds of change are blowin'
nothin' remains the same
over the ocean is music flowin'
a haunting song without a name.

—William P. Seeley, Jr.

SEASONS OF THE MIND

Today the sun I cannot see,
    A dark grey sky hides it from me,
The trees stand stark, naked of leaves,
Their umber darkness shows no reprieve
Of this weary winter ending for me.

This gloomy day reflects my soul;
Pain and sadness have taken their toll,
In this being that yearns to be free,
Of the darkness surrounding me,
I am a prisoner in agony.

I long for the warmth of the sun
To gently remind me of days to come,
When spring breaks forth excitedly
And paints the earth with colors bold
An array of beauty uncontrolled.

Spring will shout to me joyously,
"Open the door, set yourself free!"
A prisoner no longer will I be,
The prison a faded memory.

—Joyce E. Sullivan

AT DAWNING BY THE SEA

Each time I stand beside the sea —
    And watch the billows roll,
I wait in great expectancy
To see what they unfold.

I feel them lapping as they glide —
Across the gleaming sand,
And marvel at God's tremendous power
To hold this in command.

When dawn is gently breaking —
And the moon-beams cease to play,
I feel a peace within my heart
That sustains me through the day.

And watching the horizon change —
To flaming shades of red and gold,
As each wave turns to silvery mist
It's a beautiful picture to behold.

As I stand in awe and reverence —
I forget my every care,
Observing God's majestic handiwork
I meet my Saviour there!

—Odelle M. Burns

RAIN

The rain comes down in splutters against the skylight — glistening in its torrentially fat pellets.

Lulling me to sleep with its rhythmic beats against the panes;

Comforting in its steady racket.

Dedicated to my grandmother, "G-G," who is always an inspiration to me.

—April A. Phelps

*BRYCE INSPIRED

Sun ripened rocks soaring on high
    Gleam all about, invoking awed sign.

Convoluted shapes clutching at your heart
Stir imaginations, tearing them apart.

People of the past beckon us to share
Beauty and serenity, shining in the glare.

One can come search and surely here find
The sweet fruit within, hidden by rind.

This land's heartbeat thunders deep and wide
Stirring in one's soul, making fears subside.

Whoever the artist, it matters not
Embrace this glory as your chosen lot.

Passions stir, without control,
Surrounded by majesty of spire and knoll.

Tuck away memories of this special place
Shining in pink glory, as finely wrought as lace.

Return to the world, refreshed and fulfilled
Never able to forget silent music that trilled.

**Bryce Canyon National Park
in Southern Utah*

—Emily Pearl Schmidt

MY SUMMER ROSE

To the most perfect rose of all,
    Be it red, yellow or perhaps even blue.
There's one friend she can always call;
And only my summer rose knows who.

A summer rose? What is a summer rose?
After winter's last chilling wind blows,
Melting the snow, witness my summer rose.
Her rosy smile lights the spirits of the darkest roads.
No earthly flower can compare to my summer rose.
Her beauty is strength in the purest of ways,
My summer rose mocks even heaven's golden rays.

But hark, without food and quiet even the most
        perfect rose surely will wither and die.
Only with a love that is pure and true can this
        rose reach the summer sky.
To challenge the gods?
This rose would try.

Do the gods win at summer's end — and bring
        death to my summer rose, dark and doom?
Surely not, she only sleeps away all weary
        thoughts til a summer new; to born and bloom.

Her desires and thoughts only a friend really knows;
Love is the eternal food for my summer rose.

—Billy R. Skaggs

THE FINAL SHAME

My son, as we sit here in this white walled room
I realize the pain which I have caused you.
Throughout your life I never said it.
I never showed you how much that I care for you.
But as you lie here silent and lifeless, I am ashamed.
Ashamed of all the things which I have said and done to you
and all the things that I didn't say, and didn't do.
I never got to say that I was proud of you,
for all the great things that you accomplished.
That time you played in your first soccer game
and scored the goal which won the game for your team.
I was really proud, but I told you I was ashamed of you.
And now as you are on the brink of death,
I am ashamed of myself, I love you, I am proud of you.

—Steven Guilbault

A PIECE OF DUST IS WHAT I AM

It may be hard to find me, if you're looking for me, in the wind is where I'll be.

A piece of dust is what I am, never knowing where I'll land.

Can I find a place to be, when the wind sets me free, will I ever be free from the wind that blows me, where it please.

Never landing on the ground, but always being blown around and around. The piece of dust that I am.

Being trapped in the stream of the wind, as it blows me here and there and here again.

It blows me hard and it blows me soft, how I wish it will release me, the wind that blows me.

Dust is all I am, never knowing if I'll land, and when I land and think I'm free, the wind comes again and catches me.

Way up high in the sky, a piece of dust, lost in the gust of the stream of the wind that blows me.

That's where I'll be, in the wind, if you want me.

—Lisa Beryl Johnston

OF AND FOR THIS WORLD

"You're not of this world," so I've been told.
It's alright, because I've seen the heartless and cold.
Remember, "let's make peace and love, not war?"
Were you watching as men from families were torn?
We sent them off to the unknown called Vietnam.
Some came home, many didn't, but all of them were damned.
When they returned they were hated and ignored.
"Of This World," do you wanta be? I employed?

Revolutions, Germany, Vietnam, Middle East, it ain't over yet.
The good ol' USA still selling them killin' machines, you can bet.
Haven't they seen the dead, the people lie dying?
How much longer we gonna put up with their lying?
Our own government going behind our backs,
they look away from the homeless and faces with tear tracks.
We live in a nation being sold out day by day.
"For This World," you'd better hope to hell and pray.

Do you remember how we came to be the USA?
We slaughtered the Indians, then filled up the graves.
On the first Thanksgiving, who saved who?
It was the Indians taught 'em how to grow and find food.
All that history recorded and then destroyed.
Many killed, many died, as officials sat and enjoyed.
"You're not of this World," so I've been once again told.
Thank God! For in the Bible my salvation has been foretold.

—Ronald S. McNett

ENDING WITH PEACE

Crosses and Sorrows,
Stormiest Seas,
May end with tomorrows,
That sink into peace.

*Dedicated to the
Desert Storm War*

—Julie Belcher

THANK YOU VETERAN

We fight and fight
And sometimes we win
Some people die
But we still have our sin,
We pray for you day and night
Thank you for fighting
for our right!

Love,

—Ariel Maraguglio, age 9

SAILORS

Times of refrain
life and restrain
sailors walk on by

Holding their honor
with every march
a mother with her sigh

Parades of strength
life and love
controversies end

Armies march
in loyal hearts
captains orders send

Dedicated to the US Navy

—Alessandra

I WAS NOT BORN AN AMERICAN

I was not born an American,
It's what I came to be.
Free to embrace
With every race,
In melting pot of Liberty.

I was not born an American,
Yet state with pride I am.
A citizen of
This land I love,
In melting pot of Liberty.

I was not born an American,
Like you, like she or he.
In time I'll share
My countries flair,
In melting pot of Liberty,

I was not born an American,
Like me, you too can be.
While blending traits
Find equal base,
In melting pot of Liberty.

—Thelma T. Steinburg

REALITY OR CASUALTY

Who are we?
Our Ancestory?
Where are we from?
Who are we from?
Reality or Casualty?

—Robin L. Blackmon

THE EYES OF A KILLER

Sullen
dark holes
filled with black

radiating
hatred and
death

reflecting
the horror they
have seen

expressionless;
blank and
void

infinite pits
of evil
perpetuating
fear

peering, staring
caverns
almost anticipating

once again
to see
what created
them.

—Marilyn J. Bolden

A SOUL IN SLUMBER

Awaken, O' Soul
Of America.

The unborn, in silence,
Cry to live, to touch,
To know love.

Street urchins, roam.
Alone and in fear.
Fall to city vultures.

The young, bewail,
The torch, in embers,
Brightens no more, our path.

The forsaken, yearn
For yesterday, when love
Embraced the nation.

The homeless, lost.
Wandering spirits, seeking
A place in the sun.

The old and the meek
To the heavens, they plead,
Abandon us, not.

Awaken, O' Soul
Of America . . .
A Soul too long in slumber.

—Victor E. Legaspi

ABC '93

Atomic Tests — Birth Defects — Coded Clouds — Downwind
Deaths — Endless Poisoned Environment.
Fallout from five nuclear powers; Global garbage, Hydrogen
bombs, and Irradiated daily bread. Jesus Wept.
Jonah's city warning, Kilotrons of TNT in A-Plant! Lies
and Leukemia harm neighbors and kids.
Megatrons from fission — Nuclear missions, Oceans of
Plutonium. Public betrayal, Questions sidetracked. Radioactive
Heaven and Earth.
Secrecy surrounding releases, Thermonuclear Weapons —
Underground Uranium pits. Voo-Doo Economics — Waste Storage
of Leaking Poisons.
"X-Mas Island" Contamination — Also Yucca Flats. Zion
is Sowing and Reaping a Rad-Law in a "Permissible Dosage"
I Don't Want.

—Eileen Jenkins

MCNALLY'S FAREWELL

McNally sported a wrinkled brow, soulful eyes, direct somehow.
Whiskered jowls, a drinker's nose,
McNally knew he'd n'er be a rose.
Twas not always so. There once was a day when McNally was gentle,
Family man, so they say.
Before ole "Jack" had soddened his brain,
And nights in dark alleys reduced him to shame.
Before the harshness of living was etched in his face.
His arms held a woman of beauty and grace.
Long now departed, their babe in her arms.
Ah, had she returned he'd done her no harm.
Wearily he eyed the sports at the bar.
They'd find no damned answers, grow impatient and fight.
For the glow of their whiskey held promise tonight.
One sip more to steady his shaking, and then,
He'd be off in the night with his bottle of gin.
"Farewell mates" he shouted, I drink to ye all,
Tis ended for McNally, I've naught strength left to fight."
And steadily, head lifted, he went out in the night.

—Micki Cottle

TAKEN FROM . . . MY BELLY IS AGAINST MY BACKBONE . . .

We laugh with our teenagers

Who stay up until midnight and then sleep until noon
Who do their own spin cycle all in just one load
Who can never find their shoes, their glasses or their money
Who can slurp down a liter of coke all in one sitting

And we cry for those

Who hide in bunkers while bombs kill their brothers
Who have never dribbled a ball in a new pair of Nikes
Who play "Hide and Seek" in alleys just to survive
Whose tears slide down to touch an upside down smile

We laugh with our teenagers

Who munch all day from Hardees to Seven-Eleven
Who talk to two friends at once because of call-waiting
Who hug you at home and walk ahead of you at the mall
Who know every word, every movement in every music video

And we cry for those

Whose only meal is in a free-lunch line at school
Whose eyes look like bruises hiding a broken soul
Who can't remember the last time they were hugged or spoiled
And whose nightmares are in the daytime behind closed doors . . .

—Wende P. Williams

WORLD

People in worlds to come
have come to find this world as a
home for they have to live in
it So if the world has to be
changed let it begin today

—John J. Gillan

THE SOUND OF HELL

I hear the oh-so familiar sound
of gunshot
fading in my mind
I open my eyes
and I am surrounded
by horrific screams
I cover my ears, try to block it out
but my eyes don't deceive me
when I see blood trickling down people's bodies
I wish I could escape
"Get out" I hear a voice repeating
but this is the world
my home, my hell
If this is hell
Can heaven be too far away?

—Melissa S. Grundmeyer, age 16

MY WEEK . . .

Monday . . . always the same . . .
The alarm went off, the headaches came.
Tuesday, I see . . . just another day . . .
Endless chores, they just don't go away.
Wednesday . . . nope, not much better . . .
Just got a visit, from another bill collector.
Thursday . . . whew! came and went . . .
Though, I can't seem to find . . .
The T.V. remote!
Am I losing my mind?!?
Friday . . . finally here, last day to go . . .
Let's hope the time doesn't drag on slow.
Saturday . . . ah! now I can sleep . . .
Been waiting all week to catch up on Z's.
Sunday . . . last day to relax . . .
"Why me, God?" why me, I ask.

—Crystal M. Buoy

TEETERING ON THE EDGE OF INSANITY

Alone.
Trapped in my thoughts,
in a world full of people,
unable to truly connect.
Hopeless.
Unintelligible murmurings from distant pasts,
swooning and soaring into my common sense.
Logic doesn't make them go away,
for then we are left with "Why?"
Interacting with someone else just to survive.
Temporary thought paralysis;
but isolation brings them on again.
No defenses.
Hanging on to life with both hands,
straining to keep my grip,
teetering on the edge of insanity.

—Melanie M. Wright

REFLECTIONS

Yesterday feels like a long ago dream
Tomorrow seems to arrive too soon
And today just simply slips on by
But life goes on yet remains the same.

Once you watch a child's awe
At sunrise, sunset or a shooting star
Life seems different — so very bright
And the world no longer seems in strife.

Think of the children — one and all
For they should not fear for their Fall.
Now we must all stop the hate
And live in peace, else seal our fate.

—Laura Ovsanna Demurjian

MY BODY IS TO ME DEFILED

In benumbing darkness plunged he me
Brute force assault to raze life's hold
Obscene the insolent gods who abjure
To release despised body from maimed soul.

It matters not how steep the grade
How aloft exalted soars my soul
If body violate subjugate be
My wingéd soul is not my own.

The gods, more remote than men's designs
Complacent by worship of their name
Our terror, suffering, our bodily pain
They empathize not our frailties' shame.

In love's desire my heart unarmoured
Delight, embracing love requited
When impaled on violence so untoward
My flesh unsexed, my soul benighted.

From adoring trust to aimless despair
Entombed for life in weaker frame
I pilot not my careening course
from craven fear I cringe to name.

—Ellen Baudisch

DON'T WAIT 'TIL THE WAKE

Why come when I can't see you
Why speak when I can't hear,
Why touch me when I can't feel you
Why sob or shed a tear?

Why send a flower I can't smell
Why say how nice I look,
Why say I do not look my age.
Why even sign the book?

Come see me while I'm living
Come speak while I can hear,
Come touch me while I can feel you
Come smiling while I'm here.

Don't wait 'til it's all over
For then I will not care,
If you're among the mourners
I'll not even know you're there.

Good intentions are not enough
I was going to, is now too late,
Come see me while I'm living
Don't wait 'til you come to my wake.

—Gilbert L. Hilderbrand

HEART ON THE WIND

The wind blows thru the heat of summer air,
Leaves rustling, curtains billowing, wind chimes singing clear.
My heart floats on the wind, blowing here to there
To my love, in distance far, yet in spirit still so near.

Our roots now planted in different lands' soils,
But I as a tree, bending, reaching with the wind.
My leaves float as my heart, love-filled royal,
Able to soar on air to find my spirit kin.

—Stephanie R. Gutzman

BLESSINGS OF A SEASON

The air is crisp, the leaves turning gold,
Oh where is my springtime when birds sing and flowering buds unfold.

Where are those fluffy clouds against the blue sky,
The warm balmy breeze telling us that summer is nigh.

The green leaves bursting forth one by one,
Glistening brightly in the warm glowing sun.

The colorful array of sweet fragrant flowers,
The long and golden sunlit hours.

A soft gentle rain, the smell of damp earth,
Countless blessings of beauty and worth.

These are things that send my spirits soaring high,
Gifts from above that we cannot buy.

Treasures that lie so deep in our heart,
Leaving beautiful memories that have no counterpart.

Yet winter plays its part, holding many beauties to boast,
Still spring and summer are the blessings I cherish most.

*Dedicated with love to my mother, Mrs. Charlie Pope,
for her confidence and encouragement.*

—Helen Pope Bell

THE OLD BARN

An old barn yet stands,
   but a shadow of a time that used to be.
      Its glory days gone now,
         just a faded memory.

Its usefulness to man
     long since ended,
         like the barren fields that surround it
           that are no longer tended.

Wild flowers and golden rod
     grow in its empty yard.
         Ancient timbers creak and groan as if crying,
           remembering when times were simpler, yet very hard.

The northern winds are blowing now,
     another winter is in the air.
         Yet the old door stands open,
         beckoning all to share.

The field mice scurry in to build nests in the hay.
     An old groundhog has burrowed his winter home
         by the stalls where the cows used to lay.
           And a screech owl sits up in the rafters high,
              watching the busy mice as they scamper by.

Though man has abandoned this old place,
    God has touched it with His loving grace.
        He uses it now as a home for His creatures to live
          for the old barn still has its shelter to give.

—Jim Johnston

FLOWER

It's my finest hour
I am a flower
I've fed the bees
And gave the butterfly power
I'm sitting now in a vase
My aroma fills the space
My bloom is at full power
This is my finest hour.

—Betsy L. Smith

WEATHER DAYS

Rainbows fill my day,
but at night,
dark clouds hover over me.
Snow falls quietly,
dropping new opportunities,
while rain washes them away.
The sun shines bright,
signaling hope to try again.
And I remain cold,
hurricane feelings
not knowing
which way to turn.

—Sandra Glenn

SEAFARER

Where one may goeth . . .
across the deep blue waters,
and ride the sea.

In the stillness of nite,
where the darkness sets in,
and the chill winds doth
howl . . .

but never fear . . .
for your God is near.
He will always take
care of thee!

—Lillian Green

THE CACTUS

Immobile monuments
in clay pots
lime striping
white salt
dry as the desert.
Wise as God.

Bitter water runs
within the spiny puzzle.
Self breeding
it asks nothing.

We suck and search
for the nipple,
forever falling — gaping
open.
Red, sweet water
dyes the sand
as the children
pat
sandcastles.

pat. pat. pat.

—Karen Jean Barker

MEADOW WIND

Meadow wind blowing fields in spring;
 Each eddies skittish pass,
Caressing, consoling, brushing, cajoling
 The waving sea of grass.

Meadow wind lofting a fluff of seed
 That disappears from sight,
In the brilliant hue of sky so blue
 Drenched with noon day light.

Meadow wind soaring thoughts and dreams
 Remembered with smiles and tears,
On a waft of draft up a sunbeam shaft
 To keep for a thousand years!

Meadow wind sprinkling scattered seed
 As its gentle currents flow,
To flourish, nourish, enhance the earth
 Where dreams and ideas grow.

 —Edith P. Dill

A TREE

I look out of the window
 And there I see a tree . . .
Awhile ago it was beautiful
A gorgeous sight to see.

It was all dressed up in beauty
With a shimmering green gown . . .
But now the gown's all torn and blown
And brown upon the ground.

It stands all cold and naked
As it has lost its clothes . . .
And the beauty that arrayed it
In the summer months that showed.

It stands all cold and barren
Ah shivering in the wind . . .
Like it's begging for a cloak
To wrap itself up in.

 —Leah Rae Walton Nollmeyer

MORNING

The morning is quiet
 as I awaken from my night's sleep
And soon the world outside
 stirs with quiet movement

I feel at peace with myself even though
 time is revealed in the mirror
But I am pleased with the gentleness
 the years have shown by reflection

As the family rises one by one
 I listen from within my room
And I can identify each step they take
 and their destiny is apparent

I tiptoe into the kitchen to be rescued
 by my first cup of coffee
And then hideaway once more in the
 solitude of my room

I am not hiding from the day's new
 beginning and life
But savoring as the world
 gently awakens to start a new day

 —Icey E. Hagedorn

WINTER

Shadows dancing against the trees.
 The silence of the fallen leaves.
Stars glitter in the late night.
 Casting an angelic light.
Dying is the world, slowly but surely.
 Naked trees swaying obscurely.
All life has blown away,
 to come back one spring day.
Meticulously the earth freezes solid.
 Of all life, Jack Frost has quickly rid.
Children playing in the snow.
 Freezing birds not knowing where to go.
Glittering grass with frost freshly fallen,
 back to the earth. Mother Nature's been calling.
Asleep is the world we walk upon.
 It'll wake when winter is gone.

 —Corrie Alison Harrison

COLD WORLD OF BEAUTY

As I looked to the sky one bright and sunny day,
 I saw an eagle soar and hover up above.
It was a symbol of freedom, majesty, and beauty
As it beat its powerful wings with grace and confidence.

I looked into the forest of tall hardwood trees.
Here I saw life, so simple and serene;
I felt peace flow deep within my soul.
Here I could dwell eternally in pleasant harmony.

As I returned to civilization as I know it,
I observed much pain, tears and torment.
People wandering around going about their business,
Neglecting the poor and those scarred by injustice.

Why must my world be so cruel and cold?
How can we ignore the consequences of our actions?
What can I do to change the agony and corruption?
The answer: Love God, love thyself, love thy neighbor.

 —Marc Denis Sabourin

THE BLIZZARD

The sky above is dark and dreary,
 The forecast is none too cheery.
Tis a bad one say one and all,
More than a foot by nightfall.
Trees leaned as the wind blew,
Then I saw a flake, then two.
A foot was stacked by night,
I turned in and shut the light.
In the morning when I opened my eyes,
Was I in for a big surprise.
Three feet have shut my door,
I'm glad we didn't get more.
I could see no one out and about,
So no one has gotten shoveled out.
Out the window I slid with clenched teeth,
Stuck to my waist not able to move my feet.
Inch by inch I got myself unstuck,
It was like a swamp in the muck.
To the shovels I made my way,
Realizing I'd be shoveling all day.
Covered to the roof was my car,
Shoveling to it seems awful far.
Shoveling for hours and most of the day.
Everything seems back to normal or so they say.

 —Joni

THE VALUE OF LIFE

Don't they know the value of life?
Don't they know a wrong doesn't make a right?
Don't they know that within a fight; one pulls a gun, the other a knife?
  Sons and Daughters have engaged in the slaughter of their loving mothers,
  and even their fathers.
Where is the justice, does no one care?
Didn't we all learn once to share?
  The unborn child hasn't even a chance, to see the world, not even a glance.
The old folks too are afraid to go out, afraid to stay in; is there no way out?
  The people who kill; they kill for fun, only half of them even use a gun.
What has happened in the minds of our young?
  Guns, knives, and killings are fun!
Don't they know the value of life?

  —Yvonne K. Shiver

"GOOD-BYE" TO AN ALCOHOLIC

Ho hum, ho hum, . . . okay . . . ; I'll just let him drink today.
It *really* hurts, but **I'm** strong, **I** can handle it, **I'm** *not* wrong.
If I get mad, *his* daughter's there; and fits in great, cause *she* doesn't care.
For years and years, *alone*, I would cry. This, just makes it easier, to say good-bye.

Oh Lord, these words I pray, "This *'SICKNESS,'* *PLEASE*, *help* to slay."
'Hurt' and *'pain,'* . . . I'm *not* so strong; I'm . . . so . . . **alone,** my daughter's gone.
'Hurt,' . . . his daughter *too* cannot bear; she's reclused herself and will *not* share.
Now she has run away, on the sly; done so, without as much as, a . . . "good-bye."

We got her back yesterday, *why* can't I believe she'll stay.
'Talk,' . . . *he* doesn't say much, so . . . it's **me,** as all along.
I give up, I *really* swear. *What?* . . . an answer to my prayer?
Lord, *this* time, I **won't** . . . *just* **try;** I love him, . . . can't say, . . . "Good-bye."

  —Johnny 🌸"ife"

DADDY CAME AND TOOK MY HAND

I remember when I was two years old, Daddy Came and Took My Hand—
Took me to where only adults would go, that dark and frightening room
Mommy was gone and no where about, only then I wish she wasn't out—
My Only Distant Friend

I remember when I was five years old, my distant friend was ill, away she
went, I never really knew—but, I was the little adult who made my daddy's
bed—"Turn down the covers my little sweet, tuck yourself in—Daddy will be
by you in a little bit, as soon as everyone else is tucked in, too"

While my distant friend was away, everyone else went away, too, I was all
alone till noon time came—"Fix my lunch, my sweet precious girl, Daddy's
hungry, but for attention and love"—Daddy Came and Took My Hand—

I remember when I was nine years old, an adult in a child's body, sitting in
school, with an eerie feeling but didn't know what it was—That night, with my
distant friend asleep in the other room, Daddy Came and Took My Hand—

I remember when I was twelve years old, my distant friend was away at night—
All is dark and very alone, I see his silhouette in my doorway, so not to wake
up the child in the other room—Daddy Came and Took My Hand—

In my distant friend's bed I lay so cold and numb, with no one else
to hear my cry—

Oh, distant friend, why didn't you hear my cry at two? I tried to tell you in
my little voice, the only way I knew I could, words so garbled and rambling
on—No one knew our little secret when Daddy Came and Took My Hand—

I am now a young adult who is trying to survive this awful thing
My distant friend is now my best friend and only God knows—

Oh best friend, I know we need to be Nurtured—but, it will take time, and a
lot of love—I have a lot of love, and this love was never used, so let me use
it all towards a better life of loving and being close—

  —"Hutz"

REMODEL ME

Dear Lord Jesus please make me be
As much as possible,
Just like thee.
Take away the anger, worry and the grief,
Give me your wisdom, peace and relief
Help me use my life to serve you
And others, who are in such desperate need.
To plant in minds, hearts and souls
Your Holy plan of salvation,
That you may grow this seed,
Until we conquer evil,
This is what I plead.

—Vi Dykins

GOD ARE YOU LISTENING

God please listen it took me a while to
get through. I'm having trouble finding
my way back to you. Please don't forsake
me. I promise to never stray again. I
need to know that you still love me and
that I'm forgiven for my sins. I wandered
out of your fold I was lost and my
life went out of control. Since I lost
touch with you the storms of life have
been beating me down. I need to know
that you still care, God are you listening
are you still here? I've made a lot of
mistakes I've learned my lesson. I'm
sorry God for all the wrong I've done.
Please try to understand I need your
helping hand.

—Agnes Johnson

SAVED

While plowing in the field one day,
I heard a voice above me say,
"Come young man, come with your plow.
Your Master Needs you, He needs you now.

There is a weed growing in the land,
That could be the ruin of every man.
It grows in a hurry and spreads so fast,
That Christianity comes in last.

This weed, I guess you know, is sin.
You can help me save all men."
I had almost waited too late.
But I was saved, as of this date.

I left the field and took my plow.
I am saving men right now.
This blessing came to me so fast,
And I know that it will always last.

Men are still needed for this task,
Don't just wait for God to ask.
Go and do what must be done,
Because for us He gave His son.

Come, let's stop this weed of sin.
Then go to work where the weed has been.
After you have once been saved,
From there on in the road is paved.

It's up to you which road you choose.
One road you win, the other you lose.
Come with me and you will see.
The road for you is Christianity . . . .

—Mike Cordell, deceased

GOD IS THERE

Are you searching for something that you can not
see, take my hand and walk along with me.
When your cross seems hard to bear,
just remember God is there.
When ever your life feels empty
and blue, just remember God loves you.
You must remember that life is what
you make it. When you're down and out
and no one seems to care, just remember
God is there.
You try too hard to please, but as you
know it does not come with ease.
You try to smile through all your tears
and try to hide all your fears.
This does not come with ease as you know.
So we have to take things in life a
little slow. God only asks what we
believe and always do our best, and
as we do this
God will do the rest.

—Margaret Luby

GOD'S SPECIAL PLAN

I became a mother when I was just sixteen
I left you all behind to fill my wildest dream
To have a beautiful little girl and later a bouncing
Baby boy
I never realized for a minute they would bring me so
Much joy
You have always been there for me and always helped
Me through
It is hard for me to tell you this so this poem I
Give to you
I know you have my same dream but you think it will
Never come true
So now it's time I've done my share I pass it on to you
God has His plans for you and He thought it would be
Better to wait
For you He has a special plan down to that special date
So don't think He has skipped over you
And your chance has past
God knew what He was doing when He saved the best
For last

—Angel Hale

THE RIGHT-NOW-SECOND

The right-now-second is my most important gift.
It is the only time I am guaranteed.
Even though I have great future plans that will
be successful with God's help,
I must enjoy and live as if this may be my last
second.

Goodness, understanding, patience,
for me and others;
I must right now through me strive for.
So if it is my last second, I will not
have wasted my most important time.

God's Will be done,
and if he has more seconds to add to this now second,
when my life on earth is at an end;
I will have inner peace and self-satisfaction
in all my accumulated accomplishments and I will be,
without being aware,
thankful for the last right then
second.

—Carolyn Louise Gillon

READ BETWEEN THESE LINES

My heart cries out for you still
and not unlike the nightmares of our youth
when we opened our mouths to silent screams
no one ever hears.

—Rae M. Zweber

A CRY FOR HELP

I heard a cry for help, but did not listen
I saw the pain, but did not look
I touched the cuts, but did not feel
I smelled the drugs, but did not know the scent
I tasted the tears, that made it all clear

—Melissa Evans

I AM THE STORM . . .

Down I came on the village,
Black, heavy and sullen.
My lightning crackled and crashed
Like a pane of broken glass.
And my thunder boomed dreadfully.

My eerie howls and whistles
Echoed in the ears of my prey.
Afraid were the children,
Sick were the fisherman's wives.
Worry crowded into their heads.

Darkness then fell
And their terror grew more and more.
Pity seeped into my head but I fought it away,
And their fear entered my soul,
Giving me more strength.

Then morning came and I passed on,
Bringing more horror and pain.
To those below. To the people,
I am like a plague but in the eyes of nature,
I am everything.

—Corey Allan Follett

THE DRUMS OF NOVEMBER

I still recall the muffled sound
against a grey sky
and frozen ground;
the riderless horse
the Camelot years —
an eternal flame is bleeding here.

A country cries, the truth is seen
a child salutes upon the screen;
a nation mourns in watchful stare —
an eternal flame is burning there.

The years since passed will not erase
the lines,
the mem'ry of his face;
the truth cries out yet to be heard
it has spoken volumes, without speaking words.

A man to many, a hero to me
four days that will burn an eternity;
the riderless horse
the Camelot years —
an eternal flame is bleeding here.

—Kelly Scheppers

ESCAPE:

I'm being myself, and no one sees
I speak, and no one hears
I do, and it's merely expected
Experiencing a burning desire to feel alive
I search to feel connected
Immersed in a cloud of confusion
I escape into a realm of play
Camouflaging truth with laughter
The mind drifts into space
The body splits to the same dimension
Bonding with images, creating illusion
Reality fading into the dark
Identity entombed in unconsciousness
Euphoria only existing to breed
As long as my addiction I feed
The orb of discontent never ending
While my means of escape I'm befriending.

—Laurette

HE HAD A FRIEND

A friend of society he was not
There were times when he was on pot

He was a friend of mine
A heart he had
A friend he had
A world he had

All this brought under
All this brought down
Now he wears a permanent frown

He was a friend of mine
His funeral I could not attend
To his family and friends I would not bend

His mother and father could only ask why
Why their only son had to die
And become nothing but a number
To the world

—Michael A. Lomino

I'm slipping down,
slipping down to a frightened state
Afraid to talk or communicate.
The mind's transmitters and all those
wires have sent my brain in a
million fires, fires of fear and
helplessness afraid to sleep afraid to
rest. So I continue, so I continue
to slip down the slide spirals and spirals
oh it's so unkind. The grips of fear
and mind's silent screams is this life or
so it seems, I wish I could hide away
in your wood oh please oh please say
yes I could. A pair of eyes is what
I am, looking out forward to search
the land, the home, the sand, your heart
and mind please be patient, enduring and
kind. I will not hurt you, you know
that's true for I need answers to which
I haven't a clue.

—Gisele J. Aponte

129

Taking each step trying
not to pace yourself too
fast only to find no
one following

—P.O.

IMAGE

Reality or dreams
        put together
or so it seems
        by us
to appear to be
        what we are or
want to be.

Worked on
        thought about
turned over and over
Until.
perfected, so that
the want to be, the dream,
eventually,
becomes the reality.

—P.A. TurnerCobb

ATOP THIS CLIFF

Atop this cliff
where high winds blow
and blue skies meet
with sea below,
where restless waves
rush in to shore,
caressing stone
and earthern core,
where daisies dance
in crystal rain,
where high winds blow
through my golden mane,
my restless soul
finds peace again
atop this cliff
upon which I stand!

—Sharon L. Hudson

POLLUTION ABUSE

Jesus and God,
Together make one,
together make son.

Earth and space,
Together make none,
together make waste.

Why does this happen,
why in this way?

To prove a point?
No, to prove today.

Our world is dying,
and so are we.

One of God's greatest gifts,
Is destroying its only enemy:

Itself,
you and me.

—Jenni Luckman

A GRANDMOTHER'S REFLECTION

What is this little voice I'm hearing,
As I go about my daily chores?
"Grandma, grandma, please listen to me."
So many questions, why's and what for's!

No honor on earth any greater, or sweeter could be,
Than the faith and trust of a child so freely granted.
My humor and wisdom might be passed on through some ages,
With the stories I tell him of long, long agos, that keep him so enchanted.

Was there ever a companionship so close or so dear,
As with these little tykes who make things so nest and so cozy?
Today they call it talking "One on one," and I love it,
Even when the volleys of inquiries get a little nosey.

This beloved little voice with all the confidence in it,
Along with the angelic face and the busy chatter,
Wipes away the cares and sorrows of the whole wide world,
Giving me the Heavenly feeling that nothing else could matter.

—Marie Dupree

TEACHERS

You're not in it for the money; you're not in it for the fame,
Your jobs have many troubles, but you love them just the same.
Some days must seem very long—as if they'll never end,
For you must be a guiding figure, but also be a friend.
You must be a role model, and in each classroom you must show,
The proper way of learning and share everything you know.
You should be admired for your knowledge and your care,
Your courage, strength, hope, and pride, your ability to share
With every single student that you see every day.
It's not an easy task you take, from August until May.
It must get very hectic, teaching day out and day in,
And after the weekend's over, on Monday it all starts once again.
It must feel good once the year is over, and everything is through,
To know that everyone who graduates owes everything to you.
You mold a model person through the innocence of youth,
You teach them all good morals with your caring and your truth.
Just think of all the things you do, of all the kids you reach—
When someone asks you what you do, proudly say, **"I TEACH!"**

—Reed Flaherty

NO YELLOW RIBBONS

Yellow ribbons embellish each and every door,
to welcome all the soldiers home from yet another war.
Those who fought in the jungle, forever is their fight.
No welcome home, no cheering crowds, not a yellow ribbon in sight.

A coward if you didn't go, a murderer if you did,
the war has long since ended, the pain will never end.
Those who have whole bodies have mutilated souls.
There are no prostheses for hearts that are not whole.

Some died from the guns of the enemy, some from friendly fire.
What had they done that their lives should be required?
Some were missing in action, some just never came home.
Some died and were buried in the grave of the unknown.

With remorse, we do remember, who answered the futile call,
by gazing at the names etched on the crimson wall.
For the ones who did survive, no parades, no crowd, no cheers.
Left with only pain, only nightmares, only silent tears.

When songs of heroes echo, the story that they tell,
a war makes no heroes, a war can only make hell.
For them no yellow ribbons, no ribbons here at all.
The only ones who understood, are written on the wall.

—Carlotta Kosky

ABUSED

As I sit in the home of my closest friend,
I wonder if it will ever end.

When I left, he was upset with me.
He cursed, kicked, and then struck me.

He has beaten, abused me, and threatened to kill,
God only knows if he really will.

Fear rises up inside of me now.
But who can I go to and really tell?

I have no place to go and nowhere to hide,
Some people think that maybe I lied.

The beatings I took in front of my child.
I wonder who's taking care of her now.

You see: his threats he has carried out.
And that's what this poem is really about.

    —Carol Lee Nye

MY LIFE

My life is a wreck
I don't ever seem to know what to do.
I feel so cold and alone.
Alone . . . alone is what I feel.
Everything in my perfect world got flaws.
It turned ugly from beautiful, uncaring from kind.
Nothing seems the same.
Nothing at all.
Why does this have to happen to me?
Why me!
I ask of you, tell me . . . please.
Why won't someone answer me?
Doesn't anyone hear me?
Nobody cares anymore.
No one wants to listen.
Well, I'm telling you to listen!
Look at me!!!
Am I that awful to look at?
Why won't you talk to me?
Please . . . someone . . . answer me.

    —Evelyn Blankenship

UNHOLY WEDLOCK

A couple walks beside me in the airport.
"Shall I carry your coat?" he kindly asks.
"No," she snaps, "I'll carry it myself!"

I know she was his wife from the way she spoke—
In sharp, cutting, staccato syllables,
The tone of voice reserved for a faithful spouse.

In our society we would not speak so rudely
To a casual acquaintance, stranger, friend;
But there seems to be no obligation
To be civil to a marriage mate.

I wonder if she brags
That they've been married fifty years
(In armed hostility—it could not be wedded bliss.)
When did they lose the romance and awe of first love
Or the joyful interdependence of creating a love nest?

They will never be included in divorce statistics
And no one counts those partners who survive
Imprisoned, by mutual disagreement,
In a sick relationship more deadly than divorce.

    —Clela

A TEAR

A single tear rolls down my face;
It pauses at no certain place
Before it slowly moves on again.
No one knew a tear could be
Such a symbol of despair to me.
I try reaching out, but no one reaches in.

I seem to stand nowhere at all
Just watching that tear slowly fall.
If you relate to the situation shown,
Don't hold back, let it be known.
I know what it's like; I've been there before.
But think of this, "Can you stand much more?"

    —Meghann Justice, age 12

FOR TONY, DON'T GOT NO DADDY

One little boy, so small and free,
Blonde and blue-eyed—just about three.
Rambunctious, full of life is he
I thank this little one—for my heart to see,
    For Tony, don't got no daddy.

What kind of life for this child will be,
God only knows the future you see.
Will he be great and make his mark,
Or be forgotten and left in the dark?
Opportunities for God's touch, by you and me,
    For Tony, don't got no daddy.

Dirty bare feet and skinned up toes,
Talking up a storm, and no one knows
What goes on in a mind so young and small,
Or how he sees the ones, the Lord has called?
He touched my heart and made it cry,
The Lord's compassion I felt—is why.
I guess I've never felt it before,
And since I have, I want to more.
    For Tony, don't got no daddy.

    —Gwyn G. Weeks

THE STRANGER

He walks in the house, my husband,
He curses and surveys the floor.
He angrily screams "This place is a mess."
My husband's the stranger once more.

A tremble comes over my body.
"Oh God, not this man again!"
He screams out my name, demanding that I
Do something he wants there and then.

How does he turn into a tyrant,
Without true remorse down inside?
He'll say that he's sorry if I should walk out,
But not if I stay by his side.

"Don't leave me" he'd plead if I left him,
"I'm sorry for all that I said."
But stay in the house and try to be calm;
My husband's the stranger instead.

I vengefully hate the stranger.
He's destroyed so much good in my life.
If I wait for awhile, say maybe a week,
He'll realize that I'm still his wife.

To Richard, the stranger in my life.

    —Linda C. Glikin

SUNSHINE

For every teardrop that falls
a flower will grow.
And out of the shattered ruins,
love will bloom.
For Cupid's arrow is straight and true.

—Stanley D. Suski Jr.

THE SUN

Like a Phoenix rising from the ashes
its talon-like rays chasing the dark
heralding the birth of another day,

It wings across the sky
spreading its rays of life
warming and lighting the day,

Then it dives toward the horizon
and descends in a splash of orange,
A kaleidoscope of colors promising
to herald the coming of a new day.

—Jim Damon

In the land of sunny days
A walk will soothe a troubled heart
The birds will sing their lullabies
From sparrow small to meadow lark.
Perfumes course down each lovely lane
From flower rainbows which enthrall
The eyes and mind of all who care
From petals which will never fall.
When the eyes of lovers meet
They will hold their warm embrace
A little longer and their kiss
Will give the soul the time to taste.
Such wonder all about the land
And more in such wondrous ways
All one has to do is look
In this land of sunny days.

—James A. Marsters

Below that dark blue surface
Is a world all its own
To us it serves no purpose
To them they call it home

To us its wavy features
Are beautiful. Just that
It's the world of many sea creatures
That we refuse to look at

To live in peace is their dream
To ignore it is our act
To catch and sell is our scheme
But what if they don't come back?

To fish and dolphins, whales and seals
It's their only home
Is there no one left who feels
Any wrongness in their bones

Why can't we just let them be
And leave their world alone
Let them live in harmony
In the ocean, that's their home

—Pamela Turse

THE BREEZE AND WINDS

When the breeze and winds blow through the trees,
I hear the sound of evergreen leaves.

And then the wind sweeps my face,
Then I am in the wind's embrace.

When the wind sweeps the covered ground,
There are no more green leaves to be found.

But when the wind whistles and whisps, I do not know,
But perhaps it could mean rain or even snow.

And when the breeze and winds blow through the trees,
You will surely hear the whistle of evergreen leaves.

—Teresa Hemsley

THE DANCE OF THE CHERRY BLOSSOMS

Each branch swings low with its sumptuous share
Such extravagance of blossoms trilling air
Til wind with capricious abandon creates
A swarm of snow-flecked writhing snakes.

Petals fluttering in the breeze
To my delight and rapture please;
Sunlight suffusing through winsome flowers
Animates my mystical powers.

Since breath was embodied in billowy foam
Venus enamors with beauty in bloom
Flinging enchantment over bloom-laden boughs
Inflaming to ecstasy, they ravish the clouds.

Sunlight is haloed as it streams through the canopy
Sanctifies dappled ground under the tree
And the wind runs a comb through the trees'
     tousled locks
And the boughs fiercely struggle where wind
tugs at a knot.

Fashioned from an angel's wing
Suckled on sunshine in the spring
Embraced by the joy of the coming birth season
Of explosion of rapture beyond all man's reason.

Each petal bears a delicate fan
Of blood vessels, from the fairy's hand
To succor velvet pliant skin
God's immanence radiates from
     within.
Towering plumes of flowers, impaling
     themselves wantonly against the sky
Will ensnare one's whole being, he be
     possessed by his eyes;
Shamelessly preening, never loathe to display
Their beholding intoxicates, dashes dismay

A gauzy integument, sheer embodiment
of sunlight
Distracts wincing heartstrings from
     inevitable bleak night
Our journey is weary, yearnings know not
     fulfillment
Clasping heart-close such beauty
     helps endure raging torments

God victimized man when he demanded perfection
Yet interred man in a body which must yield
     to temptation
But one wonders He repented the misery he
     inflicted
And doled out earth's radiance
     so shackled souls be uplifted.

—Ellen Baudisch

132

POWER AND RETRIBUTION

When one makes a mistake, it's him
    that takes the stake.
When one loses power, it's him that starts to cower.
When one loses fame, it's him that takes the blame.
When one stands out in the rain, it's him
    that feels the pain.
When a flower blooms, is it really its doom?
The pain is as true as the color blue, as
    the color flickers, it feels like liquor.
The pain of impending doom, seems like
    never ending gloom.
As power retreats in battered defeat.
All that remains is the shattered pain.
The numbing sense feels, like the blade
    that kills, the shattered dream ends like
    a thousand moon beams.

—**Robert Norris**

A life of pain, a life of abuse
    frightened and scared I lay,
hoping and praying that I see another day.

The bruises on the surface may not stay for long
but, the way I was hurt can never be forgotten.

Without a person to care for me
    without someone's loving touch
    the pain is so unbearable
    can't anybody see how much?

I don't want to live, only to die
never was I told the truth, only lie after lie.

Told that no one would ever hurt me again,
    that I would never feel the pain,
the pain of abuse, the pain I now feel again.

The fact that I'm gone shouldn't bother them at all,
    they never loved me and never will.

All that doesn't matter anymore
    they won't have to bother with me,
for soon I'll be out of their lives forever,
    FOR SOON I WILL BE DEAD!

—**Angela Flanders**

AIDS

Trapped! I'm trapped in thy thoughts,
though I've tried to escape I know I've been caught!
I bang on these walls, my knuckles tear and bleed.
And, Oh! I've become weak, I am very, very weak.

My blood! My blood! My blood deceiveth all.
Much too clever to be trapped in skin or these walls.
Seeping, escaping into the cracks in the floor,
beyond the light of the space under the door.

The other side be chilly, my friend.
The other side, 'tis the end 'tis the end.

A deception of self.
Of riches and wealth.
The taking of a heart.
'Til death do you part.

My blood! My blood! Pure from lessons learned.
Though I've kissed innocence good-bye,
    never to return,
Youth again! I shall surely fly!

Aye, I will take flight,
dancing freely in morning's light.

—**Karen J. Buechler**

AIDS IS OUT

Aids is out
It's nothing to sneeze about
So watch out
Aids is a disease
it's usually caught by a blood transfusion
or somebody being used
Aids is out Aids is out Aids is out
watch who you date
you could make a big mistake
Aids is out tonite
you might be right by putting off this date
be sure who you date
before it's too late
Aids is a disease
you can catch it easy
it's nothing to sneeze about
so I'm watching out
cause I believe it's out there
Aids I can easily do without

—**Jerry Craig McKenzil**

LUMPS OF FEAR

Stop your chasing C-Word fear,
But check for lumps of hate.
Cast them out for those so dear
And serve a healthy plate.
Swallow shields to block the food
To PRISON cells gone bad;
Keep a kite bright happy mood,
Chasing rainbows when you're sad.
Smiles, like Angels, often weep
To hold a loved one near.
Fighting rapids, I will leap
A rushing ford to hear
Blasting horns proclaiming "HEALED" . . .
No C-Word for mankind:
Floating like feathers in a field,
Spirits free of C-Word bind.
But for now, on ships we go
Like sailors to our fate;
Riding waves against the foe,
We have no choice but wait.

—**Nancy Ford Poulin**

OUR WORLD

As I look in the past in happiness,
I see the good times and the bad.
As I look at the present I see a
    fear for the future.
As I look forward to the future, I
    wonder if I am having a nightmare!
For in the past, there was room for growth
For now, in the present, there is a
    standstill.
For in the future there is nothing—no
    love, hope, or courage.
The reason was uncalled for and
    now we are paying.
The reason was war, because two
    different countries could not
    get along.
The reason was hatred—hate is
    killing our world today and
    our future—Think about
    the *children*. The *children*
    are our future—treat them well.

—**Mollie Blount**

TENDER MOMENTS

Your jaunty walk and
    flashing smile;
Your beautiful blue eyes
    intrigue me all the while.
You hold my hands so tenderly
    and give me a gentle kiss.
You caress me with your eyes,
    that fills my heart with bliss.

I know not time nor place;
I simply know you're there,
I turn and see your smiling face,
And the wind blowing through your hair.

      —Mary Sharp

If only for a day,
    You could feel all I do.
If only for a day,
    Thoughts were not needed.
If only for a day,
    our footsteps could be shared,
    I know we could at last put faith in
    a slowly nurtured love.
If only for a day,
    Thinking didn't hurt and moods
    weren't always changing.
If only for a day,
    our love,
    our world,
    could be one.

*Dedicated to my Tommy, our day has
come. I love you with all my heart.*

      —Lauren Ann

FIRST LOVE

You seemed to think that I was great;
    And you made me laugh.
You were such a perfect date;
And you made me happy.

You never tried to kiss me,
You brought me many gifts.
You were as proper as could be;
You made my spirit lift.

You seldom asked questions,
You had a tender smile;
You made joking and teasing expressions
Yet you were gentle all the while.

Life was so easy being with you,
You gave me a special place.
I enjoyed everything with you.
With you I felt so safe.

I knew that I could walk
      with you,
Through life's many doors.
You would hold my hand and
      walk with me,
Across life's mighty shores.

      —Mary Sharp

SUCKING FACE IN A BLUES BAR

It's not just alcohol, I tell you.
It's the smell of your skin,
the thickness of your hair against my fingers,
the fact that you're a man.

Of course, it *helps* — enough Rum and Coke
makes anyone a predator,
but what you must understand is that
I too am hungry.
Some men think women don't have these needs —
Stand still.
Prepare to be enlightened.

      —Elena Rockmann

JUST ONCE MORE

Touch me, just one more touch
For I will not feel your soft hand against my face again.

Hold me, just one more hold
For I will be numb and shall never feel you against me again.

Talk to me, just one more talk
For I shall never hear your sweet voice
and the music we danced to for so long.

Look to me, just one more look
For I will never see your beautiful eyes,
the colors surrounding you,
the love inside.

Kiss me, just one more kiss
For I will never touch your lips again.

The scent of your cologne weakening
as I lose the sense of smell.

Love me, just one more love
For I will never feel the feelings
I held so deep within.

As my heart grows dim
Remember me, just one more time . . . .

      —Valerie Rose

DO YOU KNOW?

Do you know that I still care?
Do you know what I feel?
Do you know, do you know, do you know?

Do you know I think of you?
Do you know I miss you too?
Do you know I love you, though I lost you long ago?

Do you know I miss the sweetness I'm sure you had?
I miss the tenderness I know mothers have

I miss touching your face, and hearing your voice.
Do you know, do you know, do you know?

When I was a little girl, I'd sit and think of you.
I'd think about the things I'd heard you had done so well

I wish to be like you in every single way.
Just to be like my mother meant so much to me

Since you went away,
We've missed you so much.
God has the answers. Someday, I'll understand

He knows the reasons. I cannot question that.
He knows we miss you and still love you so.

Do you know, do you know, do you know?

      —Myrna Kay Bischoff

MY BELOVED MOTHER

On one cold winter's day, my beloved mother passed on her way. She said there's a door I must go through, but first there are things I must say and do. She sat me down divided her things among me and my brother. This way there won't be a fight with each other. The road I am taking is unknown, but don't worry I won't be alone. Remember I love you both and always will. I will be watching you from up on the hill. Don't mourn for me when I'm gone, for one day we'll be together you'll see. She closed her eyes and left me then, I was certain, she was on her way to Heaven.

Dedicated to My Beloved Mother, Irene D. (Hlinka) Amundson Born August 24, 1932 passed away November 10, 1991.

—**MaryJo Hines**

THERE WILL COME A TIME

There will come a time my child, when you will see and hear,
   Beauty in a flower, magic in a song, wonder in your heart,
That you have dreamed of all life long.
There will come a time my child, when you will feel a love,
You'll know when it arrives, there will be a "tugging" of your heart,
Among days of joy and laughter, too numerous to chart.
There will come a time my child, when there will be a birth,
and this you'll celebrate, like nothing else on earth. Then . . .
when things are settled . . . the babe will go away . . . but for you
the memory, will in your lifetime stay . . . and the cycle will repeat
generations after you . . . and they'll discover meaning, from life's
mysteries made new . . . and they will try to grasp the prize, to
capture it and hold it fast . . . to see if they can't run the race,
to "collar" love and make it last.
There will come a time my child, when you will see and hear,
Beauty in a flower, magic in a song, love residing in your heart,
That you have searched for all life long.

Dedicated to my children, Bethany, Shannon, Darren, and Devin All my love, Dad.

—**David R. Lessard**

A MOTHER'S LOVE

In the woods of Mississippi, eight miles north of town.
Stood a little four room house on the white sandy ground.
Big oak trees stood in the yard, with a drive-way circling through.
We swept the yard with a brush-broom, not much else we could do.

I heard my mother calling me in panic one day.
She did not know it at the time, that I had planned to run away.
I had written my brother only a week before.
Would you come and take me from this place? I can't stand it any more.

So my brother had come to get me, we would go to Wisconsin that day.
We had planned to meet upon the road if I could get away.
My mother felt there was something wrong; tho I hadn't said a word.
I knew my brother was upon the road for a car horn I had heard.

At that moment I had a choice, to leave or to stay.
And at that moment I didn't want to leave, I did not want to run away.
My mother's love came shining through, she loved me so very much.
When I was sick she was always there, with her loving tender touch.

I did not realize at the time just how much she needed me.
There was abuse in our home and I just wanted to be free.
But every time I needed her she was always there.
We had been through hard times together and she always showed she cared.

When the angels came to take my mother home in 1963.
I found out I had not known just what my mother meant to me.
I had lost my very best friend and someone that loved me so.
Now, when I think about that day, I'm so glad I did not go.

—**Oplean Duckworth**

JESSES' GONE

Lost hearts
   with voices cry,
Chasing love
   inside we die,
Pretending truth
   forgetting care,
Lost hearts
   no one prepares.

—**Ernest C. Battey Jr.**

Gentle man, lonely man, you touched me today with your tears. You revealed your heart to me. Loneliness and pain have been your plight . . . and, now alone, you trusted to expose your inner sorrow. Thank you for feeling safe with me! Your presence is a reminder of how fragile we are.

I grew today.
Bless you, old man, my friend.

—**Marilyn Chargin**

IMAGE OF LOVE

Another Time
   Another Place
Another Heart
Another Face
Another Tear
Another Sigh
Another Laugh
Another Cry
Someday a Dream
Someday a Love
I spend my time thinking
   or wishing
Star, Oh Please. Bring True
The days and nights
   of
   Loving You!

—**Jeffrey Hollingsworth**

CARING FRIENDS

Although we are far apart, you will always remain near and dear to my heart.

A little of mother, some sister added too, a little bit of brother, a friend is what I call you.

In my times of sorrow, in times of despair, I reached out and you were always there.

With your words of wisdom and faith for two. You shared a word of comfort and helped the light shine through.
Romans 15:13

—**Charles H. Lowe**

THE LITTLE FLOWER

The Little Flower just sits there,
   Her purple hair gleaming in the sun.
While little rabbits and bluejays,
Scurry, romp, and run.

The Little Flower just sits there
The wind blowing her thin waist.
While other pansies and daisies
Prance, play, and race.

The Little Flower just sits there,
Her purple hair gleaming in the sun.
While little rabbits and bluejays,
Scurry, romp, and run.

—**Sarajane Bruno**

THE WALK

I walked into the mountains today.
   To find my childhood home
      fallen, forgotten.

Cool, clear water bubbled downward
      over rocks,
      as ceaselessly as my own heart.

Memories of butter and cream
      kept cold in the stream,
      brothers, sisters, cousins splashing.

My grandmother's love
   in the porch rocker
      watching.

The sun warmed my shoulders
      as I touched the aged boards,
      the carefully chosen wallpaper
         dust under my fingertips.

GOD filled my soul, overflowed my eyes,
      exploded my heart
         and I was HOME.

I walked into the mountains today . . . .

—**Debra Stratton Rochelle**

RAINDROPS

Raindrops
   beating on my window pane
bring memories to my mind
that sear and scorch
my very soul.

Raindrops
dripping like spider webs
entwining the hurt I feel inside
with the torrent coming down.

Raindrops
dribbling like the tears I shed
when first I learned of your betrayal
when your love for me withered and died.

Raindrops
reaching downward, watering my spirit
as only raindrops can do
washing away the love I once felt.

Raindrops
disappearing down the drain
washing away sadness
and allowing the rainbow
to finally appear.

—**Willie J. Neusom**

SERENE REFLECTIONS

As warm as the skies' golden treasure,
   As gentle as the Spring's first dew
Within my soul I'll always find pleasure
Serene reflections — thinking of you

A morning dove sings for the advent of dawn,
A tune of joy for the sake of the living
Though I knew, like the dove, one day you'd be gone
Serene reflections just keep on giving

Society ignores what nature holds dear,
Abandoning logic, all reason and rhyme
Though insanity surrounds me I have no fear . . .
Serene reflections will always be mine

—**Wing**

AH, SWEET SPRINGTIME!

The outdoors are calling, and we hear the call;
   'Tis the season that beckons, "Come one and all,
The weather is luring, so come have a ball!"
   Ah, sweet springtime!

Colorful kites high above fly on a string;
Nearby we watch playful squirrels scampering,
While kiddies take turns on a favorite swing.
   Ah, sweet springtime!

Renewed field and forest rouse the sense of smell;
Pretty birds and bees have a story to tell:
As for fluttering butterflies, all is well.
   Ah, sweet springtime!

Gaze in wonder at the beautiful flower;
Watch once dormant seeds burst open with power;
Note how new leaves and green grass grow hour-by-hour.
   Ah, sweet springtime!

The sunshine gives way to light clouds and soft rain;
Then bright sun chases away all clouds again;
And sweethearts, hand-in-hand, stroll down lover's lane.
   Ah, sweet springtime!

—**Charlie F. Manuel**

NIGHT SONGS

On a clear summer's eve with the moon shining bright,
   A whippoorwill's cries pierce the quiet night.

Crickets begin chirping in unison 'fore long,
Joining together in an old mating song.

The buzz of the locust is loud and rude,
But blends in well with the evening's mood.

Hidden from view so you can't see,
Frogs start to croak way up in the trees.

And off in the distance far, far away,
The low of a cow fresh full of hay.

Owls hoot and call in a way that owls only,
Commune together in the night deep and lonely.

Oh, give me a home in the quiet countryside,
Away from the hustle and bustle.

For I cannot sleep else I can hear,
These beautiful sounds reaching my ear.

Nocturnal sounds of GOD'S perfect creatures,
Singing their night songs in melodious feature.

—**Debra Griffin**

THERE ARE THE MOUNTAINS . . .

There are the mountains—the steep, sharp inclines, the dark, vast valleys between. At some points, majestic waterfalls curtain the mountain sides, forever flowing in beauty, their powerful force incomprehensible.

There are the rainbows—each as vibrant as the other. Almost a mystical magic: a suspended, yet brief moment of peace and tranquility.

There are the oceans, like the winds, forever in motion—tides and currents forever unsettled—forever giving, forever taking, demanding complete respect and authority.

There are the rains—torrential or meek and mild. A life-giving force, a destroying force. There is beauty, there is power and fear.

There are the sun, the moon, the stars above—giving, guiding, warming, yet confined to constant paths—at times overbearing, almost unleashing powers beyond imagination.

There is love—a force as great and deep as the ocean, as mystical as the rainbows, as majestic as the mountains, forever in motion like the winds. There will be unsettling, turbulent moments. But, as these great forces have, true love will stand the test of time.

—Elizabeth Vargo

THE LYRICIST

She has no composition in the Sixties, therefore she had no song to sing. Oh, there were lyrics floating in her mind, but they belonged to someone else.
They were the lyrics of her Father set to military melodies.
She had hummed them all her life.
They were the lyrics of her fellow-travelers-in-age. Their lyrics were new, exciting, avante garde and in direct opposition to his.
In the end, his music overpowered the others.
But she couldn't sing, because she knew it wasn't her music.

It was not until his voice, his song was silenced for eternity
that she allowed herself to sift through the lyrics, the melodies.
That which was truly part of herself, she kept.
It took her a long time to write her own lyrics, years had passed.
She had one moment of regret that during an incredible decade,
when everyone was offering songs to the world, she had none to give.
But she learned that sometimes it's better not to sing just for
the sake of singing, not to compose just for the sake of having a composition.
Your copyright in life must truly be your own.

—Linda Lagasse Ferris

THE EVERCHANGING SKY

The sky is many things, a meaningful delight.
The sky can be as blue as the ocean, as dark as the night.
The sky can be filled with many colors and bright lights.
The sky is most beautiful in every shade and light.

Golden sunbeams playing on the clouds, beautiful sight.
Fluffy white clouds float in shades of blue skies.
Watching their ever changing forms most delightful.
With a little imagination one can see most any sight.

Sun in peace is glowing, brightest rays from heaven's dome is shining.
Nice to enjoy a bright clear day, beneath a calm and genial sky.
Many warnings of coming storms plainly show in the sky.
Black clouds cross the sky, thunder roars, lightning flashes.

Refreshing rain, and sunbeams, perfectly formed rainbow.
Red, orange, yellow, green, blue and violet — rainbow.
You have found the Pot of Gold, if you have found the beauty of a rainbow
Glowing sunset paints its rosy picture.

The sky is sprayed with twinkling, sparkling, jewels so very bright,
Behind clouds the moon is lurking, soon to show in brightness.
The crescent moon, the silvery moon, the harvest moon, very bright,
Most fascinating, the sky, an ever changing picture of delight.

—Ruth Boyer Gross

TRIBUTE

Of all the gifts a child's been given
The one that stands above the rest
And truly is one of the best
Is his very own grandmother.

I think of all the hurts you've healed
And tears you've dried
I couldn't repay you if I tried
But thank you, my grandmother.

—Emily Santee

VICTORIA

The love I give you has no end
I cradle you from harm
Others try to send
You're my precious daughter
No one can match your charm
You make all the day bright
A smile a thousand candles light
Your hopeful, cheerful, carefree
Character is might
Laughter from your heart
Carries any one near you
Through the dark night

—Julie Holz

IN LOVING MEMORY OF DONNA PHEGLEY

Dec. 6, 1928 — Oct. 10, 1991

The miracle I prayed for,
    Didn't come to pass that day.

On October 10, 1991
    You quietly slipped away.

I didn't get to say good bye,
    Didn't want to anyway.

I'm sure I said "I love you,"
    As they wheeled you on your way.

I wish I would have somehow known,
    That it was your last day.

I didn't know my mumbled words,
    Would be the last I'd say.

I would have told you so much more,
    And asked for your advice.

I had so much to learn from you,
    I needed you in my life.

I would have held you tighter,
    And thanked you for your care.

And asked you not to go just yet,
    There was too much still to share.

I wish I had you here right now,
    To take away the pain.

But memories of how you lived,
    Are all that now remain.

I hope that someday I can be
    Like the lady that you were.

I hope they say, "That's Donna's girl."
    She seems a lot like her.
                I miss you, Mom
                —Elizabeth J. Busch

Standing on the bank with pole in hand,
he says watch your step and don't fall in.

Spending my time with him everyday,
I hope the time will slowly wear away.

Playing checkers and letting me win,
at the beach we watch the waves roll in.

Time has passed and things have changed.
A part of my life is rearranged.

Prom, graduation, and college for me,
I know he'll be there, hoping all will see.

Looking back in my mind as I bounce on his knee,
a picture of us—my grandpa and me.
    —Ami Renata Raughton

MY GRANDFATHER'S FARM

There is a farm not far from here
    Where the ground is good and the sky is clear

This farm was started long ago
    By someone with a dream and a hoe

He dreamed of a future for his wife
    Something that would last all his life

Although it was hard work at first
    And often made him thirst

His wife and children were by his side
    And made the farm the family pride

The harvests were such a success
    That many thought his farm was the best

My grandfather now owns this farm
    And he thinks of it as his lucky charm

This place where his grandfather came upon one day,
    while the flowers were blooming in the month
    of May
        —Corey Sechler, grade 10

colorful humanity

the pages of progress
            hinge
around colorful people like you
who emanate the natural fragrance of an inward beauty

what many only emulate, you radiate
with your multifaceted uniqueness
that enriches the diversity around you

you've been discovered — not soon, not late
for your modesty could not prognosticate
what many notice and appreciate:
not just a well-trained "personality"
but a person of virtue, of cardinal quality
not a cold spot in the workplace
but the warmth of heart and soul and grace

may we strive to be more like you
who give the fabric in the quilt of attributes and hues
the strength that blends uniqueness and diversity
with culture, language, and ethnicity
who prove that no one is better than the others
that we all have needs of sisters and brothers

dedicated to Norma, my lifetime flower:
my words only reflect your constant inspiration
as my soul delights in our family garden
        —Phillip H. Duran

CELEBRATION

Birth of mornings, crystal sun.
Night surrenders as day's begun.
Spring reigns while winter succumbs.
During coronation of the equinox.

—Arnold Paulie

MESSENGERS

Walk in the dawn, dear one,
And in the blackness of the
Night's last hour —
Behold the stars.

Across the centuries
Frail ships made port,
Charted by that same
Unfailing light.

Guard safe your feet
From the foul depths
That seek to pull you down —
To devil's lair.

Reach for the stars,
To grasp the hand of God
Who sent them there —
Eons ago.

Ours is the choice —
Reach high to Heaven above —
For in those realms waits an Eternity
Of omnipotent, omnipresent Love.

—Hilda Frantz Cushwa

TODAY

Today
Is yesterday's tomorrow
And tomorrow's yesterday.
Today is the continuation
Of all the chain of events
That have happened in all
Of tomorrow's yesterdays.
In each minute of each day,
There is a new event
Or a continuation
Of a series of events,
Welded together and sustained
By the wisdom of God.

Time, whether it be yesterday,
Or tomorrow or today,
Plays its part in the portrait of life,
Being made up of a series of instances
In which there occurs an event.
Space and time can become intermingled
At any one of these moments,
But 'tis God's wisdom
That takes a series of unrelated events
And welds them all together
So that the world will not cease
To be at the end of one moment,
But will continue into a
New set of events that will
Become another and another
Of tomorrow's yesterdays . . .
Today.

—Kenneth L. Slaughter

CHRISTMAS THOUGHTS FROM A CORPSMAN

Remembering the reason why we celebrate each year,
the Birth of our Lord Jesus should bring us good cheer.
The boxes, the wrappings, the gifts we receive,
are all just small tokens of what we perceive.
"It's the thought that counts," you've heard it before
Families and friends — they are all hard to ignore.
         Stop. Let us think.
It's not what we see.
It's the feelings inside,
It's what we conceive.
Carolers, services, time that we share
Together we meet to show you we care.
The love that I know and the warmth that's inside
Bring a smile to my face that's hard to disguise.
Pray for World Peace and keep love in your heart
For All of us Servicemen that are . . .
                                     So Far Apart!

—Marty Meredith

THE END OF DARKNESS

There is an end to darkness
A dawn which begins a new day
Though the sounds of night clamor and rail
You have not lost your way

When in the midst of shadows
You believe yourself alone
Hold tightly to the Father's promises
Trust Him to lead you home.

For the Lord walks beside you
A destination well in mind
It's farther than you'd choose for yourself
And far greater than ever you'd find.

When at last you've reached safety
When the Lord has dried every tear,
You'll know your true Father
And forever hold Him dear.

—J. Daniel Litwiller

AN OFFER NOT TO REFUSE

My hand is offered in love
to take away your cares
to give you rest and freedom
and dry away your tears.

My ears are here to listen
when troubles come your way
when joy fills your soul,
I'm here in all your days.

My love is offered freely
to give shelter in life's storms,
Just call to Me for help and
I'll keep you safe and warm.

In faith, ask of Me
and you shall receive;
Open your heart to Me
and then you will be free

JESUS IS THE WAY, THE TRUTH, AND THE LIFE

—Debra Robertson

I MIGHT HAVE

Without any cause nor meaning,
And far from all you did and said,
I might one day have gone towards the light
And been quite beautiful instead.

I might one day have let you breathe your love
Which never did quite reach the ground.
Your flighty love — I might have gone so elegantly
Rather than this constant falling down.

Without any cruel demeaning,
So long as you didn't go red,
I tried to please, to kiss with all my might.
I think I was too cold, distant, too dead.

—Andrea R. Arcand

MY SUNSET OF LIFE

I was young, carefree and gay,
I had the world before me they say.
I met and married a very good wife
and together, we had a very good life.
We had our children one by one,
til there were nine and then we were done.
Now we're divorced and I have no wife,
As I stand all alone facing my sunset of life.
She took our children and I am all alone.
I have nothing I can call my own.

Darling, I get lonesome, sad and blue,
always thinking of and loving you.
To me you were always a wonderful wife.
Please remember this walking toward your sunset of life.
Divorce, isn't that an ugly word?
It's one I wish I had never heard,
It took you from me and mine,
especially our children which number nine.
But one thing I'm glad we had our joys and strife.
Before we stand alone facing our sunset of life.

—Samuel F. McNett, deceased

CONSENTED JOURNEY

Darkness came followed by nightshade,
as it lit Dad's path far beyond any grave.
It was a journey taken with his consent,
one full of God's grace and quiet intent.
Dad was in God's House, in silent meditation,
only seconds away from enlightened revelations.
"Jesus Loves Me," this Dad knows.
Mom beside him, as he heard the echos.

The nightshade led Dad to a sphere without end,
in all its beauty, the human mind can't comprehend.
It's in this sphere, the abode of the dead,
my Dad's soul was set free, his final tears shed.
Here the dead themselves do not forget.
Evidence found in blessings among our prayer sticks.

Tokens and amulets were given without hesitation.
We knew our Dad understood this Lakóta tradition.
Left as a light to comfort and guide his soul forward.
"Yes, Jesus Loves Me," and this my Dad knew,
as a loving light guided him through.
His journey here has ended, but another begins anew.
Loved by family and touched by the Lakotā Sioux.

—Cheryl K. McNett Mead

GOOD-BYE

as you came toward me
the expression on your face
told me what was on your mind.
good-bye.

because of all the fighting
despite the love behind our tears
our final words.
good-bye.

no more late night calls,
sneaking out past curfew
just to be together
good-bye.

and even though
we are no longer together,
what remains always
is my love for you.
good-bye.

—Dawn M. Sass

ALL I ASK

Hold me.
Hold me for today.
Do not promise me tomorrow.
For it may never come.
Let's not dwell on yesterday
For is it not just a glimpse in time.
Just give me today,
For tomorrow may never come.
And when tomorrow is today
That's all I'll ask,
Just hold me for today.

You hold me for today
Making no promises for tomorrow,
We talk of yesterday,
Admiring that it is not today.
You give me today.
For tomorrow is just a dream,
You give me all I ask, and more
Just holding me, today.

—Robbin

LOVE TAKES TIME

Not all love begins at first sight.
Some take a little time;
some take a lot of time.
Becoming friends is important
when you love the person;
you need to get along and
confide in one another.
Trust is, also, a needed asset.
Some people trust easily;
some people need convincing.
If that trust is broken,
it is not easily rebuilt.
You have to work on
relationships; they don't get
better without some work.
Patience is very valuable.
You can't lose it very often
without seeing some harmful effects.
Love takes time to
grow and become strong.

—Corinne Dallman-DeMoss

A SISTER IS THERE FOR YOU

A sister is a friend.
A sister's love will never end.
She will make you soup when you're ill.
She will help until you feel better.
She will write you letters when she's away
and call you every day.
She will tell you secrets you can trust.
She will never tell on you unless she must.
She will help you make cookies.
She will help bake a cake
or introduce you to Blake.
She will make the time fly by
and she will never tell a lie.
Don't you want a sister like mine!

—KristaLin McClintock

MY LEAVING PRAYER

All my life this was my home,
and so tonight I pray.
Give me strength to leave this place.
I have to go away.
How can I leave the ones I love?
This house, this land, this sky.
How can I turn my back and leave?
How can I say good-by?
Please help my feet to take a step,
and with each step I take.
Give Momma strength to watch me go.
Don't let her poor heart break.
Daddy taught me to be strong.
But he's been gone for years.
Make me brave, like he would want,
and face up to my fears.
Help me keep my family close.
My memories intact.
But most of all, in years ahead.
Please help me to come back.

—Dixie Sylvester

MOTHER

No one else could ever know,
The pain that you've been through.
When times were tough,
You were there
No matter what I'd do.

Others come and go,
On those I can't depend.
When I need advice,
Or just to talk
You're still my most special FRIEND.

Sometimes you smile,
As you watch me day to day.
Learning
As you did,
To make my own way.

I'm glad I'm here,
To learn from you.
But more than that
I'm glad
That you were here too.

Love, your daughter,
Gloria

—Gloria Terry

MY CHILD IS BORN

Into this world you came,
Benjamin Joseph is your name.
With golden hair, and eyes as blue as the sea,
Yes you definitely look like me.

As each day goes by I watch you grow,
It amazes me how much you know.
Your words are few, but mean so much,
I can still hold you, to give that gentle touch.

There's never a dull moment, when you're around,
At times you cry, what a sad sound!
But needless to say I'm glad you're here,
Loving you always, year after year.

—Elizabeth Lynn LoCoco

OUR GIFT

It's something old-fashioned, something most grand—
Not machine rationed, or woven by hand.
With purses overflowing or checkbooks galore,
It cannot be purchased in anyone's store.
Not found stacked on counters,
        or hanging on racks.
Not stuffed in big boxes,
        or placed in small sacks,
It's not only for birthdays,
        anniversaries and such—
Sometimes given too little,
        but never too much.
In any condition, even if stormy above,
It won't shrink, fade, or yellow
        but stay white as a dove.
Our gift — with best wishes —
Mom and Dad, *All Our Love*

—David McGrath

CHRISTINA'S GRAMMA

People knew her as a shy quiet little girl
who rarely ever spoke a word;
Maybe because she learned from her teachers
children were to be seen and not heard.
Right or wrong, not sharing herself with others
is the path that she did take,
Sharing only her sense of humor with life's friends,
that she would make.
She would always make people laugh,
and would give them a good time,
But she would never share her true feelings,
and to others, that was her crime.
As the years passed by she kept quiet
and held her feelings locked up inside her;
Then one day, not long ago, she finally
opened up to a special outsider.
This new friend listened to her secrets
and to the stories she had to say,
With her she shared a lifetime of knowledge
that she had learned and had tucked away.
I know all this because you see I was
that friend, she started talking to me!
She was my GRAMMA and I was her little
granddaughter, CHRISTINA MARIE.
She needs another friend now, since I
have passed on and have gone away.
Would you like to get to know her?
My Gramma's name is Carole Mae.

—Carole Mae Erickson

A friend through the passage, fear no doubt
I can't seem to reach the bridge
The bridge that declares us enemies
The other side of the passage, the voyage
Holds me from its destination
Trapped, away from light, hope, life
A crystal wine glass in the palm of my hand
I died, and reached the bridge
But it is over now
My mate can't help me
All my friends have run away from my plight
My mother loves me, and wishes me well
But has already walked, my fate, time will tell
For sometime I contemplated to not have to walk this passage
For it's dark and cold
But the child has grown
Grown to see, the world around me
  is full of glee, someday there I will be
But for now, my feet and I will continue to walk
For fear is here, my friend, with whom I can talk

—Sean DeHoney

SPENDING TIME WITH YOU

All I wanna do is spend time with you,
Sometimes you find someone who makes you feel brand new,
You enjoy his or her company in whatever you do together,
As the warmth, excitement, and devotion get better,
A beautiful everlasting friendship truly begins.

All I wanna do is spend time with you,
Weeks and months now have passed on through,
You seem to be always on my mind, and the star of my dreams,
Morning, noon, and night is filled with you constantly it seems,
Now I'm deeply and passionately in love with you.

All I wanna do is spend time with you,
After a beautiful day together you asked me to stay the night,
You were so wonderful and very good to me, we flew like a kite,
The next day our relationship became a permanent situation,
From this day forward my love and affection belong to you.

Dedicated to: Alexandre Grimaldi 323, Michael J. Johnston 3884
In memory of: Brandon Lee 330 + 317, Bryan Sherman 810,
Timothy Romei Gulf War, Mark Bannetti 1014, Bud Williams ESL.

—Kari Lundgren

THE LOVE GAME

Two hearts engage in a lonely dance
  search for love, plead for romance.
They touch, they shake, they twist and turn
never finding that for which their aging souls yearn.

That's the pain of the love game —
knowing tomorrow will feel the same.
Played by the lost who must find their way —
the lonely living day to day.

Walking down a dusty road,
unable to release their burdensome load.
There is no speed limit, nor any street signs.
A wrong turn, then a wreck — they attempt to stay in the lines.

They sit in fancy restaurants, or in a small town cafe.
No matter what they order, their bill is too high to pay.
Hard chairs, rocking tables, menus smeared with food,
cold meals, empty glasses, waiters always rude.

It's always the same in the love game —
blank face, void eyes, no name.
Never finding the right words to say —
empty souls living day by day.

—Stacey Erin Hanrahan

FAREWELL DANCE

I could dance forever if the
bossa nova I could hear, to
match my maiden's dress and
flock her aigrette with
ornaments of arid plumes and
me lady of olive sheen, we
dance about the court yard
and until farewell, farewell.

—James Mosley

FRIENDS

Friends are just strangers,
whom you haven't met yet.
Friends are people
who share the fun.
Friends are people
who share adventure.
Friends are people
male and female.
Friends are people
who share the work.
Friends are people
who share the good times,
but also share the bad times.

—Patricia Diane Hixson

PEACE OF HEART AND MIND

I wish I had a peace of Heart.
I wish I had a peace of Mind.
I wish I had some time for me.
I wish I could get rid of
  this pain in my heart.
I wish I didn't feel so
  helpless.
I wish I knew how to
  love my self.
I wish I could forget about
  all my problems.
I wish I could learn to control
  the problems in my life.
I am going to get the strength
I need to handle the problems
  in my life.

—Tammy Graham

TRUE LOVE

I love you more
  than words can say:
A debt of love
  I can ne'er repay.
And though I wish
  to be with you,
I must remain
  for a season or two.
But when the appointed
  time has come;
I'll return to you
  where my love comes from.
And never again,
  will I leave your side;
till the Lord returns
  to collect His bride.

—Charles R. Nash

LIVING AND LEARNING

As I ran toward the darkness
I couldn't resist
looking back at the sunset.
Among the vivid colors in the sky
I saw all the joy and the pain.
When I stumbled, I looked down
to see the reflection of the past.
We learn more from regret
than triumph.
Looking back once more
the light and the colors faded.
I couldn't stop them
or even slow them down.
But then, I wouldn't want to.

—Beth Hathaway Cole

TEAR OF THE MOON

Full willows whisper
In ebony of night;
Deepest cobalt blue
Spins endlessly from sight.

A cool liquid breeze
Flows viscous on my tongue —
Intoxicates my blood,
Peacefully drowns my lungs.

Gossamer mists stretch
Like cotton-candy clouds,
Rake the empty sky
Hold a pearl in their shroud.

Coyote dances
Round, with his moon dust coat
Of silver tipped fur,
Before me in the road.

And the Tear of the Moon
Falls, silver and shimmering
To the snow beneath my feet.

—Eric J. Stewart

RHYMES IN TIME

Longevity . . .
Brevity . . .
Duplicity . . . . .
Simplicity . . .
Freneticism . . .
Asceticism . . .
Rarity . . .
Asperity . . .
The Thunder . . .
The Wonder . . .
The history . . .
The mystery . . .
The same
In a Frame . . .
Avoiding intellectual slavery
With a kind of writer's bravery
So the mind's eye
Can turn a blind eye
To everything this woman can be,
But isn't.

*Dedicated to my secret heart;
now, and whenever 'Irish eyes
are smiling.' I love you.*

—Dawn Marie Nevills

THE CANDLE

I see the shadow dancing on the wall from a single candle that burns on a cold October night. The power is out. From that faint light of the candle you can see reflections of your every movement. You can hear the wind and the snow outside. The wind carries things with it as it goes. It seems so angry. It bangs things against the house, and makes it sound as if someone is at the door. The light from the candle flickers, but it still burns on. There is a few inches of snow on the ground, and by morning there will be more. The cat is sleeping on a blanket downstairs and he is not even aware of what is going on. I just sit here with a flashlight, and one single candle burning in the night with its shadow dancing on the wall.

—Stacy Paolo

DANCING, TWIRLING

She was dancing, twirling while the music played.
My heart sang a song as I watched her sway.
She was free and limber while floating on air.
She was dancing, twirling without a care.

Her graceful elegance was something to see.
She captured my heart, then surrounded me.
She danced, and twirled as the moments slipped away.
She lay on my mind through out the day.

I was happy to watch her as she went through her phase.
But I got too close, and I scared her away.
Now she's dancing, twirling, who knows where?
But in my heart, she'll forever dance there.

Dedicated to Diana

—Robert H. Gibbs Jr.

MY PRECIOUS BALLERINA

Patiently she listens and waits for the sound of the soft music to approach her and fill her soul as a cool breeze on a warm summer night.

Gently she slips her tiny feet into the shoes made of satin as the moon lights up the room and reflects the sparkle of her eyes.

Silently the wooden floor awaits the pirouettes and grande jetes that will be performed upon it as the invisible audience is in awe of her beauty and perfection.

Sweetly the blood runs through her veins and warms her body as she can hear the beat of her heart not yet pounding with the excitement of which is necessary to begin.

Peacefully she begins to hum the sweet melody of the lullaby which she sang the night before as she wondered whether the music would be there tonight and whether or not it would ever come again.

Then her song was abruptly interrupted by a voice that said, "My precious ballerina, the music does not come to you from the outer world. You must seek it from within yourself. Then you will know the true meaning of the sound."

Suddenly her heart is aroused, her soul is filled. The music has begun. Not the music known to the ears of one, but to the life inside one's self, and she gracefully begins to dance.

—Cheryl A. Boseneiler (Centerstage Dance Studio)

YOUNG DREAMS

You can hear laughter in the hall
And friends making plans to meet at the mall.
You can see two people in love hold hands
And make plans to go hear the latest bands.

You can hear the sweet whispers,
As the winds blow thru the spring flowers.
You can see love in the air,
As spring blows the leaves around.

Love afloating in the air,
Love awhistling in the breeze.
For all to see and hear.
For all to know what can be.

—Raine Marie Peoples

DREAMS —
AVENUE TO MY INNER BEING

When my watchful self is asleep,
my inner being is ever alert.
It spins an imaginative account
of my many shadowed faces.

'Tis a metaphor tailored to my
daily situations,
deepest thoughts,
hidden feelings,
forgotten hurts,
greatest joys,
and eventful decisions.

A tale from me
about me
to me.

AM I LISTENING?

—Carol Vanden Eng

YESTERDAY

Oh, how I long for the yesterday gone by,
The happy smiles of children at play,
The closeness of family ties,
Lovers walking hand and hand,
Through quiet moonlight streets,
Under shady trees, and the smell of lilacs
in the air.

Oh, where have those yesterdays gone to,
When I could feel the warm summer sun, shining
down on my face,
And feeling the fresh cool breeze blowing in the
air,
The rich clean earth at my feet with spring flowers,
breaking through,
And melodies sung so sweetly by the birds on the
wing.

Oh, what has happened to the yesterdays of long ago,
When I could embrace the cool summer rain and
feel so wonderful,
And walk barefoot through the puddles,
And hear laughter and singing, with the afternoon
picnics,
Just to see the first rainbow across the sky,
It's the quiet times I long for just to bring
me back to one more yesterday.

—Annette J. Wesgaites

ECHOES OF A DREAMER!

Tear stained words, upon a tattered page
Softly echoes a distant rage
The poet's dream, now is but a vision once told
Of how he poured out his heart and soul

To whom deaf ears, refused to hear
The falling of his silent tear
Saying once in the forest there was a tree
And when I saw, it had fallen you see

I prayed to my Lord, and Father above
Asking for only to find true love
And not to be, as a falling tree
That is alone, with only a life of poetry

Old now I write, these words of fear
And again I feel, a silent tear
Alone I think of a falling tree
I once saw in the forest you see!

—James Cotton Estep

TIME IS NOT . . .

The dreamer had a dream
as the nighttime slipped away
She dreamed about her people's lives
and why they couldn't stay
The timepiece on the mantel
told the truth of life unkind
As their faces swam before her
time was not, time was blind
She looked down at the ancient cross
she wore upon her breast
And silently walked down the road
the one she knew the best
The road to end came nearer
her burden slowly dropped
The timepiece gave one last tick
the proof that time is not
She'd carried all the burdens
an earthly mortal could endure
As He gently closed the book of life
the time for them, no more . . . .

—Michele Snyder Bock

A VIEW FROM MY WINDOW

As I gaze out my kitchen window
And watch the children at play
There comes to my mind a nostalgia
That does not go away

We moved to this house in the springtime
When our only child was a boy
For these many years we've lived here
The view from our window is a joy

The sight to the North is Woman's Club Park
A project we worked hard and long
To its few members it seemed hopeless
But how could we go wrong.

The memorial trees were planted
And terraces were made in the hill
To accommodate hundreds of people
Who came to enjoy the hill

The concerts and plays still continue
And all in the town do share
Our hopes and our dreams developed
For Colfax Woman's Club who care.

—Velma N. Cleveland

THE THINGS GOD PLANNED

When we see a housefly (yuck)
  We know that spring is here,
And though we hate the pesky things
They bring a *moment* of good cheer

For then we know the flowers will come,
And all the birds and bees;
'N butterflies, and things like that,
And green leaves on the trees

The earth will come to life again
Just as the creator planned
And some day it *will* be known,
And appreciated throughout the land!

—"The Rhymester," V. Robinson

THE FIRST ARCHITECT

I was standing at my window
  Looking off into the woods,
When I saw an ancient dwelling place
  Where a being must have stood.

A place not made by man nor beast,
  A place only made by one.
A place where its maker made everything,
  The moon, the stars, the sun.

They say that He made us from animals
  That hop around in the trees.
But I know different about the One
  Who made the apes, bears, and bees.

His name is God Almighty;
  He who made everything come to be,
He who made that ancient place,
  And He who made you and me.

He didn't make us from monkeys
  And He didn't make us unimportant.
He DID make us in His own image,
  And He gave us each a talent.

—David A. Jenkins, Jr., age 13

OUR LOVING GOD

I wonder about our loving God
  Who has stood the test of time,
Who gave to us our big round earth
  And who keeps it all in rhyme;

How he made the night and day
  So we could rest and work and play;
How he made the sun and moon
  To shine to guide us on our way;

How he made the streams and mountains
  To protect us from the storm;
How he gives us minds and wisdom
  To build a house to keep us warm;

How he put the love within our hearts
  For our neighbors all around;
How he gave to us our voices
  To make a joyful sound;

How he lived and died to show us
  How to live and not to sin
And if we are faithful to the end,
  We can spend eternity with him.

For all he has done for me,
I praise his name and thank him. Amen.

—E.L. Grapes

MY FRIEND

Let me tell you about my friend,
  He has promised to be with me until the end.
He guides me and teaches me in every way,
So I will be ready for judgement day.
Not a day goes by that we don't talk,
I've come to depend on Him as my rock.
When trouble and sorrow enter my life,
When sin surrounds me and causes strife,
I call on His name and He always hears,
He's always with me and calms my fears.
Oh the joy and comfort I feel in my heart,
to know that my friend will never depart.
He doesn't ask much and His burden is light,
My friend, have you met Him? His name's Jesus Christ!

—Barbara Whitmore

LOOK ALL AROUND YOU

Look all around you, and you will see,
  That God made this earth for you and for me.
The blue above and the green below,
  The sun, moon, and the stars that are aglow.
Look all around you, and enjoy.

Look all around you, and you will see,
That God made the grasses and the tree,
  The fleet of foot, and the fleet of wing,
Animals large and small, and the birds that sing.
  Look all around you, and enjoy.

Look all around you, and you will see,
  That God made us all equal, you and me.
The miracle of conception begins our life,
  Which can be filled with love, happiness or strife.
Look all around you, and enjoy.

Look all around you, and you will see,
  That God had made plans for you and for me.
But the way we go is up to us,
  To make something of ourselves, and not cause a fuss.
Look all around you, I implore.

—Betty Anne Kopko

TIME TO AWAKEN HUMANITY

Time to Awaken humanity;
  We've been lulled to sleep
By the enemy.

Be not whipped into conformity;
Maintain your faith and
Build your Integrity.

The last days have arrived,
Plagued by drugs, sex, and crime,
Leaving youth deprived.

Now appearing on The Scene,
The political expression, the U.N. god,
As yet unseen.

To determine God's Supremacy,
A final battle will be fought
For all eternity.

Praise belongs to Jehovah God
Who will forever rule
In universal Sovereignty.

Dedicated to the proclaiming of the Divine Name and the coming of God's Kingdom, over the earth, following the battle of Armageddon.

—Betty Manes

A THOUSAND NIGHTS OF LOVE

A thousand nights of love, now I'm alone,
wishing I was back in the comfort of the womb,
instead of constantly yearning for my tomb,
I feel such sorrow I must moan and groan.
Our love was once splendid to see,
never would I have dreamed it could end.
But now you're not even my best friend.
Did our love really die or has it just faded out to sea?
I can't help remembering the days of old,
the many ways we admired each other,
how we walked together on the beach hand in hand,
our love is still as precious to me as silver and gold.
A love I could never feel for another,
so come walk with me as we renew our love like crystals in the sand.
        —Carol Ann Nelson

LOVES RIGHTS

What right does love have to capture the soul of one?
    What right does love have to speak the words to a heart and twist the mind,
and surrender its freedom to sweet words, till all is done?
What right does love give that in even a moment of surrender only to serve
the hunger of need, only to be fulfilled, and to hunger again?
It feeds the challenge of brave men to surrender to its whims . . .
To answer to no one else but the beloved it holds,
till it has a captive mind only to seek fulfillment, to relish the soul.
Who dares to say no to the rights of a fool, totally encompassed to the love
and feverent dual?
No one, because love has a right and answers to no one, seeks only truth in
its journey of the soul.
To be immersed truly in the heart forever,
Capturing a moment embellished by adornment.
        —Cleo Olsen

FOREVER NEVER

As we continue to reach out to each other, in all that we do
    To gain some respect, and remember those who got rained on, too

And, as we come through, many of those lonely a year
Preserving our hope, even when no one seemed near

Keeping our world protected, and even our point of view
Believing, that someone really cares, in all that we do

Persistently carrying on, trusting there may be a lucky star
And, realizing there's a heavenly guidance, from a far

Determined, we stand there trying, not to fall
Knowing there's a love, a divine love, that will conquer all

And, faithfully relying on this warmth, for always and ever
Understanding this eternal strength, and to never say never

Everlasting, when there seems no where else, to turn
Comforting, always teaching, so we're able to learn

Like a butterfly, going where you please, and pleasing where you go
Painting your love, everywhere as our friend, never as our foe

Yes, you're my GOD, my love, my friend, and the truth in my heart
You are in all of my life, from the ending to the very start

From this world of blessings comes your warmth, far beyond the unknown
Giving universal love, we surely are in need of, and may call our own

Thee will truly love you for all my days, until the end of time
As you care for thee, and watch over this world, of yours and mine
        —Bobby

Young, enraged.
   What is so wrong?
Carry on.
Revise the rules, run.
Run from here.
Take some back.
There, hold on.
So little that is yours.
With your child, ready?
Give yourself again.

—Christine Fallon Kraft

the spider

My skull has eight legs
   trapping words
   in a web of hiding,
wrapping them
   neat, to place
on the ceiling
   of a great window
where it is otherwise painful
                        to look at
fermenting
      for later nourishment.

—Joe Camp III

EVERYDAY DEATH

Bloody streams
   slit from the nape
slowly ooze down
the ghastly shape.

A bludgeoned chest
heaves no more.
A dirty knife
is all it bores.

Graying skin
and lurid eyes
slowly close
as Truth dies.

—Jennifer Claghorn

            hands
      tightly balled
            fists
      felt the length
         of my body
            pain
   through every joint
            felt
       tension pulls
   every tendon taut

      grey clouds
         move
   empty stare through
      tightly held
         eyes

      pressure builds
   teeth bear down
     enamel cracks
         grind
         grind

—Kathleen O'Flinn

OLD FORT LARAMIE

The dust of marching feet, impatiently stamping hooves,
   And a by-gone era, lay inconceivably upon the ground.
Echos of commands, bartering wives with crying babes, and
Ribald barroom laughter, long since drifted to the hills.
A herd of buffalo, sounding through the now hollow structures,
Grazed off into the uncharted grasslands of extinction.
A desk, still cluttered with the important events of the day,
Now passed into decades.
Blanket-cloaked Indians, trading skins and dreams.
The lusty laugh of the redman, silenced by time.
Firearms, hanging on the walls and housed in the gun racks,
Holding secret tales of battles, some won — some lost.
Signing treaties, full of empty words and sincere hopes,
Pledging life and honor, upon soon to be forgotten promises.
Forsaken prison cells, cry out in the eerie silence to us,
Speaking of the agonies, hidden on the prairie breeze.
The breathless glimpse into the past,
Of a life we shall never know.

—Debbe Mese

FIGHTING THE FIRE

The sky was a burning red fire.
   The sea had turned to a cauldron of boiling water.
As oxygen dwindled, my lungs became a heat unbearable
and I gasped.
Forests were fluid fires on every side.
Men turned to cannibalistic beasts on a rampage.

There was no escaping the unbelievable heat of the sun
which seemed to rest upon my shoulders.
I was supporting the world and my legs were buckling.
Animals had become the superior race and the trivial
competition of dark and light was no longer.
I longed for something cold, something frozen.

I called out — I wanted to die.
Afterlife of any kind was better than this.
Riots were out of control and governments were powerless.
Men and women set aside their differences—
it was now a fight for survival and not for social status.
They realized only they could save themselves . . . and this world.

They had brought it upon themselves.

—Nicholas Little

NEW AND OLD

   One has no control over who our parents are; where one's birth
place was; or, in what part of the world one's family resides.
One doesn't know beforehand if the place where this "Birth" occurs,
is also the place where its "Future" lays.
The impact of one's "Birth-Tie" lead one's destiny, it is like a cord
that binds and interweaves.

   As a youngster we don't know that feeling of bonding one's
birth-place holds; that by starting over in a "New Country";
adapting to its culture by which-ever means it entails, thinking
one can erase its "Birth-Tie" is to no avail.
The place of "Birth" still retains a strong hold; even if by
becoming a citizen of one's new "Country" the ties can't be cut
between "New and Old."

   Dividing loyalties to both countries keep pulling on each
end, "Memories of Child-hood Years" are relived on its continent.
Through this transfer a feeling has been lost that of "Belonging,"
and it will take time again before establishing a new "Bonding."
It is like living in a "No-Man's-Land," unless one masters its
speech, one's status will stay "New," since its "Mother-Tongue"
with its heavy brogue, lays between the "New and Old."

—Bea Marie Blessing

RAINBOW OF MERCY

There's a rainbow of mercy around the throne of God
There's a rainbow of mercy upon the path my savior trod
Look to the Rainbow at the top of Golgotha's hill
Oh! The rainbow of mercy his love reaches down still

There was a rainbow of mercy around Bethlehem's stall
As the star shone down on Jesus bringing life to one and all
The shepherds and the wise men gladly heeded the call
And followed the rainbow that caught mankind's fall

There was a rainbow of mercy around that precious head
As Jesus called to his friend Lazarus come forth from the dead
And all the little children felt the Rainbow of Love
As Jesus laid hands on them saying by these ye shall be led

There was a rainbow of mercy sent down from God above
As Jesus walked the Journey that his father told him of
Mankind needs a shepherd oh, they have lost their way
Father, send them a rainbow to lead them on lest they stray

—Dixie (Ferrebee) Dawson

THE ULTIMATE ATHLETE

This is for the sports fan and you need to know,
About this player, he's neither fast nor is he slow.
When you see him with the ball, you will yell go, go, Go!
He scored a touchdown over the grave,
He slam dunks the devil with the greatest of ease,
He's the greatest of all time and not hard to please.

Everytime he comes to bat, he hits a home run,
Get on his team and always be number 1.
In tennis, he always serves an ace,
In track, he will win every race.
In golf, he gets a hole in one,
The Heavenly Father is definitely proud of his Son.

God is his manager, Heaven is his home field,
He plays for the Christian Saints with the greatest of appeal.
It's okay to be like Mike, Joe or even Steve,
But for this player all you need to do, all you want to do,
Is, unquestionably give him your heart and believe.

—Edward S. Costley

GARDEN OF ANGUISH

Our life on earth is short with worried brow
As the earth's end grows near we all have a sense of fear
Confusion of mind and battles within, where is all this to end
The homeless the helpless what's to happen to them
We all think it's bad till we've been where they've been
As the children cry from emptiness within
And their mothers look down at their child's soft skin
With tears in their eyes and no shoes for their feet
Nor food to give for the pain that they feel
The days go by and the months just fly
Oh Dear God the children still cry
Our world's in a rush and no one takes the time
To stop and think how blessed is yours and mine
If only we could open our eyes to see
How little it takes to live happily
Instead we walk by with closed eyes
And ears too deaf to hear the children's cry
They live in a garden of anguish for all to see
And if not for the grace of God so could we

—Glenda Horton

A WONDERFUL DREAM

May all the dreams you ever have come true, and may the light of happiness always be with you. May your pains all disappear to let your beautiful face be filled with a smile rather than a tear. May your heart be filled with joy, like a young child with a new Christmas toy. May God guide you in everything that you do, and let's praise the Father after each day is through. May the day come when you and I are as one, and let's praise the Father for his only son. May all the dreams you ever have come true, and may the light of happiness always be with you.

—Michael McBride

IN THE TWINKLING OF AN EYE

In the twinkling of an eye,
In the spur of the night.
Our Lord shall come,
But not to bring fright.
To take us to our Heavenly home,
Where He and I, we both
shall roam.
We shall walk along the streets
of gold,
And listen to stories untold.
I long so much to see His
face.
So I can thank Him for His
saving grace.
I can't wait to go forward,
So I can hear Him say, "My child
Look around you for great is
your reward."

—Leslie Fitzgerald, age 13

SANDS OF TIME

The one who hums the lullabye
Is pretty important, you know,
For destinies of the world
Are made by what they bestow!

The one who guides the child,
Through the formative years,
Is shaping events of tomorrow
For good — or for things to fear.

The one who steers the young person
Will be a deciding force
For what that young person becomes,
When it's done — there is no recourse.

The "Ones" I'm speaking of
Are the mothers across the land,
They have such a responsibility
That God has to lend a hand!

So it's only by diligent study,
As we take His Word line by line,
Can we expect to make an impression
On the drifting Sands of Time!

—Juanita V. Frey

ONLY PEACE FOR THE MOMENT

It was a very tender time, I looked on
    your face and smiled

You touched my lips with the soft tips
    of your fingers
The lilac blooming outside the window
    Its strong sweet smell settling
    over the sweat of our bodies

I heard your heart beating faster
    than mine
    though more softly

Your full breasts rising and falling
    in quick measure
Our energy spent for the moment,
Only peace for the moment.

        —Art Baker

LOVE

Love is a mysterious thing.
    Do you know the definition?
Well I don't think that anyone does.
Because if they did, it would be obvious to us.
    The world would be a different place.
A happy face, to guide us from place to place.
      There is one person,
      There is one soul,
Who loves the world as one whole.
Who shows love through his grace,
And through his beautiful human face.
      Can you guess who this is?
        God,
      That is the answer.
        God is love, love is God.
      The two can't be separated.
God died on a cross for our sins.
    Can you think of anyone?
Who would do something like that,
       For you.

      —Cheryse Cacia, age 13

THE PASSION CRY

We know not how God's gifted Touch
    Is passion's foil to pierce the heart:
Fierce is Love's immortal toil, yet
    With no clear reason from Above
To disclaim passion's haunting fear —
    Rising not as One is the pain!

Is it insane in Grand Design
    That we entwine? Such mood is not
Of substance thought, but of the Soul!
    In Heaven's sight the Truth in Love
Decries love's lies (a Sacred rite)
    As pristine dew in sunlight dies.

We know the deep, stark thirst of earth
    Parched of rain; the dearth of prayer
In Love's release from selfish pain;
    The throat is dry and eyes bedimmed,
While deep within "The Passion Cry"
    Goes unheard — save Love's Guardian.

Yet this Poem, sad of words gainsaid,
    Fleeting and dead, like ghostly birds
Futile flight to the blinding Light,
    Finds Passion's slave down deep inside,
With pain certain beside, while Love —
    Balm of Heart and Soul — dies denied.

      —James Buckner McKinnon

NOVEMBER SONG

He entered my life that one day in November,
that one day I shall always remember.

He came out of nowhere, this man with silver hair,
eyes and smile so kind and sweet. Why had it taken us
so long to meet?

From the onset I felt love fill my heart and knowing
from him I could never be apart. His arms so strong as he
held me tight and his kisses tender as we shared our love
in the moonlight.

My life, once empty and sad, had blossomed like the
beautiful rose, and happiness filled me as only I could
know. I marveled at this gift of love and asked, "Is this
a gift from Above?"

Perhaps we were the two ships passing quietly in the
night, trying to find our way. But now our lonely nights
had turned to sun filled days.

The final chapter is yet to be played and before the
last curtain falls, there is always one thing that I will
recall. Let the romantics have their June and Decembers,
but we will forever have our NOVEMBERS!

*Dedicated to my husband, Vince Arena, who made me
believe in myself and to never give up . . . .*

      —Susan Arena

EXPRESS

Some think it's easy and others think it's hard,
    to say a few words straight from the heart.
Express yourself and show that you care,
    and to let them know that you'll always be there.

No one said that life is fair,
    and it's okay to sometimes be scared.
To express your love and gratitude,
    will ease life's worries for me and you!

It doesn't matter what people say,
    we all need a friend day after day.
We need someone to hold our hand,
    someone who will listen and who understands.

If you need to cry don't bottle it up,
    and whatever comes along don't give up.
If you need a shoulder you can lean on mine,
    it is strong but yet divine.

Who knows what trials life will bring,
    who knows what song you will sing.
But may it be a happy tune,
    for this is what I wish for you.

To express ourselves it's a nature of life,
    may it be friend to friend or husband to wife.
To show our feelings which lie so true,
    to express that feeling that someone loves you.

One day we will be apart,
    maybe in distance but never in heart.
Wherever you go and whatever you do,
    always keep in touch because I LOVE YOU!

*Dedicated to Mary whom I admire and respect. May our
friendship last many years. Hold on to the memories
but always look ahead for many more. May God Bless
You! I LOVE YOU! Love Always, Marie.*

      —Marie C. Puggi

MUSIC

From the clear air it floats freely
over the horizon. In all its orchestral
order it brings joy to all who hear it.
A smile crosses the face of a conductor as he
leads the instruments all in a line. And
presto the instruments come to life—no longer
are they silent—but ring out with sincerity and a
calm that is unnerving and at the same time exciting.
Good food, good friends, good books and good music—
such are the joys of life. What more could a person
ask for.

—**Steve Schneider**

The time of our life goes so fleetingly fast.
You try to capture your every thought.
When you think of the future it becomes the past.
And when it's the past you've fought and lost.
Time is so precious and so short.
We take it for granted and let it fly.
Our children grow up and go away.
We wonder where those babies strayed.
Our little ones,
Our big ones,
Our big ones, little ones.
You never lose those thoughts.
You just put them away in storage
to pass on to caring listeners.
Someone finds your life as a long hard road,
just a short memory.
Memories to you that last a lifetime,
but that time has not taken away.

—**Cheryl Record**

A TIME GONE BY

TV's stereos, and Nintendo games,
what happened to the old days
when kids rode bicycles, played baseball,
and had toy trains?

The days when men were known as Mister,
and women were called ma'am.
Now everyone is a homeboy,
a dude, or a man.

Life used to be much simpler,
safer, and sane.
Drugs weren't on every corner,
causing sorrow and pain.

A time when children got high
by climbing a tree.
A time when little girls played with dolls,
and little boys skinned their knees.

What happened to families spending time together,
People getting married, and staying that way forever?
What happened to the days of morals,
ethics, and manners?
Friday night football games, cheerleaders,
and banners?

The more we move ahead
the more we should look at the past.
Remember the simple things,
because they're the things that last.

—**Dale South**

PRECIOUS MEMORIES

The thought of looking back
into the years, bringing tears
into my eyes. Thought of my
Grandmother, who's loving and kind;
my Grandfather too.
The thought of the times, I would
run to my grandmother's arms,
everytime I am scared.
She gives me so much comfort
and grandfather makes me smile
Grandparents are the special
company to share your happiness.
Those are the precious memories,
I will always cherish in my
heart forever.

—**Valerie Keesee**

PICTURES IN THE HEART

Pictures in the heart
are best of all, I think
There is a feel about them — a depth
It is as if you had found
the magic way
and stepped inside a painting
and had become a part of it.
The way you wished you might
when you were small!

A landscape on a wall
may stimulate a dream,
or resurrect some memories,
but no matter how beautiful
a canvas fades or worse
even ceases to be seen
becomes a lovely bit of furniture.

Pictures in the heart vibrate
with life — are ever fresh.
Pictures in the heart
are best of all, I think.

—**Frances McCarthy Moran**

REMINISCING

Past events make lasting impressions
Sinking deeply within: Some we like
To recall to mind as they are truly
One of a kind.

Some folks call this nostalgia since
They lie dormant like Father Time:
The good old days are long gone but
Pleasant memories live on.

The past is over yet new fields lie
Ready to explore: This gives an
Added zeal and helps us to get in on
The ground floor.

Let us learn to put our dreams, our
Fresh ideas into affirmative action,
Lest we get caught in a whirlpool or
Vacuum.

Visualize the complete puzzle coming
Into a clearer focus: This will clear
The path of objects that might even
Choke us!

—**Melvin Manwarring**

OUTSIDE LOOKING IN

On a cold rainy night
        A stranger walks the land
                Eyes filled with hunger
A constant quiver in his hand
Searching for a place to rest
        He is becoming tired and very weak
                Step by step he moves along
As his bones begin to creak
                He wanders about the night
        Not knowing where he has been
For he, will always be
        On the Outside Looking In.

—Christina Marie

STREET LIFE

Living my life day to day
    Not knowing what's going to happen
In a life of wonder and mystery
Having to take care of myself
No parents no rules
Every other kid's dream
Out here in the real world
It's not a dream
It's a nightmare
Selling drugs, getting drunk,
Getting high
Is that the way I want to die?

—Rosey Anzures, age 13

A LONELY BOY

A lonely boy,
Under the weeping willow sits.
His thoughts,
Gone with the breeze.
His heart,
Filled with sorrow,
Gives way to an unchallenged symphony
Of tears.
They do but glisten,
Upon his cheek.
His eyes reddened,
With emotional exhaustion.
His soul,
Leaving him.

—James Sacco

KING OF DRUGS

I've been here and I've been there
I've made bums out of millionaires
I'll take your last dollar or even your dimes
I'll take all your diamonds and mess up
your mind
I'll take your new car and even your house
And before I am done, you'll end up as a louse
If you just try me once, you'll see what
I mean
You can't do without me
You'll yell and you'll scream
You'll do anything to get rid of the pain
You can't do without me
My name is Cocaine
Try me just once and your ears will ring
For when it comes to drugs, I am the King

—Betty J. Barnhart

HOMELESS

Newspaper-boxes
    Trying to keep warm.
Underneath it all there's someone who's torn.
Torn from their family, their life, their home.
But no one knows why, could it be they want to
live there under that old tree in the cold and
dead of night.
Could it be they are with no care because the
street is home, and so is that can over there.
Is this the deal, all there is, garbage for a
meal?
Life isn't fair, do they need help?
No One Cares!
People walk slowly, slowly to stare
but walk fast when they start to ask,
Ask for what?
For Life.
It's Not Fair!

—Jessica Kleine

WHERE ARE THEY SLEEPING TONIGHT?

They are sleeping tonight,
    if they are fortunate,
in the shelter.

But most are not fortunate, most are forgotten
and tonight they sleep in the city's cracks.

They are drawn to the railroad tracks
and the dark areas beneath the overpasses.
They sleep beneath a tarp of plastic, a sheet of plywood.
They sleep alone, alone in a loneliness so deep . . . .

They are drawn to the railroad tracks, the overpasses,
the alleyways.
They dress in olive drab of a war they'd rather forget.
They dress in castaway clothing
they picked from dumpsters.

Tonight they sleep in the dirt
with the city's feral cats
beneath the overhang of the parking terrace.
Tonight they sleep barefoot and in fetal.

—JCD

HOMELESS

As I pull up to the traffic light
    He's stationed there again;
Standing guard on his precious corner,
Holding his cardboard sign.
"Will work for food" the scribble reads
In faded running print.
A path worn thin from pacing
On his chosen battle line.

What has he done to come to this?
What have we done to him?
Should I feel pity for his plight,
Or should I just drive on?
Perhaps tomorrow, if he's still there,
I'll roll down my window and offer him boon.
Or maybe I'll call in a pledge for his cause
If they hold another telethon.

I strain not to capture the tear in his eye.
I'd speak, but what could I say?
And just before guilt gets the better of me,
The light changes. I drive away.

—Dennis S. Martin

INTIMIDATION

Cast out "Intimidation!" It's broad — it's deep — it's high
Like a mighty crushing meteor from God's eternal sky!
All self esteem or ego are clearly, washed away —
As showers wash the hillside, in the merry month of May!

Lives grow so very lonely; Lord, let them rise again,
And lift that heavy footprint from the soul of every man!
May the spirit not be trampled by careless acts or words
That pierce the body's armor like sharp two-edged swords!

In all of God's creation, no one's perfect, no not one!
All different — but so equal! This battle must be won!
The curse, "Intimidation," can no longer wield its power,
Flow the "milk of human kindness" across each darkened hour!

—Edith P. Aase

THE TRAIL OF MEMORIES

Down the trail of memories I'd like to go again
to wander back across the years and be a child as then
I'd see my father in the field, I'd smell the new cut hay
see Mama in the garden, her bonnet bright and gay

We never had much money, our clothes were hand-me-downs
our toys were mostly make-believe, we seldom got to town
our school a country schoolhouse, we learned our A B C's
Now its windows are boarded over, the playground full of weeds

Now the family circle's broken three have gone to rest
Father, Mother and brother, their memories are blest
The old house still stands on the hill, the valley green below
The mountains stand so stately, with veils of winter snow.

If only we could go again down that trail of memories
relive our happy childhood, happy we would be
Now most of us are married, with families of our own
We tell our children stories of childhood days at home.

—Doris Moore

AM I ANY WISER

Am I any wiser than I was in years now past?
Have I grown from any lessons, and will the knowledge last?
Is the world a better place because I've been a part
of all the many people that lighten another's heart?
Could I give just a little more to help some others see
That whatever I give to others will all come back to me?
Yes I AM now wiser than I was as just a kid,
For all the things I dared to do, and More for the things I did.
Experience taught me many things then showed me how to see
The More I do for others, the More I give to Me.

Life is just as we Live it, we get what we Create,
We each have the Power, it's not just someone's Fate.
So if you've been unhappy perhaps it's time to see
That YOU create your moments by what you "Think" to be.

Knowing that your thoughts Create whatever you Expect,
Start "thinking" what you really want, No longer just neglect.
For every thought you entertain will surely come to Pass,
I know you are much wiser now, your Power acknowledged at Last.
POWER is your Energy that comes from deep within,
The same POWER that's in each of us through the very end.
So use your words Wisely, and KNOW that you Create,
Become AWARE of Who You Are, It's never just by Fate.

*Dedicated to my spirit guides and masters,
to all whose lives have enlightened mine,
and my parents for their special love.*

—Velma M. Smith

MEET TOMORROW

If I could follow my life back,
to the beginning, erase the past
I would simply, not ever be,
for all my past, has made me, me.

If I could just erase the pain
find a way to stop the rain,
I would simply not exist,
for life is not a gentle mist.

So in this life, of black and blue,
although I'd not of chosen it for you,
it's there my strengths can be found,
were only I can turn it around.

For this life has taught me well,
tomorrow may not present this hell.
Tomorrow may be the brightest yet,
for only tomorrow, I've not met.

—Cindy Squeglia

BLANK PAGES

Blank pages.
    White
        on white
            on white . . . .

Blank pages,
    with the ghosts of words,
        A hint of meaning,
            Oblique negativity.

Blank pages,
    with no past.
        no present.
            future?

Blank pages.
    White
        on white
            on white . . . .

—Steven Singer

FOR THE MOMENT

Today was a dream I
    had tomorrow
It wasn't happy, sad
or full of sorrow

I gazed upon myself
watching the many footsteps
turn into miles
In disbelief at the many
fading smiles

I listened to the seconds
disappear, forever to be
no more
I heard their slow thumping
rhythm march away into timeless
shores

Tomorrow I dreamed of
today
Into nothingness it became
another yesterday

—Genee' Renee'

THUNDERSTORM

The anger of the Gods is reaching out to me.
   Stabbing, flashing, the jagged, ragged fingers
   of fire punctuate the cries of anguish.
The deep, rumbling outbursts of rage and pain roll
   out from the heavens in defiance against the
   injustices and inhumanity in the world.
A show of incredible strength as an ancient Greek
   warrior might beat upon his breast and cry to
   the world with a mighty roar, "Alala, Alala!"
Then comes the celestial cleansing.
The flood of rain to ease and soothe and purify.
It freshens and renews the earth and the spirit.
It brings me alive again with restored courage
   and awakens new hope within my breast.
"Come! Come, O mighty storm!
Arrest my attention with your mighty roar.
Illumine my soul with your flashing light.
Wash away my bitterness with your cleansing tears.
Welcome! A thousand times, welcome!"

—Peggy Garrett

FEBRUARY ROSES

Because I forgot to prune the roses in our yard
ice now covers thick yellowed stems and snow-tipped,
withered leaves wait to fall when wind gusts blow
around the porch. I can no longer see the black petals;
they have fallen from spiked stations and become part
of the sandy soil. In the spring, they will nourish
new roses, similar to the ones I cut for you last
summer. Soft, smooth, sweet-smelling roses I placed in
water-filled, crystal bowls. The more I cut the more
they bloomed — yellow, peach and blood-red. Last
September, if I had cut away the excess growth,
clipped the heavy, green branches to their base,
the bushes would have become stronger. Now, their
decaying remains remind me of my neglect; their
thorns prod my conscience. In several weeks, the
older, yellowed stems will vie with younger, pale-red
ones for space and solace in the sandy soil. If I had
just remembered to prune the roses, I wouldn't have to
tell you how sorry I am.

—Jennifer S. Pickering

THE SEASONS OF POWER

The flowers sprout from the floor,
   and the Seven Sisters finally open their door.
The three bears have just begun breakfast,
and a girl removes her hearts cast.
   By God's grace, he is born.

The stablehouse just shed its light,
and sent His bird into flight.
For until its migration into fall,
he must be taught to crawl.
   By God's grace, he will live.

The trees have started to share their tears,
and their thoughts are overcome with fears.
Fears of his unfortunate death and pain,
fears of the impending rain.
   By God's grace, he lives.

The people have boarded their homes and moved away,
and the birds no longer come out to play.
The Devil has just shed his skin,
We cannot let him win.
   By God's grace, he dies, and we begin.

—Jason Hollingsworth

OCEANS

Calm, becalmed, roaring, roiled
   These are my attributes, driven and drawn
Destroyer of soils, driver of sails
Frothy and furious, shorelines beware
New bars? How curious! These are my wares
Of food and of life
I started the chain
So guard me with strife
Lest all be in vain.
From plankton to whales
One cell to the mammoth
I nourish the fathoms
With food for the famished.
Of saline are we
Evolved from the sea
But care not enough
And alas, will we be?

—Robert E. Steinkraus

OCEAN REFLECTIONS

I sit quietly on the shore,
   Watching waves roll in from the sea,
As I breathe-in, the ocean,
   I feel it become a part of me.
The ocean is calm,
   Like myself in the sand,
We are not so very different . . .
   The ocean out there, me on the land.
We both experience changes —
   Sunny and cloudy days,
On the ocean and in life,
   One must learn to ride the waves.
The ocean has long been a mystery,
   The unknown is what we fear . . .
Yet, when we drink of the ocean's water,
   It cleanses us, upon shedding a tear.
We are all one with the universe,
   We are one another's friend,
We need only to reach for creation,
   To have love until the end.

—Jean Hunt

AUTUMN'S AN ARTIST

Golden leaves are rustling
   Enchantments of the fall,
Their voices softly echo
A melancholy call.

Fall's kaleidoscope of beauty
Spins a lovely hue,
Crimson red, tangerine orange,
And a cloud-filled sky of blue.

A wisp of wind and nature dances
To a melody so sweet,
The gardens are decorated with pumpkins
   and gourds —
Special autumntime treats!

The moon appears round and mellow
As it beams such a golden glow,
The earth reveals a glimpse of heaven
When autumn's sent below.

Truly autumn is an artist
With a canvas brushed with color,
For this season shines a masterpiece
Outselling all the others!

—Linda C. Grazulis

THE PAST

I am old and easily neglected
When people forget about me
I feel rejected.
I have no shape
I almost have nothing
Do not get me wrong
I do have something.
Diaries and pictures
Keep me alive
Everyone remembers me
That's how I survive.
I am the only one
I am the last
No one can change me
For I am the past.

—Robyn Temple

DID HE WIN??

The feelings are heart breaking,
the thoughts are painful.
How could he do this?
I can't stop from shaking!

I used to think he used to care.
He used me, he lied, it hurt
so bad it isn't fair!

I used to sit up on his lap,
and he would act so kind,
Now it turns my stomach.
because I know now, what must
have gone through his filthy mind!

He is gone, but he has not left,
He is in my bad dreams, he is
in every dark room, in every closet
door, and in every shadow,
He took my childhood.
He might be gone, but *sometimes*
I think he has won!

—Eileen Leigh Clifford

LISTEN

Listen —
can you hear the soft
cry of sadness?
It's the unheard cry
of a mother's love.
The love, that a child
has forgotten.
As time goes by, with
no signs of caring,
The mother's cries gets
softer and less often.
But as the days of Christmas,
birthdays and Mother's
Days go by,
And the child does not
show remembrance,
The tears flow, and the
heart dies a little more.
For the mother doesn't
understand, why is she
Forgotten!

—Donna Brennan

THE BALD-HEADED DOLL

There once was a neglected little doll, without a strand of hair,
Whose home was the remote bottom corner of a toy box.
She was so much alone and friendless, way off down in there,
Since that fateful day that she began to lose her curly locks.

She was seldom ever played with, because of her handicap,
Until an ailing little girl found her lying there one day,
Picked her up and washed her dirty face, and held her in her lap,
For she likewise was bald, and had no one with whom to play.

All the little doll needed was a loving girl to be her mother,
While the cancer-stricken girl needed a miracle from above.
The doll's face began to glow, from a strange light up above her,
And reflected its healing light onto the little girl, with love.

There was a small portion of God in that little lifeless toy,
And a heart full of love in that sickly lonely little girl.
Love and God can work together, to fill a toy box with joy,
So therefore, that little girl's hair is now long enough to curl.

—E. Don Taylor

FLEETING SOLITUDE

Departure from modern civilization is essential,
for I must truly attempt to find myself;
to be alone in my inner sanctum, to contemplate.
I yearn for the pristine tranquility of the woods.
I go there.
It is a grey autumn day, ideal for the mood.
The serenity of the forest is as I had hoped,
maybe though too still, almost lifeless.
I perch on a lichen covered boulder,
basking in the vibrancy of the fall colors.
I try to ponder the future.
I try for hours, it is difficult,
for I am unaware that I'm inadvertently reflecting on the past.
Suddenly an eagle alights upon a lonesome pine.
I revel in the purity of its freedom.
He is there but for a swift moment, then gone.
I watch him slowly dissipate from view.
I then realize I had not achieved total solitude this day,
but had merely delayed it for perhaps another time and place.

—Sean Gaudet

TIGER'S HEART

There's a Tiger here, watching and waiting
time spent with stuffed animals, can't come home, debating
Love and loneliness, with music that's sad
Listening, loving, standing, pacing, just feeling bad

So empty here, curtains drawn
All waiting for you, knowing you're gone
Lonely rooms, empty chairs
My aching heart filled with despair

Empty swings, blowing to and fro
Strawberries unpicked, flowers won't grow
And they sing softly, their lonely serenade
Where laughter and blonde haired love once played

Bacon, eggs and toast on Sunday morn
Cereal crunchin', milk on her chin
Where love of life is born
Without beginning or end

And I believe the Tiger's heart is mending
Because love is what sets us free
We all need happy endings
The Tiger, little girl, and me.

—Keith W. Lindberg

BLACK WOMAN

Guilt's tenacious, and grasping fingers seek to wrap around my brain, to hold me down, and keep me in the past! But my mind will have none of it. My heart beating strong, and loud in my ears strains ever forward. The dark memories, of poverty and ignorance sit like a heavy weight upon my confidence, and determination. I know what Atlas must have felt, as he bore the weight of the world upon his shoulders. My mind, ravenous for knowledge, and light repulses the darkness, and strides onwards, and upwards. No longer willing to be coddled, as a babe in arms is lulled to sleep, by an ageless lullabye. My mind has seen a glimpse of the truth, and the light, and will not be stayed. My skin is black, but will no longer remain satisfied, by the narrow barriers the world has set for it. My eyes are brown, yet today they are able to see the silver lining in the dark clouds. My feet are tired, but determined to cross the finish line, into true freedom. My people are repressed, yet we will continue to do what we do best, that is overcome! I come from deep roots. Strong, and mysterious am I. Know me world for who I am. I am multi-layered, a sister, mother, aunt, and grandmother, salt of the earth, and bright shining light. I am black woman.

—Blondie Louise Wells

SURVIVAL

She was like a seed buried deep down in the earth,
Similar to the others yet maintaining her own worth.

The seed pushed through the ground for all the world to see,
As she began to form into the person she would be.

Like the rain had fed the seed giving birth unto the flower,
The circumstances of her life had built esteem and power.

As the hail beat down the flower and we saw its petals fold,
Life's misfortunes beat her down, her heart grew hard and cold.

The flower's life began to fade, the weather took its toll.
Anger halted any growth, resentment took control.

Piercing through the mist like the sun tow'ring high,
He would not allow her heart to wither away and die.

The sun's healing warmth revived the flower's earth.
He helped her see her strengths and reaffirmed her of her worth.

Standing tall and blooming like the flower on the plain,
She now can see reality and smiles once again.

—Kayleen Crabtree

VIVA LA RAZA!

Be proud of who and what you are. Papà always used to say. And never, hijita let your heart go astray.

"Viva la Raza!" He always used to scream. It all seems as if it were just yesterday. As I reminisce the horrid, everlasting dream.

The covetous coyote promised papà a better way. Somehow, he never saw the light of day.

I'll see you and your mamà soon, he once wrote. But it was the last I heard from him. So may I quote, "Viva la Raza!"

For the bravest man I know, my papà. Whose search for a better way of living cost him his life. If he could only see the proud woman I've become. Taking great pride in my culture and in all that I've done.

Prosperity, how sweet the sound. Lured my papà, now he is homeward bound. God forgive us from all prejudice, I pray.

Yet, I am not ashamed to say, there is only one difference, that's on the out, which is color and shouldn't count.

My color is beauty, my color is tan. And if any prejudice being wishes to comment on that note, with no knowledge of who I am, with all due respect, here is a famous quote — "Frankly my dear, I don't give a damn!"

—Sandra E. Medel

COLORS

Purple hills in smoky haze
Violet dolls with endless gaze
Silent clouds in fiery skies
Scarlet saints with reddened eyes
Golden sun in orange sunset
Amber streams from silver jet
White capped waves in bright blue wake
Speeding boats in turquoise lake
Dark green frogs in murky pool
Thoughtless men in endless duel
To destroy and not redeem
A colorful world, a rainbow dream

—Irene E. Senkiw

SPRINGTIME DEPARTURE

The sun
At first so shy
Scatters its light
Coating the earth
Of a peaceful rebirth.
But I am still stunned
By an incredible blow.
And its repercussion will follow.

The birds, warm,
Peep in alarm.
I think of the trees
And their burgeoning;
What a bad time to go.
Choice is not to be our'
But turns these moments into horror.
When it please' the Supreme Being
How drastic the adjusting.

Life imperturbable
Continues its babble.
How bitter
This tasteless sever.

—Jacqueline Ruette-Radke

MY HOME TOWN WARSAW, NORTH CAROLINA

Deep down in the heart of Dixie
lies a small little town.
A railroad is in the middle
and the streets go up and down.

Everyone's so friendly
they smile and say
"A pretty day isn't it?"
and "How are you today?"

You can tell they really mean it
by the smile on their face
And that's the way we live
in Warsaw — a truly great place!

Both young and old
are a pleasure to meet
Even the pleasant cops
who walk our streets.

We have recreation for the kids
and fellowship for the old
In our town, our wonderful little town,
We have much to behold.

—Annie Marie Grady

STARS

Have you ever gazed up at a star?
and wished you could fly to places afar?
A fantasy world, you could disappear,
no problems, no heartaches, no sorrows here!
I gaze out at stars in space, and wish
I were there, in that far away place.
I'd soar above eagles, free as a dove,
And touch that elusive, everlasting love!
I'd leave all this pain and fear behind,
I'd be that star I've been searching
To find!

Dedicated to the memory of Clovis L. Branum,
my grandfather, who passed away in November of 1991.

—Dianne Michelle

RAINY DAY

Rainy Day
Water beating on my
window . . . Falling gently on my
hands and face . . . making puddles in
the road . . . Cars splashing the little flowers in
the garden. I can see the water flowing down the
street, melting all the snow. It is watering the
flowers and trees for me. It is fun
playing games inside while it
is getting everything
wet!

—Rachael Goetz

THE TORNADO

Entering on the wings of thunderstorms,
Violet winds roll in;
Cylinder-shaped clouds begin to form,
And the wind begins to spin.

It's not known exactly why they start,
Or exactly where they'll go;
The swirling winds put fear into our hearts,
And perform a destructive show.

The roar of the wind sounds like a runaway train,
And the rain begins to flow;
The wind picked up a house down the lane,
The storm, the wind, the tornado.

—William J. Briggs

THE HURRICANE

The four winds did meet at the ocean's wet floor
and turned and churned into a watery war
The wind gods were angry at this point in space
and decided with each other to make it a race

They fought and fought all things being theirs
and lost their tempers like bee stung bears
They chased each other around a complete calm center
and struck blows of lightning while bellowing thunder

They moved as one from place to place
their battleground being laid to waste
The storm cries out the wind gods' anger
and brings to men a sense of danger

The tears of the storm flood the green earth
and cleanse away the old black dirt
The storm alone destroyed my home
and I cry out, "to what god do I belong?!"

—Allan H. Lambert

FATHER! MOTHER! LET ME LIVE!

The choice is mine! Let me live!
I cry from within my mother's womb.
You have no right to turn my bed
Into a bloody tomb!

I cannot live outside this place
That God prepared just for me to live each day,
And I could not choose another home!
So for the time appointed, please! Let me stay?

When time has come and I enter your world,
You will be proud, just wait and see.
I promise you, you'll never regret
That you choose life, and let me be.

I'll grow up fast before your eyes,
Just be a good example I could follow.
Don't worry Dad! Mom! I'll not disappoint you,
Only let me live today and you won't be sorry tomorrow.

    —Urma Cramer-Luckie

SECRET DESPAIR

Wake up screaming in the night
But the soul inside stays sleeping tight
Night turns into day, after endless day
I begin to spin out of control
My head feels as light as air
The turbulent horror of it confuses me
My senses begin to deceive me
Seeing things that don't exist
Hearing sounds inside the walls that aren't really there
Searching for someone that I can share
The secret of my despair
Robbed of my youth
It is hard to face the truth
To be neglected by my parents
Makes me feel so transparent
It makes me weary
There is nothing quite as scary
It is everlasting agony
To be neglected by my family

    —Phillip Kirschbaum

WHY DIDN'T I HAVE A CHANCE!

Here I am smaller than a teaspoon. I'm getting
Bigger and stronger everyday. But then all of a
sudden the light and warmth was taken away from me
only after three months of love and security.

I don't understand why Mommy didn't want me.
Didn't my mommy love me? Well, today is what
would've been my first birthday. My mommy just
turned seventeen last week. I now know why my
mommy didn't keep me. Her and my daddy were
sixteen years old when they decided that they needed
love and romance in their lives.

When they found out about me, they decided the best
thing to do was get rid of me. I just want them
to know that they can't have me back.
Hopefully their next child will get to live and
have a first birthday. For I wasn't one of the lucky ones.

Why didn't I have a chance?
Why Mommy, why?

*Dedicated to Fronüsch Von Polska
and to all my family with love*

    —Tonya Jo Funk

I am a shark
        fighting for my
life. The people attack me,
leaving me wounded and sad.
I need to be loved right now,
not left alone.
I feel scared and hopeless,
All alone in the dark.
        The last stab,
I'm dead.

    —Adrianne B. Cerceo

TEARS

Tear drops falling off little girls' faces.
    Rolling down sad children's cheeks.
Why have them fall for no one to notice.
    Till it's too late.
The scares
    the hurt
        Never, Never
            to go away.
They may
    fade but
        Never, Never
          will it disappear.

    —Janice F. Bashutsky

LIFE OR ABORTION?

God, the Father of Creation
Sent us to You!
With all His love and care.
But, you cast us from you
Was it hate, fear or despair?

May He forgive you
And give you a new tomorrow
As your heart fills with love and sorrow,
For all you denied us
To live, grow, learn, and to love

As sure as there's a Heaven;
And as sure as the sun shines today;
May you accept the Lord's leaven
And turn to His Ways
Learn His Commandments! *Hold fast* to
    what His Words say.

    —Annabelle Rodebaugh

REALITY?

A tear drops from her face —
A whisper is heard in silence on the wind.
The soothing voice of a mother —
The closeness of a friend.

A rose bleeds —
A clown cries —
A turtle runs —
A child dies.

A man works —
A farmer plants seeds —
A mother screams —
A teen asks for your pleads

Is this imagination —
Is this something that is meant to be?
Tomorrow, today, or the years of the past —
Is this fake, or is it just part of reality?

    —Heather Rose Felker

HAIKU

Fifteen flying birds
  gliding south for the winter
for a vacation.

HAIKU

A very tall tree
  stands alone in a forest
with no leaves on it.

—Steven D. Garner

BEYOND THE STARS

Come fly with me
  beyond the stars.
Forget the past,
just sit back and relax.

We'll fly past Mars,
the sun, and the stars.
We'll be back on earth
way before noon.

The Milky Way
will greet us, too
with falling stars
for me and you.

At the pearly gates
we will meet
to see our friends
and what they seek.

Then it's back to earth
with loving hearts
to tell the world
we've been beyond the stars.

—Kelly Leoni

SISTERS AND BROTHERS

I see you all in my face
when I look in the mirror
Oh, boy it couldn't be any
clearer! There's Kathleen
smiling, Eileen's winking
and Mary's eyes are blinking!

Barbara you're in there too
saying "Oh, it can't be true
that I'm really related to you!"
Seriously, though I'm proud to
say I love you all everyday!!!

Jimmy and John, Tommy
too, how very often I think
of you! You're in the mirror
along with the others and
want you to know how proud
I am that you're my brothers!

I see you all and thank the
Lord that I have you with me
every day even though you're
far away! We're closer than we
could ever be because God made
us part of the same family!!!

Love
Patsy
Aug'92

—Pat Ellis

THE SNOW STORM OF THE CENTURY

March thirteen, nineteen ninety-three,
We had the biggest snow storm of the century.
In the midst of snow came thunder and lightning.
I must admit it was a little frightening.
The winds blew hard through the frozen trees.
The big ones came down from the crackling freeze.
For most of us in the South, it was an uncomfortable hour.
For nine or ten days some were without power.
For so long we've prayed for snow in the South.
Maybe some wished we had hushed our mouths.
Yet, through all of this, some great things were done.
Churches began to do the things that are important to God's Son.
Beautiful things begin to happen when
People begin to share.
It makes it all worthwhile to know someone
Really does care.

—Al Thomas

WHAT IS ADVENT?

What does Advent really mean?—It's the Savior's arrival!
  Angels will sing His glory, and God's chosen will hear His call.
It's preparing for the Lord; a revived heart, mind and soul,
Giving of all diligence in morality and self-control.
It's preparing for God's Kingdom; it's God's good pleasure to give,
It dwells deep within the soul and by the 'fruits' doth live.
It's waiting for the 'True One's' coming; so all to our God, we bring;
Our prayers, praises, and our songs to honor the 'Newborn King.'
The 'lights' are trimmed and shining; reflecting the Heavenly Son,
The 'lights' glow brighter, brighter as God's will is being done!
The gifts are wrapped and waiting—filled with love, joy, faith and peace;
The gifts are all for giving to the Lord for a sure increase!
Remembering God's great gift; God's Everlasting Son!
Trying ever to please him and running the race, He's won!
Advent can be everyday; Christ is, Christ was, Christ is coming again!
"Hosanna!" Christ enters in; revived hearts are rejoicing, then!
This is the Advent message that God's children love to tell,
It's God's gift of salvation; Our Savior, The Lord, Immanuel!

—Carol Ann Ackerman

MY HOME

Today, I took a moment to be alone,
  I said a little prayer for my home;

While on my green carpet, where I laid,
I thanked my Father for what he made;

Staring at the ceiling, a lovely shade of blue,
I asked my Father "What am I to do?"

My family appears to always be in a fight,
and my home is being destroyed left and right.

My home has a roof, to protect my family from harmful rays,
which is currently being destroyed by our irresponsible ways;

A growing number of my family is dying from diseases on the spread
no cures have been found for these epidemics that rank far ahead

Some of my family don't have money for food,
while the wealthy look down on them, with a bad attitude;

Please answer my family's worrisome sobs
and provide them all with good paying jobs;

Help my family get along with one another,
even though they are all of a different color;

Father, protect the place I've called home since birth,
so I can look forward to tomorrow, at my home, called Earth.

—KariLyn J. Dolezal

HAVE COMFORT

No matter what happens, we're never alone,
There's someone who's always near;
And whene'er we need HIM, we can call out HIS name,
Where'er we may be, HE will hear!

We know who HE is, HIS name's JESUS CHRIST:
HE's our Saviour—what more can we say?
HE's an omnipresent Spirit—hence always around,
HE's only a prayer away!

—Jack G. Robb

MY PRECIOUS CHILD

My Precious, Precious child nothing is wrong,
I Loved you then, I Love you now
I've always been around.

I have just been waiting for you to come back home,
For you to just remember, how once I was your song.

But Lord, I'm very weary—my journey's been too long,
For I have failed and I have sinned,
I just can't come back home.

He Answered, In his gentle way I heard him say once more,
My Precious, Precious child I've never been away,
I Loved you then, I Love you now if only you'd believe,
The price I paid long ago on Calvary.

After a brief moment I finally realized,
That He's been here all along, it was I who had gone astray.

So I said, Lord I'm sorry, Forgive me of my sins,
Make me a new creature, I'm coming home again.

My Precious, Precious child never will I leave,
For I am the Son of God and I died to set you free,
I Loved you then, I Love you now throughout Eternity . . . .

Dedicated to Jesus Christ

—**Phyllis Huizenga**

ARE YOU DETERMINED?

Solomon was determined, to build a temple where,
The people could always come, and find God's presence there
He furnished it with gold and jewels, and kept it spotless clean,
And in Solomon's Temple, God's glory was seen.

Are you determined a temple to build?
And with God's Holy Spirit be eternally filled?
You must keep your temple, spotless, shining, clean,
Then in your temple, God's glory will be seen.

They brought into the temple, the beautiful ark of gold,
And all the priests were gathered, singing praises bold
God's glory fell upon them, in that holy place,
And they all fell down on their knees, right before his face.

Are you determined a temple to build?
And with God's Holy Spirit, be eternally filled?
Bring into your temple, God's own holy word
Then in your temple, God's voice will be heard.

You must keep your temple, spotless, shining, clean,
If you want God's glory ever to be seen,
Furnish it with praises, and God's own holy word
Then in your temple, God's voice will be heard.

*Dedicated to my wife, Kimberley, who is truly a helpmate as
God intended. To my son, Miles, a gift from God. But most
of all, the Holy Spirit, the true author of this poem.*

—**James L. Pike**

He looked up at a cloud
And heard a sound, it seemed so
loud.
He didn't know how he could
possibly stay. How?
It seemed like his time, even
though he was only five.
He was lucky to still be alive.
There wasn't anymore pain,
And nothing to gain.
He saw a bright light.
And he thought it just might,
be God.
And soon he knew that he was
right.
He saw some Angels,
And heard some bells.
And then he knew that he could
truly be happy.

—**Michelle L. Sammels**

LIFE IS A GARDEN

Good friends are the flowers,
And times spent together
Life's happiest hours;
And friendship, life flowers,
Blooms ever more fair
When carefully tended
By dear friends who care.

And if you trust your dreaming
Your faith will make it true . . .
And if you listen with your heart
He'll come and talk to you . . . .

If my "borrowed words of truth"
In some way touch your heart,
Then I am deeply thankful
To have had a little part.

In sharing these God given lines
And I hope you'll share them, too,
With family, friends, and loved ones
And all those dear to you.
So life is a garden after all.

—**Donna Rowell**

WISHES

Wishing for your dreams to come true,
When you're feeling sad or blue.
Wish any time, any where,
for anything you desire.
It could be a brown mare,
Or a T.V. extraordinaire,
Though you may not always get your wish,
it's better than being a guppy fish!

—**Melanie I. Gorscak, age 10**

THE DREAM

I dreamed a dream though wide awake,
It sped before my eyes,
It seemed so real like poems we make,
As sad as last good-byes.

The dream was filled with hopes and fears,
But surely they weren't real,
Sometimes crying, sometimes cheers,
As in life we're apt to feel.

Soon morning came, the dream had past,
I heard a soft voice call,
That was your life that passed by so fast,
It was not a dream at all.

—**Norm Veatch**

FANTASIES

In the valley of make-believe
Little gnomes talk to elves.
Realities are nil and void
And dreams are stacked upon the shelves.

Imagination fills the air
And frothy bubbles twitch the eye.
But only for a moment, then
They begin to burst and die.

Dreams are fancy visions
In a world of their own.
The secluded thoughts of one's self
Otherwise not known.

—**Katherine D. Goke**

NEVERLAND

Imagination take me there
to the place where I don't care.
No regard for what the future brings
no possessions, or material things.
Soar up, up to the sky
flying away on a natural high.
Wind through my hair, whisk me away
up to the stars, straight on 'til light
of day.
Touch down on land so very far away
a haven to rest in and just maybe stay.
Pirates and Indians, lost boys and crocks
time seems to stand still,
no tics and no tocs.
In this place that I love between sleep
and awake,
I have no fears and nothing's at stake.
For Peter, the Pan and his famous boys
protect and defend all childhoods' joys.

—**Sindee Karpel**

DREAMS

At times I dream I am a hawk
With eyes of steel and talons poised.
What creatures will I have to stalk
To keep myself alive?

Other times I am a graceful dove
With ivory wings and bodice
Spreading peace from the heavens above
Is the task I must fulfill.

What simple obligations, but of what significance!
And the harmony created is to be admired.
But there are other tasks of equal importance
That we as a union must perform.

—**Becky Wyatt**

LOOK FOR A RAINBOW

I examine all my dreams, my hopes and plans,
Some of them have, eluded my hands,
But what is a person without a dream?
Without mine, I'd surely scream.

For my family, I want the best,
To accomplish such goals, there's no time to rest.
There are roads to travel, hills to climb,
And an end of a rainbow, for us to find.

At the end of my rainbow, I don't expect gold.
As that story is so often told.
It's real happiness, that I seek,
As I move forward, and each challenge meet.

A sense of accomplishment, can be found,
With each challenge met, I'm gaining ground.
Truth and honesty will pave the way.
With it, happiness grown larger each day.

—**Ann Cook**

TO WISH FOR A STAR

Is it such a sin to reach for the stars?
"ONLY"
If you allow the stars you possess to fall
from the palm of your hands . . .
Fall, fall
        deep to the dark bottomless sea
        till the angry waves wash the fallen
        stars as sands of the sea.

Some manage to keep their sheen
While many through the beatings of the
rough sea lose their gleam.

Yet those weather beaten sand crystal stars
that glow are overlooked and neglected . . .

You look up and behold the magnificent sight
The numerous, multitudinous lights
And wish upon a star.

You look down at your feet and see the
numerous glowing sand crystals and step upon them.

Is it a sin to reach for that something that's glowing
up in the sky — that un-reachable star?
When you've got that something glowing at your feet,
Where you can reach it, touch it, hold it in your hands
and give its glow, shine, gleam . . . A VALUE.

Dedicated to my dad Arthur Spenst.
(Best dad in the world.) LA

—**Akasha Ann Spenst**

HELP ME SET AN EXAMPLE

As I lie awake in bed.
To clear the thoughts inside my head.
I struggle to keep my mind sincere.
To the only one above who can hear.
"I repent to you Lord, for my sins and ask for
guidance once again.
Help others come seek, your powerful love that's
so unique.
Keep me strong from defeat or surrender.
To Satan's corruption, and look to you, the redeemer.
Keep me on the right track.
And forgive me Lord, when I doubt and look back.
When my problems become too hard to handle.
Remind me Lord, to look to you and set an example."

—Patti J. Brogden

INDEED THIS IS WISDOM

Wisdom knows beyond the moment,
Wisdom gardens with seasons of thyme,
Wisdom plants with the sight the Lord gives them,
When life's storms make our vision near blind.

Wisdom hears the thoughts of others,
Their burdens and their fears,
Wisdom moves the heart to touch them
Wise hands, wipe up . . . fallen tears.

Wisdom wears the gentle smile,
That speaks without a sound
It's the glance of understanding
Where journey's friendships are often found.

Wisdom feels the peace of knowing,
The savior at their side,
It's the song that's softly singing,
Heaven's hymns dwell deep inside.

Wisdom extends the touch of loving,
When the foe has trodden down,
When the crippled heart stops beating,
When God's love, unlocks the bound.

—Patricia Jane Elliott

TIME AND ETERNITY

Time nourishes the essence of our existence
for which the populace searches in vain.
Time alone holds in its hand the life originally
planned.
It has no beginning nor does it end,
time is the mystical legend.
Time is the chrysalis of eternity, and therefore
time, as such, is an incomplete concept in itself,
full of possibilities which the mind of man cannot foresee.
It consists of parts only, such as seconds, minutes, days,
years, and thus it can be no part of infinite duration
or of eternity. For then there would be an infinite
duration as eternity cannot be split into parts. It is
one, just as God is one.
Time and times as conceived by the mind of man stand
never still, but are the perpetual flux, running, creeping
or trodding, rolling along like a river travels at various
speeds towards its destination. But eternity does not
move, it is still, like God, who is everywhere at one and
the same time, is still and has no need to move. Moreover
it cannot be said that time actually moves, everything
moves or stands still within it and only in this respect
can we find a connection between time and eternity.

—Leopoldine Fink

REASSURANCE

No greater peace has this land known
No deeper love to man has been shown
The finest gifts are given free
Forgiveness and mercy for you and for me.
The price is high
And some will never pay
But many are promised a glorious day.
To those that believe with all their might
The battle will be won in a single fight.
Some will lose the promises given
The rest of us will live in heaven!
For we gave our lives to Christ the King
And became His bride without a ring.

—Deborah A. Shupe

A CHRISTMAS POEM

At Christmas time we celebrate
God's gift of Salvation great,
He sent to earth His Son, Beloved
To open the gate of Heaven above.

God's Salvation lay in stable bed,
Born of a virgin as prophets said.
From His home in Heaven He came,
Men to rescue in His dear name.

Christ was born that He might die,
The price of our souls to buy.
On the cross in agony hung,
For all sin since time begun.

On the cross His life He gave.
He came to earth our souls to save.
He loved so much He gave His all
That we one day would heed His call.

He promised one day to come again,
To catch up those who trusted Him.
When we hear His trumpet sound,
Rejoicing we'll be Heaven bound.

—Clyde H. Woodward

POWER FROM THE THRONE

It's not the needs of our lives
that unlock heaven's gates,
nor the desires of our hearts
that tend to vacillate.
But the spoken word to the Father
as we bow on our knees,
and the openness of our hearts
filled with humility.
It's not the pleading,
or the bargaining across God's table,
It's not the promises we deliver
that makes God able.
It's not the Word that we have spoken
nor the deeds that we have done,
but the heart that will respond
to the pleading of His Son.
It's not the challenge, or the goal,
or the dreams we seek to claim,
though our heart's desires He recognizes,
when we seek it not in vain.
It's not the trial we encounter
that brings a miracle to his own,
but our eyes off the circumstance,
stayed on Jesus,
that brings the power from the throne.

—Sheila Moore

THE BEAST

Eight years to go, as one great
prophet has forsaw.
Death and turmoil for all that will
fall.

Mighty kingdoms that barely saw,
mass destruction for man without thought.
Listen and heed to this my sweet children,
climactic wars that will be unleashed.

Unknown to many, but some seem to think,
seven (7) years shall go this one,
upon us the great beast.

—A. Lamarge Hendrix

FOREVER SILENCE

In the black, we can only see gray
As a bird flies across the morning day
A wounded soul looking for an answer
Ever searching to find its master
Knowing that it will never find,
Even in the expanse of time

When it's done, everything fades
The memories can never be erased
If it would die even tomorrow
Would just increase their pain and sorrow
I knew of the love, once of the heart
I knew very well right from the start
At the pond when I looked down
The reflection, even it made me frown
A broken pillar lies across the ground
If there is no ear, there is no sound
Like a leaf blowing in the wind
Our life, slowly begins to dim

Everything has a beginning and an end
So goodbye, my one and only, friend.

—Martin A. Byrnes

BLACK

Black, is the color
of our skin.
It's not dark or black but
it's just a name
people say.
We have feelings just like
whites and everybody
else, but when it
comes right
down to
it,
some people don't have respect
for us. Some of you call us
niggers and things like
that, and then we
want to get
back and
attack
you
for saying that. Black is a color that
is one of a kind. While we're
around try to have
respect for us
and love us
for what
we are and not for our color.

—Rhonda Jackson

THE STARVING SOUL

These lips shift coldly to make the shape
of a far off scream inside me,
lying shapeless and unspoken yet
very much alive.
I struggle to breathe and clutch
at your heavily booted feet that sit so
evenly upon my collapsing chest.
Infinite moments of waiting
searching out your eyes, eyes that speak of walls
imprinted with the words of resistance
I lodged in vain, crumbling to dust
upon your straightened shoulders which you
hold unequal to my life.
And you, smoking a cigarette, hand held to your mouth
attempting to swallow the lies
I know you believe.

—Dominique Menzies

L E A V E S   O F   C O K E

In Miami, locoism injects
The gang! faceless monsters deify screams,
The gory night frames time in blood-red hues,
And mirrored blizzards reflect dry railed snow
Sniffed up glabrous nostrils to the brain
And oblivious there tucks death in leaves
Nestled gravely across America!
A new beginning, or is this the war?
The sickler's white razor scrapes powder lines
By row! striped hyenas siphoned through hose.
In needles alley, two guns draw hot light—
A cop gasps, purple spats graffiti walls—
Justice screams! sirens wake the woeful night,
A radio in a black and white wails with fright,
"Officer Down! MIAMI! Officer Down!"
Grave-side, melancholy drips from her eyes;
Veiled black, wife and mother, fatherless child.
Her quivering lips waft a tear to earth
With a kiss pressed gentle on one red rose—
An eternal souvenir, his keepsake!

Miami.
Miami.

—Robert H. Poulin

A CRISIS IN OUR BLACK COMMUNITY

How can we stay in good health
When we are envious of each other's wealth?
We need to quit thinking of just ourselves—
Before we destroy and kill ourselves
Can't talk to anybody these days
Because some fool is waiting to lead you astray
And it seems like decent black men
Have to watch some fool betray his so called girlfriend
Black women have to watch their backs
Because false witnesses don't keep in "tact"
Nothing but players and subs
Are what most of us are made of
Few of us have the guiding light
That will guide us night after night
No matter how much money we invest in
There is more to life than rejection and corruption
Too much back-stabbing and lying
Is the reason why we're dying
Lord come to our aid quickly
—For *there is* a crisis in our black community—

—Virgo

HE IS MORE

The man of my dreams is much more
than I prayed for.
He is much more than I ever hoped for.
He is a wonderful husband, friend, hero,
and soldier.
I could go on and on.
This man is my husband.
Thank you God for sending him to me.
Had I picked "Mr. Right" all by myself,
I could not have done better.
Help me to appreciate and love him
more every day.
Even though I didn't deserve him You gave
him to me anyway.

—Denise C. Keery

MY LOVE

We started our life on a lark,
And in this world we'd make our mark.
At first we made an unlikely pair,
But we promised to always love and care.

As a couple, we were not the best,
And many times our love was put to test.
Life with you was sometimes a struggle,
But we would always kiss, make up, and snuggle.

I never thought I would face the day,
When you had to go away.
There was pain in my heart and a tear in my eye,
Then it came time to say good-bye.

I've been told that life is not always fair,
And that God does not give us more than we can bear.
I wonder how I can go on without you,
But I must, I have, and I do.

You've been gone for over a year,
And I'm slowly getting over my fear.
But it's you, my love, I still miss,
So this poem is for you, sealed with a kiss.

—Sue Oliver

NOSTALGIC BLUE

Daybreak glows golden through dewy green leaves
and fills me with emptiness.
It's now that I miss you most,
and our mornings by the bay.

Are you watching now,
from your house on the channel,
nuzzling Fanny's purring neck
and nakedly dreaming in the sunrise?

I am with you when I close my eyes:
You smell earthy and sweet,
like the daffodils by the window.
Your olive-oil skin accepts my touch
and our kiss is unbroken as I pull you to the floor.
Sunshine-light and hot,
we make love to the dawn.

We touched lonely hearts with the caress of kindness
and woke honest passion.
But your heart belonged to another
and now he shares your morning kiss,
and now the new sun
turns my heart nostalgic blue.

—BGH

YOU ARE . . .

You are something special
Like the gift given for no reason.
You are the single flower in desert land,
Or the stepping stone in the stream.
You are the sun in the early morning,
And the brightest star in the darkest night.
You are my playmate when I'm happy,
And my protector when I'm frightened.
You are the softest pillow when I cry,
And the rock to give me courage.
You are my only love
But also my best friend.
Most importantly, you are you
And that's why I love you so.

—Jennifer A. LaPointe

IF THE MOON WERE NOT IN YOUR EYES

If the moon were not in your eyes
As a glittering pearl to a child's sight,
Perhaps cries would not be cries at all,
But stories whispered to a compassionate night.

If the moon were not in your eyes,
Blazing all but beauty for one to see,
Perhaps my gaze would turn inward,
To find a winter-soul at rest in me.

But the moon—
The moon has no mercy above;
Like stars,
No glory
Nor story of love

The beauty—
The beauty called from ancient reprise
Would be a thousand times evident
If the moon were not in your eyes.

—Bryan D. Tilt

GAYLE

She sings from another room
And her joy slips through the door
Catching my heart with a touch so sure
of my love
That my hands tremble
Waiting for the sweet, soft silence
of her entrance

Yes, yes, oh, yes, yes, yes
She says to her pleasuring
In the now of her being, treasuring
all my love
As my hands travel
Searching for the sweet, soft silence
of her entrance

She rises, leaving our bed
And, dressing for our morning tea
Taking my soul in her breath-kiss she
moves my love,
With her hands tranquil
Greeting the world with the sweet, soft silence
of her.

—Don Bessette

PRECIOUS MOMENTS

Lifting an old trunk lid
Holding treasures of time
Tears started unforbid
Pictures brought to mind

I must have dozed
Tiny garments on a line
Little ones real not posed
Precious ages of time

Years have slipped away
As times unfold
For all my eon of days
Tears of pearls still lace my soul.

—Blanche E. Evans

THINKING

I get up early every morning
When everyone is still asleep,
I spend this time with something
That is mine to keep.

It is my thoughts of yesterday
And the days to come,
I think of what I should say
And things I should have done.

I think about my family
Who all live far away,
And how nice it would be
If they all came home to stay.

I think of how the world has changed
And the people too,
Why can't we go back to yesterday,
And do what we used to do?

Like Sunday dinners together
Or picnics in the yard,
But with everyone so far away,
It is really hard.

—Joyce McFadden

DREAM AWAY AWHILE

Lay to sleep upon my heart
And dream away awhile
I bring your lips my kisses
I bring them only smiles

I guide you through my passions
They show you so much more
Than the promise of always love
That I swore to you before

Dancing slowly to our song
Your cheek upon my chest
Your other in my palm
Tender kisses all the rest

I'm sowing thoughts of myself
In your spirit, heart, and mind
Dreams of my charms around you
I'm hoping you will find

Of beauty and of virtue
I know whereof I speak
And your beauty and affection
Is all I wish to seek

—David Jay Covington

DREAMS OF A CHILD

I saw her in my dream again,
Oh so tattered and Forlorn.
She is searching, searching
for what was taken before her time.
I know that little girl just staring up at me.

Stripped away those Hopes and Dreams of one day
and when the culprit goes to hell he'll pay
For what was stolen from a child that day.
Until then that child will go on searching,
searching in her quest. I see it in her eyes.

Reflected in my mirror I see that little girl.
I must stop her searching, or I'll be denied,
Now I'm searching for what I do not know.
That little girl is part of me
And keeps me on the go . . . .

—Laura Lynn

DAY DREAMS

There are special times, special events, and treasured memories.

Everybody needs a secret to himself, that self indulging moment.

We sometimes drift along, floating down life trying to avoid the white water.

Swaying gently in a hammock, sipping a little of what makes reality worth facing.

The presence of reality temporarily subdued, never gone, only pushed aside.

Standing in a field, just listening to the bustle of a breeze through the tall grass.

The process in itself is a simple one, however, the results are inconceivably satisfying.

—Bradley Chagnon

IN THE PRESENT

Take time to smell the roses,
To hear the crunch of snow on a cold morn,
To feel the gentle breath of a child
against your cheek.

Smell the pungent odor of pine,
the perfume on the neck of
mother earth that announces
her presence and excites
the urgent passions of us all.

Listen to the laughter of
children in a group, huddled
against the world, protected
by child thoughts and the
innocence of youth.

Feel the hurt of someone's loss,
of tragedy unprovoked. Know the
compassion of one soul reaching
to another, the healing touch of
your hand on a back bent by grief.

But truly, take time to smell the roses,
To hear the crunch of snow on a cold morn,
To feel the gentle breath of a child
against your cheek.

—David H. Runyon

A DAY IN AUGUST

House-sitting in August for Trudi and Frantz — what a treat!
Two weeks with pets and paints, and a view that is hard to beat:
Vistas of blue bay and evergreen hills from their adobe home.
Mara, the dog, pulls me on her leash, when daily the hills we roam.
After our exercise we rest lazily between the cacti,
While Persian Sam entertains us with a dance a la bacti.
Across the pool butterflies and hummingbirds perform their wizardry;
— I daydream till, suddenly, Sam embraces a friend of the lizardry.
Gazing to the crest of the hill, feeling whole and free,
at this very moment I am as happy as one can be!

      —Annelis Schiebel

Panting, panting, panting
from door to door and window to window.
Stormy clouds on the rise, winds flowing ever so threateningly.

Panting, panting, panting
fear overcomes him.
Submission to all natural beings.
Terror by the acts of God.
No control over the whirlwinds.

Panting, panting, panting
now running from door to door and window to window.
Still the wind is blowing, darker, darker the clouds are forming.
He comes to me for comfort, what else can I do?
He looks at me as if to say, "I'm scared, I'm scared make everything go away."
In my lap he would be, all 90 lbs. of golden fur.
Saliva hangs from his mouth with anxiety.
The winds calm just as fast as they raged with rain.
The clouds disappear, the Heavens open the sun is shining.
Now my K9 friend may live in peace again.

Dedicated to my K9 friend, Buford

      —Michelle L Tate

AUTUMN IN CARLISLE

Autumn has come to Carlisle, Pennsylvania.
Mother Nature has flown by with her paint box,
Light-heartedly painting the trees and shrubs—
Here a dab of gold, there a patch of crimson
And some faint swatches of brown from her carelessly held palette.
The town is beautiful in its colorful robes.

Goldenrods are blooming by the Le Tort,
Vying with purple asters along the near-by Conodoguinet.
The noisy cry of blue jays ring in the cooling air
As they battle the frisky gray squirrels for seeds and nuts.
Kids coming home from school call cheerily to each other
And cries come drifting from the football field
Where the Redskins lately scrimmaged.

Dickinson College And Law School stand proudly in the autumn haze.
Leaves rustle along the street where General Washington once reviewed
        his troops,
And fall gently on the statued grave of Molly Pitcher.
A bugle call sounds faintly from the War College
Where Jim Thorpe once attended school,
And where the Hessian Guard House still stands sentry.

Have you ever seen Carlisle in the autumn?
You will be dazzled by the beauty — ever changing yet always the same.
Come visit our historic little town.
You will surely like Carlisle in any season
But in the days of fall when she is dressed in her colorful finery
You could be smitten with never-ending love!

      —Bertha Woods Greenwood

PERPETUITY

one giant crimson tulip
pushing past skeletons of weeds
brightened a forgotten flower bed
by my late neighbor's vacant house.

could it know the inner joy
and renewed hope it brought to me—
an epitome of faith and courage
in its will to live—its aloneness
would fade like fallen petals in the sun.

for pressed into my heart
that brilliant blossom cannot die;
its radiant faith-borne elegance
will add a fragrance, a breath of her,
to my life as long as I live.

—Beulahmae W. Marchbanks

YOUR OWN TREE

Plant yourself a tree, early in the
    spring.

It will make a nice place for all the
    birds to sing.

Then when you are older, and all your
    debts are paid,

You can sit back and enjoy life, just
    sitting in the shade.

And when you think how small it was,
    when you put it in the ground,

You will be glad you planted it, and
    all the peace you've found.

So while you are sitting there, and
    through its branches look,

You will know you have been paid, for
    what little time it took.

—W.L. Renfro

RAINBOWS

We're always chasing rainbows
    with hopes we'll find one day,
that pot of gold, that we are told,
exists for those who pray.

The obstacles we face in life
can keep us from our dreams,
our drive may drop, so most just stop,
that's often what it seems.

Stop right there and think a while
for if we always quit,
this life we lead, would be dull indeed,
and things would be the pits.

Dreams come true for those of us
who strive to be our best,
to quit we know, just goes to show,
we're just like all the rest.

Rainbows do exist for some
the end, that's hard to find.
If I could hold that pot of gold
for a bit, I wouldn't mind!

—Joseph H. Driscoll

THE LIGHTHOUSE KEEPER

Sing the ballad of the lighthouse keeper,
    he's just another ordinary man.
Ring the bell to awake the soft sleeper,
    lee's gust enshrouds dark the horizon's span!

Fumes tempestuous, misty tidal breath,
    anon he lumbers quick the twirling stair.
Consumes a ship in steep billowy death,
    upon steely shoals, yawns vast Neptune's lair!

Beams of light cleave the salty midnight air,
    cheers erupt far out atop the black seas!
Streams bright announce the trusty keeper's there,
    steers port, the vessel to safety swift flees!

Pause to scan the stormy waters we sail,
    be not then, my dear friends, heavy sleepers.
Because our loved one's hulls are thin and frail,
    we all must be faithful lighthouse keepers!

—Todd Charles Toth

GHOST SHIP

Calm are the waters as the breeze blows stale
Aching in the distance is the horn that wails
Thick is the fog that hides the unknown
Drawn is the scent in the breeze that's blown

Forms with no shape seem to tease the night
Misleading are the senses of sound and sight
Taunting and haunting, daunting in flight,
Deceptive is the mist that floats so white

Perched on the crest is a silhouette
Lured am I to the phantom nest
Alone I stand in this charred, crows nest
Eerie is the vision I long to forget
I sense the fury of the lifeless threat
Approaching me is the beast of death

There's no escape . . . .
                    the face I see,

There's no escape . . . .
                    the beast is me!

—Ken Flint

THE WOODEN CABOOSE
   . . . an era in time

I'm the wooden caboose that's been forgotten in time,
now I feel I'm not worth a dime.

I'm also the caboose that's arrived at night only to look
for that go "White Light."

I've traveled in snow, I've traveled in rain, I've done my
best just to maintain.

I've been a home for many a man and heard the tales
from the "railroad clan."

I've rode with the worst, I've rode with the best; the men
called "Engineers" from the east and the west.

The slack has run in, the slack has run out; my "era in
time" is surely in doubt.

I've cherished the smiling faces of all the kids as I passed
through the towns as I "once" always did.

I was "once" a part of America's Pride, the wooden
caboose with its "once" fine ride.

To look at me "once" I was shiny and new, but all
things must pass, even me, even you.

—W. Craig Hodges

OUT OF MY WINDOW

Looking at my window
I perceive sadness
clinging to the naked trees
in a cold winter city street.

Looking through my window
I envision the warm awakening
of all the people
passing along the street.

Out of my window
I want to touch your mind, your heart . . .
the life of every human being.
I run outside . . . I cry in despair . . .
Wait. Don't go away.
Peace is near . . . it's just winter time!

—Amalia Diaz-Chamorro

LOST IN THE DARK

Through passion you invaded me
and attacked.
I lie here lost in the dark
while you destroy
my body and my mind.
I feel your cold, terminal
hands strangling my future,
and I realize AIDS
is not the wrath for the wicked,
or the curse of the few.
Like the cold indifferent breath
of the night,
AIDS knows no compassion.
We are all
a part of its deadly lottery.
Don't assume your number won't come up,
because when its cold finger
touches your heart,
you may be lost
in the dark like me.

—Sarah Burlingame

SEVERED

The infinite golden ring
Broken.
Love
Wrenched like entrails
Sucked from a slain buck,
Doors crash closed
Like penitentiary cells,
Feelings
Echo in rooms stripped bare,
Curtains
Shut out light,
Coldness sleeps in my bed,
Only silence hears me sob.
The cord to future generations
Stays stillborn.
No shadow of myself
To tell the facts of life,
Or to remind the world that once I was.
This branch of life
Infinitely, viciously shorn.

—Sally Maust

All alone I'll find my way
Out of this darkness called yesterday
No longer unhappy, for surely I'll be
Without bad memories, finally free

I need only hope to guide me along
No words of inspiration from friends or song
I search without ceasing, and surely I'll find
A tomorrow of meaning, one that is kind

But searching seems hopeless, for I search to no avail
Never have I found it, no escape from this Hell.
I have failed again, and so multiply my fears
I know now it's time and cry my last tears

And though I am frightened of what is to be
I fear even more living, never free
I hope for understanding, and please remember me
And pray God forgive me, at last I am free.

—Gayla M. (Minor) Johnson

From the top of the hill I can see the Hawk
sitting on the weakened arm of an oak tree.

Our eyes meet as the wind penetrates through
my sleepy soul.

My spirit shivers as the angry darkness revives
my motivation of emotion and instinct.

Feeling the early morning dew upon my cold, bare
feet, I run to the forest for shelter.

Numbly crouching beneath the musty leaves
I cry out for understanding, comfort and being.

Through the umbrella of twig and greenery
the moonlight luminates my body,
revealing my innocence to the sky.

The Hawk and I greet again; I showing no fear
and he showing no threat.

He journeys towards the passive moon,
awakening to the Heavens that I live here on Earth
within the haunting beauty of nature.

I quietly close my heavy eyes and sleep.

—Melinda D. Michaud

MY TIME ALONE

I sit here alone and think sometimes
Of days in the past and I hear no chimes.
Tonight is different for I have enjoyed relief;
Feeling free of the causes of such a grief.

A release of stress by whatever the way
Can lead to a better life from day to day.
We all have the means to fulfill our need,
And it doesn't cost much to accomplish the deed.

Sometimes just a joke to a friend that is told,
Is all that's needed to ensure they're worth gold.
It costs nothing to have one of these at your side,
To share laughter and the many things you confide.

I have the music I enjoy that means so much,
Even though it's not shared by all as such.
They don't understand the value of this;
No cost at all for some moments of bliss.

Whatever we can do to make a better life;
Although sometimes filled with pain and strife.
It only takes a little to accomplish the goal;
Often relieving the weight from one's heart and soul.

—Betty J. Perriman

CHRISTMAS TIME
1990 DESERT STORM

Another year is almost gone, as Christmas time draws near.
The time we celebrate the birth of Christ,
Mary's baby boy so dear.
As she placed Him in the manger, the angels began to sing,
This little baby Jesus, was our newborn King.
The cattle began to low, while the baby tried to sleep,
While the shepherds in the field watched after their sheep.
The people were rejoicing over things they had heard.
Jesus the Christ child had been born into the world.
May the Spirit of Christ dwell in us all, as we celebrate
his birth.
And may there be peace over all the earth.

      —Rosie B. Sneed

COUNTRY GIVING

I sat upon my porch swing one warm, hot summer night.
I felt such great contentment as I viewed all things in sight.
I listened to the rippling direction of the stream —
I heard a conversation of a mallard drilling team.

And low, the fields before me, displayed a twinkling show.
The finale was a golden moon, in circle, all aglow.
A gentle breeze caressed me as I closed my eyes to hear —
More echoes from the country — sounds which I hold dear.

I had a talk with Jesus and praised Him for all this.
And asked that He would guide my eyes to scenes I shouldn't miss.
I no sooner asked — He answered — with a gentle purring sound —
A mama cat with kittens spoke — my squeaky swing was found.

As I stroked each little kitten and their mother too,
I felt such warmth within me as I often do.
When nature does surround me and shares her gentle touch,
I treasure magic moments — like this very much.

Now relaxed and free from stress created as the day progressed,
I know that in the arms of Jesus, I find nothing now but rest.
I know that in contentment is the way that I should live,
And when the dawn arises, I can, more, to others give.

      —Patricia A. Swisher

LOOK INTO THE LIGHT

Look into the light, don't you see your soul?
Look into the light, you shouldn't feel so old.
It is a time of confusion, it is a time of pain
I don't know if it's revolution
Can't say who's to blame
But I've got to sit and wonder of what is gonna be . . .
And I don't wanna make no guess at life expectancy . . . .

Look into the future, don't you have your crystal ball?
Look into the future man, it isn't hard to call.
Well take the facts, the scheme of life
And what it's suppoz'd to be
The fates they are as endless as the possibilities . . . .

Look into the heavens, can't you ask your God for grace?
Look into the heavens, beg forgiveness save your face?
You can live your life in goodness
Live your life with dignity
Don't do those things that cause such grief
Such pain and misery.
Let's leave this world — for children's sake —
A better place to be
It's possible, it's in our grasp . . .
It's what this self-hell needs . . . .

      —Linda M. Hansen

BIRTHDAY IN DECEMBER

The Holly & Bells, Corner Santas
and sleighs in the snow, once
the Day the Holy Child was Born,
this was Jesus' Day.

      —Dwight W. Bower

DRAW ME CLOSER

Draw me closer, ever closer
to Yourself, dear Lord, as
in distress to You I cry.
My heart is heavy and
I would ever closer draw
that You would fill my need
with Your abundant blessing.
Lift my spirits once again
to where Jesus only I see
as my dearest friend.
Could it be, my Father,
that I did not see
the life You planned for me?
My one desire is to serve Thee
in every word and deed.
Now draw me closer, ever closer
to Yourself, dear Lord.

      —Mary Alice Montgomery

LET US SING

Let us sing to the Lord and
praise His name,
Jesus who opened blind
eyes and healed the lame.
Give God the glory through
each new day,
And sing out as we walk
life's way.
Singing a happy joyful song,
Leaning on Jesus as we go along.
Asking our Lord what
He would have us do,
Jesus our Savior so
loving and true.
Come let us sing one
and all,
Always listening for God's call.
Singing and telling others of His
love,
He's daily watching us
from above.
Sing on my child He
will gently say,
As we give thanks and
humbly pray.
Sing from your heart,
And Jesus from you will
never depart.
Let us sing,
And make our voices ring.

*Dedicated to my dear husband,
Leland Tellier Sr. 38 years of
loving memories. He passed
away January 1, 1992*

      —Doris J. Tellier

171

THINGS THAT MATTER MOST

It matters not the color of
My eyes or skin or hair,
Or the kind of clothes that I
By choice may choose
Or have to wear.
It matters most that Faith
and Hope and Love can find,
Within my heart a place to meet,
For only then shall I find life
Worthwhile, my joy complete.
These are the things that matter.

—Eloise Curtis McLeod

A MEDITATION UPON DISENGAGEMENT FROM TRIVIAL LIFE ATTACHMENT

Behold the Atman
Never changing, unceasing
Guiding through Eternity
Ever present, all pervasive
All paths of seeking
Lead towards its light.
When the heart is poised
In the being of the Atman
No bonds can bind
No fetters confound
Its light in brilliance
    streams forth
No darkness can hide,
Cut free from desire
Exercising dispassion
Renouncing the pairs
    of extremes
As the water remains unmoved
As the motion of waves pass
    through it
So the Atman remains
The Atman emerges unbounded
Thoughts
    centered upon the Atman
Not to look forward to future events
Neither to await the fruits of your
    actions
Seeking contentment along the
    inward journey
In you
    will blossom
the bliss
    of the Atman.
That serene One
Absorbed in the Atman
Masters his will
He knows no disquiet
In heat or in cold
In pain or in pleasure
In honor dishonor
    He knows
        dispassion.
Let him who would climb
To the heights
    of the highest
        Union with Brahmin
Take for his path
This yoga of meditation
Then when he nears
That height of Oneness
His acts will fall from him
His path will be tranquil.

—Ellen Baudisch

FOREVER FRIEND OF MINE

Autumn is almost here, forever friend of mine
A brown-edged leaf on my green oak told me so.
Soon she will be making her soft impression on the earth
An eternal impression; It is her gift.

You are not leaving me, dear friend
Your smile has been etched upon my soul
It springs anew each time I beckon it
Defying distance; It is your gift.

The browning leaf does not go away, she assured me
Those who await her return are blinded
Her presence remains through season's changes
She is like you, friend; She is forever.

—Jeanne Marie Blystone

ADVICE

Sit down on the grass
And take caution of the pixies
Dance on the beach at night
But let only the stars and sea know.
Share the fruits of your life
With a tiny gray squirrel
And he will be your friend.
Let out a colorful phrase or two
So people know you're there.
Sleep well on a bed of feathers and silk hair
Made from that of an angel and mermaid
Remembered from a childhood dream.
Hold fast to the heart
So that clouds, the moon, and wine shall never leave.
Keep your mind open,
For if it closes,
You will be blind to all the wonders.
And always hold your soul in place
For you'll need it at the golden gates.

—Dawn M. Fago

MY RENDEZVOUS

When my days are over. When my life is through.
And it is time, to keep my rendezvous.

With loved ones who, have gone on before.
I pray God lets, my spirit soar.

I hope it soars high, glad to be free.
And I hope they are all, There waiting for me.

I hope they are waiting, There side by side.
I hope I am greeted, with arms opened wide.

To give me a hug, to hug me real tight.
To welcome me in, at the end of my flight.

When my days are over. When my life is through.
And it is time, to keep my rendezvous.

I want to be remembered, by those left behind.
As someone who cared. Someone who was kind.

One who would listen, to what others did say.
One who was contented, at the end of each day.

Someone who knew, what made living worthwhile.
Like taking the time, to make a little child smile.

Someone who loved, and tried to ease pain.
If I'm remembered this way, I lived not in vain.

—Donna B. Knoll

172

Life is like a rose
It doesn't last forever
As the petals fall, the years pass
Sometimes too slowly;
Sometimes too fast
Sometimes full of joy
Sometimes full of sorrow

But as the petals fall and the years pass
We continue to survive

A rose can not be preserved to last forever
Neither can life
So, like the rose we die

But, hopefully;
Like the rose, we live with beauty.

Dedicated to Roger and Alexis, who taught me to live life with beauty. All my love to both of you.

—**Gail Mauro**

PERSONAL EXISTENCE

As I wander the haze of reality, I wonder . . .

When the nights roll over me dark and illuminating
I feel the joy of the expectation of happiness
coursing through my blood warm blood
the expectation of wanting to let go
to let go my thoughts my love my soul
as if I would ever halt from doing so
I am from the night like a creature
of Nature allowed to roam under
the Mistress Luna yet I must
sing must scream —
who am I?

As daylight creeps into my night
obliterating my purpose of
existence the question remains
unanswered.

—**J.L. Taylor**

REFLECTIONS

As the veil of secrecy is slowly lifted,
and we stand naked before ourself —
Our essence revealed — Timeless faces appear,
contemplating what man has always known . . . .
Fascinated, the soul becomes one with time.

Destiny beats its drum
And all the people come
And all the people go —

Parasites — Eating, Digesting, Excreting all
we come in contact with. Dancing, frolicking,
then disillusioned, and confused.
Inching forward and running back
to lose that which we never had.

And all the people come
And all the people go —

Within this world we live — Choices made
long ago, not remembered. Reflections
luminate from the shadows of what might be.
A metamorphosis of a new me.
And we come & go —

—**Linda L. McDonald**

SMILING

What's in a smile? You ask.
Is smiling a form of hiding your
feelings?
Not always, one answers.
A baby smiles, as he or she sees
Someone else doing this, it is then
a learning process.
Older children smile, most of the
time, because words may fail them.
Adults smile, some out of politeness
and some because it is their nature.
Most out-going people wear a smile,
Not always.
Others smile, just as a way of
communicating with other people.

—**Fern Detweiler**

I'LL TOO—FORGET

Did you forget to give a thought?
Did you forget to care?
Thoughtfulness has disappeared,
love is lost somewhere.
Did you forget the visits?
why you don't even call,
Did you forget to tell your heart,
you do care after all?

What ever happened to respect,
there's a saying—oh, so true,
What goes around, comes around
the hurt comes back to you.
Maybe you don't realize
small things DO mean a lot,
A loving thought from you could bring
a smile—but you forgot.

So thanks for many memories
sad days, I'll ponder through,
Expect NO thoughts for anyone
I'm forgetting—just like you.

—**Doris Halpin**

TOMORROW IS FOREVER

Tomorrow never comes you know,
today is always here.
Yesterday is gone forever
as time is drawing near.

God lengthened years
then shortened them to
three score years and ten.

Tomorrow is way out yonder
beyond the setting sun,
We'll never reach the span of time
because it will never come.

We are always reaching for tomorrow
but time is out of our grasp,
no matter how long we stand and
wait tomorrow will never come.

Today is all we have the promise of,
for yesterday is forever gone.
But our promise is tomorrow
if tomorrow really comes.

—**Billie Jean Standley**

SUMMER'S GONE!

The leaves are going and I am growing
The air is colder and I am older
The water is freezing, the dogs are sneezing
The turkey's cooking but I am looking
For the wind to bring summer my way.

—**Travis D. Lund, age 9**

THE ROSE

I spied the swaying color among the weeds;
Tear-shaped dew glistened like diamonds
Upon the salmon-hued velvet petals
That arched to form plush mounds.

I felt the coolness of the dew
As around the stem I closed my hand.
"No!" I thought, "I must not pluck
This one rose that grows on barren land."

For only God could let this one survive
Where no other rose can grow.
So quickly I dropped my hand
And left this little gem to glow.

—**Wanda Hancock Rohman**

CALLING

May we meet in the mountains
where Hickory trees smell of love
and golden leaves call to souls
come together.
Where sun and cloud mingle and meander
to the depth of earth below.
Warm moist earth and crows
will call us.
The mountains we go.
Hemlock studded grove below
gentle and devoted,
holding each fallen tender leaf.
A place for crows to caw
and come to grow old.

—**Nancy Cerreta**

THE MASTER'S PAINTING

The sky is just a canvas
in The Master's skillful hand,
There He paints the clouds of darkness
or the bright sunshine so grand.

As the night gives way to daybreak
and the dawn begins to steal,
Again He stretches out His canvas
high above the barren field.

Each day a brand new painting
as grand as grand can be,
Put there, up in the sky above
for all the world to see.

He paints the clouds that bring the rain
and a sky for Winter's cold,
He sets the rainbow in the cloud
for all eyes to behold.

So look up my friend and see the work
of The Master's skillful hand,
For paintings, you will never see,
such as this in all the land.

—**Ruth C. Demetral**

ON A NICE COOL SUMMER DAY

On a cool summer day the wind in the river blows,
Some little girls wear some odd hair bows,
The soft sound of the roaring trees,
Listen to the soft rolling seas,
There is peace and no more pain,
For we all know peace will go again,
The nice bright sun is out,
So have fun and shout,
Go out and play because I will say,
It's a nice cool summer day,
Please never go away.

—**Victoria Phucas, age 10**

THE VALLEY

The valley is green with flowers,
And golden with the touch of the sun,
But it's only after it showers,
That children can have lots of fun.

The river that flows through the valley,
Is sparkling clear with delight,
The sun comes out from behind the clouds,
And gives out a radiant light.

The songbirds sing in the branches,
The animals play near the trees,
The butterflies float through the warm, spring air,
Caught up in the whispering breeze.

The house that sits in the valley,
Is red with trim of white,
A rainbow that falls near the river,
Is "oh" such a beautiful sight.

I guess that this poem's a key,
But a simple reminder to me,
That the secret of God is in my heart,
No matter where I may be.

—**Katie Uhrin**

A COLORADO SUMMER DAY

The morning dew sparkles as diamonds of light,
With more jewels than all stars of the sky;
Little sparrows awaken with the praise of joy,
Lifting their voice to the Creator on high.

Majestic mountains reaching up towards heaven,
Their presence nearly touching God's face;
In reverence and awe I stand there in silence,
Being encaptured by their beautiful grace.

A doe with her fawn nibbles on berries nearby,
Beneath the pink glow of a new summer day;
A chipmunk chatters aimlessly by an oak tree,
Trying to chase the thieving bluejay away.

Mountain goats climb upon a high rocky ridge,
As proud sentinels watching over the land;
The countryside is covered with Opuntia cacti,
As yellow blossoms grace the warm red sand.

An afternoon thunderstorm threatens overhead,
Bold lightning streaks across a black sky;
A red squirrel scampers up a rugged pine tree,
Two tiny field mice scurry for cover nearby.

A warm breeze caresses a tall stand of aspens,
Soon their leaves will be turning to gold;
Scrub oaks will ablaze the hillsides with red,
As the brilliant tapestry of Autumn unfolds.

—**Judy Ann Williams Downey**

EGGSHELL TRAIPSES

Eggshell traipses mandatory lest awaken anew
The discovery that another day is only that.
No investment continued, lost time in photo
        finish with despair.
To be gracious in defeat salves the moment
        but not reality.
Stretches of solitary offer no serenity.
Motivation fleeting and exceeding capabilities present.
Descent farther than usual as
        desolation flourishes.
But lashes raining remind me that I
        am not alone.
Remembering is the joyful base to my sadness.

      —Heather Shearer

PASSAGE INTO PARADISE

A divine messenger appeared in the night
    to carry off the lonely ones, and the meek
    who did so freely, follow

Talking to them through the Glass Harp
    weightlessly they flew a million miles
    carried away by a symphony of strings

Crystal bells chimed to the ascension
    magically transmitting hypnotic vibrations
    into sudden percussive waves of ecstasy

A piper gave to them warmth and sublime happiness
    through the breath of his soul
    penetrating to the saddest of hearts

Drifting by with flowing waves of joy
    the subtle touch of the harp
    will take them to far away lands forever . . . .

      —Paul M. Bocchetti

ANNA MARIE

Who am I danced through her head
As everyone told her Anna Marie is dead
Seeing her life as a fluke
Her managers named her Patty Duke
The years to come were hard and stressful
She wouldn't believe she was someone special
Wishing for the pain and suffering to end
Anna prayed for her family to take her back
And her life to mend
From Harry to Desi to a man she hardly knew
She fell in love with a few
But none like John
Who put her in the family way
And called her Anna til this day
Yet with an illness no one understood
Her life was still incomplete
Although she worked as hard as she could
Today with a prescription that makes her life sweet
She now feels content and complete
With her loving husband Michael
And as a proud mother of three
She can finally say happily
This is me Anna Marie.

Dedicated to the most extraordinary
woman on earth, Patty Duke.
    —Shawn Clark-Astin

LOCKED IN

The pied piper of a sort passes,
    luring all who can hear
    his dime a dozen dream songs.

But what is that to a prisoner
    locked in his pensive cell
    of quiet desperation?

What can he hear behind his bars
    but roaring rumblings
    and deafening dischords,

    Beating, booming, beating
    on hurting heart drums
    within a narrow space.

What does the passing peddler know
of caged longings and locked dreams
  wasting behind the narrow bars
    of steel reality?

    Escape   from   a   prison

    of   one's

    own   making

    is   never,   ever   easy.
    —Patricia Boney

WHY CAN'T I TELL YOU HOW I FEEL?

The pollyanna syndrome
        Was instilled
From centuries ago
        It was so willed

Society says, "Do this!"
        "Do this!"
By gosh, You'd better
        Not be amiss!

Smile when you want to frown
Don't ever, ever let anyone down.

Is that a teardrop trickling past
The painted-on smile of your mask?

Did you say yes,
        When you meant no?
How come you did this?
        You don't know?

No wonder you can't find yourself,
You're hidden somewhere on a shelf

Waiting to surface above the wall
That you have built so you won't fall.

How am I going to know
        Who you are
If you decide
        To stay afar?

Who
  are
    you?
        Please . . .
          tell
            me.

Cause I don't know if you are real,
Til you can tell me how you feel.
    —Patricia Ann Marsh

LIFE

God gives us many Blessings
He also gives us pain
The roses and the sunshine
The storm clouds and the rain.

God gives us friends and families
And lots of Love to share
With fellowship and reunions
And so glad that we were there.

God also gave us knowledge
To know right from wrong.
And to live by his commandments
As each day comes along.

We all have trials and temptations
As down "Life's" road we trod
But it sure is much easier
If we walk down that road with God

—Pauline Hoffman

MY BEST FRIEND

My Best Friend,
Will you come meet Him?
He saved me from all my sin,
He'll save you too!

He has a gentle voice
He speaks to me day by day.
We walk hand in hand,
In a special way.
With a special love
A love that lasts forever.

He carries me,
In times of trouble.

I'll live with Him forever,
He's coming back for us.
He wants to know you personally,
His name is Jesus!

—Heather M. Johnson

THE HEROES OF HEAVEN

In Heaven,
No great crowds give a cheer,
When the heroes of men
Receive their praise here.

God notices those,
Who have thoughtfully tried,
Without glory, or praise,
Or boastful pride,
To lovingly help,
Encourage and guide,
All of the people,
They come along side.

It isn't the proud,
The great or the tall,
Who will receive
The most of them all.
Of all of God's servants,
Those humble and true,
God graciously grants
The reward they have due.

—Marilyn J. Neslund

THE WRONG ROAD

Lord, you spoke to me at about the age of nine,
To me you gave a light to shine,
And I took it down into a bramble patch.
Moving so fast I felt sure I was hard to catch.
And on this road as we grow to adult,
We act like we don't care who we insult.
Of course we all think it's fine at the time,
Laughing, waltzing and drinking wine.
But the miseries untold are the results we pay,
And then we stop and think one day.
This world of fun seems less enchanted,
Because back then the seed of thought for God was planted.
So let me tell all to "do THY WILL,"
And ask "Dear Lord, Let me be STILL,"
Remembering we were out there doing our dance,
But we don't know if we'll get another chance.

—Evelyn M. Doucet

TREASURES

There are many things I prize in life
Things that help me forget every day strife:
The warmth of the sun upon my face
The feeling in church of God's Holy Grace
The pleasure of reading an absorbing book
The understanding of a friend in just a look
The feeling of awe when watching the sea
Realizing that millions of others are watching like me
The joy of laughter when sharing some fun
With family and friends when work is done
The uplift of heart when the postman appears
With notes from acquaintances I've made through the years
The sound of long-ago music on the stereo
That fills my home and me with a special glow!
The touch of my little dog's nose on my knee
That says, with effect, "Don't forget about me."
And lest I forget before the end
The fellowship I feel when meeting a friend
These are the things I will always treasure
They are the gifts of life that no one can measure.

—Verna E. Grau

A VALUED FAMILY AT CHRISTMASTIDE

Bells were tolling in Christmas day;
When little Billy Jones knelt down beside his bed to pray;

"Dear Lord, here goes with my first wish;
Please look after Benny, my goldfish.
He's been acting kind of listless,
So please make him well this Christmas.
And while you're at it, please fix Fred, my toy giraffe;
The one who always made me laugh.
While biking I dropped him and made him dead,
When the spokes of the wheel ripped off his head.

"And please take care of my Mommy;
She's been sad since dad got mad and went away.
And please help my brother Tommy; He's got a test, so please get
   him an 'A'.

"I'm at the end of my prayer, I'm just about through,
But there's one special favor I really need from you.
Even if you forget some of my other wishes which are, well, you
know, kind of dumb and silly,
Please, dear Lord, find my daddy,
And tell him 'Merry Christmas from Billy'."

—William A. Wollman

DADDY'S EYES

The wait was long from summer to fall.
The shower came loaded with gifts from the mall.
Mostly pinks but a lot of blues.
Giving LeeAnn a doubt again, looking for more clues.
All we wanted was a daughter we could call our own.
Only Nana seemed sure, but how could we have known.
Presents still came with welcomes from everywhere.
But still I refused to believe in my girl when I prepared
Finally the last day, when I heard you crying.
Only tears of a mother touched my eyes smiling.
Our sweet little girl baby, had arrived complete with Daddy's Eyes.
The joy my heart felt as she was gently placed in my arms when she
sobbed little cries.
It showed on all our faces with Derek and P.J. widening with a smile.
For finally Jasmine-Lee Sheldon completed our lives, as she gave us
most pride . . . .

Especially written for my granddaughter,
Jasmine-Lee Sheldon, November 1992   LOVE NANAXX
> **—Angie Sheldon Simard**

CHILDHOOD IS . . .

Childhood is constructing masterpieces with Legos.
Childhood is that special magic you feel when you whisper your wish
list into Santa's ear.
Childhood is roller coaster and ferris wheels, carnivals and circuses.
Childhood is endless hours playing in the sun.
Childhood is well developed imaginations and "invisible" playmates.
Childhood is skinned knees and bruised elbows.
Childhood is innocence and love.
However, sometimes childhood is . . . a dingy one-room apartment.
Childhood is no father, only men who occasionally spend the night.
Childhood is gang wars in the streets.
Childhood is cocaine sales in the halls of the apartment building.
Childhood is taking care of brothers and sisters while mother
works the night shift.
Childhood is no escape from the violence — in the streets, in the
schools, and sometimes, even at home.
Childhood is going to bed hungry and waking up to no breakfast.
Childhood is poverty and fear.
Childhood becomes adulthood.
Childhood is the future.
> **—Nancy L. Schorr**

HIGH CLIFF

Hickory nut season.
Cool afternoon breezes through my hair.
Leaves cascading as if frozen butterflies.
With silent joy I watch my father stroll leisurely
among friends not forgotten.
Devotion draws him here to see the slender beings
shake off their brilliant coppery sea.
His every step as subtle as the one before,
so as not to crush the abandoned orphans on the forest floor.
Rabbits dodge around the season's patchwork,
while the sparrow presents its familiar song.
—Sure is peaceful here, Dad. —

But the sun slowly slips behind the darkened treetops, and he
gathers the fallen hickory nuts with quick yet gentle movements.
Dinner would be waiting—
mother hoping for the basket to be full.
Being alone with my father on that glowing, autumn afternoon
was a moment both rare and precious.
Time will never diminish this memory of my father, my friend.

Dedicated to my Dad, thank you for your unspoken love.
> **—Constance Hanstedt**

THE WALL

Thousands come searching, silently, weeping,
Haunted by memories, seeking healing,
Earnestly scanning the names.

Wondering, wishing, yearning,
Always asking why
Loved ones
Lie forevermore beyond their reach.

—Judy E. Van Middendorp

SIMILE OF SADNESS

Death is like the last few days of Autumn
When the dying, rotting leaves have fallen,
And the chilling rain cries tears of sorrow
For all that has gone before.

Now no more green buds bursting to be born;
No lovely, green leaves blowing in the breeze.
No tall, young branches stretching to the skies.
This seems, then, to be the end.

But Autumn is never really the end,
When sleeping Winter wakes, Spring is nigh
With a promise of rebirth and renewal.
Death holds that promise for us.

—Dorothy Klinck Connell

GIVING UP

I ask, but "no" is always the answer.
I try, but everything ends in abrupt failure.
I reach out, but walls form in front of me.
I cry, but no one listens anymore.

I ask, less desperately, and I am received.
I try with less effort, and succeed.
I still reach out, and I am welcomed.
I still cry, and still no one hears.

I stopped asking, and nothing happened.
I stopped trying, and everything happened.
I reached out, and people were happy,
I cried and cried until there was nothing left.

—Heidi Moen

SATAN'S HORSE

The flames shot up, they licked so high;
this man walked through, unafraid to die.
Death would be impossible, he would not accept;
the prisoners looked on, full of contempt.
For Satan had sent them here;
they saw that now, oh, so clear.
This man walked past a flame-blackened corpse;
the corpse would live on, as Satan's horse.
To be beaten, kicked, and cursed.
He would carry the demon to and fro;
always in pain under that red, hot glow.
To be caged in flame at night;
in all out terror, past mild fear or fright.
This man walked through a wall of flame.
You would go blind if you saw what he became;
a lion, a wolf, whatever your fear.
It is hell to live down here.

—Kurt Adams

Crying for the fallen, a rain of tears,
Mercy pities the less fortunate and the dead.
She raises flowers in their remembrance
        for years
She forever weeps, her eyes painfully red.

Because of this she sees not with her
        eyes but heart.
Caring for all from the greatest to the
        least.
Honoring them all, she can not tell them
        apart.
From the highest king to the most wretched
        beast.

—Tom Coates

MY SOLITUDE

As I sit here in total distress,
I think of many things I want to express.
My mind seems full of things to say,
But as I begin they seem to fade away.
I feel like a King with power to spare,
But to use my power I would not dare.
Here in my solitude I sit,
Trying to make all the pieces fit.
Although I spend my time all alone,
There are things I feel I should have known.
I try to think of things that are new,
And make up my mind to what I will do.
Books I read as much as I can,
And I find things even I can't understand.
As the clock strikes eleven my hour to retire,
I warm my hands before the fire.
Who knows what tomorrow may bring,
And I'll wonder, was it worth retiring.

—Leander Wegdahl

FOOTSTEPS TO HOME

Somewhere in the Saudia Arabia Desert
Christmas, 1990

Look at the sands in these desert lands,
changing our world around us.

The wind is swift and in our eyes,
changing our paths to home.

We feel the heat upon our backs,
changing our peace of mind.

The sand is rich and dust is thick,
changing the way we live.

We rest when we can and hear the sand,
changing our footsteps to home.

We watch the dunes erode away,
changing the scenes around us.

We travel the flats and watch the sky,
changing the paths we take.

The fire dies quick when the sun is set,
changing the way we rest.

The nights are cold and the air is crisp,
the sands remain the same.

We watch the night with our lonely eyes,
seeking . . . our footsteps to home.

—SSgt. Daniel A. Swanson

HEAVEN ON EARTH

The thoughts I pray for will come true . . .
The thoughts O God will always be of you,
I pray for Thy Will Be Done and "Heaven on Earth"
To end all wars and have a new birth,
A new birth of freedom for all mankind.
The freedom we once had and hold in our mind,
As it was in the beginning without money or gold—
In Noah's day and before, the days of old.
To speak of Peace and erase rumors of wars,
And days of killing will be no more.

—Dorothy Sanders Basil

BEHIND THE FRONT

So young, yet so old.
Their bodies are worn and their minds are cold.
Everyday, to them, is the same.
Playing the war as though it's a game.

But it's not a game to them, can't you see?
There's no place to hide, but a hole and some trees.
All they can do is sit and wait
Perhaps feeling scared, perhaps . . . feeling hate.

The families at home feeling sick with dread
And fearing their "Precious," soon, will be dead.
Why can't the leaders just fight one another
And leave out our fathers, our cousins, our brothers?

So young, yet so old.
Their bodies are worn and their minds are cold.
Everyday, to them, is the same.
Playing the war as though it's a game . . . .

—Liane M. Nishioka

WAR AND PEACE

Some people find such joy in hurting others,
Why can't we live our lives in calm and peace?
After all, we are "the keepers of our brothers,"
Why can't the snipping, biting, hurtful words, just
cease!

My friend of many years, looked at me happily,
When seeing how his hateful words had hurt me.
If his insults, I had returned in kind, it would
have made no difference,
You see he has no shame, because he has no
conscience.

Why is there war, in every generation?
Sometimes even two or three.
Can't countries sit in peaceful negotiation?
And talk things over amicably?

We are all supposed to be, more civilized today
Compared to way back in the middle ages.
With heads of governments, much more intelligent
wouldn't you say?
Doesn't it seem to you, we're reverting back in
time, giving in to barbaric rages?

I am very easy going, I just hate these confrontations.
Why can't the world and everyone feel like me?
I suppose it would be boring, without some
aggravations,
But just imagine, the peace, the calm, the
serenity!

—Grace Wallstrom

ON DESERT SANDS

On desert sands, the sun goes down,
And God, I know You're here,
In spite of missiles in the sky,
And agonizing fear.

No words can say the way I feel,
Upon these desert sands,
Defending freedom, justice, peace,
For those in foreign lands.

I'll do this for America,
And those I've left behind.
So pray for me America,
And peace for all mankind.

—Anette Fehlhafer

IS THERE A WAY TO SCORE

Is there a way to score
Is there a way to win the war
If there is no way to score
Why then do we fight the war

To stop the crying in the night
Youth battling against the scene
With faces turned towards the wall
No one listening to their call

Is there a way to score at all
A way to stop the crying to the wall
Someone to listen to our call
Is there a way to win the war

Why is there no one to see
Why must life so often be
Like running down a long long
hallway with closed doors

No there is no way to score
No way to open up one door
No one to listen to our call
No way to win the war at all

—K.R. Pope

FULL CIRCLE

The war was over,
bringing all of the soldiers home,
to make new lives
for their waiting families.

A farm, with machinery to buy,
a house, to shelter
the growing family.
A school, to broaden their minds.

A church to nurture them
and prepare for the future.
Guidelines to live by
lovingly shared and taught.

All are gone their separate ways.
An empty house.
Retirement.
A stroke stops all activity.

The machinery is lined up
and moved away.
The race is done.
Now, it's God's will be done.

—Bulea Barns Rosebrook

179

A LITTLE RED ROBIN

Once upon a time way back in
the days of my teens,
I came to know a little red robin.
This was a very special little
bird. He was not afraid of me.
But it seems like he was trying
to communicate with me. Whenever
I closely approach him. He would
hop around in a circle like form,
as if he was trying to tell me
something.
But he would never fly away.
Just upon the treetop, the place
where he would stay.
The little Red Robin who came
to play.

—**Virginia McNeil**

BLUE JAY

Blue Jay near my windowsill,
what a sheer delight.
Flying in and out at will,
such a lovely sight.

They dip and fly and tumble down,
from feeders to the snow.
Using bills to crack their seeds,
they put on quite a show.

Such a lovely bird to watch,
a clown, yet brave and bold.
Their colors shining in the sun,
a wonder to behold.

What serves, in spring, as apple tree
is now both bare and bright.
For now those limbs hold feeding Jays
of shining blue and white.

I sit here at my window,
a joyous sight for me,
to see those Blue Jays cover
that bare old apple tree.

—**Sandi Chaussee'**

THE DANSEUSE DAWN

The sky is slippered with her light
So softly does she lift the night
Embracing with the gentle breeze
Chasing 'round the honey bees.

The glowworm and the firefly
Finials of the evening sky
Hidden, humbled by the dawn
She quiets even cricket's song.

She kindly wakes each hushful bird
Stillness broken, chorus heard —
Flowers weep with tears of dew
So joyous at the day anew.

Trees softened now of gnarled way
By leaves that dance and sunlit play
She peeks at children in their beds
Awakening their sleepyheads.

Dreams that filled the slumber deep
She may banish — or may keep
A precious gift is morning then
To gild the heart — to live again.

—**Pamela Mangini-Chesnick**

WILD GEESE

Across the azure sky they seem to float
These wild geese flying south
They call loud, Oh so loud
I can hear them above the traffic on land
Below the bridge high, from which I stand
Honking their farewell to all
And a hearty departure from them on their wing
Saying see you again, come spring: Come spring
It's hard so hard to see them go
You know too soon winter comes with snow: Cold snow
Yet deep in your heart you say be on your way
Don't stay
Some hunter deep is waiting to get a crack at you on wing
So safe flight my dear birds: See you again.
Come spring, Come spring

—**Margaret R. Sell**

THE EAGLE

The eagle is a very beautiful bird
The eagle will always have a companion or mate
But there is always a time when he must open his wings
He leaves his nest, his love, and his friends
But the desire to leave doesn't last too long
Before his mate cries out a sad love song
Turning around to see what's wrong
It's only his sweetheart wanting to belong
Flying so high, the freedom, but no one to share it with
At home the nest is warm and safe
Right next to his favorite mate
Even an eagle needs someone to care about him
But his search for freedom may loose his love
Should he go back to his little dove
If not, there will always be empty space
without the beauty of his mate

—**Debra Stadler**

MORNING

Sun
shines through the windowpane
only to reflect my eyes
seeing your inner plot.
Rebellion against your heart
clenching pieces of doubt
to puzzle a life
blocking glitters of warmth
freezing your cares.

stony death ghosts of love

Awakening
your sleepy eyes caress my broken (up)
body
Private moments sigh — you beckon to me.
So strong . . . striving . . . passionate . . . brave
like an eagle in pursuit
but
deep indirectly down inside your ego
a hummingbird . . . swift . . . fragile . . . tiny . . .
doubting your capture.

Dedicated to Brian Paterson Amor vincintomnia.

—**Ciss Niessen**

180

YOUNG FRIEND

Wherever you may wonder,
Wherever you may roam,
My thoughts and wishes go with you
As though you were my own.
Although you're not my real true daughter
I have learned to love you as well
As a mother can cherish a child
With a love so big I want to show and tell.
Throughout your life when you think of the past,
Please think of me with love,
With a fleeting memory of your adopted mom.
For I'll be counting all of my blessings that have
Been bestowed on me from above.

—Leona White

THE CHANGE OF SEASONS

It is difficult to look at Daddy
Because he looks right back
Yet doesn't see me,
Though he has eyes that can see.

Hello Daddy, glad to have you
Too bad the weather is cold again
It sends a chill which has no mercy
I wish this season would end,

Those summer days we took walks together
Holding hands, talking with ease
I swore your love was the sun
And your smile the gentle breeze,

It seems the summer is gone forever
These frigid days have been here so long
And now I think a storm is coming
I can tell by the gusty winds,

Good-bye Daddy, don't be a stranger
Do come back after this season ends,
For then the sun will have absorbed the winter
And the gentle breeze replaced these winds.

—Judith Couch

DAD'S LOVE FOR HIS MOTHER

Oh I wonder if Grandma is crying,
as she looks down from heaven above?
Can she see how her dear son is sighing,
for the loss of his dear mother's love.

Alone each day he walks through the fields,
seeking a comfort from all that he feels.
Then he will solemnly sit down at the creek.
For he feels only in privacy, can he weep.

But Grandma knows he's lonely and blue,
for she dearly loved her son too.
But she'll be waiting for that day,
that he will be with her forever to stay.

Tis very hard now for him to sleep,
because Russell truly wanted to keep
His mother beside him for still awhile,
that's why he'll walk that extra mile.

No I don't believe that Grandma is crying,
for now she can see that through all her trying,
She has managed to raise the perfect son,
and now she knows that her victory is won.

—Jared Baker

MY DEAR MOTHER

Oh, that each grain of sand
were but a dollar, five or even ten,
oh, that the stars of heaven were
but silver and gold in my hand,
and if the blades of grass, in an open field,
were but five hundred dollar bills.
Still, I could not repay the love
and sacrifice
of my dear mother.

Dedicated to my mother: Iris Matzen

—Matthew Fuller

A MOTHER'S PRAYER

My son, my son, I am so lonely
You moved so far away
For twenty-seven years you were here
Now you are 2,000 miles away.
Every week I call on the telephone
To hear your voice so clear
I still know you are 2,000 miles away
Thank God for the telephone
I would really feel forlorn.
I know your sweet voice will answer
He came home for my birthday in February
So we had a 10 inch snow.
He got an extra day to go
He left on an airplane
Just as before he went away.
So hurry up June 14, we'll be seeing you.
As long as you are happy
Your father and I will be too.

—Betty Richter

A MOTHER

The dainty fall of a child's footstep
Behind me while I stand,
And the tiny arms that clasp my legs,
And the touch of that trusting hand
Make joy well up within my heart,
Because I know how fair
Are the promises God gave to mothers
When He placed children in our care.

As the years roll by and the children grow,
We sometimes become quite vexed,
We may wonder how to deal with them
When our nerves are almost wrecked.
But those close and tender moments
That are part of their growing years
Help us understand that it's worth it all
When we share their love and tears.

So if God gave me a one-time choice
Of only one career or another,
The list is long and tempts me sore,
But I'd rather be a mother.

—Millie Davis

ALONE

I am lying here on this flat plane,
alone—I am left to wonder.
My hope is that you
would walk in and lie beside me.

The night comes and I dream again,
this one does not include you,
but your presence is there.
I know because the dream leaves
me feeling that I am not missed.

In it I am fighting or maybe I am just
struggling to reach for the answers.
It's unclear, but I feel it
deep in my stomach.

It's a feeling of abandonment,
like my heart is no longer there.
Even drifting out of the dream,
awakening I noticed I am alone.

—Curtis L. Coghill

ILLUSION

When we see what we see,
do we let it be?
Or, do we prod, examine,
pluck, or disturb
This expression on earth?

When we hear what we hear,
do we keep near?
Or, do we roam astray, afar,
remote, and apart
From the immediate scene?

Do we see what we see?
Do we hear what we hear?
Can we capture
the illusion,
Sight and feeling
of the joy
Above the smog and the din
of the noise?

—Constance Fitzgerald Driscoll

A SECRET PLACE

Away, alone, lonely
words to describe a place . . .
A secret place
where nobody but you can go.

Exciting, magnificent
words to describe a feeling.
A feeling that you feel at a place . . .
a secret place
a place to run
a place to be alone.

Anger, madness
words to describe crying.
Crying that you cry at a place . . .
a secret place
away from the noise of a city.

A place where you can be alone
a place where you can be yourself
a place to be . . . .

—Erika S. Knuti, age 10

FORTY 1990

The eagle,
in gossamer fashion, gliding the thermals
The dolphin,
in suspended, acrobatic watery flight rivals
The stag
an eight pointer, seemingly flying the glen
while the homosapien,
abuses and destroys in short sighted ken

Man's alter egos, the quintessence of unabridged
freedom, their survival, in paperback abridged

The eagle, for sport and spite
In telescopic sight, shot in flight
The dolphin, polluted, netted and canned
for casserole and Tabby's dinner panned
The stag, wantonly slaughtered, on bumper in proud display
of macho egos, precarious need to slay

—Jim Dahl

WHO'S THAT WOMAN

Who's that woman.
Does she have any power.
Does she have the strength to bear a child and raise it in
this world today.
Can she rule her domain or the world.
Is she able to go to war and fight among men.
Can she perform miracles.
Can she save a person from death.
Do people bow down and worship her because she's strong.
NO!!
She has no unseen power.
She raises her child the best way she can and hopes for
the best.
She can't rule the world or perform any miracles.
But given the proper motives, she can fight as well or
better than any man.
She will probably never be bowed down to and worshiped
except by her own immediate family who loves her.
All she has is a heart of gold and a smile that can warm
up the coldest room in the dead of winter.

—Natasha Monique Belton

RUBBINGS

A small plot, under the shadow of the ancient church,
The oldest were in the back, irregular and poorly tended.
Ancient barberry bushes fringed the half acre,
a backstop for the highway trash.

The stone was cut by a mason from Connecticut.
I held the parchment paper against the cold stone;
The names, dates and decorations appeared
as she rubbed hard with the charcoal.

The sandstone was old, eroded centuries before;
how had it held up to the beating of time?
The mesmerizing wind stopped short,
Reality encroached in the silent pause.

The moment gone, we looked beyond the nearby graves.
The oldest stones of all were at the small plot's edge,
remnants of families, gone now from the valley,
stark monuments to long-forgotten folk.

A path was beaten through the guardian hedge,
a shortcut to the nearby mini-mall.
The back two rows of slabs were snapped in half,
the jagged uprights sprayed with crude graffiti.

—Richard H. Thornton

NEVER STOP

Bang!
As it falls to the ground
Blood seeps out of a wound made by a bullet
It is one of the last of its kind
Yet, its life was taken as fast as a bolt of lightning

Never again will it bathe under the soothing sun
Or wash in the drops of rain
Or walk through God's beautiful land
It will never again eat a blade of grass touched by morning dew

It lays still
Footsteps approach
Men's laughter is heard.

The forest grows quiet
They mourn in sorrow for yet another life taken!

—**Mary Mahon**

WHO IS AT THE HELM

I look around and see a world in trouble.
Powerbrokers build industry and replace kings.
They hold contempt for all things in their way.
Slash down the rainforests, choke our air.
Send black billows of evil smoke into the sky.
For the dollar they will poison their very souls.
Their eyes lack the sight of earth's majesty,
    and the wonderment in all its creatures.
There is a voice for the meek animals, who are on
    the brink of extinction.
A cry for unity and of love comes from their lips.
An acceptance of all people no matter what!
A pity for the Powerbrokers who deal in death and
    create hate.
A rhythm deep in our souls plays a music that is
    harmony to the universe.
So be silent a moment and listen to the tune in your heart.
Hear not with the ear but the heart and you will
    catch the mystical beat.
Synchronousity with all that lives starts with you!

—**Christopher Miniter**

EMPLOYMENT TO UNEMPLOYMENT

Employment, happy, productive, contributing, successful, sharing,
fun, overworked, tired and the present.

Unemployed, transition, next chapter, future; fear of the
unknown, no stability and devoid of definitive answers.

Coping with the unemployment line; a number in line, dark
glasses, stereo head phones, and Time magazine, an attitude of
getting through "It" with a smile.

Feelings of loss are pervasive and insidious in terms of status,
no more kudos for a job well done, and the emotions and
introspection plague your existence in anger, depression, pain,
demoralization, discrimination, insensitivity, humiliation,
hopelessness and the character judgement from the interviewing is
limiting and taxing.

Compromising your own wants and needs. Unemployment is not
designed for individualism and is ineffective in delivery of
compensation, it plays only to that of mediocrity, truly limiting
the ability to be yourself and wanting to color outside of the
lines, truly a vision of a caged animal.

To add insult to injury, the compensation received is taxable,
from those who provide the relief. Friends unwillingness to be
available for your time in need; like as if you have the plague.
Why?

—**Linda S. Savanauskas**

ONE WISH

I wish I could cry when
he says Hi, but I didn't.
I wish I could cry when
he sticks up for me, but I didn't.
I wish I could cry when
I see him with someone else,
but I didn't.
I wish I could cry when
someone says I can't have him, but I
didn't.
I wish I could cry for he's
so fine & I can't have him, but
I didn't
But today I'm crying for
I'm dying.

—**Heather R. Castro**

Locked in a world
of darkness
I live where no
man dares to enter
Safe from the world
outside
Only I know the
tears I've cried
They see me day
after day
but they really don't
for if they did they too would
feel this God wrenching pain in
my heart.
Never listening to the feelings I
speak
Now they wonder why my voice
has grown silent.
Time has not healed me
for it has been time without
action
that has led to my despair

—**Angela R. St. Louis**

BEHIND THE MASK

Is this me or
Is it someone else,
Hiding behind a mask
Afraid to be myself?

Trapped in my seclusion
By who I want to be,
Locking myself away
For no one else to see.

The fear of rejection
Has held me to this domain,
The desire to burst out and be
Myself, driving me insane.

It will not be easy —
Change is never an easy task,
But anything must be better
Than life behind a mask.

Why should I become someone
That others want me to be?
Because no one else can play
The part of myself better than me.

—**Jessica N. Taylor**

A CHILD

There was a child that went forth each day.
Unto us he came—we taught him, loved him
And sent him forth again.

There was a child that went forth each day.
Unto those he came—they changed him, swayed him
And sent him forth again.

There was a child that went forth each day.
Unto those he came with pistol in pocket,
hatred in his heart and a bullet marked to kill.

There was a child that went forth each day.
Unto us he came—we knew not what to do with
this child that was led astray.

—E. A. Crispin

THE LOCKET

The hand encloses, holding him.
The heart whimpers at the arms so achingly empty.
A longing within engulfs the soul.
A finger strokes the gold encasing him.
Memories come to ease an unending hole.

A smiling face and laughing eyes
The completeness of holding him
Tiny hands wrapped in her hair
whispered breathing against her ears, comes in baby sighs.
Love and joy surround them in a happy pair.

The face frowns and tears well.
The rippling ache of being unable to help.
His cheeks quiver as he looks up in askance.
She reaches down pulling him into a protective shell,
as slowly they begin a comfort dance.

The finger strokes the gold
A smile crosses her face.
Emotion and remembrances of her little one.
She knows as she touches that he is being told
that to her, he is more precious than gold.

—April Dawn-Nell Irwin

IF ONLY I HAD KNOWN

A silent smile and an innocent heart
O gleaming eyes of blue,
There he stood before my eyes
the truest friend I ever knew.
He never told my secrets
and to me he never lied,
Together we shared our feelings
and emotions kept inside.
Someone to be myself with,
to make me smile instead of frown,
But on his sixteenth birthday
the story turned around.
We drank bottles of beer together
and drove as fast as the car could go,
then the car flipped over
and now he's buried far below.
O innocent heart and eyes of blue
If I had only known,
that some bottles of beer could end in such tears,
and leave me facing the world alone.

*Dedicated to Lisa Levin (teacher); Karen Ramos
(Mom); Penny Auau (good friend) Thanks for
believing in me and helping my dreams come true
and Lesley Romero and Arnel Colcol may their love last!*

—Jennifer Lynn Ramos

RESTING

She is resting now
Yes, she is resting now
Now, what should I do
if I were to die tomorrow?
Would I go the way she went?
Although, my heart is sober
and my will is strong, there
is still doubt and the feeling
of insecurity is nestled in my
heart.
Yet, I know it is best that I
let her rest.
Yet, her memory will never die,
because I will keep it alive
in my heart forever.
Therefore, it is best not to cry.
Because I am certain that she
is resting now.

—Jon Michael Costellow, age 10

OLD YELLER

There was a dog named Yeller,
Who was quite a little feller,
He'd nibble on some meat,
Which he thought was pretty neat,

His owner was not so pleased,
Even though he played and teased,
He'd suck on chicken eggs,
And bite himself on the legs,

BUT . . .
His luck turned bad,
And our story gets sad,
For now in the end,
He has an illness that won't mend,

Yeller's life is over now,
And we will miss him anyhow,
As he is laid to rest,
We'll all hope for the best.

—Bertie Langdon

GONE BUT NOT FORGOTTEN

Have you ever sat and wondered
Why the Good Lord up above —
Has taken someone from you
Someone — "You'll always love?"

When you feel sad and lonely
And the skies seem — "Oh! so blue" —
Have you often thought of someone
You could tell "your" troubles to?

And then — Like a bright star
Shining in the sky —
That someone seems to listen
And you know why!

You haven't lost him forever
For in the Heavens above —
God is taking care of
That someone you love!

And suddenly your troubles
All seem to melt away —
For "Someone Dear To You"
Is guiding you on your way!

—Mary North

Being without you near
Brings to my eye
A crystal like tear
Saying I love you
And nothing comes back
Brings sadness to my heart
That almost makes it crack
Hearing your voice echo in my ear
Brings happiness to my soul
As I recall that "I love you dear"

—Christy M Musso

TRUE LOVE

Here is a small surprise
for a special date
and though that date
is not far away
I can hardly wait.

It's something precious,
priceless and unique,
a wedding band to prove
you're fully loved by me.

This special gold ring
needs to be sized to made
fit my future husband
to be.

I know things have
moved quickly
in just a few months,
but when you find
true love
there shouldn't be
a wait.

Dedicated to my husband, Jody

—Kimberlee Vastino-Wheeler

I SAW LOVE (IN YOUR EYES)

As I drive down this road today
My thoughts so far away
Thinking of you the girl in my life

How you made my dreams come true
And with everything you do
You keep the blues so far away

How on that moon lit winter's night
We held each other tight
And at that moment I knew
I saw love in your eyes

Now the sun shines bright today
And the winds they blow away
All the troubles in my life
It was a cold winter's day
When I took you far away
So many years ago

Now we're back where we belong
And I knew I wasn't wrong
Because tonight I've seen right through
I saw love in your eyes

*Dedicated to my wife, Peggy, my
inspiration and my mom, who I miss
very much. This one is for you.*

—Jerry Charbauski

A MANIFEST OF PLEASURE

Why do I feel ecstatic to see a special smile?

(Emotions stir within.)

Why does it make my existence seem so worthwhile?

Why are cherished memories instilled inside my heart?

A smile creates an example of faith, hope, and undying

love, as it has from the very start, knowing it emanates

from that person's heart!

A smile has a certain warmth that emits a golden glow.

A smile conveys sincerity and understanding when it is on a
face I know.

A mellifluous, unique, impressive, smile that I have known for
years, not marked by lines of worry or streaked with
heartbreaking, salty tears.

Continually keep smiling in your individual, captivating
way, for it makes me feel rapturous and it really makes my
day.

—Doris R.S. Miller

JUST LAST FRIDAY

Just last Friday I saw her approaching and
she saw me   our two paths would cross and
(rosy pink annelids littered the sidewalk their
mashed broken bodies insignificant carnage everywhere and
a nervous smile played at the corners of my mouth as if
some internal gatekeeper hoisted strained gasped and
expired struggling to bear my pearly portcullis)
steadied I looked up   she was running nonchalantly
(small wonder)
fleeing the clumsy civility labored
for blind dates mildly offensive in-laws and
unwanted admirers   I laughed inside and
(gall is *bitter* love is *sweet*)
toppled her chipped and fissured pedestal a
tiny shard finding the rosy pink border of each eye hotly
brimming but
even in that moment of delicious revolt my
heart was stung by the sudden beauty of her motion the
cat-like grace of her stride.

—John D. McEntire

EASY

do you know how easy it would be
if I could talk to you and you to me
it's not your fault
nor is it mine
we have been different
from the beginning of time
when life began we were as one
as we grew older we started to run
for things to change we must make a new start
a good place to begin would be from the heart
it's a shame things changed the way that they did
but remember we didn't know better
we were just kids
a lot has been lost since we traveled the same road
we are only people in search of gold
we speak the same language
but we don't understand
could it be as easy as holding your hand
all of this however is much easier said than done
but when it does happen life is more fun

—John S. McKiernan

THE WIND CHIMES

The gentle breeze plays a twinkling song on the chimes outside my door.
It takes my weary mind back to the ocean's waving shore.
The seashells that softly tinkle their breezy little tune.
Remind me of the peaceful days of a vacation late in June.
The sandy beach was quiet and no one else was then in sight.
And I just stood there watching the waves and the gulls in lofty flight.
The timeless waves keep no daily schedule nor watch a ticking clock.
They seem to follow their own mindless churn and beat upon the rock.
Sometimes I almost envy those ever-rolling, constant waves,
And secretly yearn for unplanned days along a beach with seashells paved.

—Cheryl Barksdale

SUNLIT MEMORIES

Standing in a sunstreaked room, I gaze out the window to watch children playing tag with the wind. Above them, the sun descends over nearby houses, filling its brushes from red and orange clouds.

The cat walks through, resisting definition among the slanting shadows. It pretends an interest in a bit of floating dust, abandoning its kingly air for a moment. It stops to look at me and asks a silent question with a slight parting of its lips. I am deaf to its words and cannot answer.

A woman's voice repeats itself in my mind, echoing what was spoken long ago. My hands caress her face in retrospect. Softness and warmth under my fingers clings with ghostly persistence. "I must go," she says, "goodbye, goodbye." A tear falls, mine or hers, I do not remember. A brush, a kiss, and a thousand wishes go unanswered. She is gone.

The cat picks up its invisible crown and leaves to attend its other regal duties.

Music threads its way through the closed window, shedding most of its melody to fit through the gap.

The sun sets, painting my view with crimson and amber hues. I pull the shade and my memories go out. I leave them behind in the darkened room.

—Chris Osgood

SET

There once was a man who lived a fair life.
Yet, he knew sorrow.
Yet, he knew strife.
He toiled and labored of his own accord.
In truth he had nothing, for he neglected the Lord!

There once was a man who had all the gold.
His temper was hot.
His heart grew cold.
He struggled and worried of his own accord.
And lo, he had nothing, for he neglected the Lord!

There once was a man who lived for himself;
Striving for acceptance, fortune, and health.
He worried and fretted of his own accord.
And yet he reaped nothing, for he sowed against the Lord!

And lo, there was a man who led a humble life.
He did not curse the sorrow.
He tightly embraced strife.
And of his own accord he did not worry, nor did he fret.
For he who knows the Lord has everything when his spirit is truly set!

I Love You Mom.
This is for the disbelievers.
You know who you are.

—Dennis Dale Popham

SILENT CRIES

My spirits are slowly fading
My soul is dying from wounds of
                constant abuse.
I have been burnt by the warmth
                of the sun.
I am drowning in the tears of
                the sky.
All my strength serves as a thin line
                between life and death,
HELP ME.
Caring is all I ask.
Feed me understanding and truth,
water me with love.
Strengthen my spirits with the
                food of life.

— Peggy Plewa

THE STORM'S SONG

the trees sing
 a bittersweet song
the sky cries
 its tears are strong
the wind grows harsh
 and gives its warning
the clouds are gray
 and rain in mourning
the sun plays hide-n-seek
 with the luminous earth
it disappears and returns
 in its glow lay a new birth
the sky's tears soften
 and show a hint of blue
the air grows warm
 and sees a lush view
in circles it spins
 hovering in sheets
round and round it turns
 and the process repeats

— Sonya "Roland2" Hainstock

Looking at your childhood picture,
who would of ever thought
Did I raise you for naught.

I'm so lucky I had you for 28 years
Oh! my I can't control the tears.

Sometimes I'm up for days and
nights
How will I ever get through
this life.

I have 2 children, thank God
for that
Or else who knows where I'd be
at.

I carry the memories some good,
some bad.
My soul will forever be so sad.

Two children are with me day in
and day out.
My third one is missing, I scream
and shout.

Life is very hard but in the end,
joy comes when we'll all be
together again.

— Sharon Cashman

If one could go back to 1779,
To the tragedy at the old Opera House in London Town
Martha Ray was a victim of murder at that time.
Her death caused an old hack to pen these lines,
of the man who took her life.
   "A clergyman, O wicked one, in Covent Garden
   shot her.
   No time to cry upon her God
   It's hoped He's not forgot her."
How would one pharse those lines today
Of the woman who died 'cause to her suitor she said nay.

— Elfrida Walker

THE WHOLENESS

Tumultuous feelings pierce my internal self — screaming and writhing, endlessly searching for some . . . , any . . . , form of release.

But, the cold, steely control that sheaths my entire being — bands together, reinforcing all barriers, crunching, compacting, burying all emotion in the dreary, bleak wasteland that exists deep inside of me.

I long to find the blessed passage out of the dark core of my person, to begin the tedious journey in which I carry, drag, and thrust the heavy weight of my burdens out into the open, relinquishing them into the infinite blue sky, where magically all the immense oppressive sensations turn to diminutive, weightless bobbles that float into oblivion — forgotten except for rare, repugnant flashbacks that grow increasingly evasive with the healing hands of time.

I keep searching for the path out of this hellish turmoil, the tiniest ray of hope driving me forward — I'll continue to seek the rapturous vision of total fulfillment, elated happiness, and complete wholeness I believe can be in this existence I call my life.

— Loya D. King

A poem for a time
    when I own not one word
        nor am privy to any definition,
    when I am neither here nor there,
    when I am neither loved nor unloved,
    when I am neither at home nor homeless,

For a time
    or all of the times
    when we find ourselves wading through a stasis,
    when the pointilistic past offers no tenable image,
    when we move trepiditiously towards the fog of the future,

For a time
    when we grovel for the strong support
        or, too, just a firm hand,
            and stumble gracelessly when we find neither,
    when we cling to over-rehearsed actions
        and moral mantras

            Until we discover
                in a moment of exhaustion

                    the inescapable truth
                        of powerlessness,

                    the humbling joy
                        of grace.

— Karen Beaumont

188

What beauty does steal the night?
When your eyes become faded by cover of darkness
What words utter you in sheer delight?
A dream in a dream faded in love making
How does your eye not notice my stare?
What greatness they do glance upon
How generously you giggle and toss back your hair,
The wind blowing waves in a field on and on
When will you come into this place?
How empty this heart does seem
When will you enter with your flowing grace?
How graceless all others falter in compare
Who will you whisper to those words in your dream?
Ears all turn and wait to burn in passionate delight
Who will see a beauty so pure it is obscene?
When you become faded by cover of night . . . .

*Dedicated to Judy for her encouragement; Josué for
setting me free; and The Albany Club for their love.*

— **Elizabeth Bergeron**

THIS MUST END

Today must be the end of this love for a boy
The relationship has been total joy

The stolen days and nights filled with passion beyond belief
This must end, yet there is pain with no feelings of relief

Every stolen moment was worth the risk
This must end, it has finally come to this

Although we are many miles apart
This must end, because you are still in my heart

Due to commitments to others we love dearly
This must end, we are now beginning to see clearly

In each other we found joy, passion and love
This must end, because it is frowned on from above

Tears run down my cheeks and my heart is filled with pain
This must end, it is the end of the game

When eyes are closed and beautiful sweet memories flow
I know this must end, it is time to let go and close the door

Goodby my love, this must end.

— **Doris Moore Davis**

FATE

It took a car crash for us to meet
You couldn't walk; you couldn't speak.

They brought you to Intensive Care and assigned you to me
I cared for you day after day diligently.

I medicated you for pain
I kept you breathing
I dressed your wounds
I monitored your heart beating.

I gave you all the TLC I had to give, and
you returned it all to me on the day we wed.

It's been ten years since I've thought of those days
God I don't understand your mysterious ways.

We loved being together
Connected by the love of our hearts
Today it took a car crash to pull us apart!!

*Dedicated to the person who always inspired me to write,
through listening to her own many, wonderful verses.
The true talent of our family, my mom, Millie.*

— **Michelle L. Redd**

GREEDY YOU

Did I ever tell you
How much I like you?
I've told you I love you
Which after all should mean
Much the same thing . . .
But it doesn't.
Liking is deeper than love,
Though I'm sure I would get a lot
Of resistance on that one.
You don't necessarily have to
Like someone to love them, and
Vice versa.
How did you manage to get both
From me?

— **Rebecca G. Barbieri**

My eye is filled with
a tear of sadness
where do I go to cry?

My mind is filled with
thoughts of wrong
Why do I wonder why?

My mouth is filled with
words unspoken
Where do I go to speak?

My heart is filled with
unknown hate
Where can I go to shriek?

My body is filled with
unknown fear
Where can I go to be alone?

My world is filled with
a great loneliness
Why have I always been on my own?
WHY?

— **Kerri Hansen**

YOU, ME, WE

To there
I stare
With eyes of glass
And see that love has come to pass
The love I felt is rage inside me
A hungry rage deep inside me
That feeds upon your sight.

And when at night
I try to sleep
And pray thy Lord my soul to keep.
I lie awake and think of you
It pains me so to think of you
As I tussle in the night.

And when the night has turned to morn
Of your smile I do scorn
"Do you mock me?" I doth ask.
Is your smile a wicked mask?
But still I wait and think of we.
I daydream and think of we.
Dreaming of souls in flight.

— **Francis Lee**

SILENT TEARS

I may be smiling, but deep
  inside I'm fighting.
A heart full of sorrow, never
  looking forward to tomorrow.
Sick and tired of life, such
  madness and strife.
It's raining in my heart, when
  will the sunshine start.
Hiding lonely feelings inside, I look
  for someone to confide.
Maybe my life should end,
  because there is no way to mend,
Things done wrong.
The past is long.

—L. Rachel Carson

THE WALL

You stumble over hate
to hit the wall that's formed.
From jealousy and lies
you built it on your own.

The hurt inflicted once
just didn't seem to end,
you let the fire burn too long
and left behind the flame.

You never tried to understand
the way they lives their lives —
it didn't suit your morals
and their choices hurt your pride.

So pushing pain back and forth
will cause the hate to grow,
and building on the lies you hear
will help the wall stand tall.

—Paula Jiron Ewy

THE MEMORY

The memory is always strong
in your heart.
  Don't ever forget him and he'll
never part.
  Just hold on tight, and don't ever
let go.
  The peace will come within
someday you'll know.
  That feeling of joy, that
smiling face.
  The person is gone, but the
memory is not erased.
  No one can get them, though
you feel like they already have.
  The feelings so deep and at
times it hurts so bad.
  The loss is so great, and
the pain is so strong.
  You're so darn angry, but you
know that you're wrong.
  People live and people die,
we all have no answer,
  But the question is always why??
  So remember this poem that
I wrote here today.
  Hold on to your memories,
don't ever let them slip away.

—Alisia G. Rose

THERE ARE NO GROWTH OPPORTUNITIES IN HEAVEN

*A discourse upon Mark Twain's
"In heaven an angel is nothing special"*

Life once eternal will glide on oblivious
  With decorum and new deathless parchedness;
But this temporal life to be embraced
      no more
Its despairs and its joys, its transient fervor.

So savor deep draughts of this profane
      world's oblations;
For in heaven you're bereft of desires;
As once from this mortal coil your soul
      has departed
Your uniqueness be obliterated forever.

*"The opposite of death is desire"
Tennessee Williams.*

—Ellen Baudisch

I'M NOT HAPPY

I'm not happy with the days that pass before my eyes.
To many friends and family, by this comes as a big surprise.
This is a time in my life where everything is such a blur.
My mind dwells so far in the past,
When it should be focused on the future.
Many things have happened in my life,
That would endure you to cry.
There were often times when I asked God to take mercy,
And to allow me to die.
I haven't been raped, or beaten as a child.
Most people would consider my homelife as being quite mild.
I love my family,
And the happiness they have given me.
They themselves have made my life very satisfactory.
I think my happiness comes from within.
It is not my fears nor my ability to sin.
My unhappiness dwells on my expectation of myself.
I want to succeed in life,
Even if it means going through hell.

—Nina Kennedy, age 16

WITHOUT A FLOWER TO NURTURE

I am without a flower to nurture.
Without a bare thigh upon which to place my gaze.
Without a barrier through which I would burrow.
Without the eye whose tears I could share.
Without the arms to embrace me when I tremble.

We are of a battle-scarred heart, my body and my acts.
We are sometimes pale and incoherent.
Sometimes bitter, sometimes soiled.
Sometimes dull, sometimes jagged.
Sometimes lonely, and sometimes untimely.
But oft times rapturous, and oft times jest.

See you an old man who knows himself, but fails to
      understand his wrinkles.
See you a young man that searches for, but cannot find
      his sun, and in his acts speaks for his failure to locate.
And see you a small, cold child, eager to pass by his
      playground misfortunes, trek to the highest rungs of
      the jungle-gym, look out over the herd of young players,
      meet the gaze of his sun, and the satisfied stare of
      himself standing next to her.

—J. Andrew Parcell

COLLEGE WAS SUPPOSED TO BE FUN

Cracking the books has become number one
when coming to college it's supposed to be fun.

Studying and testing the whole semester
makes you feel like a courtroom jester.
The teachers sit up in class with a smile
with plenty of notes to last for a while.
When the mid-term arises and the papers
are due, the teacher asks, "How far are you?"
As you look up with a smile so lively and quick
"The dog ate my paper and it really made him sick."
No matter who you talk to we're all in the
same boat, studying and testing to keep us afloat.
A year into college with a degree almost there
makes the classes you need just able to bear.
With the winter comes the new fallen snow
we pray for a foot so we don't have to go.
When all the studying and testing is almost
done. You begin to realize that college was
supposed to be fun.

—Linda Geiger

PAPER

You know me like your TV.
I don't like it when you tear me out.
But you know me more like a tree.
But you think of the time you wrote your biography on me.
Ouch, the scratching of the pen.
Or the time you did your test on me.
Right now, you wrote this poem on me.
But the ripping the tearing the crumpling I hate.
Also, that English book that told you how to write a poem,
That's me!

—Jeremiah C. Moore

THE QUILL PEN OF KNOWLEDGE

My mind is an overflowing ink well.
Blue thoughts leak over the brim,
as the quill pen of knowledge dips in.
The feather pen scrawls its writ of mandamus:
"Destroy the right down deep from within us."
"Their mind is blank, no one has preset it,
let us wreak havoc and see what will happen."
"Will they live, will they die,
to see their soul dampened?"

They'll never know until it's too late,
their minds are warped and the devil's their soulmate.

—Debra J. Dickinson

A POEM

A poem is a thought,
of a fight you have fought,
or a gift you have bought.
A poem is a dream,
of a big gold shiny ring,
or a song that you will sing,
a poem is a wonderful thing.

—Brandi Susanne Hill

ODE TO A MACINTOSH

Oh, my little Mac.
It likes to give me a heart attack.
One of life's great advancements,
The personal computer enhancement.
No mind of its own,
But my consciousness alone
Cannot outwit
The Mac in a snit.
Error message.
Ah, sh—
oot!

—Michael T. Armstrong

YOUR MIND

Your mind is like a smorgasbord,
There are so many things to choose
from.
You can choose what you want,
Or you can choose whatever you see is
right for you.
Or, sample all of it & see what you like
best.
But always be careful in what you
choose,
'Cause your mind is everything to
you in life.

—Jessica B. Pister

You may wonder why I waste time
writing this crazy stuff.
To retain my sanity I think that's reason
enough.
So when I have problems and I can't
sleep at night.
In my mind I do poetry till dawn's early
light.
Worrying is dangerous and can shorten
your life.
Stress is its equal and will create
strife.
When I think about poetry and words that
will rhyme.
I dispel the problems that trouble my
mind.
You may say to yourself, "This man's not
all there."
I couldn't argue with that, no I wouldn't
dare.
As a matter of fact I would say you're
absolutely right.
If I had both oars in the water I wouldn't
worry all night.
As Joyce Kilmer had said many years ago.
It's fools that write poems.
But only God can make things that grow.

—Melvin DeHass

THE CHILDREN

The sounds of little children fill
    My troubled heart with joy,
A small girl humming to herself,
    A squealing little boy.

The love of little children fills
    My restless soul with bliss,
A flower plucked by tiny hands,
    A baby's tender kiss.

And when my soul despairs and gloom
    Beclouds my rushing thoughts,
Then sweeter is the laughter and
    The smiles of tiny tots.

God bless the little children as
    He blesses us with them,
For children are a precious gift
    That God has given men.

—Roberta E. Benedict

THE JOY OF CHRISTMAS

Christ the Holy child did lay,
    In a crib all lined with hay.
Even the cattle stood amazed,
And in awe and admire praised,
Christ the radiant babe, so small,
Born to be the Lord of all.
Wisemen traveled from afar,
Guided by the heavenly star,
On they traveled 'til they found
Baby Jesus, safe and sound.
Then, on bended knees, they hailed
Their King and then departed to tell,
That the King was here at last
And all others would surpass.
As our candle lights burn bright,
May we find the King tonight,
And as wisemen did of old,
May we let our hearts unfold;
That we too may feel His presence,
And share the joy in all its essence.

—Erma West

GIFTS FROM HEAVEN

All would I give to you,
    no thought untouched.

To the heavens would I turn,
be there no end to my reaches.

I would grasp the stars,
for they be precious jewels.

Meteors would I capture,
for they be messengers of time.

The moon would I give to you,
in all your innocence.

A comet would I take,
be it an angel from heaven.

The rings of Saturn would I give,
for these will be our sacred vows.

All would I give to you,
but there be one gift greater,
MY LOVE FOR YOU!

—David L. Forand

A CHANGE WITHIN

A dry, dusty desert is all that I see,
    A mirage and some flowers to signify me.
In the midst of myself there's water to drink,
But trusting my heart still deeper I sink.

Then blinded by sand, I cannot see clear—
My mind says again that surface will appear.
Now consider the flowers, how they toil and spin—
Yet I am the same—it's hidden within.

So I look in the mirror, the mirage is not there,
Only gray like a deadness and oddly I care.
These feelings of hopelessness cut like a knife,
But I remember the God who first gave me life.

I look up knowing Him whom I've missed for so long,
His strength is comfort and the healing is strong;
The cleansing water enters, a change deep inside—
A new life has started, now in Him I abide.

—Andrea Hernandez

REBORN

I am rested
My thoughts are straight, my mind clear
My troubles are over, my soul strong
My moods are at rest, without any fear
I am reborn, I am a deer

I fly through the forest, alone with myself
I dance in the meadows, in a small paradise
I drink from the ponds, I rest in the fields
I live by day, and sleep by night

I care for life around me, I cherish all I have
The only fear I carry near, is to return to what I was
A beast that stalks his fellow clan,
A beast that uses his might
A beast that could terrify, any day or night

This beast must be feared by all,
for it survives on making others fall
The only fear I carry near,
is being born again a man

—Deborah Anne Doran

WHERE WOULD YOU RATHER BE?

A queen in a foreign land,
    with all life's treasures at your hand.
Or with your child beside your knee,
where would you rather be?

A leading figure in the business world,
thinking fame your greatest pearl.
Your child awaits you to fill his heart with glee,
ask him, he'll tell you, where would you rather be?

A student in a classroom thick,
are you guaranteed an occupation you can pick?
Is that your lonely child I saw seated under a tree?
You don't have time you said, you are where you'd rather be?

Oh! Let's not forget your duties as a member of the church,
so you may be seen on your "Godly" perch.
She says, "Oh, Mom, I also need you spiritual-ly;
but that's okay, because I know of where you'd rather be."

Wouldn't it be better to teach your child to pray?
To lean on Christ, his Saviour, each and everyday.
Dear Mother, set that Godly example for him or her to see,
isn't that where God chose you to be!

—C. Rene Ponder

HOW A QUACKER CROAKED

Yesterday I had a bit of good luck,
I went hunting, and spoke to a duck.

He told me about his lack of fear,
For 'tis the season to hunt deer.

He told me where there was one.
He said he'd show me, just for fun.

So away we went and up, just ahead a bit,
Was the largest deer that could be imagined, an easy hit.

Just as I was about to take a shot,
The duck did quack, and off the deer did trot.

I was so mad I wanted to fight.
And that is why I had duck for dinner tonight.

— **Rev. Dixon Main**

ON THAT DARK SCARY NIGHT

From the woods that I came,
To the castle so right.
By the path to and fro,
And then it was night.
So I went inside; with fear in my face,
Oh, how I thought, "What a dark scary place."
And I wandered around with the door to my back,
AH! I screamed as I came upon that huge hulking Yak.
And he ran away baying as I recovered from fright,
I continued up the stairs on that dark scary night,
As I got to the tower and as I stood there,
Something growled from behind me that I thought was a bear.
Then I turned and my eyes beheld,
That I was to be befeld by . . . a hare!!
A hare, a hare, that gave *ME* a scare.
And I laughed haughtily at the sight.
I laughed 'til I cried with all of my might.
Then he hopped up to me and sniffed at my shoe.
Then he gobbled me up and here I am with you.

— **Amanda K. Kelly, seventh grade**

AN EMPASSIONED ENEMY

Such was this empassioned fate
A law enforcement officer ate and ate
He, not every other, had license to debrew
His coffee and antkiller once was two

Now he's overthrown
The bric-a-brac is not his own
License to murder and bring to trial
Made any licensed minister burn up and turn vile

So this is the occasion to turn to many
Occidental friendship and a turnship enclouding memory
Now this has turned backward and the exclusive right
To join foe to foe friend to friend in this equestrian fight

Jump on me tear me over and burn me up
I'll join thee in this equestrian statue meant to sup
Here we all are the superintendant of police
The next hi-jack trouble and we'll ruin your next monthly lease

So here is the police
A temper tantrum and we'll throw you a neutered release
Sorry is the income he hath made
His tailored suit is jaunty and half a spade

— **Paul R. Grosse**

THE RESTLESS RATS

Two young mousers, playing in
The cellar,
One got restless, and he began to
Holler,
'Round and 'round in circles he
Spun just like a top,
Until old momma mouser said,
"Now Rastus you must stop!
Go fetch a nest for us to rest,
Go get some food to feed us.
I'm getting mighty tired of you,
So hurry, get your speed up."
Now if they'd known what was
In store,
They would have been more quiet,
Because the old man with a gun
Was soon to start a riot.
One shot was all he needed,
And Rastus spun no more.
Two shots and momma mouser
Lie stretched out on the floor.
The moral of this little verse
Is,
Never cause a rumpus, 'cause
In the end it's you who pays,
Lay stretched out like a
Compass.

— **Cathryn Eades**

MY COFFEE

Listen, I hear it perking
It's music to my ears,
The aroma is filling the kitchen
As it has for many years

I can't stand it when it's weak
Or colored water, at its best,
I'd just as leave not have it
It's coffee I detest.

I like my coffee, strong and dark
A bit of sugar and cream,
I also like it piping hot
Unlike some other I've seen.

All who come are welcome
To sit and have a cup,
For I make it every morning
As soon as I am up.

Some will say, as they always do
It will actually curl your hair,
That it's strong enough to walk alone
Or lift you from the chair.

They say the spoon will stand upright
It will grow hair upon your chest,
It will glue the saucer to the cup
And other comments from the rest.

I don't care when they call it mud
They can laugh and joke around,
I like my coffee just this way
Perked strong and blackish brown.

— **Gilbert L. Hilderbrand**

WHAT I DREAM

    See the stars,
       Smell the air,
Be an angel up so fair.
Like the birds flying high,
Now so fine I can touch the sky.
    See the sea?
I am now free
To catch those fish and just
       To be me.

—Stephanie Ballard

HORSES

I love horses very much
They all have the softest touch
They run fast
Right on past
And they stand tall
Against their stall
They love hay
It makes them neigh
They stand and sleep
While their ponies weep

—Nicole Lynn Hoppaugh, age 9½

BIRDS

Birds! Birds! Birds everywhere!
Watch them soar, through the air!
How I wish, I was a bird,
Life would be a story untold!
Secrets no one could tell a soul,
The heavens are just at my reach,
When things got rough,
I would fly away,
and land somewhere of peace and joy!
No one would interrupt my world,
if so,
I would fly away to the farthest knoll!

—Joanne Medina

WINGS OF AN EAGLE

Wings of an eagle, how it flies so
high up in the clouds, dashing
through the sky, as the eagle
incessant so high going on its
way, without incertitude in
mind, yet having wings of an
eagle, and being called indefeasible
of being an eagle, it's not kind, there
is no fear or shame in the air,
While its wings are swift, and free
it's only fair, while the heart wonders
from place to place, from time to time,
and why call it a crime, because
the wings of an eagle get tired
and need rest, it becomes hungry,
and must eat, by doing its best,
he must defeat its only purpose
to Live, and Let die, to ride
on the wings of an eagle, and
seeking the meat of Life.

—Dee Moxley

FREE AS A BIRD

A bird of flight with great wings to fly, a
bird that soars high in the sky.
Though can you see that is no bird, for
that bird I see is only me.
Great wings to fly and balance me. I'm glad
I can fly high and free.
How could this be that I can fly so free, like
an eagle which sits proud in its tree.
I may laugh, I may love, as I jump and play.
It seems I can fly most any day, as from
past to future all my time is spent helping the
others that's the love of it.
Though can you see what I may see, how would
you picture yourself in a tree.
Maybe you'll see things as that great eagle
can see things.

—Melissa A. Green

A FROG IN MY TUB

I looked in my tub, and what did I see?
A big green frog looking back at me.
He was taking a bath, a bath in my tub,
And singing a merry rub-a-dub-dub!

I said, "Hey frog, I've worked up a wrath."
"Make yourself scarce, now get out of my bath!"
"The towels are scattered all over the room,
And the smell in the air reeks of perfume."

"I can't believe you would do this to me.
You're a very bad frog and very naughty!"
"Oh," said the frog, "my poor brain you rack,"
As he gave me the brush to scrub his back.

He continued to go on using the tub
And continued to sing a rub-a-dub-dub.
Now it has to be knowledge in my head that I lack,
Cause I took the brush and scrubbed that frog's back.

—Gloria Ann Kaminsky

MY TWO VERY IMPORTANT FRIENDS

I have two very important friends in my life,
They never let me down.
They are always here for me,
I never want to be without them.

They comfort me when I am sad or crying,
They play with me when I am happy.
They are my two very important friends,
I would be lost without them.

They can be demanding at times,
But they are allowed to be.
They can be moody at times,
But that's okay, too.

They give me strength,
They are great listeners.
I would be lost without them,
They would be lost without me and each other.

They are indeed very important friends to me,
They are my family.
My two very important friends are **Smokey** and **CJ**,
My two cats.

—Celeste A. Dewey

EXPERIENCE

Age has no phase on this word,
yell and scream, you are still unheard!
Naive attitudes in different personalities,
It makes no difference what the sexuality.

You can say it, write it, spell it,
they won't know until they feel it!
Everyday your pain is doubled,
On the other line there is no trouble.

Lack of knowledge is one deprived,
Lack of experience is nothing to hide!
Some are good and some are bad,
but that is the price to pay for something one's had!

—Jeanmarie R. Near

A BALANCE FOR ALL

I heard on the news, an oil tanker had spilled,
And all of the precious wildlife killed,
Worse than the Exxon Valdez, 25 million gallons of oil,
Leaking into our waters, and into our soil.

The rain forests are burning at an alarming rate,
Forget reforestation, it will be too late,
Soon will be gone all the trees and the parks,
Earth will only be left with man's ugly marks.

Our oceans are poisoned, some we can't even drink,
Because of the toxins we pour down our sink,
It's home to the fish that are dying as well,
As for the long term affect, only time will tell.

There is a family of bears who all live in France,
But there are only nine left, we should give them a chance,
They will all die when their habitat is lost,
Should a highway be built as them as the cost?

We can't live without trees, or live without water,
We can't live without the beautiful animals we slaughter,
We must stop this destruction, and work as one nation,
Or make a new definition for the word preservation.

—Tammy Amador

LEGACY

Conceived while they named names
I toddled as young men froze in Korea.

My teenaged eyes watched the murder of my president:
pink suit, blood-red roses, assassinated assassin.

Murder fell upon murder.
It tripped on a Nobel Prize winner,
and stumbled over a dead president's brother.

It flamed in Watts
and rained napalm in Indochina
muscling its way through 50,000 of my countrymen.

It brushed its bony fingertips against two more presidents
and a Polish pontiff,
while an aging rock star bled on a sidewalk in New York.

As murder crept by credit card into Grenada
and stormed through the Falklands and Panama
to the Gulf of Arabia
The Wall Crumbled, and the Red Bear hibernated.

Husbands rage. Children starve.

And a heavy-lidded generation
stares vacantly from behind a crack pipe.

—Sheelagh M. Schano

TOGETHER IN HEAVEN

When she closed her eyes,
she saw his face.
Was he heaven sent,
maybe a sign of grace.

The walks on the beach,
the candle light dinner.
Did we ever think it would last?
Could it last forever?

Twenty years have passed
since we've said our vows.
We are still together
back then and now.

Two stones in a graveyard
side by side *forever*
this is the way they will stay
together in heaven forever.

—Crystal Arthur

THE DECISION

Amidst the sound of battle,
The terrified soldier stood,
He had never taken a human life,
And he didn't know if he could.

As the battle fiercely raged on,
He held tight to his gun,
Fighting off the instinct,
That told the young man to run.

Bravely he raised his weapon,
And firing, a soldier fell,
He'd taken his first human life,
In this battlefield of hell.

As remorse overwhelmed him,
The young soldier understood,
He had to kill to stay alive,
No part of war was good.

—Timothy J. Luersman

Night settles on a small town
in the middle of nowhere
The hours fading away with the
sun's rays
In the house so big she sits on
the edge of her bed
The house is silent and she cannot
clear her head
The fuzziness in her mind is
driving her insane
Since the day she first got high
she has not been the same
Alone in her bedroom she begins
to cry
Bringing her hands to her face she
wishes she could die
She is yet another number added to
the ranks
Another life God created that
drugs take.

—Raquel D. Logan

SOCIAL INJUSTICE

Disabled by discrimination
Damned without justification
Disgraced by arrogance
Deprived by insolence
Deceived by hypocritical phoniness
Defeated by poverty and loneliness

—**Fran Ericksen**

MEMORIAL

Students of Beijing,
Victims of the brutal hand,
The line spoken by Lincoln
For his fallen men
Can be spoken of you in kind.
"They died that government of the people,
By the people, and for the people
Shall not perish from the face of the earth."
May you now enjoy eternal peace.

—**Vincent P. Scholten**

YUKIAH

jaw drops, book meets floor
intrigued by contrast.
personality wanders from others
chancing upon alike.

scarlet sun rises
awakening berried emotions.
new fertilized flower
spread-eagles its insides.

heart of silk brushes life
leaving penmarks of poetry.
so long, farewell
there goes my phantom.

—**Alicia Hansen**

THE TEAR

A babe is born.
Its first sound is the cry—
and the tear.
As the babe grows
it trips, it falls,
and gets up to try again—
with the tear.
A fight, a broken date,
a perfect gift—
and the tear.
Striving, trying to get ahead,
hungry bodies, a warm familiar love—
and the tear.
A new babe, a full heart—
and the tear.
The grown child being laid to rest,
the new child, with sadness and love,
and the tear goes on—
with love, joy, and sadness,
but the tear goes on.

—**Kenneth A. Davis Sr.**

"FREEDOM" BODY, MIND, SOUL

Something worth much more than gold,
That's why today it can't be sold.
Freedom to decide your own religion,
Freedom to have your own ambition.
Freedom to choose throughout the nation,
Freedom to live without segregation.
Freedom for the tall, skinny, or fat,
White, Hispanic, Asian, or Black.
We're not completely free though it may seem,
It was once said, "I have a dream."
"Let freedom ring." "Let freedom ring."
Coined by the powerful Rev. Martin Luther King.
Although it's gone and in the past,
Thank God almighty we're free at last.

—**Khot Souimaniphanh**

OUR NATIONAL TREASURE — FREEDOM

Freedom has a price they say.
Once gained, it is not set in place eternally
Like the sun, or the moon
Or other fixtures of the universe.
Freedom must needs be watched
And guarded with great vigilance.
For there are those who seek to wrest it from us,
And not by forceful means.
Today, by devious ones.
And by clever means to take it from us
If we are unsuspect.
It therefore deems most wise, that we
In guarding such a treasure
Do not forget those
Who handed down to us this treasure.
This legacy was purchased by their blood and tears.
And even lives.
Let no one forget the price.
It was paid at Valley Forge; Yorktown; Gettysburg;
the forests of Argonne, at Okinawa, Iwo Jima and
even Dak To and Saigon.

—**Laura J. Laing**

MY NATION

A Nation bound by the masses;
Melting, Burning — Up in Ashes!

A Grand Old Lady to welcome the weak;
They search for hope, long for peace and ask advice.
But Her back is turned once inside!

Assimilation, Salvation —
Hover over the land like fluffy clouds.
People see different shapes — Some don't look Up!

Discrimination, Damnation —
Roll across the land like a blanket of fog.
People can't see — Accidents happen!

Red, Yellow, Brown, Black and White;
A crayon box to paint a Rainbow.
Be careful! — Stay within the lines!

"Land of the Free, Home of the Brave!"
Battle cry of the weary white faces.
Others can sing — but are not convinced!

A Nation bound by the masses;
Melting, Burning — Up in Ashes!

—**Eric Ward**

So as in the beginning of the life of a rose so were you.
An unknown branch with the hopes and dreams of a future blossom.
Bearing the tides and winds of all that nature produces, enduring to the
end to reach its purpose.
Days and weeks and years of constant change, and alas' the branch begins to
grow. Its hopes and dreams are fulfilled along the way, as it reflects upon
the times and the things that have touched it, and in return the things
it has given of itself. And as with all, a time of harvest and change to start
again, to a new beginning, never forgetting its Creator . . . .

    —David R. Burkle

HAPPY ST. PATTIE'S DAY

The old black thorn shillelaghs, many shades of green
  eating Irish porkpies, and of course those buttered beans
Gram singing Irish ditties, telling stories of long ago
We'd all sit down and listen, our faces and hearts a glow
Dad bought us Irish potatoes, and shamrocks made of lace
you could see my Dad was Irish, by the pride upon his face
a suit of green with shoes to match, a tie and his socks too
so excited — every year — you'd think Ireland was brand new
Dad loved and believed in leprechauns, St. Patrick was his own
he would talk of County Cork, and fences made of stone
he would eat corn beef and cabbage, watch the parade the whole day through
greeting everyone he sees with, "Happy St. Pattie's Day to you."

    —Patricia Ann Craven

THE RING

Ignoring the cries that followed him, he stormed out of the house.
Glad that he had discovered her duplicity
    before it was too late.
                "Lost the ring," indeed! Such a concotion of pearls
                and opals as had graced no engagement before them!
                It must have been a flirtation with that gentleman
                    whom he knew had been eying her.
He strode through the garden
Pausing once to reflect on how happy they had been
                Sitting on that very bench last night, and he in
                    blissful ignorance.
His eyes were blinded by rage and pain; he could not see
    the glimmer of gold and opalescence
         from amidst the grass.

    —Catherine Blair

THE LEGEND OF THE DUTCHMAN'S TREASURE

There's a place in Arizona, where it's said there can be found,
  A treaure in the mountains, just outside a little town.
No one knows exactly where the Dutchman hid his gold,
They only know the story from the legend that is told.
Many, many years ago, a man was passing through,
A little town called Tucson, with possessions but a few.
He went into the mountains, in the hope that he would find,
A treasure legend told was hidden, in a long abandoned mine.
One year later he returned, claiming riches beyond measure,
He'd found at last what now is called, the famous Dutchman's Treasure.
Before he died, he left two clues as to where it could be found,
In the hills of Arizona, up above the Tucson town.
He told of a manmade window, through which the moonlight shines,
On a map he'd carved into a rock, to lead one to the mine.
Many men have gone there, in search of fortunes true.
They never found the mine, and they never found a clue.
Some say it's just a story of a poor man with a dream,
Who wanted more than anything, to see his pride redeemed.
Many say the legend is a fairy tale that grew,
But something else keeps telling me, this fairy tale is true!

    —Cheryl G. Mann

VERSERS OF LOVE

I took an oath, till death do us part;
I look for answers, within my heart;
As people fight, don't get along;
As people fear, for what is wrong;
Sometimes I feel, that I am blind,
Sometimes I feel, I must unwind;
Times play a part of my mystical life;
Time for husband, time for wife,
Answer to riddles, jokes and rhymes;
Answers to questions, all the time,
Yesterday we became one;
Yesterday was love and fun,
Years to come, years to past;
Years forever, our love will last,
I took an oath, till death do us part;
I look forever, within my heart,
Saying you love me, saying you're true;
Saying you need me, as I need you.

—Marcie Skeffington

COME HERE . . .

Come here . . .
Come walk with me awhile
And watch a sunset, share a smile.
Join me . . .
Here atop this hill.
Feel the gentle breeze?
Hear its laughter in the trees?
Now you be Jack and I'll be Jill
And race me to the pot of gold
That shines
For those who won't grow old.
See the rainbow?
Yes you can . . .
Use my eyes and try again.
View the world through eyes of green
I'll show you
All that I have seen.
Then I in turn will take your hand
And look through eyes
From where you stand.

—Sam

When we were little kids
and love was just a game
we vowed to stay together
we both would share your name.

We sat beside each other
on the bus to school each day
and when you got your license
your daddy's car became our way.

All through the years it was you
who caught me when I fell
and when I had exciting news
it was you I ran to tell.

But now that we are grown
and love's supposed to be for real
tell me dear sweet friend of mine
exactly what you feel.

Is love still a silly game
that only children play
or is our love a love
not even time can take away?

—Tracey L. Hendee

FEELINGS

Feelings, happy and sad
Sometimes feelings that make me mad.
Even shy and jealousy too.
Some make me happy like I'm just like new.

I like happy feelings always the best
'Cause happy feelings put me to rest.
Bad feelings make me real mad,
Blue feelings make me real sad.

I tell you feelings like stingy,
always make me feel dingy.
Selfish could make me greedy,
and I could not see those who are needy.

I've told you of feelings in my head,
I have feelings of lazy — don't want to make my bed!

Now I'm content and here to say,
that feelings come in various ways.

—Kimberly Owens, age 9

HIDDEN TREASURES

Searching for a lady whose destiny
is to be a positive image in society;
who has a heart filled with wisdom
and understands righteousness is the system
to help her comprehend precious life.
Never stabbing others with knives,
but letting me know every night
that everything is going to be alright.
Arrays of love that will stand forever;
she will be filled with beautiful hidden treasures.

I'm a real man,
but I realize that I need a real woman
who will provide a providence for
my emotions. Like the wind from the skies
she will remove the waters from my eyes.
Lord, I won't put pressure on this woman —
that's the sign of a heartless man.
A love that will reign forever and ever —
she will be filled with beautiful hidden treasures.

—Virgo

MY SONG

Today,
I heard a small child laugh,
How warm it felt,
How alive this small child was,
He saw a small bright yellow-gold-white butterfly,
Land by his arm,
He reached out,
And kissed it,
Ever so soft,
Then they both sang,
What a song it was,
The small child told the butterfly how to laugh,
And the small butterfly,
Told the small child how to fly,
As they both flew away,
I saw a big bright colorful rainbow,
Then in my heart,
I saw myself,
And the butterfly,
Was,
My song.

—Denis Allen Trehey

NATURAL MAGIC

Late one night
I wandered silently
along the stream,
listening to the water murmur—
and the wind whisper.

The sun was splashing colors
across the horizon,
fish were jumping tiredly
upstream . . . .

Terns flashed overhead
to protect their young,
and a young eagle landed on a rock
twenty feet ahead—

Just to watch
a human at ease.

—Kurt Kristensen

a warm blanket of words for you

keep yourself forever as beautiful
as you are today
and never let the shadows of life
portray their fantasies in your way
and if i play my part
a jester in your courts
to bring a smile onto your face
and happiness of all sorts.

and if for a moment
you alone i could share
to present myself as a
warm blanket to wear
to shield off all the troubles
in your world and see
that this life that i weave
was influenced by you, and just by you,
yourself to me

—Patrick Hunter

unfulfilled

we are forced to listen
to an untuned orchestra
for eight hours each day
        playing sour notes
from a secret score

as the conductors
        desperately accusing one another
attempt to please
a balcony of policy makers

who never notice
that silent section of professionals
        angry
        perplexed
        subdued
patiently awaiting
our signal to contribute
        notes of harmony . . . .

it could be a masterpiece
but our moment never arrives

—Phillip H. Durán

SHORT STORY

I thought my short story was simply the best.
It was so original from all the rest.
I just sat down, I created, and I wrote.
Often times in my old, ragged blue housecoat.
Then one day the mailman came to my front door,
Handing me rejection as he's done before!

—Fran LeVasseur

PRIVATE WRITER

Perched alone, the window view outside,
the writer scrawls the words that coincide.
The details unfold, spoken but not heard,
his life story is told in a single word.
He can make a pen sing — with fiction,
spending hours to mold the true depiction.
His lonely life is of his own choosing,
he views worldly strife as somewhat amusing.
But from his room, the world's a wondrous place,
he brings it to life, while leaving no trace.

—Mark W. Meyer

THERE IS POETRY IN ME, BUT . . .

I would write this poem,
    but first I must wash the kitchen curtains
    that hang sadly, grayly by the sink.
There is poetry in me,
    but I see the gnats on the August tomatoes
    that crown my pantry shelf;
    I must shoo them away.
There is much vision in my mind's eye —
    much grace to see the unseen,
            hear mute sounds,
            feel imperceptable motion,
But there is a child who cries,
    and I must attend.
There is poetry in me:
    a gift, a curse.
A conflict of what I am
    and what I am.
The ultimate response to life,
Thwarted by life itself.

—Patricia Rose

AUTOBIOGRAPHY THROUGH ALLUSION

She dreams of her Rochester, her Darcy, her Heathcliff.
But where are they?
She does not have a Thornfield to reside in.
She is blind to the moor's heather.
And what pride can she have in her name?
Let her feast as Kubla in his kingdom,
Fear is obsolete in passionless bones,
She can only welcome their love.

Take her with you.
Let her live in your dreams.
Allow her to be a Jane, a Charlotte, an Emily.
She offers little but devotion,
Yet, devotion is her greatest gift.
Take her from people's petty prejudices
Let her also be at peace and together—
Together you shall immortal be.

—Michelle Oskoui

THE SMALL LINK

We, of the world, have formed a big chain.
Be it black or white, red or brown, we learn to love.
To love my brother or sister of a different color is
my option.
I take that option, as a football player who runs with his
team's ball;
And I make my own playing strategy.
That strategy may be wrong; I have given my best and
I will not suffer for it.
If one person does suffer, I will endure with him.
The big chain we have formed ensures me that I am
But a small link.
If that link should be broken by me, I will feel more
Pain than my brother or sister.
With my soul knowing this, let me be strong;
My link may be all that keeps us together.

—Suzanne Rose

LOST INNOCENCE

As I sat in the shade of a tall oak tree,
I longed to be the children that I happened to see.
As they frolicked and laughed in the springtime sun,
how I wished to join them and partake in their fun.

But alas, I cannot join them, in their youthful ways,
for as sad as it is I've surpassed those days.
I couldn't help growing no matter how I tried,
it's no use denying, this age of innocence has died.

Although the pleasures of adulthood sometimes comfort me,
I cannot help but miss an age that again shall never be.
It seems like only yesterday my childhood truly begun,
and now before my eyes, already, this age of innocence is done.

It doesn't help by crying, or trying to drag my feet,
each time I start this battle I always reach defeat.
Even though I suspected that it would never last,
I cannot help but mourn for this age of innocence that's passed.

As I linger near the children, so carefree in their youth,
and I am here in my old age, pondering over the truth.
Although the trials of adulthood may fill me with exhaust,
I cannot join the children, for the age of innocence is lost.

—Jennifer Busby

LIGHT'S DIVISIONS

Think of us that day when we have paid in old coins
for the currency-crushing-loneliness have loosed the tongueless
gravities and served well the pirate-divorcing-planets

When I have gone tone-charted fiercely-restored in pride
to soar inside-or-out the constellations smallest whims
then you will say I am a myth outside the myths of logic

How will you answer me . . . Answer me in . . . as-you-find-me
fashioned to Time-Hushed-Sibilants
with voice-vacant-vogued as ever
then in moon-lit-words like you say
light is so careful in its division

Will you come to me when the sky is swiss-dotted
of unknown stars we never knew to speak-of
to shore down into the wind and wave
that wed so softly to bend into them
So will it be is this our unknown-speaking

If you will come to me star-proper if I should be lost
and by chance you should miss me in the moonlight
in the sounds of the willow-tree in the wind in the black night
remember as my spirit inside October and in all our ways of May

—f. Adrian Hatley

SURRENDER

Numbness settles over my mind
A broken heart beats, being
Possessed of a captive spirit
Both mirrors of a soul,
Once free and roaming
Now quiet and subdued;

What interest have I now
In this life,
Beyond that which is
Today, yet tomorrow
Fades away;

This is all I know
And no longer do I seek,
This is it—this is surrender
The surrender of my soul.

—Ernie R. Cole

RECLUSE

Are you digging your grave
child of a lost generation
For whom do you labor, who
is it you serve
Silence! Join this quest
of our last dignity
Abstinence/wrath of an entity,
singular assessment with the core
of great stature
Brought forth its dynasty of
gold laden vision unto obscure
truth . . . Disenchanted hope.
Open your garden in full bloom,
here to consummate abandonment
Was it you who sold the truth
for the price of pain and
raped dignity/Grief is dark
Self indulged incest with your
own greed, lonely in the wilds,
served by selfish needs . . . Recluse.

—D.B. Farr

OBLIVION

Huge raindrops pounding the roof
splashing in puddles curbside
lightning streaking across
the midnight sky followed
by exploding thunderclap
storm's ferocity shattering
sleepy hours lying awake
listening to heaven's war

Wondering if creeks overflowing
will wash asunder the dreams
of a lifetime amassing
its possessions coming
to naught and cascading
into oblivion forever no more

Where are the fates
when hopes are shattered
and despair rules
and life becomes
cruel no more
beckoning with siren's song?

—Daniel Rogers

EVOLVING

If we took a blade and scarred the sky,
The sun would fade and the clouds would cry.
The moon would sink (a dark forbode)
The stars would wink and all grow cold.
The grass in the meadows would surely die,
Eagles and sparrows would cease to fly.

The sea would calm and still all life,
Our hand, our palm, what a wicked knife.
The trees would grope to find the sun,
The people would hope that there would
                be none,
For the day would be so very hot,
That they would wish that they had not,
                scarred the sky.

        —Lori Bauché

THE RAVEN'S PREY

In the deep darkness of the night
I can hear them flap their wings
They are coming — coming for your soul
Their eyes are wide, their mouths are open
We hear their deafening cry
A scream in the wind
The chilling air of the night
Too dark to see them, you can't run and hide
They know where you are going
They will be there waiting, waiting to capture your soul
There's no escape — this will seal your fate
They know this is destiny
You know who you are, this prey of the Raven
And you know why they're after you
Your time is now up
The judgement is here.
You stop in the night and you hear the silence
You think you've gotten away.
But all around you are beady, black eyes
With hunger for blood . . .
Waiting to take your soul.

        —Carole A. Kritzer

OUTSPOKEN

For I am he the pebble, the outspoken one.
Suppressed and wedged between two boulders
On a rock cliff mountain side.
Struggling, tooth and nail inching my way,
Pushing away my counterparts, striving for daily light.
Muzzled and drowned by all sounds surrounded
Awaiting my time, my chance in the limelight.

Lift me and cast me aside,
To more common ground, surefooted.
Where I may recite my thoughts, my beliefs, my ideas,
Given the chance, hear this truth.
Feel the love, the hate, joys of happiness,
The anger, frustrations, the loneliness, the sadness.

Feel something then erect me to the highest pedestal.
Passing the words to every man, woman, and child,
To unite this treacherous rock cliff mountain side.

Feel nothing then cast me back,
Into the belligerent domain
From where you have plucked me from.
Suppressed and wedged never to utter another sound.

        —Zoltan Palkovits

AUTUMN

There is grace in a single leaf
lying in the hand,
separated, helpless,
feckless
to fall in gold dust
upon the land.

        —V.R. Wig

SKY VISION

Contemplating the opaque sky.
As the clouds whistle their tale.
About the orange red reflection,
that is a clue for speculation,
as the sun riles above the miles.
Where the fog is more than merry,
and the lightning is quite contrary,
and the sparrows catch your mind.
They looked . . .
Yes they seemed . . .
to be alive!!
And did they just scream?
"Don't hide from the sky."

        —Christopher Rudolph

In the heat of the summer
When the frogs and crickets
    sing no more,
As the sun sets
    for the last time,
The wind no longer blows.
Flowers and trees cease to grow;
It is time to move on
    with our lives.
We have to find ourselves
    within;
Only we can do this,
For only we hold the key
    to our soul.
No one can help;
No one can stop us.

        —Alexandre Belfield

TUMBLEWEED

Tumbleweed Body
    Skins and Bones Only

Tumbleweed Mind
Too many Rambling thoughts Intertwine

Tumbleweed Heart
Hallowed in every part

Blown here
By the cold desert wind
Blown there
By no one's particular sin

Here, there
There, here
But Always Nowhere
        in particular to go
          Tumbleweed Soul.

        —Diamond Bouaphanh

PANTHER

From the jungle, stalking rabbits he comes,
  With a sleek coat, black as the midnight sky.
Jade green eyes that burn through the jungle trees,
Hunger guiding him into the village.
To his honed senses, the man-scent is strong.

Into the hut he strides with confidence,
Seeing the children, and I with my staff.
Our eyes meet for a moment and we stare,
His eyes meeting the ground before mine.
With a growl, he slinks off into the night.

  —Forrest Burris

INDIAN TIME

Indian time makes more sense to me.
Clocks do not tick in harmony with
Mother Earth.

"Listen and observe;
There is a way and a time
For each part of being."
They taught this, but we forgot.
Lost,
We did not feel the subtle sound, smell, rhythm
That warned of danger
Or signalled spring.

Arise.
Savour the dawn.
Dedicate to the Spirit day's labour;
Listen to the beauty of its song.
Each song's time is short, and right.
When it is time to do it,
It will get done.
One should not have to rush
Through raspberries.

  —Linda L. Eagle

FROM TENTS TO TOWERS

A tent once stood on this red land;
  This land of the brave Indian band.
Here, the arrow found its mark;
  Where tears flowed in valleys dark.
There, the buffalo and deer did roam;
  Where no white man had made his home.

A tent once stood upon this red land;
  This land of the brave Indian band.
A land of grass and flowing stream;
  A land to supply the cattleman's dream.
A land of expanse for the farmer's plow;
  This land, none richer, did God endow.

A tent once stood upon this red land;
  The land of the brave Indian band.
Then suddenly there's another clan;
  A clan with a differing plan.
This brought forth the territory twins;
  The white man's tower with his wins.

A tent once stood upon this red land;
  That land of the brave Indian band.
Now the tent's part of a dream,
  Disappearing in the shadow of a towering gleam.
This red land has changed, finding statehood.
  Towers now stand where tents once stood.

  —Fran Hensley

WEATHER ANY STORM

The narrow beam glows beneath the sky
  In search of purpose, meaning, Why?

The main sail is tattered true;
Evidence of voyage gone askew.

O Captain, *"Who are you?"*
Through the waves you shall find direction
Release anchor and begin anew.

  —Sandra K. Jackson

BY THE LAKE

Ah, beauty confined.
Destination . . . ESCAPE.
  fire-flies glow
How idyllic July's kingdom
  lovely moonlit nuances
outright peaceful,
            quiet,
                    relaxing.
    silence
tranquillity unequalled
  vast wilderness
    Xanadu
  yielding zephyrs

—Deborah Lynn Trahan-Pero

WHEN DAISIES BLOOM

When daisies bloom,
I like to chase old paths
around the pasture field
where the cows used to graze;
and follow the trail
to the blackberry patch
at the edge of the field;
then wiggle my toes
in the sandy soil
of Kentucky Hills.
Let towering oaks whisper
and crows laugh;
while I zap white petals,
when daisies bloom.

—Camila Haney

SUMMER MOON

The orange yellow moon
  On that warm summer evening
Contained many secrets
And rare wisdom of ages past.

So many poets, romantics,
And songsters,
Had praised its mysterious
Beauty, their number was vast.

In the lower part
Of the eastern sky,
The large orange yellow sphere
Was full and bright,
And slowly ascending.

Gradually it traveled
Across the dark heavens,
While most of the world
Was settling in for slumber,
As their day was quietly ending.

  —Gil Saenz

SATAN'S MIRACLE

The hollowness in the child's
eyes cried out in want,
    Free Me! Free Me!
But the needle and the
damage is done.
    Innocence lost to the
predators of the streets.
    Freedom is the hand of
death.
    Childish laughter and game
lost to within the gray
concrete slab he lays upon.
    Tears of blood stain the
face.
    A voice screams out into
the night.
    "Welcome to man's doorstep!
Behold the miracles of Satan!"

—He who walked alone

MAD SALLY

She walks the streets alone
in shabby clothes hung loose
upon her shrunken frame
neglect, the passing years
are deeply etched
rough lines around her eyes.
To us who pass her by
she hurls abuse
small children laugh
and throw small stones
that find their mark
to shouts of anger
that bury deep her pain.
Mad Sal they say
and turn away
and in the rear view mirror
I see her lonely form
stumble slowly forward
and curse myself
for never having smiled

—Maureen Wilks

CHILD OF ABUSE

Airtight windows to her soul;
    they will not budge.
Unyielding as her father
    when she had done wrong.
Their tiny pristine panes,
    holding her in check.
Cryptic scribbled messages
    sealing in her pain,
as an illusion
    to the world;
keeping anger and hatred
    at bay until a
flash point is achieved.
    Uncompromising explosion
of their dazzling prisms of light,
    lying in shattered
crystalline stillness.
    A life forever changed,
left picking up the shards
    and continuing on . . . .

—Deborah Marsh Baxley

COULD YOU NOT?

Without a word you left forever,
    silently, in the still of night.
You never said that you were leaving.
    Could you not for a moment, have held me tight,
and reminisced of happy times?
    Or told me yourself that you couldn't stay?
Then reassured me of your love,
    just one more time, before going away?
A stranger called, said you were gone;
    your heartbeat ceased as I lay sleeping.
Could you not have lingered to say good-by?
    For good-byes cannot be said by weeping.

—Dianne Hamilton McGirr

JOHNNY PUSHER

It was bad from the beginning.
    My parents were apart.
I lived with my mother, who couldn't support herself let alone
    her little children.
I was only three and already I didn't like life.

I started sell'n pot around ten or eleven,
but it wasn't enough to support me and my family.
I was educated out on the street,
where I sold dope to the junkies that could afford it.
I was a rich boy then, and the big man knew it.

There was only one problem; I had started myself.
As the promotions came faster, the pressure grew stronger.
I soon found myself as deep as I had ever been.

As the time went on I found myself to be my best customer.
Sell'n the rock to my younger brothers to support my own habit.
My addiction grew readily as my supplies grew scarce.
My soul delved deep into darkness and trepidation; my own
    personal Hell!

"Punishment," for the crimes I had committed;
My life was cut short, by the bullet from my brother's gun.
I can't believe I wasted my life, WASTING OTHERS.

—Timothy J. Golliher

THE DEATH OF THE SUN

The Death of an old man is festive.
    A little boy cries,
Not crying for the old man.

The Death of a baby is awful.
The little boy cannot sleep,
Not because of the baby.

The Death of a father crumbles the roof of our home.
The Death of Mother extinguishes the fire in the hearth.
Yet the little boy fears the Death—A million years away.

The Death of the Sun
Wretched and colossal
Increasing and swallowing.
The little boy cries.

The burning hairs, skulls, and brain—shriveled up in the solar heat.
Broiling radiation—turns our stomachs out of our mouths.

Scared little boy, fears the Death—A million years away.

The Death of the Sun.
Wretched and colossal
Increasing and swallowing.
The little body fries.

—Kan Katsumi

INVISIBLE LINE

From a distance a child holds a flag.
A flag which stands for the FREE and the
BRAVE.
A flag propped up in the sand behind the
brave soldiers fighting behind the invisible
line in the sand.
The child holding the flag will hopefully be
able to one day live in a land full of love and
peace.
Where our flag can blow in the wind peacefully.
And where there will be no invisible lines in the
sand dividing a child who is now a
man.

*Dedicated to the men and
women who serve our country.
Thank-you.*

—Dawn Lovejoy

GRAY AND BLUE

He was young, so young that Spring day,
When he put on a uniform of gray,
Like his three brothers before,
He prepared to march away to war.
In his young mind he knew well,
He faced the very fires of hell.
It was with a heavy sigh,
He bid his Mom and Dad, good-by.
"I'll come back, he said, the Blue won't bury me."
"We'll pray for you, my son, and all your company."
The battles were fierce, fiercer than anyone knew,
Finally the Gray surrendered, there prevailed the Blue.
One by one three men came home, never to be the same,
War had taken a brother, John Milton, was his name.
The world seems to be the same as that Spring day,
When a young man put on a uniform of gray.
We are united as a nation, "Old Glory" still flies,
The worst of men still start the wars,
The best young man still dies.

—Myrna L. Hagy

LIBERTY REPOSSESSED

Give me your rich,
loaded with money,
with gold teeth gleaming.

Your technicians and technology,
the science of our salvation.

Keep your millions of hungry,
disease infested multitudes who bankrupt nations.

Our lady of liberty guards
against the violation
of her borders,
against the dark forces of foreign Drug Lords,
who rob the wealth of nations.

Our citizens cemented into mosaics,
inherited from a hundred cultures,
who practice democracy in reckless abandon.

Our nation suffering from too many good deeds,
policing the unwilling, feeding the insatiable,
and enduring the ineptness of leaders
who are measured in smiles.

Where is our leader born of log cabin, intellect nurtured
in the reality of our nation's poor. Oh distressed spirit.

—Rocky Lane Moore

I AM PROUD

I am proud!
I live in America, not a land of war.
When I walk down the street, I feel at ease.
At night, I sleep on a pillow with a
soothing voice.

I am proud!
Democracy is the power in force, the
guide of our country.
I can hold tight to my dreams because
of our land of the free.

I am proud!
But, maybe, some day things will change.
However, for now, I'll stay thankful
and enjoy the peace in our country.
Yes! I am proud!

—Mrs. Grace Freestone

THE AMERICAN FLAG

Before my team begins to play,
We take off our hats and start to pray.

And when I look up in the sky,
I see our country's flag held high.

The stars and stripes fill me with pride,
It makes me feel so good inside.

I pledge allegiance to the land,
Where people give a helping hand.

Where everyone works together,
To make our country strong forever.

I look up at the sky so blue,
And see our flag so brave and true.

And then I hear the umpire call,
"Come on boys, let's play ball!"

—Jonathan Simpson, age 10

IS IT POSSIBLE?

Oh, today was election day!
Over T.V. came all the news.
On our large T.V. all could see
the winner, president to be.

Some will be glad and others sad
but we will know and be relieved.
Perhaps all will give a big sigh
and hope soon our problems to solve.

Problems? Our problems — enormous!
Are they all of our own making?
None of us want to admit this
but — by and large they are our sins.

Admit — it will take many years —
perhaps two — three generations!
Let us who are living today
contribute our part. — When? — Right Away!

How can you help your country, men?
You too, ladies who wear fine clothes.
Young people, they must help, also.
Then we'll stand tall and proud once more!

—Eloise Koelling

THE SUN

When the sun comes up.
    Nobody's up.
When the sun goes down.
    Everyone's around.
But they're all in frowns.
They came to see the sun go down.
Then they're frowns.
They turn around.
To greet the sun go down.

—Tammie D. Murphy

DAY BREAK

Something happens at day break
  The earth comes alive
Sleepy eyes start to open
Birds are filling the sky
There is movement in the garden
Even under the stones
Many wonders are around us
Right here about our home
Feel the movement of a soft breeze
Playing across an open field
Murmuring in the fir trees
High on a hill
Gently whispering among the flowers
Outside my kitchen door.

—Margery Heath

GURGLING BROOK

By the gurgling brook I sat me down
with pen and pad in hand,
  And etched a sketch of God's handiwork
of water, trees, sky and land.
  And while I sat in the shady nook and
heard the song of the birds,
  My heart grew warm and silent
within and my tongue could find no
words.
  So I just sat there and very silently
worshipped the Creator of Earth,
  And drank in the beauty His hands
had made, and blessed the day of my
birth.

—Eloise Curtis McLeod

IN GOD'S COUNTRY

The Butterfly
    is not as free
        inside the acid globe.

The Trees
    are all toothpicks
        and hiker's furniture.

The Rivers
    are always on the lam.

The Birds
    have smoker's cough,
        and color.

And the Sky,
    like a dirty welcome mat,
        is not reversible.

—Brian D. Frost

FEATHERED MESSENGER

As heaven's portals opened wide
  The sunrise bathed the countryside,
It mirrored from each pane of glass
  And kissed the dew upon the grass.

Then, as it shone upon my face
  My silly heart began to race,
I whispered words of secret love
  Heard only by a morning dove.

While still at dawn of silver light
  From limb of tree the dove took flight
To lofty heights toward the west,
  My love - words tucked within its breast.

Soon gave my love's dear heart a thrill
  By perching on his windowsill
To trill my words, . . . beak opened wide,
  As sun danced o'er the countryside.

—Fran L. Grosvold-Grills

A STRING OF PEARLS

Accept these pearls and remember,
  each pearl is a moment.
Each moment is time.
Time of enjoyment and happiness.
Time of being with you.
As you finger each pearl, remember each is a
moment, cherish them as I do.
You have brought happiness to a new meaning.
May God grant me more time,
time filled with moments with you.
The beauty of each pearl,
represents the beauty of each moment.
Wear the string of pearls as beauty,
for beauty can only be worn by beauty.
The warm glow you feel from the touch of the pearls,
it's the warm glow of love I have for you.
So as endless as the string of pearls,
may our moments together be endless.

—Julian R. Plaster

A BIG CITY CHURCH

I am a big city church with a bell and a steeple.
Everyday I feel the warmness of people.
I am decorated with stained glass as well as graffiti,
giving shelter and food to the homeless and needy.

Sirens awake me in the early morning hours,
as well as the fragrant, colorful flowers.
I share in those moments of joy and happiness,
as well as the feelings of grief and sadness.

I see some people live the perfect life,
while others are carrying an inner strife—
often striving for what is right
in this beautiful city of lights.

I am a big, city church that has lived through the ages
and have seen all the possible stages.
Far from the serenity of nature,
but close to the excitement and danger.

As each year passes, so do the Masses
Singing in prayer without a problem or care—
Hoping each prayer will be heard
Because silence speaks a thousand words.

—Liziel Zapata

JESUS IS THE ANSWER

This world is filled with turmoil and sadness everywhere.
Everyone seems to be searching, longing for answers to all their cares.
Many feel rejected or hurt, and their hearts are so grieved.
The one they loved and trusted, brought more pain than they could believe.
A beloved child has rebelled and left the home empty and cold.
For some, a parent has become weak and ill or possibly left the fold.
Even little ones get very sick and often they too must die.
We don't understand, and in our pain we ask: "Why?"
Then on our knees we cry, "Oh Father, hear us when we pray."
He gently reminds us, "I am your refuge, in my arms you can stay."
Try thinking about the good times, the blessings He's given in the past.
And remember, God never changes — He is your answer — His promises forever will last.
So when your life is full of pain and you feel all alone and blue,
Look to Jesus, He loves you — will never leave you — He will see you through.

—Mary K. Dibert

A Beautiful child bestowed Viola and Jonas in the Spring of Twenty-nine.
N ow commencing their family with this gift so divine.
N o brothers were given to frolic or tease.
A comrade of sisterly love from Betty and Joan she would please.

M arriage to Bob fulfilled the desires of her heart.
A family she now would be able to start.
E ach of her children she gave distinct direction.

T o Robert, Dixie, Janis and Roberta her love and affection.
A nd her children learned the unique commitment of love.
B egetting their strength in what was dealt from above.
E ach day of our lives we will hear your laughter,
R emembering that you are at peace now and here after.

All of our love,
Your Kids

*Dedicated to our mother . . . may we forever smile
with your sense of humor, admire your courage and
cherish your love . . . .*

—Dixie Taber Cuba

LIFE

As we wander through Life, each eventful and sometimes uneventful day,
We constantly search for a better understanding of Life, we say.

The image of being worthy in someone else's eyes or just in ours, we forever strive,
Is sought by most, it gives us that constant and never-ending drive.

The never-ending hunt, in the game of Life, we play and play and play,
Takes place at the expense of others, in each and every way.

The constant searching and seeking to be accepted by all that we touch,
Leaves us sometimes feeling if it is worth it or is it too much.

The continuous meandering as we travel our course from day to day,
Affects our well-being, in many precarious ways.

The daily rituals of Life takes us away from each other, more and more,
As we navigate through the many mazes, to see what we have in store.

The searching for and accepting of the numerous roles we have to play,
Makes life challenging but sometimes burdening, make of it what you may.

The every day battles we fight with ourselves, of being hardened and tough,
Often leaves us wondering if the winning will truly be enough.

The feeling of importance and accomplishment usually keeps us on task,
Although enough is sometimes not enough, of all the things that are asked,

The numerous episodes that we face, some are happy and some full of strife,
But we bewilderedly march on, in this complex game we call Life.

—Michael Mobley

The earth spits shards of coldness
upon
a sea of snow
making the sun reflect its beauty
upon a hibernating soul
who gazes intently
towards the sky
in search of answers to whys.

—Rachel A. Kratzer

THE SPINDLY TREE

The spindly tree
stood out among the pines
So barren
it looked like a coat rack
waiting for something
to adorn its lonely branches
The reflection
on the water was so slight
not a single leaf
giving it very little size

—Marlene "Molly" Fink

AUTUMN LEAVES

Autumn leaves shone so much
brightness in the sunlight,
As the stars glow in the endless
and loneliness starry nights,
It's certainly a decorative delight,
Having seen such an incredible sight.

Autumn leaves turn their beautiful
colors,
From the splendorous green shamrocks
of Ireland,
To the golden sunlight of lemon,
That shone up the light of heaven.

—Joyce Nieuzytek

WIND

I stand in the field
Listing
And as it goes, I hear it
Hissing

It hisses like a snake
As it goes through the trees
And though I don't see it
I know it's there

I hear it
And feel it
In the air.

It's the air that we breath
Everyday, every year

It's what causes storms
The raging ones
The powerful ones
The monster ones

And no matter where you go
You'll always find it

—Jill M. LaBanca, age 12

VIRGIN SNOW

Hurried by the unrelenting hand of the north wind,
the virgin snow clamors for a place to rest.
It flutters into the uplifted arms of the trees,
blankets the nearby woods,
and cartwheels to its final resting place in the open,
unchartered field.
There it rests, as if in slumber,
awaiting its lover's kiss.
The soft caress of the night breeze causes it no alarm.
Its iridescent hues dance in the moonlight,
its innocency captivates the stars.
The pristine beauty knows no equal.
There it remains —
Virgin snow —
unaltered,
undisturbed,
undefiled.

—Cordelia B. Mueller

EBONY FROST

The frozen lake lies now in serenity
Come Spring it will be without an enemy

Icy winds encircle the barren sky
Who produces the ghostly echoes why

Towering trees stand solemnly askew
Surviving figures wrapped in soldier's blue

Eyes as indigo hardened as celluloid
Now drowning in pools of icy void

Vertebrate creatures hovering about
Breathing in and breathing out

The ritual icy death has begun
And winter's battle will be won

Absent of a bugler's call
Heroes as villains will rise and fall

Darkness will loom its iciness so austere
Until Spring returns with a majestic fanfare

—Amy Parravano

S.O.S

Iceberg starboard! Is it a mirage?
The ship of state keeps cruising . . .
Titanic choices to make . . .
Full speed ahead or,
rudder left? Rudder right?
Choppy, foamy waters.

Waves smashing hard against the hull,
cascading waters, obscuring the future.
A frozen moment; a quaking vessel, then . . .
ripped asunder, rivulets rushing in . . . higher! Higher!
It's decision time you fool!
Down with the ship of fools or . . .
Bail! Bail! Bail! S.O.S.! Survival instinct.

A child . . . a woman . . . I am not,
but, ready to die, I am not.
Lifeboat! I must have a lifeboat!
Mirage dissolves — reality —
Rather swim than sink into oblivion.
Remain afloat. Steer the course.
Steadfast decisions upon a stormy sea.

—Demetrius

KITTENS

Cute and cuddly.
Kittens are soft and frisky.
They are very playful.
Catnip toys and yarn balls are what they like to play
    with.
They like to pounce.
They love to play outside.
They claw the chairs and scratch the doors.
They hate getting baths and they especially hate
    dogs.
Kittens run, play, and fight with each other.
They like to sit on window sills.
They are very sneaky and sly.
Kittens are very curious animals.
They like to sleep all day and play.
But mostly they like to sneak around and find out
    what things are.

—Jolene Lynn Shade

A DEFINITION

The dictionary has a myriad of definitions
    For the delicate but decisive word CHARM—
The pictures we conjure, the renditions,
The emotions beset with a galaxy of reactions,
From fenial delight to heart warming spasms.
The innocent quest in a young child's eyes
Can glaze the heart with rampant delight.
The song of a whippoorwill in the cool night air,
The plea of a night owl whose resonant quadrille,
Speak to the soul and tantalize the will.
Four fuzzy legs endowed with black fur
Attached to a tight little ball of fluff,
Two floppy ears that dance in rhyme
Encompass a head compact and beguiling
Endowed with two eyes the color of onyx,
Composed by his maker to incite and delight
The hardest of hearts who see no respite
From the tragedies besetting the turmoil of life,
To revel with desire to hold in his arms
A little POODLE puppy—the persona of CHARM!

—Vivienne Bonnefil

BUTCH BEAGLE

I've been looking for a beagle for a couple of years,
    a short legged fellow with soft floppy ears.
A friend of mine, her name is Kim,
told me of a pound where we could look in.
All cooped together too crowded to move,
I spied a small bundle hiding in a blanket of blue.
My family just loved him right at first sight;
you could hold him in your palm, he was so light.
He's two years older from that happy day;
he's gotten bigger by twenty pounds, I'd say.
He follows the kids wherever they go,
he follows them in the deepest of snow.
His legs are so short, he can barely see,
but he makes it alright to check out a tree.
He sleeps through the night and part of the day,
after being outside, all he wants to do is play.
Throw him a toy and then he is off,
we chase him around; he thinks he's hot stuff.
He's so cuddly, a nice little boy,
he's our family's most lovable joy.

—Barbara Carroll Stephens

NEVER A CHAMPION

You never had the finest stock
    None from the best of bloodlines,

But you bred those dogs in tireless effort
    Always in quest of a winner.

You tramped the fields and stirred up game
    Then coaxed, scolded and guided—

Even showed them how it should be done
    With your imitation howling.

Fed and groomed them, housed them, loved them,
    Didn't sleep when they gave birth;

Clipped their nails, endured their fails—
    Your dedication was boundless.

Cleaning countless canine kennels
    A son vying for attention—

But your time and energy did have limits
    Oh, were I born a beagle . . . .

—Michael Staryak

OUR "ENERGIZED" DOGGIE GIFT

We thought you two should have a dog,
    Not any dog would do.
It should be something special,
For special folks like you.

He must not bark at nighttime
And keep good folk awake;
He must not wet upon the floor,
Or bite, For goodness sake!

On furniture he must not get,
Nor run into road.
And surely he must not get sick,
And your budget overload.

To find one dog so perfect
We'll admit was quite a chore,
But find we did, and now we hope
You'll love him evermore.

He may not be the biggest dog,
But he is cute, you'll see;
And Jeanie for the while Sam's gone,
He'll keep you company.

—Ruth Bucher Bottoms

SILENT SCREAMS

LISTEN, listen silently!

Do you not hear us screaming:
We of the forests and fields,
The sky and the deep blue sea?

We of the so, so many
Far poor, the ill, the bereaved,
The elderly or lonely?

We of other religions
Or very great frustrations
'Cause of our ethnicity?

Listen, listen silently!

—**Olde Dave**

The torture of singing
    the song of myself,
To perch and whistle
    truth of the forest—
The truth that my own colors
    blend with all others—
And the tune I whistle
    has been whistled before
    and before that

Though each morning is new,
    not the branch,
    not the tree,
    not the forest,
    not the whistling.

I've wanted to decline
    head-long
To the hard aching ground
Covered over by old death leaves.
But to suffer
    the infliction of the mind
Seems substitute
    for demise.

—**Salvatore A.V. Barreca**

TAKE MY HEART

Take my heart don't shame me
    With painful disgrace
Sin like a cancer grows
Leaves a bitter taste

Take this burden from me
We are all to blame
Burning up with anger
Feeling so ashamed

Take my soul forgive me
From this tragedy
Guilt fills my life
As I fall to my knees

Take my hand and guide me
I reach to heaven above
Abandon all regrets
With help from His love

Now my eyes are closed
Your face I still see
As I take my last breath
My spirit is set free.

—**Kim Couza**

HER GIFT

Up by Dawn reading the Word, before her daily mission;
She, so pure of heart, who accepts tasks others refuse.

The old, the ailing, the decrepit, the diseased, the troubled,
the weary, the abandoned, the dying, the dead.

She nurses, feeds, bathes, comforts, loves, and sometimes
                        Must say good-bye.

Those of us who are fools, ask questions of fools;
"How do you endure it?"
The morbidity, the pain, the constant need;
"How do you endure it?"
The sorrow of the inevitable death. Seeing, smelling, touching
the cold hand of it. Cleansing the body whose light has left it.

The answer is clear, but only to her, so pure of heart;
It is her gift, and it pleases her to give it.
And to those for whom it is the Final gift, she is honored—
Honored to prepare them for their journey Home.

—**Thacker**

WHEN I WAS SAD

Mother, you were so young to become so ill;
For the rest of my life I cannot tell you how I feel.

You almost lost your children,
From a car wreck, pneumonia, and fire in a kitchen.

Those tragedies seem so trivial today;
My heart nearly stopped as I watched yours fade away.

Dad, just when I thought we had conquered grief,
That came upon us anytime, like a thief;

You completely shattered my belief,
That parents are here forever; they are not supposed to leave.

You said, "I've been given the death sentence," as I cared for
    you and watched you deteriorate.
You were in pain and tried so hard, and my heart ached.

I wish I could still see you in the garden, down on one knee,
And Mother at the table with a cup of coffee.

I'm so glad my job was not across the country;
Life is so short; I miss you both terribly.

—**Victoria Benedict**

RSVP

Some say the wings of wild geese beat in my heart.
I know I don't live where most people live,
but won't you come for a visit?

I know a field where a million fireflies dance
and I'll hold you close when the summer-night wind
smells like childhood.

I'll show you where the memories lie in autumn-colored dust
and teach you how to find your past
in a trace of smoke from yesterday's fire.

I know how the air smells between flakes of snow
and I'll kiss you when the full moon turns the ice-covered earth
into a brittle fairyland.

I'll show you where the birds leave their footprints after the rain
and teach you how to pick your tomorrows
with the first wild onions of spring.

Some say the silent flight of owls fills my soul.
I know I don't live where most people live,
but won't you come visit me soon?

—**Judith Kaye Gibson**

This remembered as if from a dream
   Long ago and far away . . .
Ivy tangled in lattice work,
An old worn swing on a
Porch painted white . . .
The smell of wild honeysuckle
   after a summer rain . . .
A wind chime's song floating gently in the air . . .
Windows etched and frosted oval,
   set in furnished wood . . .
Doors carved and polished red in
   deep swirls and curves . . .
Tatted lace fringing sheer voile curtains . . .
Pink and white camellias floating in
   clear, crystal bowls . . .
Blue velvet pillows on moss green sofas
   plumped deep in softness . . .
Memories wrapped in fine-spun gold of a
Sweeter, finer, long-lost time . . . .

    —Dona Hough

CAMPFIRE SOLILOQUY

The rain comes down from tired skies
   And finds me lost in reverie
It strikes the earth with tiny sighs
Like whispering ghosts of memory
I sit and gaze at a vagrant blaze
That licks at a dampened stone
Your face appears with those brown eyes smiling
Over some little thing that was ours alone.
A glow of warmth sweeps over me
But soon sadness takes its place—
The Elders thought they knew what was best for you
And suddenly tore us apart
They left you troubled and confused
And me with a broken heart.
They were not aware of an everlasting truth—
That our love was tender, sweet and clean,
Burnished by the fires of youth.
It should have had a chance to live
For it was a rare and precious thing
That only God could give.

    —Abram Clement Penner

A WARM EMBRACE

Beautiful oak-tree lady
   thy sturdy, lovely, feet
plant thee firmly in place.
Thy suppliant limb's embrace
caresses me sweetly.

The radiance in your heart
glows brilliantly in your eyes.
Your branches entwine with mine,
while you kiss me softly.

Supporting me in my storm-filled hour of need —
the hurricane wind, blowing,
causing us to sway —
the added weight of thy feet and branches
comforts me, enables me to stand
more firmly to the ground.

As the sun "Apollo"
once again sheds his rays
through thy brilliant eyes,
thy heart warms mine.

    —Larry A. Makler

LIFE OF THE SUN

As it awakes, they say it's beautiful,
   It takes long to rise to height,
All through the journey, it looks as if,
It is filled with fright.
On its way down, onlookers mourn,
They say its life was nice and warm,
When it is almost dead and gone,
Once again it's complimented as
   being breathtaking,
But when that final moment comes,
Loved ones say its life was beautiful.
Finally they go to the downfall,
   and mourn and mourn for the one.

    —Jason H. Scarborough

SILENCE THROUGH TIME

Time is so silent one barely can hear
   springtime emerging again this year.
Beneath the earth silent with time
wakes crocus, forsythia, leaves on the vine.
Bird calls are music from roof top or tree
reminding us we are living and free.
Generations of growth surround us here
tradition through time year after year.
What is so silent as time itself?
A broken clock put away on the shelf?
No. Time is your gift from birth till death
when seasons of life are put to the test.
Summer, autumn, winter have passed
thus springtime adorned in beauty repass.
New life through silence in time bears fruit;
ties that bind from root to root.
Time is so silent one does not hear
earth's revolution year after year.

    —Florence N. Troll

THE STEPS

An eagle . . . soaring . . . overhead,
   Circling, slowly, wings outspread.
Eyeing life's irony from the air;
Five battered steps, going nowhere.

A split-rail fence, tumbling down,
Almost concealed by nature's gown.
Close-by a chimney made of stone,
One crumbling wall . . . almost gone,

And a giant of a tree towering near
Still holding a rope from yesteryear;
Hanging in shreds . . . a tattered thing . . .
All that's left of a treasured swing.

The old tree recalls a farm with grace,
The house kept warm by quaint fireplace.
With well-worn paths, oft traveled trails
When flowers bordered the fence of rails.

Where neighbors gathered, children played,
Bone-weary strangers, sometimes, strayed;
To the house filled with a welcome glow
And the five steps had somewhere to go.

    —M. Kaylor Williams

Count that day lost.
When it rains from sun to sun.
And planned appointed tasks are
          Put on hold.
And never done.

          —Alden Colston

PIEBERRY LANE

Pieberry Lane, wandering the woods
          and ending at my door,
Filling with such delights
          my baskets by the score.

Strawberries and thimbleberries
          of crimson and red,
Blackberries and elderberries
          that ripen high overhead.

Gooseberries so prickly
          and cranberries on highbush bend—
Then with partridgeberry to remain,
          the season you end.

          —Suzanne H. Kemp

THIS PATH

This dirt path will lead you to
          the sun,

This dirt path is filled with
loads of fun,

This dirt path will allow you
to run,

This dirt path has things that
may stun,

For I looked everywhere but
there are none,

This dirt path is the only one.

          —Adam Rainwater

IT'S THE BERRIES!

Down in the swamp
          there's a blackberry patch,
when the days get warm,
I watch and watch
as the berries ripen
and begin to fill
with juice, and get juicier still
until it's ready to spill.
Then I get my pail,
and go back down the trail
to capture this prize
for jelly, jams, and pies.
My fingers are nimble and willing,
but to my surprise,
the pail isn't filling,
and then I realize,
my willpower has failed.
They've been going into me
instead of into the pail!

          —Juanita Powell

THE FLOWERS OF LIFE

Floundering on a sandy sea of loneliness
I perceive in the distance a single splash of color
Irresistible lure for my weary soul
Impossible but true; a rose
Why has no one claimed this priceless treasure?
I will make it mine
With a single gentle tug, it is plucked
I admire its beauty
I inhale its captivating scent
Can this be what I have sought for so long?
No, for even as I marvel at this floral jewel
I feel the sting of a thorn
How can such perfection possess such blatant flaws?
In abject disgust I hurl it from me
I walk on, never deigning to look back
And in time I come to realize I was an utter fool
For every rose has its thorn
And man must realize that even beauty has its faults
I weep, for though I may search a lifetime
I fear I shall never find another rose in my desert

          —Frank Farris

DESERT GREEN

We moved a ponderosa pine
From the mountains to the desert
It survives, it flourishes
Fuller, taller each year.
They laughed at me for moving
Rocks and books and seashells
But I'm just like the pine
I need the appropriate surrounding soil
And fungus and bacteria
To survive the transplant.
My roots went much deeper than the pine's
From living 30 years in the mountains
I did prepare the new soil to receive them
Visited the new property holiday weekends for 10 years.
Found showplaces for my rocks and shells
Built shelves for my books
Surrounded the house with rocks and shells
Surrounded myself with books
The pine adapted to desert soil and temperatures
I am not the same person I was.

          —Barbara R. DuBois

ROOTS

She fell ill just as the blossoms fell
from the cherry trees outside her window and mine.
I didn't know; I savored the fragrance
drifting through the window to my kitchen.
Summer blasted its way and the leaves waned,
not waxed, in greenness, knowing.
In July she died, withering, starving,
forgetting how to eat while he watched,
unable by promise to interfere
when death was certain and to be welcomed.
December almost felled the orchard.
He leaned against the pane, a blur.
Forty years of loving to forget,
yet spring came, obscenely Green.
He shuffled out, shapeless,
not to prune or nourish, but to Cut, Burn, Uproot
the cherries from the earth.
I wash my dishes and wonder
how many roots he needs to kill
before he knows he needs to keep them.

          —Joan Leach

REINCARNATION

What of the brown leaf, tossed by the wind?
A chance to relive, its death to rescind.
It falls to the ground to mold and must;
In a year or so it turns to dust.
The dust enriches the ground beneath,
Contributing to the growth of another leaf.
And so, the cycles of Nature spin;
The dying of one, helps another begin.

—B M Perkins

HOMESICK?

The angel looked back where the golden harps
sang in the golden street,
then, smiling softly, spread her wings,
and flew with a speed so fleet
that scarce a minute had time to pass
ere she was treading earth's verdant grass.
The birds sang and the trees whispered,
the sky was blue;
clover scented the air as she folded her wings
and stepped through the dew.

—V.R. Wig

BRANDENBURG

In the woods there, he is roaming.
O does he know, that they are combing
Through the woods, both high and low?
For the wolf and the man will soon be meeting.
On his bones will the wolf be eating.
The wolf is mightier than the hunter's bow.

Why can't we love what's here and thereafter?
Man and wolf together in laughter.
What's to come is still unsure.
Wolves around there's not a plenty.
Save them before they're less than twenty.
Life's a stuff that will not endure.

—Ashley Nicholi Keys Mason

CENTRAL STANDARD TIME

To see the sky is the scariest thing,
Really see with this little-lensed eye,
But I'll keep watching for what I can't see
At least 'til the day that I die.

I will not go gentle. I'll pule, swear, and scream
Or, fight-fisted, go out with a sigh,
For wherever they send me the day after that
I really don't dare die.

There's time to sing. Tomorrow we grow old,
But fires within will keep outside the cold.
Let's go out then; you and I
Can graze on violets, hike to the stars,
Get some perspective on glaciers and Mars.
We can chase eagles and breed like race horses
(once we take care of the IRS—) . . . *!@*#$

There's so little springtime left
Before time's chariot calls.
And then, only then
We must obey. Delay.

And stand and wait to start a newer day.

—Joy-Ellis McLemore

CONCEPTS

A full moon illuminates the sky
As night enfolds me in a soft embrace.
Tree frogs croak their endless song
And cricket chirps interlace,
In symphony.
Thoughts of the day linger in my mind,
The senses desiring to retain,
The doe and fawns beyond my reach
And a foggy mist upon distant mountains,
With serenity.
How vivid the array of meadow flowers,
An artist's palette unsurpassed,
Etching the beauty upon my heart
And the wonder of a day just past,
In tranquility.

—Barbara J. Zimmerman

SUNRISE

I have revelled in the gorgeous beauty
Of many a northern sunset,
But today,
I am moving toward the sunrise!

Peeking over the trees, a soft blush of pink
Heralds the dawning of a new day,
Then gradually transforms
Into a glorious golden glow,
Ushering in the sun
To smile upon me
With its warmth and light,
As I move nearer to the sunrise!

My earthly life is destined for its sunset,
But simultaneously, as I travel,
My spiritual life is moving toward the sunrise,
The dawning of a new day — eternity!
When the glorious Son
Will smile upon me
With the light of love and peace,
As I move into the sunrise!

—L. Marie Enns

IN THE QUIET OF AN EVENING

In the quiet of an evening,
    perhaps on a front porch swing,
I'll talk with you of the stars,
    and hopefully hold your hand . . . .

In the quiet of an evening,
    smells of lilac or honeysuckle,
I'll muss your hair, and kick your toes,
    and hopefully touch your lips with mine . . . .

In the quiet of an evening,
    when whip-wills call to their own,
I'll speak of other times and other days,
    when not so lucky were we . . .
Then we'll laugh and smile,
    laugh and smile those days away . . . .

In the quiet of an evening,
    when the sun falls fast asleep,
I'll feel you breathe and hear your life,
    and then in the stillness of the night,
        we'll know we're ours . . . .

Dedicated to London. May you have
such quiet evenings . . . .

—Silas Farmer

SMELLS I LOVE BEST

Soft, velvety roses, a wondrous sight,
  With fragrances that tease and delight.
Mouth-tempting aromas of hot baking bread,
Line dried linens on a fresh made bed.
Savory bacon, frying crispy and brown,
Hot bubbling coffee, just freshly ground.
The sweet, milky odor of a new puppy's breath . . .
These are the smells that I love best.

The cool summer scent of newly cut grass,
Bringing memories of a youthful past.
Spicy pine logs and fresh Christmas trees
And hot apple cider steaming to please.
Warm, deep earth, musty with Spring rain . . .
Bright, golden scents blown o'er Kansas plain.
With many small pleasures are we all blest . . .
Among these are smells that I love best.

—Doris D. Steffen

SEASIDE JEWELS

The Master Jeweler beckoned me
to works of greatest luminosity.
I saw a golden orange fireball
so bright it blinded me,
hung midst a sea of great tranquility,
with streams of aqua shimmer
that gleamed like jeweled ice.

The softest glow of peach spread out,
shot through with blinding rays of setting sun,
a canopy of palest blue throughout,
dimmed only with black sprays of cypress
that clung along the cliffside shore.

A moment's feast was all there was.
At once the ball of glowing gold
dipped to the sea side's edge.
And suddenly a gemmed florescence
of jade's most brilliant hue
flashed blinding light and dropped
into the ocean's floor.

—Rose P. Taylor

SNORKELING

When I went snorkeling for the first time I could see,
  schools of colorful fish swimming cautiously.
Bouquets of coral decorating the sandy secrets
    below,
    and rainbows of starfish moving so slow.
As I look at all the sea's features,
    I can see the movement of the sea creatures.
When I first dive in, the cold creeps into
    my body and bones,
    as if I were entering a death zone.
I feel excited because I know,
    that I will be swimming where the manta rays
    flow.
All of a sudden my body feels tight,
    a shark passes by like a stranger in the
    night.
The sounds of bubbles fill my ears,
    and muffled sounds from above block out all
    my fears.
And as I swim ashore,
    I wish that I could go snorkeling more.

—Loren Michelle Petruny

PEQUOD

The harpooner leaned into the wind,
      his harpoon poised,
      a cobra waiting to strike.
Dark storm clouds gathered signaling
      an oncoming doom.
      Lightning lashed the sea,
      miles off in the distance.
      The steady creak of oars,
      intermixed with the groans
      of straining men.
The wind carried a smell of land,
      where there was no land.
He swallowed the bitter taste of fear,
      white spray . . . white whale.
      The behemoth rose.

—Walter E. Kirby II

MY TUGBOAT

Sittin' here on the levee
  My eyes are gettin' heavy
Laying on the cold rocks
As I look toward the docks
Watchin' that ol' tugboat
As I start to put on my coat
Such a cold but quiet night
Laying here in the moonlight
Why am I resting in this place
Thinking of your handsome face
Because I miss your touch
Though you're far away today
Wanting to remember the fun and such
Waitin' for your return someday
As down the river you slowly flow
Not knowing where you'll go
Please come back to our levee
Before my eyes get too heavy

—Margaret L. Rohlfing

We sit alone within the castle room,
  the tapestried walls illuminated,
ever so softly,
with the light of the flames
burning on the hearth,
the stone floor warmed
by the flame of our love,
and the heat of a summer night.

A zephyr from the North,
drifting gently over our embraced forms,
coaxing the flames into a flickering dance.
A brook outside,
babbling endlessly,
answering the ceaseless rustling,
of the trees outside.
We drift off to sleep,
in one another's arms,
as the flames before us
burn down to embers.

—John D. Norman

SWINGING

Because I swing high today,
Must I swing high tomorrow?
Or might I enjoy a more gentle pace
To contemplate my space or even sorrow?
For even high flying swings must dip to earth
Before being thrust back up again.

—Mary Ann Kincer

THE MOJAVE DESERT

You have been here
For a long long time,
With little change
From year to year.

Through countless ages past
These same mountains,
Caught the sun's first glow,
These same long shadows cast.

To some, you gave a wealth of gold,
Or minerals of many kinds,
To some a lingering death,
Some just stayed 'til they were old.

Boot hills testify to all who came
To love or curse you,
Little do you care,
To you, it's all the same.

For you'll be here
When all are gone
With not a single trace
Of those who came.

—Ruth S. Ozanich

A DESERT WITHOUT RAIN

Drier it grows — and barren it goes —
no rain for the need,
Silently — how silently — weeps the
fading seed.

Though no tears escape its arid,
withering heart,
Comes the anguished sigh —
Oh — Season Dry — Depart!

Harsh winds come — to the desert
they always do,
Vines, parched and scattered, divert
not the passage through.

But should a gentler breeze come
to touch the dismal land,
Would not the dormant plant lift up
its dusty hand,

And let its heart hope anew
for hence the coming rain,
Just to know the verdant flow
in tiny veins again.

But all things have their time —
and happen then they must,
Or the seed which sighs — dies —
and goes the way of dust.

—Janice Collins

THE EARTH AND ME

My soul cried out
As the last embrace faded.
Falling and falling
Fading into the darkened earth.
And the earth and I cried together
As her embers faded into nothing.
I could not save that glow,
Or nurture its dying flame.
And my life faded away like that dying ember.

I cried.

As tears put out the final flicker,
We melted into the earth as one.
Silently fading, without a single sound.
My life disappeared
I didn't care, I became one with the earth.
We felt ourselves as we entered together
A life that would never end.

—Wendi Prud'homme

spread wide your wings
red tailed hawk
cast a spell over me with your feathered cape
change me

your beady eyes are mine now
i see with precision
i do not take part in the human factor
only soar above it
like some godly glider
circling
circling

the sky has no direction
except for the moment
it holds no past to affect the present
i turn my body toward the friendly wind
zooming
zooming
i am fast
i am nothing
i am free

—Traci L.B. Galvin

THE MORNING STAR

The night was dark, black as pitch, cold,
Where were the stars, all fallen to earth.

Suddenly, a gleam of light in the eastern sky,
The sun began to rise, beautiful shades,
Rubies, diamonds, emeralds, began to appear,
In a background, pure marble.

Stars began one by one, to rise from earth,
The Morning Star appeared, stars were
leaping toward heaven, all around.

Dawn, then full light was here,
The beginning of a new day,
That would never end.

Some were still standing, crying out,
Evermore will their cry be, "Lord wait for me,"
He turned away and left, it was too late.

How sore will mankind's heart be,
This day is not far away,
Twenty-four hours, Rapture.

—Spencer Todd Neal

A FOREVER LOVE

A love that doesn't judge you for what you're not . . . but rather a love that accepts you for who you are . . . and the person you can be.

A love that helps you share your dreams, and when your dreams are shattered, inspires new dreams and hope for the future.

A love that even when the pain seems overwhelming and never ending no matter how small or big the problem . . . holds on and does endure.

A love that helps you keep your head held high and says hold on . . . tomorrow's a new day.

A love that says during the hardest times you are becoming and experimenting with who you are and who you will become.

There is only one type of forever love . . . a family's love.

I love you Mom and Dad!!

Dedicated to my mother and father who never stopped loving me.

—Jennifer Marie Deuster

ATTEMPT AT FORGETTING

As simple as a whisper perceived.
Try to forget it. Can you?

Oh, turn your head so your ear faces the spot of air from a perpendicular angle.
Now, the whisper can't provoke. The left ear does not face that spot.
And the right ear does not face that spot.
Only the hair, the eyes, the nose and the mouth face the spot.
And since these latter ones can not hear, then they can not perceive.
And so you can forget it.

Forget it, but the impression has been made; was made.
Had it been made without awareness, it may have disappeared.
But the lining of the drum felt it. The nerve transmitted it. The mind recorded it.
And the whisper with all its perceived meaning has been echoing throughout.
The eyes see. The nose smells. The mouth tastes. The hair feels.
They all sense the whisper's long gone ripple.

A whisper was thrown and it sank through the depths of life.
And the perception can only fade; the whisper has already left its imprint.
Can you really forget it?

—Anita Ohanissian

LOVE ON THE LINE

The songs they sing have such heart; the words in life you've lived.
The pain is real, the love is gone—now there's nothing but love on
the line. Each cord is strong like the pain we felt, the notes in
rhythm. Cards are dealt—Life is just there—make it happen or let
it go. It comes back through others like love on a line. It's not
made for one because it's all the same, just different players with
different rules but every one, babe, uses the same tools—There's love on
the line. I want to run, I want to hide. You're getting too close,
There's something wrong inside! Is it a feeling, is it part of the
machinery, why can't I give it a name; why can't it give a name;
why must it keep playing the same old game? All I know is I gotta run,
I gotta hide so it doesn't destroy me—this feeling inside. Am I
running away from or running to—I can't tell because now I'm with you!
Our roads are going side by side. I guess that's great, but; I want
to run away from—I think you're running to—you're looking for your
love in a bottle; in mine, it's a song! Your words will haunt me
forever; as I hope my love will haunt you. I don't think time will
heal this hurt. The only thing makes it right is I said good-bye first.
You really were a best friend; at least in my heart. A good enemy you
were in the start. There's no way you can know what I'm doing
cause I'm not even sure. Those who are close to me I confuse even more.
That's why I let no one near. I don't want them hurt by the love
I already have trying to own me; possess me. You can't hurt me because
you didn't even have the time to love me—So, forever, I'll listen for
LOVE ON THE LINE

—Sandie

AT LAST THE STREAMS RUN FREE

Seeking shelter in leafless trees
    Standing wintry thin.
    Sparrows' songs fill the air
    Notes chiming with the wind.

Wallowing in the morning sun
    In frozen earth, the hyacinth bud
    Listens to the insects' hum
    As winter retires and spring has begun.

At last the streams run cool and clear
    Leaving behind its icy shores
    These many months so drear,
    And now my heart is free.

Of winters' blasts that set me free
    I see a springtime dream
    And listen to the silent wind
    While walking nearby streams.

       —Julia Soho Margetiak

BIRTHPLACE

Back to pools of cedars and pines,
grass growing between tall trees,
wild flowers dotting borders of fields,
casting colors of red for me.

The scent of green is in the air
the firmness of earth beneath my feet,
the tin roof hovers over ancient places,
foot worn floors and memories of faces.

Images came forward from among the leaves
of tables spread, covers laid and sun
casting shadows of children's heads.

Hoe handles held with age old hands
footsteps through plowed fields,
words we once said.

Remember, drink from these secret cups
where hearts were nourished as we
grew up.

       —Faye Southerland Mobley

PARK-O-MINE

Three-quarter moon about me
    inside a wide open sky.
These feet have dragged many-a-waltz
across a grass no longer green,
but still serene and gentle to the heart.

North Bergen highlight worn to the ground,
yet Braddock is still overwhelming.
She is outdone, out-loved, but ever so
comforting this park-o-mine.

There's a lake-breeze today, with a silver
feel that's quite the dampened kind.
Sea gulls fly around a corner; around a bend.
The two white, glistening lovers dance.

My glass-felt inner thoughts rain on top
of all the light.
Dense brush is a kicking-kind of substance
alone, and winding continually.
Through and through, the mad blue/restful blue
remains against the remnants that are still
heartwarming in this park-o-mine.

       —James Wesley Duren

HOME

An old dirt road with no beginning,
    a rusted mailbox with its red flag swinging.
Many grooves and holes cover that road,
    where a big truck passed with its heavy load.
At the end and around the hill,
    there stands a house and an old grain mill.
The house itself has been abused,
    through all the years that it was used.
Where people laughed and people cried,
    where beefstew simmered and chicken fried.
That old white house grayed with time,
    but that old gray house is forever mine.

       —Vicky Abril

THE TWENTY-THIRD

You could have seen it too,
    if you'd been here with me
on the porch
this unusually warm November night.

Stark branches arching around a street—
light, halogen raindrops sparkling
and the weather-worn brown leaves danglin

                                  g

called to mind hapless victims
in some fantastic web.

I'm writing to tell you,
I've remembered her birthday.

       —Melissa Pollack

OVERCAST

If the woodland were my home
    This day would be my fancy.
The earth pulsates with radiant life
That fills my soul with rhythmic quietness.
The sun looms tucked away
There is no rain, only mist hangs all around.
The sky is cold and gray.

There upon the tranquil earth
Where nature is most pure,
And passion comes alive
I'd find freedom to think, and play all day
And trod upon damp soil.
Then, feel release from weightless life
And let my spirit uncoil.

       —Elena Maria

AWARE

This morning I saw the sun rise,
    It was a beautiful sight to behold;
It looked like a great ball of fire,
Lightly burnished with sparkles of pure gold.

There are such wonderful sights to see,
If only we would take the time to look
At what God has put here for you and me.

As I look across these hills,
Here on Farm Road, One Zero Four;
And see the trees all green, brown and gold;
The grasses are turning brown,
And the quail are walking around so bold.

The sage brush looks like silver strands,
And yes, it's Eight O'clock;
And we've been to The Farm, again.

       —Zelma Jo Harbour

It's night, the halls are quiet
The moves are soft, yet quick;
There's comfort in their bearing
As they move among the sick.

A kindly word, a blanket spread,
A hand held — true devotion,
A sip of water, a pill for pain,
They hide their own emotion.

"I'm scared," says one; "I can't sleep," another.
"Is it time for my family to arrive?"
"It hurts so much." "Is it time to get up?"
"I'm so glad to be alive."

And on they move, imparting love
No action harsh or terse.
They do what they want . . . no, are destined to do;
They are forever the nurse.

    —Shirley Holzman

WILD EYE

Wolfen eyes stare at me,
  freeing the wildness in my soul,
and the primal energies thought extinguished,
flare once again.
Of a time ago
and a freedom never realized,
I am educated;
I am enlightened in dreams of fire and ice.
In lobo's eyes I am lost and surrounded,
a willing castaway in a world unto itself;
the animal within me
is realized in these eyes;
windows of deepest longing,
mourning the wild innocence lost,
in the myriad of brutal reality.
Eyes of the wild, eyes of the free, eyes of the lost
fading away to myth and fearful rumor,
no longer needed, no longer wanted.

    —Eric Buell

INVASION OF THE BLUE-EYED NIGHT CREATURES

    I am fearfully trembling
this cool autumn night
    While beholding one
spine-tingling sight!

    Anguished moans of dismay
echo loudly right now
    Throughout Palmerville's
dark, lonely streets!

    There are creatures quite strange
on my goose-feather bed
    Shedding dandruff all over
white sheets!

    Sporting long, tousled hair
colored raven's-wing black,
    They make gestures obscene
with blue eyes!

    These could surely be monsters
from planets unknown,
    Or some KGB spies
in disguise!

    —Michael Lee Sims

THAT HALLOWEEN NIGHT

It was a clear crisp cool night;
  The silver stars were shining bright;
The moving moon was giving out all its light,
  To make that night just right.

Children were dressed in their scariest clothes;
  When out in the night darkness arose.
From many jars goodies were disposed,
  For those who were to keep from being their foes.
    —Joyce A. Mosier

TEMPEST-TOSSED NIGHT

Tempest-tossed night—
  Vanishing visions before my sight—
Surging waves wash over my brain.
Stormy images on me rain.
Taunting, sneering are the faces.
Dark and dreary are the places.
Haunting scenes only I see.
Why is he coming after me?
Running, rushing, falling, cry—
Wake to cry! Wake, don't die!
Tossing, turning, tangled in sheets—
Startled, shaken, I wake to peace.
    —Victoria L. Nightingale

GOOD NIGHT

Dark is the night,
no reason to fear,
a timeless encapture,
night upon night,
year upon year.

Night shines the heavens,
that have no end,
and breeds the dreams,
the mind will lend.

Surrender the darkness,
a colorless hue,
to dawn a new morning,
bright light fade to blue . . . .
    —M.A. Habr

THE OGRE

Deep within a cavern dark,
Where light has never shone,
An ogre sits in the murky gloom
Upon a seat of stone.
    His ears are long and pointed.
His teeth are sharply filed.
His mouth is fixed in an evil grin
Of something untamably wild.
    He listens closely to the cavern's songs,
Always lying in wait
For the careless and heedless to come along,
Staggering in their unsure gait.
    He hears their steps as they echo down
The twisting cavern's path,
Coming straight towards the awaiting beast,
Unknowing of his wrath.
    He grabs his victims with lightning speed
Then breaks them all in two,
Then gobbles down their meaty flesh,
And waits . . . perhaps . . . for you!
    —Kerschie Byerly

ONCE

Once there was love between us
Now there is only love
Once there was a flame of desire
Now there is only a flame
Once there was passion for each other
Now there is only each other
Once we dreamed of a world together
Now the dreams are of love, desire,
    and passion
And not of each other.

—Pamela R. Brazzell

LONGING

The softness of your touch,
Could you ever love me that much?

The sweetness in your eyes,
Could you assure
That it wouldn't be lies?

The innocence of your heart,
Could I ever be a part?

The uniqueness of your way,
Would you let me in someday?

—April

WHAT IS A TRUE LOVE

True love is an ever ending
love affair between a woman and
a man
True love is always wanting
to be near and never afar
to be close by to hold onto
wiping away all doubts
and fear to hold so dear
That is my love for you
and in your eyes I see
a look that tells
me it could be true

—Burl Etters

JUST STAY OUT OF HIS WAY

He's so gorgeous
With his sexy type eyes.
They sparkle like jewels,
When he looks into my eyes.
I can tell it when he walks,
And even when he talks,
That I'll always love him,
No matter what the cost.
What would I do if I didn't have him?
What would I do if I did?
Would it be different?
Would he love me?
And I ask myself over and over
If suddenly one day
Our relationship was over,
What would I do?
What would I say?
Oh! If only I could
Just stay out of his way!

—Mary Rose Green

FOR KATHY

If I could ever write a poem
as beautiful as you are to me,
I would laugh, jump, leap up
and touch the stars;
because you are the sun
burning through the clouds of my troubles,
chasing away the shadows of my doubts,
and when you shine on me
I can feel myself becoming
all the things I dream to be;
and while I don't expect a life of endless sunshine
I am thankful for the warmth you give me when you can.
And if I could ever write a poem
as beautiful as you are to me,
I would laugh, dance, and sing,
even through the rain,
and that is the poem I try for
every time I pick up a pen and paper.

—Michael Smith

THE TOIL OF MOURNING

Shall I call you up to wish you well
or seek to destroy?
You're the light which shines on
to give my sight's employ.

Obtrude, obtrude you must at last!
To spin your tiny webs, stuck in threads of the past.

And oh, this glass that shows my pain
is placed upon your feet,
I shan't walk on towards Thee.
Yet I shall not retreat.

So now place me in thy crevice
until the day I be born.
Walk on through the night, bathe ye in the day,
Speak not in thy scorn.

Send thy words to the Alter of Silence,
I call on you to pray.
I shall call on you to pray!

—Karen J. Buechler

NEVER KNOWING THE FEELING

When you come to it, You never really know.
Some dream of it;
Some wish it would just go away;
Some wish it never came.
All the time it haunts you.
You never really know,
Is it real or just your imagination?
You lay awake nights, trying to figure it out;
Days go by, soon it's months.
You see the feeling all the time never really knowing;
Will it hurt me or help me?
Will it sound crazy, When you say it out loud?
Everyone should feel it.
Sometimes it's one sided, Sometimes it's not;
One sided hurts, Two sided could hurt more;
But the feeling is always there.
Some say if you have never known the feeling,
You're a Loser; But could you,
Be The Winner!(?)

—Larry T. Dube Sr.

DEATH

Death isn't what we think it is
Death is not static
Death is an infusion of deception
Death is an emotional impulse cornered, snuffed out
Death is in our hands
Die are cast to the whim of chance
And Death eats us up
Defiant words grasp at grates
Then Death swallows you
Overcoming Death.
Serpents. Servants. An Evil Tree. Original Death.
Lies. Lies about Death.
Death as a finalized state is a lie.

—Kevin Bookey

FIRE WALK WITH ME

Tread no further on soiled ground
Shun false invitations from opaque eyes
Holograms lace the dungeon's door
and saturate senses with temptation's lies

Take refuge no longer in empty words
stripped of meaning and forsaken to fade
Identify wholly with sentient life
and shoulder the weight of a length crusade

Abandon old nonsense with defiance and rage
Unsheath wisdom's sword and wield it with light
Embrace vision's rainbow on the tail of a storm
as energy's radiance dispels the night

Let impact resound through the depths of your soul
profoundly moved by quintessence bare
Let life, death and struggle be plainly revealed
in a single expression of strained despair

The flames of the spirit, now embers of pain
ignite once more in the palm of your hand
Make dismal existence a cosmic tirade
Step into the fire and understand

—Maria A. Todisco

SEEDS

I've washed my face with the wetness of Rape.
Cleansed was I not
from the embodiment of your soul?

I've prayed for eyes to see
all the things you've given me.
Gifted was I not
from the generosity of your hand?
You've thrown me back into the land.

"MIGHT I GROW?"

I've walked my feet
without destinations complete.
Found was I not
by the eyes of contempt?
These are the things I've dreamt.

I've planted my seeds
from the malignancy of weeds.
Stunted was I not
from the growth of your womb?
I've seen you, I will return soon.

"MIGHT I GROW?!"

—Karen J. Buechler

TO GAZE UP AT THE MOON

I can see that you have fire in your eyes,
and pain inside your heart,
so many things have come.
and torn your world apart.
But don't give up,
and don't give in,
take some time and soon,
you will be able to raise your chin.
to gaze up at the moon.

*This one's for John,
a true inspiration.*

—Christy Miceli, age 14

LIBERA ME

Imprisoned by invisible walls I lived
but thought I'd broached the world's edges,
nothing beyond but chaotic seas.

Emotion could surge but so high
or control would be swept away,
a swelling and crashing of the soul
streams of thoughts effaced by violent cataracts
swirling, foaming rivers of feeling.

But I let down the walls
let in the jungle
fearing beastly rage and furious tempests.
And in rushed the tide with its shock of sorrow
yet tempered by a thing long forgotten:

Joy, bold and personal.

Oh, to be human is the strangest state—
at once vulgar and exalted
unknowing and all-knowing;
exquisite the pain can be, or the beauty.

The walls are vanquished now.
Now—let the universe in!

—Teresa Pullara

DARKNESS

Angel of Mercy
Angel of Death
Come save me from this horrible wrath
Taking over everyone
Soon all things will be gone
Now I lay here, waiting for my death
There's hardly anything or anyone left
Total silence all around
I'm hanging on my last rebound
Silent screams inside my head
I only wished I was dead
I'm not afraid of the unknown
It's better than being all alone
You scream and plea for me to come back
But there's one thing that you lack
Understanding and forgiveness for my sins
Why couldn't we have made amends
Now I'm sinking further and deeper
I can barely hear the sound of your weeping
Crying one last time for me
This is how it has to be
As I embrace the darkness that has become
I notice that I'm very numb
Grateful for this unknown place
But sad because I cannot see your face

—Nicole Laughlin

221

release

never before so close felt
this deep usonian night
        its virgin ether, through a plane
diffuse with mild headlamp light
        soul at ease upon its crest
upon black wheels
        black night, her secret beauty shown
        then undiscerned this flow of thoughts
        . . . .
        . . . .
        . . . .
        the sudden bloody slash . . . memorial flag
        a mercurial flow . . . an endless staff
bright but gripped by floods through haze
        at first alone on coke-black blouse
in shrouds of sign wounds, lost and trounce

        (soul, to the breach, anew)
                —Steve Loveland

BUFFALO WEEP

It lies below the short dry grass,
        under endless open skies,
        where clouds call from above.

The blood of bison washed down,
        the blood of Indians washed down,
        run deep within the ground.

An underground river of blood,
        runs under the hooves of cattle,
        and under the plows of steel.

It withers the souls of ranchers,
        feigning arrogance on stolen land,
screaming with fences and edgy suspicion.

It continues to drip down,
        from the veins of coyote and hawk,
it humiliates corn and hay and cane.

        The clouds call down and see,
        and cry but will not wash away,
        the sin manifest in destiny here.

—Stanley P. Reed

CARELESS WHISPER

With a careless whisper, a bond is broken
        through a single word
        a friendship ends
        the rumor is started
        a form of gossip
        but soon it changes
        to a wave of destruction

        The distorted truth
        hangs in the air
and on the tip of a sharp tongue
        it lies in wait, ready to strike
        another unseeing victim
against the rumor, there is no defense
        a soul is crushed

A broken heart lies shattered on the floor
        the deceitful lies have taken their toll
        as quickly as it came
        the rumor now fades
        but the damage remains
        as the sign of a careless whisper.

—Sally Tuffin

NO ANSWER

. . . And the ringing continues.
        "Is anyone home?"
I'm alone and it's your voice I need to hear
        to help me clear my mind.
My sadness grows deeper,
        the Grim Reaper waits by my side.
"Please pick up the phone!"
But I get no reply,
        and the ringing continues.
"Why, oh why don't you answer?"
You're my only friend and the end is near.
I need to talk, to shout, to cry,
        to hear a friend's voice say "I care."
Oh, why aren't you there?
"I'll miss you my friend," "goodbye."
As I lay on the floor, gun by my side,
        a shot through my heart, I hear a reply.
"Hello?"
And I die.

—W.D. Wisbeski

SPIRIT WARRIOR

I fight.
I dream.
        I laugh.
        Are you not the one who told me to go
        When all the worlds said stay?
        I fought your words,
        though the earth moved them to my soul.
        They buried their meaning in my heart,
        and that is when I came to know myself.
        During my journey I grew to understand.
        There along your soft spoken words
        I found strength to love,
        when shadows told me there would be none,
        Shadows had their own goodness.
        They taught me to trust.
        I am the warrior of the self.
                        I fight.
                        I dream.
                        I laugh.

—Rachel Manija Gobar

AWAKE!

Living in what you think is the flowering days,
        walking alone in the corridors of memory,
looking ahead to the vast past,
breeding dreams from yesterday's dilemma,
Are these the best you can do?
Is there an end to speak the strange tongue,
wear an old face?

Time is running through your soul.
It beats so fast.
It is not the calm day.
It is not the silent night.

Shake up your ideas.
Look towards tomorrow.
The spirits of your children
gather in a new wave.
Would you change your road?
Pour your memories
down the sink of past!

—Mohammed A. Al-Fequi

In the desert tonight a soldier sleeps
he prayed to his God his soul to keep
should he have to stand and fight
for God, country, and our way of life
cold, dead, chill of night
thunder rolls across the sky
sound of death before the dawn
the deafening beat of Hades' drums
We have waited out the calm
Now they've unleashed the storm
so let the world bear witness
to the arrogance of our races
We cannot be silent any longer
the need for a fight awakens
We felt the fires burning stronger
this desire has no patience
In the desert tonight a million soldiers sleep
Praying to their Gods, their souls to keep
In the world tonight, a million families sleep
they've prayed to their Gods, their soldiers to keep.

—Darrell Mitchell

HELPING LADY LIBERTY

What would our Lady Liberty say
If she could see across the way
And look into our prejudiced minds
All of us and all our kinds?

It doesn't matter if we're red, yellow, white or black
We're all needed to stamp out our nation's moral slack
We should all share the equal blame
For this world renowned and publicized shame

If we could look into our hearts
And find some small way to do one tiny part
One by one, by one by one
We could have this devastating problem done

Then the lovely lady could smile and say
Come to me—be safe, come across the way
But in this lifetime, I sadly fear, this will never be
For future generations, we must wait and hope, and see

We could now sow seeds of everlasting faith
The same as past seeds were sown of bitterness and hate
Then we could honestly and truly be
A great and kind nation of equality

—Lenora Caldwell

MY FREEDOM

My freedom is invisible
Against the azure sky.
And if the earth casts
Shadowed doubt, I will
Remain discrete—myself.
My freedom is invisible;
You know not where I dwell.
And if I seek some altered place,
You'll never know the why.
My freedom is invisible,
You see me here—then there.
The sound of clocks gone silent,
My spirit fills the air.
But, if by chance you see it,
Partake in pleasure rare,
And chase a moment backwards—
A spirit does not care.

—Patricia Ann Bronzo

Here stands a nation of:
 rich and poor,
 black and white,
 men and women,
 assortment and virtue.

Here stands the home of:
 the strong and the willful,
 the inventive and the free,
 the united and the brave,
 the powerful and the fearless.

Here stands a banner of:
 color and contrast,
 likeness and equality,
 culture and history,
 promise and hope.

Here stands a people:
 rich in heritage and in spirit
 wealthy in heart and intellect
 and positive in justice and in themselves.

HERE STANDS AMERICA
—Kristine M. Trozzo

VOICES OF AMERICA

Knowing the Voices of America
First I start with the Light above
Our God that Blesses America
Then Songs of America, Soar like Doves

Which Voice comes through the most?
The one with love, our Pastor's text
Our joy, the post office lady Verna
A message, by our President elect

Voices of our children at school
Such laughter with their games of life
Probably our Doctors comforting words
Nurse that says "perfect sight."

My sons say "Mom we love you!"
Daughter, "Look Mom my first cake."
Garage man tells car's running fine
Husband Gene, pleased with what I bake

Fly your flags high, the soldier speaks
Friend's voice, "Can I help you?"
Policeman that says, "Everything's O.K."
Such lovely voices that come through.

—Katrina Eller

FREEDOM

Freedom is a matter of moral excellence,
Granted to every race.
Treating all mankind with a superb dignity,
Never looking for color or face.

Freedom runs free,
With equality in mind.
Running ahead,
Not lagging behind.

Freedom has no specific boundaries,
It should be indigenous to every being.
Freedom shouldn't be desecrated,
It should be what your mind is seeing.

—Kate Turka

LET THE FLOWERS BLOOM AGAIN;
Poem on the inauguration of President Bill Clinton, January, 1993.

Let the flowers bloom again,
Let *peace* fill all the earth.
Let *justice* reign among all women and men.
Let the land know its full worth.

Let the bells ring
and the anthems swell
their message to mankind bring
that all is well.

Let *our* goal be *human good,*
an era of *conscience* among all women and men,
joined in a common sister and brother-hood.
Let the flowers bloom again.

—L.E. Ward

MY MIND TO ME A CRUCIBLE IS

Out of the indifference that immures me
Randomly pummeled by blow after blow;
I wonder what malice God must cherish
To decree his children suffer so

In the fell clutch of circumstance
I have learned to endure in submission
To acknowledge power or control
Has never been in my dominion.

Buddha taught maya could be transcended
Through acceptance of life as sorrowful
    on earth
To absolve oneself as not responsible
For worldly pain, despair and anguish in death

Still one cries out why gruesome must be
That unspeakable void, the loss of those
    of one's soul;
Must be endured, so as content God's will
Who never can know ecstasy of love between
matched souls.

But for those who urge a higher world
Wooed by sacrifice and denial
They are stealthily amassing this world's mead
To make their denial worthwhile

It matters not how beyond
    my strength
Nor how unworthy is the goal
I am dismembered, flesh still
    quivering
While still conscious is my soul

—Ellen Baudisch

A HUMANE LETTER!

There Abounds, a New Era!
In the air, coming through by HOPE,
A familiar face, and an understanding of people,
where our nation was amiss,
from much turmoil of trouble.
What our new president sees,
is a change to take place—
From the famine, to the homeless, and
the wars of the world. To perilessly omiss
and put a waiver on this disease.
A corrosion of sorts, to damn and stifle
the wrongs into a just right!
A weight of such Powers that will Be!
That by a Cohersive Human Delegation
supporting our president, we'll experience
a connection, a fusion long overdue,
by hope, understanding,
and a Power that will Be!
In a New Era *Agog!*

—Joanne G. Snyder-Haney

GRAVITY

Out of the left hand of darkness a white
neon cross florescent against the stark night.
The doors to this sanctuary are locked for
those huddled at the foot of the dream.
The dream of safety, security, warmth,
progress in the land of plenty.

Where do these shattered patrons of the dream
powered streets take their dis-ease,
their dependence, their dys-function?

Out of the right hand of darkness an unbalanced
scale administered by the blind protectors.
The doors to this sanctuary are locked for
those huddled at the foot of the dream.
The dream of wealth, justice, protection,
success in the land of plenty.

Where do these humbled patrons of the dream
powered streets take their wounds,
their chronic pain, their just demands?

—Greg Skinner

LITTLE THINGS

Such little things — words
that they could do so much damage.
And you will rue the day you used them
so lightly
these mighty little words.
You can't take them back now —
they are out
Not for the world to see
but for me to hear;
in the shower
mixed with the roar of hot water.
They will fill the silence left
by the thunder clap.
        Don't say it — no more words
        My mind teems with them
        my heart is deaf to them
        I have heard all your words
        I live with them, breathe them
        They fill my throat, choking
        like the water in the shower when I scream.

—Kelly J. Berckhan

HIDDEN STRANGER

What is it out there that feels like danger?
I feel that it's a hidden stranger.
Is it something I can not see?
Or is it someone else to be?

What is it, a person? I think not.
I feel more that it's a reason sought.
Some feelings hidden deep with-in,
to bring about a real chagrin.

What is it so deep inside,
that robs your space to decide?
Some hurtful pride,
that will only take you for a ride.

What is it this hidden stranger?
You can not hide from danger.
Only you can see the hidden stranger.
And then what . . . ?

—Diana Lynn Bucknell

THE WINDOW

As I look from my tiny kitchen window,
nothing but cornfields catch my eye.
My home, so green, the year around,
and now I behold a yellow mass.

As I left my Irish shores to voyage to,
a foreign, distant land,
I knew my reason — for marriage;
to a farmer, indeed for life.

In the midwest where I now reside,
I watch the eagle, soar high above,
and realize I too, am free, just
as it appears to be.

I come and go as a door upon a hinge,
thinking of what lies before, in the
great land of opportunity!
So I leave my window, slowly to bed,
to rest upon my pillow.

—Jennifer Young

MONSTERS IN THE DARK

As I am fast asleep
Something instinctively wakes me in fright.
Adrenalin rushes, heart pounding in fear
I clutch the covers with all my might.

Moving like a shadow in the moonlight
It stalks silently in the night.
Prowling in hunger and searching with zeal
for its next meal.

With dry throat I cannot scream
or even whisper "Who's there?"
Eyes wide in the darken room
I search frantic to know whom.

Fur coat black as coal
Twin amber eyes that glow.
Scratching at my bedroom door
It wants in. I fall to the floor.

The door opens slowly, it was ajar
my voice recovers from afar
My pulse races, I go to scream
when I hear "Meow."

Some monster, 'tis my cat.

—Tamara L. Pickenpaugh

FOR SALE

You,
Standing alone.
Where is your security?
Gone . . . .

If I offered to sell you friendship,
Would you spend your last dollar
and hold out your hand?

If I offered to sell you love,
Would you empty your pockets
and hold out your heart?

You,
Foolish man.
Where is your wisdom?
Spent . . . .

—Amanda Hore

BITTERSWEET FANTASY

i grasp i hold
sweet sanity encased in glass
i pour i watch
crystals like hourglass sand
seeping through and down
to sink
submerge
under bleak black liquid lapping gently
against a chipped china cup
i hear a tick:
the clock heralds its seconds
and still i pour
time without measure
too much too sweet
but afraid now to cease
and someone smiles nervously
and i think it might be me
who prays please god
help me stop.
time.

—Eliana Mariella Alcivar

ODE TO A STRANGER

I don't know you
But I feel your dreams
I can't show you
But it seems
A great many things are
About to stir

Within myself I always believe
I've seen the secret
I've shared the fears
You're not alone — no never — but
Always on your own
So it's that path to travel
Make it your goal to borrow
Not steal & enjoy to see
What's real & not soured
The life in me.

I Love You
You who I will never meet
I Need You
You who I have yet to greet

—Jeanne Amodeo

OLD SKIN CHILDHOOD

I never thought the day would come
That I shed my old skin childhood,
And pull the shade, and set the sun,
Adult? I guess I am one.

—David Pavelich

THE MIRACLE OF FRIENDSHIP . . .

There is a miracle of friendship
that dwells within the heart; And
you don't know how it happens or
where it gets its start . . . But the
happiness it brings you always
gives a special lift, and you
realize that friendship is God's
most perfect gift.

—Mitzie Scholl

AN ANGELIC MESSAGE
A TRUE FRIEND — HARD TO FIND

A true friend is hard to find
in the world of thine.
I want you to know,
wherever you go
North, South, East or West,
wherever you love best;
A true friend is hard to find
in the world of thine.

I want you to know,
A true friend is hard to find
In the world of thine.
Whether you are rich or poor,
Wherever you go
I want you to know,
A true friend is hard to find
In the world of thine.

Rich or poor, high or low
Wherever you go
A true friend is hard to find.

—John Marbury

FRIENDSHIP

Friendship is like a tower,
Rising far above the crowd.
And a smile is like the sunshine,
Breaking through a stormy cloud.

Friendship is like a beacon,
Burning bright for the smallest boat.
And thru the changing scenes of life,
Friendship brings us hope.

Friendship can mean so many things,
Like a tower or a beacon.
To give us strength to carry on,
In a time when we want to weaken.

Friendship is for sharing,
All of life's ups and downs.
For giving comfort to each other,
Whether it be smiles or frowns.

I hope you get some meaning,
From one little word or line.
And I hope it will last a long, long time,
This Friendship of yours and mine.

—Marcheia Darley

TO MY FRIEND:

If I had a nickel, for every sweet thing
that you've ever said or done,
or a penny for every kind thought you've had
toward me and toward everyone,
Or a quarter for every sweet card you've sent
and a dime for the thought inside,
I wouldn't need a job or an income because
I'd be the wealthiest person alive!!!

—Ed Kuypers

MY FRIEND AND ME

My friend is loud and noisy,
and I am quiet and peaceful,
My friend is wild and crazy,
and I am sweet and sane.

But when she talks, I listen,
and when she cries, I comfort,
But when she's lonely, I'm right around the corner,
and always willing to help her.

So even though we're different
or may never be together.
It really doesn't matter
cause I'll really always love her.

—Mandy

THE LOST FRIENDS

We played,
We rode bikes,
We loved the treetops too.

We talked,
We cried,
We shared our feelings through.

We sang,
We danced,
We jazzed the whole day through.

We had to move,
We felt our hearts break in two,
We became the lost friends.

Dedicated to my very best friend, Amber Hodges

—Stephanie Thomas, age 11

A FRIEND

A friend is loyal and true,
And they make you feel better when you are blue.

A friend always knows what you're thinking,
And they are your life saver when you are sinking.

A friend should never, never betray you,
And is as reliable as the morning dew.

A friend should have a big red heart,
And promise your friendship will never part.

A friend is serious, but funny,
And is more precious than money.

A friend is always there,
And they really, really care.

A friend is beautiful inside and out.
A friend forever without a doubt.

—Sabrena Pearman

ON A SUMMER'S EVE

In the midst of great pines whose aroma seems absurd
A waterfowl dares disturb the placid mercury lake
Landing on the shore, with veiny roots of conifer, and flakes
Of algae climbing to its webbed feet and fur.

Ferocious mosquitoes flailing attempts of carnal sin,
Long tempered misery without any blood,
They are driven to scream and hurl for the mud
Of our veins wherever they find the sustainer of their kin.

Too long exposed to the rigors of Leisure summer demands:
Where have the fears of leeches and the chattering blue lips gone,
Passed into the infinite or waiting to be reborn?

Still, an inch-worm will crawl across an unthreatening hand;
The sun still burns drying swiftly a swim's residue,
But only the moon, so lustrous and alone, can resurrect the summer of my childhood.

     —Bruce Wilpon

REQUIEM: A POEM FOR MY FATHER: ANTHONY JAMES CONTI

Nearly thirty years have passed
And still I remember how precious life was
When you were here, alive and leading our family.
You were my first great teacher in life,
The man most influential to me in my formative years
And during my adolescence.
I often wonder how different my own life would now be had you lived.
You were ever there to help me make major life decisions,
But since I was sixteen I have made all important choices on my own,
Grown emotionally in the process and become stronger because of it.
Your untimely death that bleak, hoarfrosted January of 1969,
Has left me with a void I rarely think about,
Because you were irreplaceable and it cannot be filled.
I know and believe that I will see you in my next life
And will prepare for that omniscient meeting in the Afterlife
With all the love, respect and understanding that I feel for you still
From this life.
I believe you are proud that I am a Writer: for you are: Especial:
My Father: Anthony James Conti . . .
And in my dreams, family photographs and my many memories you are ever alive!

     —Valerie M. Conti

MY FRIEND

Years ago I knew a man, who traveled far upon this land,
he searched the stars to find his dream, a better life, though not foreseen;
were roads of trials and error.

So on his journey he set forth, unto a vast society,
that bore the triumphs of mankind, and also tragedy.
He dealt with all the best he could, his mark on mankind yet to be;
searching always every day, for peace and harmony.

Though young and eager, full of hope, he bridged the gap from boy to man,
with honest work that made him strong . . . envisioned dreams to fill his day;
his faith stood firm in all good things, that seemed to be his way.

An older man now, growing wise, of good men's truths, of bad men's lies,
he learned to love, but yet despise;
he cherished close the innocence he'd seen in chidren's eyes.

In later years he felt the voice, of distant winds that called him home,
he traveled to the place he knew, of air so clean, and skies so brilliant blue . . .
where memories became renewed, within his aging heart.

He lived upon the forest's edge, into his dying days,
when he passed on, the eagle flew above the clouds so grey.
The winter wind began to sing unto that darkened day;
as life goes on, I'll carry forth your fading memory.

     —Stewart L. Vonada

TO SING TO THEE

Some day I'll meet Him
The Lord of our earth.
I'll lift up my voice
For whatever it's worth.
I'll sing Him my songs
Praising Him on high,
Of how much I love Him,
This will happen by and by.
He is my Savior and I'll see Him soon,
But for now I wait patiently
As I sit in my room.
There's so much love that fills my heart,
Singing my songs would be just a start.
Releasing my feelings by singing to Thee,
Is just a small part of how it will be.

—Diane B. Price

Destiny guides us all.
It leads us down a given road —
Maybe it's a bumpy path
taking us where we're supposed to be,
But like a blinded man
we must follow
And use our hands to reach out to others
for guidance, support, and love.
We learn to not always talk,
but listen, learn, and remember.
That's the way everything works out
And in the end it's all worthwhile —
We find ourselves, and others too,
new friends, companions.
We learn to trust,
and accept what's right and wrong;
to understand and learn from our mistakes.
But most important —
to believe,
especially in ourself.

—Darlene Jenkins

PRIDE

Empty canvas
Spreads before me;
Darkness stretches
Far behind me.
I see the future
In these tattered cards;
Death and Lovers,
King of Diamonds and Queen of Hearts.
Close my eyes;
I don't want to see
What lies ahead,
Waiting for me.
Try to believe
The lies they told me;
I will forget
The truths they sold me.
And in the end,
I'll return in defeat;
Broken heart, bruised pride
. . . And I will still believe.

—Lauren Collins

NOW . . . THAT'S WORSHIP

Fingers touching the velvet of a rose
Voices used kindly to speak in understanding love
Man's mind acknowledging the wonder of creation
given from above
feet walking . . . eyes seeing . . . fingers touching;
ears listening, our hearts throbbing
at the wonders GOD gave us all
Tears of joy shed at the beauty of seeing newborn life
or in beholding of a majestic mountain
Knee bent upon a sandy shore hands open
in awe of the wonderest ocean
Penetrating silence of man willing to hear
the still small voice of his GOD: from inside
Yes GOD . . . inside . . . me and you not in some beyond.

—Jeanne Vick Mills

DREAM PILLOW

Storm in the distance,
Thundering softly in the cool, gentle night.
Silent room and laughing breeze,
Curtains dance so rhythmly.

Lie upon your dream pillow and fluffy bed.
Take a journey into the night.
Go forth to the shimmering light.

View the valley with the eyes of a flying hawk.
Battlefield green and red,
Soldiers killing, dying, and dead.

Land upon this battlefield.
See the charging, silvery soldier upon his horse's back.
Feel the sharp, hollow pain as sword is driven through.

Awake to the quiet, humble, morning rain.
All is silent on this Sunday morning day.

—Stuart L. Spanier

THE KING

A high mountain meadow, right after it rains,
creeks begin to swell, as the mountainside drains.

There's a natural perfume carried on the breeze,
the fragrance of wet grass, flowers, and trees.

No artifical fragrance could ever compete,
with scents of pines that actually taste sweet.

Sunset paints the sky, and it would surely seem,
that this is the Utopia of which we all dream.

Immense beauty to the east, even more to the west,
darker, more intriguing, the sun goes to rest.

Crickets start to chirp, nightbirds begin to sing.
They are singing a lullaby, befitting a King.

This King holds riches in his eyes, not hands.
Because, beauty is the valueless wealth of land.

He wouldn't trade its worth for silver, nor gold.
Because, his wealth will survive for years untold.

That, future generations can share his treasure,
to experience its wealth, its deep inner measure.

And, feel closer to his creator and to his God,
who is The King of heavens, mountain, and sod.

—Todd Elliot Hardin

VOCATION

With such great contrivances do we
unwittingly entrap ouselves.

Be it life or enslavement some
wish they knew.

Upon closer inspection we're not alone
Yet a few
Yes the tranquil appearances of a few

Spoil the view that we haven't erred.

—Duane Vander Griend

NIHILISM'S DRIFTING ESSENCE

The trees of fall above me in my mind
Could not be mean, and yet are never kind
The golden leaf that falls upon my head
Cares not if I'm alive or I am dead.

Books stand tall upon a wooden shelf
Pulled down and read by someone like myself
Returned with only twenty pages read
I can't forget what twenty pages said.

So now I simply breathe a choke of air
Somewhere in my heart it settles there
And knowing that with every taken breath
I'm taken to an ever-knowing death.

—M. K. Vaske

BLACK

Black is a color of colors within
Where people die and burn with sin.
Black is light,
Black is dark,
Black is the smell of burnt tree bark.
Black is where demons roam,
Black is in the devil's home.
Black is hot,
Black is cold,
Black is the hearts that some may hold.
The night is black as the day is blue,
Black is witches and their stew.
Black is where skeletons rot,
Now you've heard what black is,
But have you heard what black is not.

—Billie

LIFE IS A CONTRADICTION

All the past lay before me—
leaving two roads.
All the future lay behind me—
leaving two holes.
All the mistakes lay above me—
leaving two clouds.
All the right choices lay below me—
leaving two stumps.
All my love lay below me—
dead and buried.
All my hatred lay above me—
alive and breathing.
All my friends lay behind me—
laughing and joking.
All that's left lay before me—
leaving a bunch of nothing.

—Melinda Mosocco

THE DOLL

I am a doll, I sit on a shelf,
Often I tend to sit by myself.
I look out at the world with my
Blue glass eyes, dreading the day of my demise.

I remember a time when I used to play,
But my owner got older and put me away.
I really can't smell my nose is clogged up,
I really can't feel because I'm full of stuff

But that doesn't mean that I can't be fun,
Cause I'll be the same size when my owner's 21.

So here I sit with my matted curls,
Waiting for another little girl.

—Janet Branagan

HORSESHOE CRAB

It seems very tragic but we should all pray
For the horseshoe crabs in Delaware Bay:
Prehistoric survivors, these marine lives are crucial,
But how to keep them protected is still controversial.

Limulus polyphemus is about two feet long,
And if it can sing—it must be a sad song,
For eelers and fishermen use them for bait,
And migratory shorebirds are never late

'Cause they gorge themselves on horseshoe crab eggs,
Filling their gullets right down to the dregs,
Enabling these birds to fly three thousand miles
To the Arctic each spring, with satisfied smiles!

The horseshoe crab's blood can detect contamination
Of bacteria in blood, which adds to its damnation.
It seems this crustacean gives more than is accrued:
Another example of Mother Nature being screwed.

—Ted Brohl

THE POISONOUS GRAPEVINE

The poisonous grapevine is a sight to see
It starts in every community from only a seed

Tendrils are laced with a deadly poison
The victims stand helplessly as the seed moistens

Selfishly growing the vine is controlling
All of the contacting points it is finding

Becoming aware of the mighty thrust
The victim begins to lose all trust

As lightning flashes with all of its might
The vine lashes even though not in sight

And then all at once the tendrils pounce
The victim now falls not saying an ounce

Trying to battle to kill the vine
No one will listen to give him his time

They say it was the facts that got the victim
But only one would back his efforts

Now that the victim is no longer here
The poisonous grapevine victoriously withers

But the seed is dormant for only a day
Until a new victim comes its way

—Paul Irvin Kosel

PLAYGROUND

Swings, slides and sand boxes and a teeter totter bright.
A high fence around it, and lots of green grass.
A very pretty place, a very sad and very empty place
Where are the happy voices calling to one another?
Where are the smiling faces for this pretty, sad and empty place?
Where are the children to bring life to this playground?
Where are the children to play on the grass, to swing on the swings, slide on the slides, play in the sand?
Where is the life of the playground?
Where are the children?

—Joanne Woods

BURNING RED GATES OF HELL

As I sleep an unpeaceful sleep;
I see the burning red gates of Hell.
Hotter than a branding iron;
Screams louder than man, from the burning
Red gates of Hell as they are opened.

The laugh that comes from within is beyond all man.
My hands tied with fire red ropes;
Tied to the whipping tree.
The back of my shirt torn from my body;
I feel the fire in the whip as it slices across my back.

I think about my life.
Doing for others;
What they wouldn't take upon themselves to do.
No help from anyone;
Except complaining and excuses.

Yet I lay behind the burning red gates of Hell;
As they lay on cloud nine;
Floating through the golden gates of Heaven.

—Tammy Miller

WHERE DO WE GO FROM HERE?

We are living in a world that's full of destruction
sickening minds and loads of corruption
sex drugs and teens having babies
don't they know that the daddy is a maybe
where do we go from here?

Gang violence is happening everywhere
it makes no difference
if you're here nor there
did you hear that gunshot late last night
that bullet hit a little boy
that had no sight
little did he know his days
would be numbered
as he slept and while he slumbered
where do we go from here?

I love living
I wanna live long
it won't be possible
if this goes on
where do we go from here?

—Debra Moy Harris

IN AUTUMN

In autumn, leaves on a wet sidewalk
leave ash shadows after the fall of the rain
like people in Hiroshima did
after the fall of the bomb.

—Robert B. Nejman

AGAINST THE NEVER ENDING FIGHT

A flower in the sunshine,
A blade of grass during the night,
Each are their own supporters
Against the never ending fight.

The smell of the red roses,
The comfort of no light,
The happenings of nature
Against the never ending fight.

The threatening heat of the sun,
The fear of not having sight,
Am I to win or to lose,
Against this never ending fight?

Dedicated to V. Scott Baker
8/10/66 - 4/25/88

—Denise L. Fritts

A REASON TO LIVE

Don't ever assume that it's possible
To reach that plateau of existence
Where there is nothing left to discover

Nobody will ever attain (become)
an all seeing eye
that has seen every face
heard every sound
traveled to every existing place
or touched each of the 10,000 things

Becoming is the state of life
No human ever attains the all.
And if it were possible
Still would remain the exploration
of other realities
The numbers of which are infinite.

—Beth Ann Sutton

MYSTERY OF LIFE

Clouds drawing in over the dark
murky pool.
Clouds of darkness hovering,
smothering, the soul of a fool.
As the sky nears midnight, the
waters cease to flow.
They lay dormant, waiting, waiting,
wondering who would care to know?
Look around and feel the mist
fall upon your face.
The beckoning breezes, crying a
luring cry for grace.
You wonder as you feel the
darkness envelop your very being
I look, I feel, I sense, but
what am I not seeing?

—Mary M. Price

AGEING

Oh, how I long for those days
    where it all begun.
I don't want to grow old,
    I want to stay young.

Such far-away thoughts
    run through my mind,
But I have to go ahead,
    never fall behind.

The ever-ticking of the clock
    that passes each day.
Awaits gray hair and wrinkles,
    which won't go away.

The now-gone years,
    of memories still hold.
All my laughter and tears,
    of the days grown old.

      —Maxene A. Sweat

LIFE

Life isn't always what
    you want it to be
Which all of us
will someday see
Not everything can
go our way
Each of us
has had our day
Life can be dull and boring
Life can be nice and sweet
But each and every one of us
has problems that we meet
If life doesn't go our way
Which it sometimes won't
Go start another day
And if you want to quit DON'T
So don't take a knife and end your life
Because when it's all done and through
Then you'll know what a pain
It'll be to those in life you knew

      —Sara Naughton

DOG'S LIFE

I've been born to be a dog
    Free to run around.
Here and there
Or everywhere
Visiting different places
Looking at things
That are valued to me.
Like my favorite
is the sight of a tree.
You know what I mean
So please, don't tie me up
Or tie me down
Just let me be free
To run around.
You can talk to me, to teach me
to listen and obey.
So please, as you hear people say
Don't tie him up
or tie him down.
Let him be free, to run around

      —Frank F. Polverino

RADISH

Man lives momentarily and then forever
    Peril sings sweet music and then subsides
Daydreams and day-mares are lightning
    But spirituality is like a resilient amaranth

Children ask why and then they cry — rage
    How deep is the wishing well of love!
Souls are like Jack and the Beanstalk
    Climbing invisibly from ocean unto the clouds

Love is *never* lost though it seems to vanish:
    Its bastion outshines the nova and redwood
Strong is the Spirit of God; it is never lost
    It stands strong and shines bright at the reunion

Earth is but a shadow of the divinely real.
    How sweet is its chalice of nectar
The savor shall never die but pure fulfill —
    When we shall see vividly our angels as friends.

      —Scott C. Harrison

DINOSAURS CAN EAT CHILDREN

I feel the need to scream.
    The children are suffering.
The warriors they've created are being defeated.
Their warriors are fading.
We were given the task of leading them.
We were asked to take them on a journey.
Their journey will always be.
We are losing children.
I tried to help you hear.
These words are not threatening.
These words are not prophetic.
The dinosaurs are not extinct.
They are working with the children of tomorrow.
This system needs to rekindle the spirit
of loving and learning.
The quiet screams of the children
in their seats,
ring in the ears of those who pretend to lead.

      —Nicola Battigelli

BLACK HISTORY

Give us a warning Lord, give us a sign
    Yield all our black leaders, let Christ resign

Learn all of their struggles
study their trials and their times
remember them in a positive way
instead of increasing crimes

Give us a way Lord, show us the light
give us the will Lord, give us the sight
Show us the vision to make it seem right
Give us the heart to make it through the night

Our ancestors told us
"Christ will redeem,"
from Malcolm's all righteous
to Martin's great dream

It is up to us all to learn from our past
To remember our yesterdays, and make our tomorrows last.

      —Robin Boylorn

rice-paper fans

fragile trees like silhouettes of oriental rice-paper fans
eastern ladies hiding behind paper parasols bowing
as they slip slowly in their padded feet upon the patchworked hillside
suddenly an orchid pale and lavender sprouts up from
the still lakes of so many rice-paddies like a
refrain of joyous music repeating in a song
the water of the open spaced emerald-green-and-golden pond
moving like kabuki dancers in gold-threaded silk
in harmony with the countryside-in-music of the
dancing and the orchid and the paddies and the pond
sitarist softly playing his oriental sounds
            around him so many
fragile trees like oriental rice-paper fans

    —Lisa Baden

PIGS AND PEARLS

She strings together words like a strand of pearls:
Globes shimmering in a shoreless expression
Whose luster captures time's needle threading space.

We meet, she speaks; my pigment cloven eyes cast doubt.
With clear gaze, modesty glazed, she says,
"When I write these down, the words might destroy the feeling."
Give what is left unsaid power, I infer;
Making a part of hers mine and mine a part of hers.
The miracle of her humility strikes the sty from my eye
And sets there a blue pearl gathered from the ocean of her heart.

Word nor feeling is stranded in the abyss of time
Or the blank of space, for they stand side by side
Linked in supports embrace like pearl bubbles
On a farther shore; when she releases them they form
Words grains, grown feeling, flaming points breathed to life
In simplicity, how they are meant to be, pearls of wisdom
Strewn through eternity strung to infinity.

    —Kenneth Rose

MUCK

"Sigourney, don't get muddy!" My sister yelled from the doors.
Brother, what a fuddy duddy, Sigourney thought, doing chores.

Grandpa needed her to feed the cows, pony and duck.
Climbing over hay and seed, she dallied watching calves suck.

Her legs were too short to help much with chores.
Tired of playing in the hayfort, she climbed over the barn doors.

Grandpa wasn't here and nowhere to be seen.
Five year olds don't know fear and besides cows weren't mean.

On top of a rise quacked a duck.
Shooing away flies, she climbed the muck.

But she didn't know the muck was a sewer.
"Quick, call 911" Ali cried as Sigourney sank in the manure.

Stuck up to her knees, she couldn't budge.
They pulled her free from the awful sludge.

Hosing the poop down the drain, Kevin carried her to the house.
(He'd been back the lane.) She was as meek as a mouse.

This was bad enough ordeal, but imagine our faces
And how Brad would feel the next day in the same places.

"Help, come get me, Kevin, Uncle Brian! Come help!" he was crying.
Not knowing the muck was a sewer, he sank to his knees in manure.

    —Kathy Knapp

SUNLIGHT

The sun on the wall
The light that falls
Welcomes to me this day.

The sun on the wall
Is nature's call
For me to come and play!

    —Purple Raven

SPRING IS HERE

Spring is here,
With some baby deer.
In a meadow,
Stands a doe,
With a man without a bow.
Winter has left.
It's a time of new life,
A time for playing a fife.

    —Dana A. Reed

THIS OLD TREE

Ropes on a tree
how much fun they can be
Climb'n and swing'n
with ropes on a tree

Leaves so wide
under them we hide
Branches so thick
please don't break your neck

Ropes on a tree
make my muscles heave
My mama's callin'
but I don't want to leave

'Cuz this old tree
makes my heart sing
Laugh'n and play'n
with ropes that swing

    —Kenneth Evans Ford

TREE OF TRUTH

Guess what?!
Yesterday,
I saw a wintry tree
    with seven empty nests
left
to blow in the wind . . . .

Know what?!
Today,
I saw buds on a tree
    in a cemetery
    park
hiding the spring . . . .

What else?!
Tomorrow,
perhaps I'll see a bird
    building a new nest
again
in a leafy green branch!

    —Wanda Todd

Distant Light
A Form Appears
I Cannot See
Reaching Out
A Creature Motions
To Come Close
Leery of What
Shadows of an Object
Symbols Come to Mind
Who Knows? The Meaning
Is Unclear.

—**Virginia Matheny**

LOVE

Love is the warm
    colors like red, pink and
    purple.
Love sounds like a song
    sung by Bridgit.
Love tastes like sweet
    candy from a person
    on Valentine's Day.
Love smells like roses and
    feels like a big fluffy
    pillow.

—**Danny DeGrave**

THERE'S A LANGUID STAR

There's a languid
    star studded by the
ember of night and given
devotion by the darkened
angels of
sweetness; She comes
out, and does not
erode, as she stays on the
road and is a tempting,
for the man who
pays witness, for there's a
languid star and her name
is Celeste.

—**Angus Madden**

ILLUSIONS

friends
outside
reality.
trust the

ocean.
roads to everywhere.
driving to

clouds on the beach.
always
laid back
in a sense.
far away from
origins of my past.
rain
never ceases
in this life, forming
a rainbow of hope.

—**Jennifer Glacel**

in the beginning i despaired of being able to love you
your insulation and separateness
your untouchable unreachable self
(echoes of loss in darkness)
that inpenetrable silence:

with time the core of your earth fired steam,
heat undid your seams
a glow emanated from deep embers
and melted into photographic images of youandi moments:
from sandtossed beaches under moonshimmers
intranquil seas californian mists and burnt orange canyons
ancient sequoias wailing walls postcard mediterranean history
moorish gardens and windswept patagonian grasslands
to the still uncharted geography of a child
all giving testament to the flow of time
the immeasurable depths of your patience
to delve (me alongside you) into the heart of a communal simplicity
spiraling into unknown territories
sustained by your unconditional (albeit always incomprehensible)
love.

—**Olga Hak-Jacobi**

I'M MORE CAREFUL NOW

I'm more careful now, I guess it's my age, more sensitive to life.
More sensitive to the losses in my life were I not careful.
Taking life at a slower pace, taking in the beauty of it all
as if it were my last day, no, last minute on earth.
Taking time to appreciate life more,
life and all that it is to me.
I've known love, and loss, fear, pain, excitement and more.
As I age I wonder about happiness
where is it? Did I ever have any? Where did it go?
I do remember happiness, but it left me one summer
and I can't seem to get it back.
It's raining. I see and feel the rain now
and smell it, and welcome it and appreciate it.
Sometimes the rain hides the tears of my lost self
a part of me that I know where it is but can't get back.
I'll keep on giving myself to others, risking the hurt and pain because
deep in my heart I know it really is better to have loved and lost.
I'll always believe that and bear the scars of those risks.
I'm more careful now, I guess it's my age.

—**Jeffrey D. Elliott**

LYSIS

Pale yucca roots drag memory's weight against effort's doubt and gain
    They do not serve to hold fast in storm that I might stand
        with height enough to see this day's trail or map arid terrain
So long has echo answered my stretch of voice or hand
    that I rely on silence,   defiant still demand
        at least, or at best, no new loss
            no further sudden treachery
        than infinite void wherein,   if nothing is
            Every thing can become.
The dying, dead or merely lost   windswept,   clear and free
    I look into emptiness and know
        the knower and the seer.
Evening splashes gold against cerulean arch of shoreless sea.
Suffice me this and I shall climb where no level path remains
            and no clear view but sky.
        Once I walked the canyon rim
            tasting the wind at edges of being.
    Sunset cliff falls   endless space beneath dust of boots and me
    Assured a young woman into the horizon's purple drift
            desert's wide immortality.

Dedicated to Caroline

—**Billie L. Price**

GOODBYE COUSIN EDDIE

The memory strikes me at such odd times
I see your face and I start to cry
You were so young to be trapped in life's game
Suicide seemed the only way
To put an end to all the pain you carried deep inside
I remember all the things we did
All the trouble we got in
Life is short enough — you see
And in losing you I lost a part of me
So many "what if's" pass through my mind
How could we all have been so blind
Not to see the hurt in your eyes
Or hear the pain within your sighs
You left behind many people
Who miss you so
And constantly wonder
Why you had to go

—Rhonda M. Cook

WHAT'S LIFE, MY FRIEND

Life is the land, the sea, the sky,
And the mystery of the infinite universe
That's part of it, my friend

Life is the joy, the love, the laughter,
the sadness, and somehow living through it all
That's part of it, my friend

Life is the passion, baby's birth, the bonding,
growing, learning and getting older
That's part of it, my friend

Life is the virtues, the sins, the heroes,
the villains, the thinking and moving toward death
That's part of it, my friend

Life is the walking through experience here
and everywhere, till one's energy leaves this world
. . . to somewhere else in the universe
That's the end of it, my friend

—B Hugh Maine

FAITH IN MANKIND

A happy little child he was.
He loved his cartoons, and his pup.
Happy birthdays, and Christmases, and all that stuff;
Just really made his day.

And then somewhere along the way.
Our little one grew up.
He traded in his toys, and tryke,
For a silly hat, and a fishing bite.

There were lots of friends that he did make.
But four of them would turn out fake.
He trusted them with all his heart.
And never thought they'd ever part;
From him as friends, and do him in.
But that's exactly what they did.

And so we laid our son to rest.
And day by day we do our best.
But always there within our minds,
are the memories of him.
And his faith in mankind.

In memory of our loved one, Audie Ray Wilson,
Who passed away April 8, 1990.

—Linda S. Newcombe

YEARNING

I hear you call my name in the
whispering rains.
Knowing you'll be coming my way
I can feel your wet and shimmery
Lips upon my body searching for
its sweetness that a bee would find
in its honey.
But as you slowly lay me down
to enclose in our tight net comb
There we'll find our home.

—Penny Stalnaker

REMEMBER ME

Why I'll never forget the day
We all put you away

Some of you I knew very little
Others, I didn't even know at all

Things we shared together
We thought **our** life was forever

Many Good times we had
Laughter, Joys even when we were sad.

But it is the memories that make **you** special
Because Someone at sometime told it all.

If I could see each of you today
I would have something different to say.

You say a lifetime, **is the,** short-time
When you're gone. That is forever

Let **us** not be the judge
Life is too short to hold a grudge

Now is the time to enjoy each other
Say the things today
Tomorrow . . . they **too** may be away.

—Jeanie Brungardt

THE FINAL TEAR

I've seen a million tears that
have fallen over the years of my life.
But the one that always puzzled
me, was the final tear of life.
I'd like to think it's a drop of
Holy water, cleansing the body
and soul of all sins.
Preparing them to meet their maker
on their journey's end.
I've sat by a lot of people
during their last minutes here on earth;
and the expression upon their face
is finally free of all pain and hurt.
I can't ever remember not seeing
the last tear.
It used to make me very sad,
but thinking of it differently
has made me very glad.
I know I have time to say
good-bye, and believe that
only after the final tear; they
too, are ready to say good-bye
and will no longer have to cry.

—Kathy Croy Holford

Another cloud burst
Jumping for joy in the air
To come back again.

—Michelle Ping

FRIENDS

Stars are like friends,
They light up your darkness;
And they are with you
No matter the distance.

—Leona Louise Chibante

HERE & THERE . . .

Went out this morning
To catch me a rainbow . . .
Go watch the creek flow
And follow the minnow . . .
To find where my heart goes
On a warm summer morning.
Flying free naturally
Gulls flocking to the sea.
Would they trade lives
    with me
To find where my heart
    goes
On a warm summer
    morning . . . ?

—Lori Terpenny

I'M FINE

The red pick-up drove up
    honked three times.
I ran out to the porch
    and heard the moan.

"Please help me get out,
    I can't see or walk."
The door creaked open
    Oh, what a sight.

Blood, straw, manure,
Ripped clothes and bruises
    Now, what to do
    Before he collapses.

Labored walk to the house
Clothes carefully removed,
    Into the shower
    The damage to view.

Black and blue
From his head to his feet,
    Not a bone in a place,
    Where it legally should.

Off to the doctor,
A few stitches to sew
    Pictures of bones
    Not a great view.

Back home to bed
To lie in much pain.
    No pills for this cowboy
    There's more calving to do!

—Margaret Michel

A POEM FOR WINNERS

Winners never lose
And losers never win
Dream on
Winners win by taking loss in stride
And victories too
Acceptance
Ability
A winner has to lose sometime,
    or else they aren't really human
You have to know what it's like to lose
Or else how will you appreciate it when you win
A winner understands this

Dedicated to you. Take it how it comes and don't complain.
Winners lose too. Remember that always! This poem is also
dedicated to my very close friend **LUKE SCOTT**. He has always
been there for me and I know he will always be there for
me. Luke is a winner! You can be one too.

—Leslie A. Barber

The old man held the post office door and,
    Mail in hand, grinned a crooked greeting
To a lady with fur coat and varnished hair
Who passed on with a subordinating smile.

The old man offered a cheery comment on the weather
To the contractor with muddy boots and gimme hat
Who smiled and touched his shoulder without slowing
And flung back hearty agreement on the climate.

The old man could have told the lady with the fur and hair
That he saw the Pacific in a dead clam near the Gilberts.
"Not a swell, not a wave, not a ripple. Flat, mind you!
Never like that before and never to be seen again."

The old man wanted to tell the contractor how he hunted
The woods before dawn in cold, soundless November
For deer meat that would last well nigh the winter
But settled for squirrel to go with spuds for supper.

The old man had things to say. Helpful, for the most part.
Like how it was when Martha died — so to be forearmed.
How he let things slide after that so the banker's agent
Padlocked the house and barn and took the cows.

—Robert J. Cooke

PIECES OF CARDBOARD

I find them in shoe boxes and the pockets of jeans,
    in the cushions of Dad's favorite chair,
in the car, my book, every cranny and nook,
they pop up from almost anywhere.

These thin little pieces of cardboard perplex me.
I do not understand their mystique!
They're bought, and traded, valued and rated,
from the common to the rare and unique!

My son has a million, or maybe a zillion,
I lost count of them long, long ago.
I just know that kids love 'em, can't get enough of 'em
and they take them wherever they go!

The "Card Shops" are popping up at an olympic pace,
with a lure too powerful to fight.
They'll stay there for hours, held by its powers,
"playing" sports cards from morning 'til night.

They're loved by the young, they're loved by the old,
race, creed, and religion play no part.
For each card is a treasure that evokes childlike pleasure,
whose value lies deep in the heart.

—Liz Zapp

CASUALTIES

A sadness envelopes me that cannot be shaken.
Words, paraded mockingly about me, jest in the light of foreboding uncertainty.

Or is it me?

Are mine but the only eyes that see?

Is mine the only heart burdened; ladened with the illegality of these trespasses?

Does mine need be the only voice exacting equity?

Crippling notions are these; my soul grows lame by consequence.
Stabbing at inner, cerebral peace; raping my consciousness, until
only the acerbic taste of actualities remain.

And so you wonder; the soundness of your constitution in jeopardy.
What you once were is forgotten, what you will become, unknown.

Perilous is this existence we call humanity.
Nothing remains rudimentary, and only the in-humane survive.

> —D.E. Irons

MEETING ON THE DESERT SAND

One boy born white, one boy born black, both taught to despise
the other. Each boy grew, one feeling superior, the other
feeling inferior.

Two men, one born white, one born black, met on the desert sand.
Both men carried arms for their homeland. Both men fought for a
poeple whom they thought less than either of them.

On the desert sand, the white man and the the black man began to
talk. One man had a plan, one man had a dream, for themselves and for their loved
ones left behind. They shared their hopes, their fears. They
ate together; they laughed together. They became friends.

To the homefront the black man returned. The white man did the same.
Far away from the desert sand, the two men sit
together on the pews of the same church. Their families sit
beside them.

All smile and sing. All pray for their races. All pray for peace for the peoples of the
desert sand. All praise and worship the God who made them wholly
equal.

> —Lacy Sprague

BUT NOW THAT I COULD THINK . . .

You looked at me with those condemning eyes and funny looks
calling me druggy and giving me a worthless snare
judging me by the way i look and by the color of my skin
and by the house i live in Brukdown Street
Once you even called me thief and said i was half crazy
ever since my mummy left for the greater lands

In your eyes i am only a worthless vagabond who is too lazy to find a job
i remember when i was in school trying hard to understand Shakespeare
and your friend the Mr. Ferry selected your little boy to be the main star and
i to be the master's servant

Why do you do this to me?
is it because your child's father is the well-known Justice of the peace and i have none?

i am tired of being bashed, chewed, and spited upon
don't ever cross my way again cause i am a man who has learned what loneliness means
and what emptiness is
and i will beat the drums of my fathers and dance like my ancestors and lift my head high
to stare at your face

i will not fight but only count the pace before i strike
cause now **I** am Big, Strong and Free and my bones and blood have been made and my
veins run up to my head and for the first time **I** could think, **I** could think for myself.

> —Alex P. Vega

Why can't I just smile,
instead of speaking
       unhappy thoughts —
you're unhappy also,
and just maybe, you'll
       smile back —

—Dorothy M. Bryce

CONFUSION

Confusion confuses
Bikes are ridden;
Similarity's here
In circles driven.

Insane is sane
One's in the other;
What ever you do
Don't open the cover.

Birds fly
Babies cry;
Peaceful yelling
In the sky.

Lions roar
Fish swim;
What's really lurking
Deep within.

Confusion's defined
So's a sound mind;
A sound state of confusion
Embedded in the mind.

—Mark Armstrong

BRAINSTORM

My world is made up
mega colors,
Black, blue, gray,
and so many others.

Don't peek or look
inside,
For there is where
I go to hide.

Escape I always find,
within the boundaries
of my mind.

Look if you dare,
as if you really care.

My world is made up
of mega colors,
Black, blue, gray
and so many others.

You may be surprised
at what you find,
Within the boundaries
of my mind.

Private property is what's
inside.
For there is where I
go to hide,
My space, my time, my
mind.

—Frances M. Boyd

FORGOTTEN SHADOWS

Fallen leaves and fallen angels rising stars and seraphim.

The search for love and fall to faith, destiny foregone.

Innocence conceived among the violent structures, rising
      over weathered sculptures.

From forehead to font, a trickle of truth.

Finally compelled to squeeze and strain the mystery from life.

Deep in prayer and bold conviction, feel relief in benediction.

Pale goodness and fetid darkness play and tease the aching spirit.

Looking deep and absolute, when eternity calls perhaps we'll
      hear it.

Summon those forgotten shadows, call to the fear, it is you,
      have mercy.

—V.B. Millsap, Jr.

FOREVER MY HERO

Although there are miles between us, you are always by my side,
In mind and in soul, you're someone in which I confide.
As a child you were my hero: I felt secure when I was with you,
Your strong arms to hold me, your warm, understanding eyes too.

I remember fondly, my daddy dressed in green,
Armed with badge and gun; so tall, proud and lean.
I think of you daily, my eyes well with tears,
I thank the Lord He spared you; a calming of my fears.

I followed in your footsteps; an extension of what you began,
You share in my successes and support me as only you can.
No longer a child, we reminisce of days past,
We talk, friend to friend; a friendship built to last.

I admire your strength and unselfish ways,
Your optimism inspires me, brightening even the darkest days.
There could be no better father, nor a family so blessed,
You give to us everything; your love — it's endless!

Thank you, Dad
For all the love you bestow,
I am so proud to have you as my father,
You will forever be my Hero!

—Ramona Buchlmayer

IS IT WORTH IT ALL?

So many times, I have wondered, "Will they ever get the message?
Will they understand and face life with hope and courage?"

When I started out, I was married and had help from their father.
I had done it right, just like a good woman oughta!
Somewhere along the way, the male support, I had was gone.
Distraught and confused, I was now left on my own.
To handle 4 girls—MY—That's an AWESOME responsibility!
Left with them—ALONE—I wanted to run away and be free!

Here I was, supposed to nurture, encourage, impart and share;
In the midst of a cruel world—**ALONE, "Lord, this is not fair!"**
So many things to develop and teach, so that they could grow;
And not be bitter toward men, but intelligent women in the know!

With disputes, disciplines, training and knowing who to trust;
Questions, challenges, **"I want my Daddy," "Lord, this is too much!"**

At times, we would together gain ground, at a steady pace;
Then puberty, teenage-hood, and fashions—would hit you in the face!
With their changing bodies and minds all wanting to be grown;
Facing college, new people, this world, on their own away from home.

As I listen to the reports from all others, they have encountered;
Integrity and wisdom—They got the message and I **no** longer ponder!

—Presita R. May

COLOR BLIND

I see no color in your face
I judge not by religion, nationality, or race
We are all equal in His eyes
We all must be . . . "Color Blind"

It's hard being black, and living today
Because of their skin, people are blown away

Your hair may be nappy or your hair may be straight
Realize, we're all part of the human race
I am equal to you and you are equal to me
With love in our hearts we can *truly* be free

We must live together in unity, and combine
In order to do that we must be color blind.

—Tony P., grade 6

JOY

Picking up broken pieces; Past trouble & pain
So many pieces
Expectations way too high
For this butterfly in the sky
Living life day by day; maybe not the right way
I survived; So did you
Communication is the key
To make relationships free
Free to enjoy our future
Repairing broken pieces; broken pieces of the past
Take a glue ball; throw it in the air
Let God fix the pieces of despair
It's too big a job for me; Let's enjoy life; Be free
For joy creates more joy
I sure Love my girl & boy

—Jeanne Marie Day

SILENCE

Have stepped from the darkness into the light
Saw all that is wrong and most of what's right
Men who drink heavy, and waste their lives
Hard working women who are given as wives

Children whose spirits are broken in two
Mothers that hold them and say "I love you"
Doctors and lawyers who've desperately tried
Fathers and mothers who have shamefully cried

Teachers at school who noticed the beating
Child in a corner, all alone eating
Ministers that pray for the Lord to protect
Emotional pain which no one can detect

Lost are the sons who wander the streets
Girls that call home, somewhere in sheets
Wife that obeys and never complains
Truth that is hidden in secret remains

Police who are handcuffed by citizens' rights
Brothers and sisters who can't stop the fights
Houses of filth that fall to the ground
Cries of the children, a pitiful sound

Courts that protect the rights of the wrong
Babies undernourished, will never grow strong
No laws to encourage the dreams of our youth
Held up by papers in a congressman's booth

TV and radio have tried their best
Newspapers have laid these stories to rest
Raped are the minds and hearts of our young
Where is their future, no bells to be rung

—Nick Hammerschmidt

ILLUMINATION

Let the light shine in,
Where the sun is hardly present,
Where the stars never glow
Or fade in the heaven-lit skies above.
But where the darkness
Lives throughout the night,
Where the shadows
Control the destinations of our souls,
And utter helplessness overwhelms our beings.

Let the light shine in,
Let it spread its healing rays
To the darkest spheres of our spirits,
Through the cracks of our perilous hell,
Past the slits of nightly torments.
Until, like the dew rinsing the grass,
It washes away all hostile attacks,
And defeats the night with its charm,
Dazzling the dawn with its radiance.

—Joshua Edward Rockoff

WAS LIFE A GAME?

Behind closed doors
his room remains the same.
These four walls a silent picture frame.
Racks of books and cars and toys,
all memories of boyhood joys.
Nestled in hollows once meant for eggs
rested pretty butterflies
on toothpick legs.
Rubber fins and tennis racquets,
the years of school dances and leather jackets.
Small dusty statues, green and grim,
molded of plastic were only toys to him.
Little soldiers with guns of wood
neatly displayed from where I stood.
From babe to boy to man to fame,
Oh, Dear God, who shall I blame
for his young soul's extinguished flame
when war taught him life
was not a game?

—Virginia Tabor

THE MIRROR OF MY SOUL

I see in the water a reflection;
An image of what is and might be.
To pass beyond that barrier
I give my every waking thought,
For with understanding comes ability.

I see in the reflection a truth;
An honesty that cannot be spoken.
To hear the voice of this wisdom
I deafen myself to all that is around me,
For all that is heard is not truth.

I see in the truth a vision;
A picture that binds all things together.
To hold this picture close to my heart
I blind my eyes against all else,
For deception affects first the eyes.

I see many things in the water,
None of which I may touch.
For in my selfish ignorance I wish
To think of other things; to see, to hear—
And the vision is gone.

—Neale C. Syth

A MOMENT IN BLACK HISTORY

Rosa Parks
provided the sparks
set the Civil Rights
Movement ablaze.
She defied the laws
the unjust laws
and started a national craze.
Dr. King rose to the cause
took up the torch
and marched into history.

—Paulette M. Garner

UGLY BOY DREAMS

He wakes in the morning and
prays to God, hoping the day will
be the one his dreams come true.
But he's lived a life of dreams
destroyed, and finds it hard to
live on hope alone. When he comes
home knowing the dream is done,
he cries another night in contemplation.
And when sleep has overcome,
that dream again will surely come.
And he wakes with a smile and
a prayer,
not really sure if he should care.

—Marc Sloan

The sky is falling
and no one seems to care
The earth is open
to the excess in the air
Will we be blind
to what stays behind
or look ahead without a lesson
What have we learned
in a world cut from ice
Castles in the sand
without a beach to catch the tide
Where are we going,
no one seems to know
Are we all going to pull together
when there's nowhere left to go?

—Rovert

ADOPTION DECISION

Hush little baby,
Now, don't you cry . . .
I'm sorry to say,
But yes, I lied.

You were mine,
That is true,
But I can no longer deal
With loving you.

Your father said
He'd leave me never,
But where is he now —
He's gone forever.

I look down at you,
Into your father's blue eyes . . .
I give you away,
And I start to cry.

—Linda Van Deusen

REFLECTIONS

A single tear rolled from my eye,
Fading all the memories of you.
As it rolled, it gathered all my dreams and wishes,
Then washed them away.
Like fresh blood that cleanses the dirt from a wound
That tear purified my soul;
Freeing it from your clutching talons.

—Gina M. Kowalski

AS I SIT

As I sit in the chair on the deck,
Thinking about every little speck.
I think of all I have been,
And my every dream.
And what will happen to me,
And if I will live to be eighty.
And if I will go straight to death and not be known,
Or be a millionaire with a mansion for a home.
And what will I be,
A poet or a scientist or a person in the presidency.
Or maybe just a person trying to live life,
Going through struggles and strife.
I could also not know,
And just "go with the flow."

But whatever I choose,
I know I can use.
As I sit by myself,
Like a book on a shelf.
As I sit with my life in my hands,
Hoping that it never ends.

This is what happens as I sit down,
Thinking without a frown.
And I am proud to be free,
In a country such as thee.

—Rachel Sandler

MY LITTLE HOUSE IS LONELY

My little house is lonely
as it looks back to the past.
Years it thought were moving slowly,
now it knows slipped by too fast.

Days are long, nights last forever
and its paint is cracked and chipped.
It wonders what the future holds,
what's to become of it.

There are no smudges on its doors,
where little hands had been.
No toys left out up on its floors,
it can't remember when.

It shivers when each time the wind
starts blowing from the north.
And sadly watches as the swings
start moving back and forth.

Brings to mind someone who lived there,
hears them laugh at play, but then.
Suddenly, the wind stops blowing,
and the swings are still again.

Yes, my little house is lonely.
Says a prayer it's always said.
Please God, protect and guide my loved ones,
and it bows its old grey head.

—Mae Schultz

LIFE

Cool spring days,
Hot summer nights.
Love running wild, reckless and free.
Enjoying life with all of its pleasures and pains.
Sometimes stumbling,
But others soaring like an eagle.
As we should slowly drift throughout our lives.
Clouds drift slowly across the sky
Live, love, laugh; enjoy what is ours.
Live each day as if it were our last.
What happens if there is no tomorrow?
Things change and people change,
The world will not stand still for others to catch up
Nothing ever stays the same,
It is forever changing,
Growing and moving to the beat of its own drum.

—**Elgena R. Jones**

ALWAYS A WAY OUT

Totally hip cats are surrounding me
with machine guns poised,
ready to unload their lethal lead
into my brain
causing much pain and suffering
to me and those who worship me as their selfish god.

The cats stand still and silent
waiting for me to move first towards that
which is not known to me and my constituents
hidden behind the walls of the passageways
in the felines' brains. We keep poised and
ready to slice away the inner core
of their violent and destructive thoughts
towards others.
Particularly those towards me.
I spoke forth, "These are good kitties!"
and soft they became
like flowers in the Spring.

—**Ed Wenger**

WHAT IF

One day as I was thinking sorrow,
I decided to think of tomorrow.
What if when I wake up one morning,
What if everything was boring,
What if I break a dish, what if I don't eat my fish,
What if I don't eat my food,
What if my mom gets into a bad mood,
What if I go the bed, what if I wake up dead,
What if I go to school,
What if somebody calls me a fool,
What if I throw up on the teacher's desk,
What if I have to clean up the mess,
What if I go to the nurse,
What if she hits me with her purse,
What if I don't know what I'm doing,
What if I'm in a play and the audience starts booing,
What if I get really sick,
What if Mom doesn't know which medicine to pick,
What if I can't stop worrying about tomorrow,
I might as well go back to thinking in sorrow.

—**Chantal Yanniello, 5th grade**

A TEAR, A SHRUG, A SMILE, A HUG

A tear, a shrug, a smile, a hug,
Can all express a feeling.

Although they're sometimes covered up,
We know what they're revealing.

A tear expresses sadness,
But can also spell out joy.

A shrug shows that you just don't know,
Or are simply acting coy.

A smile is a good thing,
That we happily can share.

A hug takes smiling one step further,
And really shows you care.

—**Nikki Saengchalern**

ROBERT'S RINGING

Way above the earth's shield to a place
called heaven it was a ringing of a
soul's oncoming.

Down below to a place called earth
was a man named Robert with a
calling he did not know of.

Sweet, kind, all words of love describe
But that evening before it was time
for that one last look a few
reminisces is all he took.

Of all the things in this world he
did not leave much but a presence of
his lingering touch.

Today, at the town's cemetery, is placed
a white cross in a symbol of his love
not of loss.

—**Cheryl Lee Garcia, age 16**

GROWING UP

There is an age we all must meet
When we decide to stay or retreat.
It matters not if you are young or old,
But hinges on who is weak and who is bold.
Everyone is different, that is plainly seen,
Some are nice and some are mean.
Although we know life is not fair,
We often find the injustice hard to bear.
They tell us to take life by the horns,
But they forget about the many thorns.
We are all taught the "Golden Rule"
And told to use it as a tool.
But we often find
The world is cruel and unkind.
The people too, are just as cruel,
So we dismiss this golden rule.
We find that if we wish to get ahead,
We must lead and not be led.
Why can't people live for good,
And do the things they know they should?

Dedicated to my family, friends and Kris.
Thanks for not giving up on me. Bear.

—**Cherie Gootee**

WHISPERING LOVE

Love is like a whisper in time.
Here for a moment, only to be
swept away by the current of
change in the everchanging
waves of life.
But true love is a rock in
those tides. Always there,
through the crashing force of
life. Through the gentle
splashes of the world. It
always stands strong through
the entire existence of life
itself.

—Jillian Butela

THE BUTTERCUP

You are so delicate
and fragile.
A light and beautiful
fragrance surrounds you.

The soft yellow petals
that gave you your name
Softly bend and blow
with the wind.

Moments after you are picked
on a summer's day
Your green stem
begins to wilt.

I lay you down
upon the ground
Your buds will never blossom now
But you have touched my heart.

—Dawn C. Dickinson

LIFE

I see the
crystal droplets
threatening
to fall off the blades of
grass —
dew.

I see a
long-armed
yellow
disk kissing white fluffy
pillows —
sun.

I see the
painted horizon
get
ready to say goodbye —
sunset.

I see the
large, white
ball
and its glittering friends say
hello —
moon and stars.
I've seen it all.

—Joy Ann Konarski

ODE TO JIMMY CONNORS

What is a poem if not to say
To one you admire how you feel this day;
A day to remember, to lavish, to hold,
Of a gladiator who conquered so proudly, so bold.

Into the arena like Achilles he sent
His opponent beleaguered and finally bent;
With the zither he used, he had used as a flail,
As his forehands and backhands full through did he sail.

He was like a gazelle as he moved through the air,
And like a zephyr, first here and then there.
A whirlwind of red, white, and blue hit the corners
The pride of America — his name, Jimmy Connors.

—Marie Massey

OLD MAN IN THE SNOW

There stood an old man in the swirling flakes of snow,
cold and lonely, with no place to go.
His clothes were tattered, his shoes worn;
He seemed so lost and so forlorn.

Staring out into the darkness of the night,
I knew he should be inside, but my heart cried out in fright
Suddenly, he turned and saw me standing there.
His face lit up with a glow that spread everywhere.
It brought to memory the story of the beggar come to call,
But, instead, was Jesus so strong and so tall.

As I reached out into the darkness of the night,
My heart was stilled, free of all fright.
But where the old man had stood just moments ago,
There was only a soft impression in the fallen snow.

Sadly, I turned and started to go,
When I was filled with a warm and heavenly glow.
For now I knew the old man in the snow
Really had a place; a place he could go.
For my "Beggar" had finally come to call;
In spite of my fear, from God's grace I did not fall.

—Dee Guillot

IMAGERY

Crystal clear water on a cool spring night
the stars in the sky are shining so bright
the colors of a rainbow after a warm spring shower
the smell of freshly cut grass on a hot summer's day.

As fall arrives the leaves change colors
gentle green and magnificent red
with the first snow the air is cool and crisp
even though it's cold the sun still shines.

It is a never ending cycle the snow melts,
flowers bloom, the grass is green
back again from what was to what is
soft petals from a flower bees gather their nectar.

The fresh ocean air takes away all our cares
lightning doesn't scare, it is the noise from the thunder
the breaking of a twig, the crumpling of leaves
the song of a bird, the bark of a dog.

The sun's rays burn such as the heat from a flame
gusty winds drift the sand, dunes are scattered throughout land
water freezes, ice is formed
only to be changed back to water again.

—Scott E. Yancy

DAUGHTER OF A DISEASE

Screaming, so much screaming
He is sober . . . Ha—And I am dreaming
There is no such thing as sober here
He has been drunk for my lifetime; it has been too many years
To fight it off is impossible; he is weak
The alcohol talks—I hear it speak
It says to me, "Do I make you mad?
I, the poison, have taken control of your dad!"
"No!" I scream, but my voice is silenced by the bottle
I am either hit or avoided like the road's biggest pothole
My home is the dark road—Hard to see
My dad is the car, sometimes he hits me
He hits me not physically, but with words
How terrible it hurts
I know this is a sad thing to mention
But I have to say it, I have to make you aware
When he hits me with words, at least he knows I'm there . . . .

—Holly A. Tesch

A CHILD ABUSED

Terrorized eyes — shaking body — the monster looms above menacing, screaming "How could you do such a dreadful thing? You're crazy! You're stupid! You're just like your grandfather!" Beaten, battered, pounded, bruised all over her body, the little child searches the day. She did the laundry — hung it on the line in the backyard — went to school walking four miles each way — did her best to achieve the highest grades — returned home — waited on her mother and sister — cleaned the house — ate her supper of beans boiled in water — did the dishes — all the time screaming, shouting, condemning, demeaning, downgrading poured out of the ugly mouth of her enraged, violent, brutal mother.

The little girl thought "Why does she hate me! Am I really her child? Why does she love my sister and not me? What's wrong with me?"

Blows upon blows fall on the little girl — her ears ring — pain flows over her body — her brain bounces back and forth in her skull.

—Grace Elgart

THEY TOO ARE HUMANS

I wonder why? Why everyone does stare,
For I know I am different but still I breathe the same air.
I cannot walk, or crawl, or even stand.
An' I cannot make use of my own two hands.

You see I was born a handicap an' it's different I know,
That I cannot go, where everyone else does go.
An' that sometimes makes me feel, so alone, so alone inside
That often times I've sat for hours upon hours an' cried.

Cried by wonderin' why this had happened to me.
Frightened by cold, cold, stares an' what they would see,
Would they see me as disabled, or see me as one of them,
Or would they just pass me by as if I couldn't be their friend.

I'm sure the handicapped sometimes feel no love.
But they too are gifted as special from the Lord up above.
Whether in a wheelchair, bedridden, or standin' with a cane.
They too are humans, Just the same.

So never laugh at the handicapped for it could of happened to you.
For everyone wants perfection, they want nothin' broken in two
God all I pray is for when you hear all the saddened cry
Please, Please, help the ones, so less fortunate than . . . I.

Dedicated to my brother, Ty Arron Tyson

—Ray Tyson

TO YOU, A SPECIAL FRIEND

I told you a secret
Which was my first mistake
Then, you told the secret
And problems did you make
Now, I've learned a lesson
And secrets I'll retain
Because of words I spoke
To you, a special friend

—Ernie Faison

POST-TRAUMATIC STRESS

The rush of the TERROR
Shocked his being.
It permeated like the
Black ink spilling
on the alabaster floor.
A HORROR so gripping
That reality was a
Language unknown.
Entombed in a casket
Of panic for a thousand years.
Death became so delicious,
An end to the ghastly frenzy,
Sweet dream of death.

—Betty Gianella

AT SANITY'S EDGE

the smell of sickness
is everywhere
it permeates
everything
it looms over, under
and around me
it fills me
with frustration, rage
and helplessness
it suffocates, torments
and overwhelms me
dying people
dying animals
dying things—
and me

—Barbara Coleing

IN A WORLD SO FULL

In a world,
so full of rejection,
How does one accept?

In a world,
So full of hate,
How does one love?

In a world,
So full of cries,
How does one laugh?

In a world,
So full of wrong,
How does one do right?

In a world,
So full of death,
How does one live?

—Heather Nelson

Groggy, tired and all stressed out
Reading the paper — what's it all about

Notice this column about writing a poem
When something suddenly hit down home

Hours in English class when going to school
I could compose a poem, I'm no fool

So here with paper and pen in hand
Why I'm doing this I don't understand

But, alas, what could my endeavors harm
After all, I don't expect to set off any alarms

So as I try to bring this to an end
I sit here thinking will this I really send

If read this you might some day to come
Remember it might be amusing to some

And bear in mind if you will
Groggy, tired and stressed out am I still

—**Cindy Ann Venus**

The night I died
the pen caressed the smooth paper
and robbed its soft innocence.
The body robbed of its hollow soul
and thrown to bone worms
in their deep soil planets.
The pen sleeps as I sleep
and everything is obscured inside.
Death of me and my harsh pen.
Vision implodes with its circling light spectrums
and faint echoes fill'd with laughter.
I wake quickly to this dark dream
with a grin of flesh silence.
Again I return to flight
among bright insects of the night.
In the black void above the trees,
feeling the rapture of the summer's breeze
Peering downward to the earth's liquid pools
of silvery smooth reflections
towards me.

—**Basil Bayne Whatley**

JOURNEY TO A POEM

The journey to a poem is long,
You often make turns that are wrong,
It starts with inspiration,
A very queer sensation,
That jumps into your head and sings a song.

Then you grab a pencil and start,
Beginning a true work of art,
You must find some words,
That sing out like birds,
And sound very pretty and smart.

Then you write, and you write, and you write,
And you work for a year and a night,
Lots of white-out was tipped,
Lots of paper was ripped,
But you finally have one that's just right.

Now that it's over, have fun,
But don't dare to think that you're done,
Because just count to ten,
And it's starting again,
Because no poet can think of just one!

—**Leah Rachel Berkowitz, age 11**

TOUCHING THE MIND

When you're feeling blue so far from home,
Cast an eye into your past,
See someone who cares,
Remember all you shared,
For times will come of hardship,
Dreams will fill with tears,
The someone of your past,
Is always very near.

—**Debra L. O'Connor**

THE BIRTH OF A WORK OF ART

The birth of a work of art is vague.
It is a prayer, a search of mind and soul;
A thought, a dream that will not leave,
That haunts and needles till conceived
And then fulfilled.

Creativity's an urge to share a thought,
A blurred idea to be sought
Made tangible and clear;
A spark that's energized till formed
Through sweat and labor, then transformed
Into this thing called art.

—**Ingrid Brostrom Bloomquist Pope**

COMMUNICATION

Human silence is a waste of valuable
information because we all have
something important to say.

Though one word may cause
great upheaval, it may also
bring long awaited peace.

A spoken sentence between two people
can be the creation or destruction
of a lifelong friendship.

Words are risks taken daily
for anyone who wishes to express
that which is on their mind.

—**Barbara Weglicki**

POETRY

IF POETRY
should traipse along with pentametric iambs,
why am
I even writing this unpalatable crap?

I suppose even I could digest
a few lines of perverse anapest;

Or some prosaic, unmetrical lines of
free verse.

I must be old-fashioned.
I believe that poetry should rhyme,
at least some of the time.

Should poetry make sense
in the present tense?
Is it a thought frozen in time?
Or a Universal Truth?

What is poetry?
I thought I knew.
But then, I guess, I really . . .
haven't a clue.

—**Richard Taubold**

SOLITARY CONFINEMENT

Caged w/in my skull
Trapped in a lethargy of flesh
I want to be free
        of this solitude of self

I reach out   out   out
But am stopped by bars
        of habit and indulgence

    Contemplate

Each of us
    is the loneliest person
        in the world

—Joseph F. Guzman II

AFTER THE BATTLE

How peaceful they seem,
How grotesquely peaceful.
They'll not rise to
Fight again,
They sleep together
As friend to friend.

Enemy and foe ere
The battle began
Now lying in death
Man and man
Not gallant knights,
Simple men.

No battle cry will
Rush their hearts,
Their slumber is deep
They'll forever sleep.
No they'll not rise to fight again
These pawns of other,
Weaker men.

—Edward H. Killgore, Jr.

SATISFACTION

There is no satisfaction,
    that I have ever known.
As that of helping others
when they are all alone.

A child who's lost a
parent, a Mother who's
lost a child. As a Son
that's lost in action,

or a daughter who's gone
wild. The feeling of total
loneliness, of hurt, of pain
and woe. A smiling face and an
open heart, is what they all
need so.

A word of understanding
And a shoulder to cry on.
To try to help and comfort
them, for the loved ones that
are gone. When I leave this life
on earth and go to meet your son

I hope he takes my hand
and says, "My child a job well
done."

—Linda Carter

ODE TO SILENCE

Silence! You are astonishing to hear.
You bring droll profanity to this sensitive ear,
there being no warning to your onset,
not having been announced by sob or cheer.

Silence! You breed the restive, reckless thoughts
that plague a fertile mind and offer not
one simple soothing answer for the
stark and empty world you brought.

Silence! You boldly challenge me to enter your realm
and dare me rend your mystic, mocking calm.
Oh, would that I could break your spell with cannon's roar,
but I profess a wiser way to remedy my qualm.

Silence! As poetic concepts are my goal,
I shall blithely pluck them from your pensive soul,
transcend your dreary world,
and thus give piquant meaning to your passive role.

—Lars Johnson

Encircling with warm, tantalizing embraces,
comforts in a promised ending,
The light of death is shed on reigning darkness,
captivating and held hostage,
propelled to go on by a force just as strong,
Holding an empty box where dreams were once,
shadows of regrets on heels fleeting.
So forever begins with midnight
watching day fade to night,
only hopes of yesterday's mornings,
pushing on through the recesses of a threatening self destruction.
Life has ended, but the lights are still on,
a walking, breathing corpse,
plastered smile,
pretending to be a part of the race, but not running.
Standing in place,
getting tired of going nowhere.
No comfort in the whirlpools,
where the mind once was.

—Connie Montalbano-Powers

PRISONERS' PRAYER

The time is long overdue,
    we want you to know,
what we're goin' through.

You (society), might not feel so sane,
        if you were in our shoes
facing the same old thang.

We are the prisoners, serving time behind bars,
along with rats and roaches, and physical and mental scars.
We live in a world that's often cold and dark,
with nasty food and water, which leaves another mark.

We're being oppressed spiritually, physically,
mentally, and educationally.
Now this is not rehabilitation,
but a form of dehumanization.

Lordy, Lordy, Lordy, please hear our cry,
        we'd like to see our relatives and friends,
in the free world again before we die.

We're not getting any justice,
        So Lordy, Lordy, Lordy,
bless these prison doors to open for us . . . Amen.

—Kount

THE HEART OF SPRING — DAWN

Shadows through your window fall, chased by sun's spring waking
Something in the air sets your heart on fire
And draws the flowers into blooming.
You're surprised by robins singing on your window sill
Breathing songs of life.
Gauze curtains brush against your face
Jasmine and honeysuckle spirit the morning breeze
Closing your eyes memories swell
Last night's storm now forgotten.
Earth's rebirth joins your waking soul
Lifting you flowing round and round your room.
Run your hands all through your hair
Breath deep spring's pure air
Hold this moment — it's yours forever, soundless voices say
Tears of joy bathe your face
The winter's over, you whisper softly
My heart told me so.

   —R. Clayton Lee

WHAT IS LOVE

Is it a freshly picked red rose?
Or is it an old, dried rose in a treasured scrapbook?
Is it a candlelight dinner only on birthdays or anniversaries?
Or does every dinner feel like a candlelight dinner?
Do you feel yourself staring at him with a smile on your face just thinking
  how much you love him?
Do you ever just sit and wait for him to come see you after work or school and it
  always feels like forever, like your first date?
Is it a card that says all of the things he doesn't know how to tell you —
  the many reasons why he loves you so?
Does he help you with chores you usually do alone, maybe because he loves
  you so much and wants to spend more time with you?
Is it that little gift he gives you when it's not your birthday or Christmas
  or any other special day?
Is it the places he takes you — even if *he* doesn't really want to go there —
  just because you want to go there?
Are these things love?
Or is it much, much more?

   —Corinne Dallmann-DeMoss

DREAMS OF INTIMACY

How would it feel to be completely open to another human being,
To say whatever is in your heart,
Without fear of rejection or ridicule.
To be so much at ease with one person,
That you could trust him with your innermost feelings.
To share your thoughts, your secrets, your fears, your hopes,
With someone so special, you feel you can never be close enough.

To look in this person's eyes,
And see tenderness, understanding, acceptance, desire.
To get lost in these eyes and feel the warmth of his smile
Deep inside your soul.
To feel his heartbeat become your own.

To know this man inside out.
To know him more than you know yourself.
To know his most secret desire, fantasy.
To feel his most secret dream.

This, to me, is the meaning of true intimacy.
It is yet but a fantasy,
A dream that very few people realize,
But someday, maybe, it will become reality.

   —Jackie A. Bourgeois

PEN A POEM FOR CASH

"Pen a poem for cash."
How would you like your hash?
With a taste of Mrs. Dash.
I would rather have the cash.

Everything is money, money today.
You can't do a thing today without cash.
I see some things dropping in price.
They have to drop a lot more today.

You are lucky if you have a job today.
I feel sorry for those who lost theirs.
You have to work or live with your kids.
And nobody can live together any more.

How to make a dollar today.
You have to be a "Jack-of-all-trades."
You have to be a "Mr. Fix It."
And a walking genius who knows all.

—Ruby E. Rowland

THE CLOUD MAN

By and by a cloud rolls by
It brings neither rain nor snow
Only a few more darker hours
Our joy it sours
With depression towers
And never see a rainbow
And should this thing remain unpunished
Should this cloud go on and on
What super human could you call
What mortal man could stop the fall
Of downcast shadows made by all
These clouds
But one magnificent quite unknown
Can chase them away with a wave of his hand
Watch majestic clouds unfold
Revealing color blue and bold
Look up against the sky — behold
The Cloud Man

—Ana Lee Thorn

SHOPPING

My teenager says she was born to shop
When I go with her I'm ready to drop
Standing around while she tries clothes on
Mary can model them all day long
From clothing to shoe stores she hops
Doesn't always spend money when she shops
She flits from one store to the other
Loves to go shopping with her brother
Shopping for pictures or a book
She just wants to look and look
Has never found a store that's boring
Over a grocery list she will be poring
Because with her there is no stopping
I'm now resting from a day of shopping
Us older folks don't have what it takes
We have to sit for long coffee breaks
Now there are wheelchairs in the store
So we can stay and shop some more!

—Ruth Turner

CHESS

The big dispute of the black and white,
Of Castle and Pawn, of Bishop and Knight.
White Pawn takes a move one space ahead,
Black Knight comes forward, now Pawn is dead.
Bishop to Bishop in a frightful duel,
Castle is lain in a bloody pool.
Out from the back the Queen makes her flight,
Pawns pass out in horror and fright.
The horseman rides swiftly across the board,
The other Castle takes Pawns by the hoard,
Poor Bishop doesn't have time for a prayer,
The Queen takes charge, the others in despair.
Two Kings still reigning on their own side,
Which one will fall, which one will slide?
Only one color can make it in this fight,
But who will win? 'Til another Knight.

—Cheryl Askeland

ICE

Though they're like diamonds in the rough —
I confess I have had enough —
Of New England roads just glazed with ice.
It's a pretty picture that they make —
But I'm afraid my bones will break,
And that would not be so very nice.

Now I know that ice is part
Of New England's very heart —
It's a part that I can live without.
I fear my feet will slip and slide,
And on my fanny I will glide —
Couldn't print the words that I might shout.

Come on, "Ole Sol," Shine on high,
Make that ice go "Bye-Bye,"
And put my feet again on dry ground.
My apologies to you snow-bunnies,
And to all other cold-blooded honeys,
But I'll feel better when spring comes 'round.

—J. Patricia Holohan

RURAL EDUCATION

As a small child,
I lived in a community where it wasn't
unusual to see animals that were wild.

School buses were rare,
Rural students walked and visually had
God's creative nature to share.

A beautiful stream outlined our playground,
It was easy for the teacher to locate a student
who wasn't seen around.

Lunches were carried from home in a paper sack,
Therefore, we had no lunch box to carry back.

A gymnasium wasn't to be found,
Neither was a merry-go-round.

Hop scotch, we could play,
By using nature's soil and sticks to
prepare the game each day.

Not only did we learn the alphabet,
Our teacher finally taught us not to get wet.

Our bathroom was located outside on a hill,
To lock a classmate inside was a thrill.

—Janice Edge

SHIRLEY PATRICIA

Like a fine white meadow from which your name derives,
you held sunshine for us all; sunshine all the time.
Your warmth was as radiant as the summer sun
and your smile was every bit as bright.
No matter how rocky the road, you always made it fun
to persevere from morning thru 'till night.
Even though the wheel in the sky keeps turning 'round,
your deserved rewards here on earth were never found.
Yet the goodness in your heart remained faithfully sound
and surrounding the love you spawned ran rivers of no bounds.
You relinquished self-gains for the love of your children
and I know, from your blessings, you'd have done it again.
Now you are with Him and angels so fine.
Your human saintliness is now and forever, truly divine.

In loving memory of my mother,
dedicated to my two sons,
Quinlin and Eliason.

—Sheldon Cork

MY FRIEND

My life has always been a dark and dreary place,
Until he came and took my heart and left me no trace.
I remember the day we first met,
He is a good friend, I'll never forget.
Everyone should find him and give him their trust,
For if you don't trust him in love, you'll end up in lust.
Someone evil's out to get you, and get you indeed,
My friend's out to save you and make the evil one flee.
He's my best friend and my love for him is true,
I remember before we met I was always blue.
For his father you can't live without,
Though if you find him, he'll love you without a doubt
He said in his word he'll never leave me or forsake me,
I believe in his word for he's the one who saved me.
He has a special book, a book we all should read,
And in this book it says his promises for you and me.
My friend is someone special who'll care without a doubt,
Believe me, he's one you cannot live without.
My friend is someone special, someone special to us,
He's one in a million and his name is *"Jesus!"*

—Tanisha Hernandez

BECAUSE OF A CHILD

Because of a child, I am here to share and give my time
each year.

Because of a child, I am elated to teach all I know about the
beauty God has created.

Because of a child, I will do my best, though far from perfect
I am, to show them love and lend a caring hand.

Because of their beauty and sweet innocence, I will try to
show a child the value of their existence.

Because of their smiles and joyful laughter, I hope they know
I'll remember them here after.

Because a child is a miracle of life and the key to our future,
I want to be a part and make a stand, to let them know
I understand.

Because a child is the reason to work hard each season, the
reward is mine when I look up and see the faith and
confidence they have in me.

And now I find my purpose here, to make a difference each
new year . . .

Because of a child.

—Julie E. Schantz

MOTHER

How sweet and precious are you.
Gifted am I to have you for life.
May I please now be to you, what
you've been to me,
May we turn the table
Let me now be your strength
Let me now guide your steps
Let me now be your light
Let me now give back to you
all that you've bestowed and
engraved in me,
Let me now mother love
you as you loved me, I will
now be your gift

—Maria Susanna Gallegos

HOME

Home; . . . is where you
hang your hat.
As a child, dependency in
family — the only home I knew.
The peg remained constant, on
which I hung my hat.

Life moves on, the peg is
pulled; and placed temporarily
in another notch.
Continually being moved, the
peg is worn, not fitting securely
in any one hole . . . .

Now; I lost the peg somewhere,
I don't bother looking for it.
The only places I hang my
hat are on my head, and
occasionally, when I sit down to
rest, I lay it over my face.
No peg, No place, just a chance
once in awhile to rest under my
hat; . . . Home.

—Kenneth L./Rag Poet

249

MR. PRESIDENT

In America the land of plenty
    There's much unrest and discontent,
But the thing that really troubles me
    What's my future, Mr. President.

You talk of peace and yet there's war
    What does the future hold for me,
People are fighting more and more
    I am only a child you see

I believe God will give the final test
    Only the faithful will be able to stand,
In this world with so much unrest
    But then we'll go to a better land

I will offer some prayers for you
    May your leadership be heaven sent.
Please let God safely guide us through
    Good-bye for now, Mr. President.

        —Joseph A. Thornton, Sr.

FRUSTRATED

A hurt of a man in anguished sorrow,
    heartfelt wounds that burn.
For lonely is the piper, for his song
is never heard.
Tho the King should laugh for joy,
and the lowly heart rejoice, still
there echoes "Crucify!" through
the darkness of the night.

Time spent pain, for the glory of,
"Today I am alive." is not received
by ruthless men and lovers of
the night.
Tho the fruit be sweet, and the
wine be pure, 'twill always be
a shame. For pride abounds in
jealousy, and always the night,
will hate the day.

        —Joseph C. Klimczyk

THE DEAD GET LAID

Shadow playing
    in ripped underwear
and twisted form
living nightmares
spotting the sidewalk
with blood

careless   discovery
of bruised, swollen bodies
hidden in the city trash
blank stares scanning
a street with a shrug
truths hidden . . . expendable

Daughters   dying to exact the
price of revenge
fettered to man's judgement
fallen angels destined to dye
the earth with their blood

And man wanders free
grave in his design
of the next woman's plot.

        —Moira Sullivan

You older guys leave my daughter alone,
    Do not meet at the corner, do not call on the phone,
She is far too young to satisfy your need,
She does not know where this could lead,
The attention you give, she may enjoy,
But the wrong intentions will soon destroy,
She can attract, she has appeal,
But please, her childhood do not steal,
Respect her body and for yourself do the same,
You know inside she is too young to play your game,
But you with no conscience, you feel no pain,
You have your fun and the mother takes the blame,
And mother cries and wails all night,
She must not have raised her daughter right,
You prey on your next girl, you do your bit,
And another mother becomes a misfit.

        —Sandra Kelly

REALITY

Death, decay . . . constants of eternity
Fear, dismay . . . instincts of uncertainty
    The Universe is
                    not as you believe it
        The Universe is
                    not as you perceive it

Sightless, blind . . . eyes covered by a veil
Fact, unkind . . . against your fate you rail
    Are you alive?
                    are you sure? think before you answer
        Or are you
                    a dream? whose truth is akin to cancer

Timeless, clear . . . what is not will never be
Facing, mirrors . . . all of god you'll ever see
    Your god is not
                    an omnipotent power
        It is before
                    entropy you should cower

  — Reality is only a name given to the compromise
    between what *is* and how you perceive it.

        —Robert Richards

COURAGE

we fought till the night was done
I lived to see the blood on the morning sun
can't escape the horror that has come
to the world about me

my men lie dead in the sand
as I toss down a losing hand
no one I know gives a damn
but they're coming for me

lock and load my last round
once more to hear the thunder sound
not going to die and lay down
though death pursues me

just to fight one last time
blowing wind erase this crime
fatal monument that's mine
and those about me

I have strived for all I'm worth
ready to take my place within the earth
my soul will burn on hell's hearth
but they'll have to kill me

        —Lt. Charles N. Wendt

THERE'S A GYPSY IN THE MIST

There's a gypsy in the mist
    gargling freshly-squeezed mandrake root
    with a hint of fairy dust

There's a gypsy in the mist
    practicing necromancy and sorcery
    with an acorn wand dipped in toad spittle

There's a gypsy in the mist
    changing canary yellow cacti seeds
    into a spectrum of firebreathing dragons

There's a teenager in the classroom
    drifting in the mist in order to escape
    a cauldron of tedious labor and boredom

      —Bonnie Jo Book

A FOOL'S FANCY

Frolicking funsters in bright, patterned shirts
    Sporting ties in discordant hues.
Creating mayhem, plodding about
In floppy, outrageous shoes.
Tumbling, bumbling clowns.

Jovial jesters with wild frizzy hair,
Red noses, and faces of white
Raising a ruckus. Mischief abounds.
Making us thrill with delight.
Amusing, confusing, tumbling, bumbling clowns.

Rambunctious revelers in absurd attire
Bringing laughter to all who see,
Cutting a caper, dancing around,
Stirring our yearnings to be
Masquerading, parading, amusing, confusing,
Tumbling, bumbling clowns.

      —Vickie Elaine Legg

MR. VIRGO

There was an upset in astrology
    at the discovery of a man,
an extraordinary man;
for no one knew what to call him.

Astrologers called upon
the galaxy and its stars
in hopes of finding a
way to describe him.

The moon called him INTELLIGENT
for his intellect.
The sun called him SUAVE
for his flare for style.
The stars called him UNIQUE
for his physical condition.
A comet called him COMIC
for his great sense of humor,
and the planets called him HANDSOME
for his exceeding good looks.

The description was excellent,
but astrologers wanted one word
that would mean all of these things,
so they put their heads together . . .

and found the perfect word:
Mr. Virgo . . . not just any man,
but a military man . . .
known to you as Mr. James Earl Johnson.

      —MeLinda Smith

THE COWBOY'S WIFE

She rides along by his side,
    wearing her jeans and lots of pride.
She knows her man's unique,
of his special qualities, she will speak.
His reverence for God and outdoor life,
not dwelling on hardship or strife.
Always willing to help his fellow man,
never complaining, just working the land.
Helping those critters, big and small.
In his quiet way but riding tall.
This man of the land and sky.
His woman will beside him lie.

Dedicated to my loving husband,
Robert E. McMacken.

      —Norma Jean McMacken

THIS CHILD

Oh how I wished he would sleep late
    And let me do the same
But always at the break of dawn
His busy day began

I'd sure be glad when he learned to eat
And keep his food on the tray
Cause I had to clean round his chair
Five and six times a day

The windows always needed cleaning
This was a daily thing
For he loved to watch the birds outside
And lick the window panes

And I would think "OH Happy Day"
When he picks up his toys
The fire truck and spinning top
And his little soldier boy

Lord, the silence penetrates my very soul
I stand by his crib and weep
"This Child," who always stirred at dawn
Now sleeps a dream-less sleep

      —Liz Caldwell

THE BLIND MAN

How old are you? the blind man asked,
    Of course he couldn't see
That though I was still very young,
    Life's problems had really aged me.

How old are you? I asked in return,
    He tilted his head and with a smile
He said, I'm older than my years
    These shoes have walked many a mile.

We sat in silence for quite some time
    Then I turned to him and asked,
Can you teach me what you know,
    Would that be too hard a task?

It was as if he could see my face
    As he turned in my direction,
For he gazed into my eyes
    With a questioning expression.

If I could teach you what I know
    Could you really pay attention?
After all, I am old and you are young
    And the young tend not to listen.

      —Vickie Hutchison

WHAT YOU SHOULD DO

Making amendments
Cleans the soul
As it frees you from carrying
A heavy toll.

It touches you deep
As you no longer feel
So alienated like
Before you appeal

Breaking the barriers
Is a hard step to take
But probably the best one
You'll ever make

And it's not for the other
As much as for you
Making amendments
Is what you should do.

—Jodene Stoski

HOURGLASS

It was only yesterday
That I stood so alone,
watching the stone
turn to sand,
then
back again.

Only a trick
with the hand of man,
stone to sand,
sand to stone.

Only the river knows,
as it forever flows
to the sea,
carrying with it
the mystery
of how we came to be.

Our fate,
our destiny.

—William D. Strong

WARRIOR OF THE HEART

Hearts a fire,
two swords crossed,
to protect the love,
from evil doings.

A single card,
the nine of hearts,
signifies our love,
this the card of love!

One sword to protect,
the other to glow,
glow with our radiance,
glow with our love.

So if you need me,
I'll be there,
with my swords in hand,
and my heart as our shield!

*Dedicated and written for
Bethany, the one whom I
cherish and love.*

—Chad Roberts

MY LOVE WILL MAKE IT OUT

My hope may be devoted,
But my heart is always true,
Lasting only a moment,
Is what I'm saying to you.

My mind may sometimes fail me
But my love will make it out.
I must keep my head up high,
With my self I mustn't doubt

My open heart will lead me,
And to love my path will go.
For there are some things my mind has still to find out,
But that my heart will always know.

*Dedicated to Mrs. Claire Reynold Chamberlain for
giving me this wonderful idea and for being a
great friend . . . thanks!*

—Jenna L. Gantner, age 9

LEARNING TO LIVE

In today's world mankind struggles to preserve
Clear skies, verdant trees, unpolluted land, and blue seas.
Acknowledge and protect our great natural reserve!
But wait . . . the most valuable resource of all has been missed:
Behold value beyond measure—abundances of untapped treasure,
Noble blessings that should also be cared for, not dismissed!

So don't visualize sparkling silver or glittering gold;
Rather focus on elderly dear, for they hold memories of yesteryear.
Possess patience to listen and to cherish all that's told . . .
(Rejoice!) Elderly accept you for who you are—no need to be glum.
Let them share their mind; there's no telling what you'll find!
Then, fathom their gracious gems of joy, friendship, and wisdom.

The elderly instill values of truth, discipline, and morality.
Aged expand youths' horizons; my future is as bright as ten suns!
Together, we witness a dawning age of opportunity and equality,
And hand in hand we'll share the laughs and talk away the tears.
Hear me sincerely say, "I will pass on these treasures someday.
Thank you for teaching me how to live during my beginner years!"

—Todd Sagissor, age 18

LOST HEART

Sometimes the search for happiness is endless,
Sometimes relationships are developed just to avoid loneliness,
Or maybe just to pass time,
The quest for real happiness and compatibility is hard to find,
Trying to keep a firm grip on a relationship is like trying
to hold bubbles in your hand, they may stay intact for awhile
when they touch down, or burst instantly,
Many times I get mentally and physically exhausted, peace of
mind is what I seek, no one pays attention as I speak, someone help
me please? Stop the burning that eats away at me even as I sleep,
I start to doubt life even as the ministers speak, my will to
live was once strong, now it grows weaker with every new dawn,
Dead end walls are all I find, someone help me please?
No one hears or sees my need, I'm at the point where I don't
care;
My cries fall silent, for no one cares, now I hide all of my
fears, because . . . Tears shall be no more, Pain shall be no
more, Love shall be no more, Life shall be no more.

I
SHALL
BE
NO
MORE

—Angela Albright

DREAMING

Mama, oh Mama, it's been much too long
it seems, I'd love to put my arms around you,
but instead you're in my dreams.

If dreams could really come true, I'd see
you every night, things we never did before, we
could do before daylight. I could tell you how
much I love you, how I miss you more each day
and things will never be the same, since you went
away.

Sometimes I pray to God above, to let me stay
asleep, so then I'd be with you always, never
again to weep.

I know this isn't the way it will be, so I'll
do all that I can, to make it to that heavenly place,
to walk with you hand and hand.

—Edna Plumley

FOREIGN WORLD

What is this world before my eyes?
With a bluer sky and a warmer sun
In which nothing is the same.
No more friends I once knew so well,
But a world that speaks a different tongue
And moves to a different beat.

Yes, now I remember where I am
This world is foreign to me
Yet I am here to stay 'til one day I lie in my grave.
I don't seem to fit in this world of theirs
My appearance so clearly sets me apart from them
But I know I must try to be the same as they.

I should say farewell to my beloved world
Where I spent my childhood days,
Although I am no longer in my childhood world
My heart and soul remain in the past
But now I am here so I'll say goodbye
For I know this is my home now.

—Jenny Lin

PAGES FROM A MOTHER'S HEART

My daughter, I'm thinking about you today,
And of the words I don't always say.
But they're not really needed between you and me,
You know how I feel, what others don't see.
It seems only yesterday I kissed away fears,
Rocked a cradle, sang lullabies and wiped away tears.
But those years are gone and now you are grown,
And you've made me so proud that you are my own.
Tho miles separate us and our lives divide,
My love for you will always abide.
Through good times and bad times, rough seas and mild,
You're my today's lady, my yesterday's child.
My love for you is unchanging and true
And I am so glad that God gave me you.
Flesh of my flesh, of me you're a part.
Bone of my bone and heart of my heart.
You were created in love and as such
You're unique, very special and loved very much.
God's hand selected you from the rest,
He gave you to me and he gave me his best.

—Mabel Cook

THE GIFT OF LIFE

Life Ah what a beautiful thing!
Something only God can bring.
A precious baby, girl or boy,
Nothing else can bring such joy.

The bright-eyed wonder of a child.
The teens who feel so free and wild.
Young men and women getting married.
Parents feeling busy, and harried.

The mid-life couple, kids all grown,
Talking to grandkids on the phone.
Old woman rocking on her porch,
Sunlight glowing like a torch.

What right have we to say just when,
The gift of any life should end?
The Lord gives and the Lord takes away,
It's up to Him to choose the day!

—Mary Jo Barner

OUR MOTHER

Our mother has seen hard times,
She's not had time for nursery
    rhymes.
Somehow she managed to keep us fed,
    exhausted and late she'd go to bed.
Wondering what tomorrow would bring,
    no more she wears a wedding ring.
Keeping us together was her goal,
    and at times it would seem to take
    its toll.
Though we have grown up now we know,
    down the path of life we go.
Remembering the lessons she has taught,
    thanking God for her he brought.
For without the woman we know as
    mother,
    there would never have been a
    sister or brother.

—Theresa A. Ruppert

SLEEPING CHILD

Sleeping child within my arms,
Safe and protected from life's harms.
You snuggle softly, close to my heart,
Not realizing someday we'll part.

A halo of innocence surrounds your face.
Your delicate hair is fine as lace.
Your dimpled cheeks are now at rest,
As you slumber in my protective nest.

The pink petal softness of your skin
Is satiny smooth like porcelain.
Even in sleep your grasp is quite strong.
You hold firmly to me, but for how long?

The time is short that you're totally mine,
So cling to me now like an ivy vine.
My love for you twines 'round my heart.
It will not break, even when we part.

So sleep, dear child, within my arms.
I will protect you from life's harms.
When parting leads us separate ways,
My love for you will always stay.

—Grace Burke

A WISH TO YOU

I wish upon a morning star,
    that you will not be far.
Where ever you may be,
    how often I can see,
There's a friend who cares for me.

    —Bridgett Stricklin

GRANDMA

Grandma, you're the very best
And I'm someone who should know
For down at Bishops
Where I work
I've seen them come and go.
There's been short ones
There's been tall ones
But none would ever do.
For Grandma I've got number 1
'Cause Grandma, I've got you!

*Dedicated to Grandma (Lottie) Larson,
with love from Tammy.*

    —Tammy L. Warner

ANNIVERSARY 2/21/93

I feel your arms about me
As I'm walking in the snow . . .
Such loving, precious memories.
Fifty-one years ago.

Although our years together
Were taken in a breath,
You're always with me, honey,
Though absent by your death.

Our love was never-ending;
Though we had our times of strife.
You filled my life—love, happiness.
Forever, I give thanks to God—
You chose me for your wife.

    —Hester Godwin

BUILDING MEMORIES

"Mommie, take a walk with us,"
The children begged today.
I knew that it had been too long
Since I'd shared in their play.

We left the unwashed dishes set
And headed for the brook;
They tell me there are fish out there
And we should have a look.

The fields were gold with dandelions
And fuzz balls here and there.
We stopped to blow a few away—
Into each other's hair.

We found a spot out near the brook
Where violets grow so thick
We couldn't help but listen
When they beckoned, "Come and pick!"

The days, the years, go swiftly by
But when I'm old and gray
The memories I'll treasure most
Will be those like today.

    —Martha E. Mastin

MY IMAGINATION

The future, wonderful ideas, and imaginative inventions
waiting to be made,

Sweet fragrances of my dreams and hopes,

Delightful music and the beautiful sounds of my fancies,

Sugar and spices of many delicious, exotic foods from
imaginary places,

Light and free as if I could go anywhere and do anything,

Right now my mind is hard at work.

    —Janice Goldberg

CARA'S STAR

*This is dedicated to the memory of Cara Richardson, and
all children, young and old, who now have their own star.*

There is a star for everyone large or small
    But when you are on earth you cannot see them all

They all make music of their own
Each one making its own sweet tone

You don't have to look for your star at all
For into your lap star dust will fall

My name is Cara the star said to me
And I'll be as bright as I can be

I'll twinkle and sparkle all the time
It will be the easiest star to find

A star named Cara as bright as can be
Oh! How she does shine for all to see

    —Carol Ann Marsh

MY BEST FRIEND

My Best Friend came out of the blue
Who would of thought who would of knew
She listens to my feelings and my fears
To find someone as genuine as that is very rare
Whenever we're together time just flies
And when we're not time just dies
I've said it before and I'll say it again
She truly is my best friend
I try to let her know I'll always be there
I hope she listens because I truly do care
Because friends are there all the time
Not just when everything is going fine
I miss her a lot when she's not around
A part of me is lost and I feel down
A lot of things come and a lot of things go
How we got so close I'll never know
Writing alone could never describe
Just how happy and complete she makes me feel inside
To my Best Friend I just want to say
I love it when your big brown eyes look my way

*Dedicated to my "Brown-eyed Girl." Tracy, remember Elton
John's "Your Song," well Honey this is your poem. Tracy,
by now you should know how much I truly do love you. So I
take this time to say thank you for giving me a friendship
I will cherish the rest of my life. What you and I share
is very special and rare, and no matter what I will
always love you and I'll always be here for you. I
respect you and I thank you. Love you so much, Richard.*

    —Richard Salvatore

THINGS OF NATURE

Mother nature has been the queen,
the queen of the whole world.
A world of nature and beauty.

She is the one that with a tremendous and a
fabulous skill
is able to do her will.

The ability of creation and destruction is
at her hands.

The course of nature is a mysterious one.
Is like life and death.
Nobody knows who's going to born or who's going
to die.

But whatever she decides is all right;
thus, man can predict but cannot change what nature
has laid.

—Efrain Medina-Merced

COLOURS OF REALITY

Nobody ever sees the pain I hide inside
If they could ever feel from their shallow lives

Who would they be, if they heard the truth?
Could they learn from such "wasted youth?"
You spin around . . . You spin around in me, a
whirlwind of reality, they've shown me a way
a way to feel, all the "colours," can they be real?

You think you get something for nothing? Well
let me tell you "babe" I've got news for you!
Tell me how did you feel, when they shot them dead!?
And the children screamed for their mom & dad!!
You spin around . . . You spin around in me, a
whirlwind of reality, No one can know if their
colours fade from real, but to open their eyes and heal . . .
You poor pathetic rotten soul! You'd do anything
to end the hunger your addiction knows . . . Where
will you run when your friends are out and the
fun is over cause you're down without pure colours
glowing from reality in a whirlwind like me

—Adam James Elliott

RED LIGHT

Let's make a better 1993,
I wouldn't be surprised if 1992 went down in history.
Killing each other in our society,
Someone out there would probably kill me.
Why can't we realize what we're doing is wrong,
The way we're treating the earth it won't last for long.
Saying and thinking we're smart and have knowledge,
But we can't make it in high school so how could we make it
in college.

Injecting drugs, swallowing the pill,
Just to get the money for it people will kill.
We're also judging each other by the color of our face,
Criticizing people because of their race.
Where is the red light because we need to stop,
Arguments with the citizens and the cop.

Thinking we're bold because we have a gun,
I hear people kill just for fun,
The graves are overloading and soon it wouldn't function,
After we're done with the earth it'll need to be sent to the
junction.
Can't we realize we're doing wrong not right,
It's not up to me, but for you to find that red light.

—Keon Paton, age 12

MY WISH

When I was young I wished
I was older so I could know more
about the world and what was in it.
I dreamed I could fly up into
the sky and put part of the sun
and some clouds in a jar.
Now that I'm older I now know
that
People can't fly;
Clouds are made of water,
and the sun's too hot to touch.
Daydreams were a lot better
when I didn't know so much.

—Heidi Roggenbuck

LIFE'S PASSAGES

A day is a page,
a year is a chapter.

Pages turning,
new endeavors to encounter.

Each is a challenge,
that we must conquer.

Being creased,
as a reminder.

Past pages not forgotten,
at the end of each chapter.

Our chapters may conclude,
but they will linger.

For they become memories,
in pages of another.

Dedicated to Eric, for all your
support, belief and love.
I Love You!

—Michele Casalino

THERE IS NO SOLUTION

As I sit here,
Searching through my empty soul,
I seem to wonder about my life.
What meaning is behind it?
What was I put on this earth for?
What will I accomplish?
What is the solution?

Life is a big question
That can never be answered
By any one scholar.
We try to find out
The meaning of life,
But we only seem to fail.
Can there be a solution?

I do not know what to think.
I do not know what to do.
The uncertainty of life
Seems to follow me everywhere.
What can I do?
There is no solution.

—Zelideth Maria Rivas

HEART

Bold and true, you give and take
to find it's true.

You are gentle and kind no matter
what you do. By yourself you speak
so caring. Combined to another
you are sharing. Blind to the cruel
and hate makes you crumble and
break. You loved and cherished
putting everything at stake.

You bleed through tears and heal
by faith. You seek out again
to find what's true.

Loving, caring, helping and
sharing is just the quest you do . . . .

*Dedicated to my husband, Douglas,
and my family. Thank you for
Believing in me.*

—Terri Lukonen

WITH YOU

Between you and me
Concerning the two of us,
About the love we share.
Down in our hearts,
Within the souls
Of each of us, something inside us
From the deepest parts
Of our lives, is something
Beyond friendship. Before,
In the past, we were just friends.
But now we've evolved
Into something more.
Since we've become friends
Without any warning, we've gone
Through many hardships.
At the end of all this, we are a part
Of each other's lives.
With you, in your heart always.

—Quiana Gutierrez

LOVE

Inside, an ecstatic flair
That numbs the soul within
For tears are never rare
Of a special gift that's given.

Fragile to the keeper
A heart that never mends
Like visions to a sleeper
A quest that never ends.

Should she spread her wings in flight
You'll be going round and round.
Never on a starry night
Will "love" ever be found.

A want that always requires
A feeling forever more.
A key to all desires
That will open any door.

Knowledge from the start
A tool from up above.
A warmth that would melt any heart
This heavenly wonder called "Love."

—Judy Clark

THE APPLE

She finished her salad
as I silently looked into her brown eyes.
Picking up a knife and the apple,
she looked at me and smiled.
I could only smile back,
a crooked, sly smile that was supposed to melt her heart
but, obviously, it didn't.
After quartering the apple and removing the core,
she ate, more enthused with the apple than with the salad.
Then she noticed my glances,
asked if I'd like a bite,
held the diminished quarter toward me.
I leaned forward,
sliced the apple with my teeth,
and smiled,
eating from her hand.

—Phillip Smith

THREE CHEERS FOR NETTIE

Three cheers for Nettie, the most talented cook
We recognize you at once as we take a good look
When the postman delivers the magazine for farm wives
We find a cozy corner and have the time of our lives
We look for "Nettie's Page," your best recipes then plan
Which one to try on our favorite man
For the way to a man's heart is you know how
So why delay the experiment, but do it right now
It's a challenge to try recipes, other cooks have won
In whatever contest it was they had fun
For them to be chosen the "Best in their Class"
Tempts me to produce, that when tested will pass
For it to be judged best, if I carefully measure
Thus experience the joy that gave them such pleasure
We also enjoy your creative and interesting hints
On homemaking, family living or maybe its mints
So we patiently look forward to each monthly issue
For *what's new* and the "best of everything" we wish you.

—Esther G. Fahning

FEELING

The sensuality of your touch is beyond expression
The compassion of your soul intermingles
with mine in natural harmony
It makes me wonder if you haven't always been with me
I just couldn't comprehend your existence till now
Instincts of your thoughts against mine
Tells me this love is not measured with time
I hear your voice and it's calling me
To a beautiful scene along the sea
when your emotions are running high
I feel you drift upon the tide
To another dimension far away
I sense you will return someday
I capture your attention in total delight
I enter your dreams in the still of the night
And memories of me will linger on
As long as the mutual caring is strong
Sharing Emotionally, Physically and Spiritually
Is what every human heart longs to achieve
But to accomplish this you must believe!

—Laura Dutton

YELLOW ROSE

As I sit and watch this yellow rose
The symbol of a loved one's death
I wonder how it must have struggled to survive
Only to have been cut, yet it struggles on for awhile
With all the love and care you give it
It never seems to be enough for it gives up withers and dies
Its struggles are over
Just as the loved one who has cancer
They fight with all the love in their heart and the love of their family
But cancer does not care it's a merciless enemy
An enemy which fights to destroy it does not care who you are
It eats away until there is nothing left
It is an enemy that will not be defeated
It will fade away for just awhile
Only to come back stronger
A foe we should all fear

—Michelle Friedel

MY PRECIOUS THREE

You'll never know the joy I felt as I heard each of
Your first cry,
The wonder I knew as I asked my God why?

I wanted so badly to have a child,
Even if I was young and oh so wild.

God blessed me three separate times with each of you,
I just wanted to say that I love and need you.

I listened to first words and watched you learn to walk,
I bandaged skinned knees & at you I'll never balk

One day soon you'll be grown and gone,
With your own life to live and carry on.

This world is such a mixed up mess & nothing's fair,
But when you cease fighting is when it's over — always care.

I've come across some things from which I thought I'd die,
But my heart was always on each of you — you are
my reason why.

Don't give up on Mom she believes in each of you,
Cause with the love we share together I know we'll make it through.

—Phyllis A. Archer

THROUGH A LACE CURTAIN
Of a Three-Decker House in Worcester, Massachusetts

When I was young our house stood on a hill of granite ledge.
My mother spoke the tongue of Eire
And peeled the 'taters round and round 'til naught but white was there.

In our front windows hung the most magnificent array
Of lace and tatting, cream and white,
Which filtered in the wands of light
That lit my mother's face and shot carnelian through her hair.
The parlor was my favorite room, its windows in a bay.
In winter frosts made patterns there
Which rivalled not the lace's share of splendor on display.

Fine crystal was not on our shelves but cut glass stood there tall.
Though we were poor my mother said
That lace and polish showed our class and didn't care at all.
Stern houses marching up the hill with lacy curtains at the sill
Were common on the ledge.
So elegant and intricate,
The curtains eased the homeliness of life on hardship's edge.

The years have passed. I see no lace in windows on the hill.
Our home is gone. The street is steep.
My childhood imagery is but a memory to keep.

—Lucy I. Allen

OL' SOL

As the sun chases night away,
to surround someone else's sobs and tears,
does it begin to hurry back to me
to starve my heart and feed my fears.

What vain self-conceit
to think busy ol' Sol,
having places to go,
would waste time on me.

—Vernon Judkins

CHARITY

Greeting everyone with a smile,
    With never a cross word for anyone,
Charity will always go the extra mile
    Until her work is done.

Gentle hands reach out to those in need,
    Any time of the day or night.
Never asking for praise of her deeds,
    Charity brings, to this dark world, light.

—Kattie Wilkinson

LUCK

    Luck is all I need,
to free my life from greed.

    I'd live where it was neat,
not where I had to watch what I
eat.

    I'd have pots of gold,
and clothes so I couldn't be cold.

    With luck I wouldn't have any trouble,
I could float in an air bubble.

    Life would go smooth all day
long.

    With luck, nothing could go
wrong.

—Nicole Sue Oakes

RING OF LIFE

The making of a crown —
    harvest jewels
    precious metals
Weave with nimble fingers, pale, delicate
    Be patient
Beauty blooms with each new day
    Be aware
A metamorphosis is taking yesterday's place
You are in control
    Of destiny
For these hours of creation
You are constructing
    A miracle.
Mold future memories with free hands,
Let vines, living, bind no love
But for your crown of flowers.

—Jessica Ann

When I was younger,
    People would yell at me to "Grow Up!"
And I'd just say
"I'm having too much fun!"
But eventually I had to grow up
Where am I now?

—Nick Bognar

MERRY-GO-ROUND

Bonds of silken mist I feel,
    Hazy, indistinct, yet strong as steel.
Look out past this carousel.
So much to see, I cannot tell.
I long to soar, my horse and me.
So much that I have yet to see.
The bolts that hold my fiery steed.
Tell me that we shall ne'er be freed.
Yet everyday my dream returns.
Everyday my longing still burns.
If by some chance of smiling fates
We'll rise and soar, sweet destiny awaits.

—Elja Vann

ICE-SKATING

I glide across the ice
    all is fair
I do a triple twice
    as the wind flies through my hair.
When I am on the ice
    I look around and smell the fresh air.
With the ice so smooth and nice
    I skate without a care.
I go across the ice so clear
    the ice shines like pearls
As night falls, the moon begins to appear
    As I do a few of my curls
the moon shines on me like a spotlight
    As I finish my dance with a few twirls
I realize it is time to say goodnight.

—Laura Gordon

CHILDREN AND TIME

It must be nice to be a child.
    Days are spent just running wild.
Little adventures fill the mind.
No time for worries of any kind.

Thoughts of others were never important.
With each other we were always patient.
Days were filled playing hide and seek,
Trying to count without taking a peek.

Now reality is filled with sorrow,
Never knowing what happens tomorrow.
Teddy bears are packed away
And worries are here to stay.

Oh please take me back
To those carefree days
When love was given for free
And tears were dried with a cookie.

—Pat K. Burchfield

A CHILD

A child once was I,
A child I once was.
A child is now what I have.
An adult . . . I am trying to become.

A child that is inside,
reliving memories of the past.
A child that is outside,
having to grow up too fast.
A child that stands beside,
a child belonging to a child.
An adult trying to break through,
slowly, definitely embracing the child.

A child will I always be?
An answer, I have none.
A child that calls mom,
A child I will always love.
        An adult . . .
I am trying to become.

—**Brandelynn Vincent**

HAZY SHADE

As I reluctantly peer out of
My hazy window of life,
The crystal drops of rain fall
Silently, yet harmoniously along
With my tears.
The dark rolling clouds above
Reflect my emotions
Creating a lonely shade of grey
That dulls the once bright colors.
Then suddenly the longed for sun
Escapes its captor—
Emitting warm rays of
Hopes and dreams
Colors ignite and become
Vibrant once more;
But sadly, only for a moment.
The gloomy storm of life
Apprehends its deviant prisoner—
And the rain continues to fall.

—**Kari A. Taggart**

AMERICAN CHAMP

Sweetie the American champ.
    She's a winner,
    Cause she ain't
    A dope user
    Or abuser.
    Of her body
    In any way.
She gets her sleep,
Eats what she needs,
    To keep her body
    In shape.
Knowing what is healthy
Can make her wealthy.
Leading to a better life.
Not having to think twice,
    About omitting
    What's not right,
    For her to be
    A winner in every way.

—**Felix Bourree**

Sitting by the edge of the ocean
Captivated by its endless motion
    The sun comes out and reveals the sand treasures
The little boy counts his footsteps as he measures
    For a moat that will soon float his toy boat
My back feels hot and glows a bright shade of red
    People lay around me all lifeless as if they were dead
A little girl becomes eager and bold
    Testing the waters edge to see if it's cold
As I left the beach I looked back to see
    Endless people scattered before me
There were both guys and girls walking for miles
    And I can still see their faces lit with bright smiles

—**Ken Mirocki, Jr.**

MY INNER SELF

the ability to grow within comes only from
        the power (energy) within self,
    the inner being from deep within the soul,
        the desire for this fulfillment of this
certain need will be strong for this to be so,
communitive values of self is extremely vital
for this existence of one's ability to grow and
        the soul to mature to a higher level,
    the willingness to travel will be more intense
to go deeper within finding, grasping deep into
grasping deep into embedded answers to questions
    from the soul's conscious to the conscious,
        my soul guide has guided me inwards,
    time will tell how far I will travel and
        which level of conciousness I will reach,
purposely stepping in myself, sensing, feeling, seeing —
    within timeless and limitless moments of
        going within there was beauty, peace,
tranquility, harmony of this deep inner knowing being.

Dedicated to Daphane Pickereign—(my spirit guide)
—**Peaches**

THE DESIRE OF THE LONELY

I needed you to be here for me,
    but you were not.

I needed you to hold me,
    but you could not.

He was here for me when I needed you.

He held me when I wanted you.

All I could think of all night was you.

That is all I had.

That is why I could not let him kiss me.

He held my hand, that is all I wanted.

He wanted more.

He wanted me to say one thing, "Yes."

I said "No."

Oh how I wish you were here with me,
    to hold me,
    to love me.

I count the days till your arrival and it seems years away,
    yet it is only days.

I look forward to your phone call just to hear your voice,
    just for reassurance.

—**Penny Axtell**

UNFORGETTABLE GRACE

The time has come at last.
At last utter happiness has been found.
No longer any dwelling in the past.
Peace and tranquility since you have been around.
You make life worthwhile and enjoyable.
To be with you is all that this heart desires.
Because this love for you is undeniable.
And burning for you hotter than Hell's fires.
My future now sees only you.
I cannot think of any other way to be.
All that I ever tell you is true.
Desire for you deeper than any sea.
    Please stand by my side forever,
    As I wish to leave you never.

—Darcy Metz

When I wake in the morning
you are there
in silent beauty,
asleep and dreaming —
of what, I can only guess.
I hope it is of me,
but I can not be sure
because your sleep is so deep, so peaceful.
I sometimes touch your beautiful face,
just to make sure you are not a dream,
a wonderful dream that vanishes upon waking.
And so I touch you
and you are real, so real —
yet you do not stir
because you are deep in your dreams,
unaware of my gaze upon you,
unaware of my attention, my touch, my love —
but it is there while you sleep,
and when you awaken, now and forever.

—Marc Osgoodby

MAGICAL MEMORIES

Words sit still unless brought to life,
a lot like a husband deprived of his wife.
Add a few verbs, adjectives and nouns,
now you have music with its varying sounds.

Go back in time and tap into that source,
that mind full of memories, now you're on course.
Bring back to life, those things that are stored,
for pleasures are waiting and oh so much more.

Smile, laugh, giggle and yes even holler,
You've just become a *different type scholar.*

Feed off those memories for as long as you like,
if some are unpleasant, take a different hike.
There's plenty of roads intertwined in the mind,
travel each fully and post dead end signs.

Keep mental maps to all magical places,
of harmony, joy and wonderful faces.
When down and out — always remember this,
travel any time to memory bliss.

You'll always be happy and healthy at heart,
using magical memories for a jump start.

Dedicated to Ronald H. King and my family.
For enduring and overcoming these past
four years, we are now moving mountains.
All my love — Debbie.

—D.M. Leabo/Karma Kay

A MIST

Deep within these hollowed walls
As a mist rises from my thoughts
You have captured my soul
Taking . . . giving to my delight.

Reaching inside for my broken emotion
Cupping love between your gentle hands
Drawing me within my heartbeat
Mending . . . loving to my desire.

You will conquer me once more
Tightly grasping my unspoken words
Keeping me within your breath
Touching . . . whispering my dark secrets.

As a mist rises
I am passionately embraced with you
Between the coolness and warmth of dawn
Feeling . . . touching my senses.

—Brenda S. Watson

REFLECTONS OF A FRIEND

You are there when I laugh,
You were there when I cried.
And it was no one but you
who wiped the tears from my eyes.

You always listen to my problems
and try your best to solve them;
With your warm, wonderful smile,
You make me forget them for awhile.

You know all of my deepest secrets,
as I also have shared yours.
And together we have walked
along the Atlantic Shores.

So as we wander through life apart—
Remember you are always in my heart.
And that my love for you shall never end;
For you, dearest, are my most precious friend.

—Sean R. McDonald

THERE AIN'T NOBODY LIKE YOU

There ain't nobody like you
Who can take my life
Turn it rightside up
The way you do . . .
Like an artist's palette with its many colours
And strokes of genius upon the canvas
Your gifted hand creates . . .

Harmony out of total confusion,
Expresses warmth and feeling
With your heart revealing
"Beauty,"
Gives more life to my little world
Than you've ever taken from it,
There ain't nobody like you.

I thank you for your philosophy,
For all the love you've given me,
Of never hurting but always giving
With skill and good taste
You are an artist of living,
Sunshine, laughter, passion ever after,
There ain't nobody like you.

—Janet Johnston

VALENTINE'S DAY

All hearts are filled with
Love today,
Little angels are at play;
With arrows flying through the air,
To send their love, everywhere.
So keep on thinking bright cheerful
Things; for angels have won their
Wings.
Valentines of every kind,
All red, and lovely you will find.
"So won't you be my Valentine!"

—Sharon L. Drinovsky

SERENITY

She snuggled against him,
Still euphoric
And spent with passion.

Peace and serenity
Flowed between them
As if they were one.

In tender closeness
She lost herself in him
And found completeness.

In exquisite intimacy,
Her life-long dream
Was entirely fulfilled.

—Clela

YOUR MEMORIES LIVE ON

My life is so lonely
The nights are so long
My heart is nearly broken
Since you have been gone

You're always on my mind
The tears fill my eyes
Since God called you away
To his home in the skies

It's hard to understand
Why God took you away
But you're resting in peace now
Forever with God you'll stay

The flowers placed on your grave
Remind me of our true love
There will be no more parting
In that mansion above

The rose reminds me
Of our love we had to share
For I will always love you
My darling I will always care

You'll live in my heart
Even tho you are gone
To that bright mansion
Your memories will live on

So wait for me in Heaven
For some day I'll be there too
Where forever we will be together
Where I'll never more part from you

—Peewee M. McCoy

POKER FACE

There is no pain in his eyes
And there are no tears running down his cheeks.
He's trying hard to keep it all inside;
He's making sure his emotions don't leak.
He's got to be the shoulder for the family,
So it isn't the time to show what he's feeling.
He's playing the part of a man in a movie;
A character that's extraordinarily strong and unrevealing.
And he'll play the part for the rest of the day,
Even if a chainsaw is cutting through his heart.
He'll keep on wearing his poker face,
Even if grief with claws is tearing him apart.

—Chris Donovan

DID WE EVER HAVE A CHANCE?

Thought one day we'd be together,
I was hoping that day would come fast,
It never came and I will remain alone forever,
Full of hopes, dreams, and the past,

I left my heart in your hands,
It seemed OK from what I could see,
And now I guess you don't understand,
I'm sorry I tried to force you to love me,

It's as plain as day,
That you don't feel the same,
I thought it would happen eventually someway,
But that's when I realized that love isn't a game,

I don't know what went wrong,
It's just so strange,
How we used to get along,
And now it's all changed,

Now I don't have you and that hurts more,
I'm living in a world with no romance,
Which leaves me with a question I've asked myself before,
Did we ever have a chance?

—Bernice Ann Suniga

KEY TO MY HEART

My growing love for you will never die;
I'll always give you another try.

Please don't take advantage of me,
don't make me a spectacle for others to see.

My bleeding heart can only mend one more time.
You've nearly ripped it apart so many times.

The hurt each time doesn't go, it stays.
I just forgive you and store it away.

Away in a locked chamber of my heart.
Hopefully someday the hurt will depart.

You hold the one and only key in your hand;
the key to wipe all the hurt away, do you understand?

Just whisper words of love in my ear.
And I'll hold them in my heart forever near.

I love you so much that I ache inside.
And I know it's really difficult for you to decide.

If you care just a little or maybe a lot,
please, please decide my heart's in a knot.

Forgive me when I pressure you,
how can I move on when my world's in such confusion
over you.

—Jill Ann Norris

262

INDIVIDUAL COMPREHENSION

to paint a picture with words
is to bring out the beauty of an emotion
the colors may be blurred and without boundaries
the dimensions distorted
but each makes his own reality of the scene

—Heather L. Kaeder

REALISM

I blew my breath on the windowpane and saw a patch of mist.

To this, I drew a simple picture of myself:
two eyes, a nose and a mouth.

For the first time I saw myself.

Then, it began to disappear: first the chin,
then the mouth, the nose, eyes and gradually
the head.

I returned to my nothingness.

—Ronnie J. Straw

CAPTURES

If I ever make it big:
There are all kinds of people on the street. I think if I ever make it big. I mean really, get the chance I'll make it big. I love myself, Toni the girl is hotter than butter or margarine.

I sit and wonder; I don't want to stay in tonight. I'm long and tall and want to be with you all. Something in me is burning to show them about me.

I really believe, one day I'll show them how I compare to all others.

I long for the street and the highway; I need not have all kinds of companions, just give me paper and pencil and I'll show them; wait and see.

I'll smile when the light captures me and I'll cry when the darkness appears and turns.

—Antoinette Garrick

ACTUAL EXISTENCE

I always thought that when I looked in a mirror
I was looking at myself;
An exact duplicate of me existing
but not quite alive.
I touched her and she touched me.
Her hands were smooth, cold;
a flat plane lacking vitality and feeling.
I winked at her, she winked back.
I thought she was me —
Did she think I was her?
I guess there's nothing wrong with that,
As long as she realizes that I hold the power —
The power to her longevity, her reality.
Maybe that means that I am the Creator,
And she the Created.
At the thought I stood transfixed,
What if I were wrong?
What if I am merely a reflection of her?
Then again, I live.
I guess maybe she does too.

—O'nell L. Myers

PARTING THOUGHTS

I'm floating upward, looking down.
They think they've put me in the ground,
But I have wings, and—what a view!
I think I'll stay an hour or two
To survey valley, forest, glen,
And as I do, remember when
I scarce enjoyed such scenic wonder,
For dreading when I'd be "down under."

I guess I shouldn't take for granted
That everybody, when implanted,
Will get their wings like me and fly
To frolic in the boundless sky.
Yet for those doom'd to stay "down there"
I have consoling thoughts to share.

The least you can expect when you depart
Is helping out with Nature's work of art.
You'll help a tree or shrub grow strong and tall
(Unless you're covered by a shopping mall).

—Foy Lisenby

TREASURED MOMENTS

I look down the path I once traversed,
the journey was weary, at times rough,

And now as I ponder my present state,
it still is not good enough,

I think about the many days, in many ways,
I often stumbled and erred.

Though many obstacles beset my goals,
I still have not yet been deterred.

I'm well on my way to accomplishing now
what once seemed like a lost cause,

And as each phase of my dream I complete,
I listen to the silent applause.

Even though happy I now may be,
my life is far from complete.

For I still have many things I must do,
before I lay down to sleep.

—Ralph L. Parraway

K A L E I D O S C O P E

enchanting   beauty

THE   VILLAGE   AT   MANOR   PARK

When I was young and in my prime
there was little thought of passing time,
all things in the world seemed very gay
we just whittled and pared the time away.

As I grew older I found many things awry
not always noticeable to the naked eye,
it's true that all that glitters is not gold
and we become too late smart and too soon old.

Then they gave my home a bright new name
to greatly accent its use and fame,
but the voices I hear & the faces I see
have not changed a bit, they're the same to me.

The passing of time has changed many things
I have really thought about them a lot,
it might be nice to live them over again
but I honestly think I would rather not.

—J Stanley Weinrich

DEPARTURE

What is it, this strange feeling
Upon departure from, old friend
   I'm reeling.
An emptiness grips my gut,
Slight terror rises up.

Was there something I forgot to say?
Was there some awkwardness
   When we parted ways?

There was tension as we moved to kiss,
As to which way our heads should twist.
   Left, right
Closer to the center
   Lips brush soft went her.
Bye.
Sigh.

—Courtney Spore Major

OCEAN THOUGHTS

Looking out at the distant horizon,
   as evening draws near.

A bright orange sun is slowly sinking,

into the depths of your deep blue water.

Sitting on your quiet edge,

trying to escape this emptiness inside.

A feeling of peace washes over me.

It is here that I find my perfect solitude.

Quietly I walk along your sandy shores.

Waves come crashing down upon the rocks.

Gently spraying seawater on my face.

God's majesty and splendor is all around me.

   —D.A. Baker

WHY

Why, Mama, Why
   Didn't you love us so
Did you have to make us cry

I don't understand why you had to die
And leave us all alone
Why, Mama, why

You didn't even tell us good-bye
Was it so hard to say
Did you have to make us cry

Our lives went awry
Since losing you that day
Why, Mama, why

If we could only see you, just to say "Hi"
But that cannot be
Did you have to make us cry

I will ask you once more, please do not lie
We've been in pain for so long
Why, Mama, why
Did you have to make us cry

   —Richard Jokerst

Did you really mean to hurt me?
   I thought we were something special —
that no one in the world could tear apart.
   Maybe I didn't tell you enough —
      about how much I loved you.

You made me laugh and smile, and put a fire
   in my soul that I had never felt before.
I really thought that we would be forever —
   and that you would fill the half of me
      that always seemed so empty.

But you left me — and I am alone.
I cry every so often . . . and the pain is endless.
   Did you have to come into my life?
      Just to leave me?

—Carolyn E. Belden

ABSENCE AND ETERNITY

The wise voice told you to say goodbye
   In the empty spotlight's end of your mind's stage.
Cradled hands of youth and the aged,
A bow,
And a soft kiss on the brow extending
To the depths of childhood.
You inhale the last of that sweet
Grandma smell,
And leave a tear in thanks
For all of life's yesterdays.

And the world seems so much emptier today.
The absence of one life,
But the eternity of one soul.
She is always near.
You can always find her . . .
In the scent-drenched walls of her kitchen,
In Grandpap's remembering eyes,
In a petty trinket of youth, now priceless,
And in the soul's secret family album.

   —Daniel Miller

A "GOOD"BYE TO GRANDMA

As I stand beside your bed this day
   and grasp the hand that led my way,
the strength I felt way back when
is as strong right now as it was back then.

I hold it now and I can't let go;
but as I do the memories flow.
For it's not the physical things you left.
It's the real true memories — I'll never forget.

It's the whistle I hear, the popcorn I smell.
It's things like these that I remember so well.
The smile on your face is kept in my heart
to warm up those days when I need a fresh start.

It's the faith you have shown in the Maker above —
patience, courage; but best of all love.
Going to church with you sitting near,
is a memory of mine that I'll hold most dear.

Now as my hand is drawn away,
I feel consoled cause the memories stay.
So, I thank my God for such blessings as these
for now I have memories and in them I'm well pleased.

   —Malinda Biller

THE LORD IS MY SHEPHERD

The Lord is my Shepherd; my light, and my way.
His love overshadows me by night and by day.
I'm wrapped in His mercy; secure in His care.
I abide in His presence, He's always so near.

He's with me in sunshine; He's with me in rain.
He answers my prayers again and again.
He guides me; protects me; shields me from harm.
I'm glad that in Him there is no alarm.

He is my rock; on him I depend.
He is my mediator; my guide and my friend.
He's with me in life everywhere I might go.
He'll be with me in death and in heaven, I know.

— **Bea**

GOD'S PRESENCE

I looked out my bedroom window
And the sun was shining through,
For I was sick in bed again
And feeling kind of blue.
But the light from GOD made
Me feel his LOVE for me;
And lifted my spirits to let me see,
In all things give GOD THE PRAISE.
For I knew he was close
And my spirits were raised!!
So I thanked MY LORD for what he did for me.
To let me know HE LOVED ME, you see
And I thanked the LORD for his PRESENCE
And how he made me feel,
The warmth of HIS LOVE went through my body
And I know MY LORD is REAL.

— **Edith Elaine Mohan**

WINNING THE INNER BATTLE

I know in my heart I'm bound for greatness;
I feel it every day of my life.
It calls to me from a deep, residual level
strong like a sharp, whetted knife.

It must be in the soul where its roots are lodged
so deep inside no place else could it be.
It springs forth with a burst of glorious pride,
then gets trampled and again rest within me.

And I am not still 'til it rises again,
wrestled up with anguish and mental torture.
Accompanied by prayers for forgiveness and freedom
from the demons holding on like a whore.

I believe in the innermost fibers of my being
that the power to overcome is within me.
So I'll fight the pull downward with a tireless thrust
for as long as my breath will sustain me.

I know that God's way is a winning way.
It's his will that my greatness be known
Since my only intent is to glorify him
until away from his life I have flown.

I know I'll overcome this nagging pull
for God's splendor in me is real.
It warms my heart and fires my soul.
No power can keep his glory concealed.

— **Alver Haynes Brown**

OH BENEVOLENT STRANGER

Oh benevolent stranger,
so kind, compassionate and rare.
So few would open up their heart and home
to a stranger in despair.

Oh benevolent stranger,
Other folks might think you a fool.
But you, the one with so much empathy
were thinking of the Golden Rule.

Oh benevolent stranger,
You have been so nice,
You certainly must know
that you've touched that stranger's life.

Oh benevolent stranger,
You'll get your just reward.
When you hear the Savior say,
"Well done my good and faithful servant"
Oh that glorious judgment day.

— **Allison M. Garrison**

The lightning's flashing brighter
The clouds are rolling in
"Time to wash the world, again," says God
"Try to cleanse it of its sin
I've sent them love and beauty
I've given them a home
But, the drunks lie in the gutter
And the addicts; the street roam.
There's a man, out on the corner
In his hand, he holds a knife
He doesn't know how or why, he's there
But he knows, he'll take a life.
A life that I, Myself, created
And filled with My own breath
I never gave but none of them
The right to inflict death.
So, let Me do My job, as God
And help those all I can.
And let us live in peace My friend
It will leave you, a better man."

— **Katie Abbott**

I AM

Lord, I am not a hunter—I can't shoot
ducks, deer, rabbits, possum, or quail.
I can't subdue a big bad grizzly bear,
and drag him back home by the tail.

I am not a mechanic—I can't fix
brakes, tires, cooling fans, or rotors
I can't get under an auto hood and
bring kittenish purrs to motors.

I am not a carpenter—I can't build
a house, barn, bridge, fence rail, or stair.
I can't make hammers swing, nails sing,
or do a good job of repair.

There are so many things I am not, Lord
which would fill many a long page.
Guess I am not as smart as I should be
for a guy who lives in this age;

But in spite of my shortcomings, and sins
I know I'm still one of your sheep.
This one thought fills my mind, and I commit
my soul to your keep—as I sleep . . . Amen.

— **Richard Penn**

COMPANY I HAD NONE BY MY SIDE

From dark of dawn
Till dark of night
Seven days a week
I earned my keep
Always alone in this tomb on wheels
Always so lonesome but always with great will
Below this ground I ride
Did life once dwell and not survive
From stop to stop always a cry
T'was from below it did arise
Harness this cry
Then slowly
A sigh
A tear

—Dwight W. McCollum

MOURNING

Family gathers,
    on a sacred mourning.
A fresh feeling of emptiness,
    of loss—of death.
They enter the building,
    to say good-bye.
Women cry,
    men console,
      secretly wiping tears from their eyes.
All cry.
A lonely child—confused.
    He cries.
    No one sees.
All the adults
    consoling each other.
The child, it's assumed,
    is too young to know or remember.
He's overlooked.
No one sees,
    when the child cries.

—Jon H. Travis

THE TRACK STAR THAT NEVER WILL BE

A boy at last,
One that can run so fast.
At the age of two,
A track star just like you.

When confined to a room,
You watch him zoom.
And not hit a wall,
But to stop, get stiff, and fall.

Then continue with a heart that is strong,
Shows, as if nothing was wrong.
This was the start of it all,
By catching you as you call.

To find help,
Is the right step.
So, don't take long
To sing that song.

And ease the pain,
Of a track star's fame.
If you don't know what to do,
Just remember there are a lot of
    people just like you.

—J. L. Jones

THE SEPARATION

The storm grows stronger
Thunder echoes over the beating rain
Alone in the dark, unbearable suffocation
A presence of warmth will take my fear away

Memories flash before my eyes
My judgement of events no longer matters
Only that love and warmth is shattered
And replaced by an oppressive black void

My heart cries while my face remains frozen,
With no emotion or rise in voice
I weigh decisions that are not mine to make
I pray for resolution and await the aftermath

—Robert E. Young

MARRIAGE

Look at us laughing, smiling at each other
Staring into each other's eyes
Wine glasses half full, or are they half empty
Did you smile????
Talking about old friends & new ones
My friends now, your friends then
Agreeing instead of arguing
Compromising on what to eat
Looking good for each other
Hugging like we mean it, this time around
And then I reach down to retrieve my napkin
Our eyes meet & we kiss
Nothing fancy, just a soft short sweet sensuous kiss
Looking at us now, who'd have ever thought
We're no longer married

—Meeka Muse

IT'S A GIRL

In the night they hear a small cry.
It's from a child that didn't deserve to die.
This child that cries was as healthy as any,
But the months of its life were not very many.

It had its fingers, its legs, and its eyes,
It was a girl and that's why she cries.
She would have been beautiful and full of joy,
But she'll never get the chance because she
wasn't a boy.

She would have been smart with a heart of gold,
But the days of her life she will never hold.
Because of something that was no fault
of her own.
The path of her life she will never be shown.

Her parents decided that they wanted a boy.
A little girl in their lives would bring no joy.
They decided abortion was the only way to go.
Now that special little gift they
will never know.
Now in the night they hear a small cry,
It's from a little girl that didn't
deserve to die.
She would have been beautiful and full of joy,
But she'll never get the chance because
she wasn't a boy.

—Andrea Schelling, age 14

FETAL THOUGHTS

I lie quietly, in my satin lined box,
my mind, a total blank.
I lie here quietly, ever so tightly,
waiting for them to nail each plank.
I shall laugh and love, yes, even lust no more,
my life is now a quiet tomb.
I entered this world, through my mother's womb,
I didn't ask to be here.
I was sent by God above.
I haven't asked for anything,
'cept maybe a little love.
But my mother doesn't want me,
she says she has her rights.
So I guess they'll go ahead and bury me,
and she . . . well . . .
she'll have sleepless nights.

—Richard L. Barkley

TOO LATE

What can you do,
When someone you love
Tells you they want to die?
At first you're surprised,
To hear her say such a thing.
Then you get angry.
And ask why.
She says she's tired of getting ready to take a step up,
When somebody or something ends up pulling her back.
You try and try to make her see
That life is a very precious gift.
But no matter how much you talk,
She still wants to die.
You promise not to tell,
And you end up hurting and crying.
You make yourself believe she won't do anything.
But after time goes by,
And you've tried to help her
You realize you have to tell.
But the following day
You find out she's taken her life away.

—Michelle Palacio

DAWN OF A LIFE

I, formed of only flesh and blood, will
Not hide my face, while in fetal world dwell
Warmly, securely forming, nine months and just
Beginning, feeling sensations of mother and heart beating.
Nourished by caring, protecting Mother; provided for by
Proud Father.
Loved by Parents. Family.

They hear my first cry. I come, clad in nakedness, a
New life for all to see; new world to experience.
Yearning to respond to new sensations. I, a new life,
An indifferent world; I shall find a place.

Now Given a name, a first name, and to a family belong.
A future awaits me, with joys and sorrows to endure.
Crawling, my first step, nursing and teething; being
Weaned. My first word. I will learn.

I, gift of the Creator, by the grace of GOD; I live.

Dedicated to all the millions of babies aborted over the past twenty years in the United States and in the other nations of the Earth, cheated out of life. Amen.

—Aaron R. King

FROM A VICTIM OF CHILD SEXUAL ABUSE

You are afraid to tell

So you somehow try to endure
your private hell.

But it leaves a scar on your soul

And somehow you never again feel
completely whole.

—Joy-Lynn Kenter

THE BROKEN CHILD

I've carried a secret for many years,
It's made me cry a million tears,
It was a very violent crime,
That now I hold deep inside,
It was by a person I knew well,
I trusted, and loved for throughout,
I don't show the pain I feel,
Especially to this dark cruel world,
For fear that people will see,
That broken child inside of me.

—Dora Michelle Irvin

ABJECT ANGEL

She clings to her Holy Bible
With an alcoholic's fervor
To take away the libel
Of those who did desert her
To mend past indiscretions
Of a life that was heartrending
She studies all her lessons
In the hopes she may be mending
The past and all its discontent
For deep inside she is torn
She sits with halo slightly bent
With anger for her child unborn.

—Carol Susan Pitre

A TIME AMONG GODS

It was a time among Gods
of disappointment and denial
and the government spoke to us
like one would to a small child

a time among Gods
of despair and invisible death
the nights were hard black rain
gathered in a long deep breath

a time among Gods
of icy blue fires and burning snows
the past and memory out of focus
blocked out like a murder of crows

a time among Gods
of quick bright things come to confusion
and death beyond death
and life stripped of all illusion

a time among Gods
and each world its own maker
the dinosaur had some meteor
AIDS will be our undertaker

—Steven R. Brown

GRUDGE AGAINST SPRING

The wind is blowing, yet the trees don't seem to feel any breeze.
My spirit seems to be launched in the branches of those tall, lonely trees.

The curtains flap, because the windows are open high,
Yet the house stands still and lets the wind silently die.

The bright warm sun beams down on the cold, damp earth,
Yet uncaring lies the clods of the God created dirt.

The sage grass stands so golden in the sun!
Who notices the wild array, hardly anyone.

The birds sing loudly now that winter is nearly gone,
But the flowers don't hear the sweet, descending song.

Why doesn't some of this reach me? The fever not I've felt,
Can my heart not be reached, the core not partly melt?

Or maybe it's just a grudge against the spring,
Nevertheless, God rid me of this soul-binding thing.

      —Wanda M. Shedd

It is getting cold out here
Mother nature finally coming home to reinstill beauty
where insanity roosts
Earthquake, typhoon, hurricane and fire
taking down innocent victims in retaliation
for the wounds inside her
It is getting colder out here
and while I still have a place to go inside and sleep comfortably
other lovers with voices like mine and knuckles that crack
are glad that the weather is so warm
It is getting still colder out there
and although in the womb it is a beautifully hot
I am just coming to understand that what I have founded my life on
are camouflaged rules meant to beat me down with stern faces and shaky hands
It is getting very cold out here and knowing that
what living is about is not story book fantasies I used to memorize
but drawings on the floor made with dirt
only helps me to see
that although it is very cold out here
I will always have a little bit of warmth inside

      —Erin Janelle Baker

THE BAND DIRECTOR

He quietly stands on the podium, and slowly gazes over the class,
The room is a bustling of noises, filled up with woodwinds and brass.

The sound falls to rumbling hush, as he taps his baton on the stand,
He raises his arms for the warm-up, now they're a high school band.

At last the warm-up is over, and they finally will get to play,
The music chosen for contest, which is coming in just a few days.

He cuts them off at the very next measure, and begins his hour long speech,
On how they should mark their music, because they have high goals to reach.

After the lecture is over, and they begin to play it again,
It seems they suddenly learned, and they finish the song to the end.

When he returns the baton to the stand, a smile spreads over his face,
And everyone turns to each other, as he says "Let's pick up the pace."

They play it with wild enthusiasm, and the sound that fills the room is grand,
It's amazing how his own little lecture, can seem to transform the whole band.

When they finish their second time through, they know their director is pleased,
And they quickly begin to pack up, before he says "Time to leave."

But then the final bell rings, and now he can say no more,
As instrument cases slam shut, and music sheets fall to the floor.

The room is a bustling of noises, but to him still the sound is grand,
Because he thinks to himself as they leave, **now** they're a high school band.

      —Kendra Ann Matheny

BOOBIE

I watch her wash herself, so fastidious and neat.
She misses nary a spot from her head to her feet.

Meticulous in her care; she leaves nothing to chance.
She basks in the sun, her beauty to enhance.

Her mind, bright with curiosity, weighed down by no cares.
Her eyes sparkle; her mouth twitches; a smile lives there.

How full she makes my heart at the end of the day.
The sound of her purring drives all my cares away.

She asks for so little and gives so much.
Her biggest demand, the feel of my touch.

My life would be empty, taken tit for tat,
without the love of my princess, my darling, my **BOOBIE CAT.**

— **Rob Hawley**

KITTENS

These two fresh and undisciplined
upstarts—they win and lose and win
my heart again—a dozen times a day.

Careful watchers of movement—ridiculous miscalculators,
acrobatic four legged puffs of fur and eyes, ("deadly spies"),
stretching, grabbing, rule violators.

Lurkers, peerers, pouncers, streakers, bouncers.

Nervous—calm, curious—indifferent, suspicious—trusting,
defiant—pliant.

Darting dynamos of disaster, reckless rackers of ruin,
breakers of baubles, curtain snaggers, lint baggers—
plant scatterers, flatterers.

Graceful leapers, easy sleepers,
milk lappers, shoenappers,
        soft seducers.

— **Betty Sherron**

CATS

I am a poetic person who loves cats
I wonder what the world would be like without cats
I hear the roaring of a tiger
I see a tiger stalking its prey
I want to save all the endangered animals
I am a poetic person who loves cats

I pretend that I am a tiger
I feel the urge to prowl in the jungle
I like the soft fur of cats big and small
I worry that big cats will soon go extinct
I cry when a species goes extinct
I am a poetic person who loves cats

I understand that all things must die
I say that humans and animals are equal
I try to help all animals that are in need
I hope that no more species of any animal go extinct
I dream about having a pet tiger
I am a poetic person who loves cats

— **Michael Walker, age 13**

RAIN

Rain that fosters
growing plants, takes the
creases out of pants.
    Rain that settles summer
dust, causes mildew, causes rust.
    Rain that with its
cleansing fall, washes autos,
makes them stall.
    Rain that fills the
dried-up creek, causes people's
roofs to leak.
    Rain that cools you
when it's hot, makes you shiver
when it's not.
    Rain's a mixed-up sort
of weather, pro and con all rolled
together.
    Rain is nasty, rain is
nifty, in proportion, fifty-fifty

— **Chanelsha Sue Waldron**
Tammy Joy Webb

FRIENDS

Friends are nice and kind.
Friends are warm and caring.
They help you when you need
help. All they ask for in
return is the same thing.
When your heart has been
broken your friends are
there for support. When you're
in trouble they are there
to help. Friends are forever
and should never let stupid
things come between them.
Friendship is a special gift
that boys and girls can share
with each other. Friendship is
a bond you share with each
other. Friendship is a bond
you have with people and
feelings. I should know
I have you, my friend.

— **Jodie Johnson, age 14**

TODAY AND TOMORROW

Today the weather was gray,
and if I may say, it
was a gloomy, gloomy day.
I was blue,
so I boo-hoo-hooed.
Boo-hooing got me back into
things.
Now it feels like Spring.
Outside I went and spent
my time in the garden.
Now I am gay, because the
clouds have gone away.
My daughter is home now,
a para-teacher is no easy
job from teaching all day at
school.
But she plays it real cool, gets
up early, dresses, eats and
goes right back to school.

— **Jan Will**

TOMORROW

Shallow is the night
Birds flutter and fly
The Dead Sea is in the sky
One day we all must decide

Echoes they cause the blame
Scared little children lead the way
Shouting reasons for their pain

Silent words say you're my friend
Awkward movements say the same
Life's disappointments leading us into the rain

Go to sleep, the night is almost leaving
Time will come when we least believe
And shake our fears into our dreams.

—Theresa Patrisha Spicer

GHOSTS OF THE PRAIRIE

Ya see that place
Just north of the corner
The one with the windmill
And the barn fallin' over

That's the ole Wilcoxen place
I liked to stay there as a kid
Many of life's lessons were learned there
From the kid things we did

Now it's sad to see the ole place
All grown over with weeds
Nothing left but the memories
And the wind in the trees

Just as with all things
They go with the passing of time
Everything changes over the years
But the sun continues to shine

But I'll always remember the ole Wilcoxen place
And the memories it holds so fond
But the lesson that lasts forever
Is that between friends there's always a bond

—A. Leonard Hitz

INNER INTENSITY

Look into his eyes
Notice the burning stare
His mind is set on perfection
The task at hand his only care

As he begins to practice his skill
Everything around him becomes unknown
Nothing can distract him
He has found that rare and sacred "zone"

His domain is surrounded with energy
Which radiates a contagious vibration
The only requirement is his presence
To feel the adrenalized sensation

Once affected by this drug
This stimulant in the air
There is a rebirth of power
A second wind beyond compare

I hope to someday achieve his level
So others may absorb from me
That experience of total concentration
That Inner Intensity.

—Kent Jacquay

A WAY OUT

God does not lead down dead-end streets,
Although the way seems dark and long,
When the thoroughfare appears impassable,
And everything goes wrong.

At each road's end there's a beginning,
A new song, new life, a fresh start,
So never be discouraged,
Look forward to the goal, take heart!

After you've gone as far as you can,
Your eyes can see no end,
Trudge a little farther on,
And look up to the light, my friend.

—Nancy McNew Lynn

THE STRENGTH

I've sought to acquire
a goal so dire
so when a bold, bugle blew
I've tried to find a clue
out of this thought — the weak
shall perish as we speak
I've fought the ire
in my soul, to sire
words, to inspire
war lords, to tire
over this thought — the weak
shall perish — as we speak
I've the strength, to require
at arm's length, the end to a fire
And when besieged by a few
I've cried to my mighty crew
this thought — the weak
shall perish as we speak
And; oh, it hurts to be the strength
for those who chose to fight; for the meek

—Gary Jepson

DOORS

Five doors, which one shall I choose?
One door has my heart slammed in it.
The others have pieces of my soul.
The first is full of beauty and pleasure.
The second is full of laughter and compassion.
The third is full of care and friendship.
The fourth is full of love and honesty.
The fifth is full of lust and power.
And I am caught, not knowing which to choose.
I can keep going to each door, not choosing
either, but one of these doors has given
to me a life to love.
If I knock on each door would the one
that has given to me a life to love come out
and share this life with me?
Or will all five set me free?

*Dedicated to Dean and "Heavy" for being my
life line. And to Melissa, Jaclyn, L.T.
and Kearney — the buddies I could never
live without. Or with!!*

—Nikie Guidroz

DROSS?

This, I grudge Religion as a whole,
it sets such value on the soul
that life itself seems dross.
Then man, having two lives, mimes the cat,
surfeit with surplus reasons that
                                        to lose one life's no loss.

Thus, I nudge religion: It throws shade,
for its sweet promise wars are made,
and faulty premise guides.
When the final requiem is said
a human voice promotes the dead
up to one of God's sides!

Fuss, and budge religion? Wish I might!
Does dying for a cause deemed right
another life insure?
I doubt, and will doubt with my last breath
that HE who seeks no sinner's death
commends what men endure.

—Evelyn Spore

TWO EYES

I sit and stare into two eyes
   so much can be told.
These eyes stare back
   with a small hint of sadness.
They are trying to make the world into a paradise
   yet they only see the sun through a dark cloud.

I stare into these eyes deeper, interested.
These eyes want to cry a thousand tears.
These eyes want to be filled with happiness.
These eyes belong to a young child's heart
   and a young child's soul.
They cry out to be held.
They cry out to be loved.
But the eyes of a stranger turns them away.

Stop.
Listen to the silent whisper of this child
   that no one can hear.
Maybe your shoulder will comfort this child's pain
   for once in this child's long lasting years.

—John Hamm, Jr.

THE LITTLE GOLDEN FINGER RING

An Iraqi mother bowed her head.
   She had seen the General's grin
When he said, "The children's safety is paramount."
She bowed her head again.

She scarce had gone a city block
When war planes zoomed o'erhead,
And tons and tons of mortar shells
Blew nursery walls and babies dead.

She fell face-down amid debris.
She saw a tattered piece of bunting,
And a little half-burned shoe;
A little golden finger ring
With its stone of azure blue;
A pudgy little hand, thumb and forefinger gone;
The ring finger still intact
With its ring and little stone.

They found the mother there,
Clasping the little hand
To her still and quiet breast.

—Mary S. Shepherd

UNSPEAKABLE SECRETS

I crawl into my shell
   for there's no one to tell
the secrets I know
The fear in me you've bestowed
No one will listen
to a bratling you say
But of your mistreating way
someday in judgement you will pay

—Skipper Jane

FACE AT THE WINDOW

If you look closely
   at the house in the distance,
you can see a face at the window.
Watching life go by.
Waiting, always waiting.
Never a participant in life,
but always an observer.
And if you look closer,
you will see the face at the window . . .
is mine.

—Romala Bissell

Little girl, sitting there
   in a little room, all your own
crying silently, all alone.
Stay there in your little room
safe — unknown, kid without a name.
Sit silently and hide our shame.
Remember then, no one came?
Guardian Angels that never were,
no one watching over her.
Remember mother's face you'd see
that never became reality?
Grown up now, in a grown up world,
in a little house all my own,
crying silently, all alone.
Stay inside where no one can see,
the little girl inside of me.

—Sharon Sutliff Goodin

LITTLE ONE

Little one don't be sad
   For you nothing should be so bad.
Little one there is one out there
Someone who hears your prayer.

I see you standing in the cold
There should be someone for you to hold.
Little one come in and don't feel the chill
There will be one who will hold you still.

I followed you into the dark
I saw you at the park.
I came to see you afterward
Are you the one whose cry I heard?

Little one don't be alone
I know there is so much that is unknown
In the storm you should not be unprotected
No one will leave you unprotected.

Hold the ones you love so near
Hold the ones you love so dear.
Little ones should all be held
Their fears all should be dispelled.

—Nancy Arwine

BATS, AND DRACULA

People were just starting to like us
We cute insect-eating things
When some fanged man makes a fuss
And turns into a bat
And human necks he stings.

When we would only eat a gnat
Now why would he do a thing like that?

—**Abram Racin, age 8**

MISTY

Friendly and lovable,
Cuddly and huggable.
She is a friend I would never abandon,
Because Misty is my small companion.
I just described my cat,
She is my best friend.
And I will always love her,
Until the end.

—**Melissa A. Jaryno**

KINDRED SPIRITS

Yours is a kindred spirit of a time long ago.
When the Buffalo roamed the plains.
And the Wolf was the master of the timber.
A time when you looked to the heavens and
    marveled at the stars,
And at the sun that gives life to all.
And to the moon that watches over your dreams.
To be a part of a culture that all but died
    long ago.
A way of life you long for.
And maybe someday you will find a way of life
    that suits you in this crazy world that we
    try to master.

—**Kent Stockhorst**

MEMO: TO FELLOW UNICORNS

The Unicorn is a mythical beast
Or so the experts say.
Yet the spirit of same is very real
And quite alive, even today.

It's rare, unique and splendid
With the hint of a guided air,
And a stance that strives for perfection
More than any other would dare.

My friend, you, too, have that spirit
Splendid and oh so unique:
I pray, don't try to be average,
It's the Unicorn Spirit God seeks.

Though that horn seems mere illusion
Our stance points to God above.
Though rare and unique, we've a place here.
We're created to spread God's love.

While many may laugh at this concept,
We're kept by God's own hand.
So let's act as He gives us guidance,
We Unicorns must make our stand.

—**Rose Daniels**

MY HORSE

I loved my horse and she loved me
the problem was; she wanted to be free
one day I came back home from school,
looking like a dreaded fool.
I felt like nothing, like I always feel
and went into the house to have my meal.
I opened the door and entered the hall;
my mom look at me — and started to bawl
I asked her: please oh please tell me why
you looked at me and started to cry?
She told me that my horse — was gone!
I ran outside, across the lawn.
To the barn I ran and I ran,
I even ran past the small horse van.
I wondered if I had treated her right
I wondered and pondered with all my might.
I looked down at my horse — she was finally free
I loved my horse — and my horse loved me.

—**Krista Raatikainen**

RACE FOR GLORY

It starts, in the mist frozen light,
The tensions high; the dogs ready for flight.

They all have high hopes at the start of this quest,
But, at the finish line only one can be best.

The dogs are nervous, and ready to run,
They'll all be off at the start of the gun.

Rookies, Pros, dogs are put to the test,
They'll go a long way before they can rest.

The Spirit of Adventure in their heart,
Is part of what it takes to start.

Why they run is no mystery,
Their names will go down in history.

So, while they're mushing so far from home,
One thing they remember, "There's no place
Like Nome."

—**Virginia Estes**

THE WHALE

Quietly gliding thru crystal waters,
Silent, dark depths below,
Sunlight streaked blue-green waters above.
Moving with measured grace in their vast domain,
So few gentle giants remain.

Hounded by relentless hunters throughout the ages,
Brought to the edge of extinction in bloody stages.

Amazingly gentle with our thoughtless race,
They watch with soul piercing intelligent eyes,
Letting us move amongst them; listening to their
Mysterious, musical cries.

Jumping high from out the depths,
Water cascading in jeweled rivulets down
Their seemingly endless length.
Not seeking to destroy with their awesome strength.

God is surely evident in so majestic a creature
A symbol of harmony with their environment,
A most redeeming feature.

Man, hopefully now wisely humane,
Please God, let these gentle giants remain.

—**Sharon Prince**

Kickin her over, long before dawn,
houses are dark and there's dew on the lawn.
Making my way down an uncrowded street,
no destination, no deadlines to meet.
Finally got tired of the corporate scene,
made up my mind to live out my dreams.
Leaving possessions and troubles behind,
swapping time for some peace of mind.
Humming a tune as I hit I-10,
Amarillo By Morning, I'll be there by then.
The road less traveled is my charted course,
the code of the West, my driving force.
Seeing the land from the saddle of my steed,
I'm going wherever these two wheels will lead.

—Sam

THINGS COULD BE WORSE

I have crumbs in my toaster
and scorch on my roaster;
the freezer needs defrosting
and my hair needs washing.
Thinking — it's too much to face
this bright winter day
I glanced out the window
and saw a bluejay.

Remember the sox I lost in the dryer last week
well, they re-appeared today — so to speak.
I couldn't have lost them, although they were small
they were under a stand in the back hall.
Everyone knows that I love to cook
but, so often there's rugs to be shook.
So, I think I'll just chuck it all
and read a really, really good book!

Then I received a phone call from my sister Kay
who lives down Albuquerque way.
She thanked me for a Spring bouquet
I sent her "Just to cheer her day."

—Evelyn R. Vaughn

PROBOSCIS

Some folks have a nose for news:
Others have red ones from drinking booze.
Mine, with a cold, is red from blowing.
Pinocchio's nose kept growing and growing
Durante was famous for his nose.
Without one who could smell a rose?
Eskimos kiss with the nose.
Songs are written about a turned-up or cute nose.
Dogs use their noses to bury their treasure
Also to unearth it at their leisure.
For eye glasses, you need the bridge of your nose
Remember Rudolph with his bright and shiny nose?
Without a nose, it would be hard to snore and sneeze
This certainly would the sleepers please.
Noses are symbolic of race, colour and breed.
And certainly is something we all need.
A nose decides the winner of a race,
And also divides the human face.
Santa's nose is a distinctive feature,
And a clown's nose makes him a delightful creature.

An egotist is one who's always blowing his knows.
—Allen McNally

—Dot Dougan

CHOCOLATE HEAVEN

Paint me a little picture of a great
big chocolate bar,
Hang it beside the Mona Lisa
It will come up to par.

Give me lots of chocolate chip cookies,
Empty every jar,
Let me eat my way to chocolate candy land,
I'll drive in a chocolate car.
Give me chocolate every day till I am
old and cannot see.
Make me little chocolate golf balls,
Lots of chocolate tea.

Then when I am dead and buried,
Put a chocolate Twinkie on my grave.
Send me to chocolate heaven,
The road in the chocolate place.

—Asher. Poetic Feelings Analyst

HOW

"How How How," oh how do you do it?
How would you do it? How do you feel
when you're in love.
It would be so thrilling, if you
are only willing.
You are like the stars shining
above; "How How How" How do you feel
when you're in love.
You're like a pretty flower, growing more
lovely every hour.
"How do you feel when you're
in love."
Oh know I would love to
pluck you for my own.
I could love forever, if we
could live together.
And never more would I roam
we'd live in the highest tower,
Never a one to bother How How
How I'm in Love.

—Mamie B. Ellis, deceased

MY WIFE SNORES WHEN SHE'S ASLEEP

My Wife's a great cook and her food's
good to eat; But she has this loud habit,
she snores when she's asleep.
We were once in a car with my
friend in the back. Then suddenly he
hollered, "Great Day! What Is That?" As
I laughed he leaned forward to take
a small peek. I said, "Hey! that's my
wife. She snores when she's asleep."
Once some time ago we
were talking in bed. When confronted
she snapped, "I heard what you said!"
But she had not replied, and that
was not all; she was making this
sound like an animal call. Well it
didn't take long cause the truth
I did seek. That noise was
my wife, yes snoring while asleep.
Now she's sometimes mean and
dances quite well, and she is a good
person, this I can tell. She does
much much more while she's awake on her
feet. But one thing for sure, she snores when
she's asleep.

—Marcus C. Gentry

I'm an ass with ears
A clown with real tears
A fool with no pride
And a hitchhiker with no ride.
I'm loving
Giving
Caring
and consumed with a pickled herring.
An outside opinion
would say I'm a minion
And he'd be right
unless he had the same plight.
Then I'd be a man in love.

—Dennis R. Paluso

SUNSET ON THE LAKEFRONT

Twilight arrives.
Nature dips Her brush
Into the descending palette
of glimmering primaries.

Fiery oranges, reds, & yellows
Dance & leap
Across a dusky canvas
Of dark azure.

The gentle lap of the tide
Provides the naked beach
With a liquid blanket.

Across the heavens
Jewels sparkle & shimmer
In the wake of moondust.

My love & I sit on the park bench
In Nature's theatre.
She is lulled to sleep
By the warmth of my shoulder.

—John Freiberger IV

MY SONG

I wish that everyone could share
What I have found in life to be
As inexpensive as the air,
But priceless as eternity.

So many people go through life
And never really learn to live.
They search for things in their behalf,
But fail to practice how to give.

To give one's self with all the zest
Of childhood's simple eagerness.
And seek to bring out all the best,
Is lesson one in happiness.

Real love endures the hours of grief.
It holds the key to real success;
Respects; protects; promotes belief
In God and human loveliness.

For all who seek the secret art
Of living need at first to learn
The great desire of every heart:
To love and be loved in return.

—Robert Kirk Jones

GIRL WATCHING

Firmly stepping on the pavement
Striding cross the grassy way
Hips with undulating movement
Shoulders alternating sway
Giving smiles and thoughtless laughter
Every one a latent flirt
Called by Mom a pristine daughter
Termed by me a charming skirt.

—Wade Hadley

FOR ALL TIME

Sometimes in the night
I reach out just to touch you
You laying beside me

My mate in life

I love you for no reason
I'll love you for all time

You are the one
I count on each day

My dreams are wrapped around you
My heart is in your hands

—Gloria Hood

PROMISES

To hold in my heart the love
completely,
To know in my soul the passion
deeply;

To hear in my words the honesty
dearly,
To see in my eyes the reality
clearly;

To find in my fate the struggles
endeavour,
To picture in my life the change
forever.

—William E. Free

My heart wanders through
an eternity of cloudy skies
It feels no warmth from the
imprisoned sun
Only a dark coldness of bitter
storms beating down upon it.
Its daily struggle becomes greater
though it knows the end is near
and a new beginning awaits

Soon — soon it shall feel the
warmth again, and the touch
of a tender soul
placing joy and love back into
its being
And for this it fights a constant
battle of loneliness and pain
Again.

*Dedicated to Jamie Ann Hale,
the Angel who clears my cloudy
skies away. I love you.*

—Peter Fly

ON NATURE'S WAY

It was "Hailwood-on-the-Mosey-side" between the rivers nigh,
Roaming 'mongst the thistle-down, whiskered with furtive eye,
Stretching thru the rosy-hue, glancing a silvered paw,
Striking quick the mouse it hit, Cat opened up her jaw.

Waiting in the thicket, ears to hear, and eyes to spy,
Hoof-beats — bleating — horses breathe — and distant smothered cries,
Angry men are coming, dark terror in their eyes,
"Be gentle" — sounds the wind,
"Be gentle" — sighs the pine.

Wondering in the darkness, which foe will catch my wing,
Leaving in his bloody wake, a bird that cannot sing,
Bleating — hoof-beats — horses breathe — and me with smothered cries,
"Be gentle" sounds the wind,
"Be gentle" sighs the pine.

     —Susan Gray

DOWN THE LANE

It seems like most of my life I've been going down the lane.
From the time I was 4 & the neighbor boy and I followed Dad
    down the lane.
Dad said we couldn't go, but we knew he needed us and
    sauntering in new cowboy boots sneaked down the lane.
Oh, the blisters and the scolding for two cocky four year olds
    just to follow Dad down the lane.
We rode on the mud boat and our sleds behind Dad and his tractor
    down the lane.
When Mom would have housework, you can believe I'd find something
    Dad needed me for down the lane.
We husked corn and cut corn stalks with Dad down the lane.
We earned fair money picking tomatoes with Dad down the lane.
I stole my first kiss, hiding from Dad down the lane.
I learned to drive by driving the tractor with Dad down the lane.
Years later I shared a tractor ride with my husband and Dad down the lane
I've spent my whole life following Dad down the lane.
But Dad died last week.
Now how do I go down that lane?

    —K. Clare

MY BEST AGE

I saw the night dance by, I was a fool.
While others danced right by with great delight, I felt so cold.
The warmth of hearts, lifted up in warmth of tone of voice
passed by me and left me lonely in a crowd, so all alone.
The dancing feet felt heavy on my heart, once jumped for joy, when
I was asked to dance by a new boy.
But childhood gaiety is gone and I am old.
I'll stay home and rock and there my hand will fold and say a prayer;
when I feel I can, unfold my hands and point them upward — and on high
God will catch the beam I send from hopeful fingers tilting upward
there — up to the sky.
Then my heart will sing again I know — He'll hear my prayer and send to
me a neighbor's child so full of grace, the sun will dance and radiate
upon the face upturned to me and no more will I miss the grown up
dancing feet,
I'll have the warmth of a little kiss, and little "thanks" for cookies
that I had made that day. As I placed them in the pan, all gloom would
melt away, anticipating smiles and songs of great delight and a gingerbread
man to take to bed at night, or hang upon a green and merry tree. The
evergreen will last until the cherry tree holds robins singing sweetly in their
nest,
It's then I know, what ever age I've been it was my best.

    —Dolores E. Tackett

CREATOR

Here I sit looking down on the world
No one can see me
People pass by in such a whirl
That I'm just content to sit here.
People with problems, worries, and death
People thinking of people they met
People with heartaches, with laughter, and joy
People who only feel the need to destroy.
Here I sit looking down on the world
No one can see me stare
I gaze on the creatures that I created
And am glad that I'm not there.

—Erica K. Lange

ON SECOND THOUGHT

If only God was like a tree,
That you and I could look and see,
Him standing there, with outstretched arms,
To shield and cover us from harm.

But then on second thought I know
That you and I to Him must go.
Though we can never see Him there,
He's waiting to hear and answer prayer.

He's just like love within your heart,
We know it's there, we feel the spark,
So God will always have to be,
A spirit, leading you and me.

—Helen McGirr

THE MARCH UNDERFOOT

I empower this hymn for
   the vanquished
Trampled under by life's booming strides
I will keen long the wail of betrayal
Victims bludgeoned, disemboweled by lies.

For
In his goodness God wrought man to suffer
A life sentence of sickness and loss
But no blackhearted curse he inflicted so rank
Or so crushing a heartbreak as words

Words that are stand-ins for actions
Words that are stand-ins for love
Words are now all we accomplish
There's no hand alive inside the glove.

The snake in the garden of Eden
Could not have accomplished the breach
Had God not indicted the couple
Foredoomed with affliction of speech.

The doom of humanity's great pit of despair
That one's speech be depended to impart
   full expression;
For, like appearance in Nature, words reveal
   to mislead
More obscure than disclosure one's impulses
   to action.

One's appearance more appealing
than the innermost man
Social circles repel inner ardor
Erect fences to exclude the
soul's noblest impulse
Deem words express all in
man's Nature.

—Ellen Baudisch

It's a human tragedy
when two hearts that were one
forget how they loved,

but even the angels cry
when just one of those hearts
remembers.

—Morris L. Hicks

FOR ME

For me He died on the cross,
   The nail pierced hands and feet,
And his brow was cut with thorns.

For me He cried to God on high
The sun darkened as He said,
"It's finished, Redemption work is done."

For me they sealed His tomb.
The stone was rolled away,
The empty tomb to see.

And now He sits at God's right hand
   To intercede for me!

—Hazel Jones

BATTLE

Existence is beyond our power
upon that mighty hill,
where they stand with pride
over sunlight flowers so still.

Slowly they descend
with fire-birds above,
harmony in their steps
and numbness upon their face.

Kneeling, I sing of mercy
yet they storm the stony beach,
going on and on like the sea
'God have pity they are blind!'

But when they fall upon their brothers
with piteous eyes and battled arms,
all the strength becomes weakness
when sea and sky together blend.

—Ken Bejcek

CHILDISH THINGS

I remember Jesus
When He was just a boy,
He taught me how to laugh and sing
And care with all my joy,

I told my friends what He told me,
They jeered to wound with every name,
No Beauty raised above the grave,
No Dreams untamed, He was to blame.

I threw away those childish things,
Closed eyes to plod the stone,
Somewhere along, the boy gave up,
I took my place, the man had grown.

I remember Jesus,
When they finally brought His rue,
He looked at me, my blood froze still,
I guess He grew up too.

—Adrian Dorn

CLOUDS OBSCURE THE VIEW

They were beautiful,
    My thoughts.
I searched and searched
    They are gone.
I looked and I looked
    They are gone.
How could I lose them?
Somewhere, occupying space are words
    I can not remember.
Locked in my mind
    so deep.
I think and I think
    the door does not open.
If I could find the words,
    the search
                would end.

—Judith Fuhrmann

AWAY FOR AWHILE

I've been away for awhile
A lot longer than I needed to be,
I was in the past, yesteryear
Thinking it would set me free.

And then reality hit me
It was a hard and sudden blow,
And it made me realize
That the past had to be let go.

So that I could get on with living
And really live my life,
Yes, I could cherish my memories
And still handle today's strife.

For I was not giving
Not to you, nor to myself,
My life was just a package
Sitting on a shelf.

And it was really different
Knowing that the present wouldn't last,
And I might not have a future
If I keep living in the past.

—Beverley Matchett

CHILDHOOD

Now morning is pushing back hair
    Memories strike home
Raised on elbow, I stare at stars beyond the window

So many things return to mind, with fulfilled and
strange clarity

Like letters that arrive addressed to someone who
felt

Many years ago.

—Adena M. Glover

THE BROKEN SILENCE

I know the sound of true heartache.
It isn't a banshee cry, for public display.
True heartache is something to be borne . . .
. . . not vented.

It freezes the heart; and stills the soul;
transforming everything within to a heavy leaden state . . .
. . . that never truly lifts.
    It weighs like pennies on the eyes of one
dead, and drags the body to a listlessness that
matches the spirits.
    One doesn't have the energy to wail,
or pound fists theatrically . . . for the benefit
of others.
    A true sufferer of heartache withdraws
to a dark place, like a wounded animal . . .
and conserves himself.
The forward view is one overcast with
doubt; as hour upon hour is spent
dwelling on the species of times past.
Bittersweet ghosts of embraces given,
laughter shared, and love . . . now lost.
Daily scenes are tinted in blue . . . the
color of sorrow; and *empty* skies.
The hue of deep waters, which flood the
eyes.
I know the sound of true heartache . . . the
sound of softly falling tears

—Jeff Reiner

THE BLUE WORLD

What the "WORLD" needs now is — "CRYSTAL BLUE PERSUASION," and
"SWEET, SWEET SURRENDER."
What we have now is a "BLUE CHRISTMAS," for "ELVIS," and a
"PASSIONATE, BLUE FOOTBALL," for "SWEETNESS."
Even in "SPORTS," we must not forget —
"CUBBIE BEAR BLUE," and "DODGER BLUE."
Even our "FLOWERS," are 'VIOLETS are BLUE,' and
'FORGET-ME-NOTS are BLUE.'
Even "GOD," is "MAJESTIC BLUE!"
No; WE CANNOT REST UNTIL OUR WORLD IS BETTER!
What we all need now are "BLUE SKIES" for "EVERYONE," and
"RED ROSES" for "LOVE!"
May "THE BLUEBIRD" of "HAPPINESS" smile, and
Lay it on our "WORLD" real soon, and
Carry us 'BACK TO AMERICA,' "THE LAND OF THE FREE,"
"THE HOME OF THE BRAVE," and our "FIELD OF DREAMS,"
"WRIGLEY FIELD." Out of "THE BLUE," and into "THE PINK!"

—Diana Lynn (Frybarger)

LEAVES, PAPER, BARK

Leaves, Paper, Bark for some are tools to create,
  like Shelley, Homer, Byron, Yeats
Leaves, Paper, Bark for other purpose most bemoan,
  hind bush, in pot, on porcelain throne

Dedicated to Linda, Mark,
Jamie, Christopher and Erik.

—H. Clark Anderson

PARADISE

All experiences are fed into us by living . . .
The art of understanding
Is the willingness to communicate . . .
The foundation to wisdom
Is the willingness to listen . . .
Love is universal . . .
Love is loyalty . . .
Love is the very reason for life!!
It would be wonderful if each of us
could say to one another,
I will give you
More than I need to receive.
What a beautiful paradise this would be.

—Marlene Newbold Johnson

INTO THE FUTURE

Kings and Queens,
  Scrolls and trolls still hold their own.
Books and writings continue to grow.
People still have fantasies.
They dream of deep space, dive into oceans of air,
and look to the stars for their fortune to be told.
The sun will rise and the skies darken.
There will be the early morning dawn,
and the colored setting skies.
Times will be different.
Everyone will move to a different drum beat.
There will be adventures, new challenges,
to a new and exciting frontier.
The 21st Century into the future.

—David C. Paradis

APPALACHIA

Only a day in the rest of my life.
  Only just now to look and see.
Just this moment to realize.
Molded by God's hand in eternity.

The waters, the land and sky, Behold!
Forged by the one, ages untold.
Caressed by His Spirit, mellowed in love.
Our Creator, in Heaven above.

Piled high the mountains, scooped valleys deep.
Fills winding rivers from clouds that weep.
Scattered flowers, placed man in the land.
Gift on gift from the Master's plan.

I view the splendor of this blessed place.
Drink in the beauty and feel His Grace.
I lift my hands and sing this refrain.
Appalachia, I'm home again.

—Jean Oliver Erb

I WANT YOU TO BE A QUIET GARDENER

I want you to be a quiet gardener—
  Walk freely through the bowers and brambles,
  Sure of foot,
  Poignant, purposefully
  Pause—

Choose from silver, gold, and purple
Fashion into a pointillistic garland

Then as quietly as before,
  With radiant crown,
  Poignant, purposefully
  Pause—

And know you wear my soul.

—Joseph David Bohms

KEVLAR ADVENTURES OR CANOE CACAPHONY

Heron barks signal surprise
  slip-sure the passing wings
drawn through thinner liquids arc
Across the blunted bowsprit
of direction implied
on the transient compass
of a glass canvas

Exercised like Kendo
with blunted wooden blades

Practiced like meditation
between the wind and artistic frictions

These knives cut water
in a sign language
of agility applied

Small strokes of grace delivered
in search of a blessing
Scribing traction
on impermanent media
lost in a rolling sine

—Sean Bahner-Guhin

FEELINGS OF SPRING

Long months I have waited,
  hoping for sun-warmed earth
to walk bare feet upon, spread-toed.

Woodland pathways discreetly unrolled
seasonal surprises on a Spring day
to stoop and touch, gentle-handed . . . .

Bloodroot: large-lobed leaves
holding purity in petals untainted
for warring Indians
to bleed red dye, root-bound.

Dogtooth Violet: pendulous yellow head
staining tear-dropped leaves
for a misnamed herb
to feel shame, lily-pretty.

Dutchman's Breeches: white-bloomered flowers
congregating in a shady glen
for a dress rehearsal
to greet the Trillium, three-parted.

Thus, a God-given wilderness garden
Endangered for showy hybrids, specie-improved.

—Elva Heinz

MY CLIFF

If we could go back and start again,
And retrace each smooth and rugged mile,
I would gladly do it all again my friend,
Laughingly—just for your tender smile.

Time has gone much too fast for me,
I must not forget to smell the roses.
I would like to live life completely free,
From the trials this life imposes.

But the joys in life outweigh the bad,
When I have you by my side.
At times when I have been very sad.
You made me laugh—when
    I really could have cried.

—**Mary Sharp**

MAN AND THE VOICE

One dark and stormy night,
    a little ship was lost,
Amid the tempest and the gale,
    the delicate ship was tossed.

Then tossed upon the shore it was,
    and no longer was it lost,
But torn and shattered and so alone,
    nowhere to go but home.

But home? But home?
    Yet where on earth was home?

In a kingdom by the sea,
    come away and fly with me,
    to my kingdom, by the sea.

I have no wings to fly away,
    To your kingdom by the sea.

Just follow me and trust in me,
    and we shall reach the kingdom,
    the kingdom by the sea.

—**Katie Czajka**

TARNISHED SHORES

Though dawn was spotless undefaced
    Washed by the sudsing tide
The sands along seashores glisten
In mire sea treasures hide

Gulls dive lively into the breeze
Suns warmth on waters blue
Finned tail fishes dabble smoothly
Gulls swiftly to ensue

The sleeping menace awakens
Thunderous sounds prevail
Air stenches of pollutions sting
Water grows green and stale

Evenings sunlit brilliance fades orange
Upon the tarnished shores
Seaweed wrapped litter crashing
The waves in anguish roar

The tear drops falling profusely
Upon the troubled sands
Are those of Mother Nature
As she surveys this land

—**Mary Ivie Norvell**

The pain of a poet is the wood that feeds the fire.
    The pain of a poet is your deepest desire.
The pain of a poet is every temptation.
The pain of a poet is the heart's truest sensation.

—**Jennifer McCusker**

THE EXCHANGE

"What a lovely new dress, my dear," she said.
    "The color becomes you so.
The cut of the sleeve is exactly right.
I love peau de soie, you know."

Mrs. X then demurred with a gracious blush,
"Why, I've worn it all summer long.
It's quite an old thing. I've had it for years.
I just picked it up for a song."

They smiled at each other and sugared their words,
While secretly smirking inside.
So they went on their way then, quite full of deceit.
(Each knowing the **other** had lied!)

—**Beth Guye Kittle**

THE OLD PRIVY

That little brown building at the rear of the yard
    With a half moon engraved, and a seat that is hard
Its build very sturdy to withstand nature's call
No one is exempt, it calls short and tall
In the cold of winter, a path had to be made
For each in his turn, if not they would wade
The lid of the john was held up with a hook
A catalog from Sears, through the pages you'd look
Then in case that the paper had slipped down the hole
Rip a sheet from the book, it would now save your soul
Two holers were great, if emergency came
When company was there, the smell was the same
Thank goodness for plumbing, a throne that is warm
For memories of privies, don't hold too much charm

—**Donna Dayton**

A ONCE PROUD TRADITION

Woke up this morning
    and I had myself a cup.
Walked outside to the garage
and started up my pick-up truck.

Rode downtown past the filling station;
tears rolled down my face.
A once proud service to our nation
is today considered out of place.

Where has full service gone?
Now we have self-service convenient stores.
You get out and pump your own.
The independent is fading out of existence; they
are closing their doors.

A once proud and honorable tradition
is slowly fading away.
I once had an honorable position
running a full service island Monday through Sunday.

Then one day we switched to help yourself
and all I did was collect the money.
Inside they were asking: "Will there be anything else?"
I thought the company was full of baloney.

—**Michael Vincent**

GOOD OVERCOMES EVIL

Love fills the air of hate.
Punctuality takes the place of late.

Braveness triumphs over fear.
Smiles are taking over a tear.

Sunshine prevails a storm.
Mended hearts relieve the torn.

Laughter conquers an argument.
Apologies make up for words that were not meant.

Food cures starvation.
Peace saves a ruined nation.

—Nicolette L. Flocca

PRAY TAKE MY MEANING

Adrift on a mysterious pregnant sea,
Her swollen belly slowly encompasses me.
A turbulent tide aborts my innocent sleep,
Drawing me down into the foreboding deep.

Lightning flashbacks ignite in my mind,
Illuminating a life once proud but blind.
Now drowning in aspersions of fathomless sin,
My memory forever tarnished by kin.

The menacing tempest has relentlessly pursued.
The crushing darkness and pain will not be subdued.
One last labor to breathe before I silently descend.
The pregnant sea has delivered my peace dividend.

Much later: How many months was I lost at sea,
The depth of my chasm known only to me?
I penned my first poem from my watery grave.
A life was reborn on a rhythmic wave.

*Dedicated to John Irish I (1617-1677)—England
to America 1630. And to John Irish II
(1641-1717), who wrote in his will: To my wife,
the lands of my father "Of which I was wronged
and abused about. Pray take my meaning."*

—John Irish XII

FEMMELY

Shades of womenhood
interwoven,
Intricate webbings spun,
crossing cultural and ageless boundaries.
Quilted patterns woven into a universal patchwork.

FEMMELY

One's desperate moans from deep
within bring inner strength and peace
Another's pain, shattered dreams, and
lost faith finds unyielding love through
salty tears of motherhood,

FEMMELY

Other pioneers, trudging unbroken ground
breaking barriers, bringing diversity, change
and hope,

FEMMELY

Women inner mingling, weaving sturdy bonds
creating multifarious patterns, Intermingled
tightly, quilting a stronger sisterhood

FEMMELY

—E. Gray

computer glitch
e-mail switch
printer hitch
　　the VAX is down . . .
FAX line's busy
disk drive hummmm
tape got gnarled
　　backup's gone . . .

quick the pace our modern world
if not Fed. Ex. then it's too late

—Mia Anne Nottoli (P. duVal Guillout)

INCOMING

Within my fortress black stood I,
The dome spread steely struts above:
A private ebon envelope.
All about fell incessant shells:
Pointed stalwart summit shunned their force,
Daunted might flowed from the battlements.
Concussions shook the ground:
Blinding static flash showed all in bold relief,
Surrounding frantics died by puissant whim.

Treatied into somnolence,
Shells stopped senseless self-abuse,
A new breeze sieved the air of gloom.
I peeked out,
Affirmed the peace,
And folded my umbrella.

—Douglas S. Smith

TEARS

The oceans are tears in the universe
Depression and sadness
Are only happiness in reverse

The fret of a guitar
Can create a joyful or wailful wa
Sonic sounds from a whale
Or the sheep's common baa

Years are tears of age
Death a tear humanity can't save

Raindrops are drought's tears end
Fairy dust the tear of pretend

The dew on the lawn
The tear of the earth
Jack Frost is the icy stare
It gives winter birth

Floods are tears of destruction
Goodwill is the tear of reconstruction

Glory is the tear of all who are brave
To be knighted
The tear of a knave

Fear is a tear of the unknown
Wheat is the tear that starvation has sown

The future is a tear of eternity
The past is a tear of history

Children are the tears of generations
Stillborns are the tears of frustrations

Tears are prevalent
In all emotions
The most special tear
The tear of devotion

—William C. Leppo

EMOTIONS

Emotions, spilling out,
Exploding into space;
Where do they land,
Which direction do they face.

Words that form in the mind,
Never spilling over the tongue;
Thinking, not speaking or acting.
Words being thought, songs that are unsung.

If only we were able to say
The words that are on our minds
If only we could simplify
Our emotions.

—Nancy Pothier

DISSOLUTION:

[Separation
of a thing into its parts;]
a sorted laundry explanation.
So simple, Webster.
Linen-white Paper:
[printed or written document]
folded in starched shirt formality,
on my night table, waiting
impatiently for the pen.
Children are Resillient: [elastic,
springing, flexible, supple;]
tucked into their happy-ever-after tales,
the patchwork ravels in its twentieth year.
The remnant is Financial:
[means, payment, ransom, end.]
Too fragile for a Lifetime: [duration
of an individual existence.]
Individual:
[intended for
one person.]

—D. Margaret Gambrell

SONG OF COLOR

A song is within my heart.
I feel it, sense it, but can't express
it. It is there most of the time,
to help me to feel good when I'm
in need sometimes.
I want to let the song go, but
it won't let go of me.
It's in there like a rock, and hard
as can be.
The song must be singing, because
I'm still here, it's the song of my own
heart inside of there.
Its rhythm is perfect with an occasional
off beat, but it's my song and it's playing
throughout, just for me.
The music is filled throughout my veins.
There is color of life, it's filled with
sound.
Sound you hear, the sound that gives
life, its rhythm keeps beating as you
walk your path of color with all your
eternal gifts of
life.

—Beverly E. Price

CONFUSION

Once you have experienced something so great
You can't give it up, so you wait and wait
Things just get worse, so you call it off
Then you feel bad that it happpened at all
But wait it's too late, so you curl up and cry
Cause you finally realize that he's said good-bye
Yes, you're lost without him but what can you do
This isn't obsession, just true love turned blue
Yes, people say you're young and there are other guys
And though this is true, you still want to cry
Cause they don't realize that he was the guy
Of course I knew it wouldn't last forever
But how did I know it would end so soon
I said I loved him, and he said it too
The year couldn't have been better, the year of 91-92
But then it all ended . . . .

—Jessica Devery

CONSCIENCE

Try the bottle, cigarette or a little pot.
Is it too slow of a way or not?
Hey! Little voice leave me alone.
For the answer I don't know.

Times when I want to do wrong
I say I am human, not all that strong.
Temptation is there late at night,
There are a lot of things in reach of my sight.

When my life became so complicated,
There seemed no one to relate.
Why live until tomorrow?
Again the voice says, don't end it with my sorrow.

I hear the answer is so simple;
When done so easily,
A voice deep inside of me,
Conscience! or God could it be?

—Hazel Jones

FEELINGS

How can love live spontaneous with hate
within the conscious of emotion when
people breathe to hate and live to love?
Anger and aggression control feelings,
Sadness overcomes the power to control,
Happiness touches us all.
I saw a tear wallow down the cheek of
your sacred blue pool of cries, which
has fallen from the skin of such a silky
satin of pleasure and has shattered wet
sorrow of Pain.
It crawls from your emotion.
I think I am sad, I think we all are. I am sad
but a tear falls not from scared eyes.
The fear holds me from emotion of
love and happiness, scared to face the unrealistic
reality of hiding with expression.
Confusion is mixed with understanding
of foreverness, togetherness.
Who I am should be left up to me.
I will leave it alone, as I am.

—Michael J. Saxton

EIGHTEEN TODAY — "JAY"

You are a "legal" man today!
  You no longer need to heed what I say.
But, this will not change my life's design;
For you will ever be that boy of mine.
Who has always been more man than boy and
Filled my heart with pride and joy.
So even tho today you are a man — "they say."
Let's go on as we are from day to day.
To the world go ahead and be a man
But, stay "my boy" as long as you can.
For it's not a day or a year that sets a man apart
But what is growing deep in his heart.

    —Nina Ponchak

FOR KEVIN —

Curly-headed Kevin! Now he's ten!
  With wondrous gaze he sees
The Earth spill gifts of beauty at his feet —
In shells, rocks, trees, and all of nature's
  store
He gathers, saves, collects, and treasures all!

What does the future hold for this young boy
Who holds a microscope more dear than toys
And finds in coral, sponge and whelk, exciting joys?
Will his interest lead him on to undersea adventure?
Will he hear the song of singing whales?
Or will sea-lions lure him on to California's coast?
And ensnare him in rescue studies there?

It's happy birthday time for now,
And time is yet for dreams!

The next ten years will sound the call,
Whate'er he finds to do, may he do well!

    —Betty Jean Baker

P E A C E   O F   H E A R T

This was once a place where children grew
  Where all of the sorrows and fears are kept
In this place we put our pain away, hidden
With thick doors to comfort the occupants inside.

This is where all the love and memories are
Served up like lamb chops at dinner
For it has taken many years to build it
When it was finished we were pleased at its
foundation.

To give it a sense of warmth inside of it
We filled it with noise of laughter and joy
For it protects and gives us a sense of security
Never wanting for anything on the outside

For this is the place that keeps us warm,
when the sky is cold.
Cools us when the burning eye was high in the
sky.
From our childhood to the ultimate adulthood
This place has seen many changes within it.

And when left, it gives a sense of loneliness
For it was our protector of all of the secret
treasures.
There it stands, like a skeleton of what was
For in the heart it was a home to all.

    —Ahbleza Lorraine

THE MOM

The spirit of goodness inside my child
  knows. Through her eyes, a vision from
the soul comes and goes.
Reflections and refractions pierce her
mind without restraint, and are filtered
and compacted into one big shining light.
Beaming, sometimes screaming through the
twinkles and the grin. Her upturned face
that's searching for the one to breathe
within.
Be it whispers or gentle wind, just keep
the fire going. Keep it glowing soft and
warm. It fills the hole. It fills the soul.
And the spirit of this light, shining in
her little eyes, bursts to radiate upon
the mom.

    —Laura Thomas

DREAM BIRTH

I absolutely forgot the pain-filled hours,
  and cries so agonized,
The moment I gazed upon your face
  and found the smile inside your eyes.

I spied the fuzzy top of new-found treasure
  sprinkled pink with blue and red.
I marveled at the round and golden crown
  upon a tiny, much loved head.

Magic when I held my slippery bubble
  against my wet and waiting breast.
I then forgave myself
  and all who've walked before me.
And then, forgave the rest.

Forgiveness can be free at best
  when blessed with new-found wealth.
Wealth with not yet knowing eyes,
  created by two passing souls —
  and lovingly, produced inside myself.

    —Fernando Torres

THE CHILDREN

As I looked out my window today,
  I saw some young children
Outside at play.
They were having a good time
Just playing baseball,
It didn't seem to matter to them at all,
That they were all different colors,
Almost every race,
And as I looked into each smiling face,
I thought, this is the way we all should be,
Living together in peace and harmony.
Maybe our children should rule our nations,
So if there were any altercations,
It would only be a spat,
Or maybe a little shove,
But they would end all that
With a pat on the back,
And a friendly little grin,
They would be working together again,
Showing true Brotherly Love.

    —Verda McWethy

LOVE IS

Love is the good and the bad that we share.
Love is having pain and knowing someone's
there.
Love is the changes that come from day to
day.
Love is the joy that a mother shows her
child.
Love is not made by one, but Love's made
by two.
Love is knowing that someone's there just for you.
And that the same person will pull you through.
Love is not sex, but Love is the joy.
Love is not an instrument, Love's not a toy.
Love is joy and pain, it's like sunshine
and then as rain.
If Love is all these things and Love's
even true, keep giving me all these things
and I will stay in Love with you!

—Timolyn Andionette Johns-Smith

Let Me Get You Deep
Let Me Take You Down
Down To Where All Is Light And Pure And Honest
To A Place Where Feelings Flow Like A Raging River
Where The Soul Cries Out In All Its Agony
Where The Mind Is Free From All Its Burdens
Where Tears Fall Like Gentle Rain
Take My Hand, Close Your Eyes
Open Your Heart, Your Mind
Let Me Take You There
Hear Your Own Words
Cry Your Own Tears
Feel Your Own Pain
Search Within And You Shall Find
A Place So Deep, Where Only You Can Hide
A Place With No Fear, No Madness
Drink From The Well Of Your Soul
Feed From The Harvest Of Your Feelings
Take My Hand, Lend Me Your Heart
Let Me Take You There

—Sean R. Young

Dreams are feelings that can come true,
When I sit and dream it's all about you.
My dreams consist of walking in the sand,
gazing at the stars,
walking hand in hand.
My dreams are of you holding me tight,
letting me know all is just right.

Soon after my dreams become more than just dreams,
they become deep, real, fact, it seems.
I've walked on that beach holding your hand,
and gazed at those stars as we stood on the sand.

I never did once want those feelings to come true,
I wasn't ready nor prepared,
now what should I do?
I've tried over and over again to break that tie,
but it seems you're what I want and need,
this is no lie.

So what do I do with these feelings of mine?
Go on and live life, put those dreams all behind.

—Louise M. Keple

Unleash my heart into the abandon
Of perfect passion's kissing hums
Where I, once baptized by your hair,
Now fall full through that feather echo,
Into complete—this lack of you.
Here empty where the whispers were.
Take me gasping through these sighs
To the drunken mystic bliss
Where heart-dreams dance like flicker flame.

Dedicated to my wife, Darlyn Aimee Adams
—Matthew J. Adams

BETRAYED

As you walked into my room
your tender touch, changed my mood
As you held me gently, and so near
you gently whispered, I love you dear.
I have never felt this way before
I hope our love will last forever more.
I must of been out of my mind
when I confided in you, I was blind.

But the intimacy in it must be small
since you have gone and foretold it all
the sensational feeling of being loved
out of my reach, like a flying dove
you have betrayed me once before
I am not certain, I can take any more
your love is bitter-sweet and cold
now sorrow does my heart behold
your love brings me tears of pain
from my sad eyes they drop like rain.
As a lost puppy I followed your lead
and now my dying heart, it bleeds.

—Christal Winston

LOOK BEYOND

Look Beyond What You Hear —
Look Beyond What You See —
Look Deep Within To See What Is
Within You! — Within Me!
You'll Find Your Dreams, Your Hopes,
Your Needs — All That You Can Be!
You'll Find Your Gifts & Treasures,
Your Peace & Love — That Can't Be Measured
Be Proud To Discover The Best In You! —
The Best In Me! Start To Nourish! The Good
That You Find!!! —
Don't Throw It Away & Don't Let Others
Cause Your Dreams To Stray! As They Often
Try To Do — But Realize, You're Very Proud!!!
To Be None Else — Just You!! — Just Me!!!
Take The Steps Within And Without — Keep
On Going To Be All You Can Be — Within You!!
Within Me!!!
Nourish! The Good And Let Go Of The Bad —
Let The Negative Thoughts Or People Holding
You Back —Go Away & Find A Place — Not
Within You! — Not Within Me!!!
Look Beyond What You Hear —
Look Beyond What You See —
Go Forward In The Good That's Within
To Be The Best & All You Can Be!
Within You! — Within Me!!!

—Glenda D. Davis (Dunham)

I saw the sun rise today.

I watched as it swept across your face.

I loved you deeply as you slept.

You looked so peace full out of normal life.

I wanted to reach out and touch you,
  but, for fear of spoiling this beautiful moment.
    I did not.

I drank in your beauty.
  The color of your hair.
    The smell of your perfume.
      The set of your face.

I saw the sun rise today.
  It was the most beautiful thing I have ever seen.

—**Sean M. Loftus**

MANSIONS

The darkened mansion stands alone under a
  haze-enshrouded moon in the midst of
  a thicket of trees, each borne by timeless voices
  from the past.
The remnants of a circular drive and the strewn
  ashes of ancient fireplaces speak of gatherings
  now forgotten. Cornices crumbling.
Abandoned toys and lovingly dressed dolls
  congregate in the silence; daguerreotypes of
  lost urgings and recognitions.
At last the prisms of the dawn's early light
  reflect a rainbow to be sought in the
  gentle showers of the morn
And she, at last, moves toward the last vestiges
  of the sun. Alone but for the love.

—**Cynthia A. Nevins**

TWO MOTHERS: TWO DAUGHTERS

So tenderly
Your strong fingers
Glide through my throbbing agony
For my mother,
Gently stroking my face,
Soothing my tortured soul.

Softly, I turn
To see your tears streaming through my own.
For you, my elder sister, have suffered,
  ached, and longed for your mother, too.
Remove our tears and we cry for them yet.
Put out our eyes and we can see them still.
Take away our hearts and our brains afire carry them.

From this flowing flood of feeling,
I become bonded to you.
A Sacred Covenant is born.
An unexpected gift of compassion and love:
  at once a vindication and celebration
    of your mothers lives.

The marvel of the moment is this:
  Their roots remain.
  They grow in us still.
  And like a crucifixion
  Crowning us with joy and sorrow,
  Continue to resurrect in us.

Dedicated to Edith Golden Knore Hale

—**Carolyn Mae Hale**

INFINITY

In the blink of creation
our lives were forged.
Tempered by fire, softened by love,
our paths are formed as one.
Feeling without touch,
our hearts still rejoice,
the wave of light, leads us into Infinity.

—**Grady A. Clinkenbeard**

ANGEL IN MY DREAM

There she was her skin a glow
  Natural beauty from head to toe
With eyes of blue and skin of cream
Who is this angel in my dream

I dream about us hand in hand
Walking along the shore and sand
Underneath the starry night
If I knew her we'd be so right

I feel I know her and think she's real
She must be true for my heart can feel
The warmth of her touch and tender love
I ask for your help dear Lord above

I close my eyes yet another night
Hoping and praying for her precious sight
Suddenly she appeared in a glowing light
Like a falling star in its flight

As she moved to me so very near
The pieces fit and it was clear
With hair of silk and eyes that gleam
You're the angel in my dream

—**Eric R. Figueroa**

A SMALL THANKS FROM BEYOND

The loving things that I never told you
  For Time seemed to fleet so fast,
Have come to me afresh and new,
In this wonderful land beyond Past.
As I walked down the winding trail
Behind life's gray hung moss,
The little things in life became great
While the feeble important ones got lost.
With my perspective no longer obliterated
As in the other world — it's true,
I knew that the success I'd been in life
Was because of — and for you.
In fading years if I tried your patience
And turned oft' times days to years,
I'm sure you know I regret it,
For emotions were twisted with fears.
I feared reaching the end of my journey
And walking alone on my way,
But to my joy I found you had been there
Each time you had knelt to pray.
My seat was reserved and waiting,
A land of happiness spread at my feet.
I'm grateful to you for all your thought
In preparing my Haven Of No Retreat.
So as I sit in this sublime domain,
Be happy Love, in your life so new.
I will reap the fruit of your prayers
And my Dear One — I will wait for you.

—**Mary Kay Fleming**

A GUARDING "ANGEL'S" SHINING LIGHT

Three wishes come on a beam so "bright."
Making a glow in "heaven" above. So gentle
and real like heavenly "doves." Three
"wishes" are granted and gone someday
but not in good use for God I "pray."
Three "wishes" are "granted" again, in
good use for "love," and "peace," "willing
to men." Three "wishes" are great, but
not good enough to open God's "gate."

So believe with in him or tear "apart"
in trouble or sin. So wish your "star"
and wish it "now" because if not you'll
be "hurt" somehow. So wish your
"stars" God is there, he lives "forever,"
if only we could see till never. So "wish"
it now "wish" it bright wish it on
the "heavenly light!"

—Melissa Woolsey, age 12

WHAT HAVE WE LOST

They took the Bible out of school
Now we have lost the Golden Rule.
The Ten Commandments can not be found
Have you seen them any where around?

We know when we do wrong
But there is no rule to keep us strong.
Men with guns are everywhere.
Why is it, that they do not care
And murder others unaware?

It seems so easy to learn to hate
Love we need to cultivate.
When you know someone did you wrong
And I know sometimes they do
Then try to follow the Golden Rule.

We used to learn these things in school
But the Ten Commandments can not be found
Have you seen them any where around?

—Edna L. Strahm

PATH TO HEAVEN

Struggling throughout life ripped in pain
Cry out in anguish for happiness and peace
Disturb emotion weep helplessly inflict in vain
Supreme Power embrace relationship thru grace

Stress provoke sorrow in misery suffering
Rocky road to paradise illuminate vision
Sanctify energy influence the heart veering
Holy Spirit faithfully enlighten sacred decision

Guardian Angel skillfully guide spiritual path
Divine Spirit purify conscious assist nourishment
Recognize the precious gift of energetic faith
Luxurious wealth in heaven so magnificent

Strength of courage fulfill purified love
Knowing Jesus everlasting love is forever
Consider journey the powerful spirit survive
Physical pain how amazing agony is over

Mission complete results in proper death
Saviour precede judgment Celestial is share
Animate wisdom infinite love which hath
Rest peacefully dazzlingly radiance is there

—Edith Hirsch

THE STAR

Lo, the midnight sky is dark;
When a tremulous vesper star,
Brushes by on angel wings;
   to guide them from afar;

Weary, yet tireless, in their search;
Desolate, Cold, — The journey *long!*
   Hark! Behold ye men of
      Deepest faith —
Yon glorious star's message
      in song:

   Peace on Earth —
      Good Will to Men —

      —Florence T. Griffin

ANGEL'S WINGS

Can you hear those bells ringing
   above the clouds so high.
They're ringing out the news
      another Angel is about to fly.

The jingle of the bell is heard
      as we all look toward the sound.
For it's another Angel blessed in heaven
      for his wings he has found

Peace is said to reign in heaven
      a place where all would like to go
The quiet gentle solemn music
      shall help your faith to grow

To be in heaven with the Lord
To ride those clouds pure white
The chiming bells which hail so calmly
To every Angel's great delight

I know I am a sinner Lord
      but it is known that Earth is Hell
One day I'll earn my Angel's wings
      when I hear the chiming bell

      —Rosalie A. Gamaché

A PIECE OF HEAVEN

As I compose my thoughts,
   about Heaven and earth.
I seek to realize;
   what my life, is truly worth.

With such confusement and
frustration,
as I constallate a clue,
but with complete understanding,
as my thoughts are of you.

Such a dazzling inspiration of
Heaven,
within an earthly disguise.
I see an angel, with my believing
eyes.

A beautiful Angel,
with much sweetness expressed.
My thoughts of confusement,
are now at rest.

A glamorous piece of Heaven,
a gift from God to earth,
for I now realize,
what my life, is truly worth.

—Clint Brame, Jr.

FEELINGS WITHIN

I felt like a bird, who just got out of the cage to fly.

But still like a turtle, afraid to stick my neck, or head out of the shell.

Afraid to take a chance to let oneself grow.

After being sheltered for eight years, not seeing anyone, unless
he was along.

Might have made me act like a bird, who just came out of a cage, to
try her wings to fly.

For the first time, after quite a long time.

Like a child taking her first footsteps.

Wanting to do it, but still with shaky legs afraid to try.

And be excited actions, against all odds.

I did it, I flew. Flew like a beautiful butterfly, shedding from
her cocoon.

   —Sandra A. Reed

VISION FOR VISION

My eyes can no longer see the words of this poem without glasses,
And recently, even the distant hills have become less sharp.
The accelerating inability of my eyes to focus without help
Is Nature's clear signal that youth has departed.

Deteriorating vision in middle age is entirely normal.
Still, each day, at dawn, there is short-lived optimism
That this day will not be like those preceding it.
Reality comes quickly when I am unable to make out
     the hour on the bedside digital clock.

My weakening vision foretells the demise of my physical being,
Although I stubbornly fight a rearguard action against it,
Time is relentlessly stripping me of physical skills.
Twice the training of a decade ago fails to produce improved performance.

But, while my vision declines
As the clearest indicator of the flight of physical prowess,
My vision of the world and of life itself increases.
The wisdom of age is no small thing.

   —P.F. Doyle

JACK'S LAST HURRAH

Languidly lounging across the vast horizon.
A cold white blanket betrays the thoughts of spring arriving.
Icy fields, lone patches of green.
Release your hold Mr. Frost, so that we may enjoy the first new seed.
Sun brightly shining,
the bitter cold betrays your warmth.
We long to smell the flowers, hidden underneath your windy court.
Spring beckons from afar, longingly we wait.
So near and yet:
Love's blossoming courage must dig through the treacherous
white sea.
Is it much too bitter for Prince Charming to believe?
For all you waiting princesses.
Be they young or be they old.
Trust in your patience, soon you shall have your gardens,
rich in blue and gold.
The treacherous sea of white shall compose itself into a
passive sea of green.
With warm thoughts it will be achieved.

   —Michelle F. Przybylek

THE TOUGH TIMES

No one else can see the flame inside of you,
No one else can feel the pain you do.

You can make your dreams come true,
If they could only believe in you.

So let your emotions go,
let them see the real you and only
then they'll know what's inside of you.

Let them know your true feelings,
then they'll know what you do,
to help you get through the tough times.

— Corinne Hutton

MEDICINE MAN

There is a man who comes to all,
    Relieving suffering when he hears the call
He brings himself with all his knowledge,
To battle death close to the edge
And when they arrive so few others can,
Create a peace like the medicine man.

In his eyes he feels the pain,
His magic the cure to end this rain
With more than thought the remedy gives,
Not just a cure with heart it lives
Relieve so much very few can,
Bring peace and rest like the medicine man.

He walks away to another place,
He hears a call from another face
This he knows he has done well,
Much pain has ended as many can tell
Now he will travel as fast as he can
So fly like an eagle great medicine man.

— James Carmichael

A LOVE THAT TURNED ME UPSIDE DOWN

There is a love in the world, that is in four
    dimension; when you understand this love, it
will catch your attention.

A love that is real and a love that is true;
a love that is pure, you would think it was
new. But this love been around, since the
world ever was, preparing for man to show him
this love.

If I could tell, what each letter meant; it
wouldn't describe, what God has sent.
L is for long — suffering, because love suffers
long;
O is for overcoming, when someone has done you
wrong.
V is for victorous, in defeating Satan's game
E is for enduring, and taking all the pain.

This is the love that called me out, when I
was lost in sin; he picked me up, cleaned me
off and told me we were friends.

I believed him so I'm saved by grace and things
have turned around; It's good to know a God
that loves, who turned me upside down.

— R.D.L.M. Moore

FRIENDS

Yesterday we met for lunch
    It seemed so good to see you again
For so many years you have been my dear
    friend
Memories of youth, high school and after
Our numerous antics that brought great
    laughter
Strange how the years have flown away
Leaving us struggling to cover the gray
Whatever lies ahead lets say
Our friendship is solid day after day

— Mary L. Vaughn

I WISH

I really wish I had a friend,
    To tell my troubles to.
Just one person to confide in,
When I am feeling blue.
Or someone who just checks in,
And says "How have you been?"
Is that too much to ask,
Is it really a big sin?
If this wish would ever happen,
How happy I would be.
Then life might hold new meaning,
For my new friend and me.

— Kathleen Shea Fauset

REUNION

Our hearts met
    in kindred union
remembering not
        the things of yore;

we pressed on through
        a new door.
A bouquet of companionship
    like fragrant lilacs
    filled this vase
                to overflowing.
Two hearts gathered
            the blooms
                and
    arranged them together
                    once more.

— Jeanne Lauren Morreale

WINDS OF LIFE

Your heart it is so tender
    so precious a friend are you.
You showed me a way to heaven
no one else could ever do.

Your voice it is so gentle
it sings with a sweet melody.
You whisper my name so softly
it echoes deep inside of me.

Your eyes light up my nights
with warmth they touch my soul.
So close we are in the darkness
yet still, I feel their glow.

And when the winds of life
sometime carry us far apart,
remember always, my special friend
You have a piece of my heart.

— Brenda J Collins

RIVER OF FLAMES

When I searched beneath the rubble
to find that life I had lost, I
believe the passion I once stored
has died within the frost. Then,
by surprise a beautiful dove spirits
the will to live. For my eyes began
to smolder caught in the will
to give. The force of mind begins
to flow like rivers running wild.
A wonderful dream laced in passion
at the root a curious child. What a
rush to hold her close to feel her
breath down my back. My heart
full of flames — a fury I no longer lack.
River of flames, river of flames
a sign of the power of love.

— **William Blackman**

TRUE LOVE

We lie in each other's arms,
    holding the other tight.
We kiss each other's lips,
    tenderly with love.
We look into each other's eyes,
    seeing the one we want.
We hear each other's laughter,
    filling the room with joy.
We see each other's faces,
    and feel the love filled air.
We promise each other forever,
    as we quietly pray in our hearts.
We know we are for each other,
    because true love never parts.

*Dedicated to the women who is
the inspiration of all my
poetry . . . my True Love, Julie.*

— **T.A. Heller**

INTIMATE STRANGERS

    Intimate strangers,
Who pass within the night
They may never find each other
But in their minds they're clear in sight
    Intimate strangers,
Two lives who meet as one
With a love they'll never find
That burns warmer than the sun
    Intimate strangers,
So close but yet so far
They reach to hold each other
But it's like reaching for a star
    Intimate strangers
Are sometimes caught within a stare
But they are blinded by their vision
So this moment they can't share
    Intimate strangers,
Will search through crystal screens
Trying to find the soul mate
That lives within their dreams

— **Don W. Gamble Jr.**

DESERT POOLS

I love too much; I am a river
    Surging full steam, I seek the sea,
I am too generous, a giver,
    Love will not stoop drink of me.

His feet will turn to desert places,
    Shadowless, reft of rain and dew,
Where stars stare down with sharpened faces,
    From heavens pitilessly blue.

And there at midnight sick with faring,
    He will stoop down in his desire
to slake the thirst grown past all bearing
    In pristine water keen as fire.

— **Maggie Wiley**

THE CYCLE

Compassion draws the love from us
Makes us more than what we are
Watch as it turns into something new
A passion as strong as life

Passion makes us give of ourselves
Generosity now a ruling trait
See how it turns to a different thing
Love is now stronger than life

Love is the greatest this world can see
Nothing can make us stronger than this
Notice the change before your eyes
As love breeds into contempt

The contempt burns inside of us
Its flames the fuel of burning rage
Rage transforms into hate and pain
All that remains is an empty shell

This burned out husk that holds my soul
Cries out in hopes of finding more
I look around but all I see
Is compassion drawing the love from me

— **Kurt Turner**

HOW CAN SHE THINK OF ME?

Problems of life arise and hold us sway,
    As a ship tossed on the sea — to and fro.
What variety does she face day by day,
To think of me from her past — of long ago?

She may still be in sleep, deep sleep,
My name she may no longer repeat.
How can she think of me?
As I am awakening as from sleep,
Her memory of me faded, failed to keep.
How to expect her to awaken to me,
When asleep to my remembrance — has no key.

Her sleep — being ever so deep —
Will awaken as from far away,
Gently, my name she will say,
But awakened, she will be as honey is sweet,
My name, hopefully she will repeat.

If through my poetry — she will realize,
That it is to me, she will see with her eyes.
I am in love with her.
But if thinking of me within her begins a stir,
She can't help to be . . .
In love with me.
But for the key — How can she think of me?
*Dedicated to Karol Ann. My search for her
love . . . to find her once again in my life.
To make her aware of my love for her at last.*

— **Leslie Dyck**

THE PARADOX OF JUSTICE: CAESAR DEAD? BUT, WHY?

The questions are easy, the answers are not.
  Through want of appeasement, conflict is wrought!
Sensual the knowledge presented to soul;
Wisdom the swift sledge that hammers our role
On the anvil of life span; thus crafted each mold.
In sweet incarnation love's story is told.
In cruel crucifixion is embodied His plan:
Death begets life. The God-man saves man.

If act without justice is destined to fail,
Where finds man this wisdom, if man be thus frail?
Go inward! Search long. To reason our task.
The answer so written: to receive thou must ask.
The just hand of the smithy awaits our consent.
'Tis in the fire of His love in which we are bent.

Proverbs 3:6 In all thy ways acknowledge Him:
                And He shall direct thy paths.

—Janet A. Ticknor

BLACK WOMAN

In your heart there should be no fear.
Approach me . . . Black Woman is no animal.
Remember who you are and from where you've come.
I see where you're going and must take you back.
I rise up not because I desire to be greater than you,
but because it is time to make my presence known.
As seasons change, you do likewise.
You have become that which you wish to conquer . . .
now bleeding to death from self-destruction.

You speak of overcoming the White Man,
but there's hatred toward the Brother who has done so.
You struggle with the White Man for a place in society,
but you compete with Your Own for the sake of a name.
Don't talk to me about Hardships!!!
Black Woman knows it most . . .
you see, while you struggle with the White Man
for a place in this world,
I *battle* the White Woman for a place in your heart.

—MeLinda Smith

TRIBUTE TO DR. MARTIN LUTHER KING

He climbed a mountain and talked with God.
He rests now under the silent sod.

Who slew his brother in anger and greed?
With hate the hammer, and greed the need?

Another Cain — another Abel?
One's skin was white — the other was sable.

Why was he slain? To curtain his creed?
To murder his dream? To scatter his seed?

Today from the sod and from the steeple
A Voice is calling unto its people:

"We shall overcome — we shall all be free."
The dreamer's dream made manifest is called Equality!

To fathom the depth of such a sin
One must delve beneath the skin . . .

And comprehend the hate within
Can, thus, brotherly love begin?

Dedicated to Intervention Associates, Shirley,
Janet, Alfred, Mike, Phil, Virginia and
Mary J. Drexel Home

—Thelma B. Sussman

MARK 4/12

i visit stony silence
question still nothing ask
i should leave what happened
messages i don't know you
left looked no different than i
thought paint spilled would on your
cat shot out across the room
don't you ask me who cleaned it
warmed up there wasn't much
blood i was there between the tiles

—Ginger Lorentson

TRYING

Letting your mind
  Drift through space
Looking for answers
You must find
Trying to learn
Trying to grow
Trying to find answers no one does know
Thinking and trying to be the best
Learning and growing
The path to success
Thinking and learning how to grow
Is a better reward than anyone will know

—Meghan Miller

THIS GAME OF LIFE

We must play this game of life
  with hard knocks down the road,
Encounter many ups and downs
    while carrying a heavy load.
This game is like no other
    there's no difference — win or lose,
It's how you play this game of life
    while paying up your dues.
In between our days of youth;
    childhood memories shared by all,
And though we must partake of life
    we know "who" controls the call.
This mighty introduction
    teaches us the playing goals,
Of loving, caring, sharing,
    as wisdom steadily unfolds.
If crisis should surround you
    causing depression or despair,
Try picking up the pieces —
    you will score beyond compare.
We've reached the best life offers
    as the aches and pains appear,
While rushing to fulfill our dreams
    before the golden years creep near.
In flashbacks of our lives
    through faded pictures in a book,
Of the many who played before us
    that the ravages of age have took.
So play this final game of life
    keeping faith at the golden end,
Perhaps somewhere in the great beyond
    we will play life's game — again.

—Violet Hilderbrand Kane

GRANDMA

This picture we made is to say . . .
we love you in every way.
There is no Grandma quite like you.
Some Grandmas are old and gray,
but you are here to stay.
Some Grandmas don't have much to say,
we are glad you are not that way.
Some spend all day in bed,
while others complain about their head.
You are different,
you are unique,
you are on the go every day of the week.
When we come there's so much to do.
When we squeeze you tight
we want you to know
we love you with all our might.
So when you are feeling lonely or blue
just remember **we love you!**

—Rebecca Mack
Tracy Mathewson

SOUL-IN-WAITING

You left the sanctity of the heavens
to twice make your appearance.
A warm glow from within my being
both times marked your presence.

Your soul mingling with mine
basking in the maternal experience
quenching your thirst for mortality—
the hopes, the dreams, the aspiration.

Each visit curtailed so abruptly
left me with this knowledge consoling—
a confirmation of your existence,
of a child's soul-in-waiting.

You gaze upon me now from above,
waiting for a miraculous moment
turning the next visit into a lifetime,
a life that will be heaven-sent.

—Jeanne-Marie Marquis

MOTHER

My mother is so dear to me,
and will always be for eternity.
She is my very best friend,
and always will be until the end.
She's there for the good times
and the bad,
She mostly makes me happy and
rarely makes me sad.
She tries to be so very neat,
Having her for my mother is quite a treat.
She teaches me wrong from right,
and cares for me through the night.
She is as patient as can be,
and very seldom yells at me.
She loves me in a very special way,
and helps with my problems day after day.
I love her as my mother and no one
else would do,
I hope our friendship lasts forever and
always will stay true.

—Julie Bealke, age 14

My darling one
child born from child
whom I cradled in my uncertain arms
so terrified you would break.
Or
be just a pleasant dream
on the brink of fading to reality.
Beautiful child
begotten of my creation
You are the vibrant energy of my life
the eternal spark that warms my soul
and the pride that beams from my eyes.
Even though I am young,
watching you has taught me much
the very wisdom of the ages itself.
I see that the bonds between mother and child
surmounts even the greatest tasks of life.
You — my son
make me whole
by making me
Your mother.

—Jennifer Michener

FOR THE LOVE FROM MY HUSBAND

Steve—
You came to me when I was down,
And asked me, for my hand.
I have to say, I was afraid,
Because — of the term *love.*
I never really knew what love was,
And didn't want to hurt you.
But — You were patient and understood,
And knew just what I've been through.
I want to thank you for being there,
And showing me what love is,
It's such a joyous feeling,
When it's shared, by two in love.
We have two special children
Who sometimes drive me crazy.
But I for one, will never change,
The life we built *together!*
I Love you honey, forever!
Love—Your wife and Mother of Your boys,
Barbara

—Barbara Hendrickson

I BELIEVE I'M GONNA LOVE YOU

As the morning casts a 1,000 bits of sunlight,
And they shine like diamonds on the morning dew,
I believe that every single one is mine alone to see,
Oh, I believe I'm gonna love you.

If it seems that there are special stars for lovers,
And we see them scattered across the midnight
blue,
I believe that out of all this world,
They're meant for you and me,
Cause, I believe I'm gonna love you.

I'll take you to a magic place, where no one's ever
been,
Where there's Prophets made of flowers and music
in the wind,
If you wonder why I've given you these treasures,
Because you're like no one else I've known,
I believe that as we walk thru time,
The best is yet to come,
Cause, I believe I'm gonna love you,
Cause, I believe I'm gonna love you.

—Herbert I Shockley, deceased

TOO SHORT THE TIME MY CHILD

Child you amaze me with every passing day;
A chrysalis hatching into a radiant flower.
I didn't realize the time had flown so quickly.
I am happy for you and sad for myself,
For I wanted to spend more time with you
And dream that we could remain unchanged.
Did I give you enough love and attention
Or pass on my knowledge and ideals.
Will I ever know such things in my lifetime?
I feel as a stranger to your exciting new world;
Yet, know that I love you like no other
No matter what your decisions in this life are.
And as you grow, don't look unkindly on an aging man
Who sought only to do the best he knew how.
You are my legacy, and my pride and joy.
Show the world what a special thing you are,
And what I have always known you would be . . .
A treasure of immeasurable worth.

—David Ruzicka

HOPE

What am I looking for?
I don't know.
Maybe the hand of a father
on the shoulder of his son,
Saying, "It will be alright."

Or maybe a mother's gentle stroke,
As she brushes away the tears of her child.
The sound of a bugle,
As the cavalry rushes in,
Or a miracle yet to come.

A wave from the wand
of a fairygodmother
What am I looking for that has yet to be found?
The peace in a man's eyes
As his life slips away.

Or the yell of a baby,
Just being born; or just,
Maybe a hand,
From one who can help.

—Nick Hammerschmidt

TO BE FREE

In a world of darkness,
I'm finally free.
Endless hole of depression,
will finally let me be me.

No strings attached,
that's what they say.
I was so trusting,
to believe it would be that way.

The price I had to pay was much too high,
just to live another day
I will only ask you —
why?!?

Yes, you have set me free
but I can't find the real me.
So the battle was won,
but it wasn't worth the things I've done.

Alone with my tears,
but . . . I wanted to be free.
I didn't know that the endless hole of depression,
would still have a tight grip on me.

—Andria Davis

SECOND CHANCES

Being given a second chance
to love you,
instilled new hope within me.
It created a rebirth
within the shadows and gaps
of my life . . . reestablishing wholeness.

Our second chance . . .
unlocked a stifled energy,
enhancing the meaning
of love and loving.

Just remembering . . .
I experience the love
a second chance
can bring —

—Heidi L. Plant

LIKE A FLOWER

As the white snow falls outside
my window;
I remember you lying next to my pillow.
The sun would rise and we'd wake up
into another beautiful day and you'd
smile at me and what wonderful things
you would say.
How I miss those times when only I
could call you mine;
You were so pretty, like a flower,
in the summer sky . . .
A Princess of Beauty with nothing to hide;
only hopes and dreams of a hidden
child inside;
We shared so many laughs and emotions
just like the wind and the ocean.
Now we're far apart, but I
know we can never be too far in our heart.

—Zo

DID WE EVER HAVE A CHANCE

Over time we seem to have grown apart.
Now I find you're still in my heart.
As time passes I want you even more.
I wished you had never walked out my door.

I long to be holding you in my arms.
I still love you deep inside my heart.
Our love was one I thought would last.
But now I know it's part of the past.

Sometimes I wonder if I'll make it through.
I dread every night I spend without you.
Thoughts of you still fill my head.
Could we ever be lovers again?

I guess I'll never get over you.
My love for you is strong and true.
I'll never find anyone quite like you.
I'll always long to see your eyes of blue.

Did we ever have a chance?
It's over now I guess we'll never know.
Did we ever have a chance?
I didn't want to let you go.

—Ryan Cox

DESOLATION

Show me the way back to a home,
To the life I've always dreamed of.
Show me the way back to reality,
Where fact and opinion are different.

Show me the way back to my father,
A man who I've always admired.
Show me the way to happiness,
A subject I know nothing about.

Show me the way from this desolate place,
Where life is so unpleasant.
Show me the way from my ordinary life,
That I live one day at a time.

—James A. Pratt, age 16

FRAGMENTS

My life is just fragments now . . .
Separate pieces of a puzzle
That no longer form
A recognizable picture.

Such a short time ago it all made sense.
He was the husband and I the wife
In a comfortable home—
An acceptable social unit.
My future was secure—
financially and socially,
Predictable as anything in life can be.

I am suddenly adrift . . . .

The structure of my contentment
Has collapsed,
Disintegrated in divorce.

The shattered bits are scattered,
And I cling to the fragments,
Attempting to bring the vital parts into focus,
As yet uncertain as to the value of each piece
To the whole picture that will emerge . . .
Eventually.

Now there is a new role to play—
The scorned wife
Communicating through attorneys.

And there are decisions to make—
To live in this house?
In this city or another?
To keep his name
Or revert to my maiden name
That brings no sad remembrance.
At age sixty-six I am weary
Of grappling with the weighty decisions.

I must not be afraid to love again
No matter what the risk;
But I do not know what to do
With the word "forever" any more,
And I cannot relate to "commitment."

Love, security,
Independence, companionship—
Which is more important?
Are they compatible?
Answers to those questions must be important
But beyond my reach at present.

—Clela

IF . . .

If I laid you down in a bed of roses,
would you only feel the thorns?

If I filled your life with love and joy,
would you only feel pain and regret?

If I sang you a song of love and happiness,
would you tell me I sang out of key?

If I gave you gifts of love and romance,
would you throw them away, without a thought?

If I gave you my love,
would you give me your love in return?

—Joanna Samuelson

SUDDEN SHOCK

I remember it so well, as if it were yesterday.
The day they took our boy Tommy away.
He was so young our little boy.
He was our pride, He was our joy.
I remember his eyes, as they twinkled so bright,
at everything within his sight.
So glad to know he felt no pain,
or ever knew what time remained.
Our hearts they broke, our eyes they teared,
for another day gone came another we feared.
I still will never understand,
why God came down and took his hand.
At one he learned to talk and crawl.
At two to catch and throw a ball.
At three he learned right from wrong.
At four we learned that he'd be gone.
He was so young, and yet so old.
He could be weak, and yet so bold.
It's been ten years since that day,
the day they took our dreams away.

—Sharon Floyd McCabe

A LAST GOODBYE

Why did you have to leave this way
when I never told you what I needed to say.
All of my life, you've been in my heart
but your way of parenting kept us apart.
I needed a father and I wanted you near,
to know you and love you, ever so dear.
I'd always hoped we could sit and talk,
but when things got tough, you would always walk.
This time it was different, and you're gone forever.
I won't get the chance, not now or ever

I love you — I hate you — I just don't know.
Why wouldn't you let your feelings show?

It's hard to believe I won't see you again,
and will take some time for my life to mend.
I hate that you won't get the chance
to be at my wedding and have our one dance.
And when I have children, I'll want them to know
you were someone special, you helped me grow.

The next part is hard, but I just have to try,
I'll miss you forever — I love you — goodbye!!!

—Mary Ellen LeBlanc

SOARING WITH THE GOLDEN FLEECE

Say, Fleece, My Golden Fleece, did you know I
Live true, in the energy of amour,
And when we parked had no idea! Detour???
But when we left, I was on a high;
Did you know that in Schenley Park the guy,
The gal would secure with her untamed lure,
And Spirit would contour and make cocksure
You flew with melody bye and bye?
You did not know, nor did the water urn,
That Destiny had this day decreed sharp
The fact we would indeed blend into one,
And from one another a great deal learn
About the sounds of piano, lyre, harp,
And with each other have tremendous fun!

—**Letty M. Shaw**

APPLES

In the brightest of days my heart be pure
with colors of rainbows and droplets of rain.
The nights be long, will I see you again?
For ours is a love that shall endure.

In the garden of Eden is the day we met
with luscious fruits and a serpent that deceives.
The truth be naked and our souls conceive
In the garden of Eden I met Thee, Death.

Lament ! For thy soul is broken !
Pray ! with words not spoken !
Today is the day of thy birth.
Sin shall ye not to inhabit the Earth.

Oh, Thine apples be sweet
yet sour with divinities and deceit.

—**Karen J. Buechler**

JANE

I'm just sitting here thinking
about my beautiful friend Jane.
She's the most compassionate individual alive.
Her humor lights up my life like
the sunrise on the horizon.
Jane's hugs are as warm and gentle
as a kitten sleeping in a sunny windowsill.
While cruising in the Capri with the top down,
Jane's essence surrounds us like
her hair whipping a halo around her head.
When I see her tears,
those tears are the same as mine.
You see, my friend Jane has suffered
the same loss as I have.
We both lost the love of our lives by suicide.
We are the survivors left behind.
When I see Jane's smile it makes me
realize there is life after death.
We have only been friends for a short time,
but I know we will be friends for eternity.
God has sent an angel to help me through
this tragic event in my life.
God named His angel Jane.
Thank you Jane.
I love you and your friendship.

—**Lorelei Kuhrts**

FRIENDSHIP

That flower of peace (of love — of beauty)
Its petals are as those wonderful souls
Passing through my life —
And at a glance —
Another petal drifts downward — flutters —
And somehow — magically — is spirited away
But the fragrance is everlasting.

—**Ernest A. Botti**

SET A COURSE

I finally found the love of a lifetime,
So don't ask me to let you go.
My life has been like a ship at sea;
I've been tossed both to and fro.

My younger days have passed me by,
Some experience I have gained.
The wisdom to value just one true love.
This my goal I wish to attain.

In your eyes I see a love sincere.
With your touch I feel to my soul.
Your voice brings a melody of love that I hear.
With each kiss, your love, my goal.

To share my life with you, my dear,
No longer sail alone.
I dream of the day when we'll be together —
Set a course for a life of our own.

—**Shawn Michael**

E S C A P E

Escape . . . two mortals seeking the byway
which is most still,
except for the haunting melody of night,
the cricket's song, the wind in the trees

A warm summer's day brings heat lightning
which illuminates your eyes that shine
with a strange light
Even as i lie in the niche of your arms
surrendering to the touch of your lips
pressing on mine

I fail to recognize that I have created
overwhelming excitement
succumbing to the passion you may possess
and protest, and cry a little
to your crushing caress,
fearful that i may suffer, and yet i know
that you are lost to me forever.

i have known your lips, you say mine are
sweet
until that moment that our paths crossed
i was free and idle as the summer breeze
but now escape has ripened the meaning of
love to me
Though i go where people are and find many
tasks to do
the loneliness that i face is hidden in a crowd
where none will stop to question
but will leave my young heart to wander alone
with my memories.

—**Euphemia Hungerford**

295

ABHISHEKA

I burn incense in your name
that drifts into the solemn night
entangling with the cold, cold moon
shining with an inner light.

The Regents of the Seven Winds
bear aloft my dreams of you
to levels no adept has seen
where you and I are born anew.

Our spirits dance on cosmic tides
drawn between resplendent spheres
we are forever intertwined
illuminated, crystal clear.

Beyond the gates of astral doom
a flame within your autumn eyes
between the lotus and the void
I know where true magick lies.

—Edward West

Rain streams
through the night
moonlite shines
through my window
I am awake
and I am alone
and all I can feel
is you

The mystic glow of past love,
rekindled now
by my new loneliness.
I have seen the worlds of others
but none have held
my heart like yours.

My soul drifts into
the night
and I long to find you
waiting in the rain.

—Vaelei Walkden-Brown

RHYTHMS OF THE NIGHT

Kiss me morning
kiss me night
round exotic delight.

You
have
me

With warm embraces that unite.

Soothing rhythms
tides that roll,
hearts of fire
passionate soul.

When caressed
my body explodes,
electrons ignite
finger and toes.

Suspended

like a cloud, mid-air
Body

relaxed, going no where.

—Nické -Chantalle Young

HIGHWAYS

Ribbons of Highway
Leading to everywhere — or nowhere
Each traveler molding his destination
By the route he takes

The culmination of dreams
Or by-ways of disillusion
Fulfilling all or destroying
By the choice he makes

—Nelle Hopkins

flannel

I want to be the marsupial pouch

and later
when you dress

I will be red and green

the smallest bits
from your new pajamas

hiding in your bellybutton

cozy
and close

—Joe Camp III

COCOON

Existing in a darkened room,
All exits barred and windows drawn,
Held tightly in my own cocoon,
A search for self must come to pass.

With beating heart and open hand,
To seek out one of willing mind,
And strength of spirit to understand,
That all we hunger for is nigh.

New silk cocoon, no darkness there,
To still the music that I feel,
And open windows breezing air,
Into the soul I once had lost.

Repose and laughter follow me,
Past the depth of what they see,
All happiness to enter soon,
To cradle me in love's cocoon.

—Julianne Wood

THE WATER TEST

When you think you are so mighty,
Just stop and pay some heed,
You'll be gone and soon forgotten,
Memories fade with rapid speed.

As you're bragging of your value,
Won't you try a little game?
Put your finger in some water,
Pull it out and say your name.

While your finger's in the water
You might think yourself a fool,
But as you watch the imprint
You'll not think yourself so cool.

If you think yourself important
Or take a leading role,
Pull your finger from the water,
You won't even leave a hole.

—Clarence F. Rice

WOULD YOU COME TO MY FUNERAL?

You who ignore me in school and laugh at me behind my back
You who curse my name and snicker at the way I dress
You who think I am strange because I refuse to conform
You who are my brothers and my sisters, yet you still stab me in the back
You who are my own flesh and blood, yet you choose to spill mine
I say unto you my brothers and sisters, you are hypocrites
You represent the evil in all of mankind
You have such small knowledge that you don't see that you are destroying me
You don't see that you are destroying each other
If I were to die tomorrow how many of you hypocrites would come to my funeral
You who ignore me in school and laugh at me behind my back
How can you call me friend when you didn't even know me
You who curse my name and snicker at the way I dress
How can you say that you loved me dearly and you regret my death
You who think I am strange because I refuse to conform
How can you cry and weep over my lifeless body
If I were to die tomorrow
Would you come to my funeral?

—Shane A. Blake

LIFE'S QUEST

Pick up any newspaper, turn on any TV.
Robberies, murders, wars are all you're apt to see.
I'd like to teach my sons love of life and more,
To open the happiness, fulfillment, self-esteem door.
I'm not faced with each morning light
The fear of massacre, plague or terrorized flight.
I need not worry of drought or starvation
But guidelines for you, my sons, are my deep aggravation.
In this day, when most of us married so young
It's not unusual for children to have daughters and sons.
I, though young I may be, strive for the wisdom that you may see
That the strength of a man isn't measured by biceps,
But rather that a great man often takes small steps.
Be strong like the oak. It doesn't need staking.
Learn from the willow that can bend without breaking.
Stature isn't based on physical height, respect isn't won with power and might.
Never be too old to lie on the earth, to gaze at the stars or marvel at birth.
Don't be too proud to acknowledge fear, never be too strong to show a tear.
To find the rhyme and reason of life is a quest, be insurmountable, give it your best
This world is yours from sea to sky. Be proud, my sons, eyes, ideals always high.

—K. Clare

MEMORIES IN A DOLLHOUSE

Today I brought home a dollhouse for Mom, my nieces, my grandkids and me.
A dollhouse, you ask, "Why a dollhouse?" Well, for a tomboy, let's see.
For stories, and play and tales untold, for make believe, memories and myth.
So the great-greatgrandparent generation can be known by this generation—the fifth.
Each of these pieces has its own tale-rocker, sewing machine, secretary, attic and pail.
This was just like your Great-great grandma's rocker. Many a night it was the doctor.
See Great grandpa's toothmark in the arm? Imagine him little after seeing him farm?
I'd ride the sewing machine peddle, knotting the bobbin, she'd snatch me off by my noggin'.
The secretary was just like the one Dad sold, with rounded door and a desk to fold.
When a man at the door offered Dad money, Mom didn't think it was very funny.
Believing the old piece just junk, Dad named a price he thought was just bunk.
But the man grabbed what he knew was a steal, Dad hadn't a clue as to how we'd feel.
He was a man of his word so he was licked. The secretary was gone—and were we ticked.
Now we have the toy to remember the time of keeping your word and making a dime.
Explore the attic on a cold winter's day—you'll find what *everyone* stored away.
Vases remembering flowers from cemeteries long ago, darkened portraits we should know.
Great Grandma's wicker basket filled with her dreams, old parts for milking machines.
Great Grandpa's leather harness, a wicker potty chair, old lace, a blanket of horsehair.
This dollhouse has more tales to tell, but go now. Make your own stories as well.
Go feed the pony, ride the calf, Great Grandma will scold while hiding her laugh.

—Kathleen Flaishans

HUSBAND'S PRAYER

He works hard every day,
    Rest he knows not
A peace of mind for him I pray
    For peace of mind cannot be bought.

I give him all my love
I give him children too
But, the peace of mind for which I pray
Dear Lord will have to come from you.

    —Dixie Flores

PICTURES ON THE WALL

I often sit and stare with pride
    at four pictures on the wall,
But pride soon turns to heartache
    as the teardrops start to fall.
I know I'm being selfish
    how I wish that I could touch,
Each face that I am looking at
    the ones that mean so much.

A Mom still sees that little face
    in this boy that's now a man,
It hurts to see him walk away
    and take another hand.
I know that life will never change
    I'll just cope as best I can,
If only there could be a way
    my heart would understand.

I'll still sit and stare with pride
    let my memories see me through,
I'll pretend I hear them say
    MOM — we still love you.

    —Doris Halpin

A MOTHER'S TEARS

I watched a mother, as she cried
    in despair,

Someone she loved had treated her
    unfair.

The tears came from her heart, as they
    rolled down her cheek,

Just a few kind words — she wanted
    someone to speak.

To hear them say "Mother you are the
    best,

And I love you Mother, so let those
    tears rest."

I thank you Mother, for all the joy
    you have brought,

And for all the things you gave, that
    could never be bought.

Then I knew these words she had
    heard,

Because she started to smile, never
    saying a word.

    —W.L. Renfro

A MOTHER'S THOUGHTS THROUGHOUT YEARS OF CHRONIC ILLNESS

My children's laughter, my
    children's noise.

My little girls, my little boys.

The touch of their hair, the
feel of their skin

Once more I'm alive again

Where did they come from
and why to me.

How could this miracle ever be.

When did we love one another so
much.
When did I hold them, when did we
touch.

My love for my children, their
love for me.
Was it a dream or reality.

How could they have grown
up so well, while I was
lost in the depths of hell.

Dedicated to my four most precious gifts, my children, and to my loving husband, Gregory

    —Judith A. Stephens

NUMBER THREE

Pride takes me back to yesterday
    to joy that we went through,
One precious memory comes to mind,
    the thrill of having you.
Two came before you, as you know
    but we could clearly see,
I could manage one more son
    so you were number three.

My life was filled with pleasures
    when you were here with me,
If only time could be turned back
    to nineteen fifty-three.
I've memories now to hang on to,
    for now you're quite a man,
There's someone else to take my place
    I'll have to understand.

You were the nicest son there was
    and Alan—you still are,
If ever Dad and I can help
    you know we're not too far.
Don't forget the happiness
    we shared time after time,
Each thought I have of you today
    I'm surely glad you're mine.

So Alan, be the best you can
    in life, just do your part,
Now feel the love that's hidden here
    with pride, right from the heart.

Dedicated to and written with a lot of love for my son, ALAN HALPIN

    —Doris Halpin

GAY CLEOPATRA

Dark and upward-slanted at the sides,
Those eyes behind a golden pyramid
Look sad across the Nile.
The scent of cypress stains your dusk-colored skin,
Slowly spreading in warm waters
Where Antony once sailed.
Because you knew of too much magic
And had to keep it to yourself,
An asp lies coiled between your breasts.
In your land, at perhaps a different time,
The scarcer silver claims a higher price
Than all the gold you need to wear.
Perhaps, if you had loved your own kind
The way you desired the men,
You would not have had to die.

Once, in the darkness of Egypt,
I was you.

— **Lynette Ng**

CHRISTIANS AND TROLLS: A FAIRYTALE

A brother sends me
Dark mirrors of himself on a postcard.
Barrier defining barriers
Guilt, jealousy, madness, secrets.

Fun.

Never having been to Norway
He sends a picturecard with oblique messages
Two sides, script and pictures.

Affronted by the stupid little game,
But then I decide to play, disengaged.
Out-traveling the "traveler" and Grand Wizard.

Quietly I cross the bridge, hoping to evade him
Yet let him know Christians defeat trolls.
He redoubles his efforts.

Go to Norway (where you haven't yet been, brother)
Find yourself among comrades, but remember
In Norway there are no mirrors.

— **V.P. Lombardi**

THE FATE OF A SOLDIER

Fight well young man, your time has come
Your head's been shav'd
Now you can have your fun.
For if you rely on a string o' hope
Your journey shall be pav'd
So please don't mope
For your task has just begun.
Your object can be seen afar
So you best take cover and prepare for war.
Look! He's here! He's there! He's everywhere
'guess you didn't see it comin' through the air.

You fought well young man, now your time has come
Only God forbid that blow to the head
as your weapon malfunction'd, you lost your fun.
It was a time for sorrow as you were put to bed.
Worry not 'cause I show'd utmost pride:
a pride toward a soldier for a job well done:
a pride toward a soldier who deterr'd to run!
You'll now meet "Him" on the other side
least now you won't miss out on fun.

— **Daron Gabriel Crochet**

THE SEARCH INSIDE

I search the beach amid the wonder
Not far away I hear the thunder
The sand is seeping into my boots
As I step among the rugged roots
The storm is rising, the waves are crashing
The wind and sand compound the thrashing
My body aches, my feet are sore
As I trudge along the barren shore
For what I am searching, I do not know
I continue on as it begins to snow
It's cold as Hell, my lips are chapped
Before my eyes I see the fact
I've found my goal, my life is gone
I fall and watch the dying storm
The ocean's water runs so free
The cloak of death flows over me.

— **Ned Adams**

PASSING GREY

leaves have all fallen now,
leaving behind dripping branches   unprotected.
This is not my first storm,
but I fear it is my last
For with each new day
my limbs grow weaker, and
the grey of each new season
makes life seem colder.
The bark that once sealed my soul
has begun to rust away,
melting along with Autumn's tears.
And soon snow will veil my roots,
tucking them in   keeping them warm.
I feel Winter's axe chopping
and I hear Spring's laughter approaching,
but I will not be here to greet her,
for I sense the chill of Death's arrival
choking my weathered roots.
I can no longer breathe
        the grey of a passing storm.

— **Christian W. Reynolds**

THE JOURNEY

The road was long and narrow and steep —
no gentle place a foot to keep.
And every turn embodied dread —
who knew it led to the life ahead?

And on and on the journey went
till all the light of day was spent.
The "blanket" of night one grows to hate
fell — mocking our wavering, stumbling gait.

Approaching yet another cruel bend
we were most surprised to encounter Him,
then spellbound when we saw His pen
writing "Finished" over where we'd been.

Faintest hope, long absent, stirred within
when He turned to find us watching Him.
"Your life's blueprint, when carefully read,
showed this road led to the life ahead . . . ."

New purpose given; light on the path.
Calm acceptance swallowed pent up wrath.
And on and on the journey went . . .
dread surrendered, soul content.

— **Beverly L. Ford**

Rolling Rivers Run
The foundations of our lives away.
Streams of tears carve lines into
The face we show the world.
With people, images, objects,
We try to hold back
The ravaging of the waves.
Each eventually floats away,
A consequence
Of fate.
Staccato Speeches Stream
From the minds and mouths of the young.
Pebbles moving with the current
And no action stays the words for long.
Sand Slides Slowly
Fathoms deep.
Grains never to be restored to shore.

—Hope M. Porta

CHANGE—A GOOD SIN

My chains have been released
With the key of sweat and tears
As they rattle to the ground —
Freedom, out of weakness

Pride was my strength but
My tongue swollen
Quenching my thirst with a swallow —
Poison, my lucid water

Would I let them call me Javier?
Letting my rectilinear conscience throw me
into the swollen river Seine —
Pride, my only victory

No. I changed, conformed
Accepted the higher plain and made
The best out of sin and death —
Freedom, out of strength

That is what change may provide —

—Garrett J Brown

The rain comes down hard . . . , hard,
Like the bombs that rained on Iraq.
The rain tries hard to wash up
The blood that painted the land.

The land is telling the rain:
"Stop. No need to clean anything.
The blood and the mud have mixed,
Already they are one and the same."

The rain tells the land, "Hush.
The time for crying has passed.
It's time for digging the graves,
Prepare to bury the dead."

Replies the land: "But, no need,
The bombs have already done that.
The bombs and the tombs now are
One and the same."

The rain comes down hard . . . , hard,
But not as hard as the bombs.
To walk on the ground is O.K.
The blood and the mud now are
One and the same.

—Alma-Elvira

GET THE WORLD SMILING

Our world is crying, as the rivers flow
Into the oceans, polluting everywhere they go;
Changing nature as we all know it,
Something must be done, we must not destroy it.

Life is a gift, so precious and free,
From the eagles flying high, to the tiniest bee;
We are all meant to be here and share in its wealth;
We must all stand together and nurse it to health.

We're all brothers and sisters deep down inside;
We have to love each other, it's nothing to hide;
We must live with the land, give a helping hand,
And get the world smiling again!

—Janak

ALIVE IN THE GRAY

traveling to work by train,
life can be seen beyond the pane
among the crud and garbage,
between the rot and sewage
grows life,
various shades of gleam
isolated pockets that beam
good to see
        many colors exist in the gloom
Mother Nature
        has that way of making room
for creatures of variegation
that strive even within desolation
                rain can wash you in the waste
                let him shower your hands, body, and face
                sun can reach you when it's gray
                but you have to show her the way

Hope, a flower that can grow in us; all.

—Elizabeth A. Cooper

THE STORM

The thunder makes such a loud sound,
the lightning flashes all around.

The storm is moving in real fast,
I wonder how long this one will last.

I look over the fields and see nothing but black,
it looks like night from this old shack.

I secure the windows and bolt down the door,
and pray the walls will stay hooked to the floor.

Here he comes—old Mr. Wind,
a blowin' and a blowin' and trying to come in.

Maybe we should open the old cellar door,
and climb down the ladder to the old dirt floor.

Where the home canned food is standing in a row,
the potatoes in a corner where the rafters hang low.

Get the candle ready and we'll start down the ladder.
Now I don't hear anything—wonder what's the matter?

I opened the door to just take a peek,
when I heard the old barn door creak.

Out come the cows and behind them come Rover.
I just couldn't believe it—the whole storm was over!

—Lawana Sheldon

RAVENOUS

several times today
as I lay agonizing over the silent phone
I remembered that as each hour stretched by
seventeen hundred people on the planet died of hunger
and I wondered
if the statistics in the paper were relative—
and several times tonight
as I suffered through the kisses
I remembered that in some prisons
you're lucky if you catch a rat
and I asked myself
if I couldn't be grateful for the delicacy at my side
and fall asleep

—Kara Sue Johnson

WARRIOR OF TIME

I went to seek the warrior
who rules the edge of time.
The one who seeks division
between man's heart and mind.
We journeyed through the days with countless sums,
and lost only one star.
We journeyed with demons
from the dimensions of hell,
and became demons in our own right.
We traveled to the courts of the heavenly gate,
and gazed upon His glory and light.
We traveled under the deepest of oceans,
through caverns that reach deep within.
We saw the planets and all exotic places
wrapped in man's dreams.
We watched the miracle of life begin.
After the quest
with the warrior of time,
you forget who you are.

—MaryAnn Nelson

FEAR

At times a sense of fear troubles me.
Wars within our people I see.

Disturbing racial conflicts with whites and blacks
All I hear is "Leave or I will attack."

Innocent women being raped throughout this land
Trying to forget the face of that monster-like man

Homeless people I see all around.
"Look over there, one is begging on the ground."

Political figures not doing their job
Ignoring what is important, you have to sob

Murderers being found left and right
You are afraid to walk your dog at night.

Kids doing drugs and becoming high
I ask myself "Why oh why?"

People are losing their lives to AIDS.
They slowly die with a lot of pain.

Child abuse is commonly seen.
It must be stopped by you and me.

To stop our country from breaking apart,
We must stop to look and take heart.

—Karen E. Mirbach

WHAT AM I

Pizza, cola, leg of ham,
A crass combination in a man
Fear hides behind my face
With a deep set hate for the human race
Resentment towards those I know
All the feelings I will not show
Depression behind shallow walls
Anger walks my noble halls
All in a man who will not cry
And sits here writing "What am I?"

—Phil Brown

AGAINST THE FLOW

Exerting my physical being I find no rest
I have been looked over by the best
watched to see if I would fail
how I would swim against the gale.

Behind the rock I find some peace
the waves crash over and then release
the deeper I go the smoother it flows
across my back to the next water hole.

If I endure the fate up stream
and hold in safe water beams
then against the flow I must swim
to find the destiny of my being.

—Pam Kay

THE HERMIT

A life protected by boundaries
Other than mountains or seas
The brick wall of emotion
That is beyond any seige

Emerging from his lair
Only to achieve
Raptures of life
Fulfill his only need

Mental chains and bars
The Hermit's unbreakable bonds
A mental prison
Escape can't respond

The system delivered the fatal blow
A withdrawal to a world
Where demons can't go

Imagination is the monster
It must be fed
The red-eyes of fate
Truly blood-red

Step into a world
Where an inch is a mile
A place where reflections
Are blessed with a smile

An existence
Where loneliness becomes a friend
A marriage
True to the bitter end

Dwelling can be a mental or physical state
Achievement is the shell
To which The Hermit relates

—William C. Leppo

GIFTS

As long as stars still shine all bright
Our Earth will drink their heavenly light.
The sun will glow in burning might
And make the pain of dark take flight.

Then all the things of Earth will sing
For the true gift of life they bring.
The notes upon the wind they'll fling
So all that's in the sky will ring.

And when the light's declining ray
Begins to dim and fade away
The earth will watch the end of day
And into peaceful darkness lay.

—Jennifer Stephens

ICEBERGS

We are all Icebergs drifting through life,
and spirits who dwell within us,
are a sacred cornucopia of the soul.
It is the power with which we play our role.

Titanics are the chances that happen,
but the chips we suffer are nothing,
and mixed up people as we appear,
covet past lives of previous years.

So we stay drifting in space
until we may conclude our truths.
The journey brings us to the light,
as we dance towards insight.

A thousand lives. Not enough.
Will this search ever end to
bring a spirit full to tip the glass,
as it overflows with us at last.

We know not when the end comes,
or if there is an end for us.
Then we will glide along this space
and leave the world without a trace.

—Lynn Gilbert

STREET SCENES

I was walking down the street one day
and saw a man in a red shirt.
I wondered if he had a date tonight.
I wondered if he wondered about me.

I saw a couple on a bench one day
holding hands and talking.
I wondered how they met.
I wondered if they were in love.

I went to a supermarket one day
and saw a woman yelling at her child.
I wondered if she was yelled at.
I wondered if he would yell too.

I went to a cemetery one day
and saw a women crying over a grey stone.
I wondered who she was crying for.
I wondered who would cry for her.

I left the world the other day
and I looked down on earth.
I wondered what had happened there.
I wondered what I did not do.

—Holly L. Lashbrook

THROUGH HIS EYES

With mystery and wonder, I looked at life
Through his eyes!
So much to see, visualize and fantasize in life
These I now see,
Through his eyes.
Wonderful things abide, in sight and not;
Shadowy visions take on new life,
Through his eyes!
Pure sweet visions, oh so innocent and enchanting,
Old sights with new young ideas, sparkle and flourish
Through his eyes!
Oh, to see life anew is a dream come true,
As I now see it through these young little eyes!

—J.L. Hoke

WISDOM

I look at you and wonder,
What is it like to lose,
The things I take for granted . . .
A firm step, an all conquering ambition
To take life and shape it to your destiny.

Did you, at my age,
Feel that you could resolve,
All the problems of your world . . .
With confidence and a thirst for knowledge
That brought joy for life and satisfaction.

And now, in restrospection,
Do you feel that you have found
All the answers for which you have searched . . .
Peace, contentment,
And the ability to love
That has made your life worth living,
And
Can you say
I have lived it well.

—Audrey L. Basaraba

THE SOLDIER

There was the day he had to sign
His name on the dotted line

His days of preparation were good
And he was found to be in a different mood
But the departure date was understood

As the leaving date was near
He was overwhelmed with fear

It was the day for him to leave
But how he told me not to grieve

Letters and cards were all he had to send
To his girlfriend back home who was on the mend

The first time I heard his voice on the line
I cried with rejoice for the very first time

When he stepped off the plane
I realized the waiting was worth the pain
Seeing him face to face
Made me think of my freedom and grace

Even though the miles separate us apart
He will always be close to my heart

—Stephanie Renae Hammonds

AFFINITY

The rose garden
slightly scented with earth tainted raindrops
glints with the lucent arrival.
budless branches of frosty thorns
commiserate with once concealed nose numbing frost.
a smile creeps among the weeping willows
as we follow the crackling stream
crisp with February.
a sidelong glance
a sudden stab,
briefs the present with dripping slush
Corroding a heart
upholstered in lead.

—Mary C. Beaton

SEAPORT

Seaport, wrapped, bound, in a thick unpenetrable
Blanket of mist and fog,
Like a cat curled up
On the bed, paw over nose,
Sheltered from the world
Yet tormented by a merciless
Battery of rain and ocean.
One world, no outside, just
The drapery of haze
Holding in the town, a grey cloak
Enfolding, embracing the coast in its
Clammy grip. The green, grey choppy
Waters stretching out forever, but ever coming,
Ramming grey rocks, spraying grey shore.
Fog, stifling the sun's warm rays
Keeping color at bay, always holding in the
Grey cold, never escaping,
There forever;
Always on the inside,
Looking out.

—Katherine Halstead

SHE RAISED A NEEDLE TO THE SUN

A crowd of unruly mutes surrounded us in the dark—
A warehouse in a lost city of people trying to get in
When the Leader was raised in a chair on the podium—
But She merely smiled—said nothing—then left

Some women and men in the mob asked what we should do—
Then when I said "Follow Her"—most stayed behind—
As most do—and in that other world were Her words and Sun
—And still those that came—knew not what to do—none

They were smarter than we—I knew and read what She said
As they gave us a baton encased in writing at the door—
So I went to the table where Miss Emily sat and nodded—
So I signed on the dotted line—left the crowd there

Out back—the door led to the grassy meadows once more
And I walked with Her through fields of green and things—
And where should *I* make my stand I said—looking round—
"Here" She said or "There" of course—Anywhere—but There

Where She'd pointed I saw the sacred Hill—and knew
Long ago another Queen Recluse too sat in the light of day
Talked and wrote about keeping things quiet for children—
That She said was why Cleopatra raised a Needle to the Sun.

—Bill Arnold

SHE

She walks in silence, carrying a smile;
if only to ask for her friendship,
she would walk a thousand miles.

Days, became weeks, became years ago,
brother wrote these words to she.
How could he have known,
in their short time together,
that's what she would come to be?

—Sue Martin

FALLEN IDOLS

From their pedestals they toppled,
        and broke
into shattered bits, mired as in
        clay.
The pieces too small for pasting
        back together,
with no adhesive strong enough
        to hold.

                Love alone was strong enough
                but none remained.
                Only hatred and false pride.

Tiny cracks which first appeared
                unnoticed
grew larger with each passing
                year.
Till at last the fall, that
                thunderous impact
touched the lives of all who
                knew, and grieved.

—Barbara Brown

SOME DAY IS HERE

Caring
        With my heart, my soul
I love you

Sharing

Can't imagine what my life would have
been without you
Can't imagine what it will
be without you

Trusting

A cold wind breezing
blowing throughout
My inner temperature
fallen below freezing

The blanket of your nurturing
now being removed
desperately trying

To pull your covers
back over me
Shivering, torturing
I can't seem to stop crying

For Elaine—my therapist, my "sister,"
my kindred spirit, my "friend."
Forever and always I will love you

—Vicki Maria Carter

303

A BOUQUET TO REST UPON

Love is an interesting theorum,
Prophesying that the stars,
That can combine to unite,
Lend a versatile opinion,
To capture the rainbow with also.

Love is a sparrowed smile,
The happiness that rests in peace,
The simplicity of yesteryear's bouquet,
And yesterday's measure of candid frankness,
That was meant,
To make you aware of communication.

Love rests in nature,
Love adores a separate world,
And a revering peace.
Love's quaking comedy style,
Is the rendition of the years,
As we grow older, together.

—Lisa Miller

THE NOTE

A woman lay lifeless on the sodden land,
with only this note clutched in her hand.
 To my sweet child and blooming flower,
 my life has lost its control and power,
 I feel it my fate that I must die.
 Dear sweet child don't cry, don't cry,
 if I make it there before you do keep
 loving me as I love you.
 And when the day shall happen to arrive,
 when you are no longer living or alive,
 just call out to me and grasp my hand.
 And I'll lead you to the promised land.
That note was left before her father
did die,
He killed himself no one knew why.
She awaited the day when her living was done.
So she and her father again could be one,
as she lay there limp and her body cold.
Her hand was outreached so I was told.

—Carey LeRoux

MY LOVE, MY ROSE

You're like the beauty of a rose,
 I've seen it from the start —
The seed was planted carefully,
And is embedded in my heart.
I've covered it with love and care
I've showered it with my tears,
It has weathered many a storm
Yet grew stronger over the years.
As every petal starts to unfold
I see your tenderness there —
The fragrance is your special love
I breathe it in like air.
I am the stem you lean on
That's why we need each other, you know
And we grow more beautiful
With the food of love we sow.
You're the symbol of love it stands for.
You hold all the beauty it shows
You're my favorite kind of flower,
My one, my only, Rose.

—Catherine Signerelli

My granddaughter is getting married
 what a day that will be.
She will have a gallant husband
 and a wedding jubilee.
Her gown of queenly beauty
 is a vision to behold.
She will treasure it for years to come
 as her married days unfold.
With the organ music playing
 with her friends and family
She will think of all her wedding vows
 Hope to keep them faithfully.
And with her coming honeymoon
 in California's sunny weather.
They will plan their future life anew
 with lasting love forever.

—Mary E. Hein

LOVE FOR MOTHER

Oh I wonder if grandma is crying,
 as she looks down from heaven above?
Her dear son is sighing
 for the loss of his mother's love.

He walks the fields and creek,
 for in privacy to weep.
Mother knows how lonely and blue,
 cause she dearly loved him too.

'Tis very hard to sleep,
 because Russell wanted to keep.
His mother beside him for awhile,
 he walks yet another mile.

No grandma is not crying,
 for all her trying.
She has raised a son,
 and her victory is won.

—Linda Baker

TO A KIN

My thoughts are wide
 My money is thin.
Does that stop my pride;
How can I win?

I've bought and I've spent
till there was nothing left;
Not a scrap of lint
Left for the rest.

From one kin to the next
My presents I have spread.
To them, from me;
I wish the best that could ever be.

Now the time has come;
My soul has grown numb.
With a love deeper than sin
My life is worth less than a pin.

From them, to me
I fall deep into the sea.
With the love a kin
Pulling me deeper, deeper in.

—Mary Ruth Tirpak

REACHIN FOR YOU

So many times, I'd reach to the heavens above,
Just so I could withdraw, with God's gracious love,
An knowing that somewhere, that once again,
Dear God, would send me a very special friend.

Someone I could talk to with my trials
Someone that could, always make me smile.
Someone who knows, it's just me,
With a lovin, beatin heart, ever so free

Someone who knows, my ups and downs.
Someone who knows, Jesus, I have found.
I must say this friend, is so very special you are,
That in a very short time, Joan, you became my wishin star.

An I know Jesus, has a very beautiful, an special place,
For you Joan, in his lovin heart.
An I can just see the happiness, that enlightens his face,
By knowin that in his life and mine, you're a part.

So now when I reach into the vastness of the sky.
A tear of happiness, falls from my eye.
For God has given me a gift, of friendship dedicated so very true,
When I reached to the sky. An Joan, I found You.

*Dedicated to Joan Blevins, who's my very special and loving
friend, who's always helped me thru problems I myself
couldn't mend. Joan I love you, and of course Katie too.*

　　　—Ray Tyson

LOST

When you're lost, people say the best thing to do is to stay in one place.

I'm lost in a different way, I'm a stranger with my face.

I look in the mirror at a girl with my face, but she is different; she doesn't know her place.

If I were lost in the woods, I know the best thing to do would be to stay in one place till I'm found.

As I look in the mirror I don't see myself, I try to find myself by looking around.

People say I've lost faith in God so I'm a lost soul.

Other say I'm totally hopeless; I'm lost as a whole.

But who's to say if I'm really lost or if I'm not.

In this universe we're all lost; everyone's a single dot.

There's so much more to see than simply me.

There are new worlds, new beings, and life-forms to explore.

I'm not satisfied; I want more.

I've lived my life as one, done what's needed to be done.

Everybody's worried about finding their place, where they belong.

Some find themselves by a song.

Others find themselves by talking with other people; a friend.

Still some never find themselves till their life's at an end.

I've now found myself by looking beneath the surface, we're all there.

You just have to look, and care.

　　　—Emily R. Hedges, age 13

CHANGE

trees turn gold
and bare their souls
to harshest pelts
of nature's mind

no fists are made
to ward it off
oneness with
the earth is sought

the birds that once
found shelter there
eternal flight
to flee despair

yet one day they
must yield to it
and join the trees
that turn to gold

　　　—Julie

MARY

Is there a Mary
　　Here today
Who will give her
　　Heart and life away?
Is there one who will say yes
　　No matter what the odds?
One who will bear a child
　　To be the Son of God?
Is there a woman
　　Humble as can be,
Yet strong enough to watch
　　Her Son hang on a tree?
Is there anyone
　　In our world today
Listening to what
　　Our Lord has to say?
Is there a Mary
　　Here today?

　　　—Jennifer L. Thome

TAKE ME LORD

Why not give up?
　　The blind man says;
I cannot see the light!
Why not give up?
The deaf man cries;
I cannot hear it right!
Why not give up?
The cripple does say;
In his bed, he hates to lay.
Why not give up?
A young woman sighs;
Whipped, beaten many times.

A child by far
Has a stronger will to live;
So much life left,
And so much to give.
Take me Lord;
For I am yours;
No will to live through
Any more wars!

　　　—Linda J. Thurman

TO BE ALIVE IS POWER

I embrace the wild white clouds of freedom.
The rainbow blue horizon—rich as the taste of red wine.
To dance beyond the window into a
    swirling white world.
To open myself into a vast expanse of tomorrows.
Oh! Warm me!
Welcome me into the Sunlight of myself.
Leaping clouds
I envision that to be alive is power—
Power beyond vast sky whiteness
To Encounter the Self.

    —Carolyn Mae Hale

IN GOD'S OWN LOVING HANDS

What is three months, or ninety years
Of life on Earth, with its joys, its tears,
Compared to life forever more
With Jesus Christ at Heaven's door.
Through His shed blood our victory's won,
Upon that cross, it was God's own Son.
He gave His life that we may live,
What greater love is there to give?
So, Pat and Gloria, He loves you so,
That He sent you dear Miles, just to let you know.
Now, up in Heaven your son forever lives,
His love to you, He just gives and gives.
And until you get there, our Lord demands,
Stand reassured, your son is in God's own loving hands.

    —Paul T. Ceton

THE FACE IN THE CLOUDS

As I look around to see; A face was glaring at me.

    I can't believe I've come this far; it's not the sun, the moon, or a shooting star.

My friend went to Georgia to see The Virgin Mary; He took pictures, and it was so eerie.

To think on one certain day; That Christ will come and lead the way.

He took pictures of where she had been; and where she had said, "For us not to Sin."

But people do it anyway; they curse the Lord, and then they pray.

They pray for the sick and for those that have fallen; Oh where will we be when He comes calling.

It's not really for us to say; What time, what place, or even the day.

There are all different kinds of ways we pray; which one is right, or are they all the same.

As I looked at the pictures I saw a cross; I even saw what looked to me like a face.

The face reminded me of a person I thought a lot of; someone that reminded me of how years ago things were really tough.

She passed away, it was in July; She died of cancer, and no one knows why.

Why so many diseases have come to this place; or why it has swept away so many faces.

One of these days our prayers will be answered; There will be no more diseases, not even cancer.

    —Betty Carol Cheser

I gaze up toward heaven
filled with awe.
I close my weary eyes
and see myself.
I am kneeled at the throne
encompassed by light.
I try to see the face
of my Savior,
But the brilliance of him
blinds me.
"Oh my Lord," I cry out
"let me see thy face."
My Lord reached down
and stroked my hair.
He replied "Not yet my child
Thy time has not yet come."

    —Rita A. Woodward

ANGEL WINGS

If thou would but love me
For one magic day
We would fly on angel wings
And cross the milky way

I would give thee all I have
Love thee even more
And make thee captain of my ship
And pass by heaven's door

We would dine and dance on planets
Far beyond the stars
Where I would play thee love songs
On harp and string guitars

To kiss thy moist sweet lips
And make thy every dream come true
Would mean all the world to me
If thou would love me too

    —Ellen Bouma

HOW DOES IT FEEL?

How does it feel to hate?
To enter hell through the front gate.

How does it feel to be free?
To know that we will always be.

How does it feel to be racist?
To spit in other people's faces.

How does it feel to be scared?
To live your life without a dare.

How does it feel to be content?
To know how you feel deep within.

How does it feel to be angry?
To know that you are your enemy.

How does it feel to be alone?
To be tossed aside like a little stone.

How does it feel to deny?
To always ask the question why.

How does it feel to be happy?
To look out onto the calm sea.

How does it feel to love?
To know there is a heaven above.

    —Dawn Wilmeth

I am not my self
I have lost my self
I cannot find her
I do not know who I am

It is not that I regret marriage
The union of two unto one
But part of my self
Was lost in the process

I can never rescue my true self
People would think me crazy
If I told them I am not my self
I have lost my self

Perhaps someday my self
Will find her way back to me
Until then I have this foreign self
I do not know who I am

—Patricia Dawn Doty Thomas

DID I

You reached out your hand,
    I grasped on;
You opened up your arms,
    I jumped in;
You kissed my lips,
    I undoubtedly accepted;
You asked me to walk beside you,
    I ran to keep up;
You never said your hand would fall,
    Your arms would close,
        Or your lips would dry.
Did I grasp too tight?
Did I jump too high?
Did I accept too quickly?
    For now you walk without me,
        And I run to watch you go.

—Kimberly Dugalech

I SAW YOU IN MY DREAM

Last night as I lay sleeping
I dreamed of your sweet charms
I thought you were my Darling
I held you close in my arms

I thought you said you loved me
That you would always care
But when I soon awaken
I found you were never there

Please my darling let this
Wonderful dream come true
Let me hold you in my arms
And tell how much I love you

Don't let this be a faded dream
Please help it to come true
For I will always want to hold you
Oh darling say you want me too

Just say you love and need me
Please tell me darling you care
Our lives could be so beautiful
With our love we have to share.

—Peewee M. McCoy

WEDDING DAY THOUGHTS

Each day life unfolds more of its beauty to me.
Through each quivering branch about to bloom;
Through each new born child breathing its first breath;
Through each fragment of loveliness that it seems to keep
locked in until just the right moment.
In each changing season we can experience God's inimitable
handiwork.

Some days a person can sit back and enjoy the world around
them.
Feeling secure in the knowledge that tomorrow the sun will
rise, and a new day will have begun.
Today as I walk this aisle I am experiencing the newness and
change that life has to offer me.
Starting a new life with someone I have grown to love so
very much; enabling me to enjoy life through someone else's
eyes.
At this time I too can indulge in the comfort of knowing
that my chosen partner is part of God's plan for my life.
Security then covers my soul and I anticipate each and every
moment of my new life.

—C. Skjaveland

By the light of the glistening moon,
in the cool breeze of the summer night's air
I felt her spirit serenade me.

As I do recall well,
it was a gentle touch that reached my heart
and danced the songs of joys untold.
Majestically moving with each step towards forever
the minutes slipped into hours and I knew years would follow.

I thought to myself,
if I had made this journey of a hundred lifetimes,
surely this is the place that I would call home.
So familiar was this spirit that I had never known
so familiar was the colors of the world painted about me.

As I looked closer,
I perceived that the colors were a reflection
cast about me by the world I painted for her,
strange enough I cast no form for these to follow
but was compelled by a more natural form.

In reflection on this,
I wondered what manner of creature this may be
many spirits have come and gone without touching me so?
Many such have I spoken to, but have not seen.
How is it that I have known her?

Without a glimpse of a second, as to waste
I enthralled myself back thru the mists that boarded us
"never to return to these hearts' lands," I cried out
as the rainbow engulfed us in its unceasing paths
for a moment lost to question, is but a heart laid to waste.

By the light of the glistening sun,
in the green fields where the creeks paths play
I felt her spirit serenade me.

As I do recall well,
it was the morning of her beauty shone about me
and sung of timeless dreams of yet to come
with whispers of a warmth found in no words
where two hearts would only show as one.

—Enchantment

Dedicated to Alicia Ann Tobin;
To the woman I share my
Physics book with.
    Ich Liebe Du, Ken
—Kenneth Shawn Gagne

MY MOTHER, MY FRIEND

When you have a mother who makes you smile,
A mother who helps you see how beautiful . . .
. . . the simple things in life can really be;
When you have a mother with warmth to share
and kindness to extend,

A mother who really knows you . . .
then you know you have a friend.

When you have a mother who cares about the things you try to do,
A mother you can confide your deepest thoughts and feelings to;
When you have a mother you trust in, never needing to pretend,

A mother who helps you know yourself . . .
then you know you have a friend.

I cannot count the times I've needed you,
And the equal times that you knew what to do.

You've hoped the best things possible for me,
And shared my dreams of what my life can be.

You've consoled me and told me that things will improve.
You've always convinced me to make the right move.

Yet all through this you've let *me* be *me*.
Because *me* is *you*, as I've come to see.

—Suzi Tallent

GOOD OLE DAYS

Growing up in the Fifties and Sixties was great
Hardly knew of most hardships, being a kid was great

With my cousin and I, we built soapbox cars
Roller skated up and down the streets

Snowfall came, meant no School, snow sleds
We even improvised with smashed garbage can lids

Trucks' inner tubes, we would sled for a mile
When sledding finished, there were big smiles

We knew Grandma had made something hot and warm
Hot chocolate, vegetable soup, grilled cheese fresh from the farm

We'd visit Joe's house, he had trains
Everything from his Father's imagination

Big trains, imaginary hobos, houses and people
We would have fun, it was dazzingly to our brains

Then on Sundays after Church and Dinner
Miss Mary's Soda Fountain Shop, Sundaes were a winner

Our second choice was jaw breakers or ice cream cones
At our Uncle's farm, we looked forward to home made ice cream

Of course my cousin and I would take turns on the churn
Picking peaches, blackberries, cracking nuts

This would remind us of Miss Mary's Soda Fountain Shop
Going to School we would buy two for a penny cookies

And two for a penny candies, load our pockets
With that! We would have money for School Lunch

Wearing out our knees on our jeans, shooting marbles
It wasn't odd to see patches on jeans at the knees

Being scolded from being on your knees, all the time
Every Friday we looked forward to our allowances every time

—Dicky R. Overstreet

Welcome to the show,
I just thought you ought to
know, that the victims have
arrived, it's amazing they've
survived.

Come and see the trip,
the adventure to my mind,
my soul about to rip, let's see
what treasures we can find.

We'll comb my very soul,
then we'll put it in a bowl,
mix it up, and pop it in,
let's begin, let's begin.

—William L. MacKay III

WHY DIDN'T I STAY?

Last night I dreamt
that you
Lived in a golden
shoe
And that a king who
was very keen
Picked you for his
wedded queen.
There was another
king
The two were to fight a
duel over you.
Just as the swords
started,
I jumped out of bed and
away I darted
Down to the front
door.
Then, I stopped and
thought
Why didn't I stay to dream
some more?

—Marilynn Potter

A SKATER

A jump, a spin,
a turnabout,
The cheers,
the applause,
the exuberance of the wind.
Gracefulenss in motion.
A leap in the wind;
will I fall?
The friction of the ice;
confidence in the spirit.
A rush of blood
flows into the heart.
One more minute;
Sixty seconds to be exact.
What will happen?
Do I convene?
A harrowing experience;
when will it stop?
With one final jump
I hear the crowd.
They are on their feet.
My journey accomplished
and everfelt.

—Judy Darene Oreste

A HANDLE-FREE SUITCASE

I need something without a point,
to prove there isn't always one.
And today, I should die,
to express my life,
and I can live,
instead of simple existence.
I need a spark,
and a small campfire,
but then a cooling shower,
that death may be as a confessed lie.

And, though cliché,
with all life comes death
as with rejection —
eventual acceptance.

My life seems pointless,
but who says there always is one?

Or is that something I have to prove?

—**Jennifer Parsons**

A PIECE OF VICTORY

Pick the corn
Pick the rice
Pick the cotton and make me rich
Make me lunch
Make me dinner
and make me bigger than I already am
Make me happy but don't make me mad
Do as I say and everything will be OK
That's what they want me to believe
But I won't
For I believe that the tables
will be turned one day and
I or shall I say we will
be in the lead
Because you can't force us not to have
a mind
not to think
and not to dream
But one thing we have taught you is how
to be AFRAID

—**James L. Brooks**

WHAT GOES AROUND

I.   What goes around comes around,
     this you can bet.
     We all do things to others that
     we forget.
II. But as sure as the night
     follows each day, these things
     will catch you and block your way.
III. Do unto others is more than
     a rule, life has many teachers
     in its endless schools.
IV. The things we do that cause
     others pain, these things
     will catch us and stop us
     like a clog in a drain.
V.   Sometimes we do things when
     nobody knows or we do it in
     secret where it won't show.
VI. But it will catch you sleeping
     on the sunniest day. You'd
     better beware, life
     will make you pay.

—**Johnny McNeil**

POINTED PONDERS:
A SPRING CACTUS

What lies beneath these spindles of bone?
Green skinned crevices;
Bloody red petals and sunlight blooms.

So valuable as to be protected;
With porcupine quills? Ready to be thrust.

Hidden treasures?
An unknown cure?

Tiny spears of shade from a fiery sun.

—**Ronda Collier**

A FEW THOUGHTS

Riding the Wings of the Storm
Yet, they expect you to fit in with the Norm
Hell Fire feeds their tales
Sneak out the Back Door and set Sail

It is time to leave
            Time to go

What's Flying Through
            your mind?

Is it the Immaculate
Dream of Being
The idea of Climbing out of
The Stenches of their Hate

But what can you do?
      Where can you go?

Do you want to cry?

      Maybe you want to die?

Know Why?

   Because
Everything you know

   is a Lie

—**Richard Montoya**

THOUGHTS

Wings so wide,
Legs so fast,
Canyons so deep,
Lands so flat,
Mountains so steep,
Skies so blue,
Clouds so soft,
Air so loud,
Lights so bright,
Waters so wild,
Rocks so weak,
Trees so bold,
Darkness so calm.

Love, life, joy, peace, hope, laughter,
forgiveness, Jesus Christ, Holy Ghost.

God, the Miracle, created this for His children.

Then there was Satan.

Words so stationary,
Hearts so hard,
Minds so strong,
Eyes so blind.

Thoughts are you.

—**Rebecca Kyle Tingle**

BALANCE

Deliberate and determined;
Mountain standing so rough and jagged.
With time and the elements
gentle, softer attitudes
come and settle into his being.

Savoring life's fantasies
A woman with untold sacrifices
structuring her shadow;
With love brimming follows the storm,
with her warm reviving sun.

His base, sharp edges
cutting a righteous reality
are smoothed by her astute simplicity
creating a home of love, patience and respect.
From this balance   me.

—Jane Trombley Serra

A DEEPER LOOK

I see a Utopia,
Of snow and love and joy.
You see a house,
Which isn't energy efficient.
I see children laughing and playing,
The future expanding their horizons.
You see little nuisances,
Threats to our home's precious landscape.
I hear amazing stories,
Told by people loving to reminisce.
You hear boring anecdotes,
Babbled by old people clinging to the past.
I adore the snow,
Fresh and pure it layers and cleanses the earth.
You curse the snow,
Complaining of how you must shovel it.
I love our home,
A dream come true for me.
Please look beyond the frigid exterior,
And see the warmth I see.

—Lenny Giuliano

TRANQUILITY

Miles of ebony sea
Ceasing illusively
Upon the magenta skies

Magnetic progression
Then waning still
As ivory fingers caress
Its grainy shores

Patchwork heavens
Enveloped in sullen clouds
Sparse black crystal brilliantly freckled in gold

A meandering coast
Anonymous and quiet
A cool scent of salt air
Kisses my skin

Nights breath
Cradles my soul
Utter peace —
This tranquility

—Ramona Buchlmayer

THE WOMEN'S HOUSE

Bring back the women's house
Where we can bleed and laugh and cry
together, til we run dry.
We will light a fire and be warmed.
We will tell stories and jokes
and gossip. We will sing and dance
and read poetry, and forget the life
outside the door for four or five days.
More if we're lucky.
We will stitch and sketch and write
and count, the moon's journey
and ourselves, fortunate.
We will teach our daughters.
Men shed blood together in wars.
We shed ours in joy and celebration,
In the Women's House.

—D.H. Garro

SUN RISING

The morning dew upon the plants,
reflects a rising sun dance.
The sun's brilliant colors,
shone through one another.
Purple, lavender, violet blue;
there's red, orange, and yellow,
aqua too.
So many colors in a rising sun,
you'd think it was many
but it's only one.
You'd think the colors would be there long,
lying lazily in the sky.
You didn't think that they would die.
But you're wrong.
For the colors have now faded and gone.
Oh, do not fret my friend,
It is surely not the end.
For another rising sun dance,
is just around
the bend.

—Diana LaGrandeur

MAY AT NAPLES

Many a day it seems will pass
'Til in thine arms again, at last,
With thee to see and not regress
To distant homes where now we rest.
And in some fleeting thought so glee
My hopest thou stop'st to think of me,
And tarry there on singing sands
Again and hearing gayly bands*
Wherefore we trod'st once before;
    affections giving tenderly
    I know now how thou'st thinks of me.
Those moments which we so adore
Do come to flee so fast!

*The crashing of the waves along the shore

*This moment of sweet reminisce and inspiration
came upon me at Brandy Pond, Naples, Maine,
where I had been with my dearest Samantha
several months earlier. How I longed
to walk with her again on the shores
of Manchester, Massachusetts.*

—River Conte

DECEMBER WITHOUT SNOW

Snow is melted.
December is without snow.
There's a breeze of cold winds that blow.
The winter snow has gone.
December looks like spring.
Nobody needs to be alone.
It's about time the birds begin to sing.
Christmas is around the corner,
But where is Jack Horner?
But instead it will be Santa Claus;
That is when we will stop and pause
To do a little bit of thinking,
And there will be a little bit of singing.
WHERE, O' WHERE is all the snow?
That is what I would like to know.
There might be snow at Christmastide,
Then it will be a Merry Yuletide.

—Rayola Pearl Miller

CHRISTMAS

One time I read, when I was small,
How the great ox, lodged in his stall,
At stroke of twelve on Christmas eve,
Will bow his head down on the sheave.

How all the birds and earthbound things
Can feel the beat of Angel Wings
And Shepherds watching on the plain
Hear, once more, the heavenly strain.

God, keep my faith in everything.
Please, let me hear the Angels sing.
Let all mankind, upon this night,
Bend an ear to heavenly flight.

Let us hear music, from above,
To reimbue us with your love.
For love, alone, can shed the light
To guide us through the darkest night.

—Ruth S. Ozanich

EPIPHANY

Walking barefoot over pointed pebbles,
hard at work on the path,

As a swarthy sparrow
pecks away at the corn,
spying on each other,
swallowing together,

Darkness is never the same twice,
and if lightness were foretold
it would be unbearable,

Who wants to pay the price
for this finite ride,
a juggler, a magician, a jester, a wizard,
a ticket to oz,
the precious present,

A fighter bomber fills the sky with a roar,
the sparrow lifts her head, listens,
waits till the sound has gone by,

So do I.

—Mary Jean Thompson/Stanton

WE ARE

But who could know that this speck of sand
in life's tide, could conceal so
much color from the naked eye.
Filled a heart with love and knowing.
Green trees, blue skies . . . and life.
Look oh wise years: into time's crystal ball.
Let not one moment be in vain,
For love lost is never to be regained.
Know its joys, and life will be rich and giving.
Know of what we are, that we may give the same.
Strength, secrets, — wrapped packages with
brilliant ribbons.
Inside tomorrow, parts of yesterday,
thoughts of forever.
But who could know that this speck of sand
in life's tide, could conceal so
much color from the naked eye.
We are.

—The Rose

DAY AFTER CHRISTMAS

The sun is shining on the snow below,
Ice everywhere, traffic is slow,
A chill in the air, the evening's nigh,
Soon there'll be stars, high in the night sky.

Frost on the windows, frost on the panes,
Ice on the streets, ice in your veins,
It's the day after Christmas, out
in the Colorado plains.

Soon it'll be New Year's, soon a new day,
Soon we'll be seeing the snow melt away
Spring will come and with her the thaw,
Trees will bud with leaves artists draw.

And so it goes the cycle of life,
Some in luxury, some in strife,
Nature sings her glorious song,
Life begins, again before long.

—Keith Bell

STUBBLE

The stubble peers through crusty snow
as if to test December air
and send the news to ground below
that in the ice they droop, impaired.

A crystal casket came with rain,
unwelcomed here a day ago
but stubble stands may not complain
for in the mist the jewels grow.

Their shiny rind invites the sun
to dance to music in the breeze
and finish there a task begun
of freeing diamonds from the freeze.

But is not stubble something dead
that bore its life in season past?
Can we deny that here instead
there is a life in life that lasts?

—Earl F. Fashbaugh

LOST

Lost in a cloud of a memory
A dream that will never exist
Yet somehow, it's unforgettable
Held tightly in clenched fists

Misplaced in a world of despondency
Uncertain and unlikely to change
Feeling stranded, alone, abandoned
Living a history that can't be rearranged

Wandering aimlessly without a purpose
And with no apparent direction
Striving endlessly and unsuccessfully
To reach an impossible sense of perfection

Searching for the person within
An identity smothered . . . denied
But finding only desolation
A shell with nothing inside

—Gail Lynn

MY BEST FRIEND —

We played football and baseball.
Climbed the highest tree, listened
to the same music we never knew our
destiny.
But we were friends and we
had fun, we were two of a kind.
There wasn't much we haven't done
we thought of at the time.

We've laid our army down, and our
toy guns too.
No more tree houses no Captain Kangaroo.
You were my best friend and I was yours
too.
I stayed beside you 'till the end;
Oh God what drugs can do!

It's been a while since you've been
gone I still recall the day.
What drugs you had taken took
my best friend away.

—Donald D. Smith

MISSING YOU

I've got things to say
But the distance — gets in the way
What we had, and what we are
Bridges across the distance
Hoping to reach each other
My thoughts come one after another

CHORUS:

Trying to tell you that missing you . . .
Missing you is not an easy thing to do
REPEAT:

But memories fill my mind,
Like a forest of green
There lurking the feelings, yet unseen
If I could tell you all I feel
Then I would be as you are
But my mind can't reach that far

So please believe me, when I say

Missing you is not an easy thing to do

CHORUS:
REPEAT

—Brenda LeeDee Sunstrum

No! Why should I listen to you?
You, who tells me not to do this
Not to do that
When I stand here and watch you
Do it yourself?
Why should I listen to someone,
Who says not to do what they do
Or say what they say?
Why can't I follow the truth
The example you set
When you light your cigarette
Or steal or cheat?
You want me to follow a lie
A hypocrite?
You live in a lie, and I will not have that
For me.
I will do as you say not to do
But not for you.
For me.

—Brittany Durrett

TOO LATE

I wandered through the neighborhood
painted orange with setting sun
And wondered when this wall I'd built
had really first begun.
I looked upon the flowers growing
wild under foot
And gathered all my memories that
dust the mind like soot.
What caused this wall to grow until
I could not see
The sorrow and pain of others who
seemed so close to me?
It's much too late to chip away
this stone within my heart,
And, yet, I cannot help but wonder,
"When did all this start?"
Maybe someday I will throw away
all the fear and pain
And start my life all over, for
the first time . . . once again.

—L. Parrish

THE FALLING STAR

There is a star that twinkles bright
in everyone's life. That star is,
usually, radiant, with all the brilliance
of a fine gem.

Sometimes, this star loses its
brilliance. It begins to fall into the
"BLACK HOLE" of eternity . . . As it
falls through the 'eons' of time,
it becomes lost and forgotten.

As time goes on, new stars appear,
twinkling brightly, and spreading rays of
hope for the future, as they bring the
luster back into our lives.

Once in a while, that falling star will
reappear, only for a moment, and then,
quickly vanishes into the vast universe
of life.

This falling star is known as:
"LOST LOVE"

—Valerie C. Martinez

Turning swiftly away from any warmth
    of being
Running from the darkest of shadows
    called myself
Pushing further and harder against
    love or needing
Falling deeper into this pitiful wasteland
    of despair
Moving slightly up towards a blinding
    thought of light
Knowing there should be no hiding
        if only for these feelings you
        might share

—**Tamara Jones**

RESOLUTION

From this world will I ever be free?
    From this pain causing such misery?
From the doubts that linger in me?
While my life passes through these days.

From the strangers met on the street,
from the neighbors I chance to greet.
From the top of my head to my feet,
I feel a guilt of all my frays.

From the hours passed with loneliness,
from the hopes crushed with honestness,
from the plans thwarted with bluntness,
I walk daily through this maze.

From the despair deep within me,
from the darkness, surroundingly,
from the ways called "common decency,"
I escape in a deep sleepy haze.

From the fulfillment of Bible prophecy,
from the innate knowledge given to me,
from my soul going to a destiny,
I yield to God, my life, His ways!

—**Elsie Holland Babcock Boyles**

PERILS OF A PAWN

I'd like to find the zealots,
    The ones who saved my life.
I owe them a debt of gratitude
For my expertise on strife.

Negative aspects of emotion,
The gamut I know well.
I've learned nothing about heaven
But I've experienced total hell.

I knew at once I wasn't wanted,
Even before I could state my case.
It was manifested by voice and feeling,
And, I could read it in each face.

The attention was truly effusive
Each day and every night.
Many gained their pleasures,
Although they knew it wasn't right.

Pro-choice and pro-life argued bitterly.
Who considered my possible strife?
My birth was not my decision
But I must suffer the rest of my life.

—**Daniel H. Lennox**

MAN'S INVASION

A perfect summer evening,
    Filled with wind whispering through the
    trees and the bird's serenades.
All bathed in the sunset's hues.
The magic is broken by a sleek, dark
    car racing uphill.
Then the whispers of the young couple
    next door float to my ears.
Next the sounds of a television sitcom
    break silence.
So I shut my book, which wasn't being read
    anyway, and go inside, where man blocked
    out nature.

*Dedicated to Rev. John Silbert, for
inspiring me to believe in my work.*

—**Lori King**

I have worked so long,
And yes, hard
To gain the elements of my belief.
But now
The doubters path
Comes 'round again,
And pulls me at all levels.
A little indecision in choices
Shows through me;
From foundation to peak
My self, my body, my actions, my works,
How can I maintain my foothold?
I want to be hungry:
Hungry for food, for life, for sharing,
Hungry to enjoy
Everything that comes my way.
Not just to be eating, breathing, exchanging;
I do not want
To exist
I want to live.

—**D.E. Carney**

READ TO ME

Read to me. Please read to me,
    For I have need to hear your voice.
Read of love and power,
Of sun and shower,
Of new and old,
Of heat and cold—just read!
Read our years of growing,
Read as though you are knowing,
That should you fail to read to me
I would know you had gone
Where I soon would be—just read!
We have come so far, please, don't fade out.
My sight is gone and you are deaf.
I think of you as me—myself.
You surely know my voice is weak
From yelling so, to make you speak.
Just read, dear one,
Life together is so much fun.
Read to me! You know my need;
Damn it! READ!

—**Mary S. Shepherd**

GOING HOME

She has had many lovers in the past but
  There was only one she wanted forever:
Slim of hip rippling muscles as he
  Held her and called her his own
Promising his love.
  His fickle heart exposed itself
In the arms of her close friend
  And something within her mind
Fractured—like a bad break in one's leg
  Set by an incompetent doctor—
Never to heal correctly.
  Their traitorous blood flowed together
As the gunshots pierced their flesh
  Avenged, she entered the
Asylum that she now calls home.

  —Elaine L. Sapriken

AUTUMN'S GOLDEN GLOW

The golden glow of autumn
  Presents in varied ways:
In mellow rays of sunlight
On clear September days;
Again in strollers' faces,
As they browse thru orchard . . . wood;
In river's clear serenity
Where once a green tree stood.

The gleam of harvest produce,
As it enters granary . . . crib,
Is reflective of the reaper's face
In his thankfulness, ad lib.
This special glow of autumn
In memory's golden store
May serve to warm our hearts
When winter's chill sweeps o'er!

  —Marge Toelle

SONFLOWER

(A poem about Vincent vanGogh.)

Reflected rays of hea'nly light
  Disguised his terrors and his fright.
He stood erect, head held tall,
And with bright facade, hid it all.
Dark hollow chord of great remorse
Whose bitter juices took their course
And poisoned tender seeds in bloom.
Eccentric life received no room.
Mask'd despondence and despair;
The truest feelings hidden where
Not a man could penetrate;
Not until it was too late.
Song birds pecked the bloom apart,
Tearing out his tender heart.
And with his precious gift bent down,
He fell down dead; down to the ground.

*Dedicated to my grandmother, who taught
me the magic of words, and the teachers
who never gave up teaching me how to make
the magic with words. With all my
heart . . . Tanya*

  —Tanya E. C. Fix

HEAVEN'S DOOR

I sat on the steps at Heaven's Door;
  Whipped and beaten—could take no more!
Doctors and nurses hovering above,
Their work of care and that of love.
Only God could save my shaken life;
That of being a beaten, battered wife.
Days went by, months it did seem
They cared for me, they did not leave.
If prayers were answered and I did live,
How much more could I give?
A life of beatings, God took a stand;
He chose the best and took my hand;
To walk the way into Heaven's Door;
Not to be whipped or beaten no more!

  —Linda J. Thurman

MARCH 8th

  Floating through a dark cold
place towards another world.
  She said she didn't believe
you, but you would show the girl.
  You would make her hurt so much
she wouldn't want to live.
  Ripping out her heart, destroying
her mind, no more love to give.
  But was it all worth it?
  You smile to yourself.
  To lie in your grave, your own
personal hell.
  You once called her a goddess,
but how could you have lied.
  But heroes never crumble and
a goddess does not cry.
  You shiver to yourself, you're
freezing to the bone.
  Death is the ultimate sin,
but it was your greatest pleasure
known.

  —Denise Neukum

THE RIGHTEOUS

As you hold your head high,
  You fail to see the beauty of the sky,
In your bold state,
You believe you administrate.

Let the truth be told,
You are not so bold,
In your righteous domain,
The pain still remains.

A coward tried and true,
Cowering with your blood of blue,
The jewels which you wear,
Resemble the bridle of a mare.

The perfume you pungently dispel,
Reminds me of a tainted well,
Your clothes of velvet and silk,
Curdles and churns my milk.

As you vainfully glance into the mirror,
You resemble a donkey's rear,
You disgust me with your false esteem.
It is most likely just another gust of steam.

  —Buster E. Martyn

the jury

lying in unbroken silence
he awaits his jury
only they will decide his fate
to live or die only they will know.

but soon he will know, too
he will find out when his
            heart stops,
or when his blood pulses no longer
he never had a chance to breathe
or to live, to see — anything.
it wasn't his fault
he didn't cause any trouble
yet he must die anyway
now he is gone, and the world
will never know
            this unborn child.

—**Melissa Anne Patterson**

SHADOWS

Shadows in the corners,
            EVERYWHERE!
Lurking behind the chairs,
under the bed,
            WAITING!
            FOR WHAT??
for me,
for you,
            All of us!
It'll soon catch up
We run!
We try and hide!
            No matter,
It will find us all,
It will catch up with us.
For the SHADOW we fear,
            is THE SHADOW OF DEATH!

—**Angela M. Norman**

CONTRADICTION

I am — what I want to be, and
    what I don't want to be.
I want to be — what I am, and
        what I am not.

A Contradiction; I, my mask, and me.
    Laugh, or cry, or compromise?

        Listening relentlessly,
          Looking intently,
            Understanding reluctantly,
            Crying Endlessly.
                or
        Listening and looking guardedly
          Forcing one ear and eye to close,
            Bearably blurred,
            Crying Less.

I am — what you think you see of me.
    what I think you see,
    what I know to be
  I keep to me
  Privately.
Me.

—**VieSsa Mey**

THIS IS MY LIFE

My life is a bowl of sorrow,
I wish I could fly away like a
sparrow,
away from all the hassle.

At nights I dream, I'm away from
home, to wake-up, and find I'm
all alone.

I think about what I do,
And about what I could have done,
And it makes me want to get
away from it all.

My heart is a broken glass,
who wishes it could grow as
tall as the grass.

As green as the leaves,
That lets other people live.

—**Juan Fontanez**

CONSCIENCE

    Beyond the brink of imagination,
A poor soul shrieks out in pain,
Eyes reddened from tears of guilt,
Heart pounding rapidly in fear,
Face beaded heavily with perspiration,
Thoughts running wildly,
As he flees from his conscience,
For a sinner is he.

    His innocence slashed,
With a permanent scar,
He knows what he had done,
And so he must face his punishment.

He needn't even try,
To forget his crime,
He can't forget,
He shall be punished,
By his eternal reminder,
His conscience.

—**Lindsay Morris**

THIS IS NOT A CHRISTMAS POEM

Morning lags,
pale,

over unknown snow
and vague trees,
not quite there.
Time agrees.

And the lineless sky
rides

like a sail,

flag,

a vast, still kite.

Our side
of the field
raises
five ascending willows,

whipped completely white.

—**Matt Babcock**

PIONEER O PIONEER

Shucking frozen corn at dawn
Or
Shocking droughty grain of Depression
Era
Shackled my Spirit for pioneerin'
With
John-Barley-Corn
—ahSureMom

LOVE'S PALE DREAM

Last night I dreamt of Paradise
And together we passed many sights
Your hand in mine, my soul in yours
Following footsteps to eternal streams
Bathing in their glorious waters
Basking in their ethereal glow
Yet somehow, something was not right
One of us did not truly belong
And as I passed back out of Paradise
You turned and smiled, a tear in your eye
And as I awoke, I touched my lips
And tasted the faint scent of saltwater
Where I had kissed your tear away

—Richard H. Proctor III

With hope gone, hate has grown;
I have no love to call my own.
A love had I and now it's dead
My heart now feels a cold, cold dread
I cannot bear to live each day
And know my love has gone away.
I'm so lonely that I cry.
Please dear God, just let me die.
My love is gone, my heart is cold
And I feel so very old.
Must I live another day
With hope and love both gone away?
To love and be loved not
That is my fate; that is my lot.
The day I live, the day I die
Has been predestined from on high
I cannot change one little thing.
Maybe hope returns with Spring.

—M.A. Walker

ALL ONE TOWN

Forget big people on the screen.
So dramatic not to understand.
I dream empty spaces way back home
with morning cursing at the ground,
and sundown crying to the sky.
Take it all before you go.
Hold me forever, please.

Now it's all one town
no matter which direction you may run,
and the clocks are all the same
so you'll never be left out.
Oh, you're such a lovely liar
about the way life used to be
with that person, ready made,
but you left all the love with me,
and sundown crying to the sky.
Take it all before you go
and hold me forever, please.
Sleep.

—Mark J. Shorey

A STRONGER ME!

You often said you loved me
I know you didn't mean it.
I gave you everything,
You gave me nothing.
We were once one
Now I'm alone, you're gone.
I regret the lost years I gave,
If only I could do them over.
But I can't!
I can only continue on
And I will!
Some day I will love again,
For now I will find joy and peace
Within myself.
It has made me a stronger
And a better person.
So all that I can say is thank you!
—Heather Anderson

KEEP YOUR DISTANCE

I will not lie
I will not deny
I can see it in your eyes
What you feel inside

So run and hide
And keep them inside
Never to cross over that line
For fear of what we might find

We know it's wrong to feel
The way we do
But it's a sin
To deny it too

So you keep your distance
And I'll keep mine
Praying for the resistance
That's hard to find
—Nadia Krenzel

SOMEBODY TO ME

When we first met,
You were upset.
I wished I could help
With the way you felt
But I was young
And had to sing another song.
The song I had sung
Was a lonely one,
But it was fun.
I hoped you would not run
But you did and I went on.
Now you're back and I have changed.
I am willing to let things go
But I wish I was with you.
Because it hurts not to be.
That is why you're somebody
To me.
Though I'm trying to set you free.
I cannot let you be.
It is too hard on me.
—J.W.S.

PHEASANT BABIES

My dad owned a gun but
only shot it once a year —
for the pheasants. He didn't
like the walk or the cold
or his coffee from a thermos,
but he liked his friends who
liked these things. So when he
finally un-trunked the birds
he didn't protect them
from us, since they weren't his
prize anyway. They were ours.
Before they were baked with
rice they were rocked by children;
limp pheasant babies whose
breasts seemed warm still from
the sun they had tried to reach.

—Deborah Callaghan Gannon

THE EAGLE

The rain falls
  Upon the shores of time.
    It settles,
  In puddles it does gather.

The rainbow begins
  Falling upon puddles of tears.
    It spreads,
  Widening in journey.

The silence stalls
  Hearts bound in turmoil.
    It beats,
  Singeing the edges.

The message withers
  Under weightless numbers.
    It writes,
  Carry on my friend,
  For not is despair to ruin
  But to be taught.

—Aaron J. Busch

WIND

Chasin' merry fancies
over the rolling hills.
A grasshopper passes
by on his way.
The flowers smell so good.
This day just might last forever.

The vibrance of youth
is something to behold.
With the wind at my back
I'll never get old.

A good horse and sixgun
is what a boy needs.
Men seem so ridiculous
in their suits of empty promise.
Work and worry leave little time
while today passes them by.

The vibrance of youth
is something to behold.
With the wind at my back
I'll never get old.

—Patrick Pollock

TO A ROSE

Oh, Rose with velvet petals
your beauty I behold,
Some petals white and others pink,
Still some as pure as gold.

You've reigned as queen in garden shows,
and many other places,
You've also held the spotlight
in my loveliest of vases.

Your reign as queen of summer
to a close has come, I fear.
So sleep, oh Rose, for just a while
You'll bloom again next year.

—Rose A. Kline

THE POPPY

A HUSH
of motion, never-ending labyrinth
of freeway

A RUSH
of time-frantic, time pedantic drivers,
scurrying to their own
self-immolated destiny
like maze-manipulated mice
upon a treadmill of futility
past soft, emerald slopes where

A FLUSH
of poppy-thrusting crimson and orange

A GUSH
of life-merging chlorophyll,
a green and gentle blowing,
drinks from the cornucopia of being
ignoring the iron winds
of iron ships
wheeling to nowhere

—Hank Compagnon

LOFTY

Mystified by Majestic Mountain Peaks
Boulders held Precariously in Place,
Balanced by the Force of Nature . . .

Artistic Designs
Engraved in Stone—
Deserts Vast and Still . . .

A Prairie Dog 'Neath a Cactus Quill,
Barren and Desolate
It Appears to Be.

An Oasis of Life there Decreed,
Pockets of Water
For the Mammals . . . In Reach.

A Coolant . . .
Where Creatures of Wings
Fill their Beaks.

And Fragrance of Sandlewood
Lemon and Musk . . .

And Constellations
Against Skies of Rust.

—Josiah

Like a walk in the woods,
So natural and smooth;
Like a starlit sky,
On the night of a new moon;
Like a ship on the horizon,
Ever distant and yet so near;
Like a giant, cuddly grizzly bear,
With nothing left to fear;
Like the wind in the trees,
As gentle and as free;
You're like so many wonderful
   things
That bring happiness to me.

—**Janis R. Seaman**

FROM THE HERO SERIES:

The Hero in silhouette
   Watched her quietly
As they sat side by side
On the moon-lit beach . . . .
He listened to her fear and sorrow
At leaving what had been
Her cocoon for so long . . . .
He gave her strength and courage
To welcome the new beginning.
The wishing star shone brightly as
Friendship was provided in its
Truest, kindest form . . . .

—**Dona Hough**

LOVE IN THE ATTIC

My heart weighs heavy upon
my soul;
   Hoping for happiness, I can't let
go.
   Feelings breach my tear filled
eyes;
   Memories of innocence I visualize.
   Twisted wretchedness, our love
now lies.
   Daylight memories fleeting . . . fading
fast.
   Unconscience desires leaving me
empty, it didn't last.
   Confused sorrow, mixed with despair,
   Void dreams I dared not share.
   Shadows bounding to take flight,
   Love unspoken, bridled by night.
   Maddening thoughts, cloud over
my view;
   Mythical flowers, glazed with
dew.
   Alas, the line of love and hate;
   Dreams of a dreamer, believer in
fate.
   Nothing is alike heart-filled pain;
   An unearthed battlefield;
   Stubbed growth by men past
slain.
   A wretched smile of victories that
she claimed;
   The "Just" punisher when
laying the blame.
   What a life, a life of shame . . . .

—**Tom Gabbitas**

JUSTIN

My heart bleeds the color of
red and beats the beat of a
thousand love songs as one. My
eyes show a delicate shade of
evergreen and see the sea in
which my river of thought
flows. My hands feel for the
feeling of him as if he were
within my grasp. My soul tells
as though I've been told before,
love may never tell a lie. My
mind says and says again, "Follow
your dreams, that may be an
achievement of a lifetime."

—**Tristana**

TELL ME, MY LOVE

Tell me, my love
if you could, where would you take me
would you take me to a cabin in the woods
and snuggle near a fire
or would we go to a deserted beach
and make sweet love all night
   Tell me, my love
would we be alone all night
and love each other till dawn
or would we hold each other lovingly
and fall asleep in each other's arms
   Tell me, my love
will you tell me you will always
be mine, so I can reply the same
and will you say, you will always
love me, so I may say
   I will always love you
   Tell me, my love
      is all I say true?

—**Andrea Pickler**

COME AGAIN SOME OTHER DAY

The clouds begather up on high,
   quietly murmur their deep laid plans,
Through the blowing, blustering wind,
painted on the stormy, well lit sky.

With eyes closed, the flock looks down,
with open heart, it feels its joy,
upon the streams of hopes and dreams,
next to the pretty tall Sequoia
with its reddish kissing lips,
bestows an invisible much loved smile.

Upon the twilight of romance,
in the evening of its care,
by the magic, mystic fairies,
It opens eyes, and watches down,
upon its fateful, beautiful love
and watches, too, her lovely song
wafting through the downy willows,
over the slowly lapping waters,
upon the softness of the rain,
by the fresh smelling pure white clouds.

—**Troy Van Voorhis**

OCEAN OF LOVE

I'm a ship, and you're my sea;
Depths of blue that yearn for me,
On still waters is where I'll be;
Drifting endlessly . . . .

Well, it looks like the forecast changed;
A bolt of lightning, followed by rain,
Tossing on the sea of blame;
Tossing endlessly . . . .

Seeing through tear glazed eyes;
Ghost ships sunken, lost in their lies,
Burdened by sorrow, oh Lord, I realize;
This is meant for me . . . .

Driven by dream swept winds;
Bound by untried sins, driven endlessly . . .
Guided by emotional stars, I've found the way;
Back to the still waters of your bay.
Drifting endlessly . . . .

—Angie Davidson

once upon a cloud

look, there, at that cloud array,
a wide-screen view of artistic display.
where are the words that i should say;
what turns my eyes on in this way.

dancing clouds that perform without pay;
storm clouds overhang of shadowy gray;
marshmallow clouds, animated clouds served
on a rainbow-coloured day.
clouds float unnoticed; a treasure we
betray.
i'm so sad; a silent beauty drifts astray.

to stretch myself upon a cloud,
to lose myself in that soft crowd,
i hope, i dream, i wish out loud;
to be up there, just once, once upon a cloud!

dedicated to my parents:
Willie and Francile Crossland

—Nancy J. Crossland

GREEN LIGHT, GO

Drops of rain strike the pavement
with a soft splat.
The smell of damp concrete
rises to nudge noses
as the heat of an August day
slips from the sidewalk.

Pedestrians pass by, hunched under umbrellas,
muttering to their companions
or possibly to themselves.
Blocks away, a siren wails.

Traffic on the street flows,
attuned to the signals:
green light, go; red light, stop;
yellow light, proceed with care.

How pleasant it would be to have
the "green light, go" all through life.
As it is, there is too much "caution,"
Too much "wait" . . . .

—Deanna Shuster

Who will glue together my shattered heart?
Why did we have to be torn apart?
Will my heart ever be fully healed?
When will the emptiness go and be filled?
I often sit and cry, wondering why?
Why didn't I get a chance to say goodbye?
Are you happy up where you are,
up in heaven away so far?
When I see you again up above,
will you remember our true love?
I know our God in heaven above
will give us back our eternal love.

—Angela Martinez

I'VE GOT A DATE WITH A DREAM

I've got a Date with a Dream
and I'm in love with 'em already.
Wouldcha' look at Them There Eyes.
They love me.

We were bound to meet someday.
He came like my Fairytale Prince
with the Moon in his Hand
and the Sun on top of his Head.

The Clouds be his Chariot
and I see Stars In—
In Them There Eyes . . . .
They love me.

—Jackie Moore

THE BEST DRESSED

Only in the ground, He curtly wrote.
Living Word, He is and spoke.
For my sin to the cross He went;
One bequest: a new, white garment.

Now, I'm dressed and ready for His bidding
to come up to the glorious wedding.
My steps are lighter; they have a new bounce,
while waiting for the day to be announced.

And, after the wedding consummation,
I'll be returning with that great congregation.
The groom, dressed in red; the bride, in white;
coming to earth with heaven's life.

—William Henry Williams

PEACE

Deep within my Soul,
My thoughts just ebb and flow.
Bringing up the surface tract,
Moving now, the power to act!

'Til sleep is near, the danger,
At every turn, the anger.
Moving at its preset speed,
Threatening! Its very need!

On and on, but time will tell,
That on this Earth, a living hell!
Serenity will nullify the force,
That lurks within; takes its course.

To placidly turn the mind to ease,
Calming; lulling; to apease,
The Soul, to which I always turn,
From which the lesson of "PEACE," I learn!

—Hugh Phillips, Jr. "Sam"

BRIDGES

Life brings us to many
bridges to cross & life still
goes on. The water flows under
the bridges. When we cross one
or many. The more we learn
from our pass. Remember to go
forth to move on never looking
back on mistakes. But
keep crossing many more waters
until we really come to the great
bridge that crosses the waters
to everlasting life.

—Ramona E. Hamric

THE SUNSET

Like a ball of fire falling
from the sky, it goes
behind the mountain
to hide. Behind the
mountain is a place for
fire to rest.

When the ball of fire
goes down we go
down to rest and dream
peaceful dreams.

The sunset is a warning
to tell the earth to rest as
it sets itself in the west.

As it goes to hide its
partner comes up. It's
like a night shift which
changes in a swift and
peaceful movement.

—Courtney Augustine, age 12

EAST CHINA SEA

As I look at the horizon,
Where the sea and sky meet.
The EAST CHINA SEA,
Is a sea in retreat.

EAST CHINA SEA is green and blue.
When the sun shines upon her,
She sparkles,
Like a day born anew.

She's calm and serene,
Quiet and meek.
But when she storms,
She's a sea not in retreat.

She hustles and she bustles,
With surf crashing wide.
Upon the shores of her vengeance,
Without saying why.

But when all's abated,
And the storm is no more.
She goes back to being,
The sea that I first saw.

—John Henry Jaryno

FARM MORNING IN THE SPRING

Just to hear the rooster's lusty crow
As the pink rays of the sun
Streak the eastern sky,
And hear the soft lowing of a cow,
As another day is nigh.

Then from slumber to arise,
And gaze into the east,
And see a picture painted there,
On which my eyes can feast.

There, before my wondering eyes,
Spreads a sparkling paradise,
Diamond studded, flowering sweet.
Over all from woodland near
In a cappella, coming clear,
A thousand bird songs do I hear.

—Marge

I THE STORM

Swirling darkness glittering white
Wailing wind fills the night
Clouds of powder in the air
Majestic beauty, dark but fair
Painting all with giant strokes
Covering all with mystic cloaks
Buried deep beneath the land
I bare my teeth, I make my stand
Gusting breath impending doom
In awe of forces shadows loom
Brooding giants beating down
I step into the rainbow's crown
Gazing down, a man alone
Ascending high upon the throne

Dedicated to Jenny,
an inspiration in herself

—Troy Speakman

SOMEDAY

In this life I cannot hear — but
There will be another life up there.

The angel choir will sing —
The church bells their welcome ring.

I will awake to the rooster's crow —
And hear the wind, and I will know

Love and the laughter of little children,
The tick-tock of the clock in Heaven.

There I will praise the Lord and sing.
There I will hear the bells of Heaven ring.

For in Heaven — I will be
No longer alone and I will hear my family.

My deafness will be gone forever —
I will be happy and nothing will sever

My oneness with my Lord,
For I read and know God's word.

In this life, I cannot hear — but
There will be another life for me.
— up there —

Dedicated to the deaf and hearing
impaired throughout the U.S.A.

—Ellie Tingelstad

THE ARROW OF TIME

The Arrow of Time, curved in dimension four,
　Straight in dimensions three;
Where in past ages did I dwell?
In Atlantis, now beneath the sea,
On Egyptian sand, or in Sumer's ancient land;
What was home to me?
Be it cave or palace, was it not home to thee?
Where in future times will I dwell?
Antarctic realms, now beneath the snow,
In spirit zone, or on planet unknown;
What will be home to me?
Be it spirit plane or material form,
Will it not be home to thee?

　　　　　—George W. Gingery

THE TEST

Three minutes seems
　like three years.
I feel like I'm falling,
　and there's no one below to catch me.
I can't eat,
　can't sleep.
My mind is racing,
　my heart, pounding.
My palms are sweating,
　my stomach's in knots.
What if it is?
　What if it isn't?
What am I going to do . . . .

The buzzer goes off,
　the eternal wait is over,
And it's blue.

　　　　　—Cara J. Markert

FREUDIAN SLIP

I perceived a man on a pedestal;

I was jealous and full of rage.

I thought, "Why shouldn't I be sitting there?
　Is he better than me?
　Of course not.

　　Why do people like him more?
　　What has he done?　　Nothing."

I could see nothing special about him,

Yet I wanted to be like him.

　　　　　No, I didn't . . .

I wanted to be him.

I decided that I must de-throne him,

　So I shook the pedestal until he f
　　　　　　　e
　　　　　　　　l
　　　　　　　　　l.

When I looked at his blood-soaked face

That had been smashed against the ground,

I was proud. He was off;

I could take his place,

But when I stared into his hollow eyes,

I realized that
　　　　　　He was me.

　　　　　—Christopher Martinez

MY WORLD

I write these words in simple form
yet I do not want to conform.
I don't understand how many think.
All I know I can not be as they.
My world is different from their's
for I only seek the beauty in thee.
I try and open up and be as they,
but I always come back to me.
My world and place is different
inside of me.
Mine is better from what I see.

　　　　　—Melanie Martinez

MATRIXIDE

Storing/stacking, rational practices;
　Versus bumping thugs of the world.
Cupboards/shelves, hacked by axes;
Moisture/acid, paper and film curled.

Word/number, discretely stored,
Yield to slashing power surges.
Syntax/formulae, electronic board,
Melt and drop as humidity purges.

Womb holds gnarly data of life;
Viral organisms join the attack.
Clucking librarian girds for strife;
Information spreads, stack-on-stack.

Slashing swords, ancient chaos;
Rust/mildew — Dali´ drooping stasis.

　　　　　—Richard Slick

EACH OF US

An old man sits on a bench
　motionless in the summer sun.

Staring past others
　as they make their daily run.

His spirit is living
　though all alone.

His face is lifeless
　like chiseled in stone.

What are his thoughts
　his mind is not dead.

What were his dreams
　when life was still ahead.

His days grow longer
　to only contemplate the past.

His nights grow shorter
　when he wants them to last.

Day and night
　are much the same.

Happiness is fleeting
　when few remember his name.

The bench is his home
　he has nowhere else to go.

Who will grieve
　the day he doesn't show.

The old man is each of us
　although we are not yet there.

Without our dreams
　there is only a stare.

　　　　　—C. Terry Shipp

THE FOREST

The rabbit hops through the wood
He wants to do nothing but good.

The bear would roam around for food
He really is an awesome dude.

The squirrel ran up the tree
to hide from the bumblebee.

The beaver tries to build a dam
With sticks and wood and lots of sand

The deer would run and have some fun
Until the hunter shot his gun

—**Kevin Aguirre**

CHANCES ARE

I stand now in the middle
With each side begging me.
To my left is what I've always been —
And then what I could be.

In ways I want to jump
Into the future's arms.
But I am much too happy with
The present's simple charms.

I look and see the faces
That I know as well as mine.
I know that our great friendships
Have passed the test of time.

Yet something keeps me glancing
At the ones I don't know yet.
The people who may fill my dreams,
The ones I have not met.

But if I were to stay here
And never see the light,
I may not get the chance again
To make my future bright.

Yet fear is not the answer
To why I took the chance.
And now I know that life's too short
To take a backward glance.

*Dedicated to my wonderful friends, Heather
and Summer, who have taught me the value
of true friendship.*

—**Hillary Helm, age 15**

TAKE A LOOK INSIDE

We walk with eyes wide open
Still things we do not see
For life is something special
A gift to you and me
Many things we take for granted
As we see them every day
Would we even notice
If they went away
Would we sense any absence
Or feel the empty space
To be forgotten or put aside
Leaving not a trace
Can we stop for a moment
And take a look inside
To take the time to help a friend
Or comfort a child who cries
A simple little thank-you
Or a soft I love you
Could change a life for someone
If the time we'd take to do . . . .

—**Pamela L. Reed**

THOUGHTS

Have you ever felt
So strong
That even the biggest mountain
Seemed small?

Have you ever felt
So happy
That even on a rainy day
You saw the sun?

Have you ever felt
So peaceful
That even waves breaking
Were quiet?

Have you ever felt
So loved
That even in the coldest wind
You were warm?

Have you ever felt
So contented
That the whole world
Agreed with you?

—**Rhoda Gross**

THE SPELL

Magic
Crystal Ball
Abra Ca Dabra
Incense Tannis Cannabis Moon
Enter My Love's Peaceful Mind
Cast Him Into A Feverish Dream
Which I Can Only Make Him Wake
From A Mountain He Shall Look And See
Below I Shall Appear Dressed In Purple Sadly Crying
He Shall Dive Into A Nearby Waterfall Swimming To Me
He Takes My Hand We Walk Up A Creek Slowly Barefoot
We Fly To A Faraway Star And Look Down Upon The World
He Now Knows Why I Was Crying And Looks To Me I Disappeared
Darkness Falling Sweating Gasping Unknown Spinning Lost He Wakes Frightened Remembering Our Life Together

—**Rebecca Ann LeFebre**

THE BEAUTY OF LIFE

To give birth is breathtaking
moments remembered throughout time
a miracle earthshaking
the feeling is sublime.

Babies are beautiful like doves
so very bright and pure
to have this much love
one can never be unsure
that the instinct is protection
teaching of God, love, and life
their eagerness and attention
make it worthwhile to undergo strife.

Hats off to mothers of the nation
to be commended is not a crime
to give birth is breathtaking
moments remembered throughout time.

Dedicated to my beautiful son, Cameron, born in September
of 1992, and my husband, Lazelle, for his love and support.

—Angela V. Morris

ARKANSAS

I met a man from Arkansas,
Quite a man was he.

He told me of his crazy life,
And how he came to be.

He liked to hunt and fish and spend,
his time alone.

To listen to the lonely hounds,
as they find their way back home.

To throw his fishing line out in the dark.

Then head for the biker bar for,
the rest of the night.

To wake up the next morning,
there in his bed.

WONDERING, HUM — did,
I call Idaho or is it all in my head.

—Jo Ann Nichols

CAN WE GET ALONG?

I brought you here, Ebony, in chains
In shackles then and still remain

Ivory's put-up-on Ebony, can we get along?

History prophesied manifest destiny for Ivory
Ivory's burden then must always be, Ebony

On this premise, America's systems were built
Status quo since, and Ivory feels no guilt

Can we get along, Ivory and Ebony?

Genocide by many means, Ivory's put-up-on Ebony
The gall of you to think and sing of killing Ivory

Can we get along, Ivory and Ebony?

Cease your struggle for Ebony pride, determination, and dignity
Forget education, amalgamation, and aspirations to be free

Inalienable rights, and created equal, never included Ebony
Those treasures are the sole entitlement of just-us, Ivory

Can we get along, Ivory and Ebony?

Don't be restless, resign thyself to the prophecy
Just suffer, grin, and die peacefully

Ivory's put-up-on Ebony, Can we get along?

—Ardelphia Hickey

FIRST GREY HAIR

Now on the sight of that first
grey hair,
Don't cry, Oh no do this,
Run, yes run through the street
and say,
I found my first grey hair.
I plucked it out, Oh yes I did put
it in my pocket carefully,
To save it and frame it,
Don't you see, I earned my
First grey hair . . . .

—Penny Lynn Akin

TWO SOCKS

One grey,
itchy wool, red-lined cuff,
winter ready,
right for boots.
The other; basketball elastic,
toe-holed,
dirty ankles.
You have the mates
and are probably
wearing them
now.

—Suzann Steele Saltzman

Where are we heading to today
We by-passed the past
Doing the present;

Wandering the future
Transit into the infinity;
We are on this journey
Or call it a holiday on earth.

You have a job.

We ourselves
are like individual planets;

In order to see beyond
One must look into the depth
of oneself.

—Doris Gebhardt

CLOSED WINDOWS

"I'm happy to see
that your eyes aren't sad,"
Said He to She,
In "the Elevator!"

"I'm sad, but happy
you cannot see,"
Said She to He,
In, "the Elevator!"

"For my heart's not glad,
Tho' my eyes aren't sad,
And I'm bleeding slowly
In death!"

"But, I'm happy to be
an actress you see,"
Said She to He,
In "the Elevator!"

—L. Mehner Page

⟨RING SHOWER

⟩ool rain gently falls,
Daisies bow on gentle waves;
Field birds chirp — rain gone.

—Paul E. Major Jr.

MY HONEY

I pour it on my biscuits,
I put it in my tea,
but my honey gets all over me.
My honey is so sweet, my honey
is so fine, I use it all the time,
but in the strangest places, I
always seem to find, my honey.
The cap sticks to the jar,
the honey to the spoon, if I
waited for it, I'd be here till
noon.
My honey gets on me, I can barely
get it off, but I love my honey . . .
I can never get enough.

—James F. Stewart

AGAPAO

Third grade;
For God so loved
lonely, sad, confused.
the world, he gave
Vacation Bible school
his only begotten Son,
memory verse.
that whosoever believeth
Light of understanding
in him should not
touching mind, heart.
perish, but have
Ray of hope;
everlasting life.
dawn of truth.

—Deborah Beachboard

UNPLUG

A poem a day is what they say
    Will keep away the blues.
But I'm not sure if that's the cure
    To lure you from your tubes.

Read a book and get a look
    At what it took to write.
Spend some time to pen a line
    And sign it late at night.

Or help a child, preserve the wild,
    Get riled and stop a war.
Go on a hike or ride a bike
    But don't be like a boar.

Pick up your duff, you've had enough.
    Don't take the guff you see.
Pull the rug out from the slug
    And unplug your TV.

—Ann Kemling Zweifel

ICE STORM

Jewel-tipped fingers
touching azure sky,
Lace covered mountain.

Winter storm passed by.

—Marjorie Baranski Thompson

LISTEN TO THE SONG OF LIFE

Be still, be silent and listen to the song of life
My heart throbs with anticipation of things not yet to be
The yearning and the longing of goals not realized, for
love that was never allowed to bloom
Be still and listen to the song of life
Come with me and run through the silence of the dawn
Listen to the trickle of a little brook beckoning to come and
skip the rocks
Take the wings of the morning and listen to the song of life

—Bette Mitchell

IN

In light & in darkness
In joy & in pain
In this world everchanging
I'm going insane

In love & in hate
In life & in death
In the fear of destruction
I'll spend my last breath

In good & in evil
In sainthood & sin
In only my dreams
Will I live once again

In war & in peacetime
In right & in wrong
In all of my life
I will sing just one song.

—Derrick Randolph Jennings

LIFE

        A train track is a sign
of life,
        It's very important to
stay on track,
        If you make one wrong
turn,
        You have to get on track
again,
        And take extra time to
reach your destination,
        It's hard to stay on
track,
        So sometimes you gotta
make a resting point,
        And regain your energy
for another adventure,
        So just keep on chuggin'
'till the track can't go.

—Ashley M. Jones

REMEMBRANCE DAY

Poppies are blooming.
  Poppies are big and bright.
Poppies also lay in Flanders fields.
Soldiers are dying and blood is flowing.
People are hurt and families are crying
in Flanders fields.
People are in pain and fear. Battles are
going and peace is coming.

—Melissa Johns

METEORITE OF PAIN

When I miscarried my twins
  I couldn't have dropped from a loftier height—
For to have watched my children grow
there wouldn't have been a more pleasing sight.
When I say it was all over
I couldn't have fallen any quickly through the air—
That piercing knife which ripped through my heart
there couldn't be a pain more difficult to bear.
When I knew I'd never again hold my babies
I couldn't have crashed any harder to the ground—
For to have heard their sweet voices and laughter
there surely wouldn't have been a more beautiful sound.

—Angelique Cooper McGlotten

TAWNY LION SMILES

Dawn's urgent fervour lights
Upon tawny lion smiles . . .
In a heather bound dale
'Midst misty eyed pines,
I kiss the breast
Where passion lingers . . .
Faint dew drop caress
Guides my fingers.
And no sorrow shall mark my brow
For I loved you then
As I love you now.

You . . . are sunshine reclyning
In the arc of a crescent moon . . . .

—Michael Hentges

MY DADDY

Always loving
  Always caring
Although not always showing
Always correcting
Although sometimes not for the best
I honor him as a daughter and a friend
And hope we'll be together until the unwanted end

He was my first love
And I love him more now than I ever have
He may not state his love for me
But I know it's there
For he shows it to me by his correctiveness and the
  warm, loving hugs that he gives me

Although not always joking
He's a funny man
Different from all the others
  because this one is my Daddy
And how very lucky I am to have him . . .
  . . . for my Daddy.

—Aimee Brown

TRANQUILITY

The breeze from the ocean
  The sun from the sky
The moon just visible
With the stars shining bright.
        The trees in the forest.
        The flowers on a hill.
        The rain falling softly.
        The time just stands still. ·
All the breathtaking view,
That we stand and admire,
What a magnificent sight.
For the mankind.
        We should find in its beauty.
        The peace, that we crave
        And love and laughter
        That we ourselves, can create.

—Ela Abramowicz

THE FLOWER

A flower she is to the sky
for when the sun does rise
she opens and her colors
all glow for him to see.

For him it is never like a step
into the river always changing
it is constant, her love for him
and it is what gives him strength.

As strong as war his feelings,
and with it he'd die by the blade
for any that threaten his flower
will surely meet their match.

He smiles for what is his
and bubbles with emotions
for the mirrors of his love
are the eyes of his lady.

—William H. Perks III

SNOW A HOUSEKEEPER'S DILEMMA

Befickled: bread crumbs sprinkled on the
  counter.
Diligent housekeeper that I am
Reminds me, clean the splattering
of freshest spring.
And fall the new fallen snow
with dishcloth in hand
Scrub away, away . . .
And with dustpan sweep
the well wishers salads of orchids.
And pledge the ashes to new
shiny surfaces.
Like new icicles
Droppings of changing perculiarities,
Of whether musts and stuffs.
And Oh—Oh—such results,
And rewards a new recipe
Of weather or not it does.

For my children

—Marie Snow

THE TOOTH

If I were a tooth
I'd work from 8 to 9
And get up in the morning
To be to work on time.
Oh! The horror of being a tooth
With all its cavities
And having a dentist drill in me . . .
Oh! The misery!!

—Caren Morgan

I'LL DANCE

When people start to bother me
And pry beneath my skin,
I try to smile happily
And dance a little spin.

When people start to frustrate me
And spread my patience thin,
I try to caution carefully
Before I dance again.

What people do not comprehend,
Is why I dance my jig.
I can't explain in words, my friend,
So watch me zag and zig.

—Kelly M. England

WHAT MORE CAN I DO?

A cry for help
was it heard
in the shuffle
called life?

A desperate cry
was it the last
before something precious
was lost?
Life

Will I stop?
Will I listen?
Will I care?
Will I save a life?

—John R. Yocum

T E L E P H O N E

Why don't you call?
Does it always have to be me?

I sit and wait for the phone
to ring, but it never does,
and when it does ring,
it is never you.

Waiting for the phone to ring
is very lonely.
Have you ever waited for
it to ring?

Don't you wish that you could
control the phone?
I just wish I could control
your fingers.

I would have them dial my
number.

—Dennis Wayne Cyphert

AN AFRICAN PERSON'S OPINION DURING HIS SLAVE YEARS

Invisible chains of pain still bind my legs.
After a painful beginning not wanting to live or be associated
with any white or other kind of person because of cruel
treatment. In vengence of other people.

Dying hoping no one will care.
Dying so I don't have to suffer.
Using a spear, DRIVE IT THROUGH ME!

Thank you
Well, goodbye cruel and despicable world.

—Rob Seelman, age 16

S

My right ear burrows
into warm beige brown, nestles in the
black striped fur.

I cannot hear the television
without turning up the volume
for my other outer ear to hear.

He purrs as if deliberately to interfere
with short wave too
and I am sure

you can hear him now.

From his face gazes simply
a soul.
He is sweet
his eyes are serene
and I feel calm from being, with him.

Who was he once?
I didn't think I believe in rebirth
or other lives,
but something there is that I cannot else
explain.

—Anne Ulanov

A MAN MADE HELL

Listen my people and you shall hear
A Man Made Hell, somewhere near

It's a place where blind law vomits
Accepted by Society who half the time
Don't give a damn

The steel doors show signs of welcoming all year round
The victims who come and go, minds are constantly
Homeward bound

Beds made of steel and colder than ice
Every man thinks about his time and thinks about it twice

The "slop" provided a dog wouldn't eat
While the man, sips on his coffee in his black seat
In the next room a cheese eater is getting his head beat

Incarcerated for their crime
Justice feels they must pay it in time
Now it's merely a question of time
For they'll all be graduates from a College of Crime

Society! You call this rehabilitation, Hell
This is merely a Man Made Hell
It's a prevention for chaos so you say
Beware this place of Justice is
A Man Made Hell

You never know, this place may become your home some day
I suggest, you value your freedom and stay away
You'll never get in a Man Made Hell

—Dicky R. Overstreet

CLAY

A Small Child — A Baby — is a Gem —
A Blessing and a Joy!!
Whether it be Girl or Boy.
Clay —
Like a piece of Clay —
Clay —
Can be molded —
And — if molded —
With lots of LOVE — Some learning and PLAY —
Chances are —
THAT —
That child is going to turn out OK

   —Scotty

LESSONS IN LOVE

I can see our love was meant forever. Time has passed.
Though years we've crossed, I know we'll always be together.

There were times I felt you slipping, but I caught you in my grasp.
This love we have is so strong, And I know that it will last.

Suddenly you said you were leaving, Now I'll be left alone here . . . waiting.
How can I live when the love of my life, is ever-so-slowly fading?

My love held nothing meaningful, Then you entered my silent world.
Giving your love and yourself, Making sure I was secure.

And now I think of you often, I think of you everyday.
Somehow I respect your decision, I'm not the type to force you to stay.

And though my soul is hurting, I'm going to pass this test.
I'll be strong with you in my heart. You taught me your best.

   —Wade Wyckoff

THE FUTURE???

Our Children today are the future tomorrow
We try to protect them from disappointments and sorrow.
There's still so much racial tension in our schools today
Partly because the parents are teaching them that way.
The preschoolers do not know that there is a difference in their skin
They only know that the one sitting next to them is their best friend.
But as they get older and learn how their parents were raised,
They turn against that friend, the one who gave them so much praise.
But all the while they want to continue their friendship in the way they once had
And yet they do not want to upset their first love, their Mom and Dad.
Their parents had told them that people of a different color were once and outcast
And that accepting one as an equal is a thing that will come to pass.
With attitudes like that, our world is taking two steps back
When we should concentrate on forward progress, and form a positive pact.
So let's teach our children that the color of your skin is God's creation
And focus on more important things that's killing our young generation.
That dreadful topic is AIDS and it doesn't discriminate.
It will affect all colors, whether you are a drug addict, gay, or straight.
So let's put all of this racial pettiness behind
And come up with a cure for AIDS, while we still have time.
We need our young ones to be sensible and stay with one mate
Because without them, there will be no future date.

   —Janis L. Robinson

About The Authors

Authors are listed in alphabetical order by name or pen name.

NED ADAMS resides in Greenwich, Connecticut. His education includes: Brunswick School. His interests include: sports. He is a member of the Greenwich Blues Hockey Association. **His comments:** I've never found school entirely interesting. During class, I look out the window and my poetry just forms. I usually do a rough copy on my binder... 299

SHANNON HEATHER ALBRIGHT resides in Winslow, Illinois. She is in the 11th grade in high school. She works on a cruise ship and plays softball. **Her comments:** In everyone's life, as well as mine, friendship and personal experiences of some kind play a key role as sources of inspiration for me.. 36

Shannon Heather Albright

ALESSANDRA is the pen name for **ALESSANDRA LOREN REISS (Ali) (Sandi),** who resides in Lake Hiawatha, New Jersey. Her interests include: music, art, and writing. Her occupation is with topiaries (dried flowers). She had **The Gulf War** published in **Treasured Poems of America. Her comments:** Inspiration comes natural to me through many experiences in life. I often write about love, romance, and world events. It's a spiritual gift that comes from within. This poem was dedicated to the U.S. Navy...................................... 121

Alessandra

MOHAMMED AHD AL-KADIR AL-FEQUI resides in Dhahran, Saudi Arabia. His education includes: B.Sc. in chemical engineering, Faculty of Engineering, Cairo University, 1976. He is a technical writer and editor in Saudi Aramco. His memberships include: Syndicate of Engineers (Cairo), Kuwait Environment Protection Society, Literature Club in Eastern Province (Saudi Arabia), and Modern Literature Association (Cairo). His publications include: **Rhythms on Environmental Strings** (poetry in Arabic) published in Kuwait, 1992; **Corrosion** published in Kuwait, 1987; and **Petroleum Industries** published in Kuwait, 1985. His awards include: Arab Tongue, 1st Prize, KFAS, 1985; Supreme Council of Youth, Egypt, poetry award, 1975; Supreme Council of Youth, Egypt, poetry award, 1974. **His comments:** Environment is my source of inspiration. I wrote more than 25 poems on environmental problems (in Arabic). Also, I wrote 30 poems about the experiment of leaving Kuwait and getting lost in the Arabian Desert during Iraq's invasion

Mohammed Ahd
Al-Kadir Al-Fequi
of Kuwait.. 18, 222

Dorothy A. Allen

DOROTHY A. ALLEN resides in Arlington, Texas. Her education includes: twelve years plus modern management classes and computer courses. She is a secretary who enjoys writing, bowling, and quilting. **Her comments:** Most of my themes are "faith" and "family," since it is these sources that have inspired me to write poetry. I am a mother of 5 children and grandmother of 5 children... 43

H. Clark Anderson

H. CLARK ANDERSON is the pen name for **HARRY ANDERSON,** who resides in Milford, Connecticut. His education includes: BA in English, University of New Haven, 1970; MS in education, So. Connecticut St. University, 1973. He is a computer analyst who enjoys fishing and classical music. **His comments:** Poetry—Where else can so little say so much? I appreciate the free gifts given to all of us. After a hundred sunrises, the next is always better.. 279

CRYSTAL JUNE ARTHUR resides in Marion, Ohio. She is a student at River Valley Jr. High School. She enjoys music, football, and basketball. **Her comments:** I am fifteen years old and this is the first poem I have ever written... 195

DALE H. BROOKS resides in Shelbiana, Kentucky. His education includes: Shelbiana Grade School, 1st through 8th grade; graduated from Millard High School, Millard, Kentucky, in 1976. His interests include: helping to ease others hurt and pain through his poetry. He is a member of the Shelby United Methodist Church. **His comments:** My poetry is always written from emotions of the way I truly feel. I am often inspired by family members and close friends, from their experiences or what they wish to happen. May God bless them all... 103

Ramona Buchlmayer

RAMONA BUCHLMAYER resides in Riverside, California. She is a deputy sheriff in Orange County, California. She is a member of Peace Officers for Christ. **Her comments:** My poems are truly inspirations of the heart and reflections of my soul. They are derived through my own life experiences. My husband, Joel, and my parents, Ira and Ramona Essoe, greatly inspire me through their love, inner beauty, and support. I thank the Lord for blessing me with the ability to breathe life into mere words.......... 22, 238, 311

Karen J. Buechler

KAREN J. BUECHLER resides in Strathmore, Alberta, Canada. Her education includes: high school graduate and 1 year of art college. Her interests include: painting, sculpting, and playing and learning music.......... 133, 220, 221, 295

CHARLOTTE J. BYERLY resides in Herndon, Pennsylvania. She is a housewife who enjoys custom framing, crafts, the piano, and the organ. **Her comments:** I have had many sources of inspiration including God's love, my husband, and my four children. I do custom poetry which people ask me to write for a father or husband, etc. My daughter, a free-lance artist, does the poetry in calligraphy and then I frame it. A very unique gift...........75, 80

Charlotte J. Byerly

WILLIAM J. COLE (nickname — "Bill") resides in Freehold, New Jersey. His education includes: Associate Degree in psychology, Brookdale Community College, Lincroft, New Jersey; 1 year at Seton Hall University, South Orange, New Jersey. He works part-time at a nursing home. He loves jazz and wants to take trumpet lessons this year. He belongs to Brookdale Alumni Association and Nursing Home and Service Employees Union. **His comments:** My interest in jazz music inspired me to write this poem in addition to my great respect for the memories of some of the deceased jazz musicians... 10

William J. Cole

KIM COUZA resides in Macomb, Illinois. She graduated from Western Illinois University. She is a special education teacher who enjoys photography and music. **Her comments:** Many of my poems have been used as lyrics and set to music...210

Kim Couza

URMA CRAMER-LUCKIE resides in Tampa, Florida. Her education includes: 4 years at Jamaica Bible College, graduate; E.K.G. tech.; attended advanced career training in New York. She is a resident counsellor and is interested in songwriting, poetry, writing short stories, singing, sports, family life, and travelling. She is a member of BCM International. **Her comments:** There are many sensations in my innermost being, and deep feelings about so many things in life just waiting for me to express them in words of beauty, strength, and strong emotions. My failures and triumphs as a person, my religious beliefs, and my family inspire me...159

Urma Cramer-Luckie

DORIS MOORE DAVIS resides in Killeen, Texas. She is a graduate of Central Texas College and an alumni of Norfolk State University. She is a registered nurse, certified in geriatrics and loves acting. Her memberships include: Vive Les Arts Theater, Antioch Baptist Church, and 19th St. Black Horse Chapel. She had **Ultimate Possession** published in **Indian Oaks Newsletter,** 1991. She won a 1st Place Blue Ribbon for **Advantages of Being Black and Female** in 1984. **Her comments:** My inspiration comes from the love I have for people and their feelings. I can not remember when I was not writing poems. I close my eyes and the words come. Poetry is therapy..189

Doris Moore Davis

SEAN DEHONEY resides in Houston, Texas. Education includes: GED. Occupation is in sales and interests include: music and creative writing. Publications include: **Once There Lived, Final Signs,** and **Something That Is,** all published in **Summer's Treasures,** 1993. **Comments:** My inspiration comes straight from the heart and from the origin of pain and change.....................................143

MICHAEL L. DUBLIN, SR. resides in Raleigh, North Carolina. He studied political science at Shaw University, Raleigh, North Carolina. He is a minister with the Church of Christ and prevention specialist, Drug Action, Inc. (substance abuse). He is president elect—Board of Directors of Healthy Mothers/Healthy Babies Coalition of Wake County. **His comments:** This poem is inspired by the hardships suffered because I'm of African descent, being male in the 90's and the expectations of perfection for ministers. I have discovered that my real significance in life is a personal relationship with God through Jesus Christ... 32

Michael L. Dublin, Sr.

DRICE DYKHOUSE resides in Osseo, Michigan. His education includes: country grade school. He has worked as a farmer, factory worker, and gardener. He is a member of the Chapman Memorial Church of the Nazarene. **His comments:** I am now at age 85 living in a nursing home. Poetry still comes to me! I recite it often for the entertainment and enjoyment of the other patients here. I meet 4 days a week with a group here for Bible study and prayer!.. 21

Drice Dykhouse

JANICE EDGE resides in Dowelltown, TN. She has a B.S. Degree in elementary education. She is a retired teacher due to health at 43. She is a member of the Women's Missionary Society and the Retired Teacher's Association in DeKalb, County, Tennessee. She had **Best of West** published in the **Smithville Review** (weekly), 1983-84. She won the DeKalb County's Outstanding Teacher Award, 1971-1972; Dekalb West Outstanding Teacher, 1984; and Outstanding Retired Teacher, 1988. **Her comments:** After winning three Outstanding Teacher Awards, I was thankful for my primary years as a student in a rural community with no conveniences.....................................248

Janice Edge standing outside her first school, June Bug School

DAVID J. EMSWILER resides in Socorro, New Mexico. He is a proud father of Landreth, Anastacia, and Christian. **His comments:** Special thanks to my mother who inspired me to "Peel the onion, son.".................................... 68

David J. Emswiler

ANETTE FEHLHAFER resides in Utica, Nebraska. She has a degree in elementary education with a major in elementary education and literature. She is a teacher who enjoys writing poetry and children's books. **Her comments:** This poem, **On Desert Sands,** was written during Desert Storm, after watching, along with many other Americans, the day by day account of the war. It was written on behalf of those who were sent to this land, foreign to them, to defend freedom, justice, and peace, and return home safely to America.....................................179

JUANITA (NITA) V. FREY resides in Waco, Texas.. 149

Juanita (Nita) V. Frey

BETTY GIANELLA resides in Waco, Texas. Her education includes: Baylor University, North Texas State University, and Oceanside College; two Bachelor of Arts Degrees and graduate studies. She is a former teacher and art center museum chairman. Her memberships include: charter member of the National Museum of Women in the Arts, Washington, D.C.; The Art Center; The Symphony Association; Hillcrest Baptist Medical Center Auxiliary, and Historic Waco Foundation. She was chairman of The Art Center in 1987-88; listed in Who's Who in Education in 1975; president of The Council for Exceptional Children in 1970. Her publications include: **Lady of Loveliness, Credo,** and **Call It an Adventure,** all published in **Poetic Voices of America,** 1993. She was a winner in a creative writing contest in 1960. **Her comments:** Poetry is a mode of expressing the creativity in my being.......... 243

Betty Gianella

LYNN GILBERT resides in Bridgeport, Connecticut. Education includes: B.A. from Stirling University, Scotland; graduated in 1990. An aspiring writer with great interest in theatre and film. **Comments:** Being Scottish, Scotland and the people of Scotland are a great inspiration to me. Having now lived in America, this inspiration has deepened, accompanied by the experience of living in the most powerful western nation. Both countries have unique spirituality which is a strong theme in my work.. 302

RACHEL MANIJA GOBAR resides in Pittsburg, Kansas. **Comments:** "Each thing in the world—the animals, the plants, the sky and stars and lightning—has a power behind it that makes it do what it does. What you can see is only a little of the whole thing. The power is the spirit part. Some people can learn to reach the spirit part of something, and they become its shaman. There is power in everything!" James L. Haley. "When love beckons you, follow him, though his ways are hard and steep." Khalil Gibran..... 222

Rachel Manija Gobar

KATHRYN RACHELLE GORDY resides in White Deer, Texas. She graduated from White Deer High School in May of 1990 and attended Amarillo College from September of 1990 to May of 1991. She has been attending Clarendon Jr. College for nursing since January of 1992. Her interests include: reading and arts & crafts. She is a collector. **Her comments:** I wrote my first poem at 10 years old. Feelings, thoughts, and circumstances were my inspiration...................................... 47

JEANNE HALEY resides in Hopatcong, NJ. Her education includes: B.A. from New Jersey State College at Montclair; graduate work at New York University and Rutgers. She is a tutor who enjoys crafts, collecting hair receivers and candlewick crystal, and playing the piano. Her memberships include: past president of Ladies Auxillary of the Firemen of the State of New Jersey; Ladies Auxillary of the Sussex County Fire Department; Women's Auxillary of Defiance Eng. Co. #3 of Hopatcong; editor of **Firemen's Monthly** in the 1980's. She had a poem, **Ode of a Tour** published in **Rolling Together** in 1985 and a book, **Life With Mother,** published in 1990. **Her comments:** I've always enjoyed writing. My son, a journalism major, shares this interest. I consider writing in a format a challenge and so enjoy doing so.. 54

Jeanne Haley

DEBRA MOY HARRIS resides in Dallas, Texas. Her education includes: Susan Miller Dorsey High, Los Angeles, California; California Institute for Law Enforcement and Management. She is a security officer for the Dallas Morning News. Hew awards include: Business Woman of the Week, 1991; Student of the Month (Security School Law Enforcement), 1987; and Valedictorian of Security School graduating class, 1988. **Her comments:** I am a freelance poet who gets inspiration from life itself. I've written over 100 poems entitled, **Paths of Life.** I have three beautiful children, Doyle III, Granville III, and JuNene, who have inspired me to write such poems as, **My Son,** and **My Daughter.** My poetry comes from within. I express love, my love for God, and my love for my parents. I not only like expressing my wants and needs through my poetry, but also the wants and needs of others. One day I hope to publish my first book of poetry so that the world may see life for its beauty and pain, as I have expressed through my poetry.................... 231

Debra Moy Harris

JAKE HERRERA resided in Longmont, CO. He was a high school graduate. He was a counselor who enjoyed music, art, and eagles. He was paralyzed from the waist down and always dreamed of being a disc jockey. **Comments:** Jacob, my brother, who passed away November 10, 1992, was a very special person. He came from a very dysfunctional family and got involved with the wrong people, but the last 10 months of his life he got away from drugs and alcohol. He was counseling kids, working, and helping people. He made an impact on a lot of people... 97

Jake Herrera

ARDELPHIA HICKEY resides in Los Angeles, California. Her education includes: honor student graduate, Summa Cum Laude, Los Angeles Southwest College, Associate of Arts Degree in Journalism, 1982-1983. She is a volunteer community political and social activist. Her interests include: activities relating to bringing about core systemic changes in the political and social systems in America. This will in turn bring about fairness, justice, peace and harmony for future generations. Her awards include: Who's Who Among Students in American Junior Colleges, 1982-'83; National Dean's List, 1982-'83; Sixth Place in editorial competition of the annual conference of the Journalism Association of Community Colleges, 1982-'83; and numerous awards for academic achievement, appreciation, recognition, merits, and commendations. **Her comments:** My theme is social responsibility and commitment to quickly bring about parity among all Americans. I am inspired to bring forth a renewed trend of thought and commitment because, Americans, blinded by their individual and collective greed and hipocracy, still just "Don't Get It." Still, they do not heed the last words of John Brown on the Negro Question, "The end of that is not yet.".......................................28, 325

Ardelphia Hickey

MARGO HINTON resides in Pittsburgh, Pennsylvania. She has a B.S. in education, health and physical education. She is a physical education teacher, scholarship athlete, and enjoys basketball, writing, etc. She is a member of NAFE (National Association for Female Executives); NAFT (North Allegheny Federation of Teachers); Campaign for a New Tomorrow; NAACP; etc. **Her comments:** My inspiration comes from my perception of reality. The poetry that I write transcends many circumstances that affect my inner spirit. My poems express my message to the planet and beyond. The themes of my poetry come from experiences that have affected me deeply.......................... 20

JEAN HUNT resides in Fresno, California. She has a high school diploma. She produces her own cassettes for special occasions. She also loves to dance and sing. She had **Roger** published in **Western Poetry Round-Up** in 1993. **Her comments:** I began writing poetry a year ago. My main inspiration comes from God, as well as my love of people. My poems are all from the depths of my soul...155

Jean Hunt

HUTZ is the pen name for **ANNE MARIE BOWEY**, who resides in Atwood, CO. She grew up with the name of Hutz, short for her maiden name. She has had 12 years of schooling and is currently working on a business degree in finance. She is a real estate processor who enjoys children and the outdoors. She is a member of Help for Abused Partners and past secretary of the Board of Atwood Men's Club. **Her comments:** This is dedicated to my family. My son was 2 months old when at the time I was feeding him, and while he clung to my finger, I began to realize that this poem needs to be written and not kept in the back of my mind. My family is now close and open minded as to living again!...127

RACHEL JENKINS resides in Lenoir, North Carolina. She was born in Kenosha, Wisconsin and raised in the foothills of Lenoir, North Carolina. She is 18 years old. She enjoys recorded music and singing into her stereo-microphone along with Whitney Houston's **I Will Always Love You.** She enjoys cooking, art, writing poetry, and collecting rings and things........................ 92

Rachel Jenkins

JOSIAH is the pen name for **KHALID ABDULLAH**, who resides in Oceanside, California. He was born of Cherokee and African roots in Alexandria, Louisiana, and reared in Texas where he cut his teeth on the music of the Cajun and Caribbean communities in which his young life was submersed. After a number of years in the performing arts of the Los Angeles and San Francisco area—acting in movies and television series, dancing and singing in theatre productions, he turned his full energies into his "true love," i.e., composing and performing his own music and poetry—delighting audiences young and old. For over a decade he has devoted his energies to teaching the youth how to utilize music to bring about better health, personal growth, higher levels of understanding and communication, — and a more peaceful and humane coexistence with each other and the earth. **His comments:** The inspiration for poetry and song come from God, my experiences in life, and the beauty and natural balances within this creation and the possibili-

Josiah

ties in each of us..318

BETTY ANNE KOPKO resides in Porcupine Plain, Saskatchewan, Canada. Her education includes: grade 12; courses completed in computer literacy and office procedure and accounting. She is presently working as a photographer and correspondent for Hudson Bay Post-Review, (weekly), Hudson Bay, Saskatchewan. She is a member of the Saskatchewan Wildlife Federation and Porcupine Plain Board of Trade. Her publications include: **Winter Frost** published in **Where Dreams Begin,** 1992; **Merry Christmas** and **Teachers,** both published in **Wind in the Night Sky,** 1993. **Her comments:** A poem is from the heart. A feeling that comes gushing out and is put into words. A poem is something that can not be said, otherwise to its full meaning, sometimes sad, sometimes happy, but very expressive and picturesque...... 146

Ingeborg Kraehmer

INGEBORG KRAEHMER resides in Connelly, New York. Her education includes: teacher's college in Leipzig, Germany. She escaped Communist East Germany in 1955 with her husband and three children. After a stop in West Germany, they traveled on to the United States. They eventually settled down after a few years in Wappinger Falls, living there for 27 years. Her family grew to include two more children, a total of 4 boys and 1 girl. She is 60 years old and has been a widow for 12 months. She never has enough time in a day to do all the things she wants to do. She is presently working as a manager in a party goods store, mostly 8 to 10 hours a day, loving every minute of it. She is always on her feet, once in awhile baby-sitting. Her children, 4 boys ranging from 38 to 21, and one daughter 36 years old, are very close. She also has 3 grandsons and 3 granddaughters. She belongs to the Reformed Church on New Hackensack Road, a wonderful congregation. She loves to travel, cook, and bake. She hardly watches T.V. She enjoys writing, especially letters to old friends and one of her single boys who lives in San Diego, California. Her youngest son lives with her, and has graduated from Dutchess Community College. She also writes poems and songs. Her mother was still in East Germany when she passed away last year. **Her comments:** My inspiration comes from listening to the church choir then writing poems. I have many friends at our Reformed Church. I am leaving my home of 27 years and moving to Port Ewen. Later this year, I hope to make my first visit back to Germany since we left in 1955. A woman's life around the world. The big new step to the life in the USAS started in Port Ewen, and after 32 very exciting years, back to Port Ewen. Hopefully, with some years of happiness until God will let me rest in peace............. 64

Jill M. LaBanca

JILL M. LaBANCA resides in North Haven, Connecticut. She is 12 years old and has attended elementary through the sixth grade. Her interests include: reading, writing, dancing, and civic work. Her memberships include: student council, church lecture, religion teacher's assistant, and library aide. She had **My Father** published in **Shoreline News** in 1985. Her awards include: Youth Service of the Year Award, 1992; Summer Library Reading Program, 1988-1989; and North Haven Middleschool Read-a-thon, 1992. **Her comments:** I enjoy writing poetry because it's a way of expressing my feelings. Reading about characters is my source of inspiration because they help my imagination. I like to visualize things deeper than they appear to other people. I try to observe everything to get new topics.......... 110, 208

Ben Larsen

BEN LARSEN resides in N. Logan, Utah. His education includes: 9th grade at North Cache Middle School. He played high school football and baseball. He plays guitar in a band and enjoys writing. His interests include: skiing, basketball, and soccer........ 28

MARY V. MAHON resides in Park City, Utah. She is a sophomore at Park City High School, Park City, Utah. She is a competitive junior tennis player. **Her comments:** My poetry is inspired from thoughts on real life experiences.......183

Mary V. Mahon

PAUL E. MAJOR, JR. has had 14 years of education. He works in international relations/life acceptance short works. **His comments:** Haiku is a disciplined poetic art of Japan. The control of form is relaxing and challenging for the author. My inspiration to pursue this type of poetry is the people of Japan and their ability to relate to life's simplest of pleasures...........326

Paul E. Major, Jr.

BETTY LOU MANES resides in Salem, Missouri. She has a 12th grade education. She has a cleaning business and enjoys reading, writing, and photography. **Her comments:** My inspiration comes from New World Translation of the Holy Scriptures, American Literature, and an article from Destiny Magazine. My themes are accurate knowledge, survival, and sovereignty.............146

Betty Lou Manes

CHERYL G. MANN resides in Clinton, North Carolina. She has a high school education. She is a housewife and would like to become an author. She won the Golden Poet Award in 1989. **Her comments:** All of my poetry is written in rhythm and rhyme. There are many different things that inspire me, from the loss of a loved one, to legends and tales. Basically, I am inspired by life and its experiences. My themes speak for themselves.................197

Cheryl G. Mann

JAMES A. MARSTERS resides in St. Louis, Missouri. He has a high school education. His interests include: chess, photography, karate, and painting. He is a member of the U.S. Chess Federation. He had **Fragments** published in hardback in 1991. **His comments:** My inspiration for writing comes from poverty. My father died when I was 5 years old, and my mother died when I was 16. Under the dominance of an alcoholic, nomadic, stepfather, I had lived in 5 states by the time I was 9 years old. The streets were my mentor—their garbage, my food—their people, how not to be. I have been married 36 years (November) with three fine boys and 6 grandchildren. As of May, I have worked at the same job for 30 years. I started writing at 16. My book, **Fragments,** ends in 1986 when I was 44 years old—A noticeable point of my later work, brevity, as people have so little time to read. This book comes through Winston Derek of Nashville, Tennessee................ 132

James A. Marsters

JERRY CRAIG McKENZIL resides in Marion, Ohio. He has a high school education and a certificate for auto body in vocational ed. He is disabled and a lyricist. He has three songs recorded for **Hollywood Gold Album.** They are: **Aids Is Out,** 33 1/3 record, 1986; **Pusher,** 45 rpm, 1985; and **Wise Men Say,** 45 rpm, 1985. He received a royalty payment for **Aids Is Out** in 1986. **His comments:** My poetry is educational.. 133

JAMES BUCKNER McKINNON resides in Seattle, Washington. His education includes: B.A., Henry M. Jackson School, 1983, University of Washington, Seattle, Washington; over a dozen military schools; American Operatic Laboratory, Los Angeles, 1946-1950. He is retired from the U.S. Navy and is a writer/researcher. His memberships include: U.S. Naval Institute; The Retired Officers Association; The Fleet Reserve Association; International Platform Association; American Mensa, Ltd., Kentucky Colonel, 1976; and the International Poet's Society. His publications include: **Cutting Off the Drug Serpent's Head** published in **Proceedings,** October, Vol. 115/10/1,040, 1989; **Nuclear Survival—"It All Boils Down To Food"** published in **The Christian Science Monitor,** March 21, 1979; and **Tax Reform** published in **The Page** and **The Seattle Times,** April 15th, 1978. His awards include: The International Poet of Merit Award (IPS), 1992; Award for Poetic Achievement (APA), April 20, 1989; The Wilmer Culver Memorial Award (Alumni Fictioneers), October, 1979. **His comments:** Concerns—Man's inhumanity to man: the entire course of human conduct is directed by the value people place upon what others consider and believe of them—usually, they are all wrong!....... 23, 150

CONNIE MONTALBANO-POWERS resides in Whitefish, Montana. She has a Bachelor of Science Degree in Nursing (BSN) from Chico State University, California. She is a registered nurse who enjoys hiking, gardening, guitar, and reading. She is a member of the Oregon State Poetry Association. **Her comments:** I never thought of my writings as categorical. I just write from the darkest depths of my soul and farthest recesses accessible to my mind. Sometimes, I write pages, other days I can't even find a pen. My poetry is usually dark and most of what I write I feel, if I don't I may self destruct.. 246

MR. D. is the pen name for **LOUIS J. DeCRESCENTIS,** who resides in Brighton, Colorado. His education includes: 1955 high school graduate; B.A. in 1959; and a M.A. in 1981. He retired in June, 1993 as a special education teacher. His memberships include: church, N.E.A., and C.E.A. His awards include: Colorado Award Nominee, 1990; and District #14 C.T.A. Lion's Award, 1992. **His comments:** My inspiration comes from nature and children, and many years working the soil as a farmer...................................... 56

Mr. D.

LIANE MIKIE NISHIOKA resides in Torrance, California. She is a student at CSU, Long Beach as an English education major. She hopes to become a high school English teacher. She belongs to the Koto String Society. She had **The Old Tree** published in **Word Power**, 1990, and **Forever Immortal You Are, Dad** published in **Poetic Voices of America**, 1993. She won the Young Writer's Award in 1990, and 2nd Place in the Reflections Contest, 1991. **Her comments:** I wrote this poem after reading Stephen Crane's **The Red Badge of Courage** and thinking about the men who have fought in wars in the past and the present......179

Liane Mikie Nishioka

Mary Ivie Norvell

MARY IVIE NORVELL is a former member of Christian Writers Association in Sacramento, California. She now resides with her husband, Glenn, in Ocala, Florida where she is a member of Writers Independent Network. Having an unquenchable passion for writing for as long as she can remember, she fuels the flame of that passion by pulling out old journals of her life, and travels both here, and abroad. Poring through the memories hiding within the confines of the old pages, she rewrites them, bringing about a brightness to the faded glow of times past, into a blazing newness for today's readers. Her persistence is paying off. She currently has several poems and a short story being published. While living in Sacramento, she studied writing under the expert direction and motivating teachings of Bud Gardner at American River College. The writing techniques acquired through Mr. Gardner's classes, and workshops have instilled within her the encouragement and determination that have now launched her into a full time career as a free lance writer. As a long time member and discussion leader with Bible Study Fellowship, and an active member of her church, Mary has chosen to go into the field of Christian Writing. She weaves into her crisp, clean writing skills, flickers of hope, and enthusiasm with which to kindle breathtaking excitement for every reader. She and her husband like to travel. As lovers of nature, they like to hike and walk, whether it be through the mountainous woods of Yosemite National Forest, the sandy shores of Bodega Bay in northern California, surveying the ruins of Saint Andrews, Scotland, or the beautiful rolling hills through the horse country of Ocala, Florida, she will always find something about which to write......280

MIA ANNE NOTTOLI (P. du VAL GUILLOUT) resides in University Heights, Ohio. Her education includes: B.A. in English, John Carroll University, Sept. 1992; currently working on M.A. in English, degree expected by 1995. She is a publications specialist and teaching assistant at the Center for Community Service, John Carroll University. She is in Who's Who Among Students in American Universities and Colleges, 1992. She had work published in **Celebrations!, Moments In Time,** and **American Poetry Annual,** all in 1993. Her awards include: Outstanding New Broadcaster, 1992, W.U.J.C. 88.7 F.M.; John Carroll Scholarship; John Huntington Scholarship; and Who's Who Among American High School Students, 1985 & 1986......281

Mia Anne Nottoli

HUGH PHILLIPS, JR. "SAM" resides in Denver, Colorado. His education includes: Newport High School, Newport, Arkansas; Aviation Cadet Class 55-D; many tech. schools and off-duty colleges in the USAF; University of North Dakota. He is a retired USAF Major and a certified flight instructor, a guitar player, and a poet. **His comments:** I grant the pleasure I realize from poetry to all experiences throughout my life. Achievements, failures, losses, pride and the emotions gained, all serve the inspiration of every "thought." I strive to lend the essence each deserves, sincerely! I do not seek poetry; it seeks me!......76, 321

Hugh Phillips, Jr. "Sam"

Norma Lou Quiring

NORMA LOU QUIRING was born in Buhler, Kansas, the granddaughter of Russian Mennonite immigrants of Dutch descent who immigrated to the United States from Ukraine in 1874 so that they might have religious freedom. In June, 1932, her family moved to Hutchinson, Kansas. The difficult and painful years of the Great Depression (1930's) and World War II (1940's) followed. After graduation from high school at the age of 17, she worked as a telephone operator for Southwestern Bell Telephone Company in Hutchinson, Kansas. Through the years she worked in various capacities, including work as a legal and medical secretary/transciptionist. For nearly six years she was employed as Scharf, Levi and Associates, a cardiology group in Kansas City, Missoui as a medical transcriptionist. She played the xylophone in the rhythm band during a program her first grade class presented to their mothers. She made her soprano soloist debut at the age of 14. She studied voice with Alice Moncrieff of Lawrence, Kansas and Hardin Van Deursen of the Kansas City Conservatory of Music. She attended Hutchinson Junior College and Colorado University in Boulder. While a student, she became a member of Sigma Alpha Iota, national honorary music fraternity. Her principal musical interest is sacred music and the majority of her singing has been in churches. She also enjoys singing the lieder of Franz Schubert. Artistic ability was manifested early in childhood and many happy hours were spent in this endeavor. She never studied art formally. In the 1970's, she met artist Franz Pollak, a native of Steyr, Austria who fled the Nazi invasion in 1938. He became her mentor and they exhibited their pictures together. The writing of poetry developed late in life although there was a very brief transitory interest in childhood. The poetry expresses strong emotional feelings and thoughts. Some of the poetry was composed during wakeful night hours and later put into writing. An avid lover of birds and animals, she takes pleasure in having parakeets and cockatiels as friends and pets. She has participated in many rescues. "To God be the glory, great things He has done!".. 14

Heather Shearer

HEATHER SHEARER resides in Regina, Saskatchewan, Canada. She has a Bachelor of Science Degree in Nursing. She is a registered nurse in an Intensive Care Unit. Her interests include: dancing, traveling, all sports, cooking, reading, 19th Century films, and playing the piano. Her memberships include: Sons of Scotland Benevolent Society; chairperson of P.R. for Scottish Society of Regina; Social Committee member at work; and involved in pet therapy with the Humane Society of Regina. She had **Why Nurses Are Leaving the Workforce: A Telephone Survey** published in an in-house document of the Saskatchewan Registered Nurses Association in 1986. **Her comments:** My usual source of inspiration is love's demise. I'm most prolific when I'm infinitely sad...175

Mary S. Shepherd

MARY S. SHEPHERD resides in Picayune, Mississippi. Her education includes: Tulane University and University of New Orleans, Louisana, Jr. status. Her interests include: painting in oils, acrylics, sand, and writing poetry. Her memberships include: Slidell Louisiana Artists League; Live Poets of Slidell, LA.; and Friends of the Library of Slidell, LA. She received the XYZ Service Award (Xtra years of zest) as teacher of senior citizen art, Slidell, LA, 1973-1980; Best of Show, Mississippi Coin and Mineral display, in 1970. **Her comments:** My poetry interests are in the use of words to show deep interest in life as it is today. I am 83 years old. I have traveled extensively in Central America, and I love life. Much of what I write is lively, funny, and has some rhyme. Sometimes I cry when I read **El Sacrahocas Mother, Am brays Mother's Cry,** or **Little Golden Finger Ring**.................8, 271, 314

HERBERT I. SHOCKLEY was born on January 19, 1932, in Hazelton, PA. His mother was of English descent and his father was of Indian descent. His father's mother was a full blooded Cherokee Indian. He loved art and began by creating cartoons at a very early age as he admired the magic of Walt Disney. Known for its beautiful mountains and valleys, the Hazelton area provided him with ample subjects to capture on canvas. He also liked painting still life & people, attempting to capture their mood and personality. He excelled in art in high school and his senior year he was the first recipient of the annual award the Hazelton High School presents to the most outstanding High School senior student. The painting he received it for was of a friend of his sitting in a big overstuffed chair titled, **Lazy Day.** After graduation in 1949, his mother passed away. Not knowing what he wanted to do, he worked in the Hazelton area for a few years. He moved to San Francisco and fell in love with the area. While there, he got the inspiration for many of his paintings. He moved back East and in 1955, opened his own sign painting business in his hometown of Hazelton. During this time he got involved with the Hazelton Chapter of Barbershoppers and

continued on next page

loved singing. He also took up table tennis and basketball. He belonged to the Hazelton Art League and kept in close touch with the arts and his high school art teacher. She encouraged him to paint more. After painting for many years, he was invited to have his own art show at the Hazelton Art League in 1979. At that show he sold 18 paintings, mostly of local scenery and historic landmarks. He was awarded the first ever Service Award in 1990 from the Art League. It was truly an honor for him. His love of life and genuine sincere personality touched every person he met. Art came natural to him and he never pursued it further than a high school diploma. In 1967, he started working for St. Regis Paper Company in Hazelton as a graphic artist. He worked there for 26 years. He worked his way up to becoming a graphic art manager the last ten years he was there. During that time, the company changed from St. Regis to Princeton Pkg. Inc. He passed away on December 2, 1992, and shortly after that, Princeton Pkg. became Bemis. He was the last art director there............292

JACKIE SISTO resides in Geneva, Illinois. She is a junior in high school. Her interest is in nursing. She is in cheerleading and track in high school. **Comments:** This poem was written when Jacki was 14. Her mind never seems to stop working and she felt like putting an occasional "nightmare" on paper. Jackie is now 16............108

Jackie Sisto

ANNIE SMITH resides in Rockville, Maryland. Her education includes: high school—Academy of the Holy Cross in Kensington, Maryland; college—currently a sophomore at Stonehill College, North Easton, Massachusetts. She is president of the English Society at Stonehill College and a member of the Stonehill Theater Company............ 66

MARY ANN WAGNER STEIRER resides in Port Richey, Florida. She is a graduate of Springfield Technical Institute, Springfield, Massachusetts in nursing. She took her state board exams in Boston, Massachusetts. She is a nurse who enjoys aerobics and walking. She takes jazz and tap dancing and performs on stage every June. She relaxes by playing her organ music. She is a member of the A.N.A. She won a Who's Who in Poetry from **World of Poetry** in 1979, and Poetry Hall of Fame in Tampa, Florida, in 1979. **Her comments:** I have 37 poems published in various anthologies in the U.S.A., as well as Canada. I get inspired in poetry when I walk, which I love to do, or play my music on my organ. Many ideas for a poem come to me then. My sister, who is very interested in what I do, is my greatest supporter............ 77

Mary Ann Wagner Steirer

RUDOLF STOBER resides in Lansing, MI. His education includes: German and English; construction engineering. He is a bar owner. His is a member of the Michigan Amateur Softball Association, and was inducted in Michigan Hall of Fame, 1985. **His comments:** For my friends, I write speeches and eulogies; to my wife and children, I write essays. Frank Dilloughby, Honored Colonel, known poet, resides in Kentucky, encouraged and inspired me to write poems. I have been in the bar business for 29 years. I had to overcome and absorb, deceit and rude treatment. I felt humbled in more ways than should be written. I have seen my daughter in the same condition. I found myself. The shock inspired me to write this poem............35, 44

Rudolf Stober

BRENDA LEEDEE SUNSTRUM resides in North Vancouver, British Columbia, Canada. Her education includes: high school diploma and basic psychology. She is a reservations agent and enjoys music and the outdoors. **Her comments: Missing You** was written after leaving home and living across the country...313

Brenda LeeDee Sunstrum

JENNIFER JILL TAYLOR resides in Stratford, CT. She is a home schooled high school freshman. She is actively involved in her church youth group and in hospital volunteer work. She is working toward her black belt in karate and swims on a local swim team. She loves horseback riding, playing the piano, singing, reading, and especially writing. **Her comments:** I have wanted to be a writer ever since I could write. I already loved reading, and found creating my own stories and poems exciting and fun. I come from a large family of seven and have received much encouragement from them. Nature really inspires a lot of my work and I like to compose poems with meaning. I feel that I am dedicated to writing and hope to continue it throughout my life...100

Jennifer Jill Taylor

J.L. TAYLOR resides in Fairbanks, Alaska. Education includes: graduating senior in English at University of Alaska Fairbanks, (B.A.), 1994. Occupation is a radio disc jockey. Interests include: native arts and film. **Sky City** published in **Poetry: An American Heritage** in 1993. **Comments:** As a Native American (Cherokee), I find my inspiration thru traditional sources, like nature and the world around me and the people and animals in it. Many of my themes deal with raw, uncensored emotions dealt with in a brutally honest manner. I also use the Alaskan wilderness as a backdrop for fiction and poetry...173

DORIS J. TELLIER resides in Oakwood, Illinois. She is a high school graduate. She has been writing poetry since she was 16. She is now a senior citizen who enjoys singing. She also takes care of a 91 year old lady at night. She is chaplain in the American Legion Auxillary, and president of the senior citizen meals they have in Muncie, Illinois. She had **In Memory** published in 1975. **Her comments:** I always pray and ask God to give me the words I should write, then I thank Him. My other poem, **In Memory,** was about my mother and was in our family's history. My older sister wrote about our ancestors in her book. I have a scrapbook of some of my work since high school...171

Doris J. Tellier

GLORIA J. TERRY resides in Crawfordsville, Indiana. She has a high school education. She is a secretary who enjoys writing, crafts, cooking, target shooting, and refinishing furniture. She is a volunteer at family crisis center, New Hope Christian Church. She had **Dad** published in **Fountain County Neighbor** in 1992. **Her comments:** I enjoy writing about my true to life experiences and those people who are so very special to me. Daily life is an inspiration in itself, if we choose to see it...142

Gloria J. Terry

J.E. TURACHAK is the pen name for **JASON ERIC TURACHAK,** who resides in Barton, Ohio. He is a graduate of Martins Ferry High School and attended Kent State University. He is a customer service clerk whose interests include: computers and communications. He is a member of the United Food and Commercial Workers Union, Local 23. **His comments:** My writing has always been an outlet for me. My inspiration is derived from day to day life and my themes are typically ones of love both lost and found. My friend once saw a smudge on an original and commented, based on the content, that it was a tear... 18

RAY TYSON resides in Stewartstown, Pennsylvania. He is 29 years old. He is gifted in poetry and has touched many hearts. He writes poems for people, especially for them.....................................243, 306

KATIE UHRIN resides in Mount Pleasant, Pennsylvania. Her education includes: 6th grade, Blessed Sacrament Cathedral School. Her interests include: reading, basketball, and tennis. She is a member of the Greensburg Racquet Club Riding School. **Her comments:** I like to write poetry because my poems can make the people that I give them to feel better. I also become closer to the people and objects that I write about..174

CYNTHIA HOLLEY WARREN (LEE) resides in Axton, Virginia. She is a part time student at Patrick Henry Community College and Danville Community College in the engineering program. She is presently employed at Tultex Corp. in Martinsville, Virginia. She is active in management team concept at her place of employment. **Her comments:** My poetry reflects my innermost feelings. Love inspires my imagination to boundless limits. What is love but a dream. For this dream I thank the man of my heart.......................21, 78, 98

Cynthia Holley Warren (Lee)

BOBBY WELLS, JR. resides in Donna, Texas. His education includes: Weslaco schools throughout childhood; May, 1993 graduate of Weslaco High School. He collects African and Indian artifacts and beads, and enjoys drawing and swimming. His memberships include: National Honor Society; student council; yearbook staff; honor band; U.I.L. Prose; Poetry; Group Improv.; One-Act Play Save The Manatee Club; Save A Turtle Club; and the National Wildlife Federation. His awards include: National Written & Illustrated Book Contest Winner, Top 100 of 7,500 entries, 1991; American Legion Texas Boys' State, 1992; and "Most Talented" for W.H.S. Sr. personalities, 1993. **His comments:** Being an only child, I have more time on my hands than most children my age. I use this time to stare high up into the heavens above and think about the beautiful world around me. My own thoughts become my companions, and my companions become my inspiration to write. A dear friend by the name of Daniel Peña inspired me to create this piece entitled, **Thinking.** Although we only met last year, I feel he has come to know me just as well as any other. And as I grow through life learning

Bobby Wells, Jr.

different things each and everyday, I shall always give thanks to my companions that walked with me through the wilderness of the world. After all, the best mirror I could ever look into, is the smiling face of an old friend. I also enjoy traveling and blending together with different cultures. Above all this, I strongly look forward to becoming a famous addition to the Hollywood scenario by working my way up to stardom and being a famous actor in movies some-day.. 77

Index of Authors

Authors are indexed under name or pen name that appears with their poem.

Aase, Edith P., Minnesota............................ 153
Abbott, Katie, New Jersey........................... 265
Abbott-Wagner, Betty, Pennsylvania............. 118
Abel, Ben, British Columbia, Canada............. 104
Abramowicz, Ela, Quebec, Canada................ 327
Abril, Vicky, Wyoming.............................. 218
Ackerman, Carol Ann, South Dakota............. 160
Adams, Diane, California............................. 10
Adams, Kurt, Michigan.............................. 178
Adams, Mary Ann, New Mexico............. 41, 44
Adams, Matthew J., Minnesota..................... 284
Adams, Ned, Connecticut........................... 299
Adkins, Maurice, California......................... 29
Aguirre, Kevin, California........................... 324
Ahbleza Lorraine, California........................ 283
ahSureMom, Washington............................ 317
Akin, Penny Lynn, New York....................... 325
Albright, Angela, Iowa.............................. 252
Albright, Shannon H., Illinois...................... 36
Alcivar, Eliana Mariella, New York................ 225
Alessandra, New Jersey............................. 121
Al-Fequi, Mohammed A., Saudi Arabia........ 18, 222
Allen, Dorothy A., Texas............................. 43
Allen, Lucy I., Massachusetts...................... 257
Allen, Samuel Blaine, Ohio......................... 95
Alma-Elvira, California.............................. 300
Amador, Tammy, Texas.............................. 195
Amodeo, Jeanne, New Jersey....................... 225
Amunson, Patricia Capps, Wyoming.............. 106
Anderson, H. Clark, Connecticut................... 279
Anderson, Heather, British Columbia, Canada.... 317
Anderson, Tara L., Massachusetts................. 40
Anna Lee, Pennsylvania............................. 116
Annetia, Alberta, Canada........................... 113
Anzures, Rosey, California.......................... 152
Aponte, Gisele J., Wisconsin....................... 129
April, Oklahoma..................................... 220
Arcand, Andrea R., Wyoming...................... 141
Archer, Phyllis A., Nebraska....................... 257
Arena, Susan, Mississippi.......................... 150
Armstrong, Mark, Massachusetts.................. 238
Armstrong, Michael T., Ohio....................... 191
Arnold, Bill, Florida................................. 303
Arnold Paulie, North Carolina..................... 140
Arthur, Crystal, Ohio............................... 195
Arwine, Nancy, Washington........................ 271
Ashall, Frank, Missouri............................. 28
Asher, Poetic Feelings Analyst, New York....... 273
Askeland, Cheryl, California....................... 248
Atkins, Cynthia, Oregon............................ 54
Audino, Frank L., Rhode Island.................... 70
Augustine, Courtney, Arizona...................... 322
Aull, Gerald .S., Sr., Wisconsin.................... 35
Aunt Linda, Illinois................................. 62
Axtell, Penny, Kansas............................... 260
Ayers, Mary E., West Virginia...................... 50
Babcock, Matt, Idaho............................... 316
Baden, Lisa, Missouri............................... 233
Bahner-Guhin, Sean, New York..................... 279
Baker, Art, California................................ 150
Baker, Betty Jean, Indiana.......................... 283
Baker, D.A., New Jersey............................. 264
Baker, Erin Janelle, California..................... 268
Baker, Jared, Missouri.............................. 181
Baker, Linda, Missouri.............................. 305
Ballard, Stephanie, Massachusetts................ 194

Ballis, Jean P., North Carolina..................... 44
Bangura, Bernard, Massachusetts.................. 30
Barber, Leslie A., Ontario, Canada................ 236
Barber, Wanda L., Louisiana........................ 119
Barbieri, Rebecca G., New Jersey............. 110, 189
Barker, Karen Jean, North Carolina............... 125
Barkley, Richard L., Colorado...................... 267
Barksdale, Cheryl, Alabama........................ 187
Barner, Mary Jo, Pennsylvania..................... 253
Barnhart, Betty J., West Virginia................... 152
Baroi, Suranjan K., California...................... 31
Barr, Jack, West Virginia............................ 56
Barreca, Salvatore A.V., Pennsylvania............ 210
Bartelson, Sue, Indiana............................. 65
Barton, Rebecca A., Illinois........................ 37
Barton, Rolanda, Texas............................. 46
Basaraba, Audrey L., British Columbia, Canada...... 302
Bashutsky, Janice F., Saskatchewan, Canada.......... 159
Basil, Dorothy Sanders, West Virginia............ 179
Bassett, Pamela T., Alberta, Canada.............. 30
Bastian, Zane, Pennsylvania....................... 76
Batcha, Chris, Pennsylvania........................ 42
Battey, Ernest C., Jr., Rhode Island............... 135
Battigelli, Nicola, Ontario, Canada............... 232
Bauché, Lori, British Columbia, Canada.......... 202
Baudisch, Ellen, New York...
..................................123, 132, 172, 190, 224, 277
Baxley, Deborah Marsh, Georgia................... 204
Bea, Oklahoma...................................... 265
Beachboard, Deborah, Washington................ 326
Bealke, Julie, Minnesota........................... 292
Beaton, Mary C., New Jersey....................... 303
Beaumont, Karen, Wisconsin....................... 188
Beebee, Robert, Nebraska.......................... 38
Bejcek, Ken, New Brunswick, Canada............. 277
Belcher, Julie, Ohio................................. 121
Belden, Carolyn E., Ohio........................... 264
Belfield, Alexandre, West Virginia................. 202
Bell, Heather Marie, Kansas........................ 53
Bell, Helen Pope, Georgia.......................... 125
Bell, Kathy Sue Hicks, Tennessee.................. 40
Bell, Keith, Colorado........................... 63, 312
Bell, Roni, New York................................ 113
Belton, Natasha Monique, New York.............. 182
Benedict, Roberta E., New York.................... 192
Benedict, Vickie, Indiana........................... 88
Benedict, Victoria, Indiana......................... 210
Benjamin, Ann H. Womer, Ohio.................... 14
Benn, June, Idaho................................... 70
Benson, Alvin K., Utah......................... 12, 45
Berckhan, Kelly J., California....................... 224
Bergeron, Elizabeth, New York..................... 189
Berghoff, Andrea, An Original, Michigan......... 67
Berkowitz, Leah Rachel, Pennsylvania............ 245
Bernstein, Charles, California...................... 68
Bessette, Don, New York............................ 165
Bettger, M. Marie, Washington..................... 66
BGH, Florida.. 165
Biermann, Eileen O., Missouri..................... 114
Biller, Malinda, Ohio............................... 264
Billie, Wyoming..................................... 230
Binder, Sara, Indiana............................... 21
Birch, Mary, North Carolina........................ 92
Birks, Joanne, New York............................ 69
Bisbano, Julie A., Rhode Island.................... 14
Bischoff, Arley M., Washington..................... 72

Bischoff, Myrna Kay, Washington......................... 134
Bissell, Romala, Michigan.............................. 271
Blackman, William, Wisconsin.......................... 290
Blackmon, Robin L., California......................... 122
Blagg, Shirley, West Virginia.......................... 82
Blair, Catherine, Massachusetts....................... 197
Blake, Shane A., South Dakota......................... 297
Blankenship, Evelyn, Missouri......................... 131
Blathers-Craig, Lolita, Wisconsin..................... 41
Blessing, Bea Marie, Texas............................ 148
Bloom, Janna, Ontario, Canada........................ 33
Blount, Mollie, Georgia............................... 133
Blue, Justin, California.............................. 63
Blystone, Jeanne Marie, Pennsylvania................. 172
Bobby, Washington.................................... 147
Bocchetti, Paul M., New York.......................... 175
Bock, Michele Snyder, Kansas.......................... 145
Bocook, Heather, Illinois............................. 43
Boecker, Aileen, Iowa................................. 53
Bognar, Nick, Virginia................................ 258
Bohms, Joseph David, Illinois......................... 279
Boland, Hugh T., Wisconsin............................ 27
Bolden, Marilyn J., Michigan.......................... 122
Bolen, Lisa, Maryland................................. 75
Boney, Patricia, Georgia.......................... 40, 175
Bonnefil, Vivienne, Maryland.......................... 209
Book, Bonnie Jo, New Jersey........................... 251
Bookey, Kevin, Oregon................................. 221
Bopp, Joseph V., New Jersey........................... 63
Boseneiler, Cheryl A.,
     (Centerstage Dance Studio), Illinois......... 144
Botsford, Megan, Kansas............................... 15
Botti, Ernest A., Massachusetts....................... 295
Bottoms, Ruth Bucher, New York........................ 209
Bouaphanh, Diamond, Alabama........................... 202
Bouma, Ellen, Alberta, Canada......................... 307
Bourgeois, Jackie A., Ontario, Canada................. 247
Bourree, Felix, Mississippi........................... 260
Bower, Dwight W., Ohio................................ 171
Boyd, Frances M., New Jersey.......................... 238
Boyles, Elsie Holland Babcock, Georgia................ 314
Boylorn, Robin, North Carolina........................ 232
Brame, Clint, Jr., Oklahoma........................... 286
Branagan, Janet, New Jersey........................... 230
Branam, Heather, Florida.............................. 80
Brauher, Oneta, Michigan.............................. 42
Brazzell, Pamela R., Indiana.......................... 220
Brennan, Donna, Maryland.............................. 156
Brewer, Doris Hartsell, Virginia...................... 96
Brewer, Jeni, Illinois................................ 74
Brewster, Steven G., Oklahoma......................... 87
Briggs, William J., Kansas............................ 158
Brogden, Patti J., Tennessee.......................... 163
Brohl, Ted, New Jersey................................ 230
Bronzo, Patricia Ann, Connecticut..................... 223
Brooks, Dale H., Kentucky............................. 103
Brooks, James L., New Jersey.......................... 310
Brown, Aimee, Michigan................................ 327
Brown, Alver Haynes, New Jersey....................... 265
Brown, Austin Wayne, Georgia.......................... 54
Brown, Barbara, New York.............................. 303
Brown, Bonnie S., Pennsylvania........................ 50
Brown, Garrett J., Maryland........................... 300
Brown, Phil, New Jersey............................... 301
Brown, Steven R., Rhode Island............. 9, 16, 267
Brown, Violet, Missouri....................... 61, 92
Brungardt, Deb, Kansas................................ 35
Brungardt, Jeanie, Kansas............................. 235
Bruno, Sarajane, New Jersey........................... 136
Bryant, L. Elizabeth, Massachusetts................... 13
Bryant, Lolly, California............................. 78
Bryce, Dorothy M., Virginia........................... 238
Bryla, Leonard, California............................ 64
B., Sonny, Louisiana.................................. 51

Buchlmayer, Ramona, California............... 22, 238, 311
Bucknell, Diana Lynn, Alaska.......................... 225
Bue, Geoffrey S., Wisconsin........................... 44
Buechler, Karen J., Alberta, Canada...
.... 133, 220, 221, 295
Buell, Eric, Prince Edward Island, Canada............. 219
Buoy, Crystal M., Kansas.............................. 123
Burch, Jim, Texas..................................... 118
Burchfield, Pat K., Wisconsin......................... 258
Burgette, Jerica Elisabeth, Tennessee................. 73
Burke, Grace, Pennsylvania............................ 253
Burkle, David R., Washington.......................... 197
Burlingame, Sarah, Massachusetts...................... 170
Burnett, Audrey V., Ohio.............................. 60
Burns, Odelle M., South Carolina...................... 120
Burris, Forrest, Oregon............................... 203
Busby, Jennifer, Oklahoma............................. 201
Busch, Aaron J., Massachusetts........................ 318
Busch, Elizabeth J., Indiana.......................... 138
Butela, Jillian, Pennsylvania......................... 242
Byerly, Charlotte J., Pennsylvania.............. 75, 80
Byerly, Kerschie, Ohio................................ 219
Byrnes, Martin A., Pennsylvania....................... 164
Cabral, Richard, California........................... 7
Cacia, Cheryse, Utah.................................. 150
Cacioppo, John D., New York................... 69, 117
Cagle, Elaine Ash, Georgia............................ 67
Caldwell, Lenora, West Virginia....................... 223
Caldwell, Liz, Indiana................................ 251
Calton, Ray A., Utah.................................. 86
Cameron, Roy L., Alabama.............................. 115
Camp, Joe, III, Michigan.......... 26, 39, 43, 148, 296
Campbell, Allen J, Iowa............................... 74
Campbell, Jennifer Elizabeth, New York................ 115
Carlson-Sega, Amber D., California.................... 53
Carmichael, James, Ontario, Canada.................... 288
Carney, D.E., Ohio.................................... 314
Carpenter, Lynne A., Kansas........................... 38
Carreon, Cheryl Daniels, Texas........................ 101
Carrozza, Anna, Tennessee............................. 64
Carson, L. Rachel, Connecticut........................ 190
Carter, Linda, Arkansas............................... 246
Carter, Vicki Maria, Michigan......................... 303
Casalino, Michele, New Jersey......................... 255
Cashman, Sharon, California........................... 188
Castro, Heather R., California........................ 183
Caylor, Douglas L., California........................ 63
Cerceo, Adrianne B., Pennsylvania..................... 159
Cerreta, Nancy, Connecticut........................... 174
Certo, Dorothy Marta, New Jersey...................... 71
Ceton, Paul T., Michigan.............................. 307
Chaffin, Melba, Texas................................. 12
Chagnon, Bradley, California.......................... 166
Chaney, Krista, Illinois.............................. 25
Chapman, Lydia, New York.............................. 56
Charbauski, Jerry, Mississippi........................ 186
Chargin, Marilyn, California.......................... 135
Charles, Leah, Arizona................................ 32
Chaussee', Sandi, Wisconsin........................... 180
Chavez, Sindy,   New Mexico......................... 60
Cheser, Betty Carol, Kentucky......................... 307
Chibante, Leona Louise, California.................... 236
Childs, Maryanna, OP, Ohio............................ 9
Christina Marie, Rhode Island......................... 152
Christofferson, Shiril, Utah.......................... 38
Cialkoszewski, Gina, Wisconsin........................ 64
Cito, Jean, New Jersey................................ 55
Claghorn, Jennifer, Georgia........................... 148
Clare, K., Michigan........................... 276, 297
Clark, Jeanette, K., Rhode Island..................... 107
Clark, Judy, Quebec, Canada........................... 256
Clark, Sheila Raye, Minnesota......................... 72
Clark-Astin, Shawn, Pennsylvania...................... 175
Clausen, Dorothea, California......................... 46

Clela, California........................ 131, 262, 294
Cleveland, Velma N., Iowa............................. 145
Clifford, Eileen Leigh, Colorado.................... 156
Clinard, Mary, North Carolina....................... 36
Clinkenbeard, Grady A., Texas....................... 285
Clouse, Catherine M., Michigan...................... 49
Coates, Tom, New Jersey.............................. 178
Cochran, Lee Joseph, Washington..................... 106
Coggeshall, Sharon Rae, Hawaii...................... 111
Coghill, Curtis L., Arizona......................... 182
Cole, Beth Hathaway, Wyoming........................ 144
Cole, Ernie R., Indiana............................. 201
Cole, William J., New Jersey........................ 10
Coleing, Barbara, Ontario, Canada.............. 23, 243
Collier, Ronda, Arizona............................. 310
Collins, Brenda J, Hawaii........................... 288
Collins, Charles W., Sr., Florida................... 107
Collins, Janice, Virginia........................... 216
Collins, Lauren, Virginia........................... 228
Colston, Alden, Texas............................... 212
Compagnon, Hank, California......................... 318
Connell, Dorothy Klinck, Pennsylvania............... 178
Conover, Matt, Utah................................. 105
Conte, River, Massachusetts......................... 311
Conti, Valerie M., New York......................... 227
Cook, Ann, Texas.................................... 162
Cook, David M., (Cooky), Alberta, Canada............ 51
Cook, Mabel, Washington............................. 253
Cook, Nicole L., Alberta, Canada.................... 90
Cook, Rhonda M., Illinois........................... 235
Cooke, Robert J., New York.......................... 236
Cooper, Elizabeth A., Connecticut................... 300
Cooper, Jerry W., Ohio.............................. 115
Cooper, Linda M., West Virginia..................... 100
Copeland, J.D., Texas............................... 84
Cordell, Amber, Mississippi......................... 96
Cordell, Mike, Mississippi.......................... 128
Cork, Sheldon, Alberta, Canada...................... 249
Cormier, Doreen M, New Brunswick, Canada.... 29
Costellow, Jon Michael, Kentucky.................... 185
Costley, Edward S., Maryland........................ 149
Cote, Andy, Maine................................... 39
Cottle, Micki, North Carolina....................... 122
Couch, Judith, New York............................. 181
Couch, Kathryn B., Georgia.......................... 32
Couza, Kim, Illinois................................ 210
Covington, David Jay, Texas......................... 166
Cox, Ryan, Colorado................................. 293
Crabtree, Kayleen, Washington....................... 157
Craft, Marion Armstrong, Texas...................... 64
Cramer-Luckie, Urma, Florida........................ 159
Craven, Patricia Ann, New Jersey.................... 197
Crawford, Lynell, Massachusetts..................... 107
Crew, Carol Jean, Iowa.............................. 55
Crewe, Karen Ann, New Jersey........................ 22
Crispin, E. A., Colorado............................ 185
Critzer, Kelly, Virginia............................ 21
Crobaugh, Emma, Florida............................. 6
Crochet, Daron Gabriel, Louisiana................... 299
Cromeans, Cindy L., Texas........................... 58
Crossland, Nancy J., Texas.......................... 321
Cuba, Dixie Taber, Missouri......................... 207
Curran, S.T., Michigan.............................. 117
Cuschera, Teri, California.......................... 32
Cushwa, Hilda Frantz, Maryland...................... 140
Cutkomp, Gladys B., Iowa............................ 49
Cyphert, Dennis Wayne, Maryland..................... 328
Czajka, Katie, Texas................................ 280
Dabrowski, Linda, Wisconsin......................... 29
Dahl, Jim, California........................... 16, 182
Dallman-DeMoss, Corinne, North Dakota... 141, 247
Dames D.F., North Carolina.......................... 113
Damon, Jim, California.............................. 132
Dana, A. Charles, Texas............................. 36

Daniels, Rose, Ontario, Canada...................... 272
Dannenmann, Otto K., Wisconsin...................... 12
Dapul, Gina Elaine, New Jersey...................... 98
Darley, Marcheia, Florida........................... 226
Davidson, Angie, Wyoming............................ 321
Davis, Andria, Pennsylvania......................... 293
Davis, Doris Moore, Texas........................... 189
Davis, Geneva, Indiana.............................. 46
Davis, Glenda D. (Dunham), Maryland................. 284
Davis, J. Scott, Tennessee.......................... 81
Davis, Kenneth A., Sr., Oregon...................... 196
Davis, Millie, South Dakota......................... 181
Davis-Hurst, Lin, Illinois.......................... 8
dawn marie, Illinois................................ 108
Dawson, Dixie (Ferrebee), Ohio...................... 149
Day, Jeanne Marie, Alaska........................... 239
Day, Marlis, Indiana................................ 50
Dayton, Donna, Utah................................. 280
DeGrave, Danny, West Virginia....................... 234
Deguire, Kimberly L., Ontario, Canada............... 43
DeHass, Melvin, Oklahoma............................ 191
DeHoney, Sean, Texas................................ 143
de La Rochelle, Francois, Florida................... 117
Demetral, Ruth C., California................ 17, 116, 174
Demetrius, California............................... 208
Demurjian, Laura Ovsanna, Massachusetts............. 123
De Natley, Beryl B., California..................... 99
Denman, Amanda J., Pennsylvania..................... 41
Dennick, Bradley, Washington........................ 10
Detweiler, Fern, Ontario, Canada.................... 173
Deuster, Jennifer Marie, Wisconsin.................. 217
Deutschmann, Mildred, Illinois...................... 35
Devery, Jessica, Pennsylvania....................... 282
Devontine, Julie E., California..................... 72
Dewey, Celeste A., Colorado......................... 194
DeWitte, Denelda, Indiana........................... 85
Dial, Margaret M., North Carolina................... 26
Dianne Michelle, Oklahoma........................... 158
Diaz-Chamorro, Amalia, California................... 170
Dibert, Mary K., Pennsylvania....................... 207
Dickinson, Dawn C., Maryland........................ 242
Dickinson, Debra J., New York....................... 191
Dill, Edith P., Florida............................. 126
Doerig, C., New Brunswick, Canada................... 39
Dolezal, KariLyn J., Minnesota...................... 160
Donovan, Chris, Ontario, Canada..................... 262
Doran, Deborah Anne, New York....................... 192
Doran, Melissa, New Hampshire....................... 48
Dorn, Adrian, Washington............................ 277
Doucet, Evelyn M., Virginia..................... 37, 176
Dougan, Dot, Ontario, Canada........................ 273
Downey, Judy Ann Williams, Colorado................. 174
Doyle, P.F., British Columbia, Canada............... 287
Drinovsky, Sharon L., Iowa.......................... 262
Driscoll, Constance Fitzgerald, Massachusetts....... 182
Driscoll, Joseph H., Michigan....................... 168
Dube, Larry T., Sr., California..................... 220
Dubé, Violet, Ontario, Canada....................... 118
Dublin, Michael L., Sr., North Carolina............. 32
DuBois, Barbara R., New Mexico...................... 212
Du Bose, Grady, Texas............................... 24
Duckworth, Oplean, Mississippi...................... 135
Duffy, Mary A., New Jersey.......................... 89
Dugalech, Kimberly, Michigan........................ 308
Dunbar, W. Channing, III, Massachusetts............. 77
Dunn, Mary, Colorado................................ 93
Dupree, Marie, Washington........................... 130
Durán, Phillip H., Washington................... 138, 200
Duren, James Wesley, New Jersey..................... 218
Durrett, Brittany, Tennessee........................ 313
Dutton, Laura, North Carolina....................... 256
Dyck, Leslie, Pennsylvania.......................... 290
Dyer, David E., Connecticut......................... 40
Dykhouse, Drice, Michigan........................... 21

Dykins, Vi, Indiana	128
Eades, Cathryn, Pennsylvania	193
Eagle, Linda L., New York	203
Eaton, Autumn H., Texas	43
Ebell, Kathleen Pieters, Texas	73
Eckerle, Philip A., Michigan	13
Edge, Janice, Tennessee	248
Edgington, Byron, Iowa	111
Edwards, Clare, Florida	83
Edwards, T.M., Tennessee	105
Eiring, Kris, Wisconsin	111
Elena Maria, Pennsylvania	218
Elgart, Grace, Florida	243
Eller, Katrina, Colorado	223
Elliott, Adam James, California	255
Elliott, Jeffrey D., West Virginia	234
Elliott, Patricia Jane, Massachusetts	163
Ellis, Mamie B., Iowa	273
Ellis, Pat, New Jersey	160
Ellis, Paul D., West Virginia	23
Emerson, Barbara Weaver, Texas	38
Emswiler, David J., New Mexico	68
Eng, Carol Vanden, Wisconsin	145
England, Kelly M., Connecticut	328
Enns, L. Marie, Alberta, Canada	13, 213
Erb, Jean Oliver, Ohio	279
Ericksen, Fran, South Dakota	196
Erickson, Carole Mae, British Columbia, Canada	142
Esch, Lee, North Dakota	15
Esposito, Gina Marie, Pennsylvania	15
Estep, Helen Gibson, Tennessee	98
Estep, James Cotton, Indiana	145
Estes, Virginia, Alaska	272
Etters, Burl, Illinois	220
Evans, Blanche E., Florida	166
Evans, Helen M., Illinois	25
Evans, Melissa, Texas	129
Evans, Walter A., Illinois	56
Everett, M.L., Indiana	111
Everson, Bret, New York	101
Ewy, Paula Jiron, New Mexico	190
Fago, Dawn M., New Jersey	172
Faher, Michael, Pennsylvania	99
Fahning, Esther G., Minnesota	256
Faison, Ernie, North Carolina	243
Fama, Gloria, Pennsylvania	50
Farmer, Silas, Indiana	213
Farr, D. B., California	201
Farris, Frank, New Hampshire	212
Fashbaugh, Earl F., Minnesota	312
Fauset, Kathleen Shea, Illinois	288
Fechhelm, Constance, Wisconsin	59
Fehlhafer, Anette, Nebraska	179
Felker, Heather Rose, New York	159
Ferris, Linda Lagasse, Missouri	137
Field, Deborah, Rhode Island	113
Figueroa, Eric R., California	285
Fink, Leopoldine, Ontario, Canada	163
Fink, Marlene "Molly", Wisconsin	208
Fitzgerald, Leslie, Texas	149
Fix, Tanya E. C., Alberta, Canada	315
Flaherty, Reed, Missouri	130
Flaishans, Kathleen, Michigan	297
Flanders, Angela, Massachusetts	133
Fleck, Rebecca E., South Carolina	81
Fleming, Mary Kay, Florida	285
Flint, Ken, New York	168
Flocca, Nicolette L., Illinois	281
Flores, Dixie, Kansas	298
Fly, Peter, Hawaii	275
Fogleman, Pat, Oklahoma	96
Follett, Corey Allan, Newfoundland, Canada	129
Fonda, Sheridan, Florida	20
Fontanez, Juan, New Jersey	316
Forand, David L., Vermont	192
Ford, Beverly L., Kansas	299
Ford, Kenneth Evans, Oregon	233
Ford, Sandra K., Georgia	106
Ford, William R., Jr., Michigan	90
Fossa, Aimee D., New York	113
Fox, Fred, New Jersey	15
Francis, Shawn W., Massachusetts	25
Frazier, Carlotta, Indiana	71
Free, William E., Georgia	275
Freeman, Freda, South Africa	6
Freeman, Judy, Ontario, Canada	76
Freestone, Grace, Mrs., Iowa	205
Freiberger, John IV, New York	275
Frey, Juanita V., Texas	149
Friedel, Michelle, Illinois	257
Fritts, Denise L., New York	231
Fritz, Diane S., Iowa	115
Frost, Brian D., Ohio	206
(Frybarger), Diana Lynn, Illinois	278
Fuhrmann, Judith, Illinois	278
Fuller, Matthew, Michigan	181
Funk, Tonya Jo, Missouri	159
Gabbitas, Tom, Wyoming	320
Gadwah, Joslyn, Connecticut	11
Gagne, Kenneth Shawn, Wisconsin	308
Gail Lynn, Arkansas	313
Gallegos, Maria Susanna, Colorado	249
Galloway, Cat, North Carolina	54
Galloway, Richard L., Mississippi	35
Galvin, Traci L.B., Colorado	216
Gamache, Rosalie A., Colorado	286
Gamble, Don W., Jr., Mississippi	290
Gamrell, D. Margaret, Mississippi	282
Gannon, Deborah Callaghan, Wisconsin	318
Gano, Candace, Alberta, Canada	19
Gantner, Jenna L., New Jersey	252
Garcia, Cheryl Lee, Texas	241
Garner, Paulette M., Virginia	240
Garner, Steven D., Virginia	160
Garofalo, Lisa, New York	28
Garrett, Peggy, New York	155
Garrick, Antoinette, Louisiana	263
Garringer, Robert W., Sr., Pennsylvania	88
Garrison, Allison M., Texas	265
Garro, D. H., New Jersey	311
Garton, Dana M., Wisconsin	19
Gaudet, Sean, Virginia	156
Gebhardt, Doris, Ontario, Canada	325
Gebo, Mary, Maine	52
Geiger, Linda, Maryland	191
Genco, Denise Marie, Kentucky	74
Genee' Renee', South Carolina	153
Gentry, Marcus C., Illinois	273
Gerhardson, Helen, Minnesota	31
Gianella, Betty, Texas	243
Gibbs, Robert H., Jr., New York	144
Gibson, Dana L., Missouri	89
Gibson, Judith Kaye, Missouri	210
Gilbert, Lynn, Connecticut	302
Giles, Käthe, Saskatchewan, Canada	44
Gillan, John J., New York	123
Gillon, Carolyn Louise, Michigan	128
Gingery, George W., Colorado	323
Girsdansky, Michael B., New York	11
Giuliani, Anna, Ohio	51
Giuliano, Lenny, New Jersey	311
Giusti, Tana, New Jersey	59
Glacel, Jennifer, California	234
Glass, Bonnie L., Illinois	66
Glass, Ervin, Indiana	91
Glazewski, Kimberly, Wisconsin	22
Glenn, Sandra, Illinois	125

Glikin, Linda C., New Jersey............................ 131
Glover, Adena M., Missouri.............................. 278
Gobar, Rachel Manija, Kansas.......................... 222
Godwin, Hester, Washington.................... 11, 254
Goetz, Rachael, Colorado................................ 158
Goke, Katherine D., Wisconsin.......................... 162
Goldberg, Janice, New Jersey........................... 254
Golliher, Timothy J., Indiana............................. 204
Goodin, Sharon Sutliff, Pennsylvania.............. 271
Gootee, Cherie, Wyoming................................. 241
Gordon, Laura, Ohio.. 258
Gordy, Kathryn Rachelle, Texas......................... 47
Gorscak, Melanie I., Ohio................................. 162
Goudie, Renée C., Alberta, Canada.................... 114
Grady, Annie Marie, North Carolina.................. 158
Grager, Micha, Pennsylvania............................... 17
Graham, Tammy, Tennessee............................. 143
Grail, Tabatha, New York.................................... 25
Grapes, E.L., West Virginia............................... 146
Grau, Verna E., New York................................. 176
Graves, Hazel McNeal, Ohio............................... 53
Gray, E., California.. 281
Gray, Samantha, West Virginia............................. 8
Gray, Susan, Wisconsin................................... 276
Grazulis, Linda C., Pennsylvania..................... 155
Green, Charles E., Jr., West Virginia................. 73
Green, Judy R., California.................................. 82
Green, Lillian, Michigan................................... 125
Green, Mary Rose, Georgia.............................. 220
Green, Melissa A., Kentucky............................. 194
Greenwood, Bertha Woods, Pennsylvania........... 167
Gregg, Katharine, Maine...................................... 7
Gregory, Theatta Mae, California...................... 119
Griend, Duane Vander, Washington................... 230
Griffin, Debra, Texas...................................... 136
Griffin, Florence T., Massachusetts.................. 286
Grimes, Mary, Iowa.. 33
Gross, Rhoda, Alberta, Canada......................... 324
Gross, Ruth Boyer, Pennsylvania..................... 137
Grosse, Paul R., Vermont................................. 193
Grossman, Alma, Wisconsin............................... 48
Grosvold-Grills, Fran L., Ontario, Canada......... 206
Gruber, Patricia A., Ohio................................. 118
Grundmeyer, Melissa S., Oklahoma.................. 123
Guidroz, Nikie, Louisiana................................ 270
Guilbault, Steven, Connecticut......................... 121
Guillot, Dee, Louisiana.................................... 242
Gutierrez, Quiana, Wisconsin........................... 256
Gutzman, Stephanie R., Colorado...................... 125
Guzman, Joseph F., II, California.............. 21, 246
Habr, M.A., Indiana... 219
Hadley, Wade, North Carolina........................... 275
Hagedorn, Icey E., California........................... 126
Hagen, Betty J., Wisconsin................................ 52
Hagy, Myrna L., California............................... 205
Haines, Sarah B., Connecticut............................ 91
Hainstock, Sonya "Roland2", California............ 188
Hak-Jacobi, Olga, Illinois............................... 234
Halberstadt, Carol Snyder, Massachusetts............ 8
Hale, Angel, Alabama...................................... 128
Hale, Carolyn Mae, Kansas..................... 285, 307
Haley, Jeanne, New Jersey................................. 54
Hall, Roger, Florida.. 75
Halpin, Doris, New York....................... 173, 298
Halstead, Katherine, New Hampshire................ 303
Hamilton, Denise R., West Virginia..................... 15
Hamm, John, Jr., Ohio..................................... 271
Hammel, William G., New Jersey......................... 49
Hammerberg, J.M. Bennett, Illinois...................... 24
Hammerschmidt, Nick, Ohio............ 24, 239, 293
Hammonds, Stephanie Renae, Virginia.............. 302
Hamric, Ramona E., West Virginia.................... 322
Haney, Camila, Kentucky................................. 203
Hanrahan, Stacey Erin, Indiana....................... 143

Hansen, Alicia, Washington.............................. 196
Hansen, Kelley, Colorado.................................. 62
Hansen, Kerri, Kansas..................................... 189
Hansen, Linda M., West Virginia....................... 171
Hansen, Merle C., California............................. 114
Hanstedt, Constance, California........................ 177
Harbour, Zelma Jo, Texas................................ 218
Hardin, Todd Elliot, Missouri........................... 228
Harding, Elizabeth, North Dakota....................... 48
Haroutunian, Jan, Massachusetts........................ 68
Harrer, J. Jeff, Utah... 93
Harris, Alice R., New Jersey............................ 101
Harris, Anne, Montana...................................... 58
Harris, Debra Moy, Texas................................ 231
Harris, Janet M., Washington........................... 103
Harrison, Corrie Alison, Tennessee.................. 126
Harrison, Scott C., Washington......................... 232
Hase, Karl E., Colorado..................................... 73
Hatley, f. Adrian, North Carolina...................... 201
Hawersaat, Kelly Majors, Florida....................... 98
Hawley, Rob, Maine... 269
Hayden, H.E., Louisiana.................................... 39
Haynes, Terrence D., New York.......................... 99
Head, Edith F., Texas.. 91
Heath, Margery, Washington............................ 206
Heath, Roxanne T., New Mexico....................... 118
Heaton-Blouin, Nancy, Oregon........................ 101
Hedges, Emily R., Oregon................................ 306
Heefner, Reginald Lee, Pennsylvania.................. 78
Hegle, Mary, Arizona.. 55
Hein, Mary E., Michigan.................................. 305
Heinz, Elva, Washington.................................. 279
Heller, T.A., Pennsylvania............................... 290
Helm, Hillary, New York.................................. 324
Helms, Kelly B., Wisconsin............................... 71
Hemsley, Teresa, California.............................. 132
Hendee, Tracey L., Michigan............................ 198
Hendrickson, Barbara, Minnesota..................... 292
Hendrix, A. Lamarge, Arkansas........................ 164
Hensley, Fran, Arkansas........................ 116, 203
Hentges, Michael, Alberta, Canada.................... 327
Herbert, Maria E., South Dakota........................ 85
Hermann, Kay M., Iowa..................................... 87
Hernandez, Andrea, California.......................... 192
Hernandez, Tanisha, California......................... 249
Herrera, Jake, Colorado.................................... 97
Herring, Cynthia J., Texas................................. 13
He who walked alone, New York......................... 204
Hiatt, Randall C, Iowa..................................... 116
Hickey, Ardelphia, California.................... 28, 325
Hicks, Morris L., Texas.................................... 277
Hilderbrand, Gilbert L., New York........... 123, 193
Hill, Brandi Susanne, West Virginia................. 191
Hill, Victoria, New Jersey........................ 23, 74
Hillius, Chantel M., North Dakota...................... 92
Hines, MaryJo, Washington.............................. 135
Hinton, Margo, Pennsylvania............................. 20
Hirsch, Edith, Texas....................................... 286
Hirstine, Marijo, Iowa.................................... 105
Hitz, A. Leonard, Kansas................................. 270
Hixson, Patricia Diane, Iowa............................ 143
Hodges, W. Craig, Georgia............................... 168
Hoffman, Linda, Ohio...................................... 105
Hoffman, Pauline, Pennsylvania....................... 176
Hoke, J.L., Indiana... 302
Holbrook, Jamie L., Wisconsin........................... 62
Holford, Kathy Croy, Indiana........................... 235
Hollingsworth, Jason, Florida.......................... 155
Hollingsworth, Jeffrey, Oklahoma.................... 135
Holm, Matthew A., Missouri............................... 80
Holohan, J. Patricia, Massachusetts.................. 248
Holz, Julie, Washington................................... 138
Holzman, Shirley, British Columbia, Canada........ 219
Homan, Cindy Jentho, Texas.............................. 72

Hood, Gloria, California.................................... 275
Hopkins, Nelle, Florida.................................... 296
Hopkins-Woodcock, Linda Faye, Mississippi....... 72
Hoppaugh, Nicole Lynn, New Jersey.................. 194
Hore, Amanda, Arkansas.................................. 225
Horton, Angela Holloway, North Carolina.......... 20
Horton, Glenda, Texas..................................... 149
Hough, Dona, Florida.............. 48, 211, 320
Houghton, Joanne, California............................ 39
House, Carol, Washington................................ 19
Howard-McGraw, Amie, Oregon........................ 76
Hudson, Sharon L., Mississippi........................ 130
Hughes, Gina M., Texas................................... 58
Huizenga, Phyllis, Washington.......................... 161
Hulley, Gloria A., Iowa.................................... 82
Human, Elisa E., West Virginia......................... 86
Hungerford, Euphemia, New York...................... 295
Hunt, Jean, California...................................... 155
Hunter, Margaret Ethelyn, Michigan.................. 55
Hunter, Patrick, Georgia.................................. 200
Hurley, Hazel, West Virginia............................ 103
Huskins, Cindy E., Massachusetts..................... 31
Hutchison, Vickie, Indiana............................... 251
Hutson, Jane, Oklahoma.................................. 51
Hutton, Corinne, Manitoba, Canada................... 288
"Hutz", Colorado... 127
Iaccino, Elaine, New York................................ 33
Iannotti, Maria L., Massachusetts..................... 81
Imrie, Judy, Ontario, Canada........................... 103
Irish, John, XII, West Virginia.......................... 281
Irizar, Eugenia Garcia, New York...................... 31
Irons, D.E., Pennsylvania................................. 237
Irvin, Dora Michelle, Arkansas......................... 267
Irwin, April Dawn-Nell, New Mexico.................. 185
Iverson, Patra Jo, Wisconsin............................ 50
Jackson, Beverly, Arkansas.............................. 74
Jackson, Karen, Indiana................................... 106
Jackson, Rhonda, Georgia................................ 164
Jackson, Sandra K., Iowa................................. 203
Jacquay, Kent, Indiana.................................... 270
Janak, Colorado... 300
Jantzi, Heather L., New York............................ 112
Jaryno, John Henry, New Jersey....................... 322
Jaryno, Melissa A., New Jersey........................ 272
Jaygee, California... 33
Jayme, Wyoming.. 65
JCD, Utah.. 152
Jenkins, Darlene, South Carolina...................... 228
Jenkins, David A., Jr., Pennsylvania.................. 146
Jenkins, Eileen, North Carolina........................ 122
Jenkins, Rachel, North Carolina....................... 92
Jennifer Lynn, Indiana.................................... 95
Jennings, Derrick Randolph, South Carolina...... 326
Jepson, Gary, Minnesota.................................. 270
Jessica Ann, Arizona....................................... 258
Jex, Hedy Schwarzhaupt, California................... 21
Jillian Lonely, New York.................................. 42
Johannes, Reneé Lyn, Maryland........................ 64
Johnny, ⚘"ife", New York................................ 127
Johns, Melissa, Alberta, Canada....................... 327
Johns-Smith, Timolyn Andionette, Louisiana....... 284
Johnson, Agnes, Tennessee............................... 128
Johnson, Amanda, Iowa................................... 41
Johnson, Carol A., Kentucky............................ 84
Johnson, Denise K., Ohio................................. 59
Johnson, Gayla M. (Minor), Indiana.................. 170
Johnson, Heather M., Illinois............................ 176
Johnson, Jodie, Louisiana................................ 269
Johnson Kara Sue, Minnesota........................... 301
Johnson, Lars, Wisconsin................................. 246
Johnson, Linda S., Florida............................... 95
Johnson, Marlene Newbold, North Carolina....... 279
Johnson, Thernell, South Carolina..................... 46
Johnson, Vicki, Wisconsin............................... 100

Johnston, Janet, Canada.................................. 261
Johnston, Jim, Pennsylvania............................ 125
Johnston, Lisa Beryl, Texas............................. 121
Jokerst, Richard, Illinois................................. 264
Jones, Ashley M., New Jersey.......................... 326
Jones, Elgena R., Kentucky.............................. 241
Jones, Hazel, Colorado.............. 27, 277, 282
Jones, J. L., California.................................... 266
Jones, Kelly R., Florida.................................. 76
Jones, Kristine, New York............................... 86
Jones, M. Shane, Georgia................................ 33
Jones, Richard, New York................................ 56
Jones, Robert Kirk, Kentucky.............. 22, 275
Jones, Tamara, California................................ 314
Joni, New York.. 126
Jontz, Clyde W., Iowa..................................... 91
Jordan, Alice, Mississippi............................... 112
Jordan, Joey, Alaska...................................... 29
Josiah, California... 318
Joyce, Anna Jess, Nevada................................ 21
Judkins, Vernon, Washington........................... 258
Julianne, Wisconsin....................................... 65
Julie, Ontario, Canada.................................... 306
Justice, Meghann, West Virginia....................... 131
J.W.S., California... 317
Kaeder, Heather L., Minnesota......................... 263
Kaminsky, Gloria Ann, Texas........................... 194
Kane, Violet Hilderbrand, New York......... 119, 291
Kania, Christine, New Jersey........................... 16
Kapadia, Malika, New York.............................. 17
Kapellusch, Andrea, Wisconsin........................ 12
Karpel, Sindee, New York................................ 162
Katsumi, Kan, Massachusetts........................... 204
Kay, John Oliver, California............................. 42
Keenan, Robin, Nebraska................................ 74
Keery, Denise C., Massachusetts....................... 165
Keesee, Valerie, Tennessee.............................. 151
Kegelmyer, Jimi D., New York.......................... 114
Keithan, John, OAF, Massachusetts................... 59
Kelley, Barbara, Maine................................... 50
Kelly, Amanda K., Florida............................... 193
Kelly, Angela, New Jersey............................... 26
Kelly, Sandra, Ontario, Canada........................ 250
Kelly-Pereira, Anne, Australia......................... 71
Kemp, Suzanne H., New York........................... 212
Kennedy, Nina, Georgia.................................. 190
Kennelly, L., New Mexico................................ 10
Kenneth L./Rag Poet, Illinois........................... 249
Kenter, Joy-Lynn, New Mexico......................... 267
Keple, Louise M., New Jersey.......................... 284
Kessinger, Alvin Ray, Indiana.......................... 80
Killgore, Edward H., Jr., Mississippi................. 246
Kimber, Dave, Pennsylvania............................ 102
Kimble, Wendy J., Michigan............................ 51
Kincer, Mary Ann, Kentucky........................... 216
King, Aaron R., North Carolina........................ 267
King, Lori, Pennsylvania................................. 314
King, Loya D., Oregon.................................... 188
King, Robert J., Ohio...................................... 17
Kingery, L. Bruce, Ed.D., Michigan................... 6
Kingwood, Dave L., British Columbia, Canada........ 8
Kirby, Walter E., II, Texas.............................. 215
Kirschbaum, Phillip, Illinois............................ 159
Kittle, Beth Guye, West Virginia....................... 280
Kleine, Jessica, Pennsylvania........................... 152
Klimczyk, Joseph C., Ohio............................... 250
Kline, Rose A., Pennsylvania........................... 318
Knapp, Kathy, Michigan.................................. 233
Knoll, Donna B., Kansas.................................. 172
Knuti, Erika S., Virginia.................................. 182
Koelling, Eloise, Wisconsin............................. 205
Konarski, Joy Ann, New Jersey......................... 242
Kopko, Betty Anne, Saskatchewan, Canada........... 146
Kosel, Paul Irvin, South Dakota........................ 230

Kosky, Carlotta, Missouri.............................. 130
Kount, Illinois.. 246
Kowalski, Gina M., Michigan.......................... 240
Kraehmer, Ingeborg, New York........................ 64
Kraft, Christine Fallon, Massachusetts............... 148
Kram, Diane, North Dakota............................ 86
Kratzer, Rachel A., Pennsylvania..................... 208
Kremers, Kathleen M., Nebraska..................... 112
Krenzel, Nadia, California............................. 317
Kristal, Nicole, California............................. 19
Kristensen, Kurt, Alaska............................... 200
Kritzer, Carole A., West Virginia..................... 202
Kuegle, Peter F.X., Manitoba, Canada............... 26
Kugland, Nathan, California........................... 102
Kuhrts, Lorelei, Missouri.............................. 295
Kuppinger, Steve, California........................... 88
Kuypers, Ed, New Jersey.............................. 226
LaBanca, Jill M., Connecticut................... 110, 208
Lafleur, Alice R., California........................... 43
LaGrandeur, Diana, Washington....................... 311
Lagrone, Heather Louise, Connecticut............... 89
Laing, Laura J., New York............................. 196
Lakin, Pat Ellin, California............................ 27
Lambert, Allan H., Louisiana.................... 90, 158
Lame, Vicki, Texas..................................... 68
Lane, April, Tennessee................................ 104
Langdon, Bertie, Oregon............................... 185
Lange, Erica K., Colorado............................. 277
Lannan, Kelly, Colorado............................... 85
Lansing, Clara E., Ohio................................ 116
LaPointe, Jennifer A., Michigan...................... 165
Larsen, Ben, Utah..................................... 28
Lashbrook, Holly L., Michigan........................ 302
Laughlin, Nicole, North Carolina..................... 221
Laura Lynn, British Columbia, Canada............... 166
Lauren Ann, New Jersey............................... 134
Laurette, Illinois...................................... 129
Laykish, Pinky, Pennsylvania......................... 38
Leabo, D.M./Karma Kay, New York.................. 261
Leach, Joan, Utah..................................... 212
LeBlanc, Mary Ellen, Colorado....................... 294
Lee, Elina E., California............................... 93
Lee, Francis, Mississippi.............................. 189
Lee, Mindie, South Carolina........................... 69
Lee, R. Clayton, Texas................................ 247
LeFebre, Rebecca Ann, Colorado..................... 324
Legaspi, Victor E., California......................... 122
Legg, Vickie Elaine, Indiana.......................... 251
Legge, J.C., Ohio...................................... 101
Leigh, New York....................................... 70
Lennox, Daniel H., Massachusetts.................... 314
Leoni, Kelly, California................................ 160
Leppo, William C., Pennsylvania............... 281, 301
Lerner, Jean M.S., Illinois............................ 92
LeRoux, Carey, Missouri.............................. 305
Lessard, David R., Arizona............................ 135
LeVasseur, Fran, Florida.............................. 200
Leverette, Tamika Lushonna, North Carolina....... 80
Libby, Terre, Maine................................... 89
Liddell-Hackett, Wendy L., Colorado................ 92
Liebich, Carl, Wisconsin.............................. 10
Liinamaa, Liisa, Ontario, Canada..................... 42
Lin, Jenny, California.................................. 253
Lind, C.W., (Jr.), Iowa................................ 12
Lindberg, Keith W., Iowa.............................. 156
Lisenby, Foy, Arizona................................. 263
Little, Nicholas, Alberta, Canada..................... 148
Litwiller, J. Daniel, Missouri......................... 140
Locke, James A., Michigan............................ 89
LoCoco, Elizabeth Lynn, Ohio........................ 142
Loftus, Sean M., Massachusetts...................... 285
Logan, Raquel D., Kansas............................. 195
Lohre, Jo Jo, South Dakota........................... 83
Lombardi, V.P., Pennsylvania......................... 299

Lomino, Michael A., California........................ 129
Long, Blair C., Connecticut........................... 114
Long, Charles A., Wisconsin.......................... 67
Long, Darcy Erin-Marie, California................... 112
Long, Robert, California............................... 11
Lorentson, Ginger, Iowa............................... 291
Lovejoy, Dawn, Minnesota............................ 205
Loveland, Steve, Michigan............................ 222
Loveless, Ila, Texas................................... 56
Lowe, Charles H., Michigan........................... 135
Luby, Margaret, Connecticut.......................... 128
Luckman, Jenni, Iowa................................. 130
Luersman, Timothy J., Ohio.......................... 195
Lukonen, Terri, Tennessee............................ 256
Lund, Travis D., Tennessee........................... 174
Lundgren, Kari, California............................. 143
Lynn, Nancy McNew, Texas........................... 270
Mack, Rebecca, Michigan............................. 292
Mackay, William L., III, Colorado.................... 309
Madden, Angus, California............................ 234
Maglaris, Bettye, Pennsylvania....................... 14
Magnuson, Karin L., Massachusetts.................. 32
Mahon, Mary, Utah................................... 183
Main, Dixon, Rev., Arizona........................... 193
Maine, B Hugh, Texas................................. 235
Maiwald, Trudy, Wisconsin........................... 60
Major, Courtney Spore, New Jersey.................. 264
Major, Paul E., Jr., FPO AP........................... 326
Makler, Larry A., Indiana............................. 211
Malfi, Patrick Terrence, New York................... 104
Mallette, Lynette, New York.......................... 7
Malone, Tammy L., Massachusetts.................... 41
Mandy, North Carolina................................ 226
Manes, Betty, Missouri................................ 146
Manes, Erica, Arkansas................................ 80
Mangini-Chesnick, Pamela, Pennsylvania............ 180
Mann, Cheryl G., North Carolina..................... 197
Manuel, Charlie F., North Carolina................... 136
Manwarring, Melvin, Texas............................ 151
Maraguglio, Ariel, New Jersey........................ 121
Marbury, John, Ohio.................................. 226
Marchbanks, Beulahmae W., Montana................ 168
Marge, Ohio... 322
Margerison, Brenda, British Columbia, Canada....... 106
Margetiak, Julia Soho, Pennsylvania.................. 218
Markert, Cara J., California........................... 323
Marquis, Jeanne-Marie, Wisconsin.................... 292
Marsh, Carol Ann, California.......................... 254
Marsh, Patricia Ann, Mississippi...................... 175
Marsters, James A., Missouri.......................... 132
Martin, Dennis S., Maryland.......................... 152
Martin, Linda (Ryan), New York...................... 42
Martin, Sue, Colorado................................. 303
Martinez, Angela, California........................... 321
Martinez, Christopher, Colorado...................... 323
Martinez, Melanie, New Jersey........................ 323
Martinez, Valerie C., Nevada.......................... 313
Martin-Litch, Francoise, Ohio........................ 53
Martyn, Buster E., Ontario, Canada.................. 315
Mascena, Marie, Rhode Island........................ 99
Mason, Ashley Nicholi Keys, Florida................. 213
Massey, Marie, Texas.................................. 242
Massie, Shirley, Pennsylvania......................... 61
Massimino, Mary, West Virginia...................... 57
Mastin, Martha E., Mississippi........................ 254
Matchett, Beverly, New Brunswick, Canada.......... 278
Matheny, Kendra Ann, Texas.......................... 268
Matheny, Virginia, West Virginia..................... 234
Mathews, Ann, Texas.................................. 99
Mathewson, Tracy, Michigan.......................... 292
Matsey, Nancy L., West Virginia...................... 96
Matzen, Iris, Michigan................................ 116
Mauro, Gail, New Jersey.............................. 173
Maust, Sally, Pennsylvania............................ 170

Mauthe, Barbara, Wisconsin.................... 56
Maxwell, S.E., New Jersey........................ 61
May, Cathy, Idaho.................................... 102
May, Presita R., Illinois.......................... 238
McBride, Michael, Wyoming.................... 149
McCabe, Sharon Floyd, Massachusetts.... 294
McCartney, SueAnn, Missouri.................. 70
McClellan, Toni, Texas............................ 7
McClintock, KristaLin, Missouri.............. 142
McCloskey, Burr, Illinois........................ 10
McCollum, Dwight W., Mississippi.......... 266
McCoy, Peewee M., Iowa................ 262, 308
McCusker, Jennifer, Pennsylvania.......... 280
McDonald, Janice, Ontario, Canada........ 66
McDonald, Linda L., West Virginia.......... 173
McDonald, Sean R., West Virginia.......... 261
McDowell, Maggie, Florida...................... 7
McEntire, John D., Texas........................ 186
McFadden, Joyce, Ohio............................ 166
McGirr, Dianne Hamilton, New York........ 204
McGirr, Helen, Ohio................................ 277
McGlotten, Angelique Cooper, New Jersey........ 327
McGrath, David, New York...................... 142
McGuire, Judith R., Oklahoma................ 70
McKenzil, Jerry Craig, Ohio.................... 133
McKiernan, John S., Rhode Island.......... 186
McKinnon, James Buckner, Washington........ 23, 150
McLaughlin, Kendra, Pennsylvania.......... 113
McLemore, Joy-Ellis, Texas.................... 213
McLeod, Eloise Curtis, Ontario, Canada.... 172, 206
McMacken, Norma Jean, Wyoming.......... 251
Mcnab, Deborah L., Georgia.................... 111
McNeil, Johnny, Mississippi.................... 310
McNeil, Virginia, Mississippi.................. 180
McNeil, Wendy L., British Columbia,
    Canada.................................. 73, 98
McNett, Ronald S., Texas........................ 121
McNett, Samuel F., Texas........................ 141
McWethy, Verda, Oklahoma.................... 283
Mead, Cheryl K. McNett, Texas.............. 9, 141
Medel, Sandra E., Texas.......................... 157
Medina, Joanne, California...................... 194
Medina, Melinda M., California................ 78
Medina-Merced, Efrain, Georgia.............. 255
Meeks, Louise M., Connecticut................ 118
Menzies, Dominique, British Columbia, Canada.. 164
Mercade, Fran Singley, New Jersey.......... 30
Mercurio, Varda, Indiana........................ 18
Meredith, Marty, North Carolina.............. 140
Mese, Debbe, Colorado............................ 148
Metz, Darcy, British Columbia, Canada.... 261
Mey, VieSsa, Manitoba, Canada.............. 316
Meyer, Mark W., Washington.................. 200
Miceli, Christy, Wisconsin...................... 221
Michaud, Melinda D., Virginia................ 170
Michaud, Tami, Wisconsin...................... 58
Michel, Margaret, Wyoming.................... 236
Michener, Jennifer, New Jersey.............. 292
Mihalko, Robert, Pennsylvania................ 114
Milburn, Ruth Wylie, Illinois.................. 21
Miller, Daniel, West Virginia.................. 264
Miller, Doris, R.S., Pennsylvania............ 186
Miller, Laura Lyne, California................ 78
Miller, Lisa, New York............................ 305
Miller, Meghan, Ohio.............................. 291
Miller, Rayola Pearl, North Dakota.......... 312
Miller, Sidney, Iowa................................ 110
Miller, Tammy, Iowa.............................. 231
Mills, Jeanne Vick, Oklahoma................ 228
Mills, Philip W., Colorado...................... 76
Mills, Rebecca J., New York.................... 82
Millsap, V.B., Jr., Virginia...................... 238
Miniter, Christopher, Connecticut............ 183
Mirbach, Karen E., New Jersey.............. 301

Mirocki, Ken, Jr., New York.................... 260
Mitchell, Amy S., Virginia...................... 13
Mitchell, Bette, New Jersey.................... 326
Mitchell, Darrell, Texas.......................... 223
Mitchell, Tammie, Pennsylvania.............. 81
Mobley, Faye Southerland, North Carolina.... 218
Mobley, Michael, North Carolina.............. 207
Moen, Heidi, New Hampshire.................. 178
Mohan, Edith Elaine, Maryland................ 265
Monda, Kimberly, California.................... 104
Montalbano-Powers, Connie, Montana...... 246
Montgomery, Mary Alice, Illinois............ 171
Montoya, Richard, Oregon...................... 310
Moore, Doris, Idaho................................ 153
Moore, Edna E., West Virginia................ 30
Moore, Jackie, Arkansas.......................... 321
Moore, Jeremiah C., Texas...................... 191
Moore, Patricia, California...................... 60
Moore, R.D.L.M., Connecticut................ 288
Moore, Rocky Lane, North Carolina.......... 205
Moore, Sheila, Georgia............................ 163
Moore, Steven Wendall, Alabama............ 23
Moran, Frances McCarthy, New York........ 151
Morgan, Caren, Washington.................... 328
Morgan, Marie E., California.................... 20
Morgan, Sandra, Pennsylvania................ 111
Morreale, Jeanne Lauren, Michigan.......... 288
Morris, Angela V., California.................... 325
Morris, Lindsay, Wisconsin.................... 316
Morrow, Rocky, Oregon.......................... 81
Morsch, Samantha, Missouri.................... 15
Morse, Sayward, Nebraska...................... 68
Mosier, Joyce A., Ohio............................ 219
Moskovito, Gloria Mae, California............ 53
Mosley, James, Pennsylvania.................. 143
Mosocco, Melinda, Virginia.................... 230
Moxley, Dee, Maryland............................ 194
Mr. D., Colorado.................................... 56
Mueller, Cordelia B., Massachusetts........ 208
Muldowney, Katie, Wisconsin.................. 82
Murano, Juana, Massachusetts................ 69
Murphy, Tammie D., West Virginia.......... 206
Muse, Meeka, California.......................... 266
Muska, Brian P., Wisconsin.................... 88
Musso, Christy M, Alabama.................... 186
Myers, O'nell L., California...................... 263
Nash, Charles R., Arkansas...................... 143
Naughton, Sara, Missouri........................ 232
Nazario, Tony, Florida............................ 100
Neal, Spencer Todd, Kentucky................ 216
Near, Jeanmarie R., New York................ 195
Neergaard, Janis, New Mexico................ 69
Neighbors, Geraldine, Indiana................ 95
Nejman, Robert B., New York.................. 231
Nelson, Albert, New Jersey...................... 72
Nelson, Carol Ann, Pennsylvania............ 147
Nelson, Heather, California...................... 243
Nelson, MaryAnn, Minnesota.................. 301
Nelson, Paulette, Pennsylvania................ 6
Nelson, Raymond Clark, New York.......... 52
Neslund, Marilyn J., Florida.................... 176
Neukum, Denise, New Jersey.................. 315
Neusom, Willie J., California.................... 136
Nevills, Dawn Marie, Ontario, Canada...... 144
Nevins, Cynthia A., New York................ 285
Newcombe, Linda S., Tennessee.............. 235
Ng, Lynette, Massachusetts.................... 299
Nichols, Jo Ann, Idaho............................ 325
Niessen, Ciss, British Columbia, Canada.... 180
Nieuzytek, Joyce, New Jersey................ 208
Nightingale, Victoria L., Louisiana.......... 219
Nishioka, Liane M., California.................. 179
Nissen, Martha J., Texas........................ 24
Nollmeyer, Leah Rae Walton, Montana...... 126

Norman, Angela M., Indiana........................ 316
Norman, John D., Michigan........................ 215
Normandin, Diane, Ontario, Canada.................. 96
Norris, Jill Ann, Indiana........................ 262
Norris, Robert, Idaho........................ 133
North, Mary, Illinois........................ 185
Norvell, Mary Ivie, Florida........................ 280
Nottoli, Mia Anne, (P. duVal Guillout), Ohio.... 281
Nugent, Michelle V., Ontario, Canada.............. 75
Nye, Carol Lee, Pennsylvania........................ 131
Oakes, Nicole Sue, Wisconsin........................ 258
O'Connor, Debra L., South Carolina.............. 245
O'Dell, Ray, Florida........................ 60
Oesterreich, K.A., Ontario, Canada.............. 18
O'Flinn, Kathleen, California........................ 148
Ohanissian, Anita, Pennsylvania........................ 217
Olde Dave, Wyoming........................ 210
Oliver, Sue, Maryland........................ 165
Olsen, Cleo, Montana........................ 147
O'Malley, Nancy, Florida........................ 45
Oman, Tracy Naughton, Pennsylvania.............. 65
O'Masters, Patrick, Ohio........................ 63
Oreste, Judy Darene, California........................ 309
Osborne, Deanna, California........................ 30
Osgood, Chris, Tennessee........................ 187
Osgoodby, Marc, New Jersey........................ 261
Oskoui, Michelle, California........................ 200
Overstreet, Dicky R., New York.............. 309, 328
Owens, June, Florida........................ 7
Owens, Kimberly, Louisiana........................ 198
Ozanich, Ruth S., California.............. 216, 312
P., Tony, New Jersey........................ 239
Pacheco, Christina, Nebraska........................ 83
Page, L. Mehner, Wisconsin........................ 325
Palacio, Michelle, Texas........................ 267
Palkovits, Zoltan, Massachusetts.............. 62, 202
Palmitier, Gloria J., Wyoming........................ 110
Paluso, Dennis R., Pennsylvania........................ 275
Pam Kay, Wyoming........................ 301
Pantalena, Vickie, Connecticut........................ 63
Paolo, Stacy, Minnesota........................ 144
Paradis, David C., Maine........................ 279
Parcell, J. Andrew, Iowa........................ 190
Parlier, R. Wayne, North Carolina.............. 19
Parravano, Amy, Rhode Island........................ 208
Parraway, Ralph L., Texas........................ 263
Parrish, L., Colorado........................ 313
Parsons, Jennifer, Virginia........................ 310
Pasquino, Anthony Jason, Florida.............. 66
Paton, Keon, New Jersey........................ 255
Patterson, Melissa Anne, Mississippi.............. 316
Paugh, David L., West Virginia........................ 51
Pavelich, David, Wisconsin........................ 226
Pavlina, Rosemary, Indiana........................ 54
Payne, Lee, Pennsylvania........................ 75
Payne-Norris, Mary M., Florida........................ 85
Pazehoski, Jeanne M., Pennsylvania.............. 110
Peaches, New York........................ 260
Pearman, Sabrena, Nebraska........................ 226
Peary, Alexandria, Iowa........................ 9
Penn, John, New Jersey........................ 15
Penn, Richard, Arkansas........................ 265
Penner, Abram Clement, California.............. 211
Peoples, Raine Marie, Kentucky........................ 145
Perkins, B M, Florida........................ 213
Perkins, Gregory, New Jersey........................ 30
Perkins, Jay, Michigan........................ 47
Perks, William H., III, New York........................ 327
Perriman, Betty J., Kansas........................ 170
Petrovic, Michelle, New Mexico........................ 90
Petruny, Loren Michelle, Connecticut.............. 215
Phelps, April A., Massachusetts........................ 120
Phillips, Hugh, Jr., "Sam", Colorado.......... 76, 321
Phucas, Victoria, Texas........................ 174

Pickenpaugh, Tamara L., California........................ 225
Pickering, Jennifer S., Utah........................ 155
Pickler, Andrea, Maine........................ 320
Pierce, Linda Williams, Mississippi.............. 45
Pierpont, Stacy, New Mexico........................ 86
Pierritz, J., Illinois........................ 10, 12
Pike, James L., Texas........................ 161
Ping, Michelle, Illinois........................ 236
Piper, Michael, Iowa........................ 100
Pister, Jessica B., California........................ 191
Pitman, Jody Kauffman, Indiana........................ 65
Pitre, Carol Susan, Ontario, Canada.............. 267
Plant, Heidi L., Vermont........................ 293
Plaster, Julian R., Wisconsin........................ 206
Plewa, Peggy, New Jersey........................ 188
Plumley, Edna, North Carolina........................ 253
P.O., California........................ 130
Pollack, Melissa, New York........................ 218
Pollock, Patrick, Ohio........................ 318
Polverino, Frank F., New Jersey........................ 232
Ponchak, Nina, Pennsylvania........................ 283
Ponder, C. Rene, Nevada........................ 192
Pope, Ingrid Brostrom Bloomquist, Connecticut...... 245
Pope, K.R., British Columbia, Canada.............. 179
Popham, Dennis Dale, Texas........................ 187
Porta, Hope M., Ohio........................ 300
Porter, Maureen, California........................ 108
Posk, Jeremy Francis, Massachusetts.............. 14
Posner, Joseph, Florida........................ 62
Pothier, Nancy, Ontario, Canada........................ 282
Potter, Marilynn, Illinois........................ 309
Poulin, Nancy Ford, Florida........................ 133
Poulin, Robert H., Florida........................ 164
Pounds, Eddie, California........................ 36
Powell, Juanita, Colorado........................ 212
Pratt, James A., Idaho........................ 294
Price, Beverly E., Arkansas........................ 282
Price, Billie L., Quebec, Canada........................ 234
Price, Diane B., North Carolina........................ 228
Price, Jay, Alabama........................ 31
Price, Mary M., Ohio........................ 231
Prince, Sharon, California........................ 272
Proctor, Richard H., III, Indiana........................ 317
Prud'homme, Wendi, New York........................ 216
Przybylek, Michelle, F., New York........................ 287
Puggi, Marie C., Pennsylvania........................ 150
Pugh, Paula, Alabama........................ 103
Pugliese, Miriam, New York........................ 28
Pullara, Teresa, Florida........................ 221
Purple Raven, West Virginia........................ 233
Quinn, Liz, Pennsylvania........................ 47
Quiring, Norma Lou, Missouri........................ 14
Raatikainen, Krista, Ontario, Canada.............. 272
Racin, Abram, West Virginia........................ 272
Ragan, L., Rhode Island........................ 65
Rainwater, Adam, Illinois........................ 212
Ramos, Jennifer Lynn, Hawaii........................ 185
Randall, Tanisha Hamel, Mississippi.............. 39
Rasor, Ruby, Montana........................ 103
Raughton, Ami Renata, Alabama........................ 138
Re, Michael A., New Jersey........................ 16
Reader, Graham, Alberta, Canada........................ 14
Record, Cheryl, New York........................ 151
Redd, Michelle L., West Virginia........................ 189
Reed, Dana A., Tennessee........................ 233
Reed, Donna A., Tennessee........................ 33
Reed, Pamela L., Iowa........................ 324
Reed, Sandra A., Pennsylvania........................ 287
Reed, Stanley P., Colorado........................ 222
Reeder, Stephanie, Florida........................ 100
Rehbein, Tiffany L., Montana........................ 112
Reid, Maureen, New Jersey........................ 71
Reidland, Donna, Texas........................ 25
Reiner, Jeff, New Jersey........................ 278

Remesoff, Leissa, Alberta, Canada................ 16
Renfro, W.L., Texas.................... 168, 298
Renfroe, Susan G., Florida.................... 61
Resh, Harold P., Maryland.................... 30
Reynolds, Christian W., New Jersey.................... 299
Reynolds, Donna, Tennessee.................... 49
Rhoades, Miriam, Arkansas.................... 52
Rice, Clarence F., West Virginia.................... 296
Richards, Charles, Michigan.................... 72
Richards, Jamey, Alberta, Canada.................... 106
Richards, Robert, Ohio.................... 250
Richter, Betty, Illinois.................... 181
Ricker, Ida A., New Hampshire.................... 62
Ricky Bruce, California.................... 114
Rikoun, Polina, California.................... 11
Ritchey, Charlotte Harvey, North Carolina...... 98
Rivas, Zelideth Maria, New Jersey.................... 255
Robb, Chelsea L., Washington.................... 89
Robb, Jack G., California.................... 161
Robbin, Massachusetts.................... 141
Roberts, Chad, Ohio.................... 252
Roberts, June, Tennessee.................... 105
Robertson, Debra, Alabama.................... 140
Robinson, Janis L., Texas.................... 329
Robinson, V., "The Rhymester", Michigan........ 146
Rochelle, Debra Stratton, North Carolina........ 136
Rockmann, Elena, New York.................... 25, 134
Rockoff, Joshua Edward, New Jersey.................... 239
Rodebaugh, Annabelle, Arizona.................... 159
Rogers, Daniel, California.................... 201
Rogers, Gale, Kansas.................... 99
Roggenbuck, Heidi, Wisconsin.................... 255
Rohlfing, Margaret L., Florida.................... 215
Rohman, Wanda Hancock, Arkansas.................... 174
Roop, Scottye, Montana.................... 33
Rose, Alisia G., Indiana.................... 190
Rose, Kenneth, Georgia.................... 233
Rose, Patricia, Pennsylvania.................... 200
Rose, Richard E., Oregon.................... 97
Rose, Suzanne, Wyoming.................... 201
Rose, Valerie, Oregon.................... 134
Rosebrook, Bulea Barns, Ohio.................... 179
Rothermel, Joan, Pennsylvania.................... 40
Rourke, Wendy C., Massachusetts.................... 69
Rovens-Beedle, Susan, Illinois.................... 49
Rovert, Ohio.................... 240
Rowe, Marda, California.................... 106
Rowell, Donna, North Carolina.................... 161
Rowland, Ruby E., Florida.................... 248
Royer, Ronnie Rhea, Arkansas.................... 61
Ruark, Madge Lay, Michigan.................... 6
Rudolph, Christopher, New Jersey.................... 202
Ruette-Radke, Jacqueline, New York.................... 158
Runyan, David H., Iowa.................... 166
Ruppert, Theresa A., Texas.................... 253
Ruzicka, David, Nebraska.................... 293
Sabourin, Marc Denis, Ontario, Canada............ 126
Sacco, James, Ohio.................... 152
Saengchalern, Nikki, California.................... 241
Saenz, Gil, Michigan.................... 203
Sagissor, Todd, Wyoming.................... 252
Saltzman, Suzann Steele, Texas.................... 325
Salvatore, Richard, New York.................... 254
Sam, Illinois.................... 198
Sam, Wyoming.................... 273
Sammels, Michelle L., Michigan.................... 161
Samuelson, Joanna, Massachusetts.................... 294
Sandie, Pennsylvania.................... 217
Sandler, Rachel, Iowa.................... 240
Sands, Paulette, Florida.................... 53
Sanghvi, Hrishabh, California.................... 113
Santee, Emily, Pennsylvania.................... 138
Sapriken, Elaine L., Alberta, Canada.................... 315
Sass, Dawn M., Florida.................... 141

Sausen, Carol A., West Virginia.................... 84
Savanauskas, Linda S., Massachusetts.................... 183
Savich, Elisabeth, M., North Carolina.................... 23
Savino, John T., New York.................... 36
Saxton, Michael J., Texas.................... 17, 282
Scarborough, Jason H., Georgia.................... 211
Schaffer, Jeanne, New Jersey.................... 108
Schano, Sheelagh M., Pennsylvania.................... 195
Schantz, Julie E., Indiana.................... 249
Scharmen, Audrey Y., Maryland.................... 11
Schelling, Andrea, Wyoming.................... 266
Scheppers, Kelly, Maryland.................... 129
Schiebel, Annelis, Oregon.................... 167
schierl, shari, Wisconsin.................... 14
Schmidt, Ann-Marie, New Jersey.................... 45
Schmidt, Emily Pearl, California.................... 120
Schneider, Steve, North Dakota.................... 151
Scholl, Mitzie, California.................... 226
Scholten, Vincent P., South Dakota.................... 196
Schorr, Nancy L., Pennsylvania.................... 177
Schultz, Mae, Minnesota.................... 240
Scoby, T. Hawk, Washington.................... 96
Scott, Terri, New York.................... 57
Scotty, Ohio.................... 329
Scrivano, John, California.................... 84
Seaman, Janis R., Missouri.................... 320
Searle, Helen, Illinois.................... 112
SEBS, Virginia.................... 83
Sechler, Corey, Pennsylvania.................... 138
Seeley, William P., Jr., Pennsylvania.................... 120
Seelman, Rob, New York.................... 328
Sell, Margaret R., Ontario, Canada.................... 180
Senkiw, Irene E., Michigan.................... 158
Serra, Jane Trombley, Michigan.................... 311
Shade, Jolene Lynn, Pennsylvania.................... 209
Sharp, Mary, Texas.................... 134, 280
Sharp-Van Buskirk, Lori, Pennsylvania.................... 38
Shaw, Letty M., Pennsylvania.................... 295
Shawn Michael, Indiana.................... 295
Shea, Texas.................... 91
Shearer, Heather, Saskatchewan, Canada.................... 175
Shedd, Wanda M., Alabama.................... 268
Sheets, Juanita Russell, Iowa.................... 58, 59
Sheldon, Lawana, Wisconsin.................... 300
Shepard, Cristie, Texas.................... 62
Shepard, Shirley, Texas.................... 45
Shepherd, Mary S., Mississippi.................... 8, 271, 314
Shepherd, Tammy J., Arkansas.................... 115
Sherron, Betty, Alabama.................... 9, 269
Shey, Indiana.................... 26
Shipp, C. Terry, Louisiana.................... 323
Shipp, Vivian, West Virginia.................... 37, 104
Shiver, Yvonne K., Mississippi.................... 127
Shockley, Herbert I, Pennsylvania.................... 292
Shorey, Mark J., Colorado.................... 317
Shupe, Deborah A., Pennsylvania.................... 163
Shuster, Deanna, Missouri.................... 321
Siconolfi, Anthony J., New York.................... 91
Siders, Jerry D., Texas.................... 48
Signerelli, Catherine, New York.................... 305
Silvia, Lee Lannan, Rhode Island.................... 119
Simard, Angie Sheldon, Ontario, Canada............ 83, 177
Simmerman, Kelli R., Illinois.................... 93
Simmons, Randall K., Kentucky.................... 61
Simpson, Jonathan, North Carolina.................... 205
Sims, Michael Lee, Texas.................... 219
Singer, Steven, Pennsylvania.................... 153
Sisson, Al, North Carolina.................... 55
Sisto, Jackie, West Virginia.................... 108
Sjöberg, David W., Florida.................... 86
SJones, Oklahoma.................... 24
Skaggs, Billy R., Mississippi.................... 120
Skeffington, Marcie, Iowa.................... 198
Skinner, Greg, Washington.................... 224

Skipper Jane, Colorado........................... 271
Skjaveland C., Alberta, Canada....................... 308
Slaughter, Kenneth L., Missouri....................... 140
Slick, Richard, Pennsylvania....................... 323
Sloan, Marc, California........................... 240
Smith, Annie, Maryland........................... 66
Smith, Ann T., Michigan........................... 6
Smith, Betsy L., Pennsylvania....................... 125
Smith, Denise, Virginia........................... 66
Smith, Donald D., West Virginia....................... 313
Smith, Douglas S., Tennessee....................... 281
Smith, Jean Carr, New Jersey....................... 25
Smith, MeLinda, Massachusetts........... 18, 251, 291
Smith, Michael, North Carolina....................... 220
Smith, Phillip, Indiana........................... 256
Smith, Velma M., California....................... 153
Sneed, Rosie B., Tennessee....................... 171
Snow, Marie, Ontario, Canada....................... 327
Snyder-Haney, Joanne G., Pennsylvania............. 224
Solls, Ronald J., California........................... 55
Souimaniphanh, Khot, Texas....................... 196
South, Dale, Georgia........................... 151
Spanier, Stuart L., Kansas....................... 228
Sparks, Robert Eugene Christopher, Jr.,
    Indiana........................... 87
Sparks, Linda L., Colorado....................... 88
Speakman, Troy, Colorado....................... 322
Spenst, Akasha Ann, Tennessee....................... 162
Spicer, Theresa Patrisha, Colorado.................... 270
Spivey, James E., Texas........................... 102
Spore, Evelyn, Wisconsin........................... 271
Sprague, Lacy, APO AE........................... 237
Spriestersbach, Jill, Ohio........................... 115
Squeglia, Cindy, New York....................... 153
Stadler, Debra, New Jersey....................... 180
Staggs, Sean T., Kansas........................... 82
Stalnaker, Penny, Florida........................... 235
Standley, Billie Jean, Texas....................... 173
Stark, Kathy, Wisconsin........................... 90
Staryak, Michael, New Jersey....................... 209
Stearns, Stephen C., California....................... 119
Steffen, Doris D., Texas........................... 215
Steinberg, Thelma T., Massachusetts................. 121
Steinkraus, Robert E., New York....................... 155
Steirer, Mary Ann Wagner, Florida.................... 77
Stephens, Barbara Carroll, West Virginia........... 209
Stephens, Jennifer, Alabama....................... 302
Stephens, Judith A., Ohio........................... 298
Stevens, Aliza, California........................... 68
Stevens, Austyn M., New Jersey....................... 119
Stewart, Eric J., Illinois........................... 144
Stewart, James F., Connecticut....................... 326
St. Louis, Angela R., North Carolina................. 183
Stober, Rudolf, Michigan....................... 35, 44
Stockhorst, Kent, Missouri....................... 272
Stohl, Johan, Michigan........................... 7
Stone, William, Iowa........................... 86
Story, Sherman, "Dewayne", Missouri................. 108
Stoski, Jodene, Manitoba, Canada................. 252
Strahm, Edna L., Indiana........................... 286
Straw, Ronnie J., Wisconsin....................... 263
Stricklin, Bridgett, Tennessee....................... 254
Strong, William D., Ohio........................... 252
Struse, Terry L., South Dakota....................... 17
Stuckey, Annelle, South Carolina................. 48
Sullivan, Joyce E., Indiana....................... 120
Sullivan, Moira, New York........................... 250
Suniga, Bernice Ann, California....................... 262
Sunstrum, Brenda LeeDee, Ontario, Canada...... 313
Suski, Stanley D., Jr., Wisconsin................. 132
Sussman, Thelma B., Pennsylvania................. 291
Sutton, Beth Ann, New York....................... 231
Swan, Brian, Connecticut........................... 16
Swanson, Daniel A., SSgt., California............. 178

Sweat, Maxene A., Utah........................... 232
Swisher, Patricia A., Pennsylvania................. 171
Sykes, Wanda, West Virginia....................... 57
Sylvester, Dixie, Idaho........................... 142
Syth, Neale C., Idaho........................... 239
Tabor, Virginia, California....................... 239
Tackett, Dolores E., Kansas....................... 276
Taggart, Kari A., Utah........................... 260
Tallent, Suzi, Texas........................... 309
Tate, Michelle L, Kentucky....................... 167
Taubold, Richard, New York....................... 245
Taylor, Burton, New York........................... 32
Taylor, David, Ontario, Canada....................... 105
Taylor, E. Don, Texas........................... 156
Taylor, Jennifer Jill, Connecticut................. 100
Taylor, Jessica N., West Virginia................. 183
Taylor, J.L., Alaska........................... 173
Taylor, Lennice-Marie, Oklahoma................. 93
Taylor, Rose P., California....................... 215
Taylor, Teoma, California........................... 20
Tellier, Doris J., Illinois........................... 171
Temple, Robyn, Texas........................... 156
Teploff, Alexandra, New Jersey....................... 52
Terpenny, Lori, California....................... 236
Terry, Gloria, Indiana........................... 142
Tesch, Holly A., Ohio........................... 243
Thacker, Oklahoma........................... 210
The Rose, Ohio........................... 312
Theroux, Jennifer, Washington....................... 85
Thomas, Al, Georgia........................... 160
Thomas, Laura, Kentucky........................... 283
Thomas, Patricia Dawn Doty, West Virginia.......... 308
Thomas, Stephanie, West Virginia................. 226
Thome, Jennifer L., Indiana....................... 306
Thompson, Marjorie Baranski, Connecticut............. 326
Thompson/Stanton, Mary Jean, Iowa.................... 312
Thorn, Ana Lee, Kentucky........................... 248
Thornton, Joseph A., Sr., Ohio....................... 250
Thornton, Richard H., New York....................... 182
Thurman, Linda J., Wyoming........................... 306, 315
Ticknor, Janet A., Wisconsin....................... 291
Tidwell, Kristy, Tennessee....................... 118
Tilt, Bryan D., Utah........................... 165
Tingelstad, Ellie, Minnesota....................... 322
Tingle, Rebecca Kyle, Mississippi................. 310
Tirpak, Mary Ruth, Ohio........................... 305
Todd, Wanda, South Dakota....................... 233
Todisco, Maria A., New York....................... 221
Toelle, Marge, Wisconsin........................... 315
Tonita, Stacey, Saskatchewan, Canada................. 29
Tootle, Charles H., Florida....................... 110
Torgerson, Chelsey A., Idaho....................... 54
Torian-Taylor, Kathleen, California................. 16
Torres, Fernando, California....................... 283
Toth, Todd Charles, Pennsylvania................. 168
Townsend, Geoffrey, Pennsylvania................. 31
Townsend, Margaret E., Mississippi................. 108
Trahan-Pero, Deborah Lynn, Ontario, Canada.......... 203
Travis, Jon H., Iowa........................... 266
Trehey, Denis Allen, Iowa....................... 198
Tristana, Alaska........................... 320
Troll, Florence N., Pennsylvania................. 211
Trozzo, Kristine M., Pennsylvania................. 223
Trunecek, Stacey, Kansas........................... 105
Tuffin, Sally, Ontario, Canada....................... 222
Tunstall, Stacey L., Pennsylvania................. 80
Turachak, J.E., Ohio........................... 18
Turdo, Mike, Connecticut........................... 22
Turka, Kate, Pennsylvania........................... 224
Turner, Kurt, California........................... 290
Turner, Ruth, California........................... 248
TurnerCobb, P.A., Illinois....................... 130
Turse, Pamela, New Jersey....................... 132
Twitchell, Shelly, Nevada....................... 59

Tyson, Ray, Pennsylvania..................... 243, 306
Uhrin, Katie, Pennsylvania............................... 174
Ulanov, Anne, New York................................... 328
Urguhart, Catherine, Japan............................... 14
Utecht, Delores, Nebraska................................ 85
Vadino, Pearl, Ohio... 95
Van Arsdale, Lorrie, New Jersey...................... 104
Van Deusen, Linda, New York........................... 240
Vangi, California.. 9
Van Middendorp, Judy E., Iowa........................ 178
Vann, Elja, Tennessee..................................... 258
VanOrman, Sandra, Washington........................ 71
Vanovcan, Dorothy, Ontario, Canada.................. 19
VanVleit, Phyllis, New York.............................. 101
Van Voorhis, Troy, Indiana............................... 320
Vargo, Elizabeth, Wisconsin............................. 137
Vaske, M.K., South Dakota............................... 230
Vastino-Wheeler, Kimberlee, New York............. 186
Vaughn, Evelyn R., Iowa.................................. 273
Vaughn, Mary L., New York.............................. 288
Veatch, Norm, Iowa.. 162
Vega, Alex P., New Mexico............................... 237
Velez, Anthony J., Massachusetts..................... 5
Venus, Cindy Ann, Wisconsin........................... 245
Villa, Yvonne M., California.............................. 35
Vilsmeyer, Victoria M., Washington................... 81
Vincent, Brandelynn, Idaho.............................. 260
Vincent, Michael, Mississippi........................... 280
Virgo, South Carolina.......................... 164, 198
Virostko, Josh, Illinois.................................... 26
Vonada, Stewart L., Pennsylvania...................... 227
Wade, Joyce Lane, Texas.................. 22, 83, 88
Waldron, Chanelsha Sue, Colorado.................... 269
Walkden-Brown, Valelei, Alberta, Canada.......... 296
Walker, Elfrida, Illinois................................... 188
Walker, M.A., New York................................... 317
Walker, Michael, California............................... 269
Wallstrom, Grace, Ohio................................... 179
Walton, Leslie K., Utah.................................... 45
Ward, Eric, Hawaii.. 196
Ward, L.E., Michigan....................................... 224
Warner, Tammy L., Illinois............................... 254
Warren, Cynthia, Virginia.................... 21, 78, 98
Watkins, R.G., Texas....................................... 46
Watson, Brenda S., Ohio.................................. 261
Webb, Tammy Joy, Colorado............................. 269
Webb, William B., California............................. 102
Weber, Barbara, Florida................................... 28
Weddell, Cindy, Ohio....................................... 70
Weeks, Gwyn G., Georgia................................. 131
Wegdahl, Leander, Oregon............................... 178
Weglicki, Barbara, Ontario, Canada................... 245
Weiner, Glee Stevens, Minnesota...................... 93
Weinrich, J Stanley, Wisconsin......................... 263
Wells, Blondie Louise, Texas............................ 157
Wells, Bobby, Texas.. 77
Wendt, Lt. Charles N., North Dakota.................. 250
Wenger, Ed, Illinois.. 241
Wesgaites, Annette J., Pennsylvania.................. 145
West, Clarence, Michigan................................. 73
West, Edward, Florida...................................... 296
West, Erma, Ohio.. 192
Westover, Judy, Iowa...................................... 46

Whatley, Basil Bayne, Tennessee...................... 245
Wheaton, Rebecca L., New Jersey..................... 36
White, Erma L., Utah....................................... 90
White, Kristopher, California............................ 60
White, Leona, Indiana...................................... 181
Whiteside, W.A., Kansas.................................. 8
Whitmore, Barbara, Oregon.............................. 146
Whitsel, Marcia (Shank), Pennsylvania.............. 41
Widman, Jan, Ohio.. 20
Wig, V.R., Wisconsin........................... 20, 202, 213
Wiley, Maggie, Mississippi............................... 290
Wilkinson, Kattie, Alabama.............................. 258
Wilks, Maureen, New Mexico............................ 204
Will, Jan, Florida.. 269
Williams, Altha B. Davis, Colorado................... 95
Williams, Johnny Laronn, North Carolina........... 24
Williams, Kari Anne, Georgia............................ 44
Williams, Misha Renee', Tennessee................... 25
Williams, M. Kaylor, Arkansas.......................... 211
Williams, Wende P., West Virginia..................... 122
Williams, William Henry, Georgia...................... 321
Willis, Elizabeth C., Massachusetts................... 22
Wilmeth, Dawn, Texas..................................... 307
Wilpon, Bruce, Illinois.................................... 227
Wilson, Christine, New Mexico.......................... 8
Wilson, Pam, Colorado.................................... 75
Wing, Hawaii... 136
Winston, Christal, Idaho.................................. 284
Wisbeski, W.D., New Jersey............................. 222
Wisehart, Mickey B., Ohio................................ 52
Wolf, Hedy, California...................................... 48
Wolff, Sonia, California.................................... 18
Wollman, William A., New Jersey...................... 176
Wood, Charlotte, Oklahoma.............................. 29
Wood, Julianne, Illinois................................... 296
Woodburn, Mechelle Lively, West Virginia.......... 63
Woodruff, Charlyn P., South Carolina................. 78
Woods, Edmond C., Ohio.................................. 102
Woods, Joanne, New York................................ 231
Woodward, Clyde H., California......................... 163
Woodward, Rita A., California............................ 307
Woolsey, Butch, Pennsylvania.......................... 58
Woolsey, Melissa, Pennsylvania....................... 286
Wright, Melanie M., North Carolina................... 123
Wyant, Mark L., North Dakota.......................... 49
Wyatt, Becky, North Carolina........................... 162
Wyckoff, Wade, Pennsylvania........................... 329
Yancy, Scott E., California................................ 242
Yanniello, Chantal, Arizona.............................. 241
Yocum, John R., Pennsylvania........................... 328
Yost, D. Helene, Colorado................................ 40
Young, Jennifer, Illinois.................................. 225
Young, Nické-Chantalle, Colorado..................... 296
Young, Robert E., Arizona................................ 266
Young, Sean R., New Hampshire........................ 284
Z, Texas.. 293
Zapata, Liziel, California.................................. 206
Zapp, Liz, Texas... 236
Zieger, Barb, Saskatchewan, Canada................. 91
Zimmerman, Barbara J., Tennessee................... 213
Zweber, Rae M., Wisconsin..................... 41, 129
Zweifel, Ann Kemling, California....................... 326

134821